Unity 6 Shaders and Effects Cookbook

Fifth Edition

Over 50 recipes for creating captivating visual effects in Unity and enhancing your game's visual impact

John P. Doran

‹packt›

Unity 6 Shaders and Effects Cookbook

Fifth Edition

Portfolio Director: Rohit Rajkumar
Relationship Lead: Neha Pande
Program Manager: Sandip Tadge
Content Engineer: Shreya Sarkar
Technical Editor: Tejas Mhasvekar
Copy Editor: Safis Editing
Indexer: Manju Arasan
Proofreader: Shreya Sarkar
Production Designer: Aparna Bhagat
Growth Lead: Lee Booth
Marketing Owner: Nivedita Pandey

First published: June 2013
Second edition: February 2016
Third edition: June 2018
Fourth edition: October 2021
Fifth edition: July 2025

Production reference: 1020725

Published by Packt Publishing Ltd.
Grosvenor House
11 St Paul's Square
Birmingham
B3 1RB, UK.

ISBN 978-1-83546-857-9

www.packtpub.com

For Johanna, my little game designer in the making, and to my wonderful wife, Hannah, my co-op partner in this great adventure. May our lives always be filled with love, learning, and the joy of creating together.

— John P. Doran

Contributors

About the author

John P. Doran is a passionate and seasoned technical game designer, software engineer, and author who is based in Songdo, South Korea. His passion for game development began at an early age. He graduated from DigiPen Institute of Technology with a Bachelor of Science in Game Design and a Master of Science in Computer Science from Bradley University.

For over a decade, John has gained extensive hands-on expertise in game development, working in various roles ranging from game designer to lead UI programmer in teams ranging from just himself to over 70 people in student, mod, and professional game projects, including working at LucasArts on *Star Wars: 1313*. Additionally, John has worked in game development education teaching in Singapore, South Korea, and the United States. To date, he has authored over 10 books pertaining to game development.

John is currently an Instructor at George Mason University Korea. Prior to his present ventures, he was an award-winning videographer.

This book would not have been possible without the unwavering support of my wife, Hannah, and my daughter, Johanna. Your love, patience, and encouragement mean everything to me.

A special thanks to everyone at Packt, especially Neha, Shreya, Arul, and Mark, for your patience, guidance, and invaluable feedback throughout this journey. Balancing a full-time job, a PhD, and writing this book has been no small feat, and I deeply appreciate your flexibility and support in making this project a reality.

About the reviewers

Alejandro Diaz is a seasoned game programmer with extensive experience in remote and international environments. Specializing in mobile game development, he excels in mechanics, systems, UI design, and optimization. Alejandro's career includes significant contributions to renowned projects such as *Roller Coaster Tycoon Touch*. His strong foundation in Unity development and interest in shaders and effects make him a valuable contributor to projects exploring these technical areas. With proficiency in creating tools for game designers and managing complex development systems, Alejandro continues to shape the future of interactive experiences.

Shailja Shrivastava is a game developer and software engineer with extensive experience in Unity, Unreal Engine, and multiplayer game architecture. With a background in backend development, networking, and rendering optimizations, she has contributed to various game projects across mobile, web, and console platforms. She has worked with multiple publishers worldwide and has experience developing API backends, CI/CD pipelines, and AR applications. Her expertise also includes shader programming, gameplay mechanics, game optimization, and server-side development.

Obinna Akpen is a senior Unity developer with over 6 years of experience, specializing in Unity, C# scripting, and shader development. He has worked on multiple successful titles, including *Who Dies First*, a globally acclaimed mobile game with millions of downloads and top chart rankings. Obinna is known for his strong grasp of game mechanics, delivering immersive gameplay and polished experiences. A former e-sports champion, he thrives under pressure, adapts quickly to challenges, and actively mentors aspiring developers, fostering growth in the game development community.

Table of Contents

Part II: Advanced Shader Effects and Geometry Manipulation

Chapter 6: Using Vertex Functions

Part III: Performance Optimization and Fullscreen Effects   253

Chapter 8: Optimizing Shaders   255

Chapter 9: Creating Screen Effects with Fullscreen Shaders   281

Chapter 12: Developing Advanced Shading Techniques   419

Preface

Unity 6 Shaders and Effects Cookbook is your guide to mastering shader creation and post-processing effects in Unity 6. With Unity 6 making **the Universal Render Pipeline (URP)** the default render pipeline used, this edition of the book has been rewritten with a focus on URP and **Shader Graph**, ensuring that you are equipped to create shaders using Unity's latest rendering technology.

You will start your journey by exploring URP's built-in post-processing features, learning how to enhance your game's visuals without writing custom scripts. From there, you will dive into Shader Graph, creating your first shaders and learning how surfaces interact with light. As you progress, you will explore texture mapping, vertex functions, and advanced transparency effects using grab passes, all of which help bring your game world to life.

This edition introduces **Unity Muse**, a generative AI tool that simplifies texture creation, alongside deeper coverage of physically based rendering (PBR), lighting models, and fullscreen shaders. You'll learn how to optimize shaders for performance, implement dynamic screen effects such as night vision and old film filters, and use **HLSL** and **ShaderLab** to create fully customized shading techniques. The final chapter explores high-end rendering with HDRP, helping you create shaders suited for AAA-quality visuals.

Each chapter is designed to build your skills step by step, but you can also jump into specific topics to quickly learn a new technique. Whether you're a game programmer, technical artist, or an experienced Unity developer looking to deepen your shader expertise, this book will give you the knowledge and practical recipes to create stunning effects in Unity 6. So, let's get started!

Who this book is for

Unity 6 Shaders and Effects Cookbook is designed for game developers who want to create shaders from scratch or enhance their projects with custom visual effects in Unity 6. It is especially useful for game programmers, technical artists, and aspiring developers who already have a solid understanding of Unity and are looking to deepen their skills in shader creation with Shader Graph, ShaderLab, and HLSL. This book assumes familiarity with Unity's interface and basic workflows, and is best suited for those at an intermediate level or higher in their Unity development journey.

What this book covers

Chapter 1, Using Post-Processing with URP, explores how screen shaders in URP can refine a game's style while introducing key shader concepts.

You will learn how to enable and configure post-processing, apply grain, vignetting, and depth of field for a filmic look, use bloom and motion blur for dynamic effects, and adjust scene tone through color grading. The chapter concludes with using fog to create immersive atmospheres, ideal for horror games.

Chapter 2, Creating Your First Shader with Shader Graph, introduces common diffusion techniques in modern shading pipelines, focusing on how light interacts with surfaces to enhance realism in 3D graphics.

You will be introduced to Shader Graph in Unity, a visual tool that enables shader creation without writing code. By the end of the chapter, you'll be able to create basic shaders, define adjustable properties, and use Shader Graph to execute fundamental visual operations in Unity.

Chapter 3, Working with Surfaces, takes a deeper dive into surface materials in Shader Graph. Mastering surface materials is essential for creating visually compelling and optimized shaders in Unity.

This chapter begins with a simple matte material and progresses to more advanced effects, including holographic projections.

Chapter 4, Working with Texture Mapping, teaches you how to apply and manipulate textures in shaders to enhance visual quality and create dynamic effects. The chapter covers UV manipulation for scrolling textures, blending multiple textures for richer materials, and implementing transparency for realistic surfaces. By the end of the chapter, you will be able to animate textures and modify shader properties at runtime using C#.

Chapter 5, Enhancing Realism: Unity Muse and Physically Based Rendering, explores PBR and how Unity Muse, a generative AI tool, simplifies the creation of realistic materials and textures.

The chapter covers how light interacts with surfaces, the role of PBR in achieving realism, and how to fine-tune materials using Muse's refinements menu. By the end, you will be able to apply PBR principles, create reflective surfaces, add transparency, and bake lighting for optimized visual fidelity.

Chapter 6, Using Vertex Functions, explains vertex functions and how shaders can be used not only to define an object's appearance but also to modify its geometry in real time. The chapter covers accessing vertex data, animating vertices, and using shaders to create deformations without altering the underlying mesh. By the end, you will have hands-on experience with extruding models, implementing a snow shader, and simulating volumetric explosions.

Chapter 7, Using Grab Passes, delves into grab passes, a powerful technique for capturing and manipulating the background scene within shaders to create advanced transparency effects. Unlike simple transparency, which only reveals what's behind an object, grab passes allow for refraction, distortion, and dynamic interactions with the background.

The chapter covers using grab passes to draw behind objects, implementing a glass shader with stained-glass effects, and creating a water shader for 2D games to simulate animated distortions.

Chapter 8, Optimizing Shaders, explores shader optimization techniques to ensure performance-friendly rendering across different platforms. We will break down key elements that impact shader performance, including reducing memory overhead, optimizing calculations, and how to best leverage Unity's built-in variables.

You will learn how to profile shaders, adjust precision types (fixed, half, or float) for better memory management, and refine lighting calculations to suit lower-end hardware.

Chapter 9, Creating Screen Effects with Fullscreen Shaders, teaches you how to create fullscreen shaders to apply effects directly within Unity, gaining full control over real-time rendering. Unlike Unity's built-in post-processing stack, fullscreen shaders allow developers to craft custom visual effects such as depth-based effects and color correction from scratch.

This chapter explores the depth buffer, demonstrates how to create Photoshop-like blend modes, and teaches you how to adjust brightness, saturation, and contrast dynamically.

Chapter 10, *Gameplay and Screen Effects*, builds on concepts from *Chapter 9*, *Creating Screen Effects with Fullscreen Shaders*, focusing on creating specific screen effects that completely change how a game feels. You will learn how to create an old movie screen effect, complete with film grain, scratches, and sepia tones, and implement a night vision effect, commonly used in FPS games, while also learning about using sub-graphs to break up complex effects and the **Custom Function** node, which will allow us to write High-Level Shader Language (HLSL) code directly within Shader Graph.

Chapter 11, *Understanding Lighting Models*, explores how lighting models determine the way light interacts with surfaces in shaders. You will learn how to create custom lighting models, including diffuse shading, toon shading, and Blinn-Phong specular reflections, while also adding shadows and multiple light support. By the end, you will understand how to control light reflection and shading effects, enabling you to create both realistic and stylized materials.

Chapter 12, *Developing Advanced Shading Techniques*, delves into advanced shader development by writing .shader files, combining ShaderLab and HLSL for greater control over rendering effects.

You will learn how ShaderLab structures shaders, handling rendering properties, passes, and tags, while HLSL is used to define the vertex and fragment shader logic. By leveraging both, developers can push the boundaries of graphical effects, crafting unique materials that go beyond Shader Graph's capabilities.

Chapter 13, *Utilizing the HDRP*, introduces the High-Definition Render Pipeline (HDRP). Unlike URP, which prioritizes efficiency, HDRP is designed for powerful hardware such as modern consoles and high-performance PCs. This chapter will guide you through Shader Graph techniques in HDRP, focusing on implementing a glowing highlight system and portal shaders to create dynamic visual effects.

To get the most out of this book

To get the most out of this book, you should have experience working with Unity and some scripting knowledge (C# is fine). While no prior experience with shaders is required, familiarity with Unity's rendering system will help you grasp the concepts more easily.

This book is written using **Unity Editor version 6 Preview 6000.0.7f1**, but the techniques covered should work with future versions of Unity with only minor adjustments.

Software/hardware covered in the book	OS requirements
Unity 6000.0.7f1	Windows, macOS, or Linux (any)

If you need to access older versions of Unity for compatibility reasons, you can download them from the Unity download archive: `https://unity.com/releases/editor/archive`.

If you are using the digital version of this book, we advise you to type the code yourself or access the code via the GitHub repository (link available in the next section). Doing so will help you avoid any potential errors related to the copying and pasting of code.

Note that the author acknowledges the use of cutting-edge AI, such as ChatGPT, with the sole aim of enhancing the language and clarity within the book, thereby ensuring a smooth reading experience for readers. It's important to note that the content itself has been crafted by the author and edited by a professional publishing team.

Download the example code and asset files

You can download the example code and asset files for this book from GitHub at `https://github.com/PacktPublishing/Unity-6-Shaders-and-Effects-Cookbook`. In case there's an update to the code or assets, it will be updated on the existing GitHub repository.

We also have other code bundles from our rich catalog of books and videos available at `https://github.com/PacktPublishing/`. Check them out!

Download the color images

We also provide a PDF file that has color images of the screenshots/diagrams used in this book. You can download it here: `https://packt.link/gbp/9781835468579`.

Conventions used

There are a number of text conventions used throughout this book.

`CodeInText`: Indicates code words in text, database table names, folder names, filenames, file extensions, pathnames, dummy URLs, user input, and Twitter handles. For example: "Above the frag function, add the `CalculateAlphaFade` function to handle edge fading."

A block of code is set as follows:

```
GameObject explosion = Instantiate(explosionPrefab) as GameObject;
Renderer = explosion.GetComponent<Renderer>();
Material = new Material(renderer.sharedMaterial);
renderer.material = material;
```

When we wish to draw your attention to a particular part of a code block, the relevant lines or items are set in bold:

```
struct appdata
{
    float4 vertex : POSITION;
    float2 uv : TEXCOORD0;
    float3 normal : NORMAL;
};
```

Bold: Indicates a new term, an important word, or words that you see on the screen. For instance, words in menus or dialog boxes appear in the text like this. For example: "Drag and drop **Global Color Tint** onto the graph. Below it, create a **Vertex Color** node to access the vertex color data from the model."

Warnings or important notes appear like this.

Tips and tricks appear like this.

Sections

In this book, you will find several headings that appear frequently (*Getting ready*, *How to do it...*, *How it works...*, *There's more...*, and *See also*).

To give clear instructions on how to complete a recipe, use these sections as follows:

Getting ready

This section tells you what to expect in the recipe and describes how to set up any software or any preliminary settings required for the recipe.

How to do it...

This section contains the steps required to follow the recipe.

How it works...

This section usually consists of a detailed explanation of what happened in the previous section.

There's more...

This section consists of additional information about the recipe in order to make you more knowledgeable about the recipe.

See also

This section provides helpful links to other useful information for the recipe.

Get in touch

Feedback from our readers is always welcome.

General feedback: Email feedback@packtpub.com and mention the book's title in the subject of your message. If you have questions about any aspect of this book, please email us at questions@packtpub.com.

Errata: Although we have taken every care to ensure the accuracy of our content, mistakes do happen. If you have found a mistake in this book, we would be grateful if you reported this to us. Please visit http://www.packtpub.com/submit-errata, click **Submit Errata**, and fill in the form.

Piracy: If you come across any illegal copies of our works in any form on the internet, we would be grateful if you would provide us with the location address or website name. Please contact us at copyright@packtpub.com with a link to the material.

If you are interested in becoming an author: If there is a topic that you have expertise in and you are interested in either writing or contributing to a book, please visit http://authors.packtpub.com/.

Join our community on Discord

Join our community's Discord space for discussions with the authors and other readers:

https://packt.link/gamedevelopment

Share Your Thoughts

Once you've read *Unity 6 Shaders and Effects Cookbook, Fifth edition*, we'd love to hear your thoughts! Scan the QR code below to go straight to the Amazon review page for this book and share your feedback.

https://packt.link/r/1835468578

Your review is important to us and the tech community and will help us make sure we're delivering excellent quality content.

Download a free PDF copy of this book

Thanks for purchasing this book!

Do you like to read on the go but are unable to carry your print books everywhere?

Is your eBook purchase not compatible with the device of your choice?

Don't worry, now with every Packt book you get a DRM-free PDF version of that book at no cost.

Read anywhere, any place, on any device. Search, copy, and paste code from your favorite technical books directly into your application.

The perks don't stop there, you can get exclusive access to discounts, newsletters, and great free content in your inbox daily

Follow these simple steps to get the benefits:

1. Scan the QR code or visit the link below

https://packt.link/free-ebook/9781835468579

2. Submit your proof of purchase
3. That's it! We'll send your free PDF and other benefits to your email directly

Part 1

Foundations of Shading and Rendering in Unity

The world of real-time rendering is built on shaders — specialized programs that define how objects appear in a game. Unity 6 has shifted its default render pipeline to Universal Render Pipeline (URP), making Shader Graph a key tool for developers looking to create stunning visual effects. This part introduces the fundamental building blocks of shaders, helping you establish a strong foundation in shader development.

We will begin with post-processing effects in URP, exploring how Unity's built-in screen shaders can be used to refine a game's style. Without writing custom shaders, you will learn how to apply grain, vignetting, depth of field, bloom, motion blur, color grading, and atmospheric fog to achieve cinematic visuals. From there, we will introduce Shader Graph, a visual tool that allows developers to create shaders without needing to write HLSL code.

Once you understand the basics, we will dive into surface materials and texture mapping, where you'll learn how to define material properties such as diffuse color, transparency, and reflectivity. We will explore UV mapping, blending multiple textures, and animating texture properties using C# to create dynamic visual effects. The part concludes with Physically Based Rendering (PBR), where we will explore how light interacts with surfaces in a realistic way and how Unity Muse, a generative AI tool, can assist in rapid material creation and refinement.

By the end of this part, you will have a solid grasp of Shader Graph fundamentals, texture mapping techniques, and PBR principles, equipping you with the knowledge needed to move into advanced shader effects and real-time geometry manipulation.

This part has the following chapters:

1

Using Post-Processing with URP

Custom shaders allow you to fine-tune visuals, achieving a unique look for your project. This book focuses on writing shaders and effects, but it's worth noting that Unity's **Universal Render Pipeline (URP)** provides built-in solutions for common visual enhancements. Prebuilt shaders like the Standard Shader and configurable lighting and shadows offer a solid foundation.

For quick and effective visual improvements, URP's integrated post-processing features provide effects such as bloom, depth of field, color grading, ambient occlusion, and motion blur. These can enhance your game's aesthetics without requiring additional coding while offering insight into how shaders work. URP applies these effects via screen shaders, which not only save development time but also introduce key shader concepts.

This chapter covers enabling and configuring post-processing in URP, using grain, vignetting, and depth of field for a filmic look, applying bloom and motion blur for dynamic visuals, and exploring color grading to adjust scene tone. We conclude by using fog to create immersive atmospheres, ideal for horror games.

By leveraging URP's post-processing tools, you can refine your game's style, experiment with effects, and gain a deeper understanding of professional-quality rendering. In this chapter, we will be covering the following recipes:

- Setting up post-processing
- Achieving a filmic look with grain, vignetting, and depth of field
- Simulating realistic effects with bloom and motion blur
- Enhancing the atmosphere with color grading
- Creating a horror game look with fog

Technical requirements

For this chapter, you'll need **Unity Editor version 6 Preview 6000.0.4f1**. The instructions should remain mostly applicable in future URP-based projects. The sample project was created using the **Universal 3D Core** template, which includes URP preconfigured but is otherwise minimal, requiring additional content.

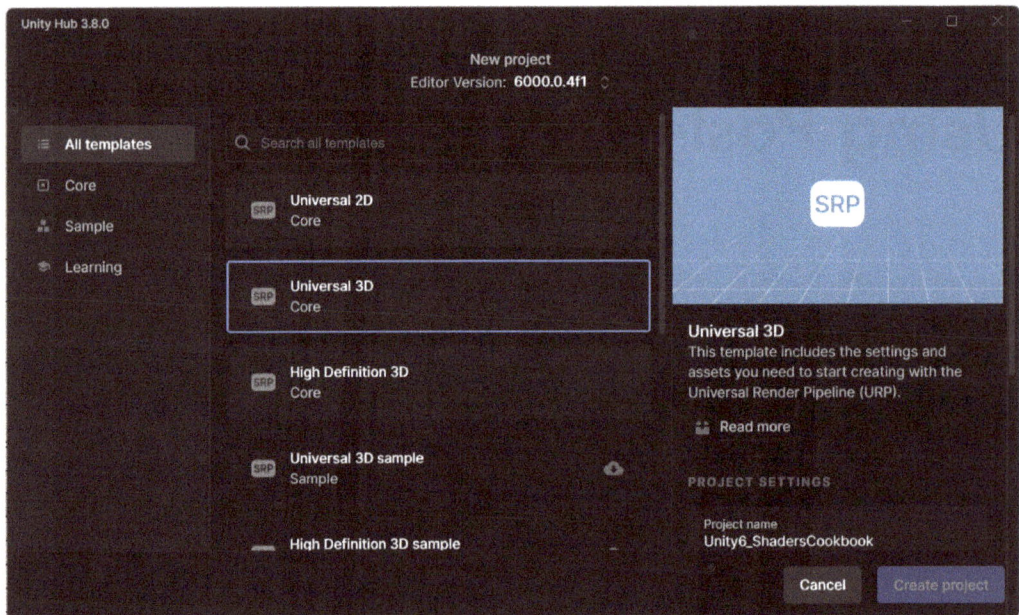

Figure 1.1 – Universal 3D Core template

The provided code files for the book on GitHub include a Unity package named Chapter1_StartingPoint.unitypackage, located in the Unity Packages folder (https://github.com/PacktPublishing/Unity-6-Shaders-and-Effects-Cookbook/tree/main/Unity%20Packages). This package contains a basic scene and assets necessary to experiment with post-processing techniques. All recipes in this chapter rely on this environment to demonstrate their effects.

Setting up post-processing

In this recipe, you'll learn how to set up a Unity project and enable post-processing effects in a URP project. Once enabled, you'll gain greater control over your game's visual style.

Earlier editions of this book used the Built-in Render Pipeline, requiring the post-processing stack from the Package Manager. However, URP includes post-processing by default, simplifying setup and allowing you to apply effects quickly.

Getting ready

To begin, launch Unity and create a 3D template project. This chapter requires an environment to observe post-processing effects. If you prefer to use the scene on its own within your own project rather than working directly from the example code, you can import the Chapter1_StartingPoint.unitypackage (found in the Unity Packages folder) which includes a basic scene and supporting assets.

For those using the example code, open Chapter 1/Starting Point from Assets/Chapter 01/Scenes folder from the **Project** window. If all goes well, you should see something like this in the **Scene** view:

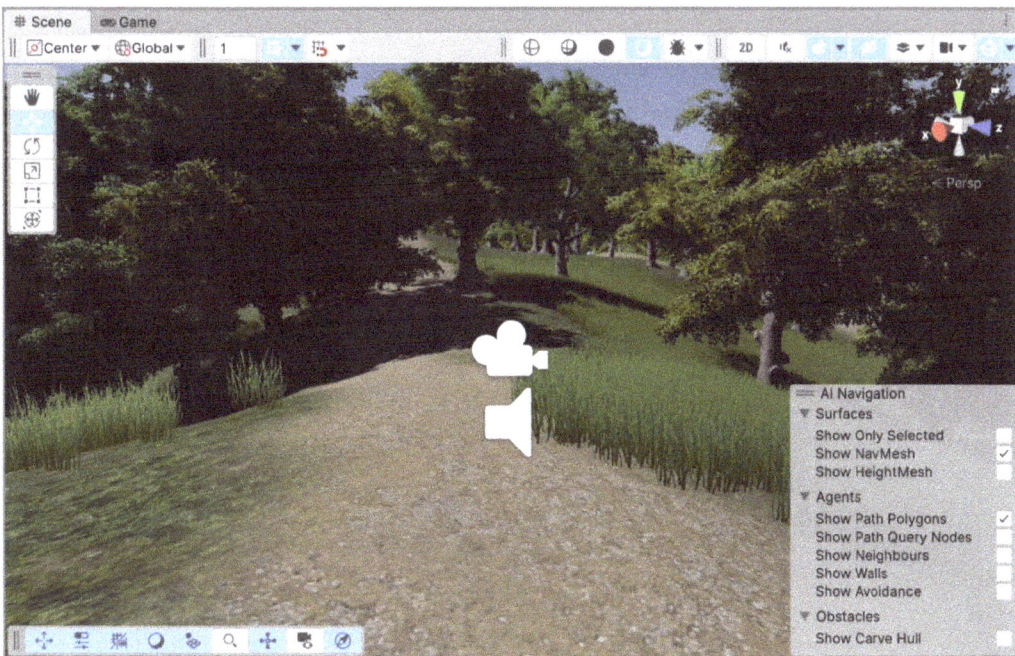

Figure 1.2 – Starting Point scene

This is a simple environment that will allow us to easily see how changes that have been made with post-processing effects can modify how things are drawn on the screen.

> Note
>
> If you are interested in learning how to create the environment we are going to be using here, you can check out one of my previous books, *Unity 5.x Game Development Blueprints*, (2016) also available from *Packt Publishing*.

How to do it...

To get started, follow these steps:

1. Select the object in your scene with a camera. In this case, go to the **Hierarchy** window and expand the **FPSController** object. From there, select the **FirstPersonCharacter** object.

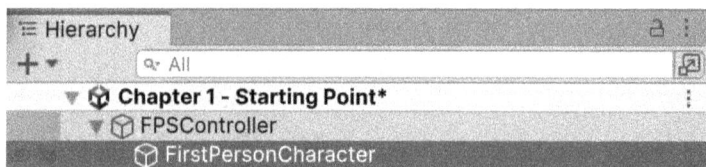

Figure 1.3 – Selecting the FirstPersonCharacter object

2. Next, go to the **Inspector** window. From there, scroll down to the **Camera** component and check the **Post Processing** option.

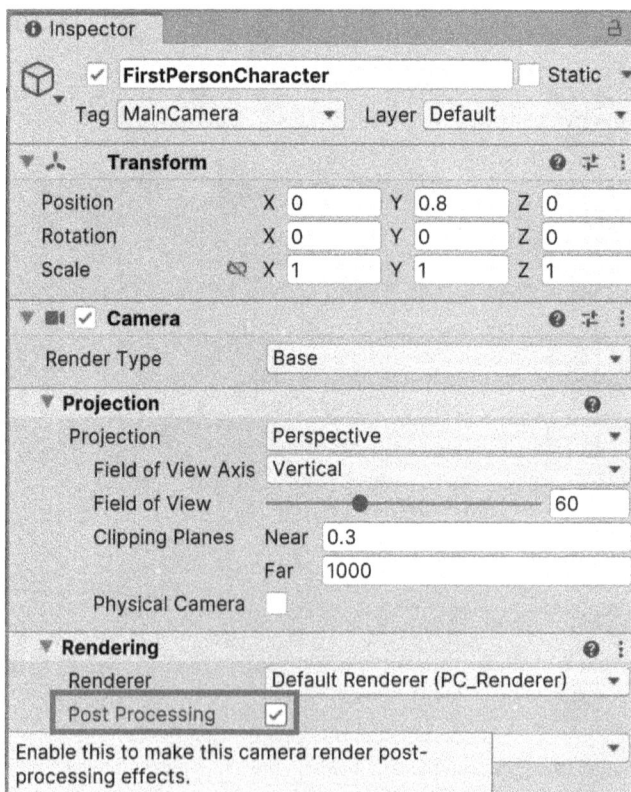

Figure 1.4 – Enabling Post Processing

3. From the top bar, select **GameObject | Volume | Global Volume**. This will add a new object to the **Hierarchy** window.

How it works...

Enabling **Post Processing** on a camera activates post-processing effects for that camera. If your project has multiple cameras, ensure this option is enabled for each one.

Unity's **URP** uses the **Volume** framework for post-processing, allowing effects to be applied globally or within specific areas. A **Volume** defines a space in the scene where post-processing settings take effect. Global Volumes apply to the entire scene, while Local Volumes affect only designated areas.

To set up post-processing, create an empty **GameObject** and add a **Volume** component. When Post Processing is enabled on a camera, it will use the settings inside the assigned volume. Since we are using a **Post Processing**, its **Mode** is set to **Global**, meaning it has no boundaries and affects all cameras in the scene.

At runtime, URP evaluates all active **Volume** components, using the camera's position and volume properties to determine their impact on the final scene rendering.

Achieving a filmic look using grain, vignetting, and depth of field

Now that we have finished setting up our project to utilize post-processing, we can create our first **Post Processing Volume Profile**. A **volume profile** is an asset that contains the settings URP uses to render a scene.

One of the most common appearances people like their projects to have is that of a film. This is used quite frequently in titles such as *Red Dead Redemption 2* (2018) and *The Last of Us Part II* (2020). It's also used quite effectively in *Resident Evil Village* (2021), as its creators aimed to emulate the cinematic horror atmosphere that the game is based on.

Figure 1.5 – Final result of the filmic look

Getting ready

Make sure you have completed the *Setting up post-processing* recipe before starting this one.

How to do it...

Follow these steps to get a filmic look using grain, vignetting, and depth of field:

1. First, we must create a new volume profile by going to the **Project** window. From there, right-click within the Assets/Chapter 01 folder and then select **Create** | **Rendering** | **Volume Profile**.

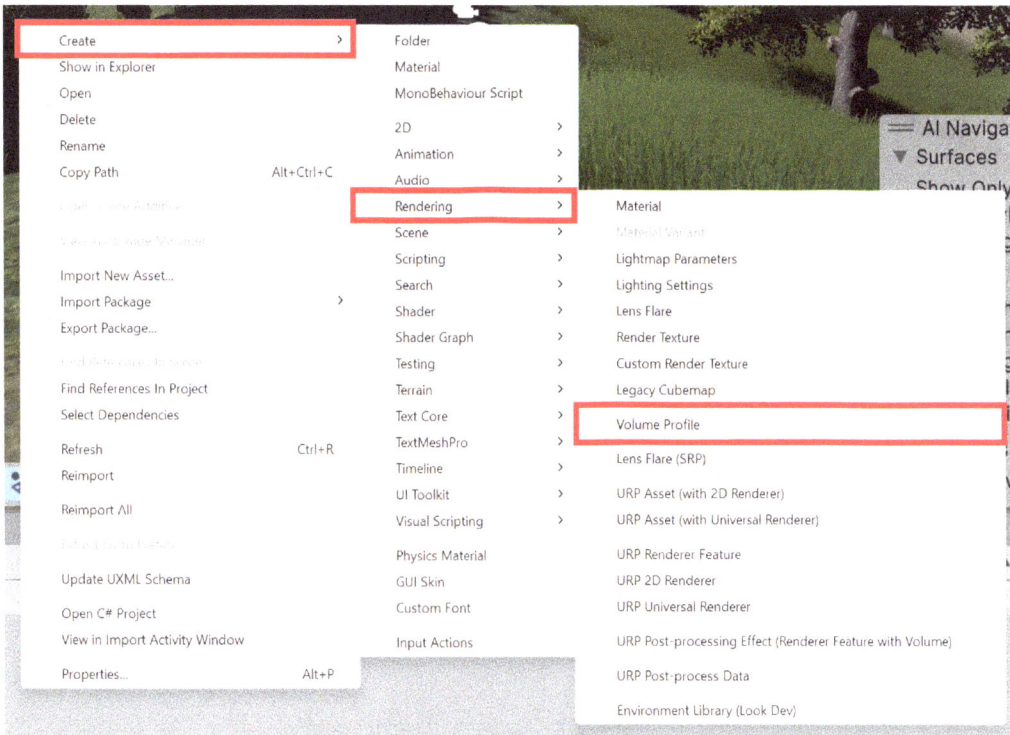

Figure 1.6 – Creating a volume profile

2. Once selected, we can rename the item. Go ahead and set the name to `FilmicProfile`.

> **Note**
>
> If you don't enter a name correctly, you can rename an item from the **Project** window by clicking on the name and then clicking it again. Alternatively, you can right-click on the item and select **Rename** or hit *F2* on your keyboard with an item selected.

3. Then, from the **Hierarchy** window, select the **Global Volume** object and drag and drop the **FilmicProfile** object into the **Volume Profile** section of the **Inspector** window by dragging and dropping it from the **Project** window over the property and then letting go.

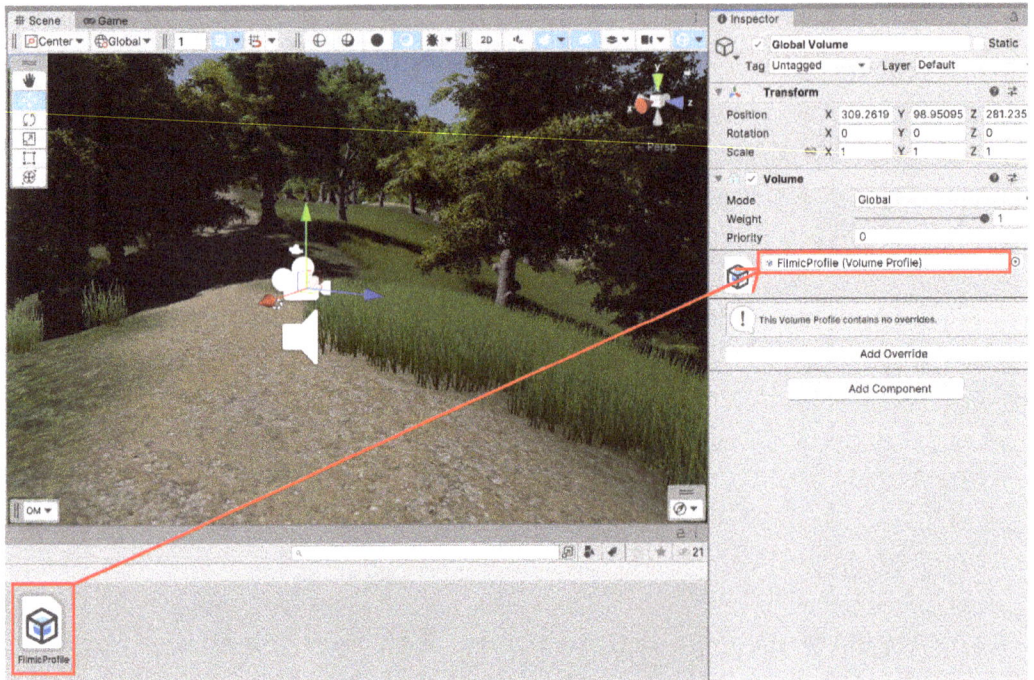

Figure 1.7 – Assigning the filmic profile

Note

Alternatively, you can also click on the **New** button, which will automatically create an object for you with the name of the scene. This method works well if you only want to have one profile. However, since we are going to be using several profiles over the course of this chapter, I wanted to ensure that you know the entire process by doing it manually.

4. Once the profile has been added, we should see an **Add Override** button appear. Click it and select **Post-processing | Film Grain**.

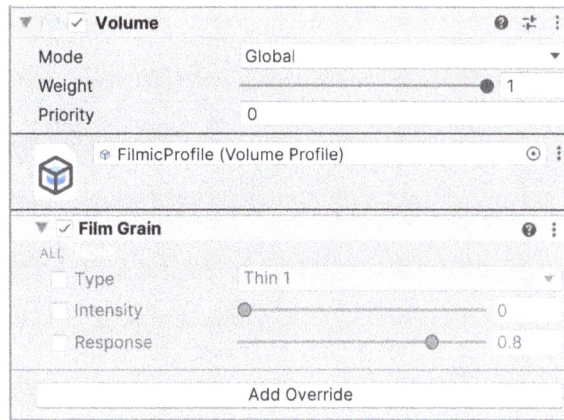

Figure 1.8 – Adding the Film Grain effect to post-process volume

By default, all options will appear grayed out. To activate any of the options, you need to click the checkbox on the left side of each option. You can also quickly enable or disable all options at once by clicking the **All** or **None** options, respectively, located at the top-left side of the override that we just added.

5. To view the changes in a way that resembles the finished game, switch to the **Game** view by selecting the **Game** tab. Next, check the **Intensity** option and set it to 1.0. Then, check the **Type** property and set it to **Medium 1**. Afterward, hit the **Play** button to see a representation of what the tweaks have done:

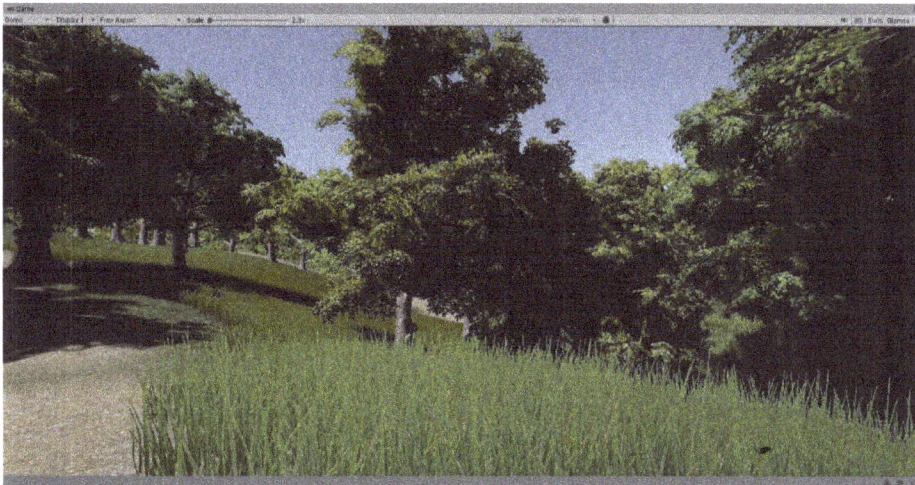

Figure 1.9 – Result of the Film Grain effect

You will notice that the screen has become much fuzzier than before.

6. We want to have a more subtle effect here, so we will decrease **Intensity** to 0.2 and set
    Type to **Thin 2**:

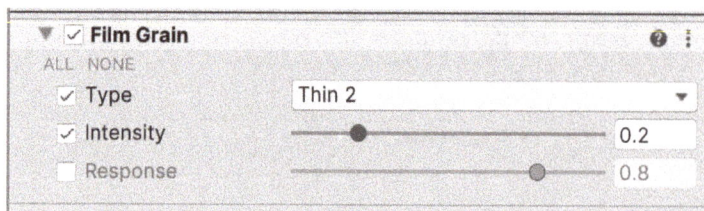

Figure 1.10 – Altering the Film Grain effect

This will alter the grain effect so that it looks like this:

Figure 1.11 – Altered result

Note

Unlike how users typically work in Unity, due to Post Processing Profiles
being asset files, you can modify them while playing your game and, upon
stopping the game, the values are still saved. This can be useful for tweaking
values to achieve the exact look that you're after.

The next property we want to tweak is the **Vignette** property, which will add blackened
edges around the screen.

7. Click on **Add Override** and select **Post-processing** | **Vignette**. Open the properties, enable the **Intensity** property, and set it to 0.5. Afterward, enable and set **Smoothness** to 0.35:

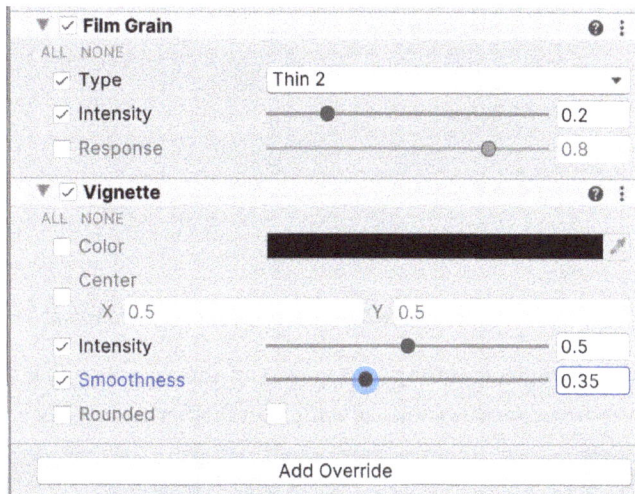

Figure 1.12 – Creating a vignette effect

Adding this effect will make the screen look like this:

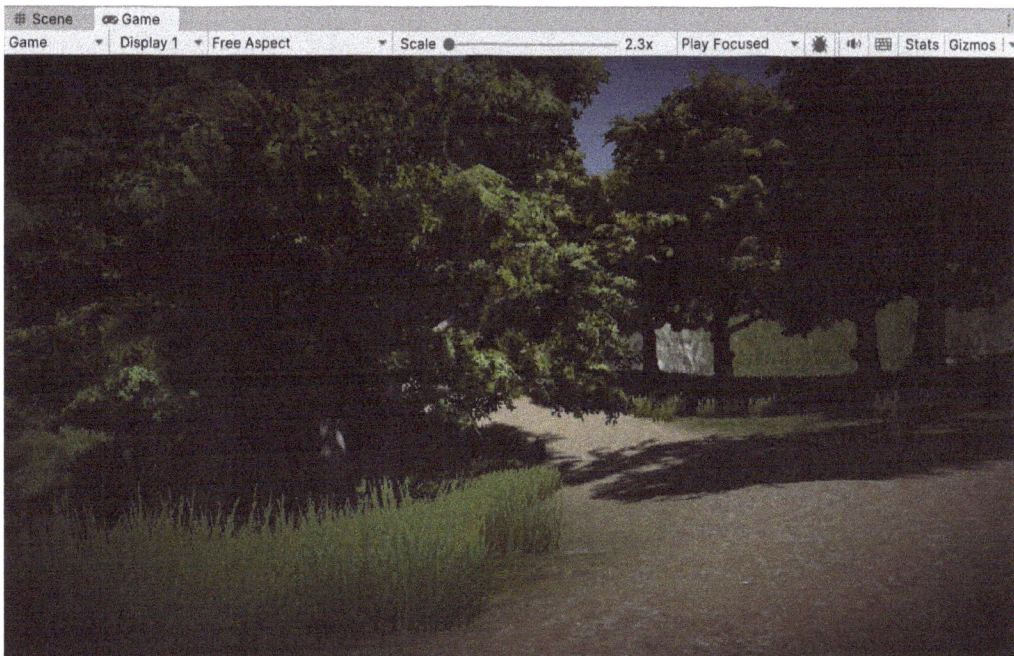

Figure 1.13 – Visual of vignette effect

8.   Next, select **Add Override** again and, this time, select **Post-processing** | **Depth of Field**. Check the **Mode** property and change it to **Gaussian**. Then set the **Start** property to 20:

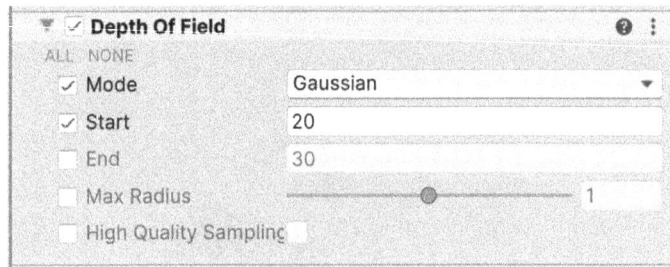

Figure 1.14 – Setting Depth Of Field values

Afterward, if you look at the **Scene** view, you should notice that while things in front of the player are perfectly visible, as things get further away, they are now blurred:

Figure 1.15 – Result of depth of field effect

Now, if we go into the game itself and move around, we should see our filmic look in action:

Figure 1.16 – Final result of the filmic look

And with that, we now have a scene that looks much more like a film than what we had to begin with!

How it works...

Each time we add an effect to a post-processing volume, we are overriding what would normally be put onto the screen.

If you've been to a movie theater that still uses film, you may have noticed how there were little specks in the filmstock while the film was playing. The **Film Grain** effect simulates this film grain, causing the effect to become more pronounced the more the movie is played. This is often used in horror games to obscure the player's vision.

Note

For more information about the **Film Grain** effect, check out
`https://docs.unity3d.com/Packages/com.unity.render-pipelines.`
`universal@7.1/manual/Post-Processing-Film-Grain.html`.

In the film world, vignetting can be an unintended effect of using the wrong type of lens for the type of shot you are trying to achieve or the aspect ratio that you are shooting for. In game development, we typically use vignetting for dramatic effect or to have players focus on the center of the screen by darkening and/or desaturating the edges of the screen compared to the center.

Note

For more information about the **Vignette** effect, check out
`https://docs.unity3d.com/Packages/com.unity.render-pipelines.`
`universal@17.0/manual/post-processing-vignette.html.`

The **Depth Of Field** setting determines what is blurry and what isn't. The idea is to have items of importance in focus while items in the background are not. In this version, we are using Gaussian, which is the fastest and best mode of the depth of field effect to use for lower-end platforms.

Note

For more information about the **Depth of Field** effect, check out
`https://docs.unity3d.com/Packages/com.unity.render-pipelines.`
`universal@17.0/manual/post-processing-depth-of-field.html.`

Simulating realistic effects with bloom and motion blur

The **bloom** optical effect aims to mimic the imaging effects of real-world cameras. In real life, when a camera captures bright lights, the light can bleed over into adjacent areas, creating a glow around the edges of bright objects. This effect can make scenes look more vivid and dynamic, as it simulates the way cameras and the human eye perceive intense light sources. The bloom effect is very distinctive and is often used in games to create a magical or ethereal atmosphere. You've likely seen it employed in areas of a game that are magical, heaven-like, or otherworldly. Popular titles such as *Cyberpunk 2077* (2020) and *Final Fantasy XV* (2016) make extensive use of bloom to enhance their visual storytelling and immerse players in their fantastical worlds.

Motion blur is another effect used to mimic real-life camera behavior. It simulates the blurring that occurs when objects move quickly within the frame, replicating the effect seen in both cinematography and real life. This effect can make fast movements appear smoother and more realistic, enhancing the sense of speed and motion. Motion blur is commonly used in action-packed games to provide a more immersive experience and to visually communicate the intensity of fast-paced sequences. Recent games such as Marvel's *Spider-Man 2* (2023), developed by Insomniac Games, and *Forza Horizon 5* (2021), developed by Playground Games, use motion blur to great effect, making their high-speed action sequences more dynamic and engaging.

By combining bloom and motion blur, developers can create visually stunning and more lifelike scenes, enhancing the overall gaming experience.

Figure 1.17 – The final result of using bloom and motion blur

Getting ready

Make sure you have completed the *Setting up post-processing* recipe before starting this one.

How to do it...

To add the bloom and anti-aliasing effect, follow these steps:

1. First, we must create a new volume profile by going to the **Project** window. From there, right-click within the `Assets/Chapter 01` folder and then select **Create | Rendering | Volume Profile**.

2. Once selected, set the name to `RadiantProfile`.

3. From the **Hierarchy** window, select the **Global Volume** object. In the **Inspector** window, locate the **Volume** component and assign the profile property to our newly created profile.

4. Afterward, select the **Game** tab (if it hasn't been selected already) to see the results of the changes we are about to make.

5. In the **Inspector** window, go to **Volume**, select the **Add Override** button, and select **Post-processing** | **Bloom**. Check the **Intensity** property and set it to 12. Afterward, check and set **Threshold** to 0.5:

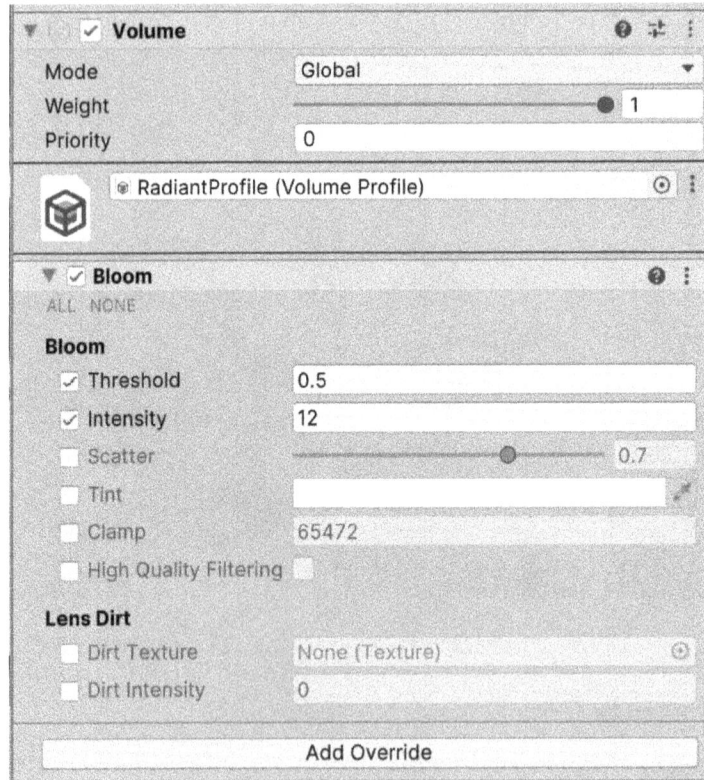

Figure 1.18 – Adding a Bloom effect

This will give us the following effect:

Figure 1.19 – Visual of the bloom effect

6.   In the **Inspector** window, go to **Volume**, select the **Add Override** button, and select **Post-processing** | **Motion Blur**. Check the **Intensity** property and set it to 0.5. Afterward, check and set **Clamp** to 0.2:

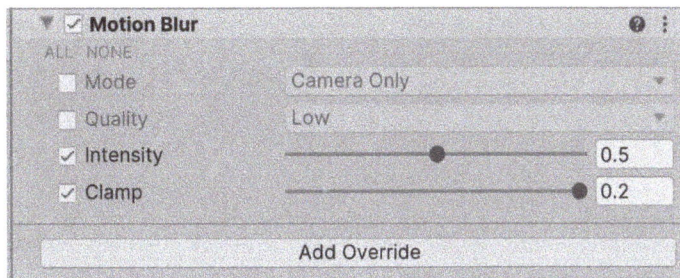

Figure 1.20 – Adjusting the Intensity and Clamp values of Motion Blur

7.   Afterward, save your scene and hit the **Play** button to check out your project:

Figure 1.21 – The final result of using bloom and motion blur

You should notice that whenever you turn the camera, there will be a subtle blur effect.

How it works...

As we mentioned previously, the bloom filter will make bright things even brighter while adding a glow to lighter areas. In this recipe, you may have noticed that the path is much lighter than it was previously. We can do this to ensure that players will follow the path to get to the next section of gameplay.

Note

For more information about **Bloom**, check out `https://docs.unity3d.com/Packages/com.unity.render-pipelines.universal@17.0/manual/post-processing-bloom.html`.

Motion blur attempts to simulate the effect of motion in real life, where objects moving quickly within the frame appear blurred. This effect occurs because the camera (or the human eye) cannot capture the fast-moving objects in sharp detail, resulting in a smeared appearance. Motion blur can make fast movements appear smoother and more natural, enhancing the overall realism and immersion in a game.

When a game character or object moves rapidly, the display may struggle to render each frame with perfect clarity, especially at lower frame rates. Motion blur helps mitigate this by blending frames together, creating a trail of blur that mimics the natural way our eyes perceive motion. This can be particularly effective in action-packed sequences, racing games, or any scenario involving high-speed movement.

However, it's important to use motion blur judiciously. While it can enhance realism, excessive use can lead to a loss of visual clarity, making the game appear overly blurred and reducing the sharpness of the scene.

Note

For more information about **Motion Blur** and what each property means, check out `https://docs.unity3d.com/Packages/com.unity.render-pipelines.universal@17.0/manual/Post-Processing-Motion-Blur.html`.

Enhancing the atmosphere with color grading

One of the best ways to easily change the mood of a scene is by changing the colors a scene uses. One of the best examples of this can be seen in *The Matrix* series of films, where the real world is always blue-tinted, while the computer-generated world is always tinted green. We can emulate this in our games by using color grading:

Figure 1.22 – The final result of using color grading

Getting ready

Make sure you have completed the *Setting up post-processing* recipe before starting this one.

How to do it...

To add color grading, follow these steps:

1. First, we must create a new volume profile by going to the **Project** window. From there, right-click within the Assets/Chapter 01 folder and then select **Create | Rendering | Volume Profile**.

2. Once selected, we can rename the item. Go ahead and set the name to ColorGradingProfile.

3. From the **Hierarchy** window, select the **Global Volume** object. In the **Inspector** window, locate the **Volume** component and assign the profile property to our newly created profile.

4. Afterward, select the **Game** tab (if it hasn't been selected already) to see the results of the changes to be made.

5. Select the **Add Override** button and select **Post-processing | White Balance**. Check the **Temperature** property and set it to 30. Afterward, check and set **Threshold** to 0.5.

6. Select the **Add Override** button and select **Post-processing | Color Grading**. Check the **Hue Shift** property and set it to -20 and the **Saturation** property to 15.

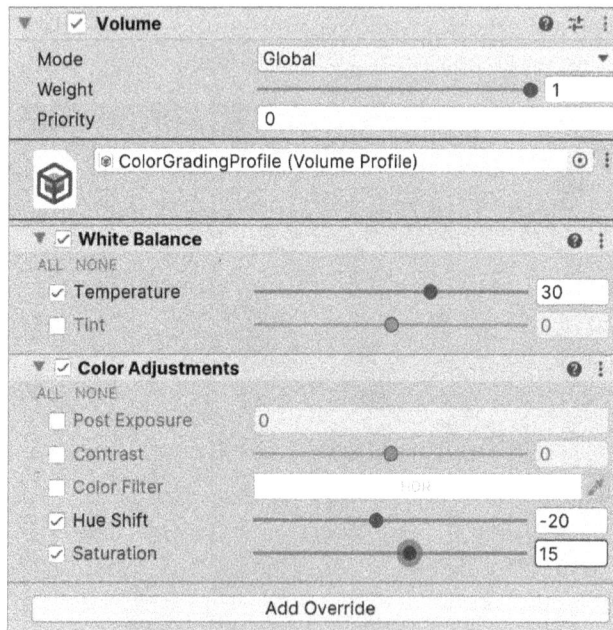

Figure 1.23 – Adjusting the properties of Color Grading

From the **Scene** view, you may see some changes; but to get a better feel dive into the game and move around to see what it looks like when playing it:

Figure 1.24 – The final result of using color grading

Notice how the previously very green environment is now much warmer and more yellow than before. Using techniques like this, environments can simulate different times of the year, such as fall, with minimal effort when it comes to creating new art assets.

How it works...

White balance attempts to correct the color cast in your scene so that objects that appear white in real life also appear white in your game. This adjustment compensates for the color temperature of the light source, which can range from the warm tones of incandescent lighting to the cool tones of daylight. In our case, we are shifting the temperature to make the game have warmer tones than it would normally.

Note

For more information about the **White Balance** effect, check out `https://docs.unity3d.com/Packages/com.unity.render-pipelines.universal@17.0/manual/Post-Processing-White-Balance.html`.

Color adjustments modify the hue, saturation, and brightness of the colors in your scene. These adjustments are vital for correcting any color discrepancies and achieving the desired look and feel for your game. You can enhance the vibrancy of certain colors, tone down others, or completely shift the color palette to fit a particular mood or theme. In our case, we shifted the hue to move all colors slightly toward the opposite side of the color wheel. We also increased the saturation, which made the colors more vibrant.

Note

For more information about the **Color Adjustments** effect, check out
`https://docs.unity3d.com/Packages/com.unity.render-pipelines.`
`universal@17.0/manual/Post-Processing-Color-Adjustments.html`.

Creating a horror game look with fog

One of the genres of games that best utilizes the features of the post-processing stack is the horror genre. Using things such as depth of field to hide scary objects, as well as static to make the screen more menacing, can help set your game firmly in the right place and provide the mood you are going for.

Figure 1.25 – The final result of our horror look

Getting ready

Make sure you have completed the *Setting up post-processing* recipe before starting this one.

How to do it...

To add color grading, follow these steps:

1. First, we must create a new volume profile by going to the **Project** window. From there, right-click within the `Assets/Chapter 01` folder and then select **Create** | **Rendering** | **Volume Profile**.

2. Once selected, we can rename the item. Go ahead and set the name to `HorrorProfile`.

3. From the **Hierarchy** window, select the **Global Volume** object. In the **Inspector** window, locate the **Volume** component and assign the profile property to our newly created profile.

4. Unlike the previous settings, though, the fog settings are located in the **Lighting** window, which can be accessed by going to **Window** | **Rendering** | **Lighting Settings**.

> Tip
>
> You may see the **Lighting** window open as a separate window on your screen. If you would like, you can drag and drop the top tab into another section of the Unity Editor to dock it to another section. I place it next to the **Inspector** window so that I can easily switch between the various options.

5. From there, select the **Environment** option at the top. Scroll to the bottom until you reach the **Other Settings** option. Once there, check **Fog** and set the **Color** property to a value that is close to the skybox to help the fog fade into the background of the environment. I used the following settings:

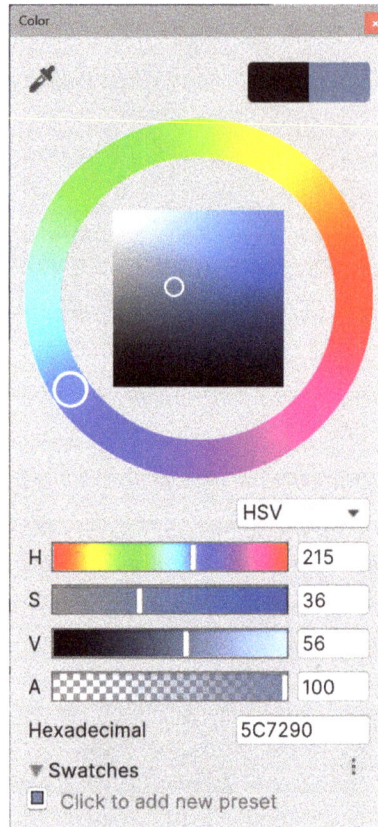

Figure 1.26 – The Color menu

Note

If you know the hex values of the color from your graphic editing software, such as Photoshop, you can just type it in the **Hexadecimal** property of the **Color** window, but I just clicked on the eye dropper and then clicked on the skybox.

6. Next, confirm that **Mode** is set to **Exponential Squared** and set **Density** to 0.03:

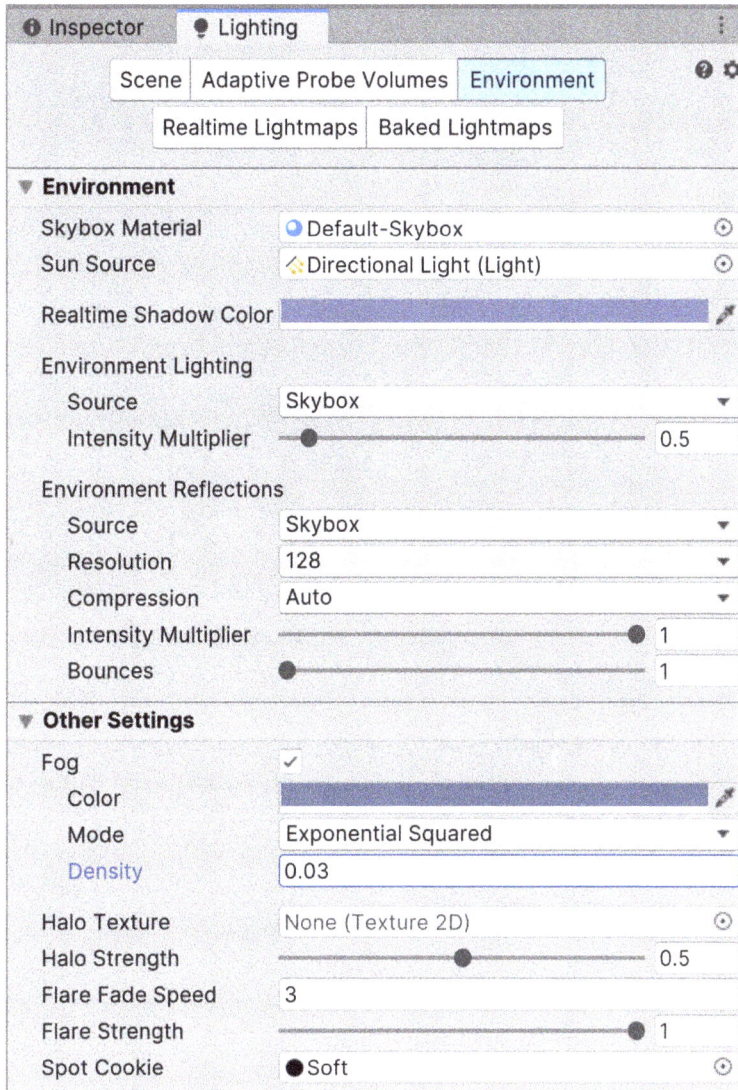

Figure 1.27 – Enabling Fog in our scene

As you can see, it's already much more spooky than it was previously, but there are still more options that we can change:

Figure 1.28 – Visual of fog in our scene

7. Go to the **Project** window, and select the Assets\Settings folder. From there, select the **PC_Renderer** object. From the **Inspector** window, go to the **Screen Space Ambient Occlusion** component. Afterward, change **Intensity** to 2 and **Radius** to 20:

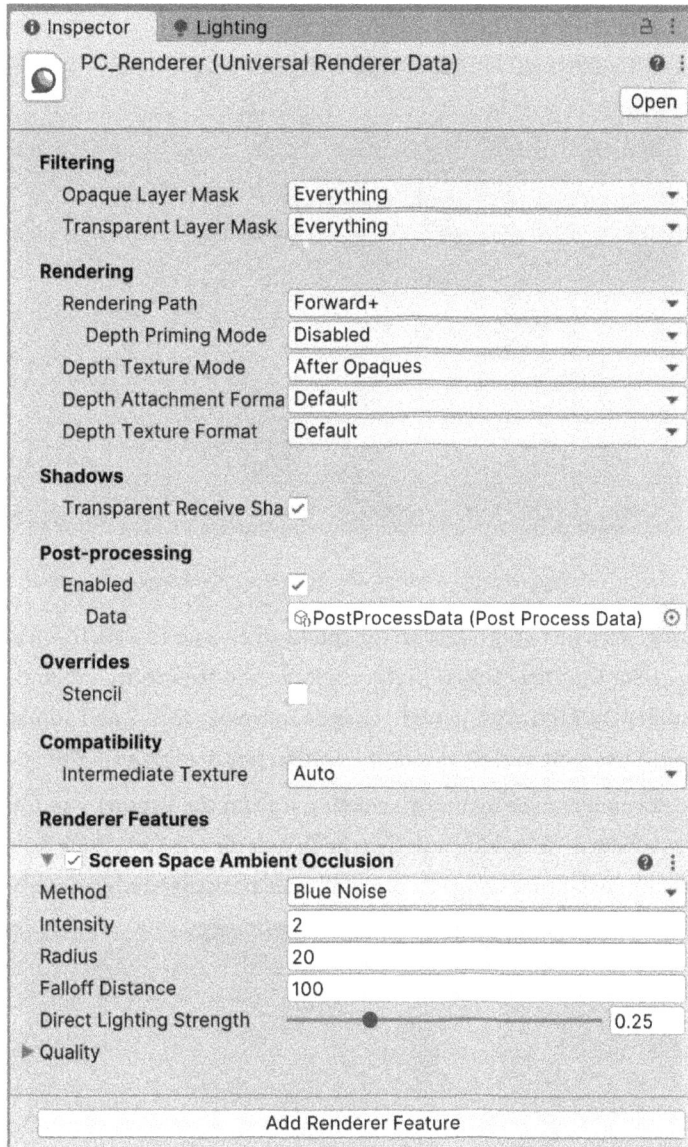

Figure 1.29 – Adjusting the Screen Space Ambient Occlusion effect

This will provide us with the following visual change:

Figure 1.30 – Viewing the Screen Space Ambient Occlusion effect

8. Lighting often has a big effect on the theme of a scene as well. If you are using the example map, select the **Directional Light** object in the **Hierarchy** tab and, from the **Inspector** tab, under the **Light** component, change **Intensity** to 0.5 and adjust **Color** to something darker. (I used the same color that I used in *step 5*, with a HEX of 5C7290.)

9. Open HorrorProfile again by selecting it from the **Project** window and then go to the Assets\Chapter 01 folder and then the **Inspector** window. Click the **Add Override** button and select **Post-processing | Depth of Field**. Check the **Mode** property and select **Gaussian**.

Figure 1.31 – Viewing the depth of field effect

10. Click the **Add Override** button and select **Post-processing | Shadows Midtones Highlights**. Check the **Shadows** property and drag the trackball on the slider at the bottom section to the left until the values are at 0.63:

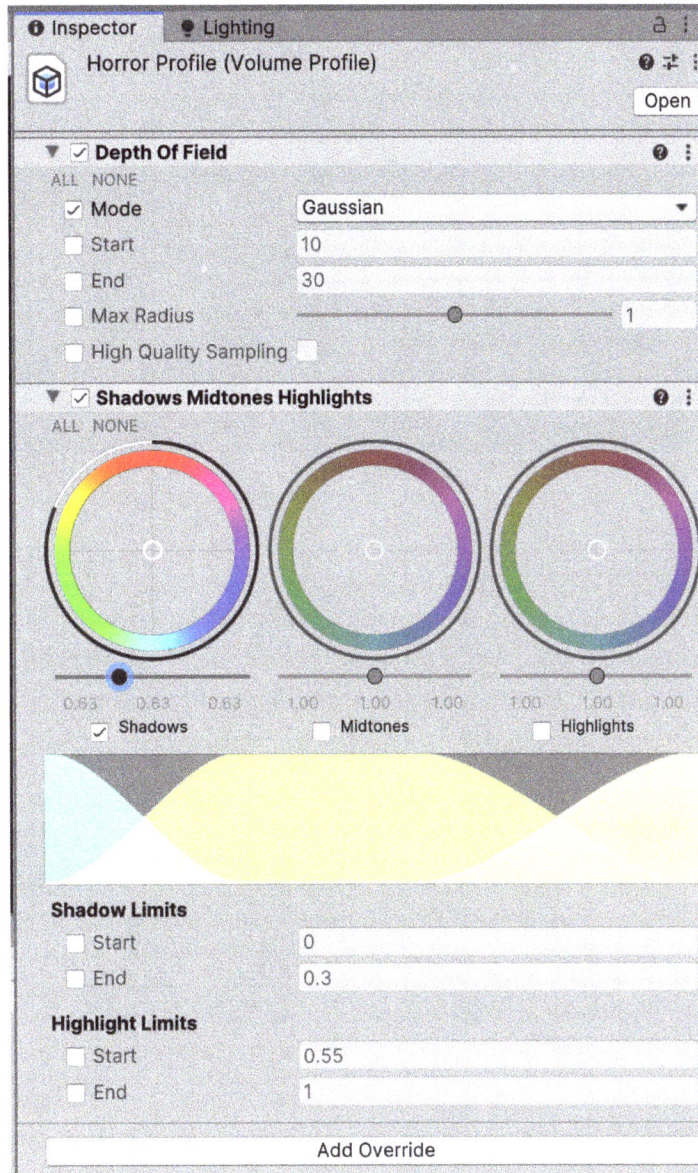

Figure 1.32 – Adjusting Shadow lightness

11. Save your game and then start it to see the effect of all of these changes:

Figure 1.33 – The final result of our horror look

How it works...

Ambient occlusion is a shading and rendering technique that's used to calculate how exposed each point in a scene is to ambient lighting. In this instance, the **Ambient Occlusion** option will calculate areas that should have additional shadows. Since our scene is filled with trees, this will make the undersides much darker than they were previously.

> Note
>
> For more information about the **Ambient Occlusion** effect, check out `https://github.com/Unity-Technologies/PostProcessing/wiki/Ambient-Occlusion`.

We previously used depth of field in the *Achieving a filmic look using grain, vignetting, and depth of field* recipe, so I'll refer to that explanation instead, but shadows, midtones, and highlights adjustments allow you to fine-tune the tonal balance of your scene, ensuring that the darkest areas, mid-level tones, and brightest parts of your image are all visually pleasing and coherent. In our case, we are making our shadows even darker than they would normally be. These adjustments are crucial for achieving a polished, professional look and can be used to create a specific mood or enhance the overall visual quality of your game.

Note

For more information about the **Shadows Midtones Highlights** effect, check out `https://docs.unity3d.com/6000.0/Documentation/Manual/urp/Post-Processing-Shadows-Midtones-Highlights.html`.

If you are interested in looking into the other options that post-processing has in URP, check out `https://docs.unity3d.com/6000.0/Documentation/Manual/urp/add-post-processing.html`.

Join our community on Discord

Join our community's Discord space for discussions with the authors and other readers: `https://packt.link/gamedevelopment`

2

Creating Your First Shader with Shader Graph

This chapter explores common **diffusion** techniques in modern shading pipelines. In 3D graphics, light interacts with surfaces differently based on direction and viewing angle, adding realism through shaders—specialized programs that simulate light behavior. For instance, a wooden and metal cube may share the same model but appear distinct due to their respective shaders.

In this chapter, you'll be introduced to **Shader Graph** in Unity, a visual tool for creating shaders without writing code. Whether you're new to shaders or have limited experience, this chapter provides the foundation to understand how shaders work and how to customize them. By the end of the chapter, you'll be able to create basic shaders and execute fundamental visual operations using Shader Graph.

In this chapter, we will be covering the following recipes:

- Implementing a simple Shader Graph
- Adding properties to a shader
- Using properties in a Surface Shader

Technical requirements

For this chapter, you will need Unity Editor version 6 Preview 6000.0.4f1. This chapter's instructions should work with minimal changes in future versions of the editor in projects that utilize the **Universal Render Pipeline (URP)**. The chapter's sample project was created using the Universal 3D Core template.

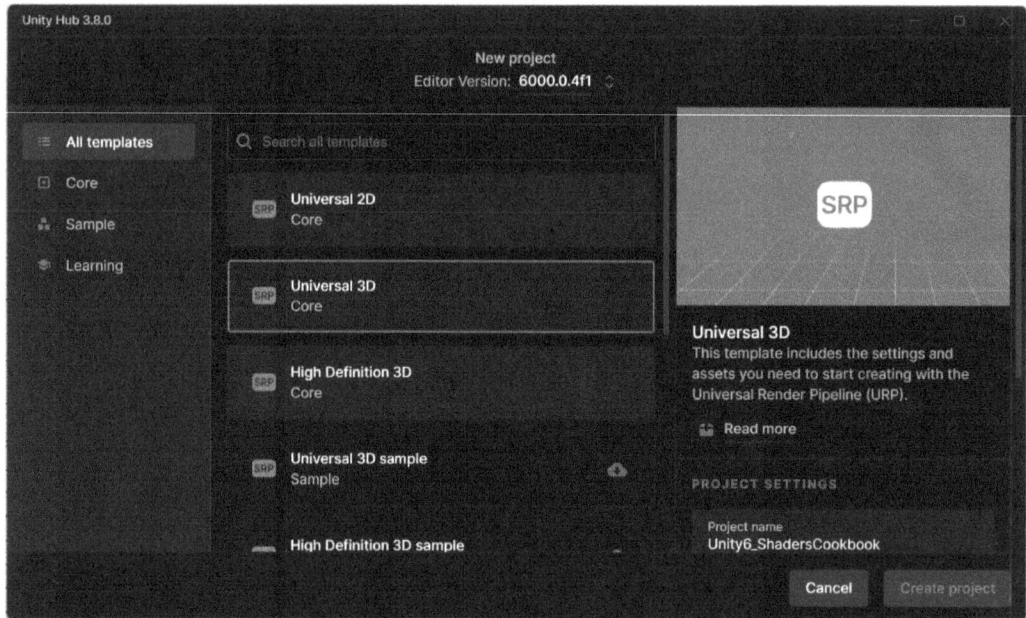

Figure 2.1 – Universal 3D Core template

The code files for this chapter can be found on GitHub at https://github.com/PacktPublishing/ Unity-6-Shaders-and-Effects-Cookbook. The necessary files for this chapter are organized in the Unity project in a folder named Chapter 02 (https://github.com/PacktPublishing/Unity-6-Shaders-and-Effects-Cookbook/tree/main/Unity6_ShadersCookbook/Assets/Chapter%20 02) on GitHub.

Implementing a simple Shader Graph

In Unity, **GameObjects** gain functionality through components. Every GameObject includes a Transform component, and additional built-in or custom components (via MonoBehaviour **scripts**) define behavior and appearance. **Renderers** determine an object's visual representation, with MeshRenderer being common for 3D models. While an object typically has one renderer, it can contain multiple materials, each wrapping a shader—the core element in 3D rendering.

With Shader Graph, creating shaders is more intuitive, allowing visual shader development without coding. This tool is particularly useful for projects using URP or the **High-Definition Render Pipeline** (HDRP).

The relationship between shaders, models, materials, and objects can be illustrated as follows:

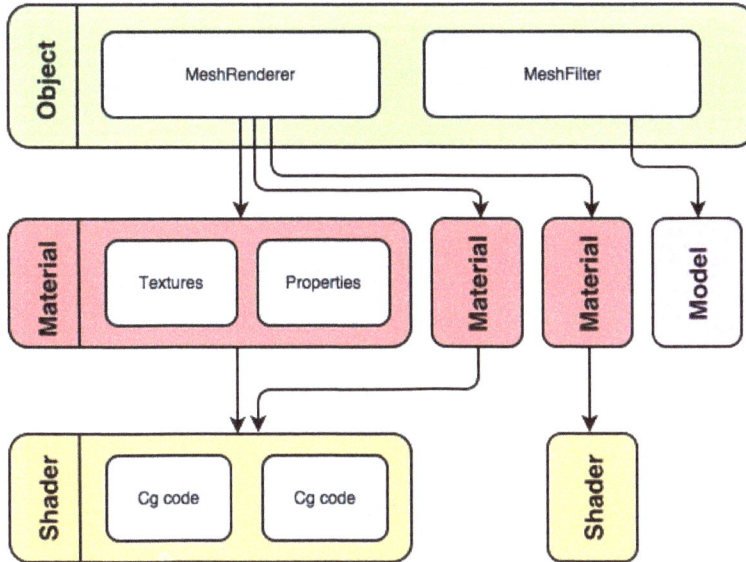

Figure 2.2 – Relationship between shaders, models, materials, and objects

Note that the preceding diagram mentions **Cg** code. While Cg is the default for the built-in renderer, URP and HDRP use HLSL code. However, with Shader Graph, you can create shaders without directly writing HLSL code.

Understanding the differences between these components is essential for comprehending how shaders work and effectively using Shader Graph to create them.

Getting ready

Before we create our first shader using Shader Graph, let's create a small scene for us to work with:

> **Note**
>
> If you are using the Unity project that came with this cookbook, you can open the `Chapter 02/Scenes/Starting Point` scene located at `https://github.com/PacktPublishing/Unity-6-Shaders-and-Effects-Cookbook/tree/main/Unity6_ShadersCookbook/Assets/Chapter%2002/Scenes` instead of completing the *Getting ready* section as it has been set up already.

1. Create a new scene by navigating to **File** | **New Scene**. A dialog window will appear, asking which template should be used. Select **Basic (URP)** and then click on the **Create** button.

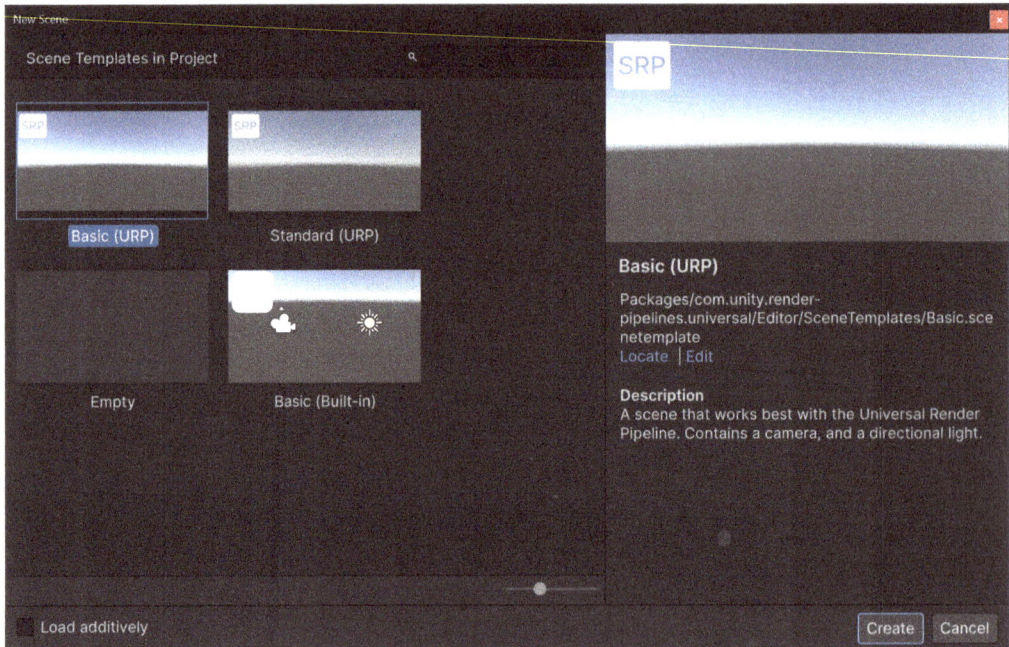

Figure 2.3 – Creating a Basic (URP) scene

2. Create a plane that will act as the ground by going to the Unity Editor and selecting **GameObject** | **3D Object** | **Plane** from the top menu bar.

Figure 2.4 – Creating a plane

3. Select the plane in the **Hierarchy** window and then go into the **Inspector** window. Right-click on the **Transform** component and select **Reset** to reset the position of the object to (0, 0, 0), which is the center of our game world.

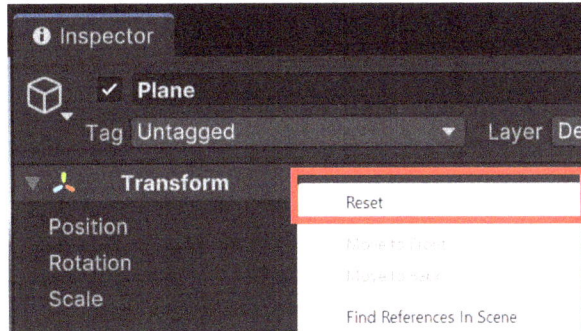

Figure 2.5 – Resetting the Transform component

4. You can then double-click on the object in the **Hierarchy** window in order to center the camera in the **Scene** view to the location.

5. Create a sphere by going to **GameObject | 3D Object | Sphere**. Once it has been created, select it and go to the **Inspector** window. Change the position to (0, 1, 0) so that it is above the origin of the world and the previously created plane.

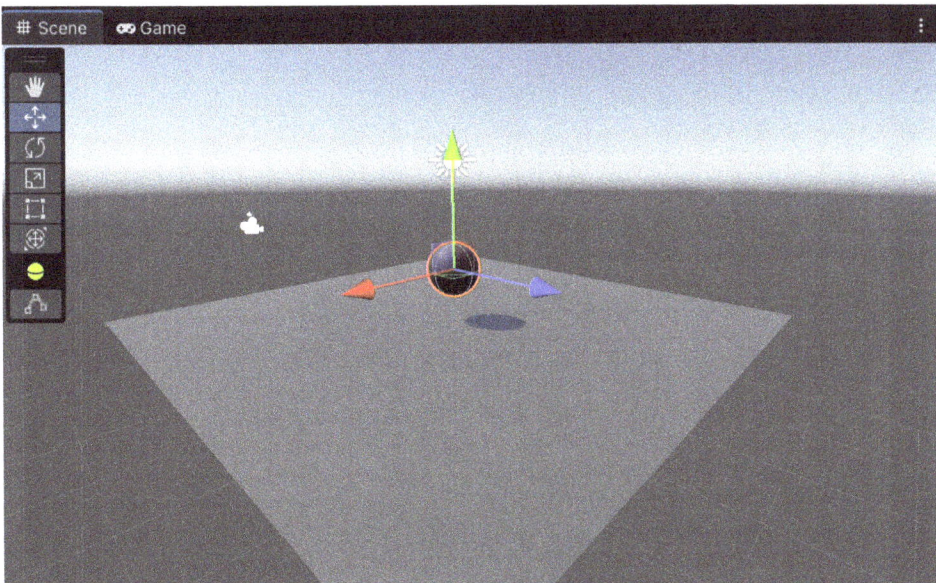

Figure 2.6 – Creating a sphere

6. Create two more spheres and place them to the left and right of the first sphere at positions (-2, 1, 0) and (2, 1, 0), respectively.

> Note
>
> One quick way to do this is to duplicate the objects by pressing *Ctrl + D* while having the object selected in the **Hierarchy** window. You can rename the objects via the top text box in the **Inspector** window.

7. Confirm that you have a directional light (it should be listed in the **Hierarchy** window). If not, add it by selecting **GameObject** | **Light** | **Directional Light** to make it easier to see your changes and how your shaders react to light.

8. Create a folder for organizing your Shader Graphs. In the **Project** window in the Unity Editor, right-click and select **Create** | **Folder**. Rename the folder Chapter 02.

9. Inside the Chapter 02 folder, create three more folders: Scenes, Shaders, and Materials.

10. Save this scene so you can use it as a foundation for other recipes later on.

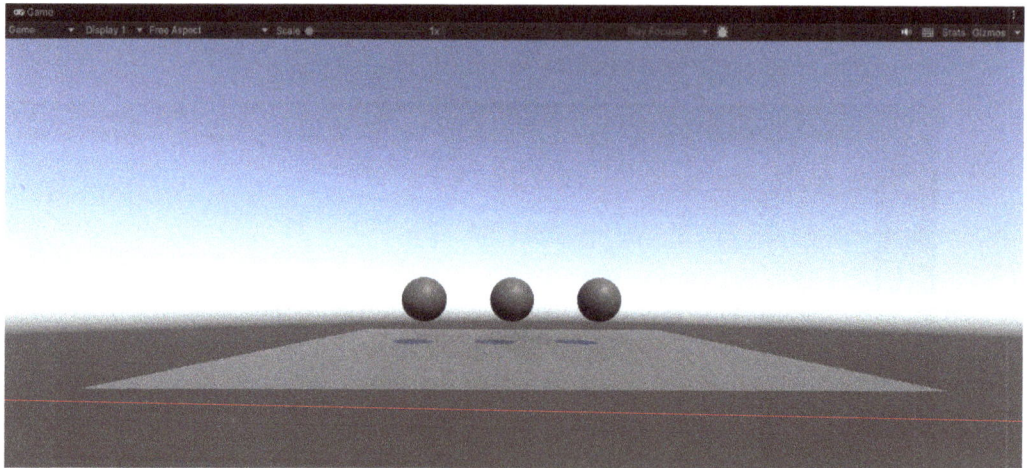

Figure 2.7 – Final starting point

How to do it...

With our scene set up, we can start creating our first shader using Shader Graph:

1. In the **Project** tab, right-click on the Shaders folder and select **Create** | **Shader Graph** | **URP** | **Lit Shader Graph**. Name the new shader StandardDiffuseShader.

The Lit shader type is a **Physically Based Rendering (PBR)** shader that simulates realistic lighting effects. It supports features such as reflections, shadows, and advanced material properties to achieve high-quality visuals.

2. Double-click on **StandardDiffuseShader** to open the Shader Graph editor. This will launch a visual interface where you can create and edit your shader.

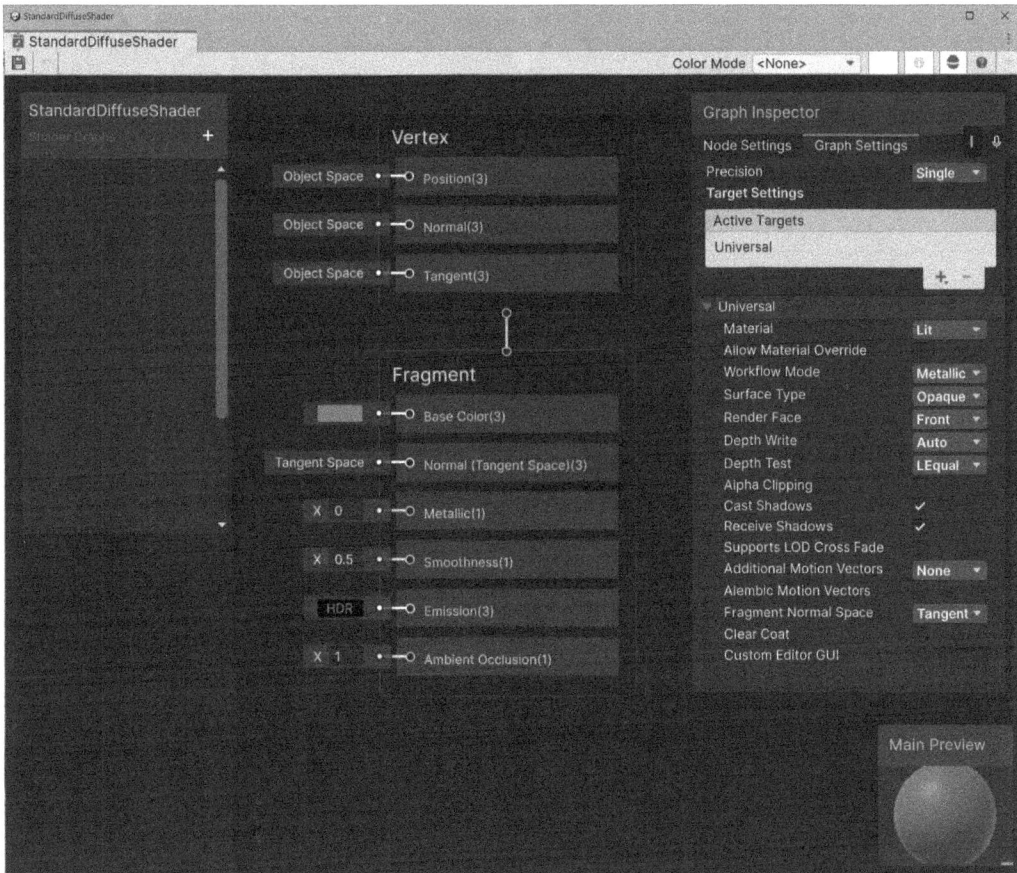

Figure 2.8 – The Shader Graph editor

In the Shader Graph editor, you'll see a default setup with the **Master Stack**, which is split into the **Vertex** and **Fragment** contexts.

The Shader Graph window features several key elements, including **Blackboard**, **Graph Inspector**, and **Main Preview**. Each of these components can be repositioned within the workspace to suit your preferences.

The **Blackboard** (the area on the top left) is where you manage shader properties and organize them for easy access. **Graph Inspector** provides detailed settings for the nodes and properties within your Shader Graph. **Main Preview** offers a real-time visual representation of how your shader will look when applied to objects in your scene.

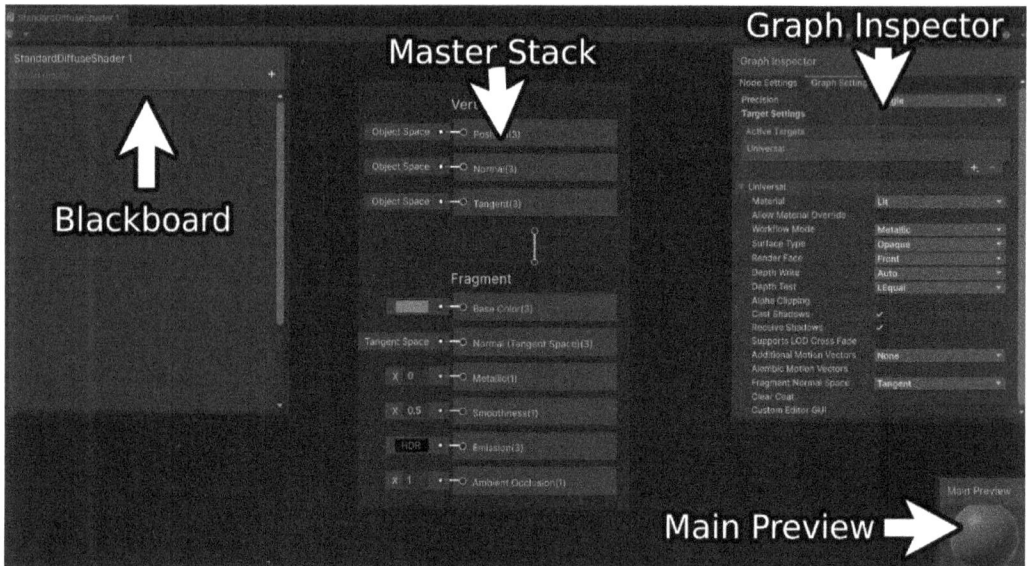

Figure 2.9 – Location of Shader Graph elements

Tip

The top right of Shader Graph has buttons that will let you toggle the visibility of the different elements. If you'd like to turn off **Blackboard**, **Graph Inspector**, or **Main Preview**, that is where you can easily do it.

When you resize the Shader Graph window, these elements will automatically anchor to the nearest corner, ensuring they remain accessible and well-organized regardless of the window size.

Note

To move within the Shader Graph editor, you can use the mouse wheel to zoom in and out, and you can hold the middle mouse button and drag to pan the graph. Alternatively, you can also use *Alt* + left mouse button.

3. From the **Blackboard**, underneath the shader's name, you'll see some greyed-out text that says Shader Graphs. Double-click on it and it'll become editable. Change the text to Shader Graphs/Chapter 02 and press *Enter*.

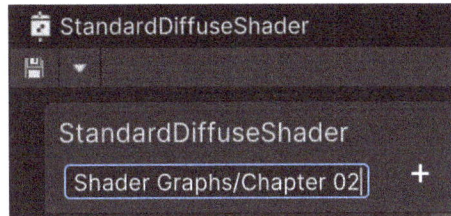

Figure 2.10 – Changing the Shader's location

This will change the path of our shader graph, making it easier to find the appropriate one depending on what recipe we're working on.

4. Save the Shader Graph by clicking on the **Save** icon (icon that looks like a floppy disk) in the top-left corner of the Shader Graph editor. This will compile your shader.

5. Exit the Shader Graph and return to the Unity Editor. Create a new material by right-clicking on the Materials folder and selecting **Create | Material**. Name it StandardDiffuseMaterial.

6. In the **Inspector** window, select the **Shader** dropdown and choose Shader Graphs/ Chapter 02/StandardDiffuseShader (or your custom path if different). This assigns your shader to the material.

7. Drag StandardDiffuseMaterial from the **Project** tab onto the spheres in your scene or onto the **Inspector** tab of the objects to assign the material.

Figure 2.11 – Assigning the material

> **Note**
>
> To make it easier to read relevant properties, I clicked on the arrow to the left of the component's name to condense the properties from the **Inspector** window.

How it works...

Shaders control how surfaces interact with light, creating various visual effects. In Unity, shaders are encapsulated within materials, which are applied to renderers on GameObjects.

After creating a shader in Shader Graph, it is saved, compiled, and assigned to a material. For example, we created `StandardDiffuseMaterial` using `StandardDiffuseShader`. Applying this material to spheres in our scene showcases how the shader interacts with lighting and the environment.

Maintaining a structured project is essential. Organizing assets into folders for shaders and materials keeps the project manageable. A simple test scene with a ground plane, spheres, and directional light provides an effective environment for shader visualization.

With Shader Graph, we can adjust visual properties like color, transparency, and reflectivity by modifying nodes. These changes are instantly reflected in the scene, enabling real-time feedback and an iterative design process.

Shaders are integral to graphics rendering, controlling how surfaces interact with light to create various visual effects. In Unity, shaders are encapsulated within materials, which are then applied to renderers on GameObjects.

After creating a shader with Shader Graph, the shader is saved and compiled, ready to be used in materials. In our example, we created a material named `StandardDiffuseMaterial` and assigned our custom shader, `StandardDiffuseShader`, to it. Applying this material to the spheres in our scene allows us to see the shader in action, demonstrating how it interacts with the scene's lighting and environment.

By adjusting nodes in the Shader Graph editor, we can change how the shader affects the material's appearance by altering its color, transparency, reflective properties, and so on. These changes are immediately reflected in the scene, providing real-time feedback to us allowing us to easily iterate on our design.

Adding properties to a shader

The properties of a shader are crucial for the shader pipeline as they allow the artist or user to assign textures and tweak shader values. Properties enable you to expose GUI elements in a material's **Inspector** window, providing a visual means of adjusting shader parameters without the need for a separate editor.

Getting ready

Let's see how this works in our current shader, `StandardDiffuse`, by creating some properties and learning more about the syntax involved. For this example, we will refit the shader we created previously. Instead of using a texture to create the visuals, the shader will only use a color and some other properties that we will be able to change directly from the **Inspector** window:

1. Start by duplicating `StandardDiffuseShader`. You can do this by selecting it from the **Inspector** tab and pressing *Ctrl + D*. This will create a copy called `StandardDiffuseShader 1`. Go ahead and rename it `StandardColor`.

2. Next, create a new material (`StandardColorMaterial`) and set the shader it uses to the `Shader Graphs/Chapter 02/StandardColor` selection.

3. Assign the material to the spheres in our scene:

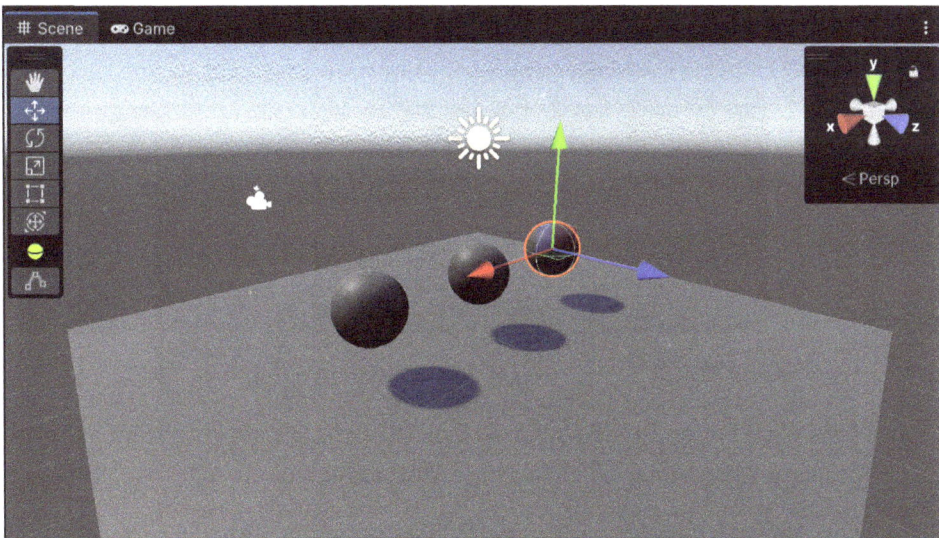

Figure 2.12 – Assigning the material

The project should look the same as what we had in the previous recipe since we are using a duplicate of the previous shader.

How to do it...

With Shader Graph, we can visually create and manage shader properties without writing code. Here's how you can set up and modify shader properties using Shader Graph:

1. Double-click on StandardColorShader to open the Shader Graph editor.

2. From the **Blackboard**, click the + button in the **Blackboard** on the left-hand side of the menu to add a new property. Select **Color** and leave its default name of Color. This will create a color property that you can use to change the color of the material.

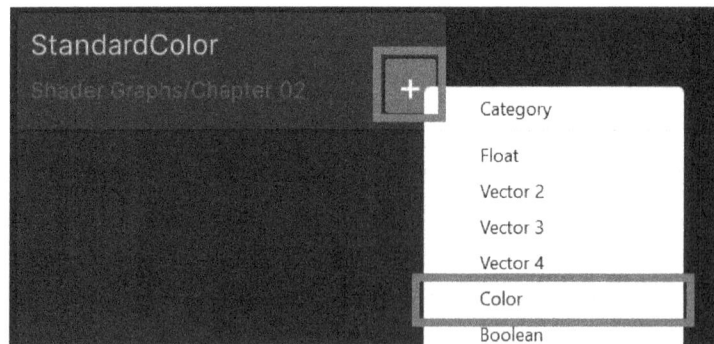

Figure 2.13 – Creating a color

3. Drag the **Color** property from the **Blackboard** to the graph area and connect it to the **Base Color(3)** input of the **Master Stack** node under the **Fragment** section.

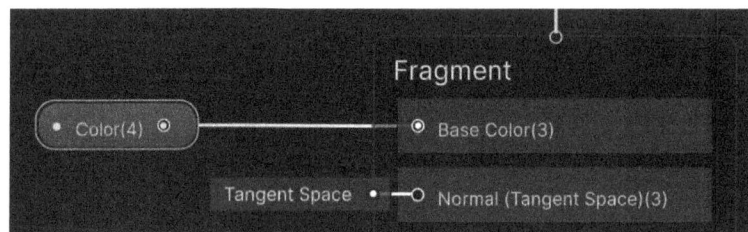

Figure 2.14 – Connecting a color

4. Click the + button in the **Blackboard** on the left-hand side of the menu to add a new property. Select **Float** and give a name of Glossiness.

   This property functions as a standard floating-point variable, allowing you to input numerical values in the **Graph Inspector**. Additionally, you can enhance usability by converting it into a slider, setting a custom range for more precise control.

5. With the **Glossiness** property selected, on the right-hand side, go to **Graph Inspector** and note the properties that are listed. Change **Default Value** to 0.5 and change **Mode** to **Slider**. Note the **Min** and **Max** values of 0 and 1.

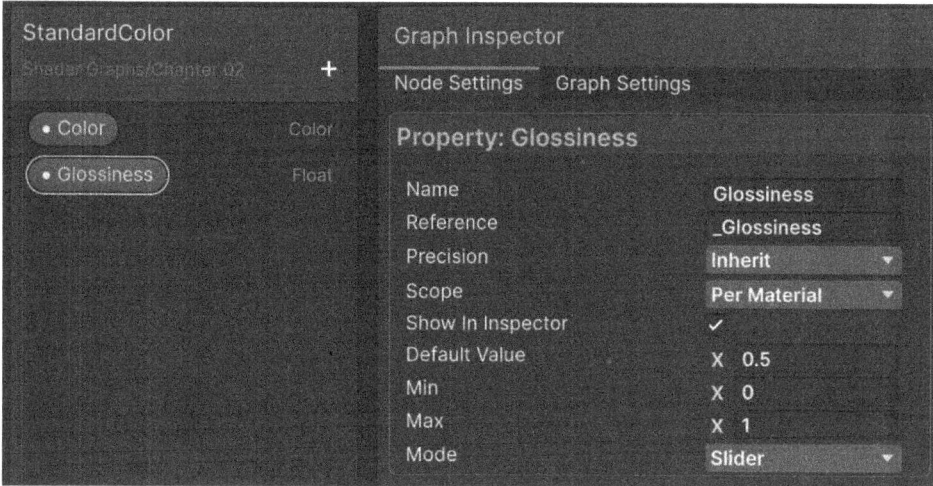

Figure 2.15 – Creating the Glossiness property

6. Drag the **Glossiness** property from the **Blackboard** to the graph area and connect it to the **Smoothness** input of the **Master Stack** node under the **Fragment** section:

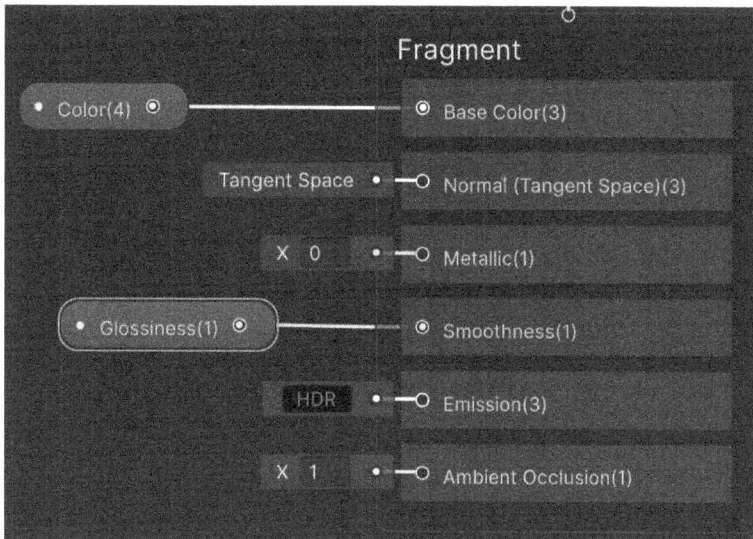

Figure 2.16 – The Shader Graph editor

7. Save the Shader Graph by clicking on the **Save** icon that looks like a floppy disk in the top-left corner of the Shader Graph editor. Return to the Unity Editor.

8. At this point, you should notice that the **Surface Inputs** section has properties for both items we created:

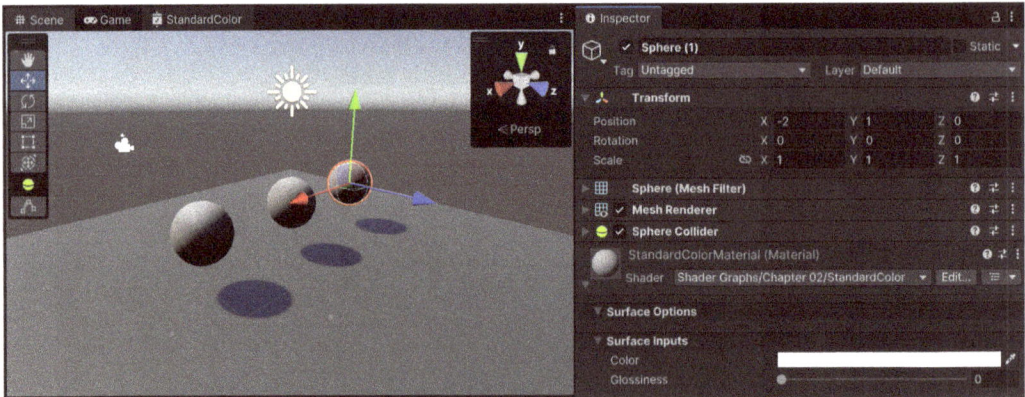

Figure 2.17 – Properties are visible

If we change the values, we should see all of the items with the material attached to it change:

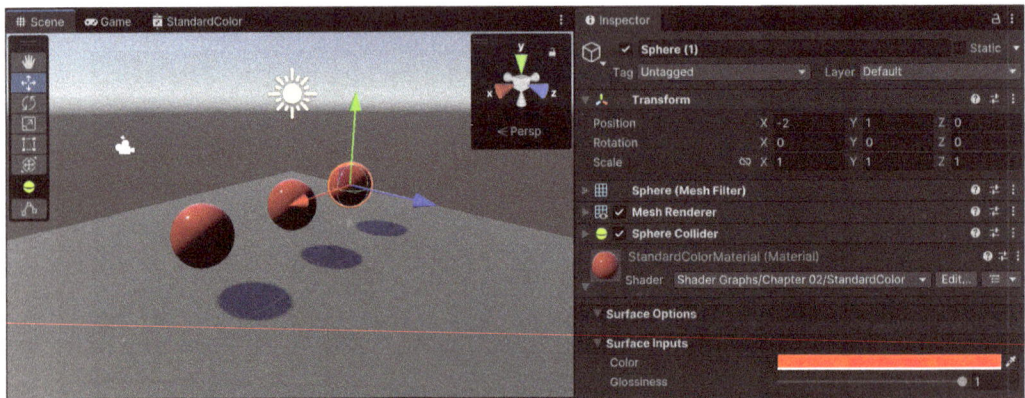

Figure 2.18 – Adjusting material properties

How it works...

Shader properties in Shader Graph allow you to create flexible, customizable shaders by exposing parameters that can be adjusted directly within the **Inspector** window.

The **Blackboard** in Shader Graph is the primary interface for managing shader properties and allows you to rename properties, change their default values (which is what they will be set to upon first being created), and categorize them for better organization.

When we select a property in the **Blackboard**, the **Node Settings** menu allows us to define several useful properties that will be used by us over the course of the book. For instance, the **Reference** property is how we can access our properties via code as we will see later.

> Note
>
> Default values are only set the first time a shader is assigned to a new material. After that, the material's values are used. Changing the **Default Value** property will not affect the values of existing materials that use the shader. This is a good thing, of course, but often forgotten. So, if you change a value and notice something not changing, this could be the reason why.

You can create various types of properties such as colors, textures, vectors, and floats directly from the **Blackboard**. By default, the **Show in Inspector** property is turned on when we create a property, so properties defined in the **Blackboard** are exposed in the material's **Inspector** window, making it easy for artists and developers to tweak shader parameters without diving into the shader code.

Shader Graph supports a wide range of properties, each serving a different purpose. Some of the most commonly used properties are as follows:

- **Float**: Numerical properties for scalar values such as the glossiness we used earlier; the range includes a min and max value for sliders in **Inspector**
- **Vector**: Useful for representing directional data or multi-component values such as positions or normals
- **Color**: A property for setting colors, often used for albedo, emissive, or tint colors
- **Boolean**: A true/false property, often used for toggling shader features
- **Texture2D**: Allows for texture input, enabling the use of image files to define surface details

Once properties are created in the **Blackboard**, they need to be connected to the shader's logic through nodes. In this example, we directly connected the property to the **Master Stack**; in the next recipe, we will be using additional nodes to perform more complex actions. By exposing these properties to the material's **Inspector** window, you make it easy for artists and developers to fine-tune the appearance and behavior of shaders in real time, enhancing both the creative process and the efficiency of shader development.

Using properties in a Surface Shader

Now that we have created some properties in Shader Graph, let's hook them up to the shader so that we can tweak the value and make the material process much more interactive. Shader properties allow users to tweak shader values directly from the material's **Inspector** window, providing a flexible and user-friendly way to adjust shader parameters without modifying the shader code itself.

Getting ready

For this recipe, we will refit the shader we created previously. Instead of using a texture to create the visuals, the shader will only use a color and some other properties that we will be able to change directly from the **Inspector** window:

1. Start by duplicating `StandardDiffuseShader`. You can do this by selecting it from the **Inspector** window and pressing *Ctrl + D*. This will create a copy called `StandardDiffuseShader 1`. Go ahead and rename it `ParameterExample`.

2. Next, create a new material (`ParameterExampleMaterial`) and set the shader it uses to the `Shader Graphs/ParameterExample` selection.

3. Assign the material to the spheres in our scene:

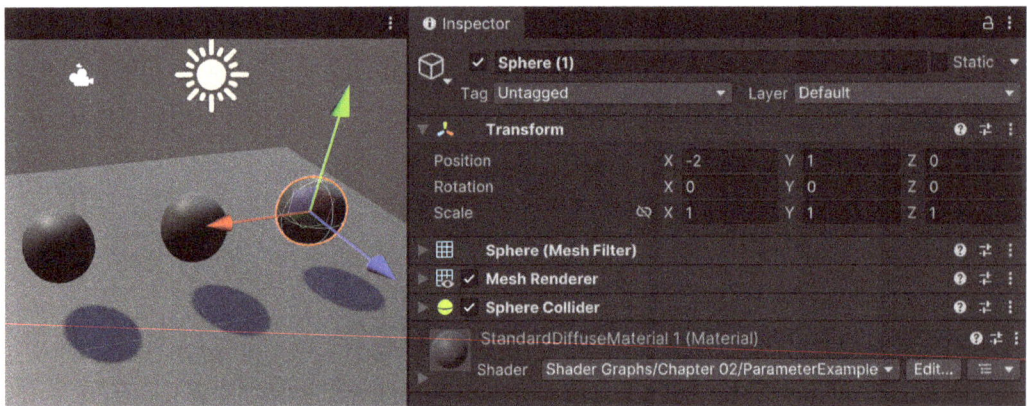

Figure 2.19 – Assigning materials

How to do it…

The following steps show you how to use the properties in a Shader Graph:

1. Double-click on `ParameterExample` to open the Shader Graph editor.

2. Click the + button in the **Blackboard** on the left-hand side of the menu to add a new property. Select **Color** and leave its default name of `Color`.

3. With the **Color** property selected, on the right-hand side, go to **Graph Inspector** and note the properties that are listed. Change **Default Value** to white by clicking on the color box. Change the color mode from **HSV** to **RGB** and **0** to **1.0** and then set the values to 1, 1, 1, 1, or just type in the FFFFFF **Hexadecimal** value.

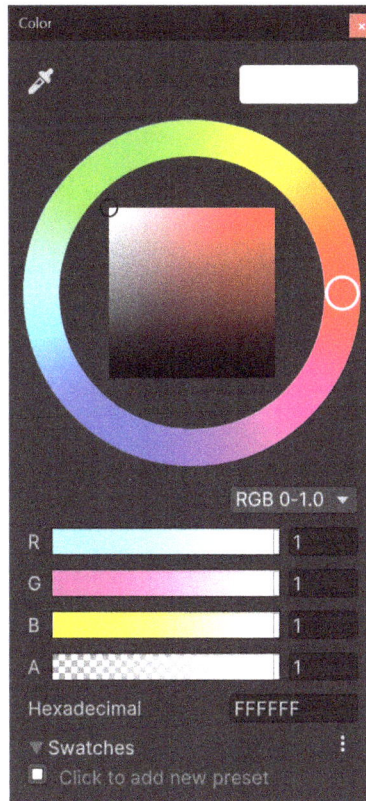

Figure 2.20 – Setting white color

4. Click the + button in the **Blackboard** on the left-hand side of the menu to add a new property. Select Color and set the new color's name to AmbientColor. With the **AmbientColor** property selected, on the right-hand side, go to **Graph Inspector** and note the properties that are listed. Change **Default Value** to white in the same manner as the above steps.

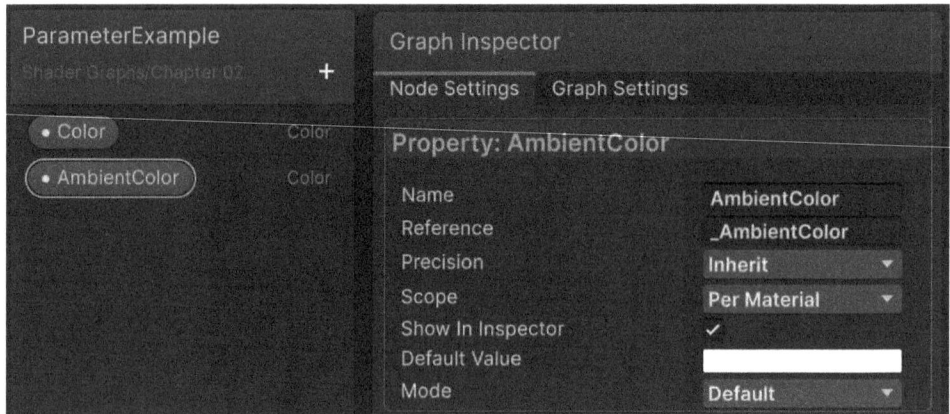

Figure 2.21 – Setting AmbientColor properties

5. Next, drag **Color** and **Ambient Color** out into the graph. To the right of their placement, right-click and select **Add Node**. In the menu that pops up, type Add, select the node (**Math | Basic | Add**), and press *Enter*.

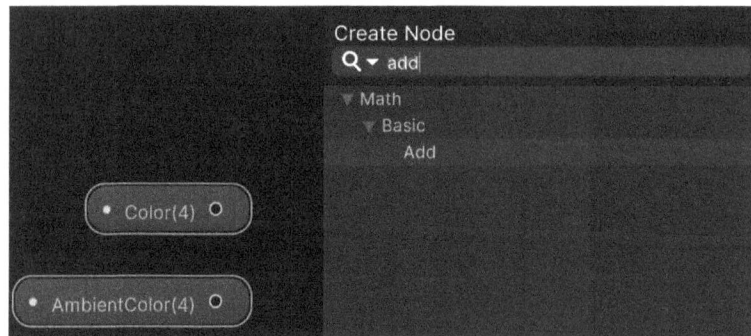

Figure 2.22 – Creating the Add node

Note

If you need to move your nodes around, you can click and hold the mouse button to create a selection box to highlight multiple nodes and move them around.

6. Connect the output of the **Color(4)** node to the **A** input of the **Add** node and the output of the **AmbientColor(4)** node to **B**.

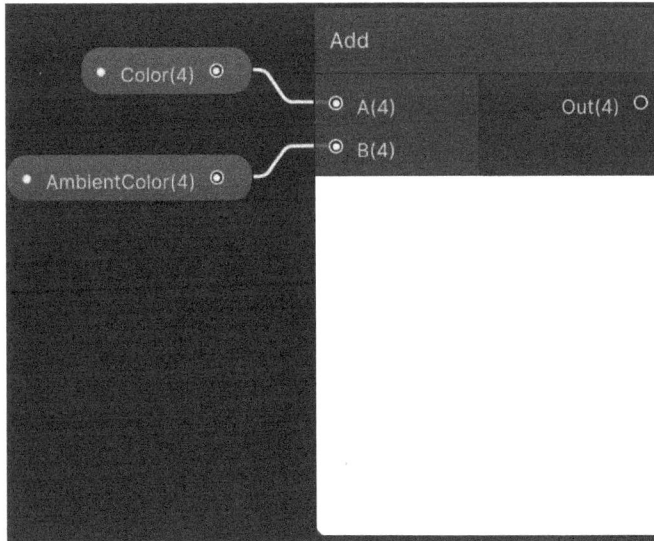

Figure 2.23 – Color + Ambient Color

7. Click the + button in the **Blackboard** on the left-hand side of the menu to add a new property. Select **Float** and give a name of SaturationPower.

8. With the **SaturationPower** property selected, on the right-hand side, go to **Graph Inspector** and note the properties that are listed. Change **Default Value** to 2.5 and change **Mode** to **Slider**. Change the **Max** value to 10.

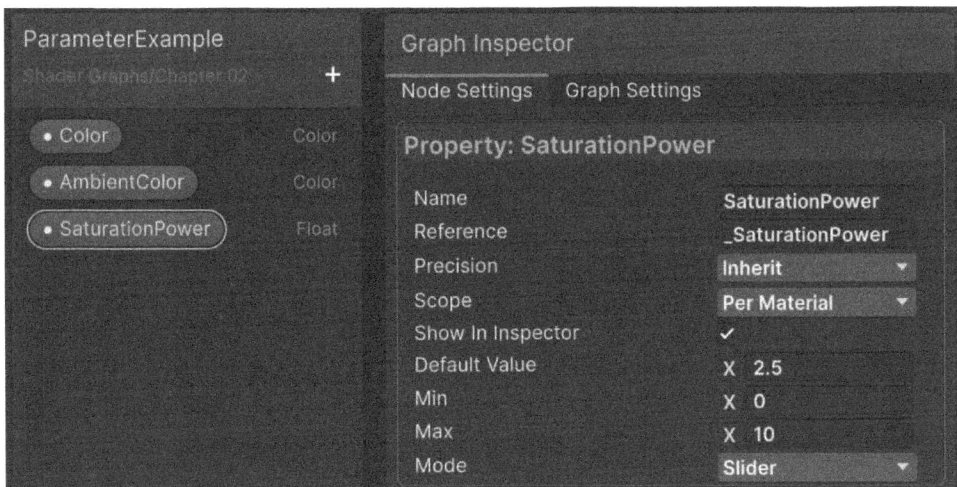

Figure 2.24 – SaturationPower setup

9. To the right of the **Add** node, right-click and select **Add Node**. On the menu that pops up, type Power, select the node (**Math | Basic | Power**), and press *Enter*.

10. Connect the **Out** of the **Add** node to the **A** input of the **Power** node. Then drag the **SaturationPower** node onto the graph. Connect the **SaturationPower** node output into the **B** of the **Power** node. Finally, connect the **Out** of the **Power** node to the **Base Color (3)** input of the **Fragment** of the **Master Stack**:

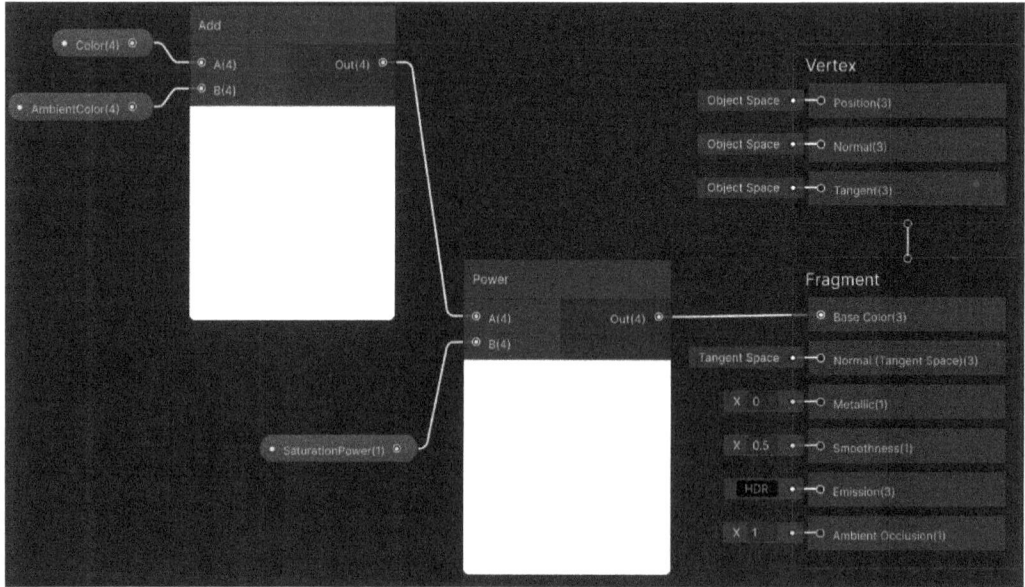

Figure 2.25 – Power node setup

Note

The **Power** node will perform the equivalent math function of power. So, the **A** argument is the value that we want to raise to a power, while the **B** argument is the power that we want to raise it to.

To find out more about the **Power** node, we can look at the node library that Shader Graph has available at https://docs.unity3d.com/Packages/com.unity.shadergraph@17.0/manual/Power-Node.html. This can also be accessed by selecting any node in Shader Graph and pressing the *F1* key.

11. Save the Shader Graph by clicking on the **Save** icon (the icon that looks like a floppy disk) in the top-left corner of the Shader Graph editor and return to the Unity Editor.

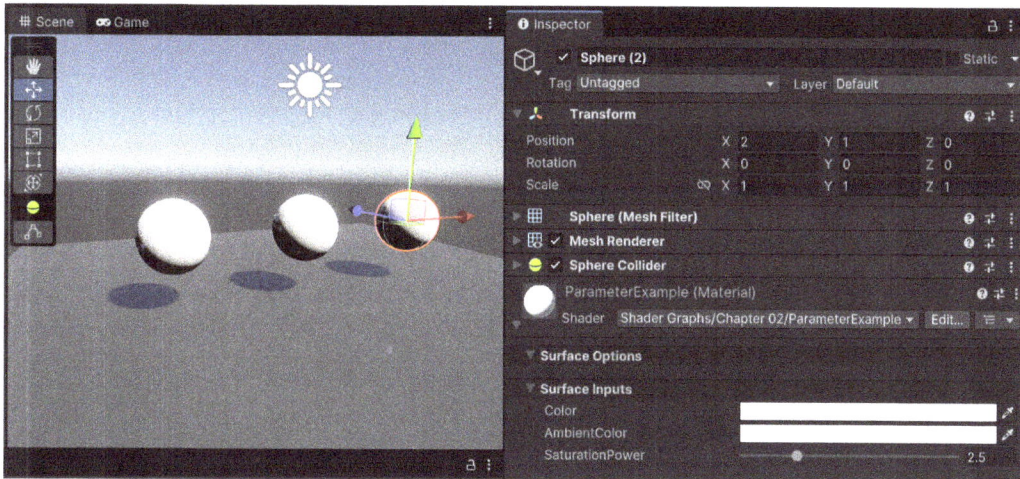

Figure 2.26 – Default settings

12. After doing this, modify the parameters of the material and see how it affects the objects within the scene.

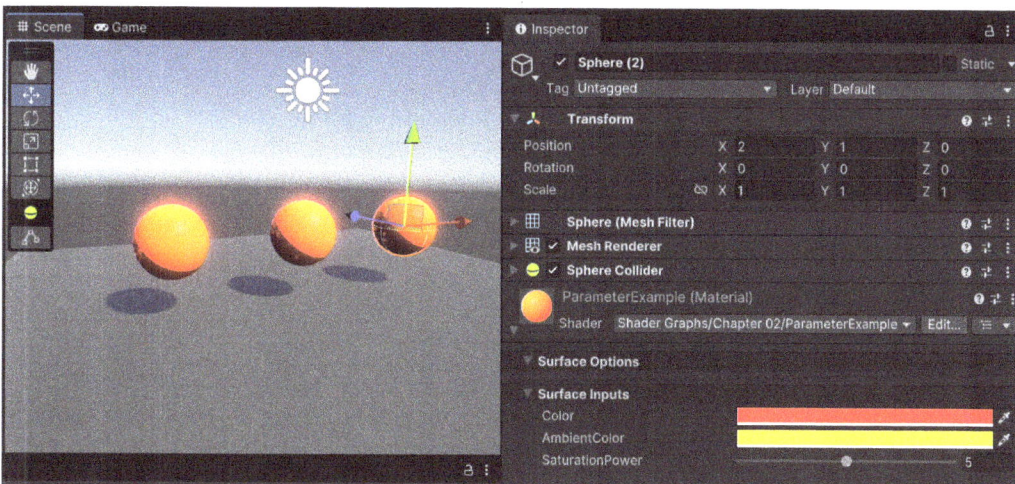

Figure 2.27 – With adjusted colors

How it works...

The **Color** property sets the base color of the material. This property is exposed in the **Inspector** tab, allowing users to change the color dynamically. Similarly, the **AmbientColor** property defines an additional color that can be added to the base color, and it is also exposed for real-time adjustments. These two properties are combined using an **Add** node, which adds the two colors together, resulting in a combined color that reflects both inputs.

A unique aspect of this shader is the SaturationPower property. This property acts as an exponent that modifies the intensity or saturation of the combined color. By feeding the combined color into a **Power** node, with SaturationPower as the exponent, the shader can dynamically adjust the color's intensity and saturation based on the slider value provided in **Inspector**. This allows for fine-tuning the visual effect, making it easy to achieve the desired look.

The final output of these operations is connected to the **Base Color** input of the **Master Stack** node, which determines the overall color of the material.

By exposing these properties in the material's **Inspector** window, we were able to tweak the shader parameters in real time, receiving immediate visual feedback. This makes it easy to adjust the material's appearance without diving into the shader code. The combination of these properties and nodes allows for the creation of dynamic visual effects, providing a high level of control over the final output.

> Note
>
> Materials are assets. This means that any changes that are made to them while your game is running in the editor are permanent. If you have changed the value of a property by mistake, you can undo it using *Ctrl + Z*.
>
> For more info on what materials being assets means see the note in the *Scrolling textures by modifying UV values* recipe in *Chapter 4*.

3

Working with Surfaces

Surfaces were introduced in *Chapter 2, Creating Your First Shader with Shader Graph*. This chapter explores them in greater depth. Creating a shader using surface inputs involves two key steps:

First, you have to specify certain physical properties of the material that you want to describe with characteristics like diffuse color, smoothness, and transparency using Shader Graph nodes (e.g., Color, Smoothness, and Alpha).

Secondly, the output from these nodes is connected to the **Master Stack**. The **Master Stack** processes these properties based on the lighting model and graph settings, determining how the material interacts with light.

Mastering surface materials is essential for creating visually compelling and optimized shaders in Unity. By effectively using Shader Graph, you can enhance visual quality and immersion in your projects.

We'll start with a simple matte material and progress to holographic projections.

In this chapter, we will be covering the following recipes:

- Implementing diffuse shading
- Accessing and modifying packed arrays
- Creating a shader with normal mapping
- Creating a holographic shader

Technical requirements

For this chapter, you will need Unity Editor version 6 Preview 6000.0.7f1. This chapter's instructions should work with minimal changes in future versions of the editor in projects that utilize the **Universal Render Pipeline** (**URP**). The chapter's sample project was created using the **Universal 3D Core** template.

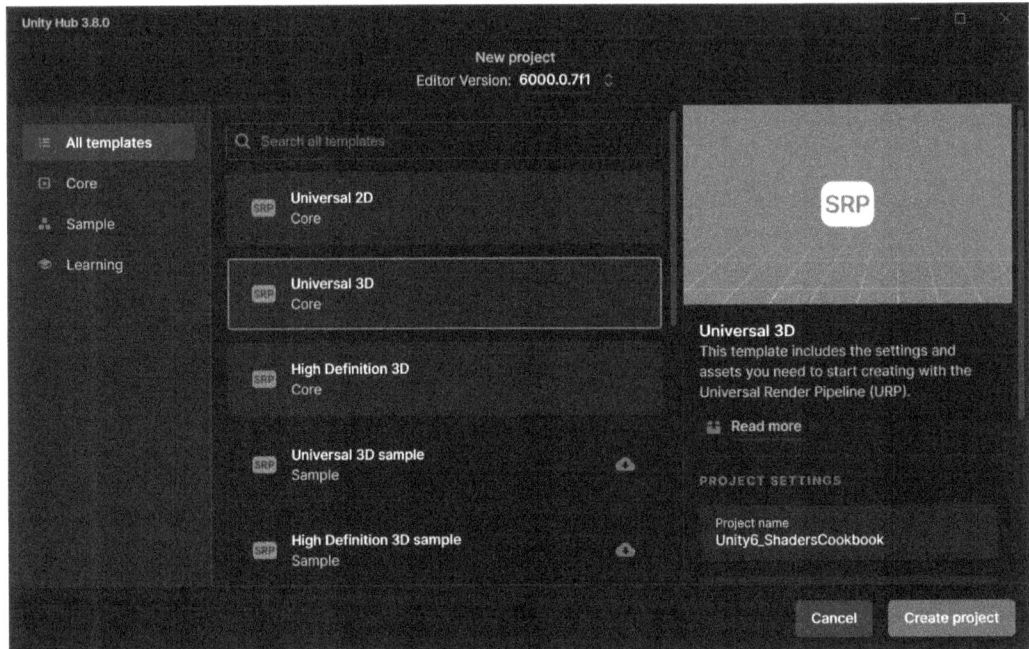

Figure 3.1 – Universal URP project

The code files for this chapter can be found on GitHub at https://github.com/PacktPublishing/ Unity-6-Shaders-and-Effects-Cookbook. The necessary files for this chapter are organized in the Unity project in a folder named Chapter 03 on GitHub (https://github.com/PacktPublishing/ Unity-6-Shaders-and-Effects-Cookbook/tree/main/Unity6_ShadersCookbook/Assets/ Chapter%2003).

Implementing diffuse shading

Before we start our journey into texture mapping, it is important to understand how diffuse materials work. Certain objects might have a uniform color and smooth surface but are not smooth enough to shine in reflected light. These matte materials are best represented with a **diffuse shader**. A diffuse shader is a type of shader used in 3D graphics to simulate the way light interacts with a matte surface. It models how light is scattered in many directions when it hits a rough surface, giving the object a consistent color regardless of the angle of the light source. In the real world, pure diffuse materials do not exist; however, diffuse shaders are relatively cheap to implement and are largely applied in games with low-poly aesthetics, so they're worth learning about.

A quick way is to start with Unity's default Shader Graph and edit it to remove any additional texture information.

Getting ready

Before starting this recipe, you should have created a Shader Graph before and be familiar with its layout. For instructions on creating a Standard Shader Graph, look at the *Implementing a simple Shader Graph* recipe of *Chapter 2, Creating Your First Shader with Shader Graph*, if you haven't done so already.

How to do it...

With our scene set up, we can start creating our diffuse shader using Shader Graph:

1. In the **Project** tab, right-click on the Shaders folder and select **Create | Shader Graph | URP | Lit Shader Graph**.

2. Name the new shader SimpleDiffuse and double click on it to open Shader Graph.

3. In the **Blackboard** (left side), double-click on the grayed-out **Shader Graphs** text and change it to Shader Graphs/Chapter 03.

4. Then click the + button and choose **Color**. You should see the property show up. Leave the default name of **Color**.

Figure 3.2 – Creating the Color property

5. With the newly created **Color** property selected, we can now go to **Graph Inspector** on the right side and set **Default Value** to white (RGBA = (1, 1, 1, 1)) by double-clicking on the box with its value.

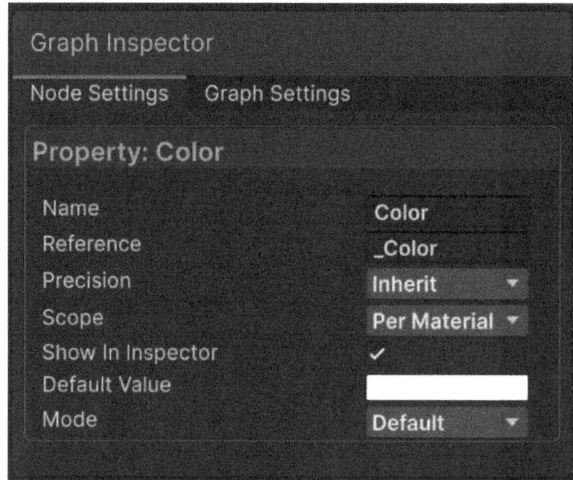

Figure 3.3 – Color property default value

6. Drag the **Color** property from the **Blackboard** to the graph area and connect it to the **Base Color(3)** input of the **Master Stack** node in the **Fragment** section.

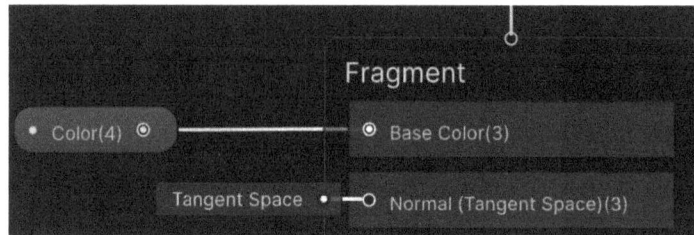

Figure 3.4 – Assigning the Color property

7. Next, in **Graph Inspector**, switch to the **Graph Settings** section. From there, ensure that **Material** is set to **Lit** and **Surface Type** is set to **Opaque**.

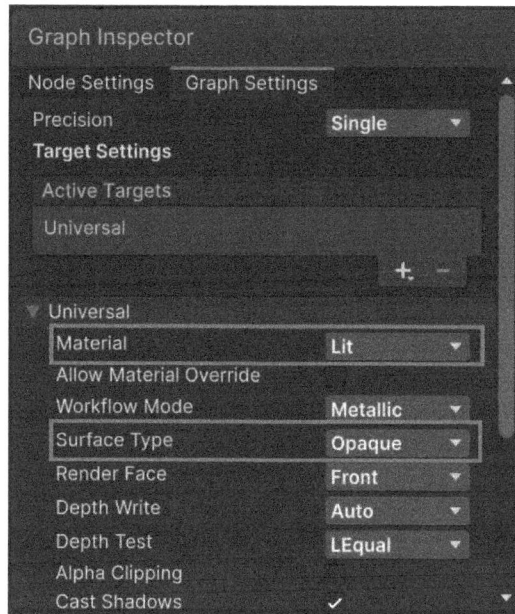

Figure 3.5 – Verifying graph settings

8. Save the Shader Graph by clicking on the **Save** icon that looks like a floppy disk in the top-left corner of the Shader Graph editor and return to the Unity Editor.

9. Next, create a new material (`SimpleDiffuseMat`) and set the shader it uses to the `Shader Graphs/Chapter 03/SimpleDiffuse` selection.

Tip

To quickly create a material based on a certain shader graph, you can right-click on the shader graph, select **Create** | **Material**, and then move it to our `Materials` folder.

10. Change the color to something different, such as red, by clicking on the window next to the **Color** property in the **Inspector** window while it's selected.

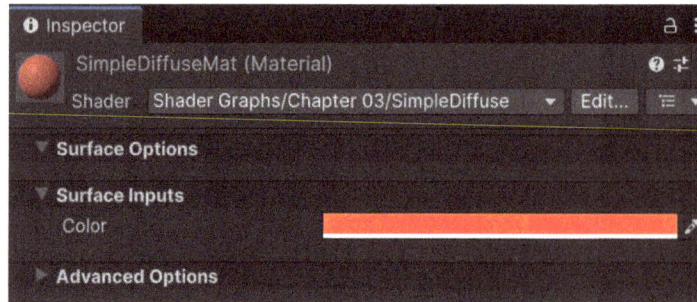

Figure 3.6 – Creating a Color property

11. Then, create a new scene by going to **File** | **New Scene**. From the template menu that pops up, go ahead and create a **Basic (URP)** scene and click **Create**.

12. Go into the Models folder of this book's example code and bring the bunny object into the scene by dragging and dropping it from the **Project** window into the **Hierarchy** window.

> **Note**
>
> You can double-click on an object in the **Hierarchy** window to center the camera on the object that's been selected.

13. From there, assign the **SimpleDiffuseMat** material to the object:

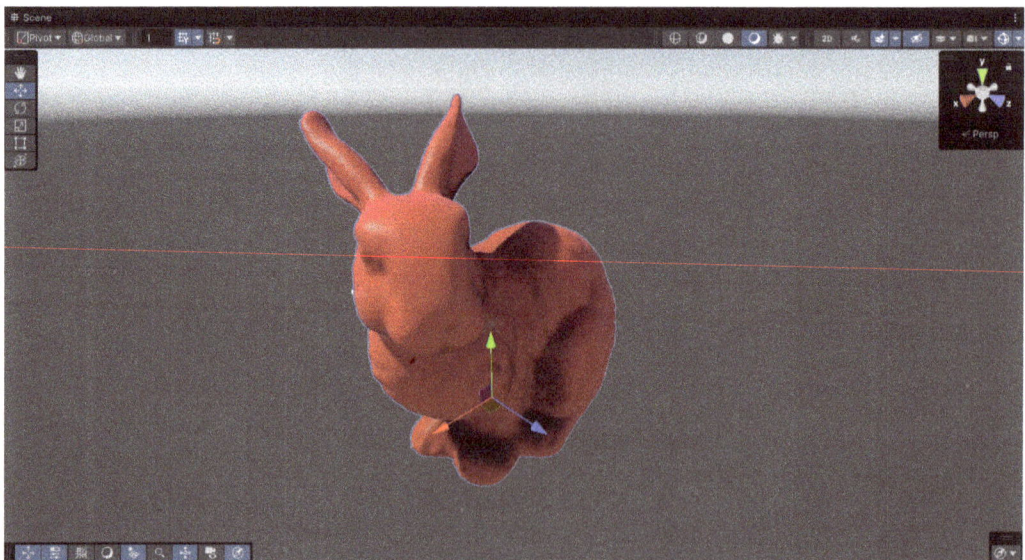

Figure 3.7 – Assigning the simple diffuse shader

How it works...

Shader Graph allows you to visually communicate the rendering properties of your material to the lighting model. In this example, we set up a simple diffuse shader by defining a color property and connecting it to the base color of the shader. Shader Graph handles the rest, ensuring that the material behaves correctly under different lighting conditions.

By following these steps, you created a basic diffuse shader using Shader Graph, which simulates how light interacts with a matte surface.

Accessing and modifying packed arrays

Packed arrays are data structures that store multiple elements in a compact, contiguous block of memory. Loosely speaking, the code inside a shader has to be executed for at least every pixel on your screen. This is the reason why GPUs are highly optimized for parallel computing; they can execute multiple processes at the same time. This parallel processing philosophy is also evident in the standard type of variables and operators available to us when creating shaders. Understanding these variables and operators is essential, not just so that you can use the shaders correctly, but also so that you can write highly optimized ones.

Some of the more advanced usages of variable concepts that you'll find are **packed arrays (vectors)** and **swizzling**. We'll also talk about the concepts of **smearing** and **masking** in the *There's more...* section of this recipe:

- **Packed arrays (vectors)**: In shader programming, packed arrays are variables that hold multiple values. In Shader Graph, they are represented by Vector2, Vector3, and Vector4 nodes. For instance, Vector4 is a type of packed array that contains four values, which can represent components such as color channels (red, green, blue, alpha) or spatial coordinates (x, y, z, w).

  To create a vector, right-click in the graph area, select **Create Node**, and choose the appropriate vector node. For example, select Vector4 to create a vector with four components. To access individual components of a vector, you can use the **Split** node. This will break the vector into its individual components (x, y, z, w or r, g, b, a).

- **Swizzling**: This is the process of reordering or selecting specific components of a vector. For instance, you can take the red, green, and blue components of a color vector and form a new vector without using its alpha component.

Swizzling in Shader Graph can be achieved using the **Combine** node or directly through vector component manipulation.

For example, if you want to create a Vector3 node from the red, green, and blue components of a Vector4 color, use the **Split** node to break the Vector4 node into components, then use a **Combine** node to reassemble them into a Vector3 node, or after doing some manipulation, as we will do in the following example.

How to do it...

In this example, we will create a shader that transitions between two colors over time utilizing a sine wave. We'll use swizzling to manipulate the red channel data and create a visually appealing effect:

1. In the **Project** tab, right-click on the Shaders folder and select **Create | Shader Graph | URP | Lit Shader Graph**.

2. Name the new shader PackedArraysShader.

3. Double-click on PackedArraysShader to open Shader Graph.

4. In the **Blackboard** (the panel on the left), double-click on the grayed-out **Shader Graphs** text and change it to Shader Graphs/Chapter 03.

5. Then click the + button and choose **Color**. You should see the property show up. Leave the default name of Color.

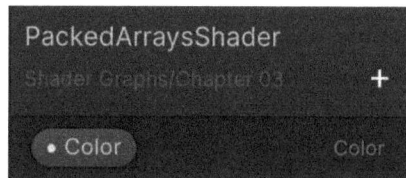

Figure 3.8 – Creating the Color property

6. With the newly created **Color** property selected, we can now go to **Graph Inspector** on the right side and set **Default Value** to something that has less than half of its value in the red channel (I used RGBA = (0, 1, 1, 1)) by double-clicking on the box with its value. This is because we will be adding to the red channel later on after we split it up.

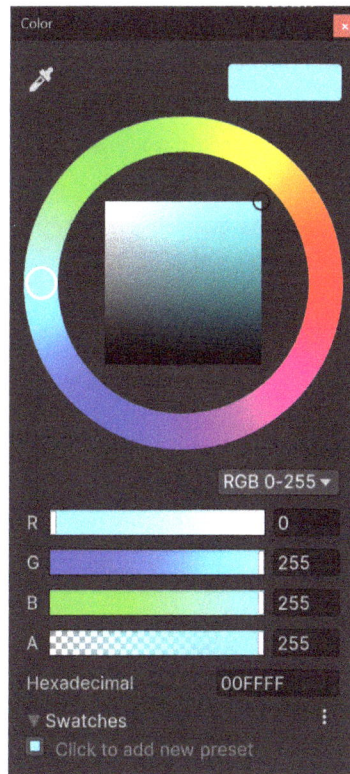

Figure 3.9 – Setting Default Value of the Color property

7. Drag the **Color** property from the **Blackboard** to the graph area. Click and drag from the **Out** of the **Color (4)** node and create a **Split** node to break the color into its **R**, **G**, **B**, and **A** components.

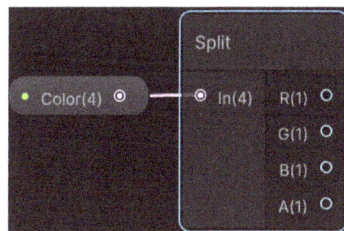

Figure 3.10 – Splitting the Color property

8. Right-click above the **Split** node and select **Create node**. From there, select **Sine**. To the left of it, create a **Time** node. Connect the **Sine Time** output to the **In** of the **Sine** node. You should see the **Sine** value start pulsing from black to white repeatedly. Then, to the right of the **Sine** node, create an **Add** node. Set the **A** to the **Out** of the **Sine** node. Set the **R** of the **Split** node to the **B** of the **Add** node.

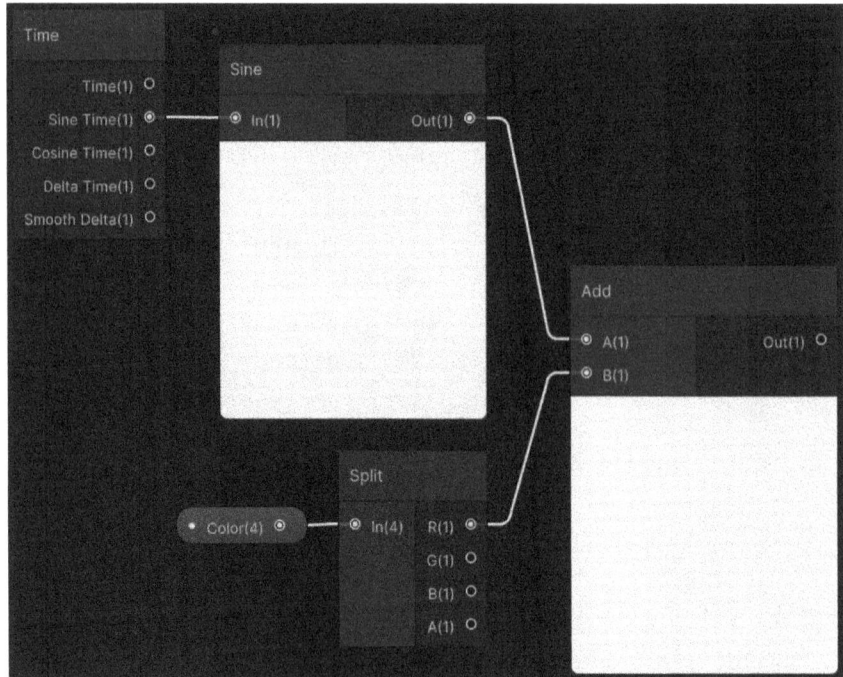

Figure 3.11 – Using Sine to change over time

9. To the right of the **Add** node, create a **Combine** node. From there, connect the **Out(1)** of the **Add** node to the **R** channel. Then, connect the **G**, **B**, and **A** values from the **Split** node to the **Combine** node. Finally, connect the **RGB(3)** output from the **Combine** node to **Base Color(3)** of the **Master Stack** under the **Fragment** section.

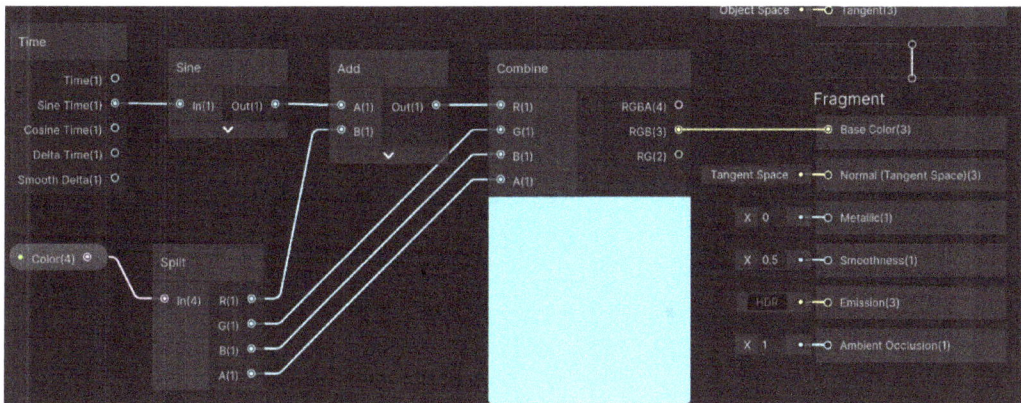

Figure 3.12 – Combining the values and assigning the result

Tip

Each node with a preview window has a toggle arrow (∧) that you can use to hide or preview what each node looks like. In the preceding screenshot, I toggled off the **Sine** and **Add** nodes to make it easier to see the connections between the nodes.

10. Save the Shader Graph by clicking on the **Save** icon that looks like a floppy disk in the top-left corner of the Shader Graph editor and return to the Unity Editor.

11. Next, create a new material (PackedArraysMat) and set the shader it uses to the Shader Graphs/Chapter 03/PackedArrays selection. Change the color to something different, such as red, by clicking on the window next to the **Color** property in the **Inspector** window while it's selected.

12. If you are continuing from the previous recipe, assign the newly created material to bunny; otherwise, bring in an object to see the result of the material. If your **Scene** camera is in a better position than the game's camera, select the **Main Camera** game object and then select **GameObject | Align with View**. Then hit the **Play** button to see the result of the shader at runtime.

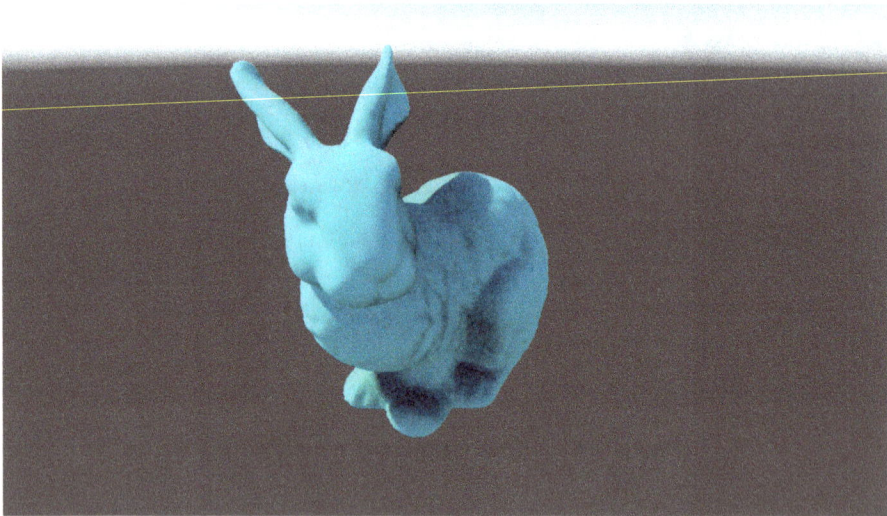

Figure 3.13 – Shader result

How it works...

The custom color effect shader demonstrates the power and flexibility of accessing and modifying packed arrays (vectors) to create dynamic visual effects.

The **Color** property represents the primary color input for the shader. This color is split into its individual red, green, blue, and alpha components using the **Split** node. The **Sine Time** output of the **Time** node generates a sine wave based on the elapsed time, which produces a value that oscillates smoothly between -1 and 1. This sine wave is used to create a pulsating effect by adding its value to the red component (**R**) of **Color**.

The modified red component (original red value plus the sine wave) is combined with the unchanged green and blue components using the **Combine** node to form a new Vector3 value that is a Color (RGB) vector in this case. This creates a color that pulsates over time in the red channel while the green and blue channels remain constant.

By combining these elements, the shader produces a dynamic visual effect where the color of the material smoothly transitions between two states, creating an engaging and visually interesting appearance.

There's more...

While we saw a simple example of how to break out packed arrays, there are several other ways to manipulate these properties. For instance, here are some other techniques and terms related to packed arrays that are useful:

- **Smearing**: Smearing is when a single value is copied to all fields of a vector. For example, setting all components of a Vector3 node to 1 results in (1, 1, 1). In Shader Graph, this can be done by connecting a single float to multiple inputs of a **Combine** node.

  For instance, to create a Vector3 node where all components are 1, create a **Float** node with a value of 1, then connect it to all three inputs of a **Combine** node set to output a Vector3 node.

- **Masking**: Masking in Shader Graph can be performed using the **Swizzle** node. This node allows you to rearrange or select specific components of a vector. This involves modifying specific components of a vector while leaving others unchanged, for instance, setting only the red and green components of a color vector and leaving blue and alpha as they are.

Creating a shader with normal mapping

Every triangle in a 3D model has a *facing direction*, which determines how it interacts with light. Represented as an orthogonal vector, this direction influences shading where adjacent triangles with different facings reflect light differently. For curved objects, this is a problem: it is obvious that the geometry is made out of flat triangles.

To address this, shading is basSed on *normal direction* rather than facing direction. Vertex normals, stored alongside UV data, define how light reflects at each point. As you will see in the *Adding a texture to a shader* recipe in *Chapter 4, Working with Texture Mapping*, vertices can store data; the normal direction is the most used information after the UV data. A normal is a unit vector (length = 1) that indicates the direction a vertex is facing.

Each point within a triangle has an interpolated normal direction, blending vertex normals to create the illusion of a smooth surface, even on low-polygon models.

The following screenshot shows the same geometric shape rendered with different per-vertex normals:

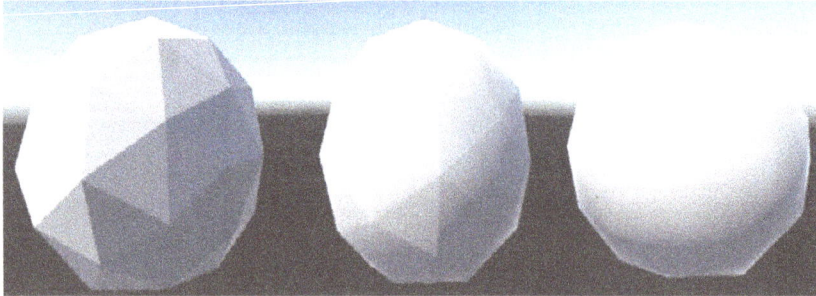

Figure 3.14 – Same shape with different per-vertex normals

On the left, the normals are orthogonal to the face represented by its vertices; this indicates that there is a clear separation between each face. On the right, the normals are interpolated along the surface, indicating that even though the surface is rough, the light should reflect as if it's smooth. It's easy to see that even though the three objects in the following screenshot share the same geometry, they reflect light differently. Despite being made out of flat triangles, the object on the right reflects light as if its surface were curved.

Smooth objects with rough edges are a clear indication that per-vertex normals have been interpolated. This can be seen if we draw the normal directions stored in every vertex, as shown in the following screenshot. Note that every triangle has only three normal directions, one at each vertex, but since multiple triangles can share the same vertex, more than one line can come out of it:

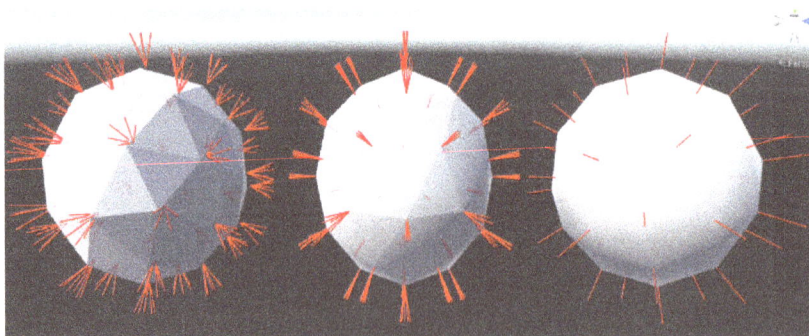

Figure 3.15 – The normal directions for each vertex

Normal mapping has largely replaced calculating normals directly in shaders. Similar to texture mapping, normal maps provide precomputed normal directions using an additional texture, often called a bump map.

In a normal map, the *red*, *green*, and *blue* (RGB) channels represent the *X*, *Y*, and *Z* components of the normal direction. Various tools can generate normal maps:

- **CrazyBump** (`crazybump.com`) converts 2D images into normal data.
- **ZBrush 4R7** (`pixologic.com`) and **Autodesk Mudbox** (`autodesk.com`) generate normal maps from 3D sculpted models.

While creating normal maps is beyond this book's scope, these links provide a starting point. However, Unity makes the process of adding normals to your shaders quite an easy process using Shader Graph. Let's see how this is done.

Getting ready

To get started, follow these steps:

1. Create a new scene by selecting **File** | **New Scene**.
2. Choose the **Basic (URP)** template and then select **Create**.

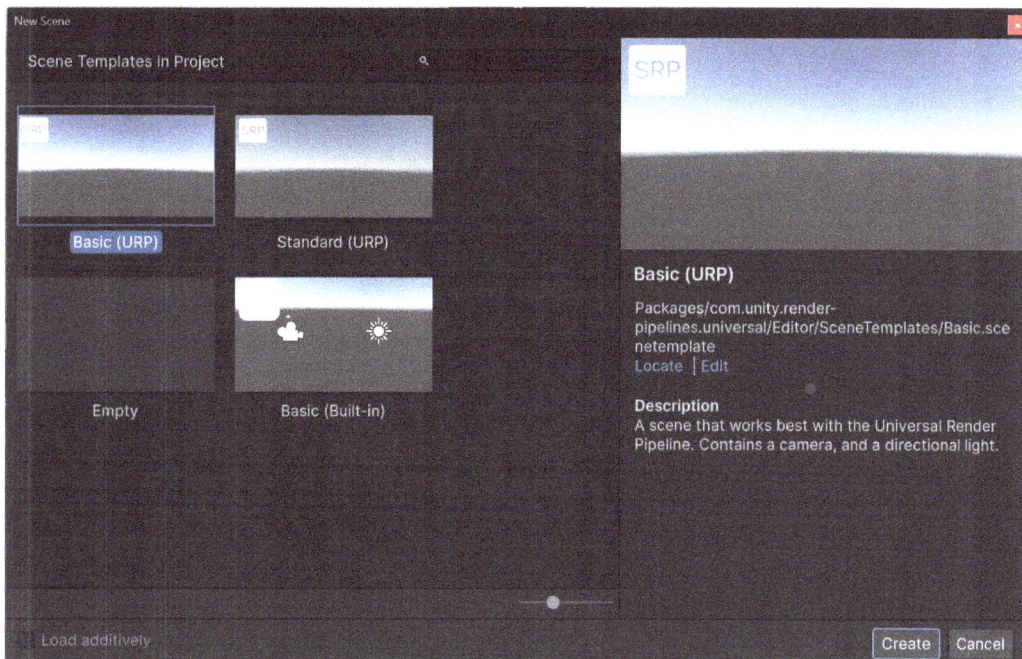

Figure 3.16 – Creating a Basic (URP) scene

3. Create a sphere game object by going to **GameObject** | **3D Object** | **Sphere**.

4. Double-click on the object in the **Hierarchy** window to bring the object into focus in the **Scene** view.

5. Create a new Shader Graph file (NormalMapShader) and a material (NormalMapMat).

6. Assign the material to the sphere that was created in *step 3* in the **Scene** view. This will give us a clean workspace where we can look at the normal mapping technique.

Figure 3.17 – Assigning NormalMapMat

You will need a normal map for this recipe; there is one in the Unity project included with this book. The example normal map included with this book's content is shown here:

Figure 3.18 – Figure showing the normal map texture

You can see it for yourself by going to the Assets/Chapter 03/Textures folder under normalMapExample.

How to do it...

The following steps show you how to use the properties in a Shader Graph:

1. Double-click on NormalMapShader to open the **Shader Graph** editor.

2. Click the + button in the **Blackboard** on the left-hand side of the menu to add a new property. Select **Color** and give it the name of Main Tint.

3. With the newly created **Color** property selected, we can now go to **Graph Inspector** on the right side and set **Default Value** to green (I used RGBA = (0, 1, 0, 1)) by double-clicking on the box with its value.

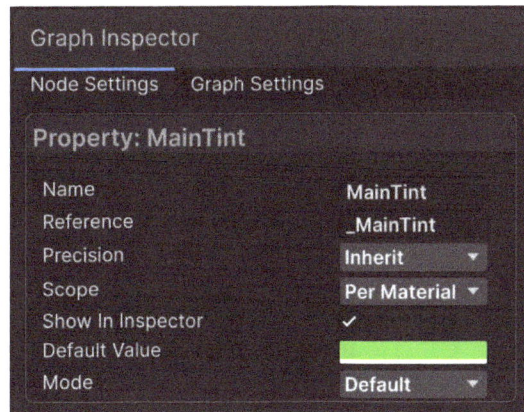

Figure 3.19 – Main Tint default setup

4. Click the + button in the **Blackboard** on the left-hand side of the menu to add a new property. Select **Texture2D**, and give it the name NormalTex.

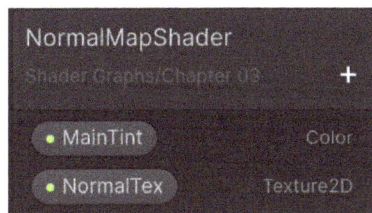

Figure 3.20 – NormalMapShader properties

5. With the newly created **NormalTex** property selected, we can now go to **Graph Inspector** on the right side and set **Default Value** to our `normalMapExample` texture by either dragging and dropping it in or by selecting the circle and selecting it from the **Select Texture** menu. To make it easier to find, you can use the search bar at the top by typing in `normalMap`.

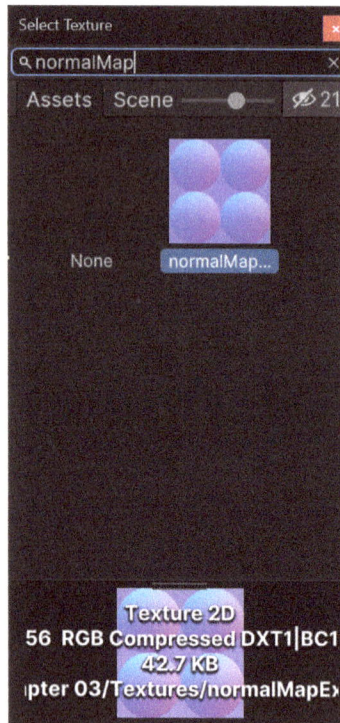

Figure 3.21 – Selecting the normalMap texture

6. Drag the **MainTint** and **NormalTex** properties into the graph.

7. Right-click in the graph area, select **Create Node**, and search for **Sample Texture 2D**. Connect the **NormalTex** property to the **Texture(T2)** input of the **Sample Texture 2D** node.

8. To the left of the **Sample Texture 2D** node, create a **Tiling And Offset** node and connect it to the **UV(2)** input of the **Sample Texture 2D** node.

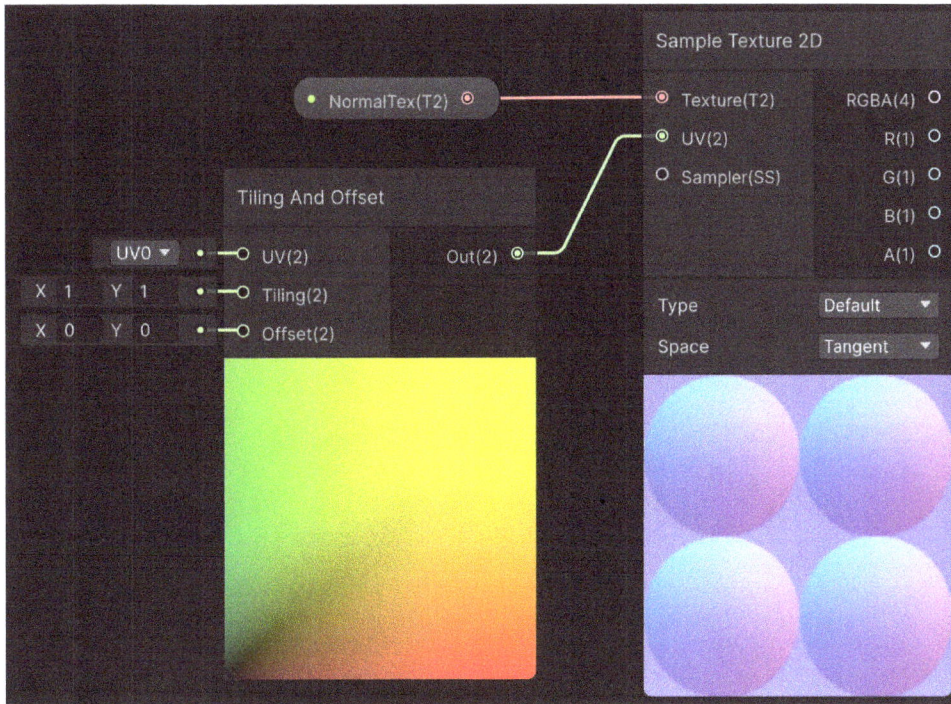

Figure 3.22 – Setup for the Sample Texture 2D node

9. To the right of the **Sample Texture 2D** node, right-click and create a **Normal Unpack** node. Connect the **RGBA (4)** output of the **Sample Texture 2D** node to the **In(4)** input of the **Normal Unpack** node.

10. Connect the **MainTint** property directly to the **Base Color(3)** input of the **Master Stack**.

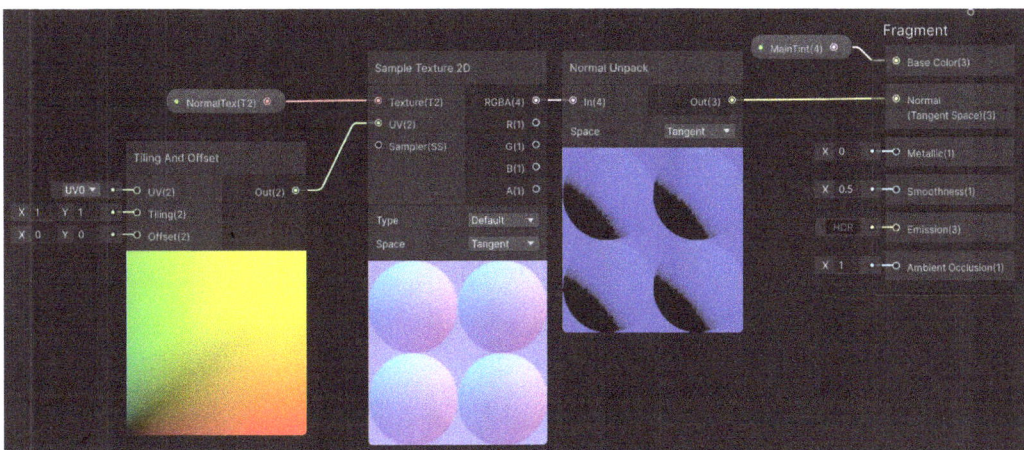

Figure 3.23 – Connecting the Normal Unpack node

11. Save the Shader Graph and close the editor.

12. Select the **Sphere** object in the **Hierarchy** window and then, from the **Inspector** window, assign the **NormalTex** property if needed by dragging and dropping the value in.

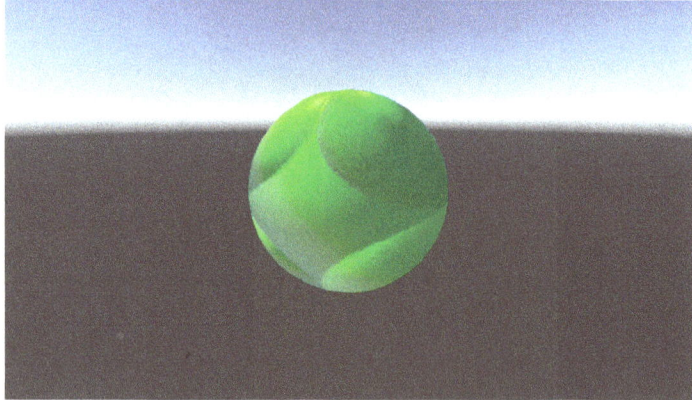

Figure 3.24 – Assigning the material to the sphere

13. You may notice some changes, but it may be hard to see what is going on visually. Open Shader Graph again and under the **Tiling And Offset** node, change the **Tiling(2)** property to 10, 10.

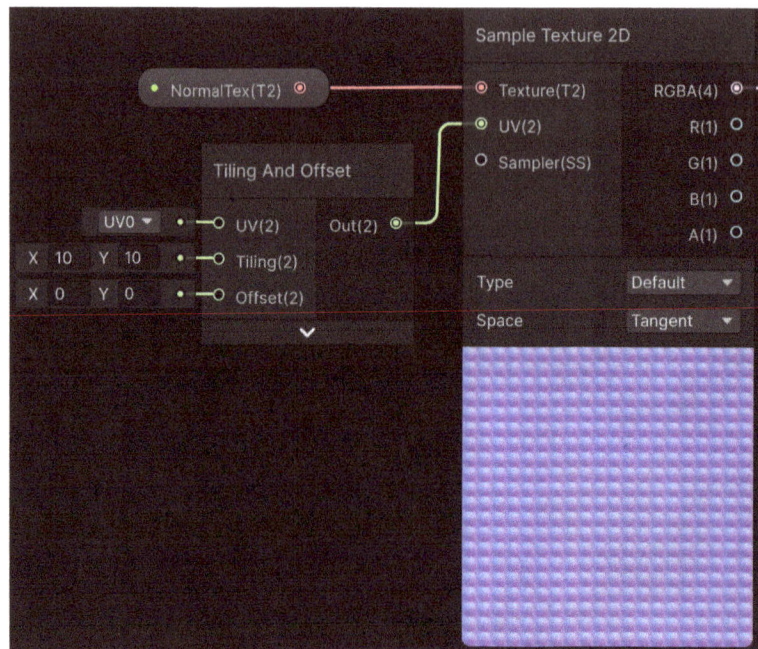

Figure 3.25 – Increasing the Tiling(2) value

14. Save the shader and then return to the Unity Editor.

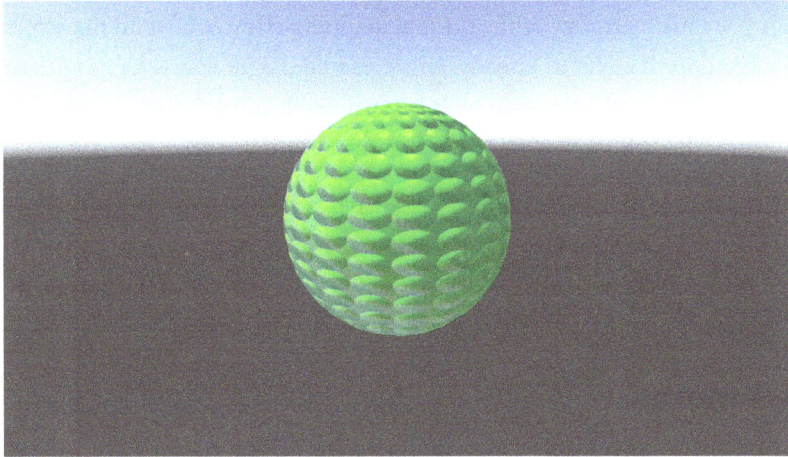

Figure 3.26 – Result from our tiling modifications

This way, you can see that the normal map was duplicated 10 times throughout the sphere on the *x* and *y* axes instead of only once.

The following screenshot demonstrates the result of our normal map shader:

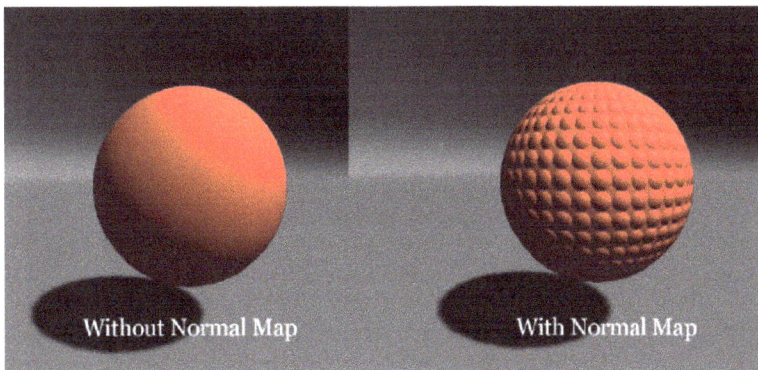

Figure 3.27 – Result of the normal map shader

Note

Shaders can have both a texture map and a normal map. It is not uncommon to use the same UV data to address both. However, it is possible to provide a second set of UVs in the vertex data (UV2), which are specifically used for the normal map.

How it works...

The math you must perform for the normal mapping effect is beyond the scope of this chapter, but Unity has done it all for us already. It has created the functions for us so that we do not have to keep doing it over and over again. This is another reason why Shader Graph can be an efficient way of writing shaders.

The math required for normal mapping is handled by the Shader Graph nodes. The **Normal Unpack** node converts texture data into normal vectors, which are then used by the shader to modify the way light interacts with the surface. Adjusting the intensity of the normal map modifies the normal vectors to create more or less pronounced surface details.

There's more...

You can also add some controls to your normal map shader that let a user adjust the intensity of the normal map. You can do this by modifying the x and y axes components of the normal map variable and then adding them together:

1. In the **Blackboard**, add a new property of type **Float** named NormalIntensity.

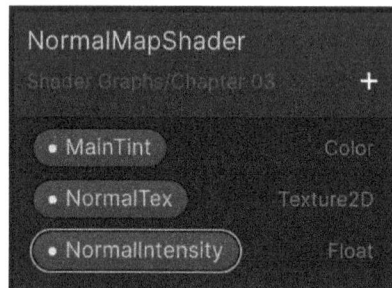

Figure 3.28 – Adding a NormalIntensity value

2. From **Graph Inspector**, set **Default Value** to 1. From there, set **Mode** to **Slider** and then set the **Min** value to 0 and **Max** to 3.

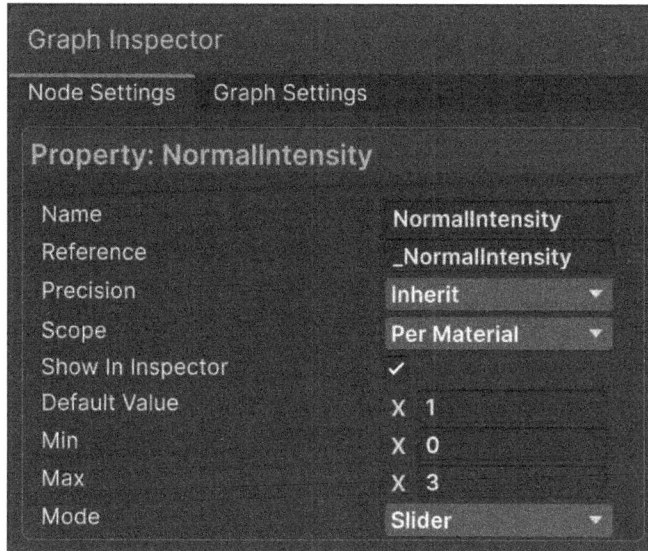

Figure 3.29 – NormalIntensity default setup

3. Drag the **NormalIntensity** property into the graph.

4. To the right of the **Normal Unpack** node, remove the connection from the **Out(3)** node by selecting it and pressing the *delete* key.

5. Then, create a **Split** node and connect the **Out(3)** node of the **Normal Unpack** node to the input of the **Split** node.

6. To the right of the **Split** node, create two **Multiply** nodes. Connect the **NormalIntensity** node to the **A** input of both **Multiply** nodes. In one **Multiply** node, connect the **R** output of the **Split** node to the other input, and in the other **Multiply** node, connect the **G** output of the **Split** node to the other input.

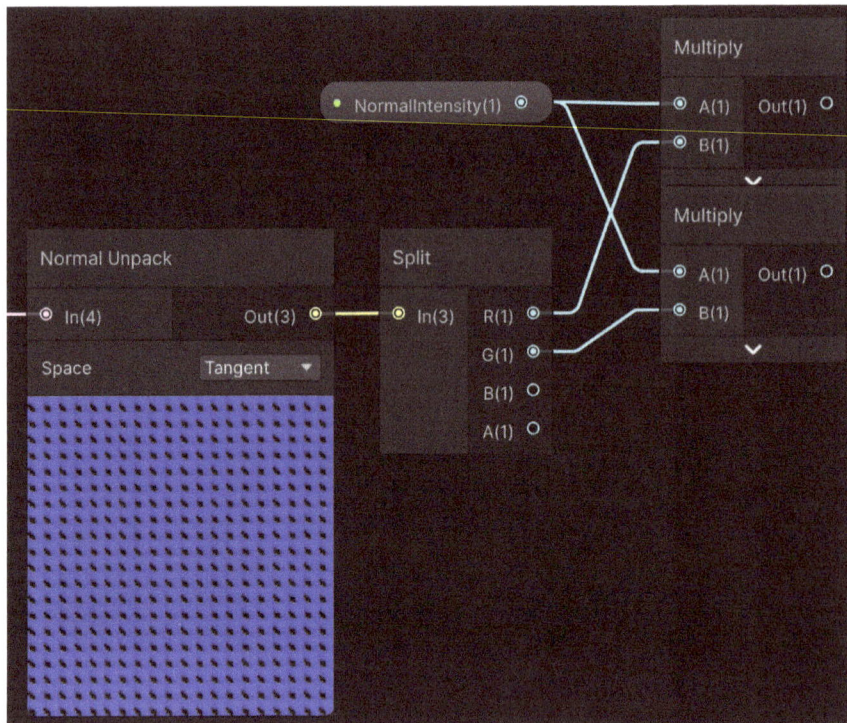

Figure 3.30 – Multiplying the R and B values by Normal Intensity

7. To the right of the **Multiply** nodes, create a **Combine** node. Connect the output of the multiplication between **Normal Intensity** and the **R** channel to the **R** input of the **Combine** node. Connect the output of the multiplication between **Normal Intensity** and the **G** channel to the **G** input of the **Combine** node. Finally, connect the **B** output of the **Split** node to the **B** input of the **Combine** node.

To make it easier to see the connections between nodes, you can double-click on any connection to create what's called a **Reroute** node. This allows you to click and drag to adjust where the line will be seen. For example, in the following screenshot, I used this to ensure that the **B** connection does not pass between the **Multiply** nodes, making it clear that the **B** value from the **Split** node and the **Combine** node is the same.

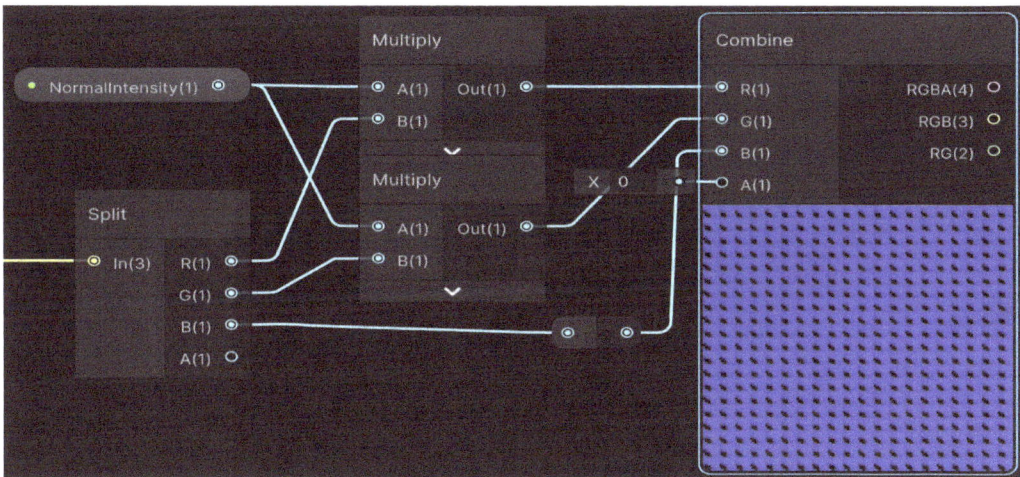

Figure 3.31 – Combining the result

8. To the right of the **Combine** node, create a **Normalize** node. Connect the **RGB** output of the **Combine** node to the input of the **Normalize** node. Finally, connect the output of the **Normalize** node to the **Normal (Tangent Space)(3)** input of the **Fragment** section in the **Master Stack**.

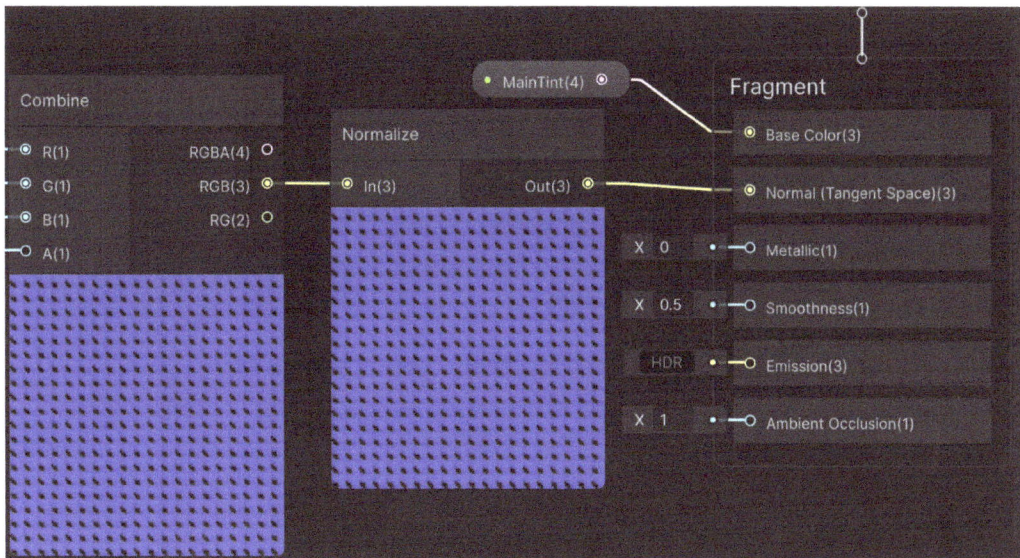

Figure 3.32 – Normalizing and assigning the Normal value

Now, you can let a user adjust the intensity of the normal map in the material's **Inspector** window.

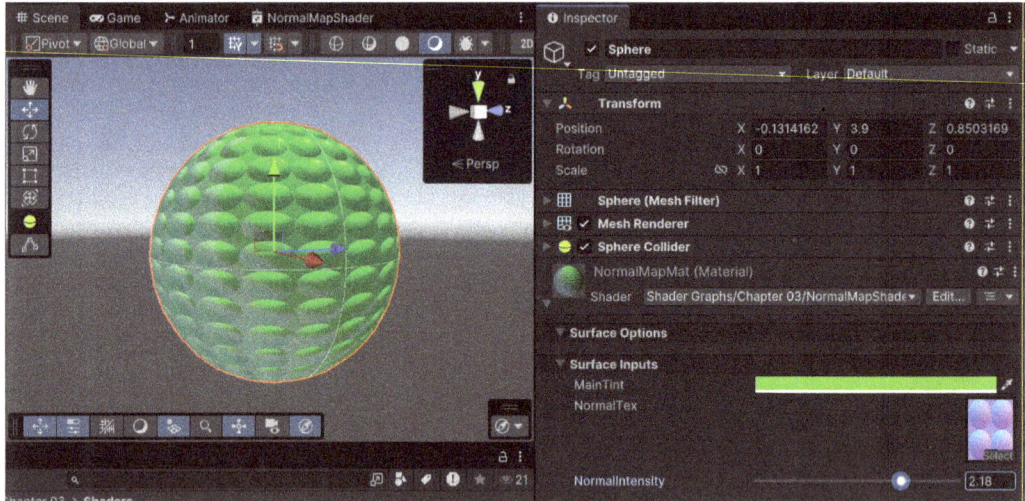

Figure 3.33 – Result of the recipe changes

The following screenshot shows the result of modifying the normal map with our scalar values:

Figure 3.34 – The result of adjusting the normal map intensity

Note

Normal vectors are supposed to have lengths equal to one. Multiplying them by `NormalIntensity` changes their length, making normalization necessary. The **Normalize** node will take the vector and adjust it so that it is pointing in the correct direction but with a length of one, which is what we are looking for.

Creating a holographic shader

More and more space-themed games are being released every year. An important part of a good sci-fi game is the way futuristic technology is presented and integrated into gameplay. There's nothing that screams futuristic more than holograms. Despite being present in many flavors, holograms are often represented as semi-transparent, thin projections of an object. This recipe will show you how to create a shader that simulates such effects. Take this as a starting point: you can add noise, animated scan lines, and vibrations to create a truly outstanding holographic effect.

Getting ready

Create a shader called `Holographic`. Attach it to a material (`HolographicMat`) and assign it to a 3D model in your scene:

Figure 3.35 – Bunny model with the holographic material attached

How to do it...

1. In the **Blackboard**, add a new property of type **Color** named `Rim Color`.

2. From **Graph Inspector**, set **Default Value** to cyan by setting the colors to (0,1,1,0.5).

Figure 3.36 – Setting the cyan color

3. In the **Blackboard**, add a new property of type **Float** named `Rim Effect`.

4. From **Graph Inspector**, set **Default Value** to 0.25. From there, set **Mode** to **Slider** and then set the **Min** value to -1 and **Max** to 1.

5. From **Graph Inspector**, go to **Graph Settings** and set **Surface Type** to **Transparent**.

   We will use the dot product to figure out where the edges of the screen are and create the rim effect of the hologram.

6. Create a **Normal Vector** node and a **View Direction** node. These will provide the world normal and view direction vectors, respectively.

7. Create a **Dot Product** node and connect the outputs of the **Normal Vector** and **View Direction** nodes to its inputs. This will calculate the dot product between the view direction and the world normal.

8. Create a **One Minus** node and connect the output of the **Dot Product** node to its input.

9. Create a **Multiply** node. Connect the output of the **One Minus** node to the **A** input. Drag and drop the **Rim Effect** property into the graph and then connect the **Rim Effect** property to the **B** input.

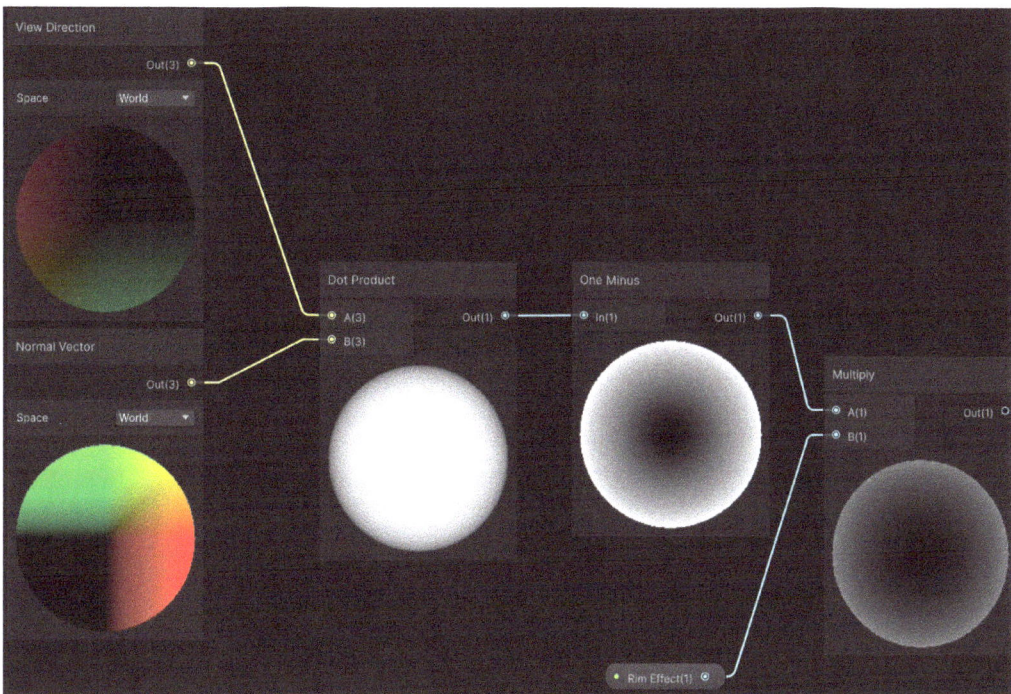

Figure 3.37 – Creating the rim effect

10. Drag the **Rim Color** property above the **Multiply** node. To the right of it, create a **Split** node and connect the **Out** output of the **Rim Color** node to the **In** input of the **Split** node.

11. To the right of the **Split** node, create a **Combine** node. Connect the **R, G**, and **B** properties from the **Split** node to the **Combine** node. Then connect the **Out** output from the **Multiply** node to **A** input of the **Combine** node. Then connect the **Out** output of the **Multiply** node to also connect to **Alpha** input of the **Fragment** portion of the **Master Stack**.

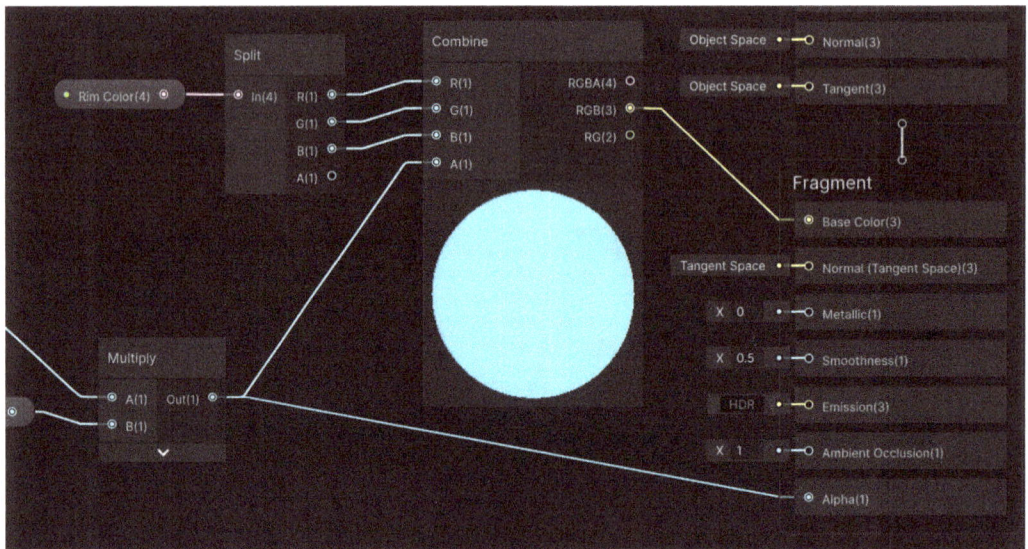

Figure 3.38 – Adding color to and combining the result

12. Save the Shader Graph and return to the Unity Editor.

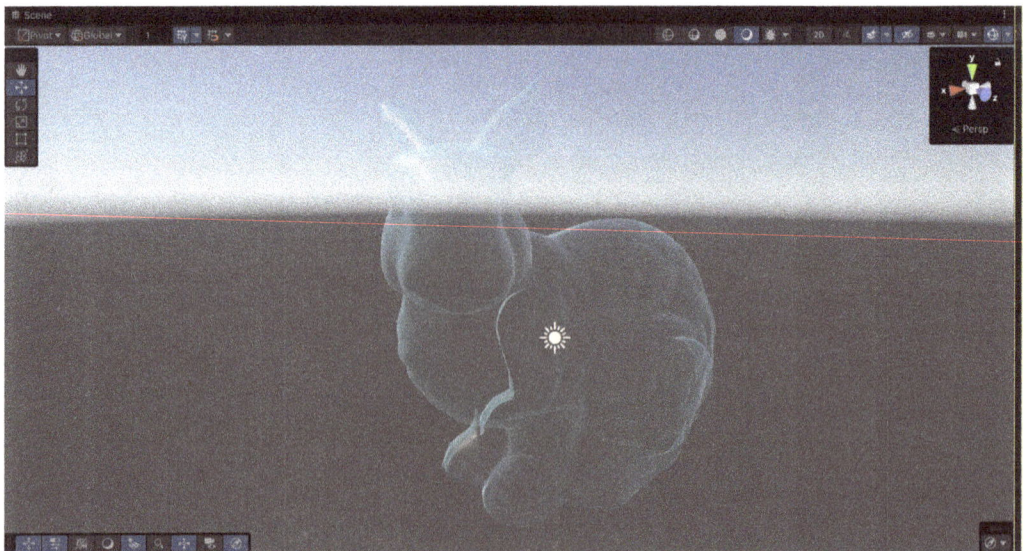

Figure 3.39 – Original result

You can now use the **Rim Effect** slider to choose the strength of the holographic effect.

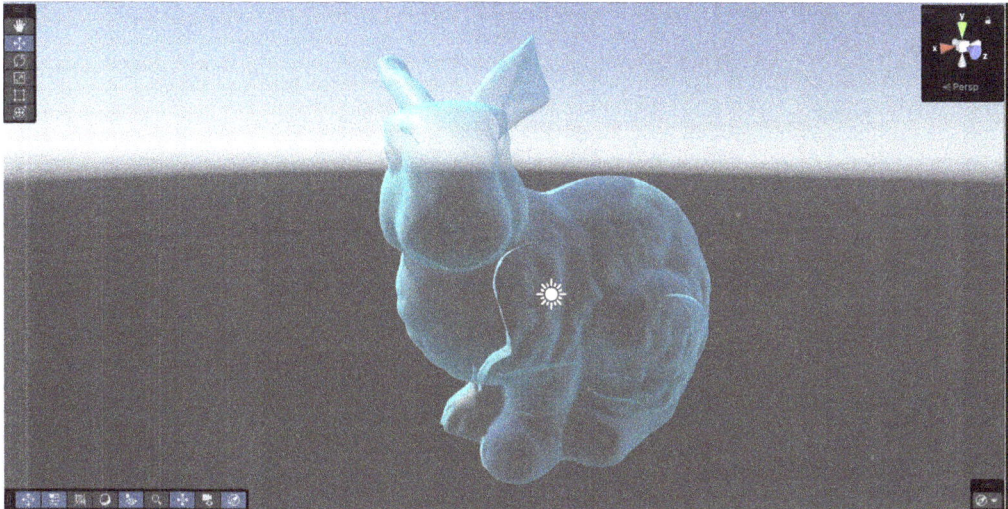

Figure 3.40 – Adjusting the Rim Effect slider

How it works...

This shader works by creating a rim effect that shows only the silhouette of an object. The rim effect is controlled by the dot product of the view direction and the world normal. When these vectors are orthogonal (90 degrees), the dot product is zero, and the rim effect is strongest. By adjusting the **Rim Effect** property, you can control how much of the rim effect is applied, giving you control over the visibility and intensity of the hologram.

There's more...

This technique is very simple and relatively inexpensive, and yet it can be used for a large variety of effects, such as the following:

- The slightly colored atmosphere of a planet in sci-fi games
- The edge of an object that has been selected or is currently under the mouse
- A ghost or specter
- Smoke coming out of an engine
- The shockwave of an explosion
- The bubble shield of a spaceship under attack

In *Chapter 11, Understanding Lighting Models*, we will explain how reflections are calculated using the dot product and why the dot product is widely used in so many shaders.

By following these steps, you will have created a holographic shader using Shader Graph, enabling you to add futuristic visual effects to your 3D models.

Join our community on Discord

Join our community's Discord space for discussions with the authors and other readers:

```
https://packt.link/gamedevelopment
```

4

Working with Texture Mapping

Textures (an image or a pattern) can bring our shaders to life very quickly as they can help us to achieve very realistic effects. **Texture mapping** is the process of applying a texture to the surface of a 3D model to give it color, detail, and realism. It involves wrapping the 2D texture around the 3D object using coordinates that map points on the texture to points on the object's surface.

Texture mapping is a crucial technique in 3D graphics and game development for several reasons. Firstly, it enhances realism by allowing 3D models to look much more realistic. By applying textures, you can simulate intricate details such as skin, fabric, wood grain, metal, and more without needing to model these details geometrically. Secondly, using textures can significantly enhance performance. Instead of modeling every small detail, which increases the number of polygons and computational load, textures can provide these details with minimal performance cost.

Additionally, texture mapping provides artistic flexibility. Artists can create detailed and varied appearances for 3D models through textures, allowing rich visual experiences without altering the geometry of the models. Moreover, textures can be animated or modified at runtime to create special effects such as waves, flowing water, changing colors, or dynamic surfaces, enhancing the visual dynamism of a scene. Lastly, textures allow 3D models to be reused with different appearances by simply changing the texture applied, which is resource-efficient in terms of both storage and rendering.

In this chapter, we will see how you can use textures to animate and blend, and how to use C# code to modify properties at runtime to manipulate what a shader does.

In this chapter, we will be covering the following recipes:

- Adding a texture to a shader
- Scrolling textures by modifying UV values
- Creating a transparent material
- Packing and blending textures
- Creating a circle around your terrain

Technical requirements

For this chapter, you will need Unity Editor version 6 Preview 6000.0.7f1. This chapter's instructions should work with minimal changes in future versions of the editor in projects that utilize the **Universal Render Pipeline** (**URP**). The chapter's sample project was created using the **Universal 3D** Core template.

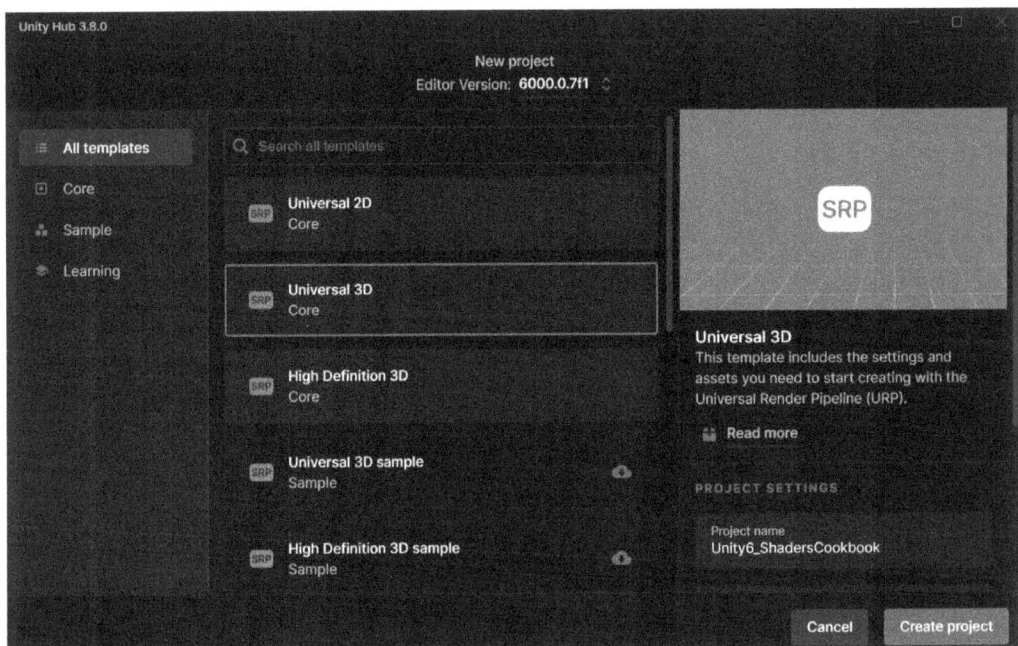

Figure 4.1 – Universal URP project

The code files for this chapter can be found on GitHub at https://github.com/PacktPublishing/ Unity-6-Shaders-and-Effects-Cookbook. The files for this chapter are organized in the Unity project in a folder named Chapter 04 (https://github.com/Packtublishing/Unity-6-Shaders- and-Effects-Cookbook/tree/main/Unity6_ShadersCookbook/Assets/Chapter%2004) on GitHub.

Adding a texture to a shader

In order to effectively use textures, we need to understand how a 2D image is mapped to a 3D model. As mentioned earlier, this process is called **texture mapping**, and it requires some work to be done on the shader and 3D model that we want to use. Models, in fact, are made out of triangles, which are often referred to as polygons; each vertex on the model can store data that shaders can access and use to determine what to draw.

One of the most important pieces of information that is stored in vertices is the **UV data**. This consists of two coordinates, *U* and *V*, each of which ranges from 0 to 1 to get the full extent of the image. They represent the *X,Y* position of the pixel in the 2D image that will be mapped to the vertices. UV data is present only for vertices; when the inner points of a triangle have to be texture-mapped, the GPU interpolates the closest UV values to find the right pixel in the texture to be used. The following diagram shows you how a 2D texture is mapped to a triangle from a 3D model:

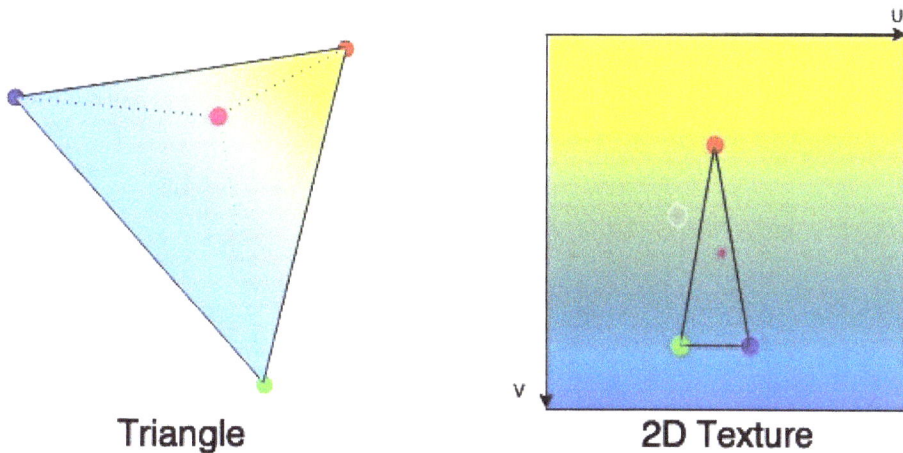

Figure 4.2 – How UVs are projected to a polygon

The UV data is stored in the 3D model and requires modeling software to be edited. Some models lack the UV component and therefore cannot support texture mapping. For example, the *Stanford bunny* that we used in the last chapter was not originally provided with one.

Getting ready

For this recipe, you'll need a 3D model with UV data and its texture. They both need to be imported to Unity before starting. You can do this simply by dragging them to the editor. In the sample code for this chapter that's provided with this book, you can find the basicCharacter model in the Chapter 04/Models folder, which, by default, has UV information embedded in it, so that when we attach a material, the basicCharacter model will draw the texture using that information.

How to do it...

With our scene set up, we can start creating our diffuse shader using Shader Graph:

1. In the **Project** tab, right-click on the Shaders folder (creating one if needed) and select **Create | Shader Graph | URP | Lit Shader Graph**. Name the new shader TexturedShader.

2. Double-click on TexturedShader to open the Shader Graph.

3. In the **Blackboard** (the panel on the left), double-click on the grayed-out Shader Graphs text and change it to Shader Graphs/Chapter 04.

4. Then, click the + button and choose **Texture2D**. The property should appear. Change the name of the property to Base Texture and press *Enter*.

Figure 4.3 – Creating the Base Texture property

5. With the newly created **Texture** property selected, we can now go to the **Graph Inspector** on the right side and set **Default Value** to the texture you'd like to use (I'm using skin_man, which you can download from the sample code for this book) by either dragging and dropping it from the **Project** window or by clicking on the button on the right-hand side and then selecting the skin_man image from the menu that pops up.

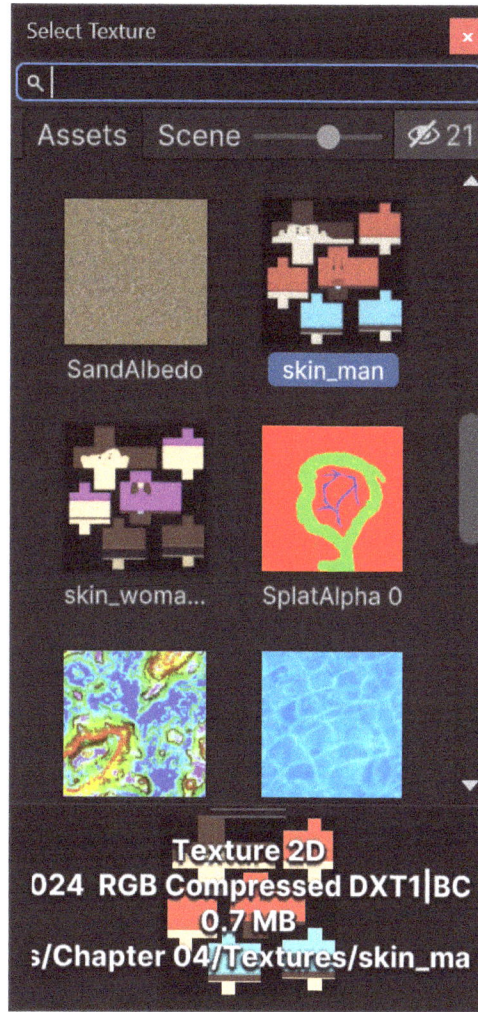

Figure 4.4 – The Select Texture menu

After selecting the texture, you should see it set inside **Default Value**:

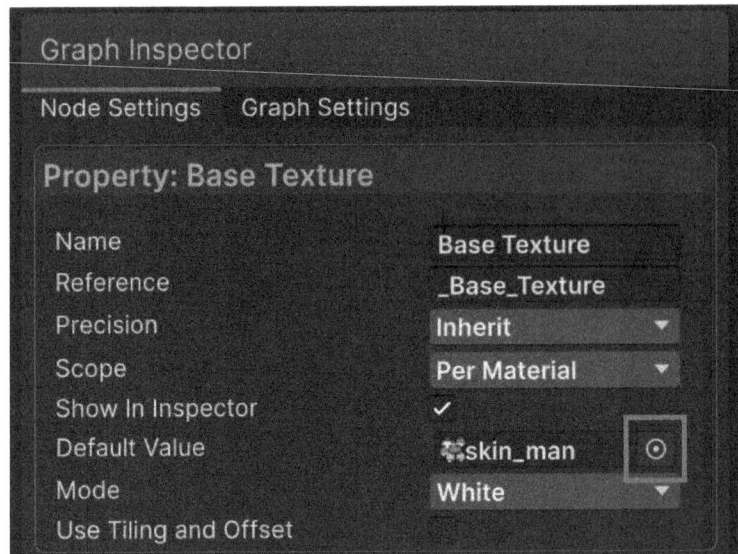

Figure 4.5 – Base Texture property default value

Note

The textures and model used in this example were created by Kenney Vleugels and Casper Jorissen. You can find these and many other public-domain game assets at https://kenney.nl/.

6.   Drag the **Base Texture** property from the **Blackboard** to the graph area.

You'll notice that by default we are unable to directly connect this to the **Base Color(3)** input of the **Master Stack** node in the **Fragment** section, so we will need to sample the texture instead.

7. Drag from the output of the **Base Texture(T2)** node and, from the menu that pops up, type in Sam and you should see the **Sample Texture 2D** option pop up. Select it to create the node. Then, connect the **RGBA(4)** output of the **Sample Texture 2D** node to the **Base Color(3)** input of the **Master Stack** node in the **Fragment** section.

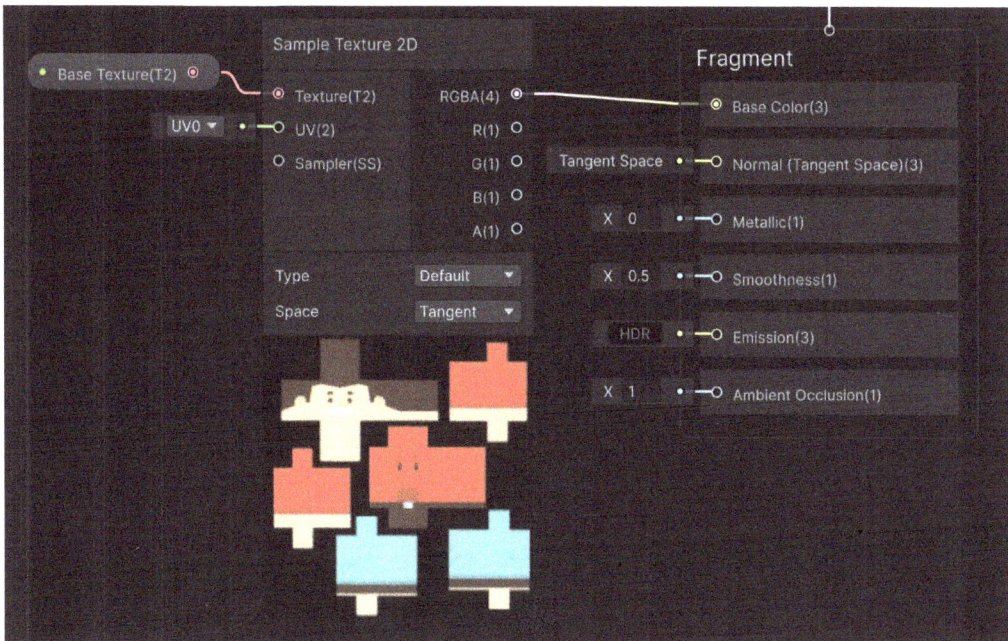

Figure 4.6 – Connecting the Sample Texture 2D to the Base Color

8. Save the Shader Graph by clicking on the **Save** icon that looks like a floppy disk in the top left corner of the Shader Graph editor and return to the Unity Editor.

9. Next, create a new material (TexturedMat) and set the shader it uses to the Shader Graphs/ Chapter 04/TexturedShader selection.

10. Then, create a new scene by going to **File** | **New Scene**. From the template menu that pops up, go ahead and create a **Basic (URP)** scene and press **Create**.

11. Go into the Models folder of this book's example code and bring the model object into our scene by dragging and dropping it from the **Project** window into the **Hierarchy** window.

> Note
>
> You can double-click on an object in the **Hierarchy** window to center the camera on the object that's been selected.

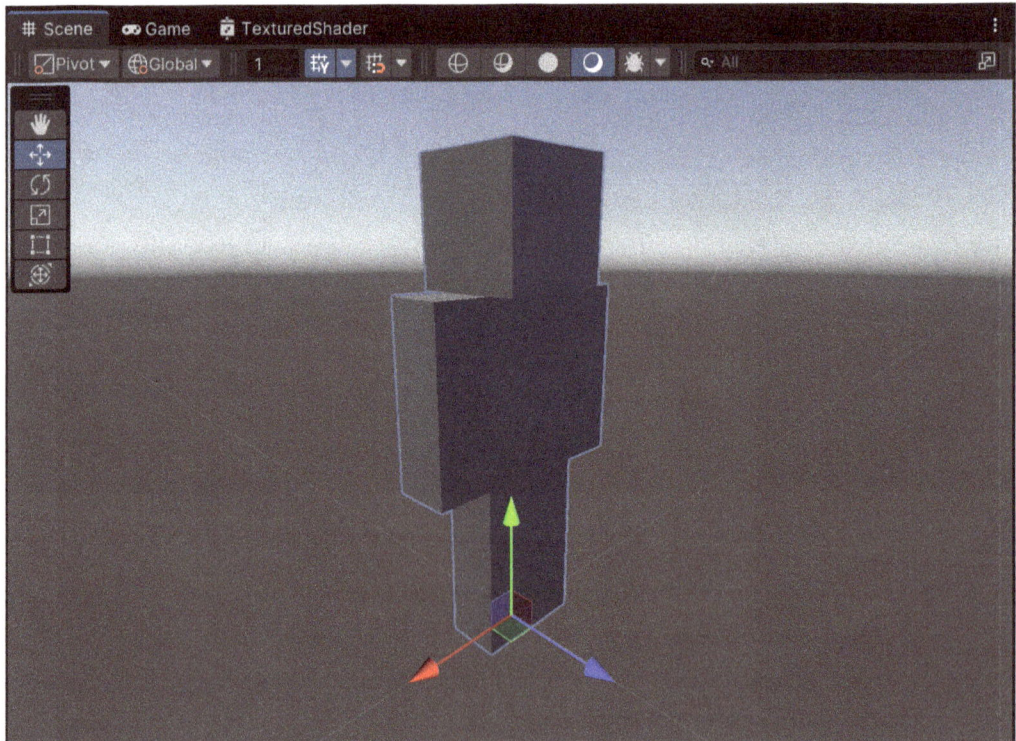

Figure 4.7 – Placing the character in the scene

12. From there, assign the **TexturedMat** material to the object. Note that the model consists of different objects, each of which provides direction to draw in a particular place. This means you will need to drop the material on each part of the model (ArmLeft1, ArmRight1, Body1, and so on); trying to apply this to only the top level of the hierarchy (basicCharacter) will not work:

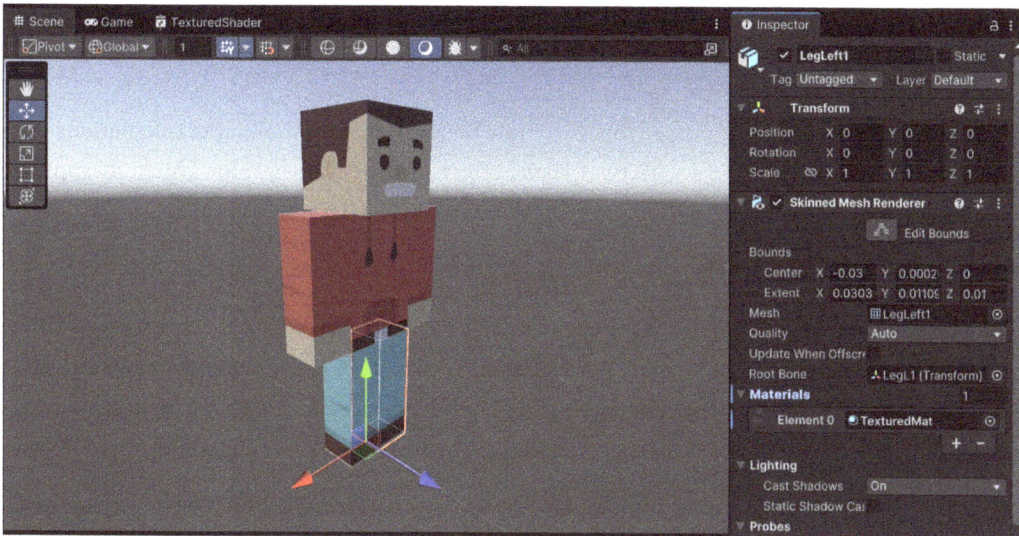

Figure 4.8 – Assigning the TexturedMat Shader

13. It's also possible to change what the object looks like by changing the texture that's being
     used. For instance, if we use the other texture provided (`skin_womanAlternative`) on the
     material, we'll have a very different-looking character:

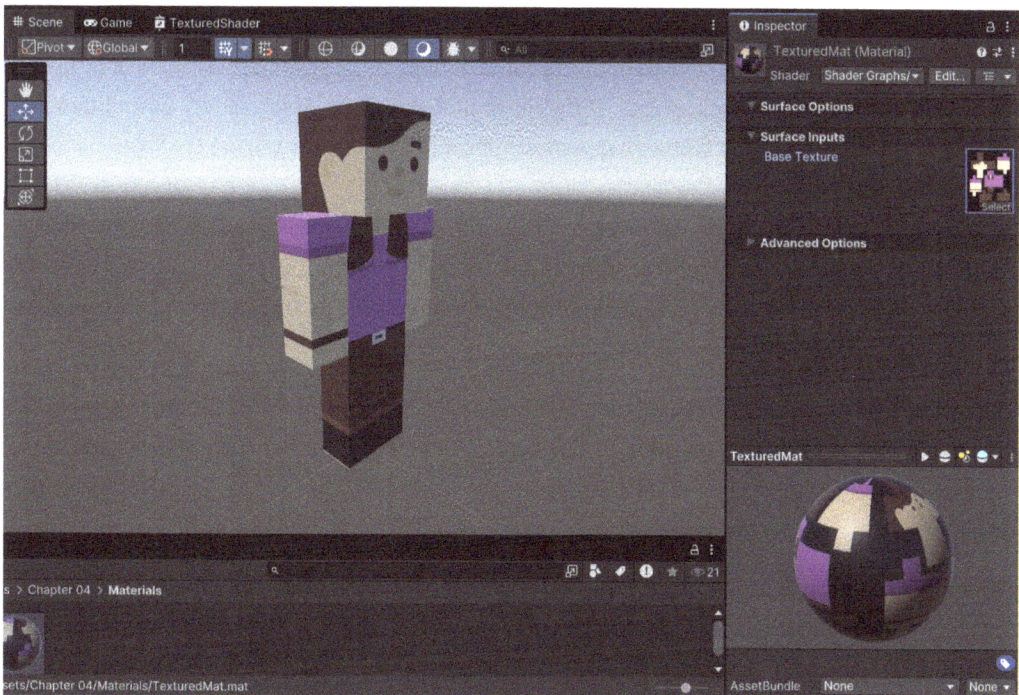

Figure 4.9 – Changing the texture

This is often used in games to provide different kinds of characters with minimal cost.

How it works...

The **Texture Sample 2D** node is used to incorporate texture data into the shader calculations. This node is essential for creating a variety of visual effects in real-time graphics, such as applying detailed surface textures, normal maps, or other image-based data to 3D models.

Since we will be using it so often, here is a breakdown of how the node works.

The **Texture Sample 2D** node requires a texture asset to be connected to it. This texture can be any 2D image, such as a diffuse map, normal map, or any other type of texture map. The node includes a **Sampler** property, which determines how the texture is read. This includes settings for filtering (e.g., bilinear and trilinear) and addressing modes (e.g., repeat and clamp).

The node uses UV coordinates to sample the texture. UV coordinates, which we represent as 2D vectors, map points on the surface of a 3D model to points on the 2D texture. UV coordinates can be manipulated before being fed into the **Texture Sample 2D** node to create effects such as scrolling textures, tiling, or distortion.

> Note
>
> As mentioned previously, the U and V coordinates go from 0 to 1, where (0,0) and (1,1) correspond to two opposite corners. UVs can go beyond [0..1] and can be used this way to tile textures. Different implementations associate UV with different corners; if your texture happens to appear reversed, try inverting the V component.

The **Texture Sample 2D** node retrieves color data from the texture based on the provided UV coordinates. Each **texture pixel** (**texel**) contains color information that the node outputs. The texture's color data typically includes multiple channels (e.g., RGBA), which can be accessed individually or together.

The primary output of the **Texture Sample 2D** node is the sampled color from the texture. This can be used directly as a color value in the shader. Depending on the texture type, additional outputs such as alpha or individual color channels might be used for further calculations (e.g., using the alpha channel for transparency or using a specific channel for masking).

The output from the **Texture Sample 2D** node is often combined with other nodes in the Shader Graph. For example, it can be mixed with colors, used in lighting calculations, or modified by mathematical operations. By manipulating the sampled texture data, a wide range of effects can be achieved, such as bump mapping, parallax mapping, and procedural texturing.

There's more...

When you import a texture to Unity, you are setting up some of the properties that will used by the **Texture 2D** file. The most important is **Filter Mode**, which determines how colors are interpolated when the texture is sampled. It is very unlikely that the UV data will point exactly to the center of a pixel; in all other cases, you might want to interpolate between the closest pixels to get a more uniform color.

The following is a screenshot of the **Inspector** tab of an example texture:

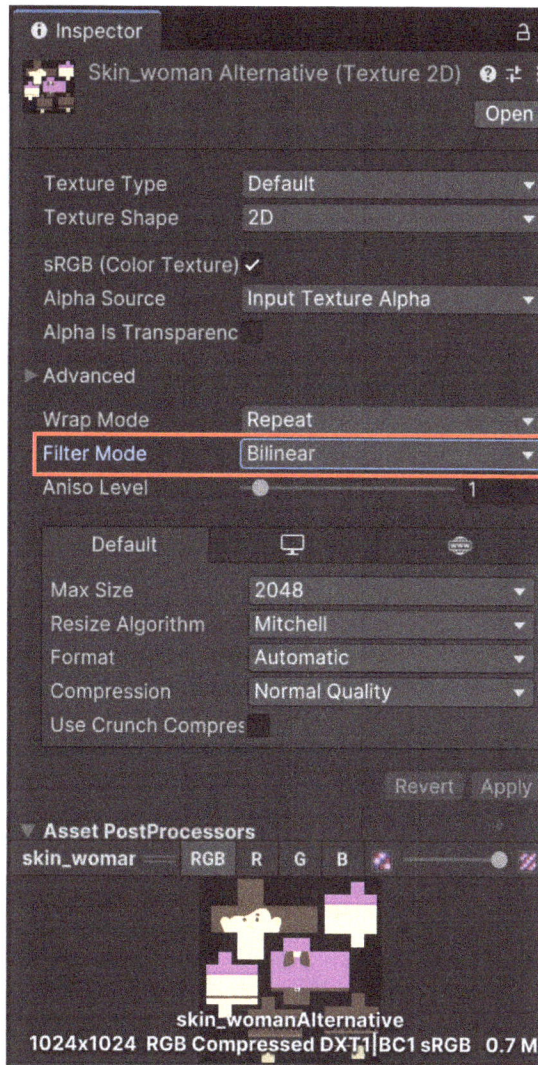

Figure 4.10 – The location of Filter Mode, set to Bilinear

For most applications, **Bilinear** provides an inexpensive but effective way to smooth the texture. However, if you are creating a 2D game, **Bilinear** might produce blurred tiles. In this case, you can use **Point** to remove any interpolation from the texture sampling.

When a texture is seen from a steep angle, texture sampling is likely to produce visually unpleasant artifacts. You can reduce these by setting **Aniso Level** to a higher value. This is particularly useful for floor and ceiling textures, where glitches can break the illusion of continuity.

See also

For a complete list of the options available when importing a 2D texture, you can refer to the following website: `https://docs.unity3d.com/Manual/class-TextureImporter.html`

Scrolling textures by modifying UV values

One of the most common texture techniques used in today's game industry is the process of allowing you to scroll the textures over the surface of an object. This allows you to create effects such as waterfalls, rivers, and lava flows. It's also a technique that is the basis of creating animated sprite effects, but we will cover this in a subsequent recipe of this chapter. First, let's see how we will create a simple scrolling effect in a Surface Shader.

Getting ready

To begin this recipe, you will need to create a new Shader Graph file (`ScrollingUVsGraph`) and material (`ScrollingUVMat`) in a similar manner to how we've created our shader files previously. This will set us up with a nice clean shader that we can use to study the scrolling effect by itself.

How to do it...

In this example, we will create a shader that transitions between two colors over time utilizing a sine wave. We'll use swizzling to manipulate the red channel data and create a visually appealing effect:

1. In the **Project** tab, right-click on the `Shaders` folder and select **Create | Shader Graph | URP | Lit Shader Graph**. Name the new shader `ScrollingUVsGraph`.

2. Double-click on `ScrollingUVsGraph` to open the Shader Graph.

3. In the **Blackboard** (the panel on the left), double-click on the grayed-out Shader Graphs text and change it to Shader Graphs/Chapter 04.

4. Then, click the + button and choose **Texture2D**. The property should appear. Change the name of the property to Base Texture and press *Enter*.

5. With the newly created **Texture** property selected, we can now go to **Graph Inspector** on the right side and set **Default Value** to the water texture example from this chapter by either dragging and dropping it from the **Project** window or by clicking on the button on the right-hand side and then selecting it from the menu that pops up.

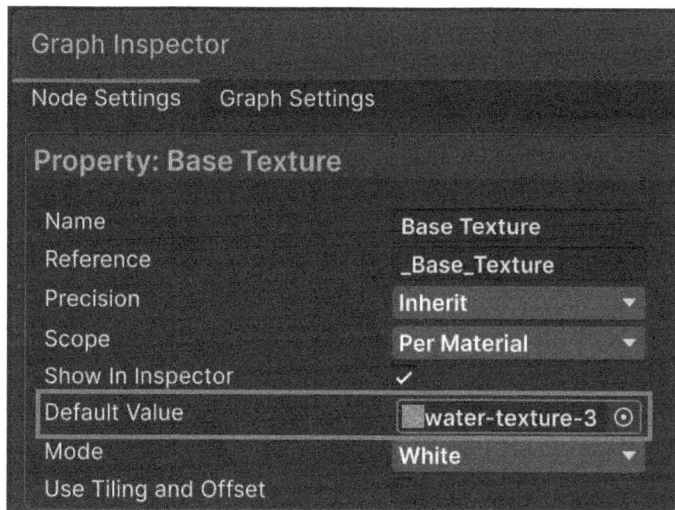

Figure 4.11 – Assigning the Base Texture's Default Value

6. In the **Blackboard**, add a new property of type **Float** named X Scroll Speed.

7. From **Graph Inspector**, set **Default Value** to 0.25. From there, set the **Mode** to **Slider** and then set the **Min** value to 0 and the **Max** to 10.

8. Then, right-click on the **X Scroll Speed** variable and select to **Duplicate** it. Rename the duplicate Y Scroll Speed.

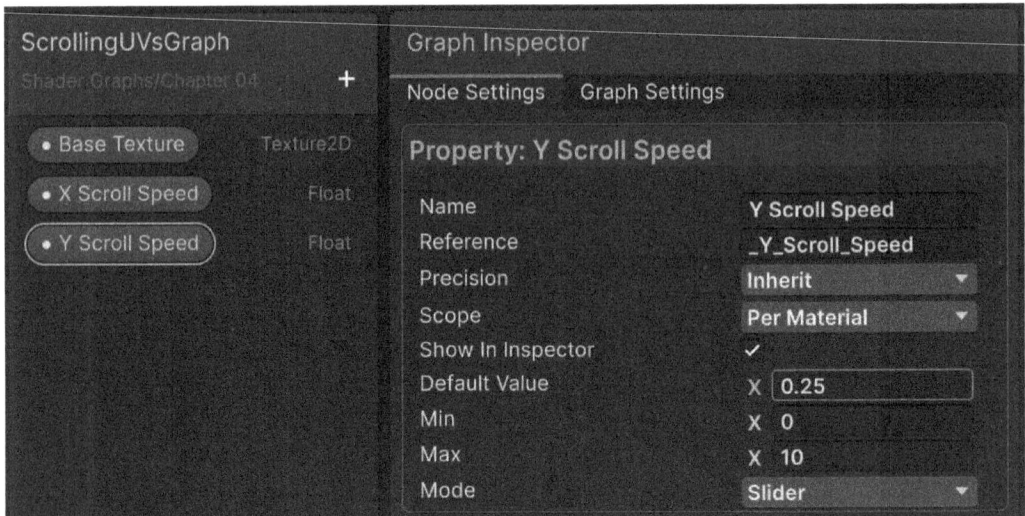

Figure 4.12 – Setting the Default Value Y Scroll Speed property

9. Drag the **Base Texture** property from the **Blackboard** to the graph area.

10. Drag from the output of the **Base Texture(T2)** node and create a **Sample Texture 2D** node. Then, connect the **RGBA(4)** output of the **Sample Texture 2D** node to the **Base Color(3)** input of the **Master Stack** node in the **Fragment** section.

This gets us to somewhere similar to our previous recipe; now we can adjust the UVs to move the object.

11. To the left of the **UV(2)** input, create a **Tiling And Offset** node and connect **UV(2)** to **Out(2)**.

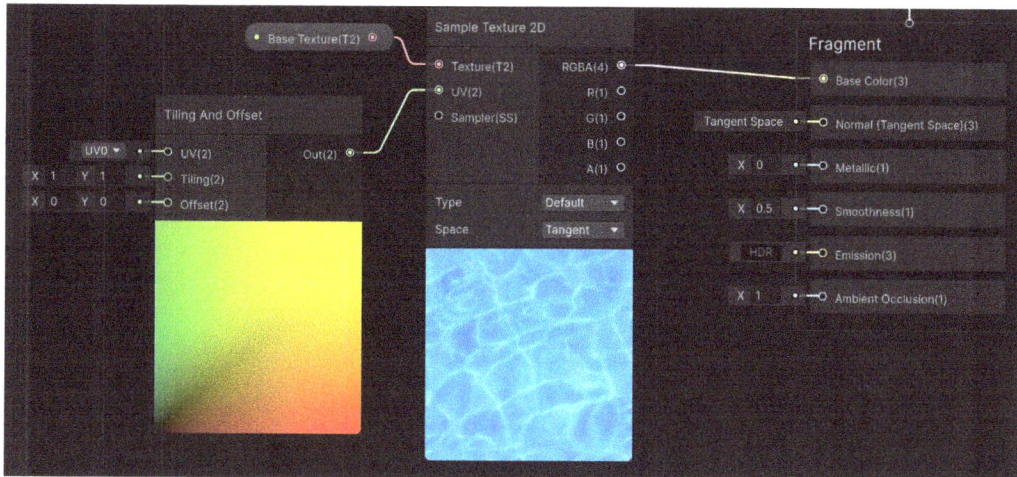

Figure 4.13 – Connecting the Sample Texture 2D node to the Base Color input

12. First, drag and drop the **X Scroll Speed** and **Y Scroll Speed** variables from the **Blackboard** into the graph area. Next, create two **Multiply** nodes to the right of these variables. Connect the **A** input of the first **Multiply** node to the **X Scroll Speed** and the **B** input of the second **Multiply** node to the **Y Scroll Speed**.

13. Now, create a **Time** node and connect its **Time** output to the **B** input of the first **Multiply** node and the **A** input of the second **Multiply** node.

    This setup multiplies both the **X Scroll Speed** and **Y Scroll Speed** values by the current game time. Since these are single float values and the **Tiling And Offset** node requires a **Vector 2**, we need to create a **Vector 2** to hold these values.

14. Right-click to the right of the **Multiply** nodes and create a **Vector 2** node. Connect the output of the first **Multiply** node to the **X** value of the **Vector 2** node, and the output of the second **Multiply** node to the **Y** value of the **Vector 2** node. Finally, connect the **Out(2)** of the **Vector 2** node to the **Offset(2)** input of the **Tiling And Offset** node.

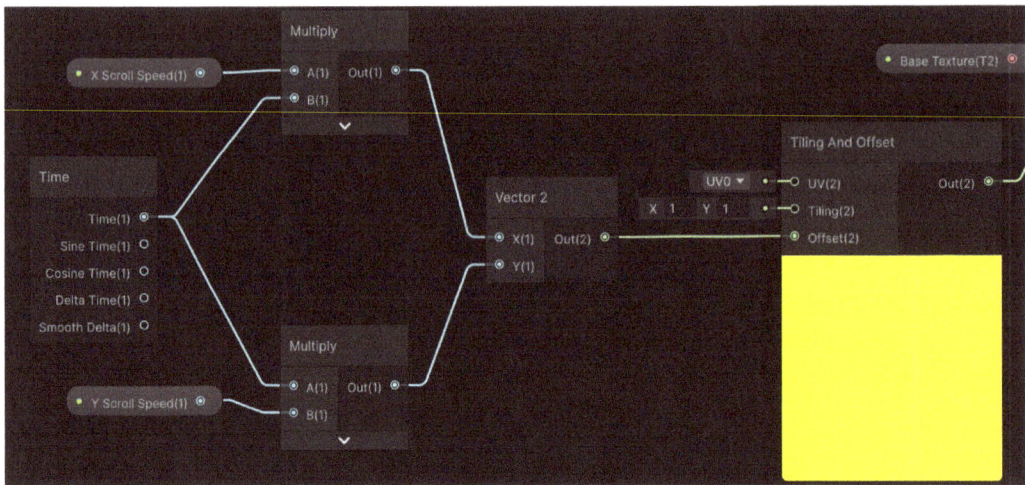

Figure 4.14 – Connecting the offsets to the Tiling And Offset node

At this point, you should see the **Sample Texture 2D** node moving according to the **X Scroll Speed** and **Y Scroll Speed** values you provided. Feel free to adjust these values to observe how they affect the final visuals of your shader.

15. Save the Shader Graph by clicking on the **Save** icon that looks like a floppy disk in the top left corner of the Shader Graph editor and return to the Unity Editor.

16. Next, create a new material (ScrollingUVsMat) and set the shader it uses to Shader Graphs/Chapter 04/ScrollingUVsGraph.

17. After this is created, we need to create an object that can use the shader. From a new scene, go ahead and select **GameObject | 3D Object | Plane** and drag and drop the **ScrollingUVMat** material onto it.

18. To make it easier to see once we play the game, select the **Main Camera** object from the **Hierarchy** window, and then, in the **Inspector** window, change the **Y** Position to 2.

19. Once the above changes are applied, go ahead and play the game to see the shader in action:

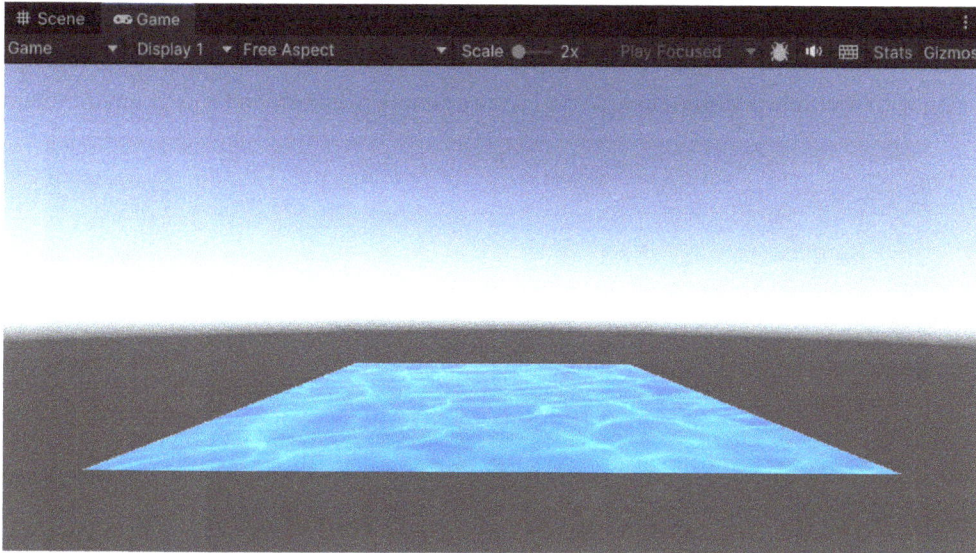

Figure 4.15 – The scrolling UVs shader attached to a plane

While it is not visible in this still image, you will notice that in the Unity Editor, the object will now move on both the *X* and *Y* axes! Feel free to drag the **X Scroll Speed** and **Y Scroll Speed** properties in the **Inspector** tab to see how the changes affect how the object moves. Also, feel free to move the camera to make it easier to see if you would like.

Note

As discussed in the *Using properties in a Surface Shader recipe* in *Chapter 2*, materials are assets. This means that when you modify a variable on a material during gameplay, the value remains changed even after playing the game unlike most objects in Unity, which are instantiated in memory and revert to their original state when the game stops running. Any changes made to assets are written directly in the file itself as it is modified so it will be persistent.

This persistent nature of materials means that adjustments made in the editor or via scripts during gameplay will be saved. This can be particularly useful for developing and testing, as you can tweak visual properties in real time and immediately see the results without needing to reset parameters each time.

However, this also requires caution. Since changes to materials are saved permanently, unintended modifications during gameplay can lead to unwanted visual changes. If you have changed the value of a property by mistake, you can undo it using *Ctrl + Z*.

Pretty cool! With this knowledge, we can take this concept much further to create interesting visual effects. The following screenshot demonstrates the result of utilizing the scrolling UV system with multiple materials in order to create a simple river motion for your environments:

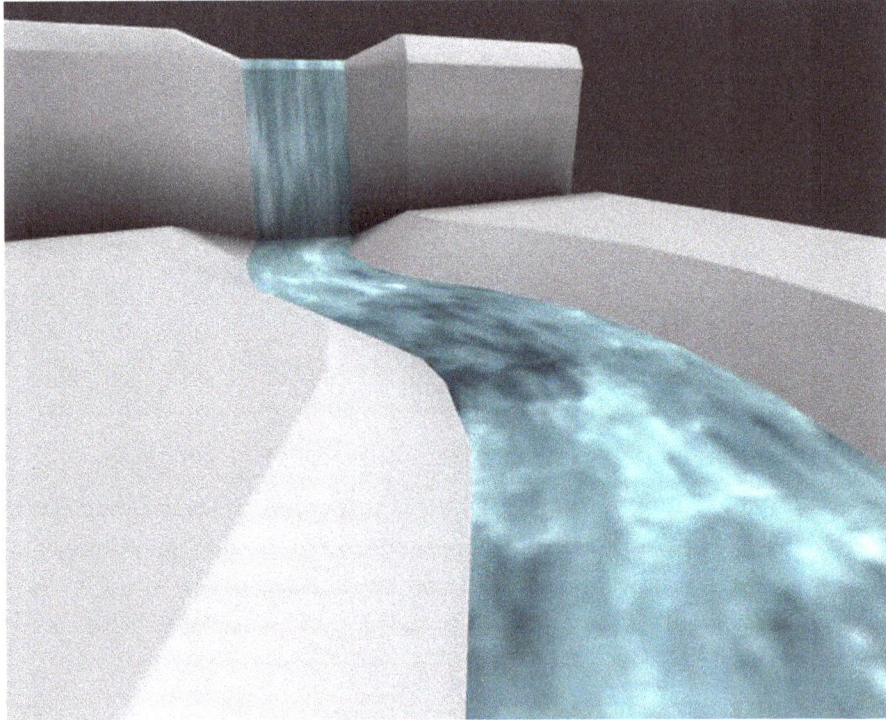

Figure 4.16 – A simple river using scrolling UVs

How it works...

The scrolling system starts with the declaration of three properties: **Base Texture**, **X Scroll Speed**, and **Y Scroll Speed**. **Base Texture** allows us to store the texture we wish to modify while the scroll speed properties allow users to control the speed of the scrolling effect. At their core, each of the three properties are values passed from the material's **Inspector** tab to the Shader Graph. For more information on shader properties, see *Chapter 2, Creating Your First Shader with Shader Graph*.

Once we have these float values, we can use them to offset our UV values in the shader. This process begins by placing the **X Scroll Speed** and **Y Scroll Speed** variables into the graph and connecting them to **Multiply** nodes. These nodes will scale the scroll speed by the current game time.

The **Time** node outputs a float value representing Unity's game time, which we then connect to the **Multiply** nodes, which tells us how much the texture should be offset by. We previously used the **Time** node in the *Accessing and modifying packed arrays* recipe in *Chapter 3, Working with Surfaces*, but there, we used the **Sine Time** output, which produces oscillating values between -1 and 1, which are ideal for creating periodic or cyclical effects such as pulsating lights or rhythmic movements. In this case, we use the **Time** output, which continuously and linearly increases over time, making it a great asset for scrolling textures or time-based changes.

Next, we need to convert these single float values to a **Vector 2** since the **Tiling And Offset** node requires a **Vector 2** input. Finally, we connect the output of the **Vector 2** node to the **Offset** input of the **Tiling And Offset** node.

The **Tiling And Offset** node is crucial in this process as it handles the UV coordinates of the texture. The **Tiling** component scales the texture, while the **Offset** component shifts the texture's UV coordinates. By connecting our **Vector 2** node to the **Offset** input, we dynamically adjust the UV coordinates based on the scroll speed and game time, causing the texture to scroll.

This effectively creates a dynamic UV offset based on the scroll speed and the game time. By adjusting the **X Scroll Speed** and **Y Scroll Speed** values in the material's **Inspector** tab, you can control how fast the texture moves along the *x* and *y* axes, respectively. The texture's movement is a result of continuously updating its UV coordinates based on the scaled time value, creating the effect of the texture scrolling across the surface.

Creating a transparent material

All the shaders we have seen so far have something in common: they are used for solid materials. If you want to improve the look of your game, transparent materials are often a good way to start. They can be used for anything from a fire effect to a glass window. Unfortunately, working with them is slightly more complicated. Before rendering solid models, Unity orders them according to the distance from the camera (Z ordering) and skips all the triangles that are facing away from the camera (culling). When rendering transparent geometries, there are instances in which these two aspects can cause problems. This recipe will show you how to solve some of these issues when it comes to creating a transparent Surface Shader. This topic will be revisited in detail in *Chapter 7, Using Grab Passes*, where realistic glass and water shaders will be provided.

Getting ready

To get started, you should have already completed the *Adding a texture to a shader* recipe in this chapter. Afterward, follow these steps:

1. Create a new scene by selecting **File** | **New Scene**.

2. Choose the **Basic (URP)** template and then select **Create**.

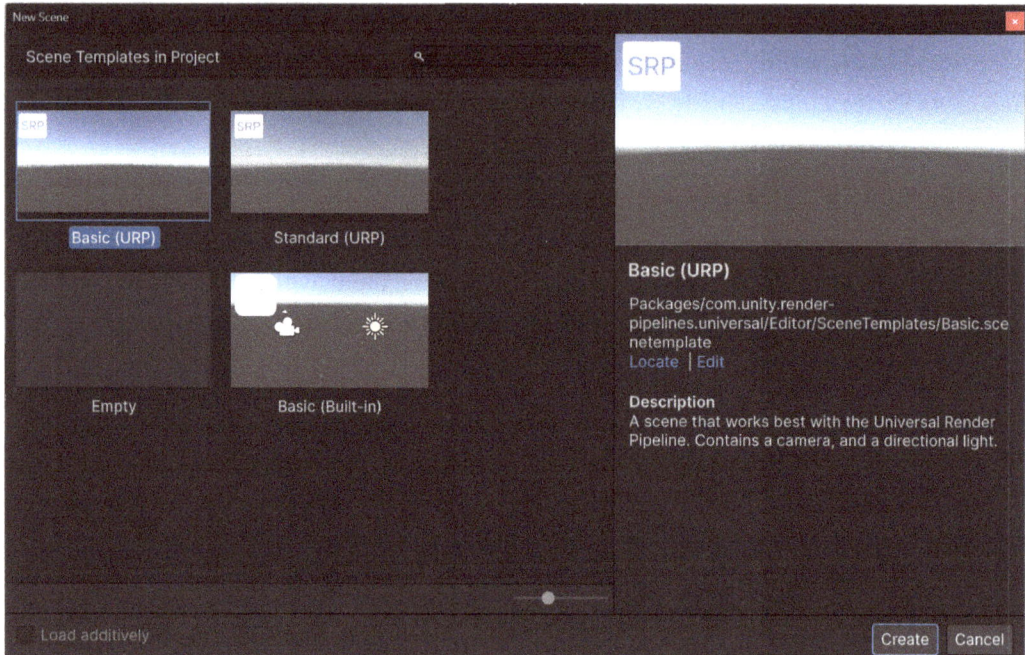

Figure 4.17 – Creating a Basic (URP) scene

3. Create a quad game object by going to **GameObject** | **3D Object** | **Quad**.

4. Double-click on the object in the **Hierarchy** window to bring the object into focus in the **Scene** view. If the quad is invisible on your screen, rotate your camera around until it can be seen. We will also need several other non-transparent objects to test the effect:

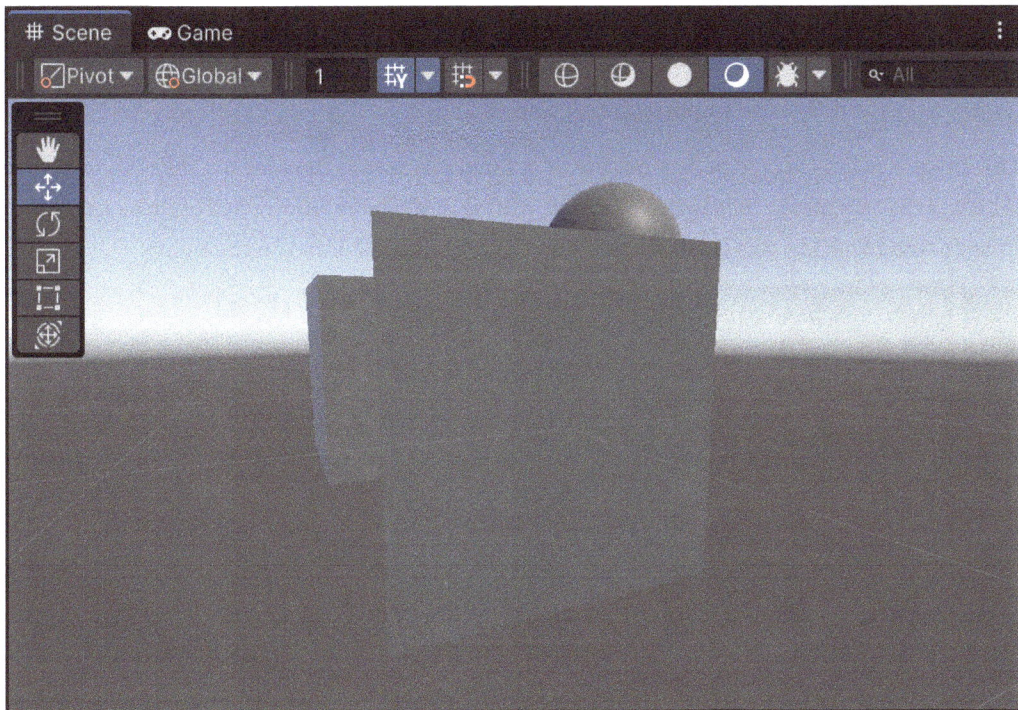

Figure 4.18 – Default scene setup

5. Once you've moved the **Scene** view camera so that you can see the objects, go ahead and select the **Main Camera** in the **Hierarchy** window and then go to **Game Object | Align with View** so that when you play the game, the screen will look the same as it does in the **Scene** view.

In this example, we will use a PNG image file for the glass texture, since it has support for an alpha channel that will be used to determine the transparency of the glass. The process of creating such an image depends on the software that you are using. However, these are the main steps that you will need to follow:

1. Find the image of the glass you want for your windows.

2. Open it with photo editing software, such as **GIMP** or **Photoshop**.

3. Select the parts of the image that you want to be semi-transparent.

4. Create a white (full opacity) layer mask on your image.

5. Use the selection previously made to fill the layer mask with a darker color. White is treated as fully visible, black will be treated as invisible, and gray will be somewhere in the middle.

6. Save the image and import it into Unity.

The image used in this recipe is a picture of stained glass from the *Meaux Cathedral* in France (https://en.wikipedia.org/wiki/Stained_glass). If you have followed all of these steps, your image should look like this (**RGB** channels on the left, and **A** channel on the right):

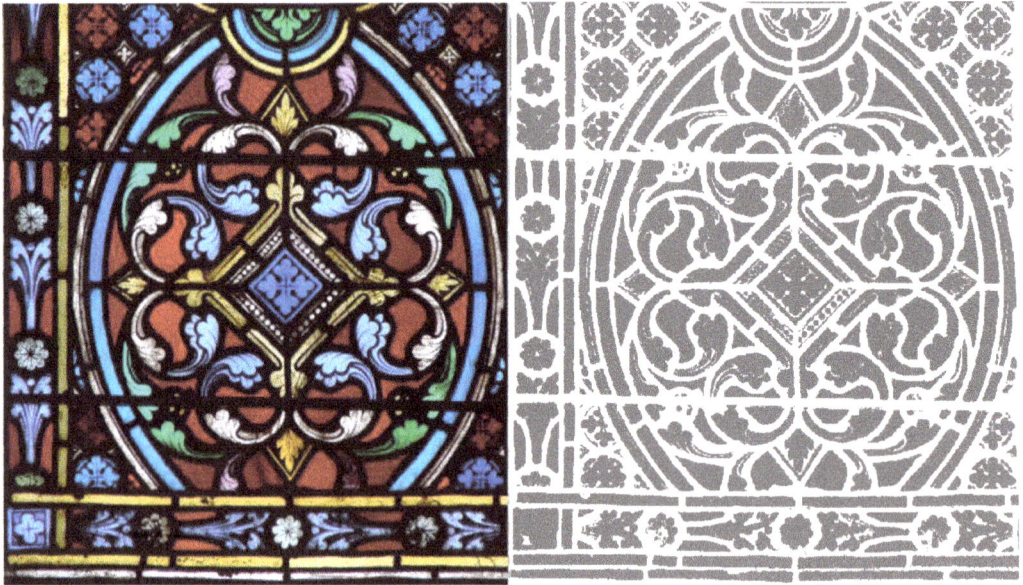

Figure 4.19 – Sample image used in our recipe

You can also make use of the image file provided in the example code for this book in the Chapter 04/Textures folder (Meaux_Vitrail.psd):

1. From the Chapter 04/Shaders folder, duplicate our **TexturedShader** graph and rename the new shader TransparentShader.

2. Open the Shader Graph editor and, from the **Blackboard**, select the **Base Texture** property. From the **Graph Inspector** on the right side, set **Default Value** to your image with transparency.

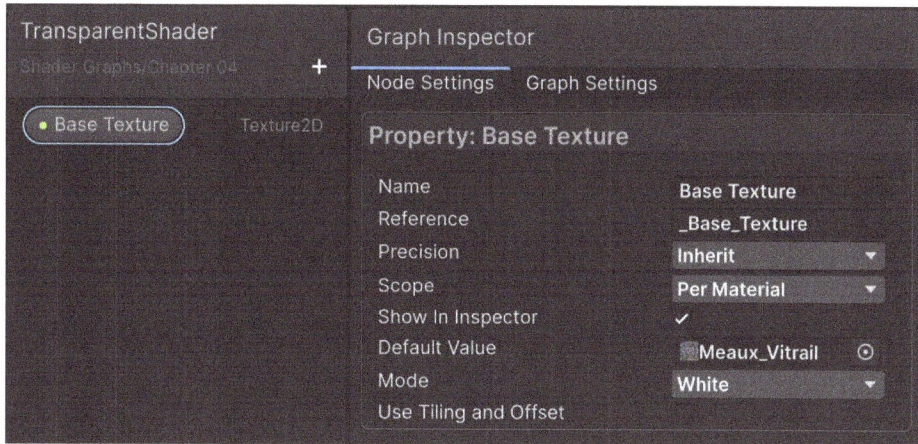

Figure 4.20 – Creating Base Texture properties

3. Save the Shader Graph and close the editor.

4. Next, create a new material (TransparentMat) and set the shader it uses to the Shader Graphs/Chapter 04/Transparent selection.

5. Select the Quad object in the **Hierarchy** window and then drag and drop the material on the object to assign it.

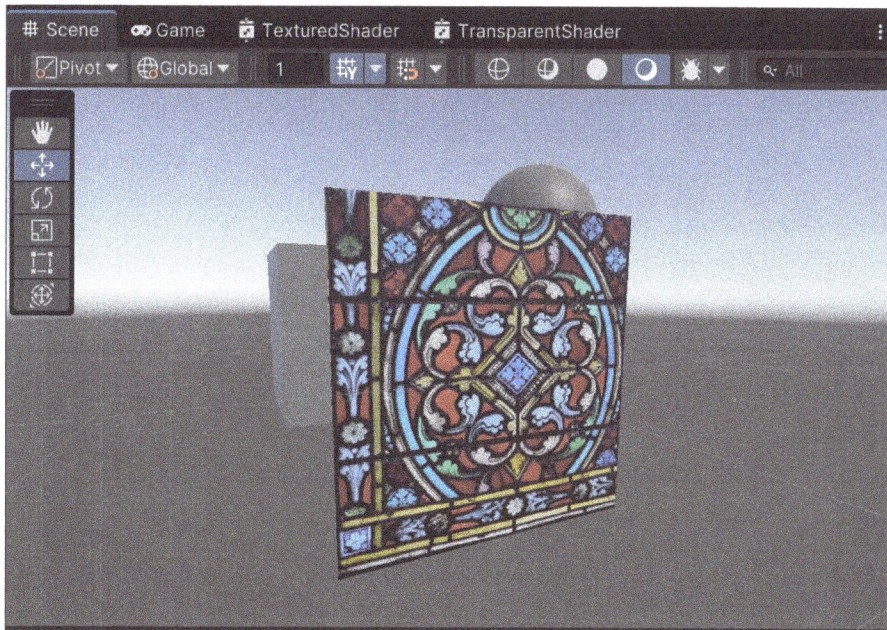

Figure 4.21 – Glass without the transparency effect

As we would like to see behind this, we can make adjustments to the shader to do exactly that.

How to do it...

The following steps show you how to use the properties in a Shader Graph:

1. Double-click on TransparancyShader to open the **Shader Graph** editor.

2. Go to **Graph Inspector**, and click on the **Graph Settings** tab. Change the **Surface Type** to **Transparent**. Ensure the **Blending Mode** is set to **Alpha**. Then, set the **Render Face** to **Both**.

   You should notice that now there is a new channel (Alpha) that was added to the **Fragment** part of the **Master Stack**.

3. Connect the **A(1)** output from the **Sample Texture 2D** node to the **Alpha(1)** input of the **Fragment** part of the **Master Stack**. For clarity's sake, after making the connection, we can create a redirect node by either right-clicking on the connection and selecting **Add Redirect Node** or by selecting the connection and pressing *Ctrl + R*.

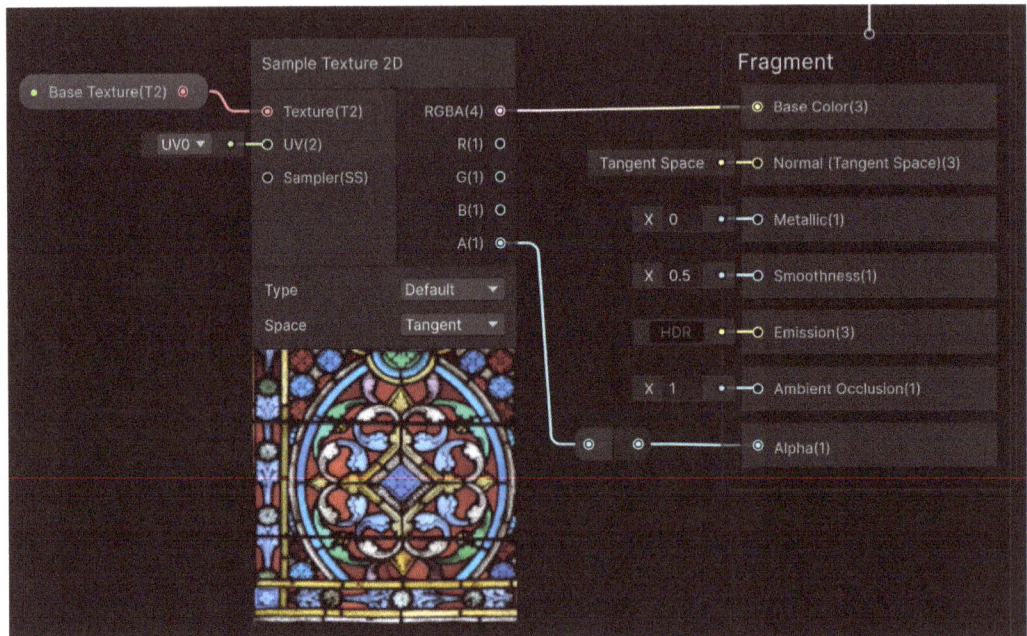

Figure 4.22 – Creating a redirect node for the Alpha

This node is merely for aesthetic purposes but makes it easier to follow the path, so I try to use it when needed.

4. Save the Shader Graph and close the editor. If you look at the material, you should see where we added the gray, there is transparency!

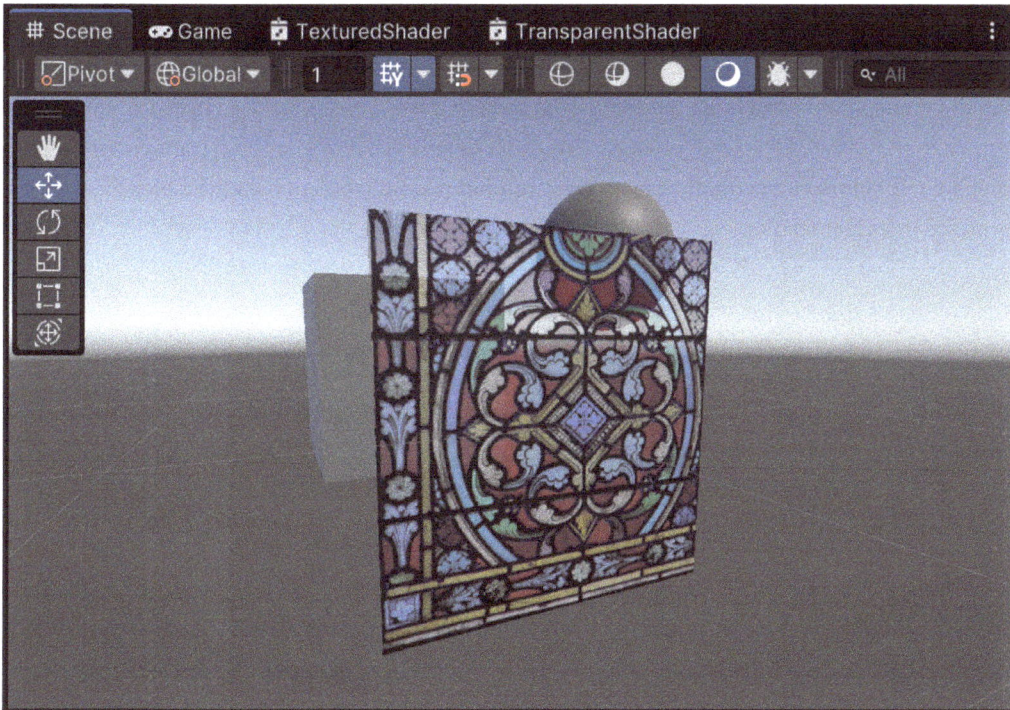

Figure 4.23 – Example of the transparency effect in use

Notice that you can now see the cube and sphere behind the glass. Perfect!

How it works...

Transparent objects are handled differently than opaque objects in Unity for efficiency reasons. When rendering opaque objects, Unity draws them starting with the closest object. This approach is efficient because any object behind the closest one is obscured and does not need to be drawn at all. This leads to a performance gain since fewer objects require rendering.

Transparent objects, however, require a different approach. They need to blend their color with the color of objects behind them based on their alpha value. This process is called **alpha-blended transparency**.

First, all opaque objects are drawn before any transparent objects. This is crucial because transparent objects need the background to be already drawn to blend colors correctly.

Second, Unity uses a queue system where shaders are assigned a queue number. Shaders with lower numbers are drawn before those with higher numbers. If we were writing shaders using code, we would need to specify this number manually, but Shader Graph handles this assignment automatically by default.

Finally, transparent objects are rendered from back to front. Objects furthest from the camera are drawn first, followed by closer objects. This order ensures that overlapping transparent objects blend their colors correctly. If objects were rendered from front to back, the blending would produce incorrect results.

Note

The fact that the Transparent queue is rendered after Geometry does not mean that our glass will appear on top of all the other solid objects. Unity will draw the glass last, but it will not render pixels that belong to pieces of geometry hidden behind something else. This control is done using a technique called *ZBuffering*.

One thing that's important to note is that transparent objects don't receive shadows in Unity. Transparent objects can cast shadows by rendering the object as opaque in a shadow pass, which is what is done when **Cast Shadows** is enabled (which it is by default in Shader Graph).

The last concept introduced is **Blend Mode** which when set to **Alpha** will take all the pixels from this material to be blended with what was on the screen before according to their alpha values. Without this directive, the pixels will be drawn in the correct order, but they will not have any transparency.

There's more...

If you would like to set the queue number, select **Material** and, under **Advanced Options**, change the **Queue Control** property to UserOverride. This will enable the **Render Queue** property to be set from what the shader provided or customized. Unity has provided us with some default render queues, each with a unique value that directs Unity when to draw the object to the screen. The built-in render queues that are shown under the **Render Queue** property are called Geometry, AlphaTest, and Transparent; however, Unity also has Background and Overlay defined. These queues weren't just created arbitrarily; they actually serve a purpose to make our lives easier when writing shaders and interacting with the real-time renderer.

Refer to the following table for descriptions of the use of each of these individual render queues:

Render Queue	Description	Render Queue Value
`Background`	This friend or queue is rendered first. It is used for skyboxes and so on.	1000
`Geometry`	This is the default render queue. It is used for most objects. Opaque geometry uses this queue.	2000
`AlphaTest`	Alpha-tested geometry uses this queue. It's different from the `Geometry` queue as it's more efficient to render alpha-tested objects after all of the solid objects have been drawn.	2450
`Transparent`	This queue is rendered after the `Geometry` and `AlphaTest` queues in back-to-front order. Anything that's alpha blended where the shaders don't write to the depth buffer should go here, for example, things such as glass and particle effects.	3000
`Overlay`	This render queue is meant for overlay effects. Anything rendered last should go here, for example, lens flare.	4000

Table 4.1 – Render queues and their usage

Packing and blending textures

Textures are not only useful for storing loads of data or pixel colors, as we generally tend to think of them, but also for multiple sets of pixels in both the X and Y directions and RGBA channels. We can actually pack multiple images into a single RGBA texture, and use each of the R, G, B, and A components as individual textures by extracting each of these components from the shader code.

The result of packing individual grayscale images into a single RGBA texture can be seen in the following screenshot:

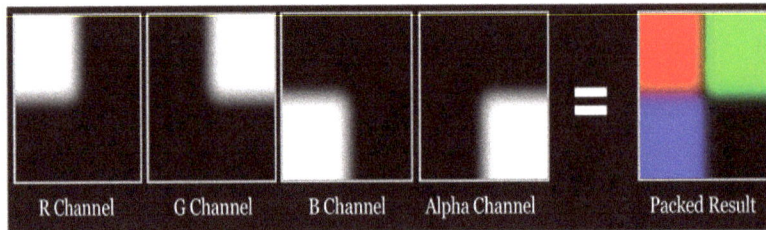

Figure 4.24 – Packing

Why is this helpful? Well, in terms of the amount of memory that your application takes up, textures are a large portion of your application's size. We can, of course, reduce the size of the image, but then we would lose the detail of how it can be represented. So, to begin reducing the size of your application, we can look at all of the images that we are using in our shader and see whether we can merge these textures into a single texture. Using a single texture with multiple images in it requires fewer draw calls and less overhead than separate files. We can also use this concept to combine irregularly shaped textures (that is, those that are not squares) into a single one to take up less space than giving them their own full texture.

Any texture that is grayscale can be packed into one of the RGBA channels of another texture. This might sound a bit odd at first, but this recipe is going to demonstrate one of the uses of packing a texture and using these packed textures in a shader.

One example of using these packed textures is when you want to blend a set of textures together onto a single surface. You see this most often in terrain shaders, where you need to blend into another texture nicely using some sort of control texture or, in this case, the packed texture. This recipe covers this technique and shows you how to construct the beginnings of a nice four-texture blended terrain shader.

Getting ready

Let's create a new shader file in your Shaders folder (TextureBlending) and then create a new material for this shader (TextureBlendingMat). The naming convention is entirely up to you for your shader and material files, so try your best to keep them organized and easy to reference later on.

Once you have your shader and material ready, create a new scene in which we can test our shader. Inside the scene, place the `Terrain_001` object from the `Chapter 04/Models` folder and assign the **TextureBlendingMat** material to it:

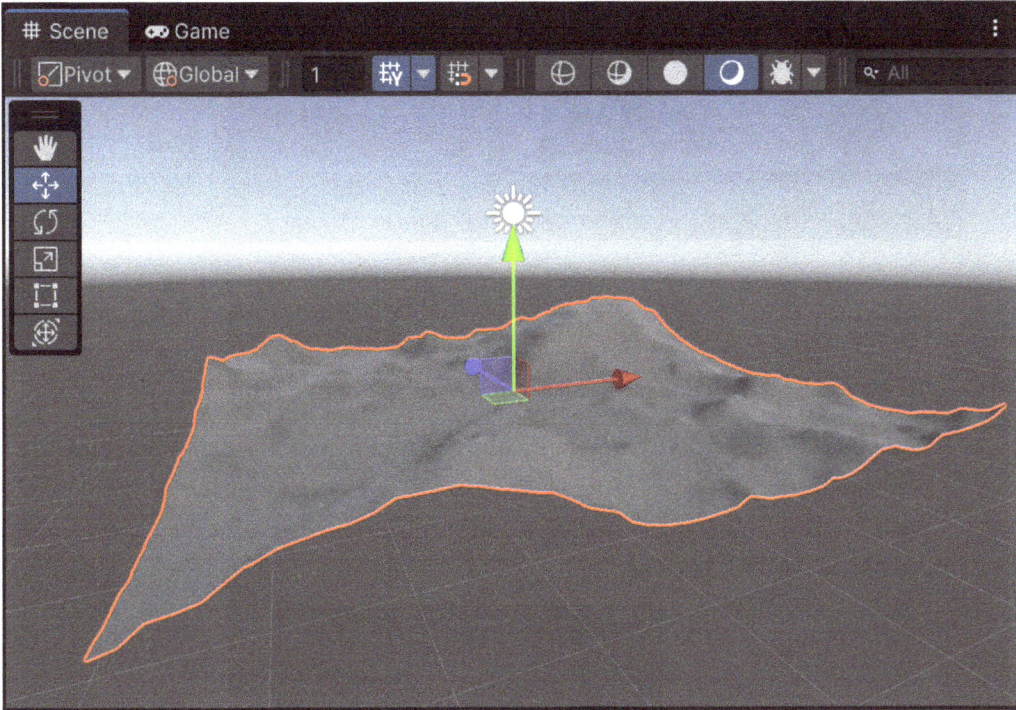

Figure 4.25 – Terrain with material applied

You will also need to gather up four textures that you would want to blend together. These can be anything, but for a nice terrain shader, you will want grass, dirt, rocky dirt, and rock textures. You can find these assets in the `Chapter 01/Standard Assets/Environment/TerrainAssets/SurfaceTextures` folder in the example code for this book.

Finally, we will also need a blending texture that is packed with grayscale images. This will give us the four blending textures that we can use to direct how the color textures will be placed on the object surface.

We can use very intricate blending textures to create a very realistic distribution of terrain textures over a terrain mesh, as shown in the following screenshot:

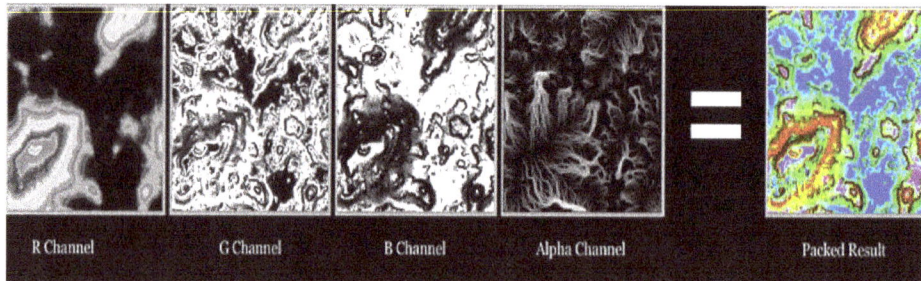

Figure 4.26 – Example of blended textures

How to do it...

To get started, let's first add some properties that we will use in this graph:

1. In the **Blackboard**, add a new property of type **Color** named Diffuse Tint. Create two other **Color** properties named Terrain Color A and Terrain Color B. Then, we will create five Texture2D variables called Red Channel, Green Channel, Blue Channel, Alpha Channel, and Blend Texture.

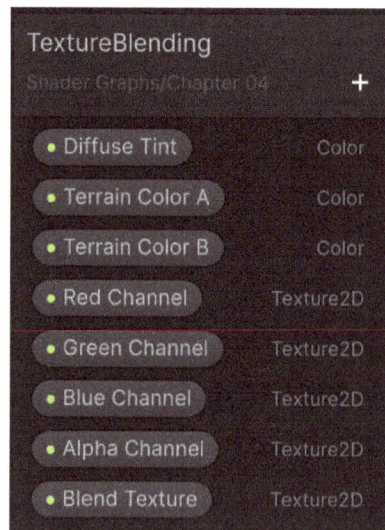

Figure 4.27 – Properties for the TextureBlending shader

2. To start, drag out the **Blend Texture**, **Red Channel**, and **Green Channel** textures to the graph. Then create three **Sample Texture 2D** nodes and connect the **Texture(T2)** input to each of them.

3. Next, we need to create a **Lerp** node. The **Lerp** node is used to blend between two values (**A** & **B**) based on a weight factor (**T**). In shader programming, it's commonly used to smoothly transition between textures, colors, or other values.

4. Connect the **RGBA(4)** output of the **Red Channel** texture's **Sample Texture 2D** node to **A** of the **Lerp** node, and it will convert to the **Vector4** version.

5. Then connect the **RGBA(4)** output of the **Green Channel** texture's **Sample Texture 2D** node to **B** of the Lerp. Finally, connect the **G(1)** output of the **Blend Texture's Sample Texture 2D** node to the **T(1)** of the **Lerp** node. To make it easier to see the connections, I created two reroute nodes.

6. To make it easier to see the result of the **Lerp** from the **Blackboard**, select **Blend Texture**, set the image to `TerrainBlend`, and then set **Red Channel** to another texture; I used `CliffAlbedoSpecular`. If all goes well, you should see something like the following:

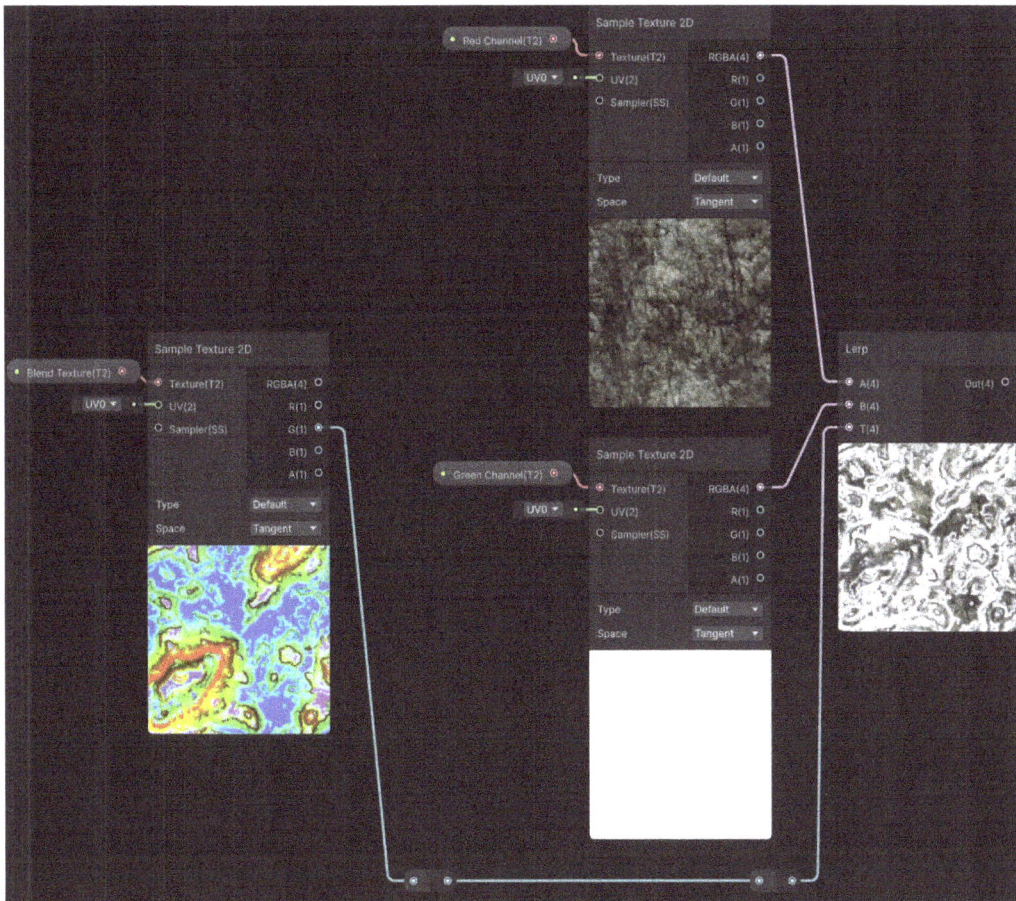

Figure 4.28 – Lerping B and G channels

Here, we can see the green texture is being painted on top of the red texture where there is green in the blend texture image.

7. To make it easier to see the result, set **Default Values** of the other channel textures (I used GrassRockyAlbedo for green, GrassHillAlbedo for blue, and SandAlbedo for the alpha channel).

8. Drag and drop the **Blue Channel** texture to the graph and add a **Sample Texture 2D** node to get its data. Then create another **Lerp** node and connect the **Out(4)** of the first **Lerp** node into **A** of this newly created one. Then, connect the **RGBA(4)** output of the **Sample Texture 2D** connected to the Blue Channel texture to **B(4)**. Finally, connect **B(1)** from the **Blend Texture's Sample Texture 2D** node to **T(4)**. If all goes well, you should see the grass texture being used where blue is on the blend texture:

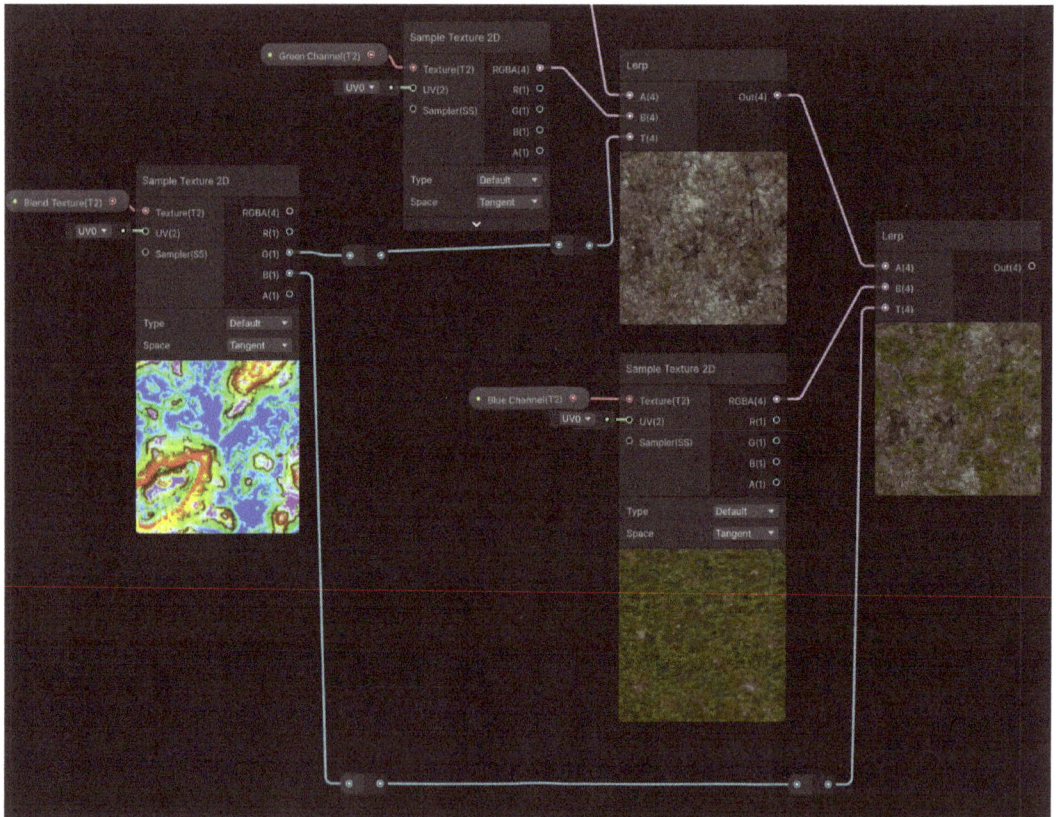

Figure 4.29 – Lerping to the B channel

9. Finally, we need to do the Alpha channel. Drag and drop the **Alpha Channel** texture to the graph and add a **Sample Texture 2D** node to get its data. Then, create another **Lerp** node and connect the **Out(4)** of the last **Lerp** node to **A** of this newly created one. Then, connect the **RGBA(4)** output of the **Sample Texture 2D** connected to the **Alpha Channel** texture to **B(4)**. Finally, connect **A(1)** from the **Blend Texture**'s **Sample Texture 2D** node to the **T(4)**. If all goes well, you should see the sand texture being used in various places of the blend texture:

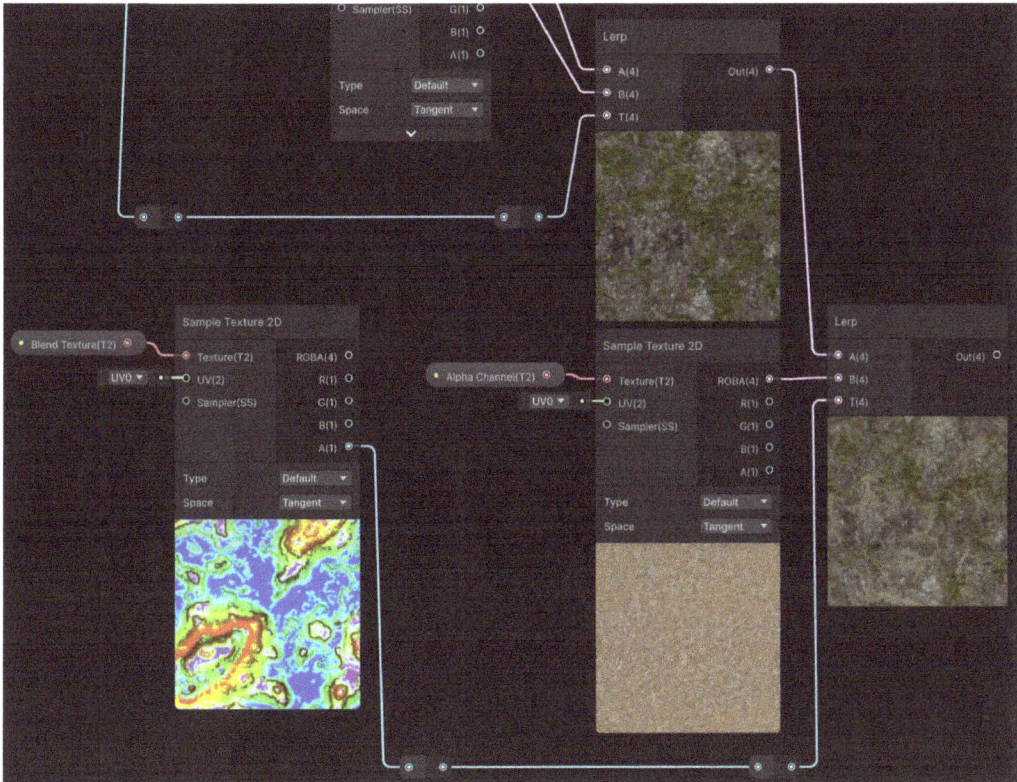

Figure 4.30 – Lerping to the Alpha channel

10. Finally, connect the **Out(4)** of the **Lerp** node to the **Base Color** of the **Fragment** section of the **Master Stack**.

11. Save the Shader Graph and return to the Unity Editor. You may notice the material may still be all white. To use our default values, you can click on the three-dot button in the top right of the **Inspector** window with the material selected and select **Reset**.

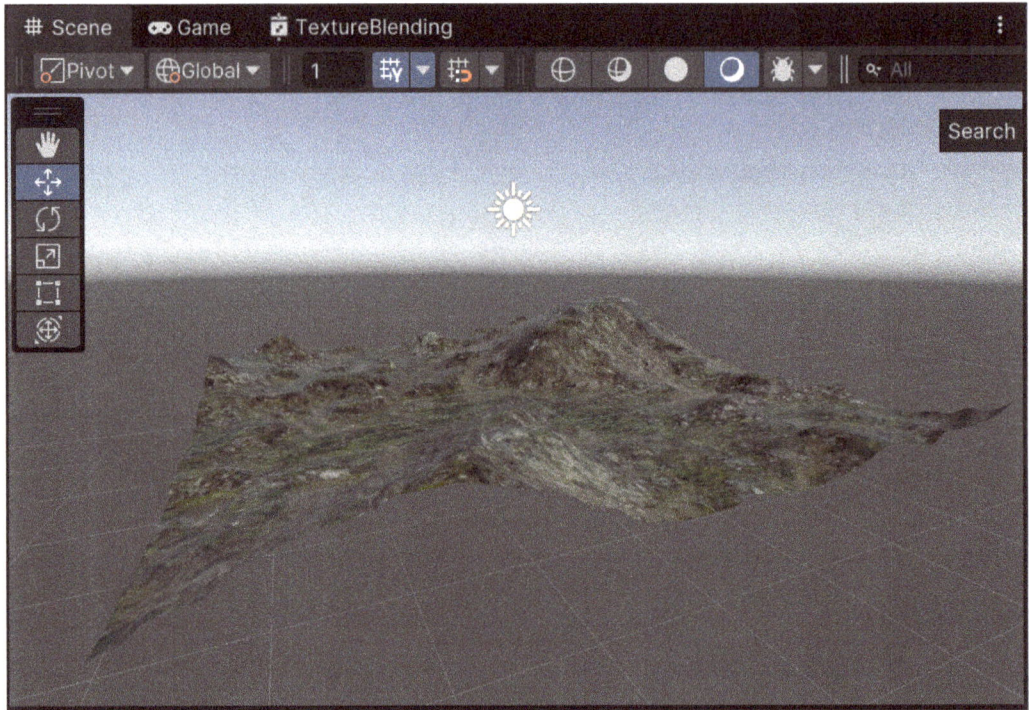

Figure 4.31 – Blended Textures result

This is great, but we currently aren't using the R channel. Next, we multiply our blended texture by the color tint values and use the red channel to determine where the two different terrain tint colors go:

1. In the **Blackboard**, change the values of **Terrain Color A** and **Terrain Color B**. I used white for A and red for B.

2. Remove the connection of the final color to the **Base Color** by selecting it and pressing the *delete* key.

3. Create another **Lerp** node. Connect **A** to **Terrain Color A** and **B** to **Terrain Color B**. In **T(4)**, connect the **R(1)** channel from our **Blend Texture**'s **Sample Texture 2D** node.

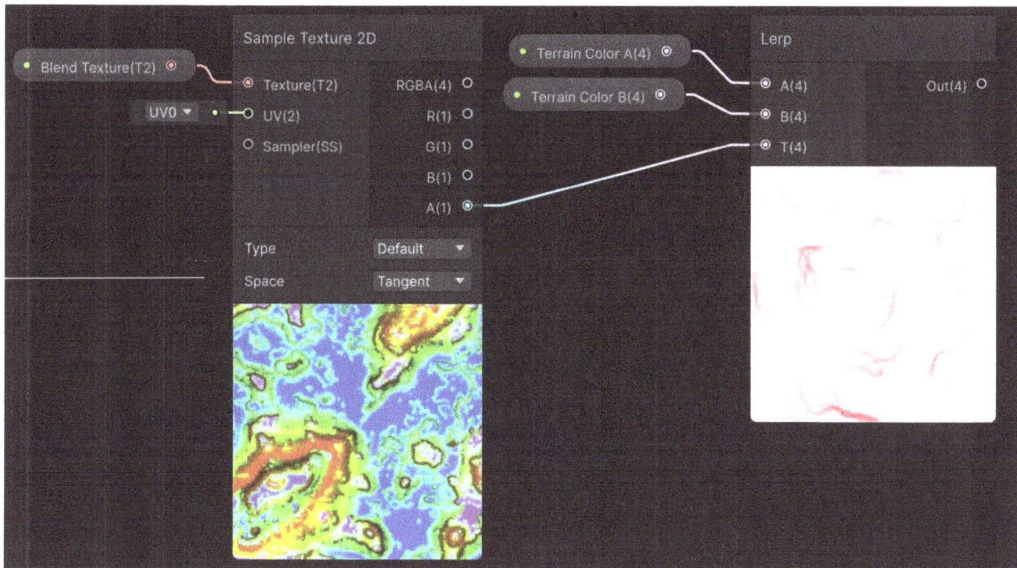

Figure 4.32 – Terrain Color Lerp

4. Next, create a **Multiply** node. In the **A** slot, place the combined color **Lerp** output. Then, connect the output of our newly created **Lerp** into **B**. It is possible with multiplication to have invalid values, so, to the right of the **Multiply** node, create a **Saturate** node and connect the **Out** from the **Multiply** node to the **In** of the **Saturate** node.

5. Drag and drop the **Diffuse Tint** color onto the graph. Create another **Multiply** node and, in the **A** slot, put the output of the **Saturate** node. Then, in the **B** slot, put the **Diffuse Tint**. Finally, connect the **Out** of the final multiply to the **Base Color** of the fragment part of the **Master Stack**.

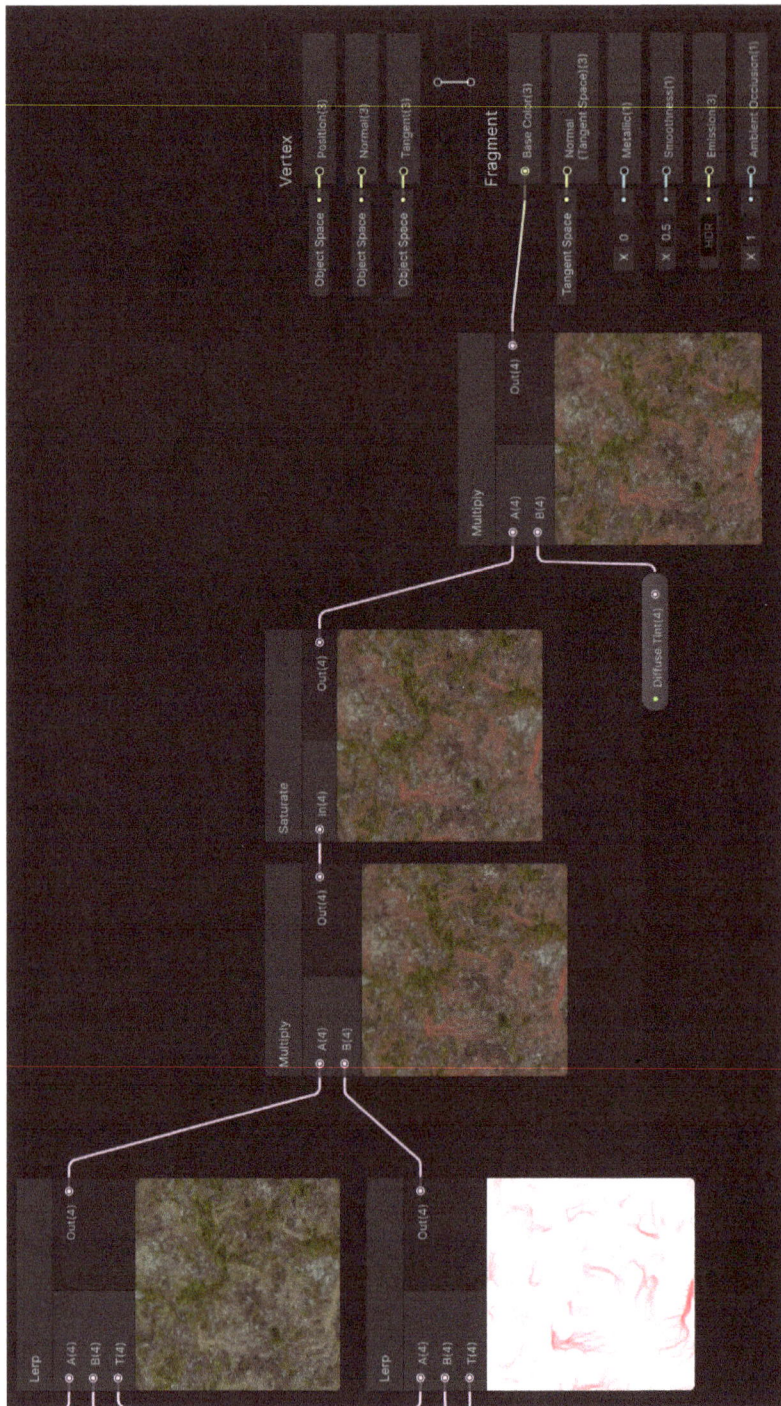

Figure 4.33 – Connecting the final Multiply node to the Base Color node

6. Save the Shader Graph and return to the Unity Editor, resetting the material if needed.

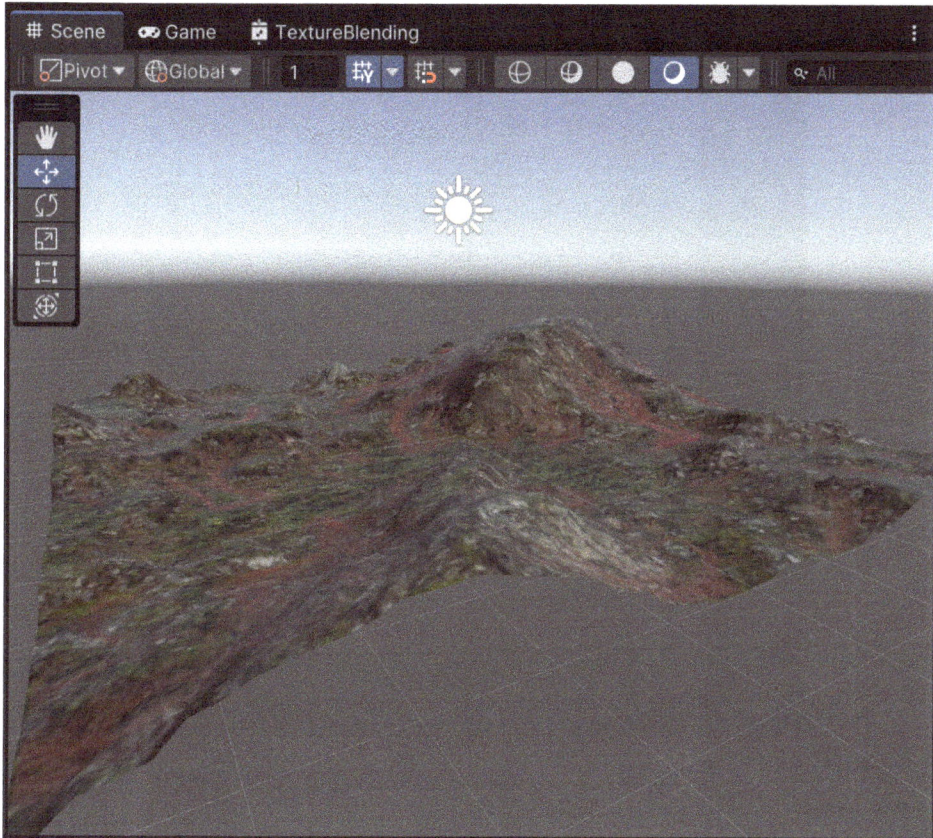

Figure 4.34 – Final result

And with that, we can now see the colors being used as well!

This effect can be taken even further by using different textures and terrain tinting to create some great-looking terrains with minimal effort. The result of blending together four terrain textures and creating a terrain tinting technique can be seen in the following screenshot:

Figure 4.35 – Further example of the blended textures

How it works...

This might seem like quite a few nodes, but the concept behind blending is actually quite simple. For the technique to work, we have to employ the **Lerp** node that calls the built-in `lerp()` function from the **CgFX** standard library. This function allows us to pick a value between argument one and argument two, using argument three as the blend amount:

Function	Description
`lerp(a,b,t)`	This involves linear interpolation: $(1-t)*a+b*f$ Here, a and b are matching vectors or scalar types. The t parameter can be either a scalar or vector of the same type as a and b.

Table 4.2 – Usage of the lerp() function for linear interpolation

So, for example, if we wanted to find the mid-value between 1 and 2, we could feed the 0.5 value as the third argument to the lerp() function and it would return 1.5. This works perfectly for our blending needs, as the values of an individual channel in an RGBA texture are single float values, usually in the range of 0 to 1.

In the graph, we simply take one of the channels from our **Blend Texture** and use it to drive the color that is picked in a **Lerp** node for each pixel. For instance, we take our grass texture and dirt texture, use the red channel from our blending texture, and feed this to the **Lerp** node. This will give us the correct blended color result for each pixel on the surface.

The shader code simply uses the four channels of the **Blend Texture** and all the color textures to create a final blended texture. This final texture then becomes the color that we can multiply with our diffuse lighting.

Creating a circle around your terrain

Many **real-time strategy** (**RTS**) games display distances (range attack, moving distance, sight, and so on) by drawing a circle around the selected unit. If the terrain is flat, this can be done simply by stretching a quad with the texture of a circle. If that's not the case, the quad will most likely be clipped behind a hill or another piece of geometry. This recipe will show you how to create a shader that allows you to draw circles around an object of arbitrary complexity. If you want to be able to move or animate your circle, you will need both a shader and a C# script.

Getting ready

Despite working with every piece of geometry, this technique is oriented to terrains. Hence, the first step is setting up a terrain in Unity, but instead of using a model, we will create one within the Unity Editor:

1. Let's start by creating a new shader called RadiusShader and the respective material, RadiusMat.

2. Create a GameObject to represent your character; we will draw a circle around it later on.

   From the menu, navigate to **GameObject** | **3D Object** | **Terrain** to create a new terrain.

3.   Create the geometry for your terrain. You can either import an existing one or draw your own using the tools available (**Raise/Lower Terrain**, **Paint Height**, **Smooth Height**):

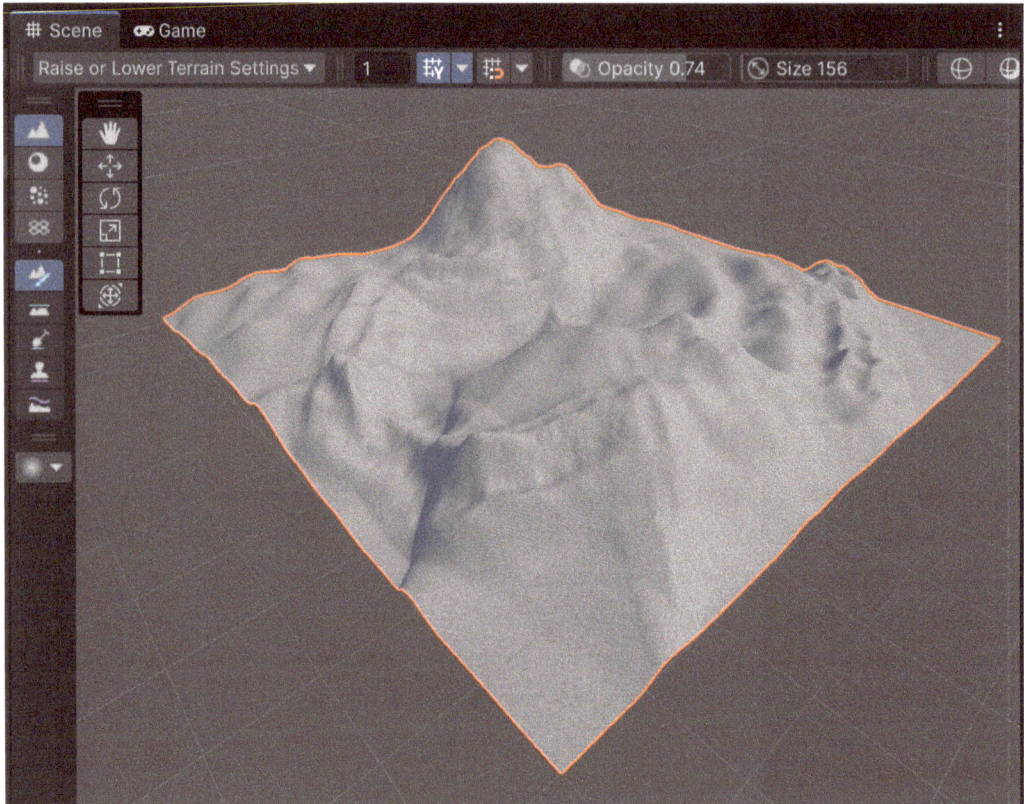

Figure 4.36 – Terrain example

Terrains are special objects in Unity, and the way texture mapping works on them is different from traditional 3D models. You cannot provide _MainTex from a shader as it needs to be provided directly from the terrain itself. To do this, you will first need to go to the **Raise or Lower Terrain** dropdown and select **Paint Texture**:

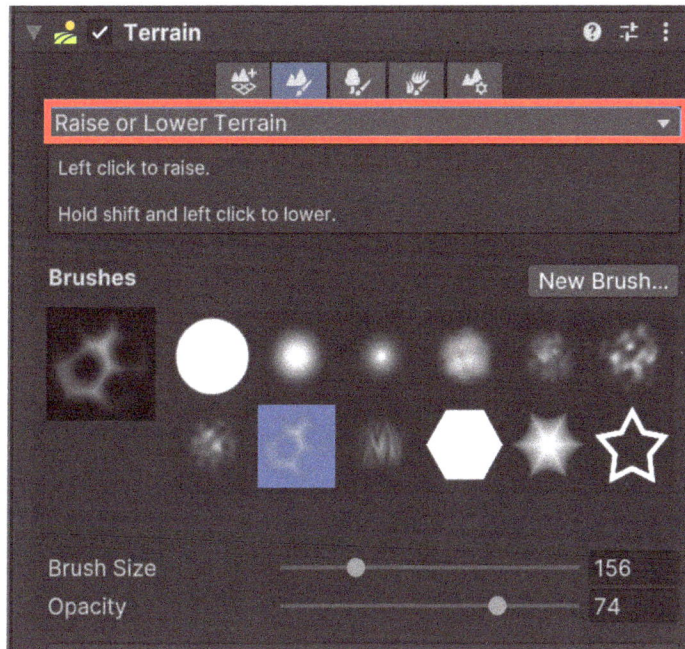

Figure 4.37 – Adding Paint Texture

4.   Afterward, in the **Terrain Layers** section, select **Edit Terrain Layers...** and then **Add Layer**. Select a material and apply it:

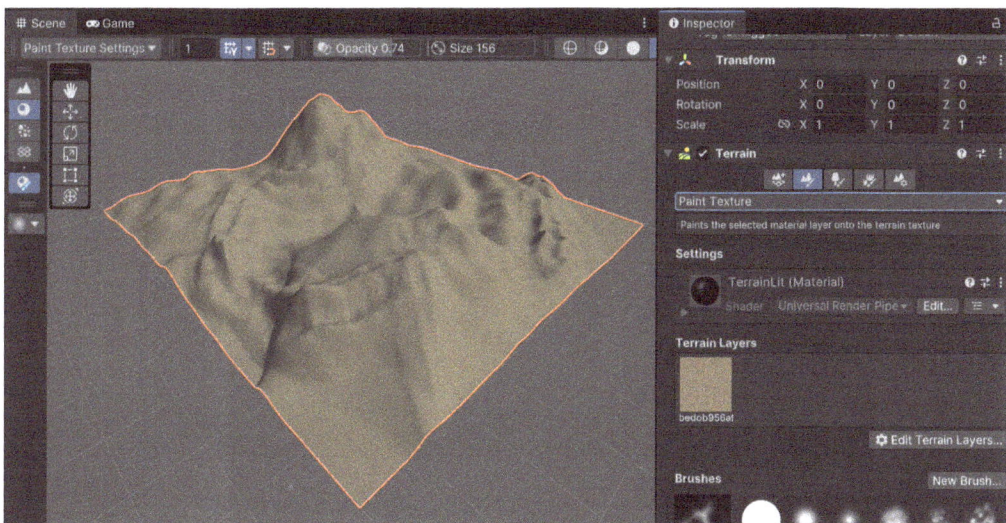

Figure 4.38 – An example of the terrain with the initial texture

Note

The creation of a terrain isn't covered in this book, but if you would like to learn more about it, check out the following link:

`https://docs.unity3d.com/Manual/terrain-UsingTerrains.html`

5. Now that the texture is set, you have to change the material of the terrain so that a custom shader can be provided. From the **Terrain** settings, change the **Material** property to the **RadiusMat** material:

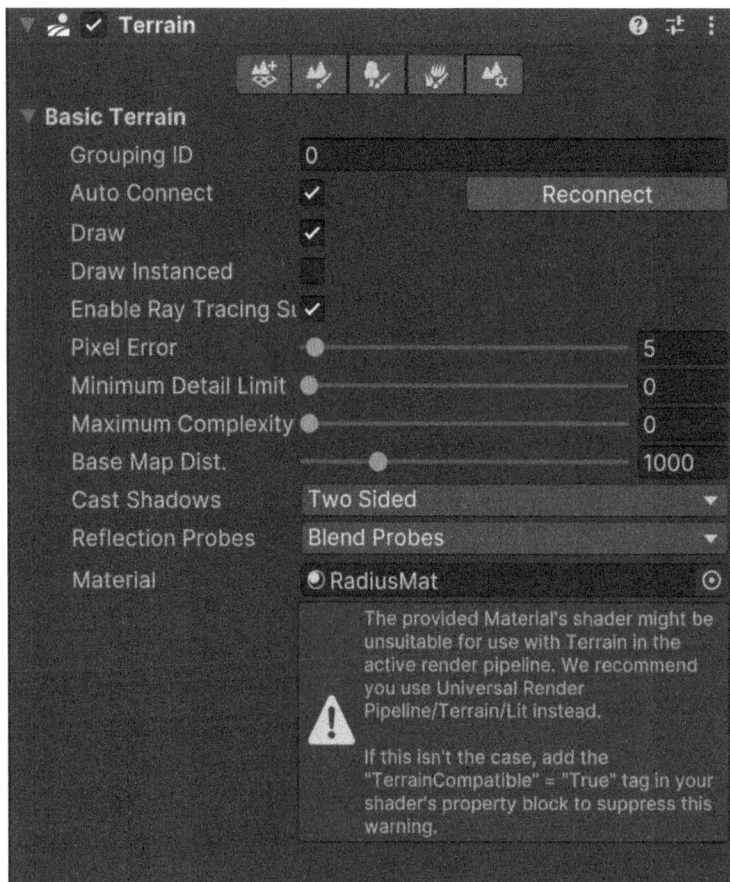

Figure 4.39 – Applying the RadiusMat property

You are now ready to create your shader. As you can see, there is a warning in the preceding screenshot stating the shader may be unsuitable for use with terrains. You can simply ignore that warning about it possibility not working. If you would like to remove the warning, after finishing this recipe you may add the tag to the property block after compiling the Shader Graph code; but it is not necessary.

How to do it...

With our scene set up, we can start creating our diffuse shader using Shader Graph:

1. Double-click on the `RadiusShader` to open the Shader Graph.

2. In the **Blackboard** (the panel on the left), double-click on the grayed-out Shader Graphs text and change it to `Shader Graphs/Chapter 04`.

3. Then, click the + button and add the following properties in the **Blackboard**:

   - **Center** (Vector) with the default value, `(500,0,500,0)`.
   - **Radius** (Float) with the default value, `100`.
   - **RadiusColor** (Color) with the default value of red `(1,0,0,1)`.
   - **RadiusWidth** (Float) with the default value, `10`.
   - **Splat0** (Texture2D) as the main texture of the terrain. Uncheck the **Show in Inspector** property and ensure the **Reference** property is set to `_Splat0`. `Splat0` is often the default texture used for the base layer of the terrain, providing the foundational look and feel upon which other textures can be layered.

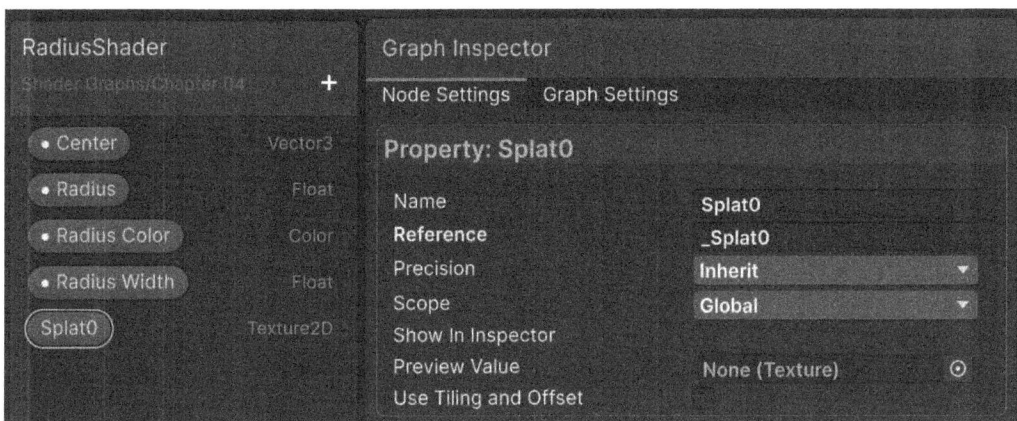

Figure 4.40 – Creating the Splat0 property

4. Create a **Position** node and ensure the **Space** is set to **World**. Below that place drag and drop the **Center** property. To the right of those nodes, create a **Distance** node.

5. To the right of that, create two **Comparison** nodes. Under the dropdowns, set the top one to **Greater** and the other one to **Less Or Equal**. To both **Comparison** nodes connect the **Distance Out(1)** as the **A** value. For the top one, drag and drop the **Radius** property into the graph and assign that as the **B(1)** value.

6. Create an **Add** node and add **Radius** and **Radius Width**. Connect that output to the second **Comparison** node.

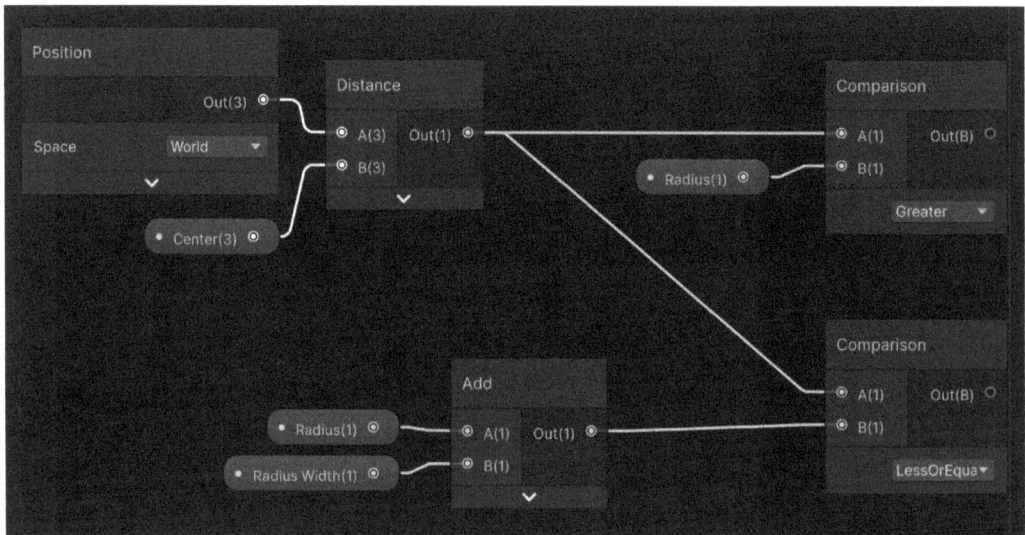

Figure 4.41 – Creating the two comparisons

7. To the right of both of those **Comparison** nodes, create an **And** node. Connect the output of each of the comparisons to the **A** and **B** of the **And** node. When both of these conditions are true, the result of the **And** node will be 1, otherwise it'll give us 0.

8. Create a **Lerp** node. Drag and drop the **Splat0** node into the graph and create a **Sample Texture 2D** node connected to it. Connect the **RGBA(4)** of the **Sample Texture 2D** node to the **A** of the **Lerp**, then connect **Radius Color** to the **B** node, dragging it out from the **Blackboard**. Finally, connect the **Out(4)** of the **Lerp** node to the **Base Color(3)** in the **Fragment** section of the **Master Stack**.

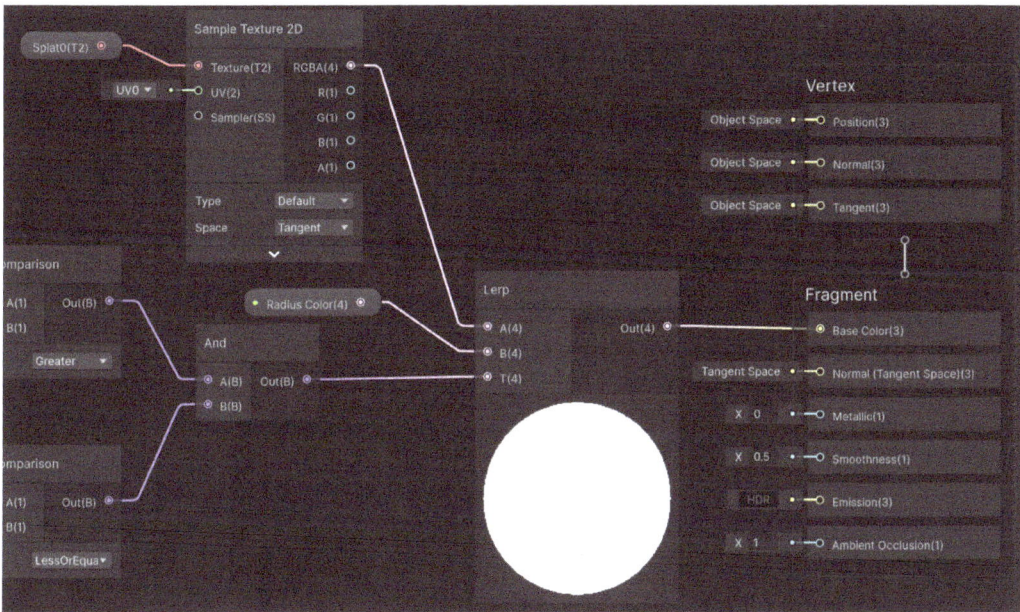

Figure 4.42 – Connecting the Lerp to the Base Color

9.   Save the Shader Graph and return to the Unity Editor.

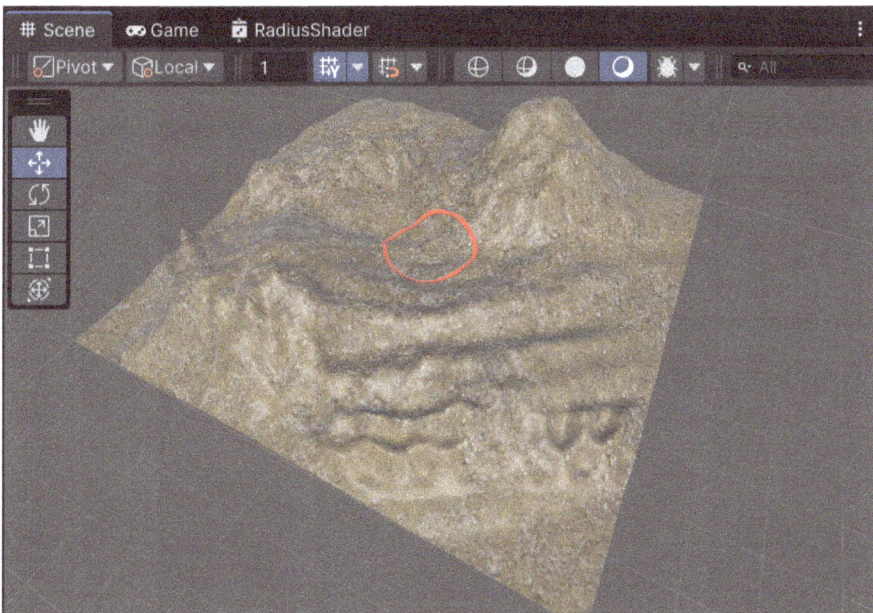

Figure 4.43 – RadiusMat's default look

How it works...

The relevant parameters to draw a circle are its center, radius, and color. By adding the **Position** node to our shader, we are asking Unity to provide us with the position of the pixel that we are drawing expressed in world coordinates. This is the actual position of an object in the editor.

In our Shader Graph, we first calculate the distance from the point being drawn and the center of the radius, and then the graph checks whether it is between *Radius* and *Radius + Radius Width*; if this is the case, it uses the chosen color. If not, we then will utilize the **Splat0** texture, which is something that is created by Unity's terrain system, but the **Splat0** texture only defines the first texture that the terrain may have. If you wish to have multiple textures on your terrain object, you'd need to use *Splat1-3* as well and lerp them with each of the four channels of another Texture2D with a reference of _Control, like in the *Packing and blending textures* recipe earlier in this chapter.

You can see a video going through the process of adding the other Splat textures and adding holes to terrains for things like tunnels here: https://www.youtube.com/watch?v=kmPj2GmoMWo&t=1454s.

There's more...

This is great, but you'll probably also want to change where the circle is at runtime, which we can do via code. If you want the circle to follow your character, other steps are necessary:

1. Create a new `MonoBehaviour` script called `SetRadiusProperties`.

2. Since you may wish to see this change both in the game and outside, we can add a tag to the top of the class saying to execute this code while in the editor, in addition to when the game is being played:

    ```
    [ExecuteInEditMode]
    public class SetRadiusProperties : MonoBehaviour
    ```

3. Add these properties to the script:

    ```
    public Material radiusMaterial;
    public float radius = 1;
    public Color color = Color.white;
    ```

4. In the Update() method, add these lines of code:

```
if (radiusMaterial != null)
{
    radiusMaterial.SetVector("_Center", transform.position);
    radiusMaterial.SetFloat("_Radius", radius);
    radiusMaterial.SetColor("_Radius_Color", color);
}
```

5. Attach the script to the object you wish to have the circle drawn around by locating the object in the **Hierarchy** window that you want to draw the circle around, then select the object to highlight it.

6. In the **Inspector** window, scroll down to find the **Add Component** button. Click **Add Component** and either type (SetRadiusProperties) or find it in the list of available scripts. Finally, click on your script to add it to the object.

7. Finally, drag the RadiusMat material to the **Radius Material** slot of the script:

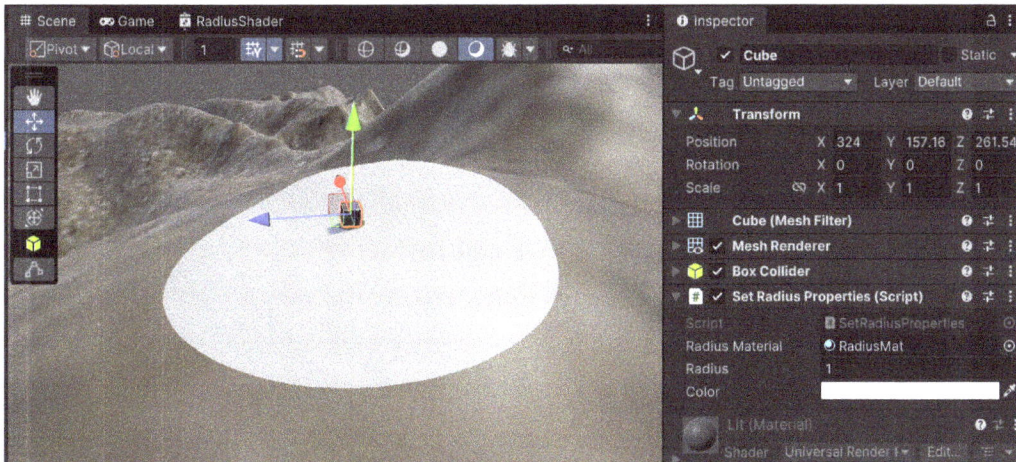

Figure 4.44 – Default options with the cube attached to it

You can now move your character around, and this will create a nice circle around it. Changing the properties of the Radius script will change the radius as well.

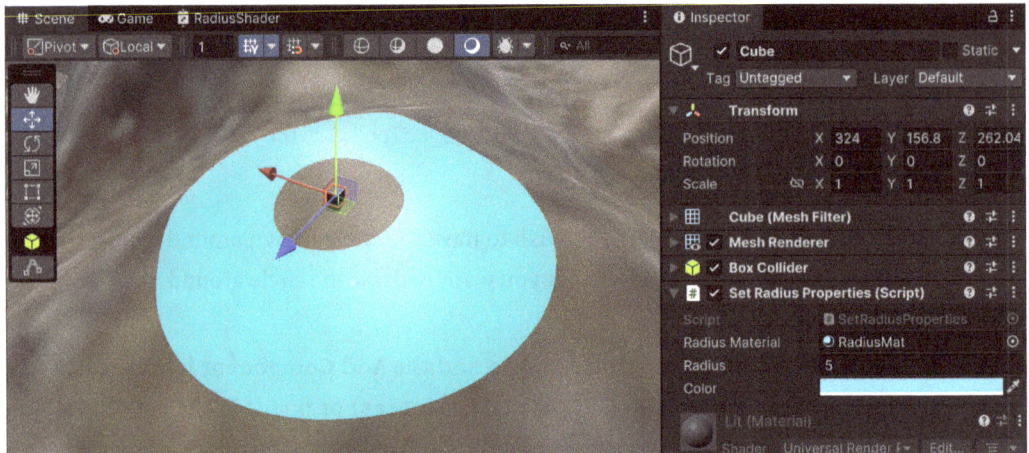

Figure 4.45 – Tweaking the properties of the SetRadiusProperties component

5

Enhancing Realism: Unity Muse and Physically Based Rendering

Creating realistic visuals in game development requires high-quality materials that accurately simulate how light interacts with surfaces. Traditionally, achieving this level of realism requires extensive manual work, but new tools like Unity Muse are revolutionizing the process.

Unity Muse is a generative AI-powered tool designed to streamline asset creation, allowing developers to rapidly generate high-quality textures and materials using simple text prompts. With Muse, artists and developers can prototype and refine visuals quickly, making it an invaluable addition to any workflow. In this chapter, we will explore how Unity Muse enhances Physically Based Rendering (PBR) by generating materials that behave realistically under different lighting conditions.

Introduced in Unity 5, **Physically Based Rendering** or **PBR** is a shading model that simulates how light interacts with materials in a physically accurate way. Unlike traditional shading models, which rely on approximations, PBR mimics real-world material properties, ensuring consistency under different lighting conditions. Despite this, the term PBR has been widely used in marketing campaigns and is more of a synonym for state-of-the-art rendering than a well-defined technique.

Unity implements PBR through its **Standard Shader**, which allows developers to define material properties using physically meaningful parameters. Unlike traditional Surface Shaders, which provide flexibility without enforcing real-world constraints, the Standard Shader ensures that materials follow the laws of physics. This results in more realistic reflections, shadows, and overall material behavior.

While PBR ensures that materials behave realistically, the lighting system in Unity determines how these materials appear in different environments. Light reflects off surfaces, interacts with rough or smooth materials, and contributes to the overall realism of a scene.

All the lighting models we will encounter in *Chapter 11, Understanding Lighting Models*, are simplified descriptions of how light behaves. The most important aspect of these models is efficiency—real-time shading is computationally expensive, so techniques such as Lambertian or Blinn-Phong are compromises between performance and realism. While these models allow for fast rendering, they do not capture the full complexity of real-world light interactions, particularly with PBR aspects such as how **global illumination** (**GI**) simulates how light bounces off objects and affects nearby surfaces. However, accurately calculating light interactions in real time is computationally expensive. Unity provides optimized solutions that approximate GI while balancing performance and visual fidelity. Some advanced features, such as reflections, require additional user input to fine-tune which we will discuss.

By the end of this chapter, you will have a better understanding of what PBR is, how it works, and how it can be utilized through several shader examples, leveraging Unity Muse for enhanced creativity and prototyping.

In this chapter, we will cover the following recipes:

- Utilizing generative AI for texture creation
- Utilizing the refinements menu on Muse materials
- Understanding the metallic setup
- Adding transparency to PBR
- Creating mirrors and reflective surfaces
- Baking lights into your scene

Technical requirements

For this chapter, you will need Unity Editor version 6 Preview 6000.0.07f1. This chapter's instructions should work with minimal changes in future versions of the editor in projects that utilize the **Universal Render Pipeline** (**URP**). The chapter's project was created using the **Universal 3D Core** template.

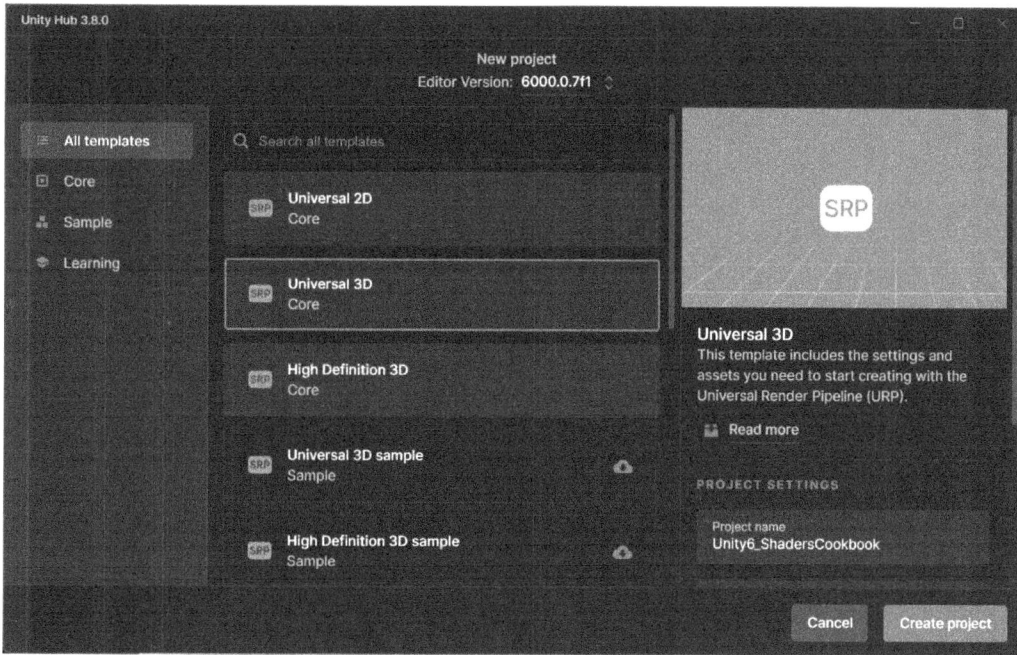

Figure 5.1 – Universal 3D (URP) project

The code files for this chapter can be found on GitHub at https://github.com/PacktPublishing/ Unity-6-Shaders-and-Effects-Cookbook. The files for this chapter are organized in the Unity project in a folder named Chapter 05 (https://github.com/PacktPublishing/Unity-6- Shaders-and-Effects-Cookbook/tree/main/Unity6_ShadersCookbook/Assets/Chapter%20 05) on GitHub.

Utilizing generative AI for texture creation

With Unity Muse Texture, developers can explore the use of generative AI to create game-ready textures. Through simple natural language input, you will learn how to instantly generate textures in various styles directly within the Unity Editor, enhancing the visual quality of your projects.

Getting ready

For the next two recipes, you will need a Unity Muse subscription. At the time of writing, a free 15-day trial is available, allowing you to test its features and determine if it is worthwhile for you. It is advisable to have a project ready before starting the trial to fully utilize the time and complete these recipes effectively.

1. In your web browser, visit the Unity Muse website, at `https://muse.unity.com/en-us/account`.

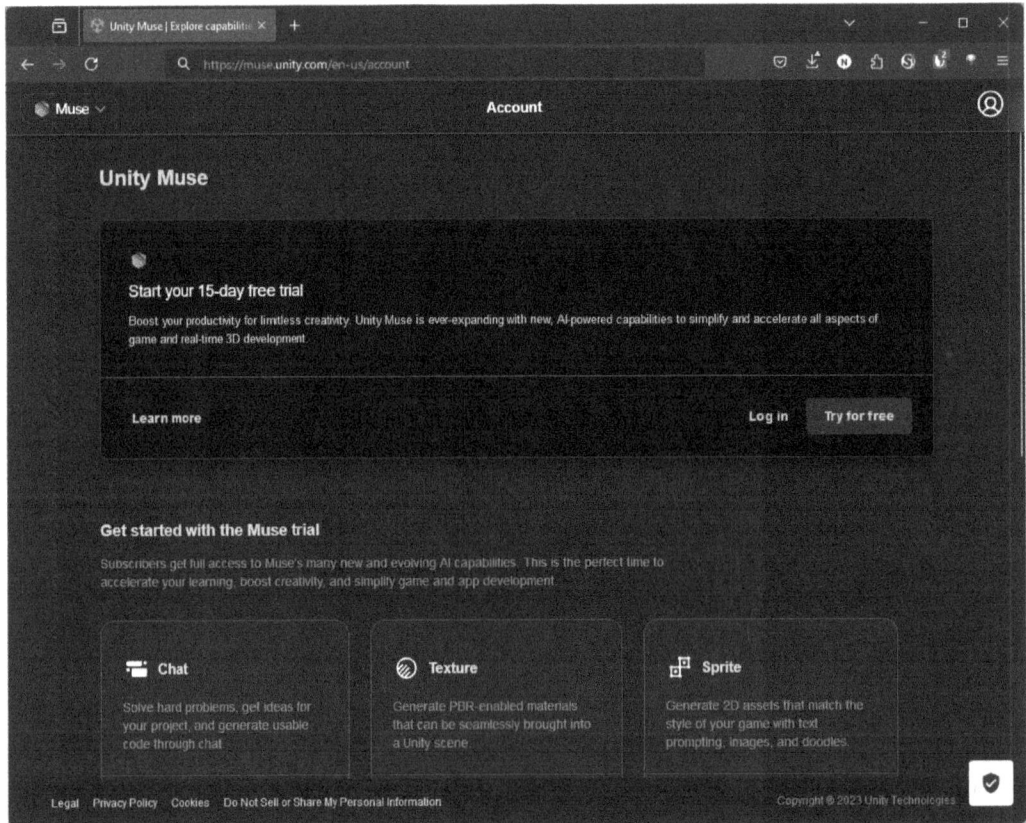

Figure 5.2 – Unity Muse sign up page

2. At the top of the page, you can either **Log in** or click on the **Try for free** button.

3. Once you start your subscription, we can now add the Unity package for **Muse Texture** to our project. Scroll down to the **Texture** section and click on the **Learn more** button.

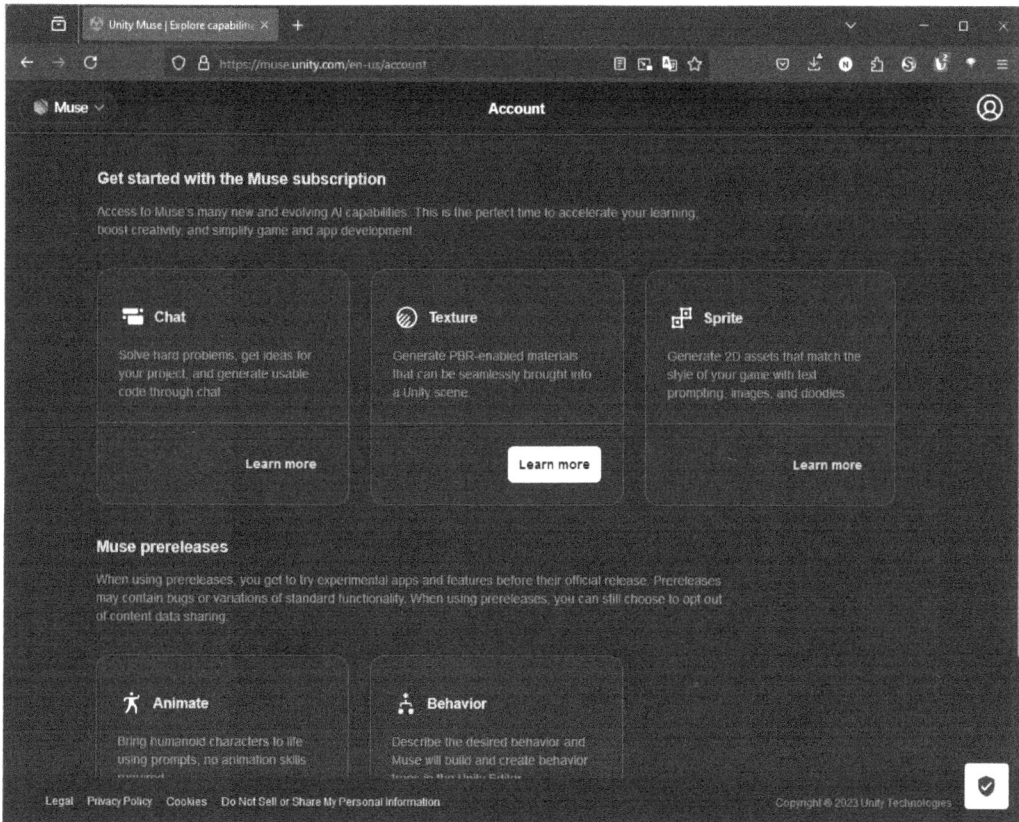

Figure 5.3 – Learn more about Muse Texture

4. There, you'll see a link where you can click **install the Muse Texture package**.

5.   If you have your Unity project open, click it and it should download it automatically for you, though you may need to allow the site to open links for you.

However, if you have issues, you can also download it manually. From the Unity Editor, open the **Package Manager** by going to **Window | Package Manager**. In the **Package Manager**, select **Unity Registry** and, then from the menu, scroll down to **Muse Texture Tool** and select it. Then, click **Install** in the **Package Manager** to complete the installation.

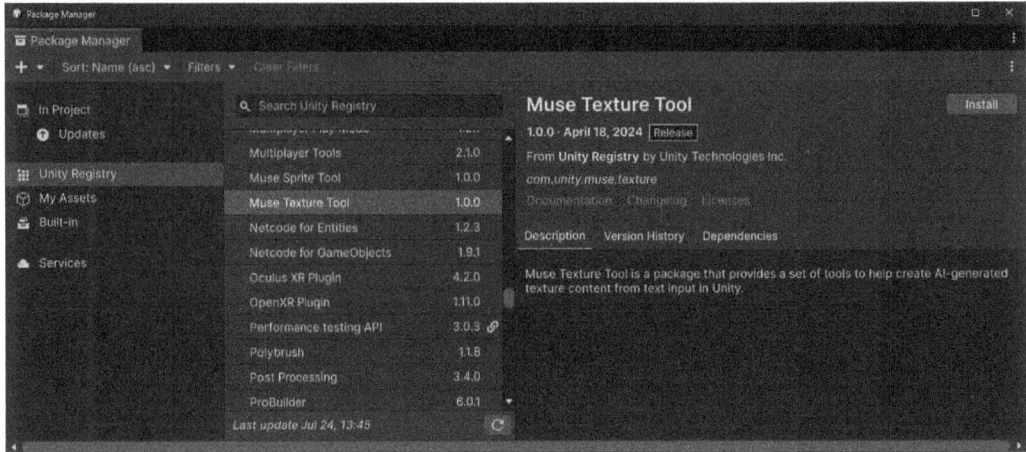

Figure 5.4 – Installing Muse Texture Tool via Package Manager

If all went well, you should see a **Muse** menu added to the top menu bar:

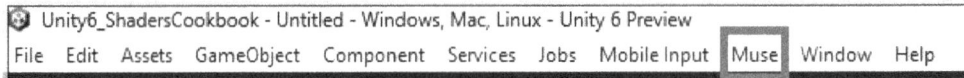

Figure 5.5 – Muse added to the menu bar

How to do it...

Now that Muse has been added to our project, we can now generate a texture from it:

1.   From the menu bar, select **Muse | New Texture Generator**.

If you see a window like the following one, you'll need to click on the **Start your subscription** button and start your subscription to use the service.

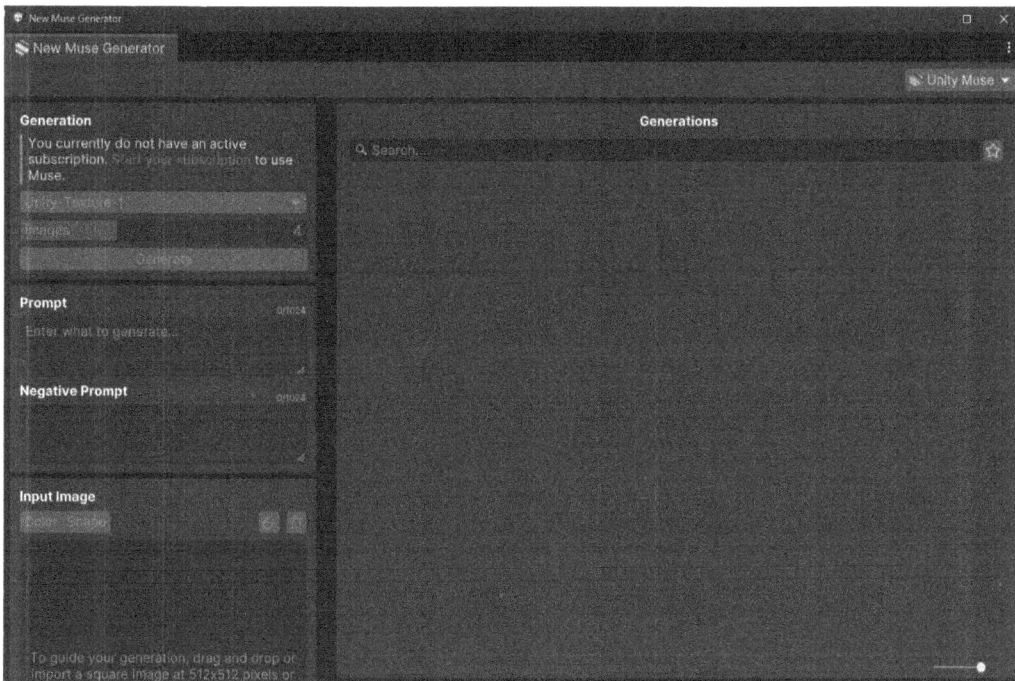

Figure 5.6 – Muse Generator before Subscription is Active

Tip

If you are part of multiple organizations, you can change which one is being used for Muse by going to the **Project Settings** menu, going to the **Muse** section, and, in the **Account** section, setting the **Select your organization** option.

2. Once your subscription is recognized, you should see the menu like this:

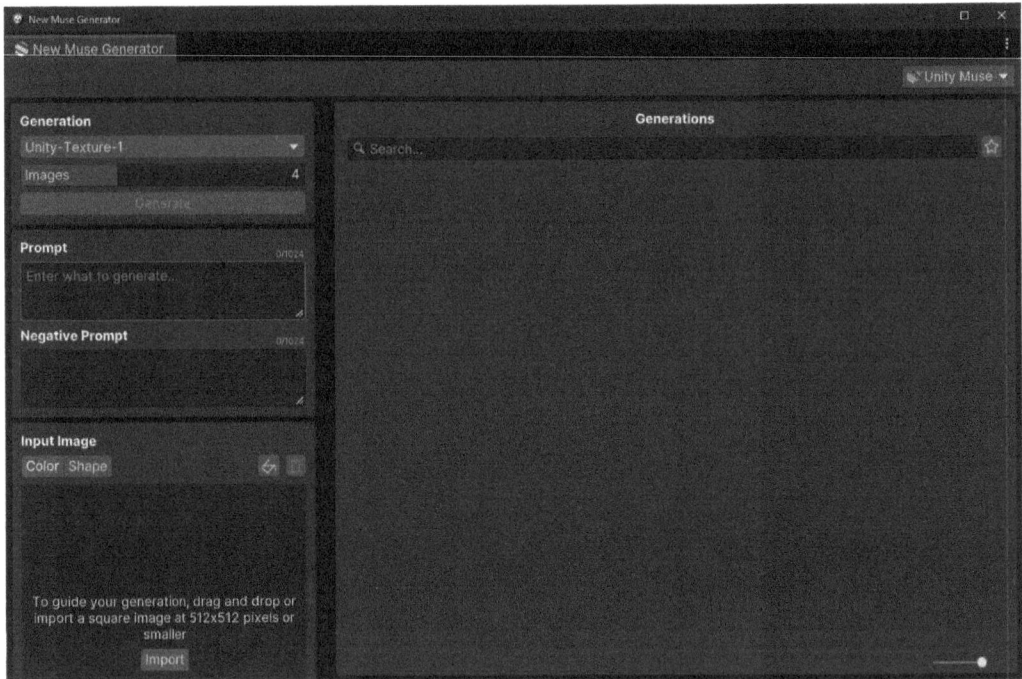

Figure 5.7 – Ready to Generate

Inside the **Prompt**, type in a description of what you'd like to create. For example, suppose we want to update the textures we used in the original area from *Chapter 1, Using Post-Processing with URP*, and apply new textures to the scene there. For instance, maybe we could redo the dirt path texture that we are using.

3. In the **Prompt**, we will put rough dirt mixed with small gravel, and in the **Negative Prompt**, we'll put smooth surfaces, large rocks, vegetation, water, footprints.

When you put in a **Negative Prompt**, you're letting Muse know what it is that you don't want. It guides the AI away from certain features that you're not interested in.

4. Under **Generation**, you'll see there is a slider called **Images** that we can drag to choose how many images we want to be generated when we click **Generate** so we have more options to pick from, as they'll have variations. We can leave it at 4 or increase it to up to 10. In the future, it will cost money for each generation, but at the time of writing, it is free for subscribers, so I'll increase it to 10. Hit **Generate** and wait for the textures to be created.

When it finishes, you may see something like the following:

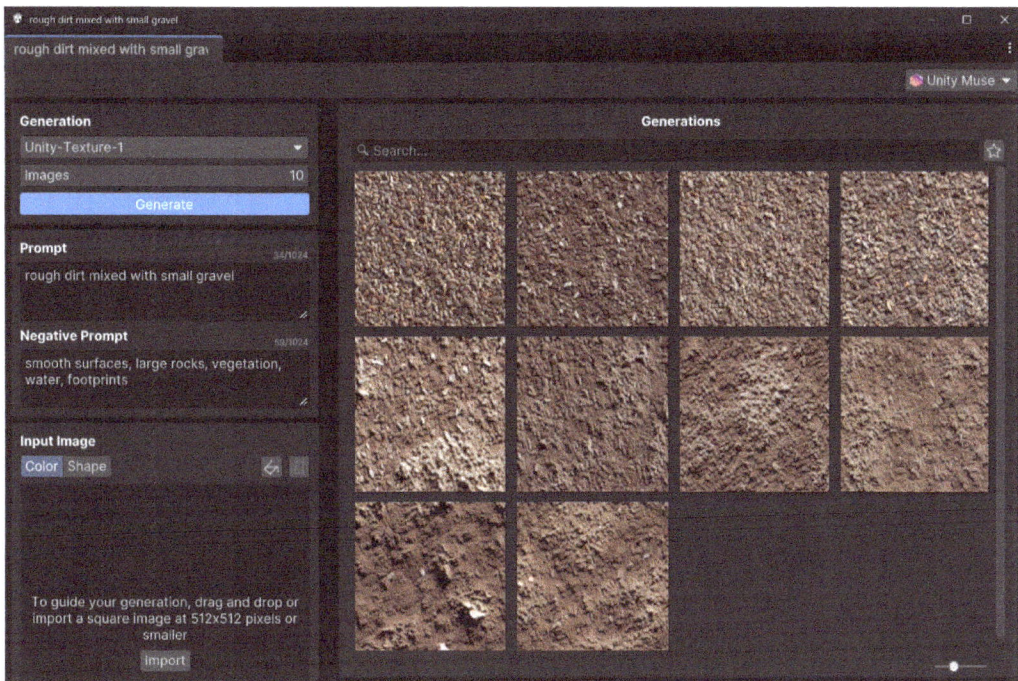

Figure 5.8 – Some generated textures

Note

To make it easier to see all the choices that are generated in the bottom right of the **Generations** section, there is a slider at the bottom right that can be dragged to adjust the scale of the images shown.

This is a great start, but perhaps the colors aren't close enough to what I like, and maybe too much variation for what is meant to be a muted texture.

One way we can improve the selection of images is to provide an image you already have as input that is close to the image you envision or have in mind. This image will be able to guide the tool to provide outputs that are closer to what you have in mind.

5. To make the selection of images that will be output closer to the original image, we can go to **Input Image** and click on **Import**, selecting the `SandAlbedo` image from the `Assets\ Chapter 01\Standard Assets\Environment\TerrainAssets\SurfaceTextures` folder and generating again.

    You'll notice that the newly generated images are much closer to the provided image. We can use the **Strength** property to increase or decrease the effect of this image on the AI's output.

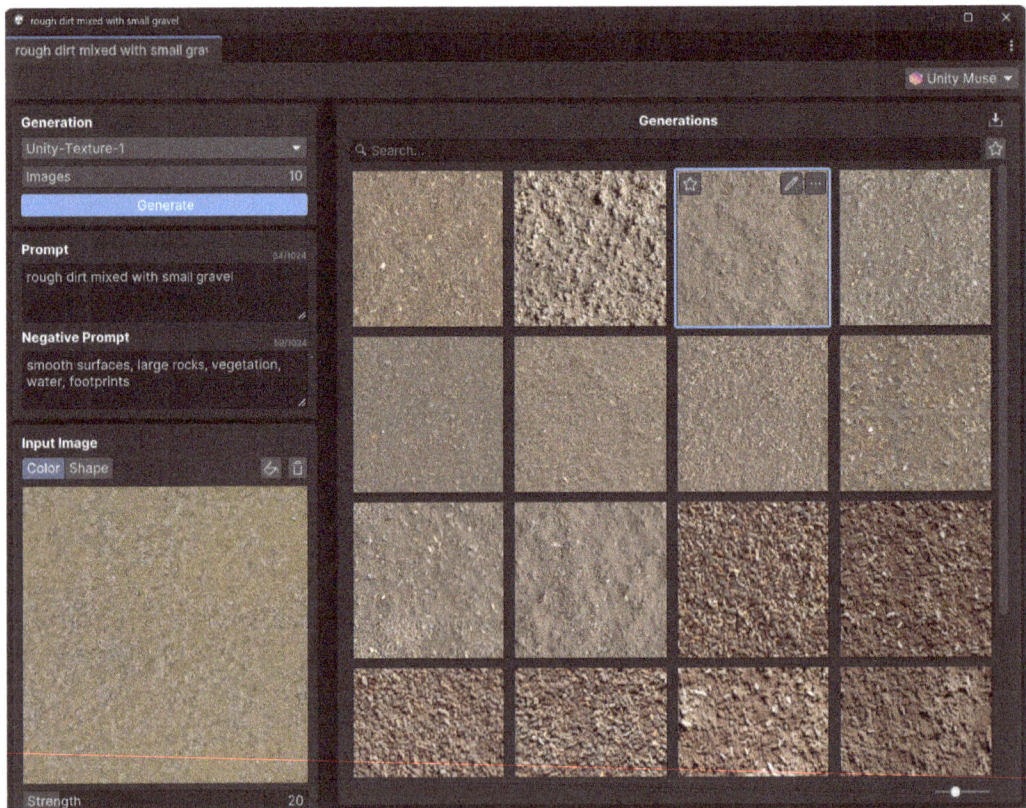

Figure 5.9 – Using Input Image

6. If you find one that is close to what you would like, you can right-click on it and select **Set as Reference**, and it will use it as the **Input Image** instead.

7. When you select the image that you like the most and want to work with, we can increase its resolution by right-clicking on it and selecting **Upscale**.

8. Then, when you are finished, right-click on it and select **View as PBR Material**.

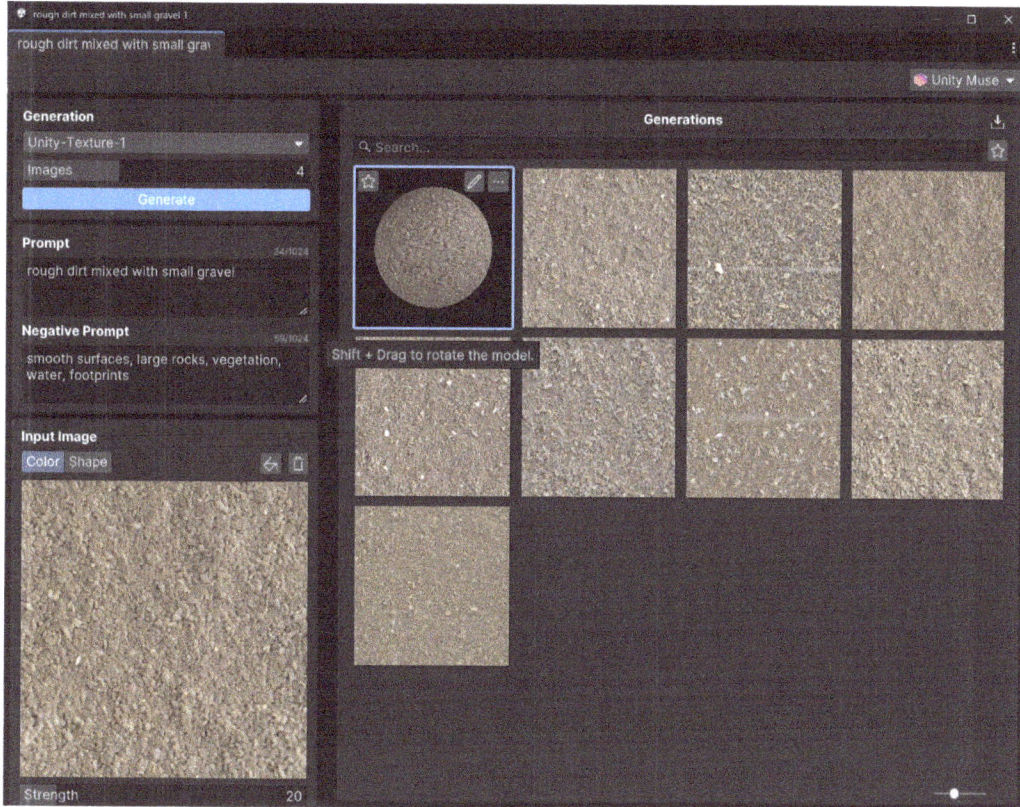

Figure 5.10 – Converting to PBR

This will allow you to see how it will look when attached to an object and will be covered in more detail in the next recipe.

9. When finished, drag and drop the material to the `Chapter 05\Materials` folder in your **Project** window (creating it if necessary) and you'll see that it has created the material as well as a folder with all of the maps needed for this object.

10. For neatness, I will drag and drop the `RoughDirt…` folder into the `Chapter 05\Textures` folder.

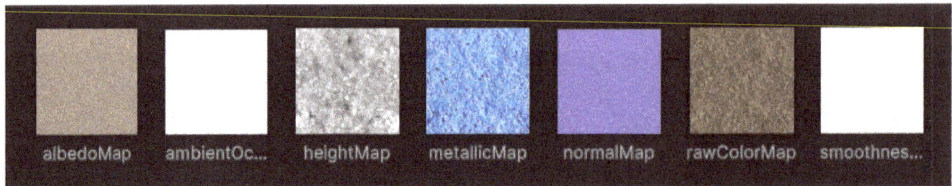

Figure 5.11 – All the maps that were created

How it works...

Unity Muse leverages generative AI to streamline the texture creation process, making it accessible and efficient for developers. By providing natural language input, Muse interprets the description and generates a variety of textures that align with the specified parameters. This capability allows rapid iteration and the exploration of different visual styles directly within the Unity Editor, significantly enhancing the creative workflow.

The texture generation process begins with the user defining a prompt that describes the desired texture. Muse then processes this prompt and generates multiple texture options based on the input. To describe the texture you want to generate, use keywords instead of instructions. For example, use `marble tile` instead of `generate a marble tile texture`.

To ensure the separation of concepts, enter multiple keywords separated by commas. For example, inputting `velvet blue upholstery` generates blue velvet upholstery, while `velvet, blue upholstery` generates velvet that is tinted a bit blue.

Users can further refine the generated textures by adjusting settings such as the number of generated images and providing negative prompts to exclude unwanted elements. To exclude specific elements from generated textures, enter keywords that describe the elements to exclude in the **Negative Prompt**. The keyword can be a color, shape, or texture type. To ensure the separation of concepts, enter multiple keywords separated by commas.

Tip

To avoid double negatives, don't use no in the Negative Prompt. For example, if you want to generate a green fabric and you don't want any red in it, enter green fabric in the **Prompt** and red in the **Negative Prompt**, not no red.

Additionally, Muse provides an option to import reference images, guiding the AI to produce textures that closely match the visual characteristics of the provided reference. This feature ensures that the textures are not only high-quality but also tailored to the specific needs of the project.

Utilizing the Refinements menu on Muse materials

Unity Muse allows us to manipulate the various aspects of 3D surfaces it generates within Unity. In this recipe, users will look at each of the texture files that can be adjusted in the **Refinements** menu and see how we can regenerate areas of a generation to have more precise control over the final output.

We will then see how we can fine-tune several key material properties, including the **Tiling**, **Height**, **Metallic**, and **Smoothness** of the object.

Getting ready

Just like the previous recipe, you will need a Unity Muse subscription. At the time of writing, a free 15-day trial is available, allowing you to test its features and determine if it is worthwhile for you. You'll want to follow the same steps as the previous recipe before getting to this one.

How to do it...

Once you've signed in to Muse, perform the following steps:

1. First, generate some images that you'd like to alter. I'm going for a bronze tiles prompt. One way to make the shapes more consistent with each other is to give them a pattern to work with. Go to the **Input Image** section and select **Shape**, you can select **Pattern** and select a pattern you'd like to use as a basis. As usual, increasing the **Strength** will increase how much that image will be used to influence the resultant images. When you are ready, go ahead and click **Generate**.

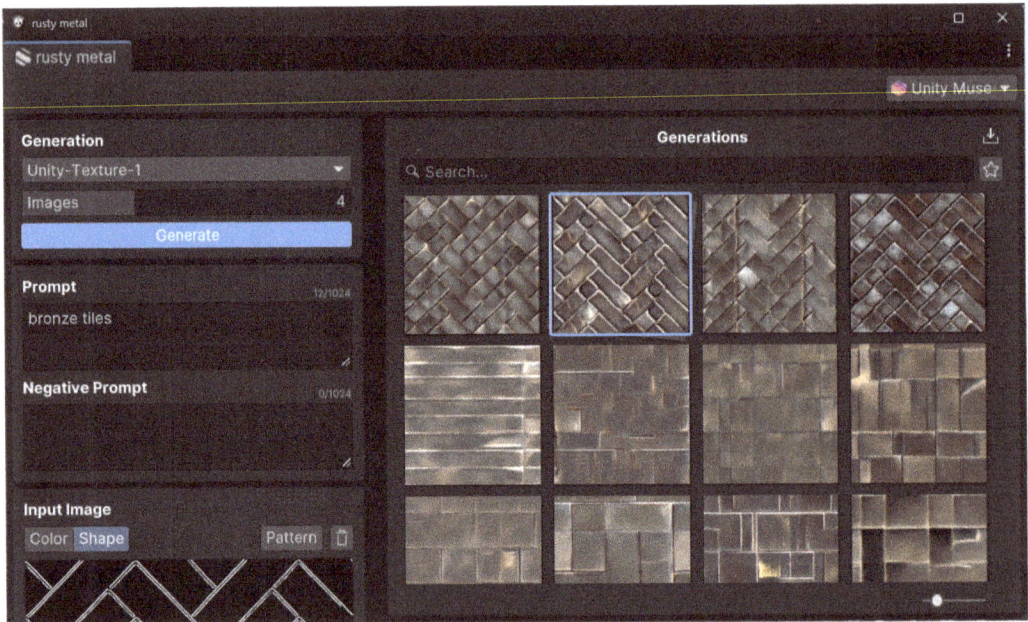

Figure 5.12 – Generating bronze tiles

2. I found an image that I like, but there are some issues that I'd like to fix. To do that, double-click on the image to open the **Refinements** menu.

3. From here, click on the **paintbrush** icon or press *2* and then start drawing on the areas that you'd like to be regenerated. In my case, I'm looking at areas that look incorrect to me.

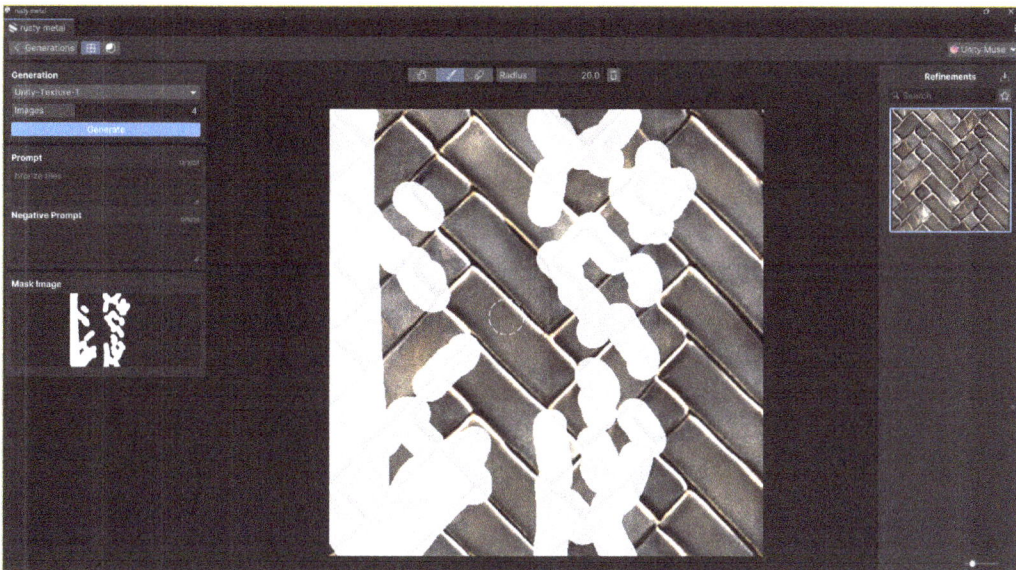

Figure 5.13 – Selecting what to regenerate

The next time we hit **Generate** again, it will only redraw these sections.

4. When you are finished making refinements, right-click on the image that you'd like to use and select **View as PBR Material**. Then, click on it to move to the **PBR Canvas**.

5. At the top, you'll see a menu that currently says **Sphere**. If you click it, you'll see other options you can use to preview the material. I'll select **Cube** to make it easier to see, as this will likely be something we'd use for a floor. You can also change the lighting to see how the material will look in different areas; for instance, I'll change it to **Inside** if we were doing a dungeon area.

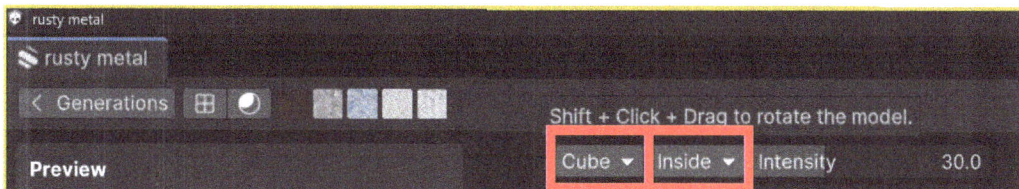

Figure 5.14 – Changing the PBR Canvas visuals

6.   On the left, you'll see **Preview**; we'll set the **Tiling** to 2, 2 to make it easier to see how well the texture repeats itself, which would make it easier to see what we'd need to redraw. Below that, we'll see the **Maps** section, which will allow us to change the **Height**, **Metallic**, and **Smoothness** values of the material. In my case, I increased the **Height** to add variation between the grooves of the tiles, adjusting how the normal map will affect the object, increased **Metallic** so it reflects things better, and increased the **Smoothness** as well.

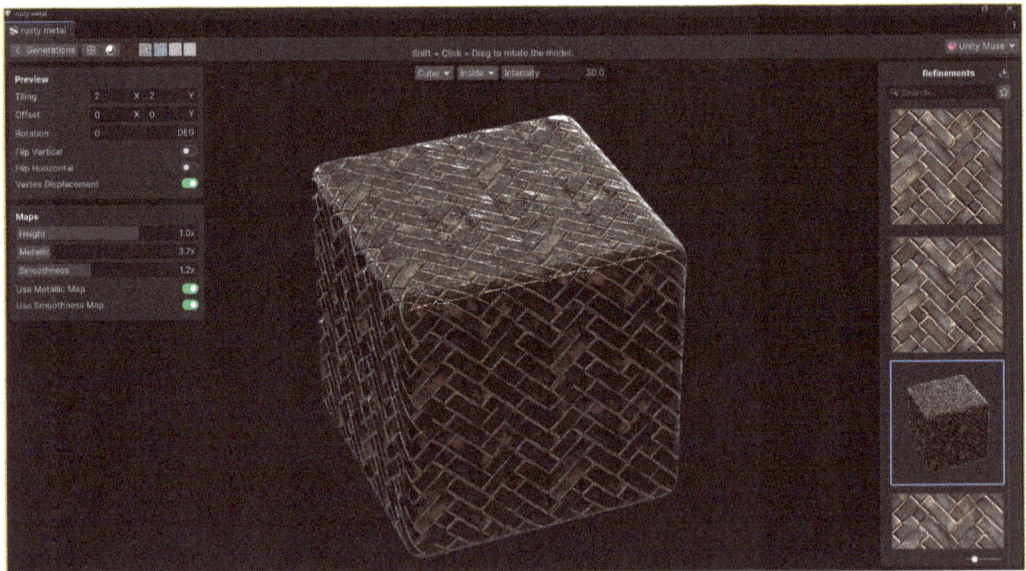

Figure 5.15 – Adjusting Maps

7.   When you are finished, drag and drop the material into the **Project** window.

8.   Create a new scene and add a plane object (**Game Object | 3D Object | Plane**). Then drag and drop your newly created material to the plane.

9.   Once you've finished, note that we can tweak all of the material properties inside of the **Inspector** window. Note that I increased **Tiling** to 4, 4 to make it easier to see.

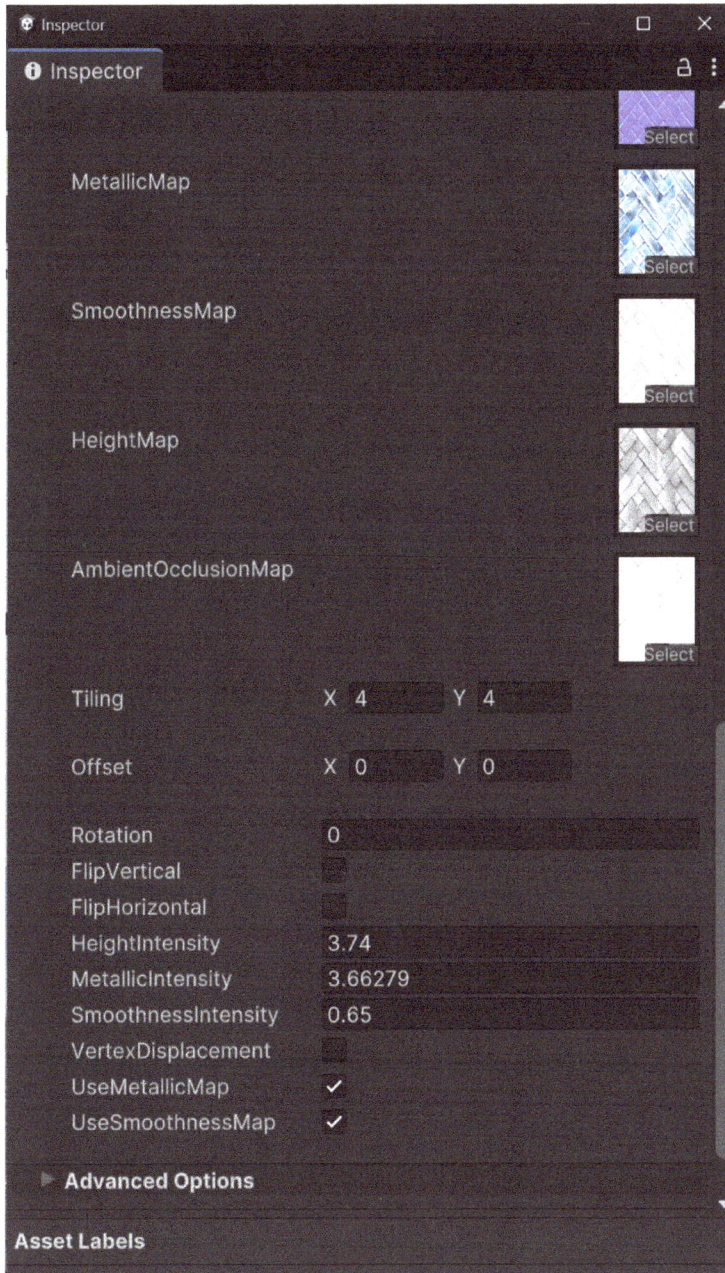

Figure 5.16 – Adjustments via the Inspector window

Once you've finished, you should be able to see your material with the settings the way you created it.

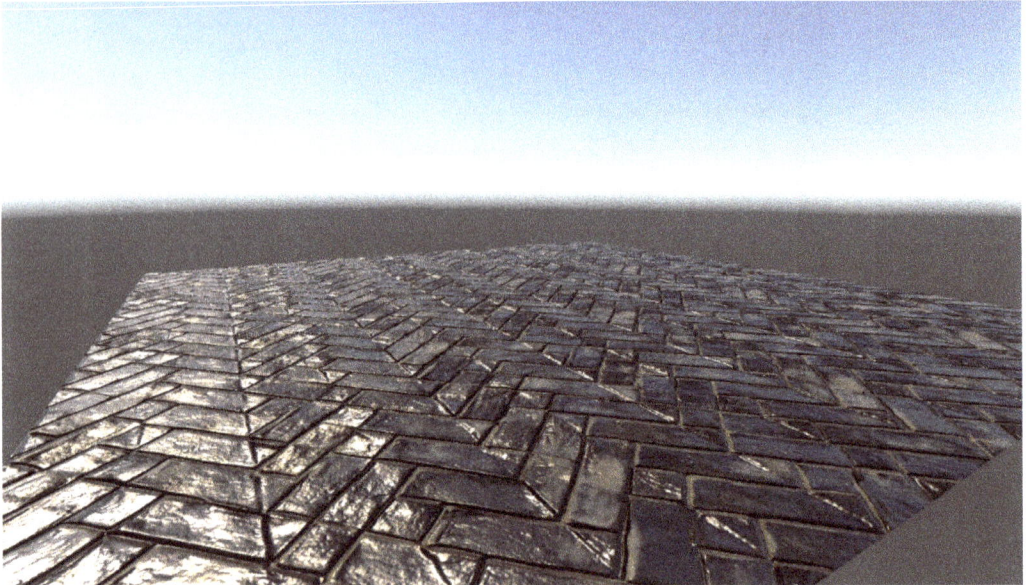

Figure 5.17 – Final result

How it works...

Unity Muse enables us to refine and manipulate various aspects of 3D surfaces directly within Unity. The process begins with generating an initial image based on prompt and pattern selection, ensuring consistency and control over the initial design. Once the image is generated, we can open the **Refinements** menu to make targeted adjustments. This is done by selecting areas to regenerate, allowing precise control over the final output.

The refined image can then be viewed as a PBR material, providing a realistic preview of how it will appear on different 3D objects. We can choose different preview shapes, such as a sphere or cube, and adjust the lighting to see the material in various environments.

In the **Maps** section, we can fine-tune several key material properties:

- **Tiling**: This refers to how the texture repeats across a surface. Adjusting the tiling allows you to control the scale of the texture pattern. For example, increasing the tiling values makes the texture repeat more frequently, which is useful for large surfaces where you want to avoid visible stretching or low-resolution textures.

- **Height**: This map controls the perceived depth and surface variation of the material. Adjusting the height can add realistic details, such as grooves between tiles or the roughness of a stone surface. By increasing the height, you create a more pronounced 3D effect on what would otherwise be a flat texture.

- **Metallic**: This property determines how metallic the material appears. A higher metallic value makes the surface reflect light more like a metal, contributing to a shiny, reflective appearance. Adjusting this can help differentiate materials such as metal from non-metal surfaces, adding to the realism of the scene. We will talk about this in greater detail in the next recipe.

- **Smoothness**: This controls the clarity of reflections on the material's surface. Higher smoothness values result in clearer and sharper reflections, making the surface appear more polished. Lower values make the surface look rougher and more diffused. Adjusting smoothness is crucial for materials such as polished floors or glossy tiles, where reflections play a significant role in their appearance. We will talk about this in greater detail in the next recipe.

Finally, customized materials can be applied to objects within a Unity scene. By dragging and dropping the material onto a plane or other objects, users can further tweak the material properties in the **Inspector** window, ensuring the texture seamlessly integrates into their project.

Understanding the metallic setup

Unity's URP Lit Shader provides two different workflows for PBR shaders: the **metallic workflow** and the **specular workflow**. These workflows are selectable in the material's **Inspector** window through the **Workflow Mode** property and cater to different material needs.

The metallic workflow exposes the **Metallic** property and the **Smoothness** property. The **Metallic** property defines how metallic the surface appears, ranging from 0 (non-metallic) to 1 (fully metallic), while the **Smoothness** property determines how smooth or rough the surface is, affecting the sharpness of reflections.

In the specular workflow, the **Specular** property replaces the **Metallic** property. The **Specular** property defines the reflective properties of the surface using a color value, and the **Smoothness** property remains to control the surface's roughness.

Smoothness and **Roughness** are opposites of each other, so a **Smoothness** value of 1 means a **Roughness** value of 0 and vice versa. You can generally get the same result no matter which shader you use, so it mostly comes down to personal preference.

These workflows represent different ways in which you can initialize PBR materials. One of the concepts that has driven PBR is the ability to provide meaningful, physically related properties that artists and developers can tweak and play with. The properties of some materials are easier to represent, indicating how metallic they are. For others, it is more important to specify how they reflect light directly through their **specularity**. This recipe will show you how to use the metallic setup effectively. It's important to remember that the metallic workflow is not just for metallic materials; it is also a way of defining how materials will look according to how metallic or non-metallic their surface is.

Despite being presented as two different workflows, the metallic and specular setups are generally equally expressive and just require us to set the **Workflow Mode** to switch between them.

Getting ready

This recipe will use the default URP Lit shader, so there is no need to create a new one. Follow these steps:

1. Create a new scene by going to **File** | **New Scene**. Select the **Basic (URP)** scene and then hit **Create**.

2. Create a new material (MetallicMat).

3. From its **Inspector** window, make sure that **Universal Render Pipeline/Lit** is selected from its **Shader** drop-down menu.

4. You will also need a textured 3D model. The basic character we used previously (basicCharacter, which is located in the Chapter 04/Models folder of the project) will work perfectly. Drag and drop it into the scene. Afterward, drag and drop the **MetallicMat** material onto each of the parts of the character. Also, assign the texture for the material (skin_man or skin_woman, both of which are located in the Chapter 04/Textures folder) to the **Base Map** property, which will assign the base colors that will be used in each area of the object according to the UVs:

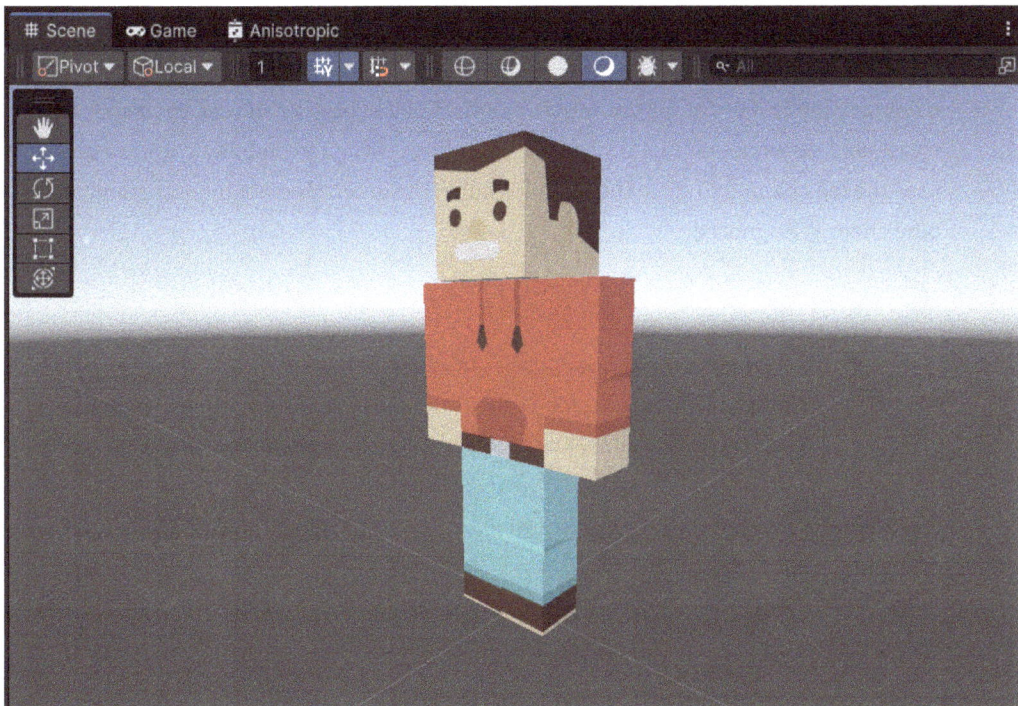

Figure 5.18 – Setup for the scene

How to do it...

Two main textures need to be configured in the URP Lit Shader: **Base Map** and **Metallic**. To use the metallic workflow effectively, we need to initialize these maps correctly. Follow these steps:

1. The **Base Map** should be initialized with the unlit texture of the 3D model, which we did in the *Getting ready* section.

2. To create the **Metallic** map, start by duplicating the file for your **Base Map**. You can do this by selecting the map from the **Project** window and pressing *Ctrl + D*.

3. We will then need to open the file in an image editor of your choice.

Note

For those wanting a free option, I've found **PhotoPea** (https://www. photopea.com/) to be a solid choice for a web-based version with ads. You can also consider **Paint.net** (https://www.getpaint.net/) if you are working in Windows or **Gimp** (https://www.gimp.org/).

4. Use white (#ffffff) to color the regions of the map that correspond to materials that are made of pure metal.

5. Use black (#000000) for all the other regions. Shades of gray should be used for dusty, weathered, or worn-out metal surfaces, including rust, scratched paint, and so on. Unity uses the red channel to store the metallic value, the green channel for occlusion, and the blue channel is ignored.

> Note
>
> For more information on how the shader uses channel packing check out: `https://docs.unity3d.com/Packages/com.unity.render-pipelines.universal@17.0/manual/lit-shader.html#channel-packing`.

6. Use the alpha channel of the image to provide information about the **Smoothness** property of the material.

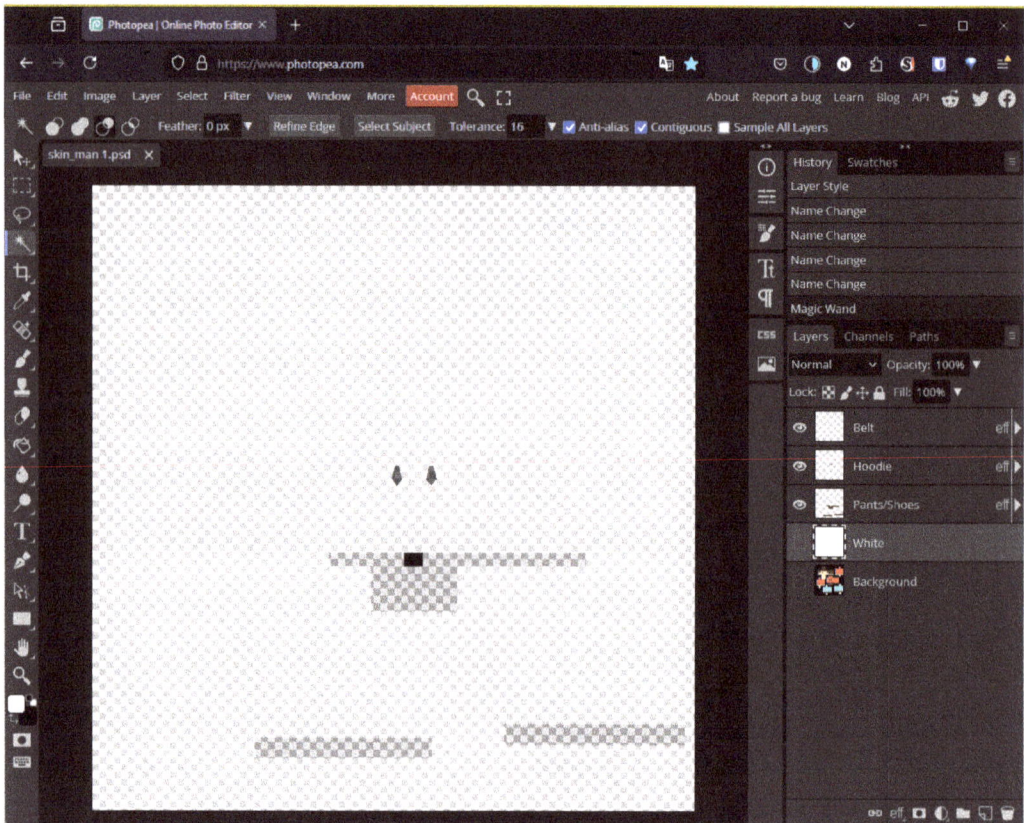

Figure 5.19 – Creating the metallic map

For our simple character, the belt and the little ends of the hoodie are the only parts we need to be metallic, but I also added a little bit to the character's pants and shoes as well with 20% opacity. I've also made the opacity 55% for the hoodie, with the belt having a higher opacity of 100%.

For those who don't have photo editing software or want to just have the completed version, it is included in the sample code for this chapter in the Textures folder.

7. Once you've finished, export your image, go back to the Unity Editor, and assign the **Metallic Map** to the material. The **Metallic** slider will disappear as these two properties are now controlled by the map. You may use the **Smoothness** slider to provide a modifier for the map you've provided:

Figure 5.20 – Final result

How it works...

Metals conduct electricity and reflect light in a way that makes them shiny. This is because metals reflect most of the light that hits them (70-100%), and the light they don't reflect is absorbed, giving them a dark, non-shiny appearance. Insulators, on the other hand, reflect only a small amount of light (about 4%) and scatter the rest, making them look more diffused and less shiny.

In the **URP Lit Shader**, purely metallic materials have dark non-shiny parts, and their shiny reflections are determined by the **Base Map**. For non-metallic materials, the non-shiny parts are determined by the **Base Map**, and the shiny highlights are influenced by the color of the light.

By following these principles, the metallic workflow combines the **Base Map** and shiny reflections, ensuring physically accurate behaviors. This method also saves space and speeds up performance, though it gives you less control over the appearance of your materials.

See also

For more information about the metallic setup, you can refer to these links:

- **Calibration chart**: How to calibrate a metallic material: `https://docs.unity3d.com/uploads/Main/StandardShaderCalibrationChartMetallic.png`.

- **Quixel megascans**: A vast library of materials, including textures and PBR parameters. While free for Unreal-Engine projects, it is possible to get a subscription to use with Unity as well (`https://www.fab.com/sellers/Quixel`).

- **PBR texture conversion**: How traditional shaders can be converted into PBR shaders (`https://marmoset.co/posts/pbr-texture-conversion/`).

- **Substance Designer**: A node-based software for working with PBR (`https://www.adobe.com/products/substance3d/apps/designer.html`)

- **The Theory of Physically Based Rendering**: A starter guide to PBR (`https://marmoset.co/posts/basic-theory-of-physically-based-rendering/`).

Adding transparency to PBR

Transparency is such an important aspect in games that the URP Lit Shader supports different ways of achieving it. This recipe will be useful to you if you need to have realistic materials with transparent or semi-transparent properties. Glasses, bottles, windows, and crystals are good candidates for PBR transparent shaders. This is because you can still have all the realism that's introduced by PBR but with the addition of a transparent or translucent effect. If you need transparency for something different, such as UI elements or pixel art, there are more efficient alternatives. These alternatives were explored in the *Creating a transparent material* recipe of *Chapter 4, Working with Texture Mapping*.

Important note

To have a transparent URP Lit material, changing the alpha channel of its **Base Map Color** property is not enough. Unless you set its **Surface Type** property, your material will not appear transparent.

Getting ready

Let's start this recipe by creating a shader and its material and importing a special texture. Perform the following steps:

1. Create a new scene by going to **File** | **New Scene**. Select the **Basic (URP)** scene and then hit **Create**.

2. Create a new material (TransparancyMat).

3. From its **Inspector** window, make sure that **Universal Render Pipeline/Lit** is selected from its **Shader** drop-down menu.

4. Assign the newly created material to the 3D object that you want to be transparent (I'm using the bunny from our sample code):

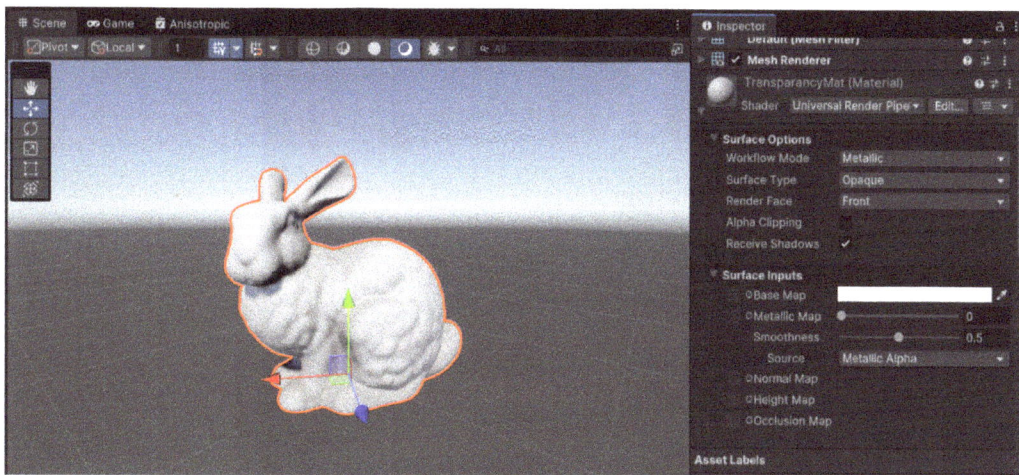

Figure 5.21 – Recipe setup

How to do it...

The URP Lit Shader provides three different types of transparencies. Despite being very similar, they have subtle differences and are used in different contexts.

Using semi-transparent materials

Some materials, such as clear plastics, crystals, and glass are semi-transparent. This means that they require all the realistic effects of PBR (such as specular highlights and Fresnel refraction and reflection) but allow the geometry behind an object with the material attached to be seen. If this is what you need, follow these steps:

1. From the material's **Inspector** tab, set **Surface Type** to **Transparent**.

2. The amount of transparency is determined by the alpha channel of the **Base Map** color or the **Base Map** texture (if any). If you click on the box to the right of the **Base Map** section, you'll bring up a **Color** menu. Adjusting the **A** channel will make the item more or less visible.

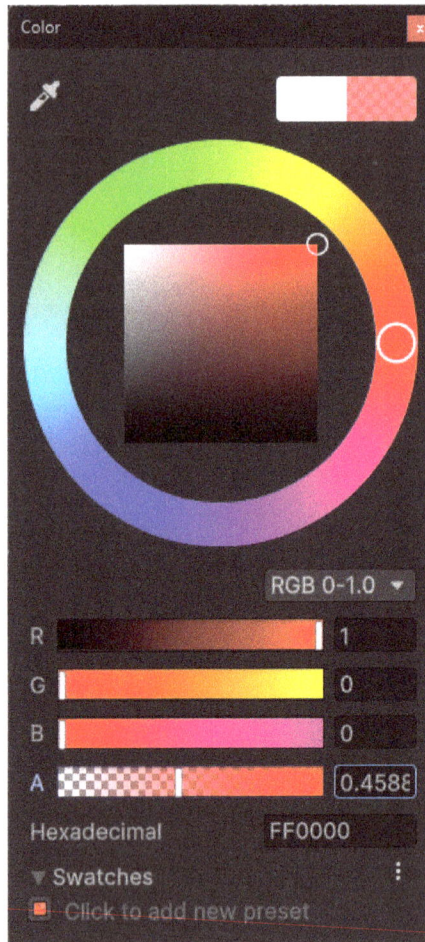

Figure 5.22 – Assigning a transparent color

3. Set the **A** channel to 0.46 to create the desired effect. Since the value is less than 1, we should see a semi-transparent effect; the closer to 0, the more transparent it will be.

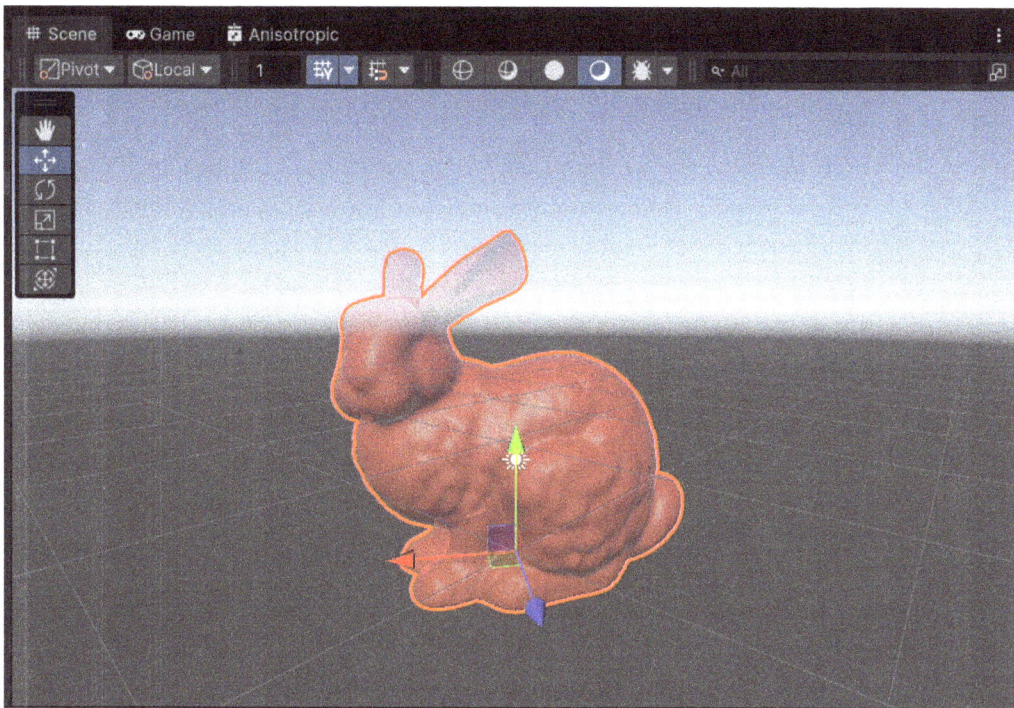

Figure 5.23 – Result of altering the alpha

To give an example of how this effect works at different alphas, the following screenshot from the Unity calibration scene shows four different highly polished plastic spheres. From left to right, their transparency is increasing (the alpha values are decreasing). Note that the last sphere is fully transparent but retains all the added effects of PBR.

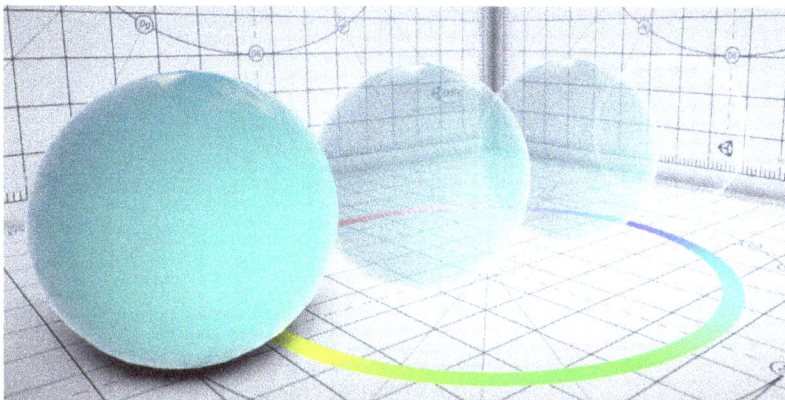

Figure 5.24 – Transparent rendering mode – alpha effect

The **Transparent** surface type is perfect for windows, bottles, gems, and headsets.

Important information

Note that many transparent materials don't usually project shadows. On top of this, the **Metallic** and **Smoothness** properties of a material can interfere with the transparency effect. A mirror-like surface can have the alpha set to zero, but if it reflects all the incoming light, it won't appear transparent.

Creating fading objects

Sometimes, you want an object to fully disappear with a fading effect. In this case, specular reflections and Fresnel refraction and reflection should disappear as well. When a fading object is fully transparent, it should also be invisible. To do this, follow these steps:

1. From the material's **Inspector** tab, uncheck the **Preserve Specular** option.

2. As we did previously, use the alpha channel of the **Base Map** color or texture to set the final transparency.

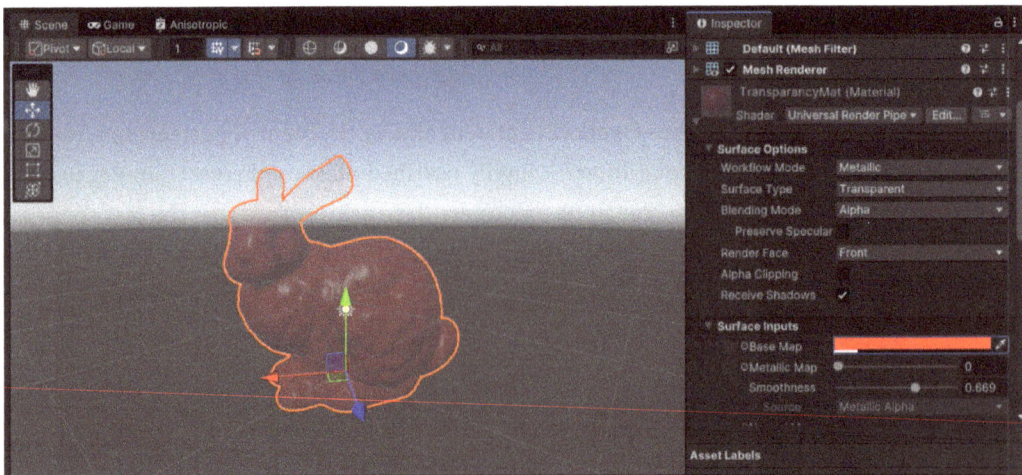

Figure 5.25 – Unchecking Preserve Specular

To give an example of how this effect works at different alphas, the following screenshot from the Unity calibration scene shows four fading spheres. From left to right, their transparency is increasing (the alpha values are decreasing). As you can see, the last one on the right is almost invisible:

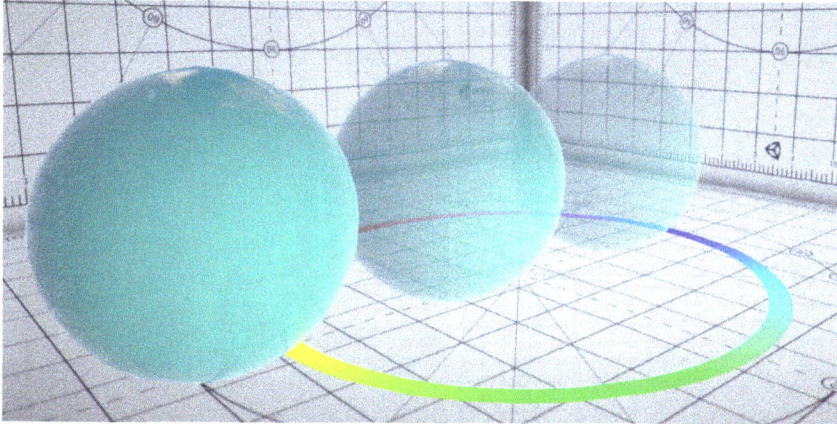

Figure 5.26 – Fade rendering mode – alpha effect

This rendering mode works best for non-realistic objects, such as holograms, laser rays, faux lights, ghosts, and particle effects.

Creating solid geometries with holes

Most of the materials that are encountered in a game are solid, meaning that they don't allow light to pass through them. At the same time, many objects have a very complex (yet flat) geometry. Modeling leaves and grass with 3D objects is often overkill. A more efficient approach is to use a quad (rectangle) with a leaf texture. While the leaf itself is solid, the rest of the texture should be fully transparent. If this is what you want, then follow these steps:

1. From the material's **Inspector** window, check the **Alpha Clipping** property.

2. Use the **Alpha Clipping Threshold** slider to determine the cutoff threshold. All the pixels in the **Base Map** texture with an alpha value less than or equal to **Alpha Clipping** will be hidden.

The following screenshot, taken from Unity Official Tutorials on PBR (`https://www.youtube.com/watch?v=fD_ho_ofY6A`), shows you how the effect of cutouts can be used to create a hole in the geometry.

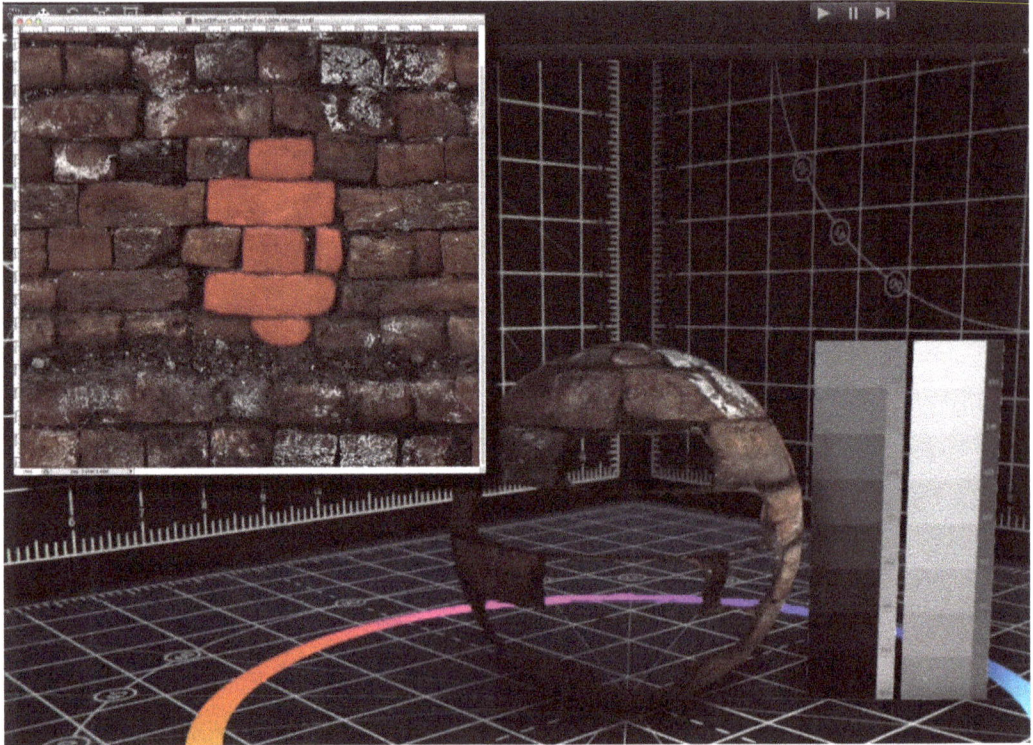

Figure 5.27 – The effect of the cutout rendering mode

It's worth noticing that **Cutout** does not allow the back of the geometry to be seen. In the previous example, you can't see the inner volume of the sphere. If you need to do this, you need to create a shader and make sure that the back geometry is not culled. A simple way to see something in **Shader Graph** is by going to the **Graph Settings** and checking **Two Sided**.

Creating mirrors and reflective surfaces

Specular materials reflect light when objects are viewed from certain angles. Unfortunately, even Fresnel reflection, which is one of the most accurate models, does not reflect light from nearby objects correctly. The lighting models we examined in the previous chapters only took light sources into account; they ignored light that is reflected from other surfaces. With what you've learned about shaders so far, making a mirror is simply not possible.

GI makes this possible by providing PBR shaders with information about their surroundings. This allows objects to have not just specular highlights, but also real reflections, which depend on the other objects around them. Real-time reflections are very costly and must be set up and tweaked to work. When done properly, they can be used to create mirror-like surfaces, as shown in the following screenshot:

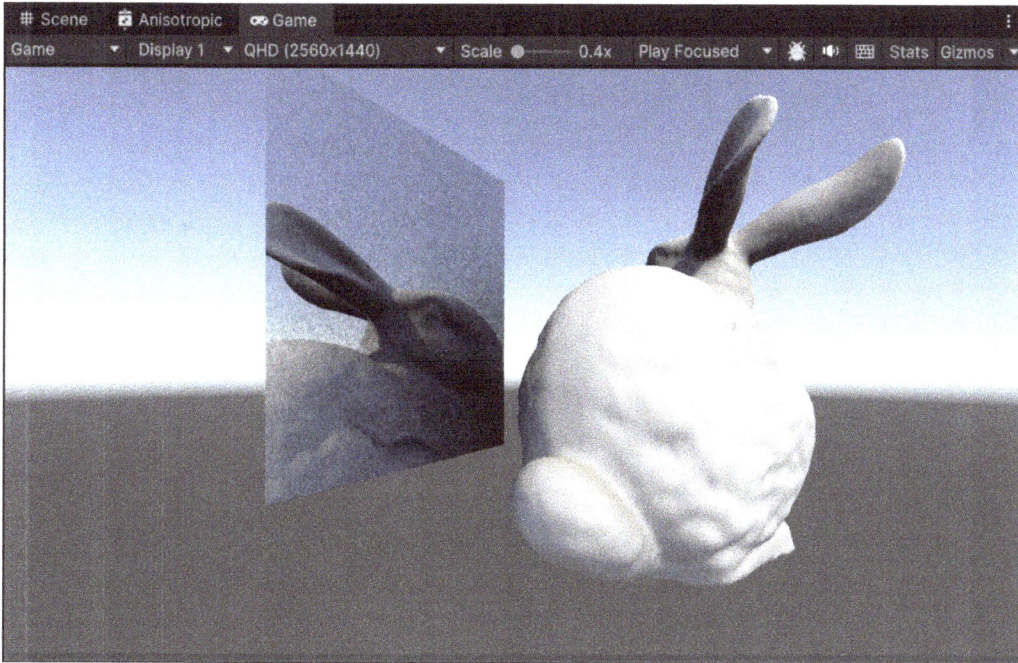

Figure 5.28 – Mirror-like reflection

Getting ready

This recipe will not feature a new shader. Instead, most of the work will be done directly in the editor. Follow these steps:

1. Create a new scene and place an object(s) into the scene to be reflected. I used the bunny model that's located in the Chapter 03/Models folder.

2. Create a quad (**GameObject | 3D Object | Quad**); this will serve as a mirror. I've scaled it up to (10, 10, 1), moved it to (-3, 3, 6), and rotated it to -60 in the Y axis to make it easy to see.

3. Create a new material (MirrorMat) and attach it to the mirror.

4. Create a new reflection probe by right-clicking on the Quad and selecting **GameObject | Light | Reflection Probe**; then, place it in front of the quad:

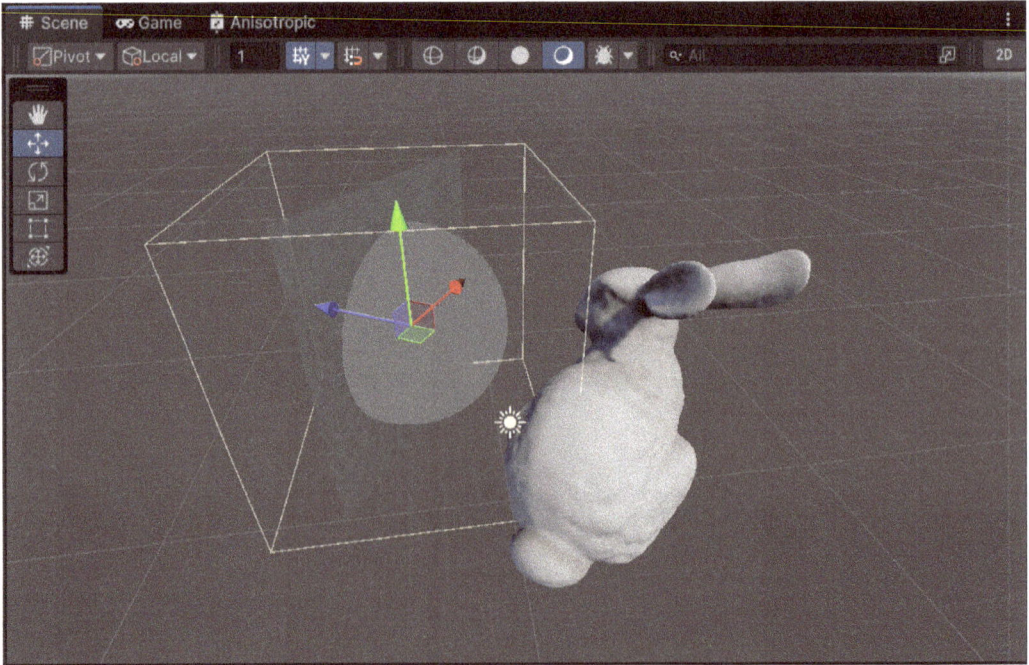

Figure 5.29 – Recipe setup

How to do it...

If you followed the preceding steps correctly, you should have a quad in the middle of your scene, close to a reflection probe. To make it into a mirror, some changes need to be made:

1. Double-check that the shader of the material is set to **Universal Render Pipeline/Lit** and that **Surface Type** is set to **Opaque**.

2. Change its **Metallic Map** and **Smoothness** properties to 1. You should see the material reflecting the sky more clearly in the **Inspector** view. However, in the main scene, you may see the material within the **Scene** view change to still not show the bunny.

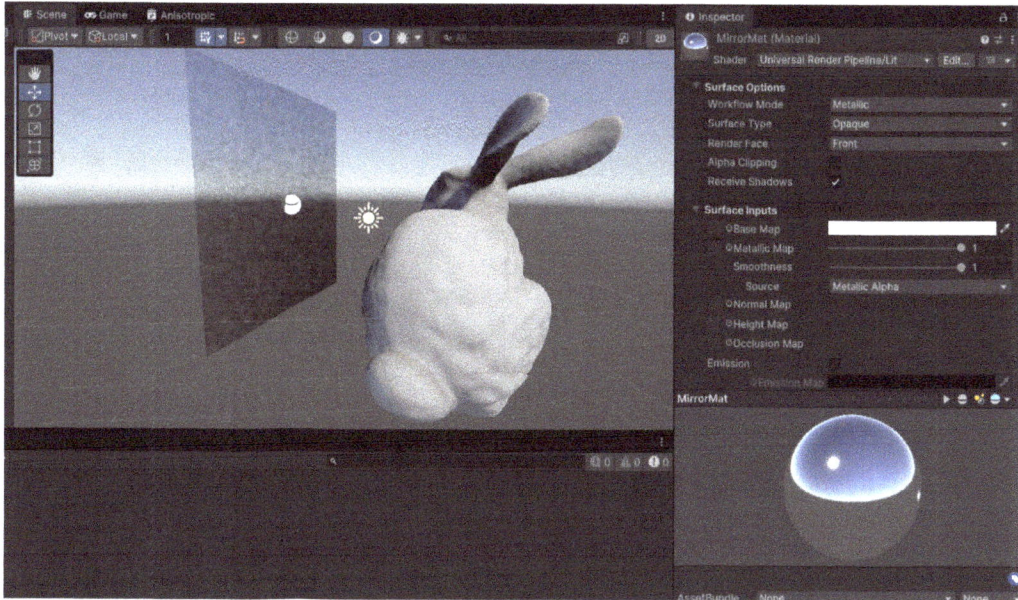

Figure 5.30 – Adjusting Metallic and Smoothness properties

3. Select the reflection probe and change **Type** to **Realtime** and **Refresh Mode** to **Every frame**. Also, make sure that **Culling Mask** is set to **Everything**.

4. To enable real-time reflection probes, we will need to go to the project settings (**Edit |
Project Settings**), and then, under **Quality**, under **Rendering**, go to **Realtime Reflection
Probes** and check the box.

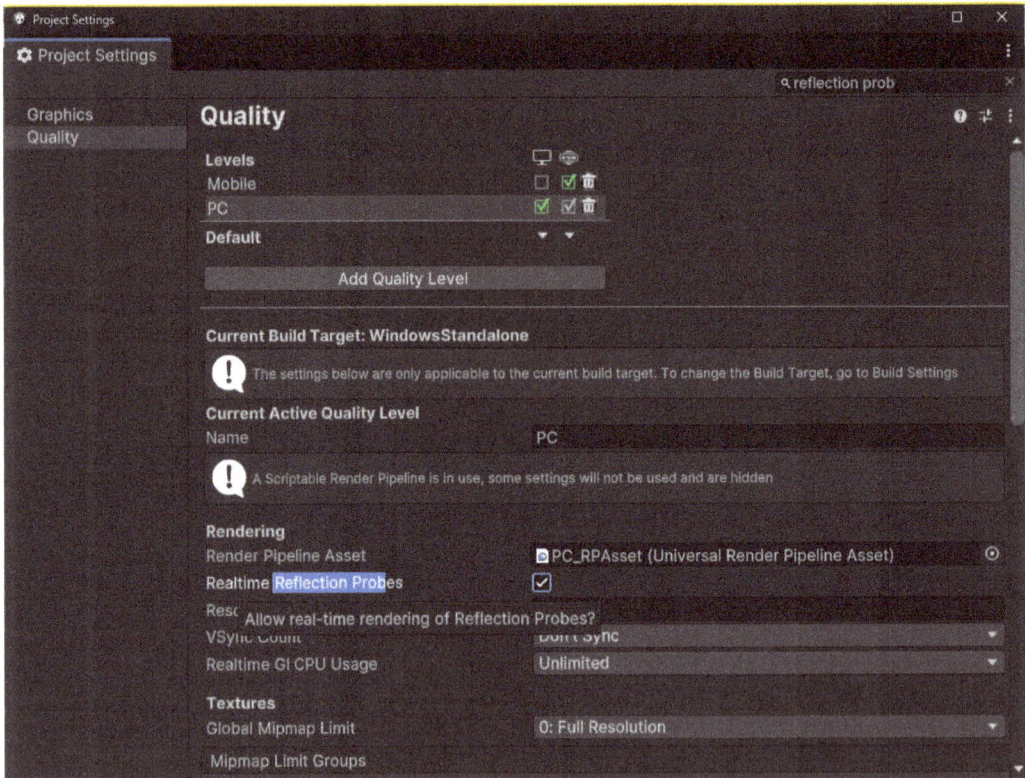

Figure 5.31 – Enabling Realtime Reflection Probes

5. Next, check the **Box Projection** property and then change its **Box Size** and **Box Offset**
properties until it is in front of the quad and encloses all the objects that you want to
reflect (I used 100,100,100 for the **Box Size** and 0,0,0 for the **Box Offset**).

6. To make the item clearer, under **Cubemap Capture Settings**, change **Resolution** to **2048**.

Your reflection probe should now be configured.

Using these settings, you should see something similar to this:

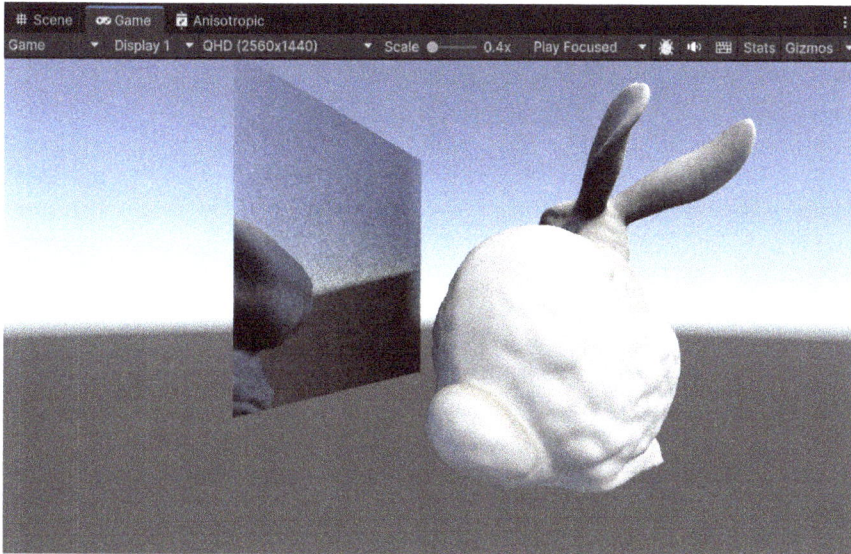

Figure 5.32 – Mirror image is now working

You may notice that the bunny seems larger in the reflection compared to what's beside it. This is partially because we've scaled the image earlier; but also, if your probe is being used for a real mirror, you should check the **Box Projection** flag. If it is used for other reflective surfaces, such as shiny pieces of metal or glass tables, you can uncheck it.

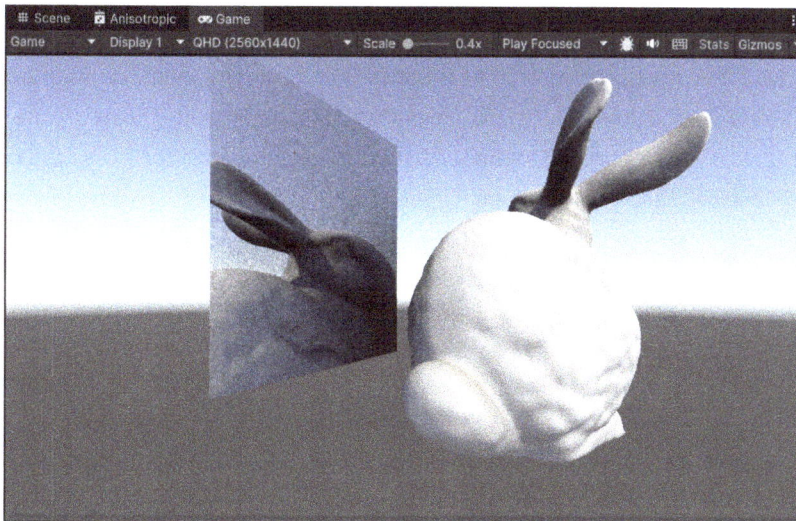

Figure 5.33 – Mirror after Box Projection

How it works...

When a shader wants information about its surroundings, it is usually provided in a structure called **cube maps**. Loosely speaking, cube maps are the 3D equivalent of 2D textures; they represent a 360-degree view of the world, as seen from a center point.

Unity previews cube maps with a spherical projection, as shown in the following figure:

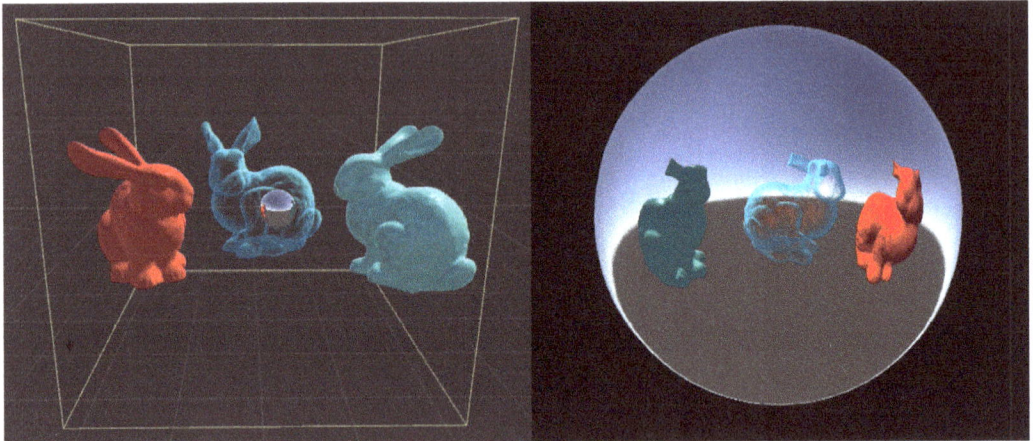

Figure 5.34 – Cube maps example

When cube maps are attached to a camera, they are referred to as skyboxes, since they are used to provide a way to reflect the sky. They can be used to reflect geometries that are not in the actual scene, such as nebulae, clouds, and stars.

The reason why they are called cube maps is because of the way they are created: a cube map is made up of six different textures, each one attached to the face of a cube. You can create a cube map manually or delegate it to a reflection probe. You can imagine a reflection probe as a collection of six cameras, creating a 360-degree mapping of the surrounding area. This also gives you an idea as to why probes are so expensive. By creating one in our scene, we allow Unity to know which objects are around the mirror. If you need more reflective surfaces, you can add multiple probes. You don't need to do anything else for the reflection probes to work. The URP Lit Shaders will use them automatically.

You should notice that when they are set to **Realtime**, they render their cube map at the beginning of every frame, which is very computationally expensive, which is why it's disabled by default.

There is a trick to make this faster; if you know that part of the geometry that you want to reflect does not move, you can bake the reflection. This means that Unity can calculate the reflection before starting the game, allowing for more precise (and computationally expensive) calculations. To do this, your reflection probe must be set to **Baked** and will only work for objects that are flagged as **Static**. **Static** objects cannot move or change, which makes them perfect for terrain, buildings, and props. Every time a static object is moved, Unity will regenerate the cube maps for its baked reflection probes. This might take a few minutes to several hours.

You can mix **Realtime** and **Baked** probes to increase the realism of your game. Baked probes will provide very high-quality reflections and environmental reflections, while real-time probes can be used to move objects such as cars or mirrors. The *Baking lights into your scene* recipe will explain how light baking works.

See also

If you are interested in learning more about reflection probes, you should check out these links:

- **Unity manual about the reflection probe**: `http://docs.unity3d.com/Manual/class-ReflectionProbe.html`
- **Box projection and other advanced reflection probe settings**: `https://docs.unity3d.com/Manual/AdvancedRefProbe.html`

Baking lights into your scene

Rendering lighting is a very expensive process. Even with state-of-the-art GPUs, accurately calculating the light transport (which is how light bounces between surfaces) can take hours. To make this process feasible for games, real-time rendering is essential. Modern engines compromise between realism and efficiency; most of the computation is done beforehand in a process called light baking. This recipe will explain how light baking works and how you can get the most out of it.

Getting ready

Light baking requires you to have a scene ready. It should contain geometries and, obviously, lights. For this recipe, we will rely on Unity's built-in and Universal Render Pipeline features so that there is no need to create additional shaders or materials. We will be reusing the map that we used in *Chapter 1, Using Post-Processing with URP*. For better control, you might want to access the **Lighting** window. If you don't see it, select **Window** | **Rendering** | **Lighting** from the menu and dock it somewhere that is more convenient for you.

How to do it...

Light baking requires some manual configuration. There are three essential, yet independent, steps that you need to follow.

Configuring the static geometry

Follow these steps to configure the static geometry:

1. Identify all the objects in your scene that do not change position, size, and material. Possible candidates include buildings, walls, terrain, props, trees, and others. In our case, it will be all of the objects aside from FPSController and its children.

2. Select these objects and check the **Static** box from the **Inspector** window, as shown in the following screenshot:

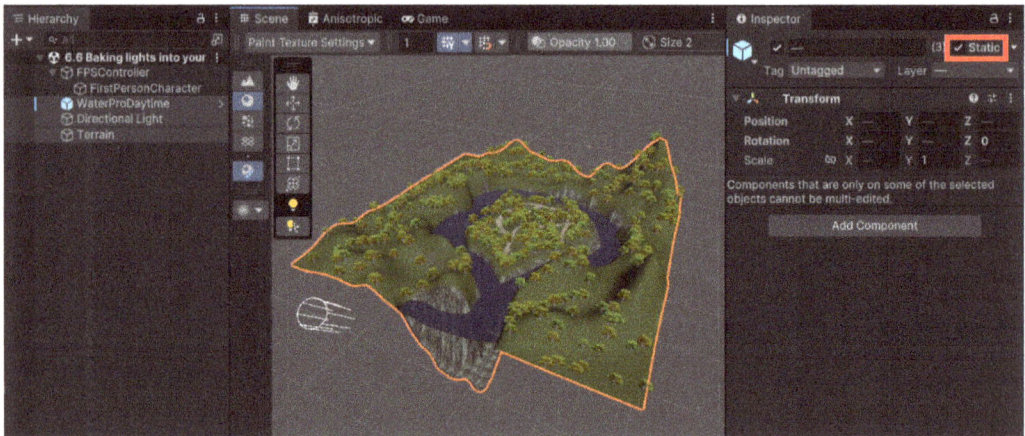

Figure 5.35 – Setting the Static property

If any of the selected objects have children, Unity will ask if you want them to be considered static as well. If they meet the requirements (fixed position, size, and material), select **Yes, change children** in the pop-up box.

> Tip
>
> If a light qualifies as a static object but illuminates non-static geometry, make sure that its **Baking** property is set to **Mixed**. If it will only affect static objects, set it to **Baked**.

Configuring the light probes

There are objects in your game that will move, such as the main character, enemies, and the **non-playable characters (NPCs)**. If they enter a static region that is illuminated, you might want to surround it with light probes. To do this, follow these steps:

1. From the menu, navigate to **GameObject | Light | Light Probe Group**. A new object called **Light Probe Group** will appear in the **Hierarchy** window.

2. Once selected, eight interconnected spheres will appear. They can be manipulated by selecting the newly added **Edit Light Probe Group** tool in the **Scene Tools Overlay**. Click and move them around the scene so that they enclose the static region that your characters can enter. The following screenshot shows an example of how light probes can be used to enclose the volume of a static office space:

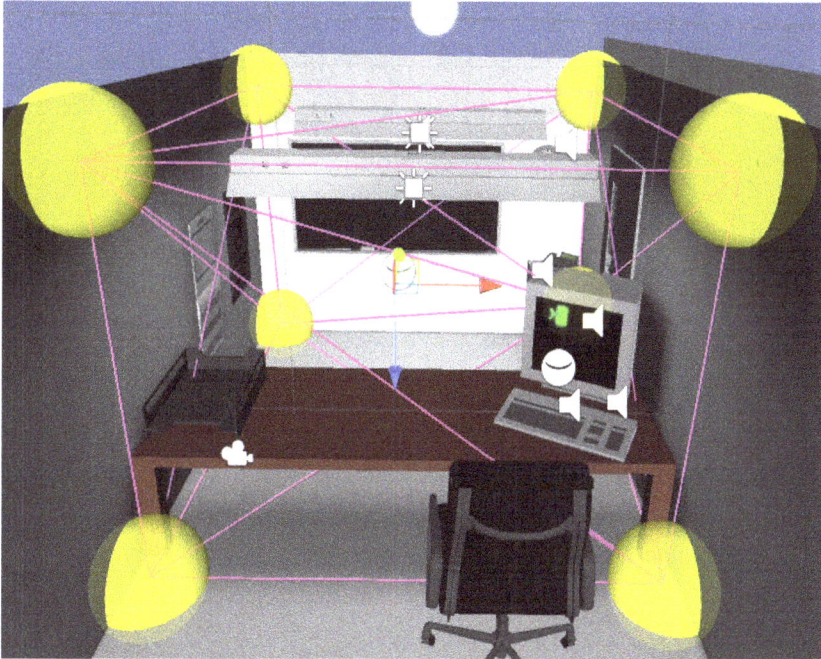

Figure 5.36 – How light probes can be used to enclose the volume of a static office space

For our example, it would just be the center area that the player can enter:

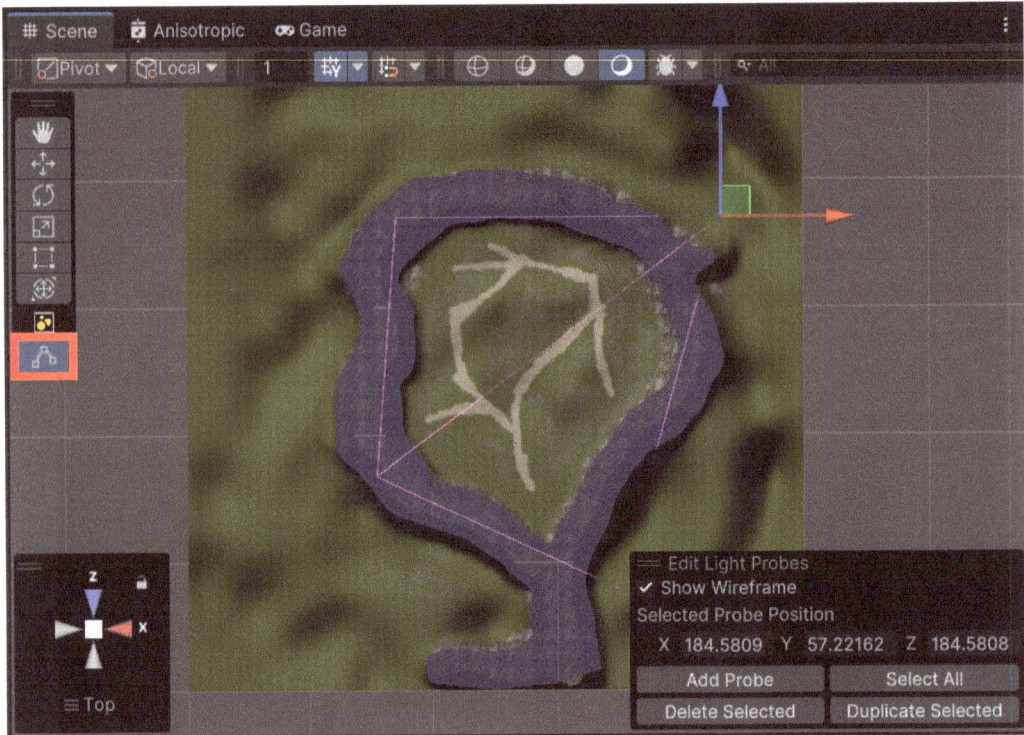

Figure 5.37 – Adjusting the size of Light Probe Group

3. Select the moving objects that will enter the light probe region.

4. From their **Inspector** window, expand their renderer component (usually, this is **Mesh Renderer**) and make sure that **Light Probes** is not set to **Off** (see the following screenshot):

Figure 5.38 – Ensuring the Light Probes property is not set to Off

Deciding where and when to use light probes is a critical problem; more information about this can be found in the *How it works...* section of this recipe.

Baking the lights

To bake the lights, follow these steps:

1. First, select the lights you'd like to bake. From the **Inspector** window, confirm that **Mode** is set to **Baked** in the **Light** component:

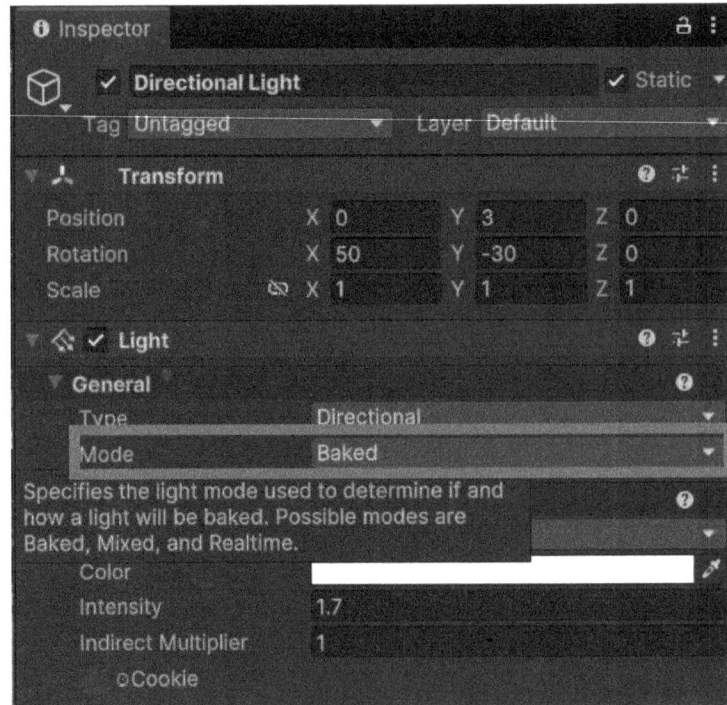

Figure 5.39 – Setting the light's Mode to Baked

2. To bake the lights, open the **Lighting** window by going to **Window | Rendering | Lighting**. Once you're there, select the **Scene** tab. Then, click on **Generate Lighting**.

> Tip
>
> Light baking can take several hours, even for a relatively small scene. If you are constantly moving static objects or lights, Unity will restart the process from scratch, causing a severe slowdown in the editor.

How it works...

The most complicated part of rendering is transporting the light. During this phase, the GPU calculates how the rays of light bounce between objects. If an object and its lights don't move, this calculation can be done only once as it will never change during the game. Flagging an object as **Static** is how to tell Unity that such an optimization can be made.

Loosely speaking, light baking refers to the process of calculating the GI of a static object and saving it in what is called a lightmap. Once baking has been completed, the lightmaps can be seen in the **Baked Lightmaps** tab of the **Lighting** window:

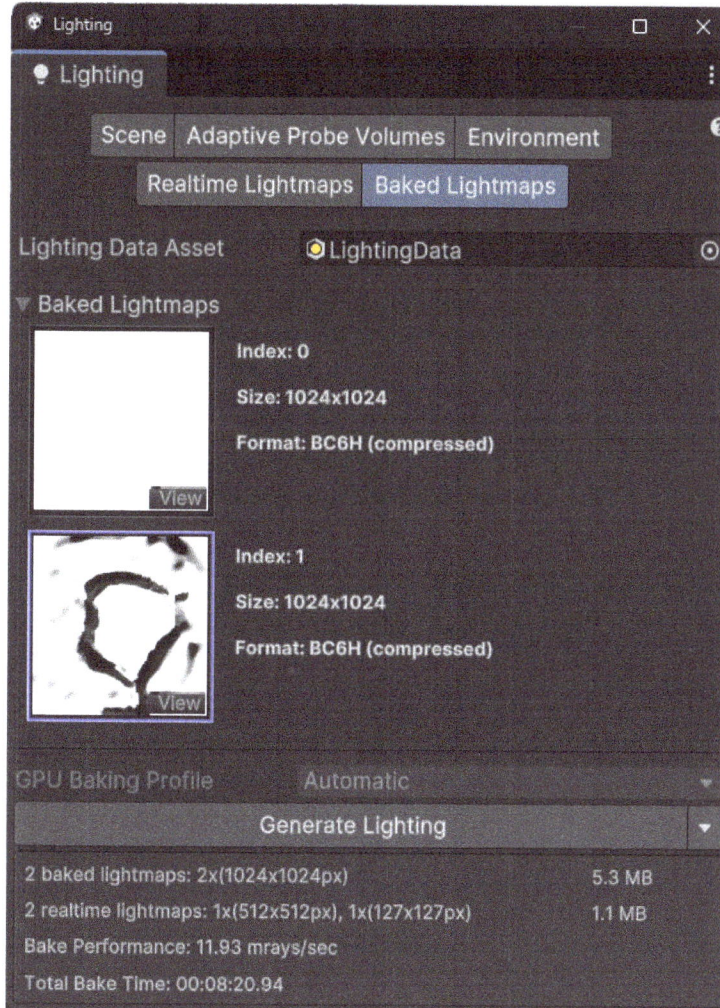

Figure 5.40 – The Baked Lightmaps menu

Clicking on the **Open Preview** button will allow you to see the other maps that were generated, including the **Baked Directionality** map:

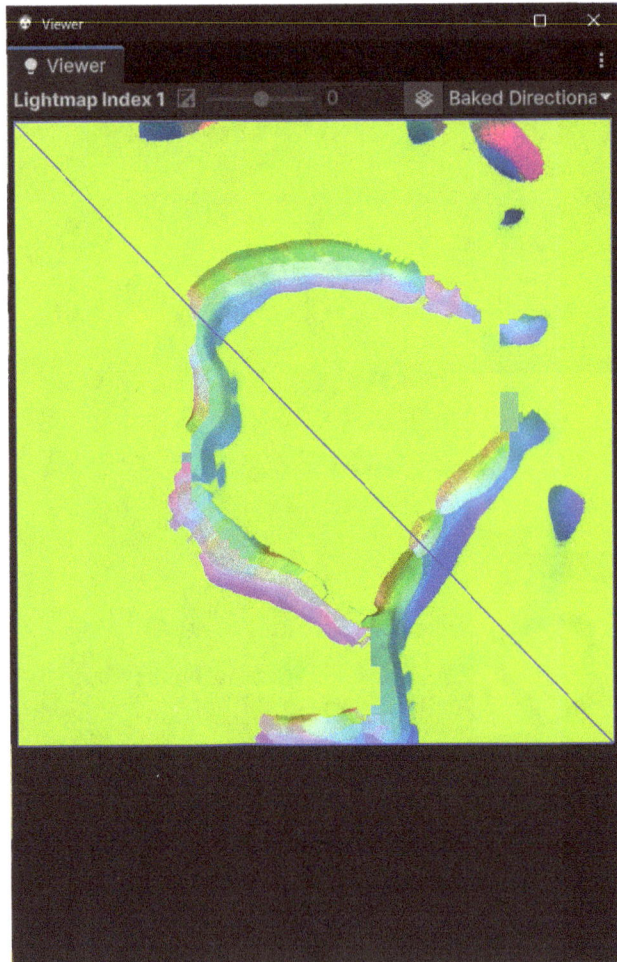

Figure 5.41 – A Baked Directionality map

Light baking comes at a great expense: memory. Every static surface is retextured so that it already includes its lighting condition. Let's imagine that you have a forest of trees, all sharing the same texture. Once they have been made static, each tree will have its very own texture. Light baking not only increases the size of your game but can also take up a lot of texture memory if used indiscriminately.

The second aspect that was introduced in this recipe was light probing. Light baking produces extremely high-quality results for static geometries but does not work on moving objects. If your character is entering a static region, it can look somehow detached from the environment. Its shading will not match the surroundings, resulting in an aesthetically unpleasant result. Other objects, such as **skinned mesh renderers**, will not receive GI, even if they're made static. Baking lights in real time is not possible, although light probes offer an effective alternative. Every light probe samples the GI at a specific point in space. A light probe group can sample several points in space, allowing GI to be interpolated within a specific volume. This allows us to cast a better light on moving objects, even though GI has only been calculated for a few points. It is important to remember that light probes need to enclose a volume to work. It is best to place light probes in regions where there is a sudden change in light conditions. Similar to lightmaps, probes consume memory and should be placed wisely; remember that they only exist for non-static geometry.

Even while using light probes, there are a few aspects that Unity's GI cannot capture. Non-static objects, for instance, cannot reflect light on other objects.

See also

You can read more about light probes at: `http://docs.unity3d.com/Manual/LightProbes.html`.

Join our community on Discord

Join our community's Discord space for discussions with the authors and other readers:

`https://packt.link/gamedevelopment`

Part 2

Advanced Shader Effects and Geometry Manipulation

With the foundations of Shader Graph established, this part explores advanced effects that modify both appearance and geometry. Traditional shaders define how an object looks, but vertex shaders allow us to modify the shape of objects in real time, unlocking effects such as animated deformations, procedural geometry, and dynamic movement.

We will also explore grab passes, a technique that captures and manipulates the background scene within a shader. Unlike simple transparency, which only reveals what's behind an object, grab passes enable refraction, distortion, and advanced visual effects, commonly used for materials like glass and water.

By the end of this part, you'll have a deeper understanding of modifying vertex data and leveraging background information within shaders, expanding the creative possibilities for your projects.

This part has the following chapters:

- *Chapter 6, Using Vertex Functions*
- *Chapter 7, Using Grab Passes*

6

Using Vertex Functions

The term shader originates from the fact that **C for Graphics (Cg)** is mainly used to simulate realistic lighting conditions (shadows) on **three-dimensional (3D)** models. Despite this, shaders are now much more than that. They not only define the way objects are going to look, but they can also redefine their shapes entirely. If you want to learn how to manipulate the geometry of a 3D object via shaders, this is the chapter for you.

In *Chapter 2, Creating Your First Shader with Shader Graph*, we explained that 3D models are not just a collection of triangles. Each vertex can contain data that is essential to render the model itself correctly. This chapter will explore how to access this information in order to use it in a shader. We will also explore in detail how the geometry of an object can be deformed simply by using Cg code.

By the end of this chapter, you will have seen several different ways that you can manipulate the geometry of a 3D object via shaders rather than by manipulating the mesh of the object itself.

In this chapter, you will work through the following recipes:

- Accessing a vertex color in a Shader Graph
- Animating vertices in a Shader Graph
- Extruding your models
- Implementing a snow shader
- Implementing a volumetric explosion

Technical requirements

For this chapter, you will need Unity Editor version 6 Preview 6000.0.07f1. This chapter's instructions should work with minimal changes in future versions of the editor in projects that utilize the **Universal Render Pipeline (URP)**. The chapter's sample project was created using the **Universal 3D Core** template.

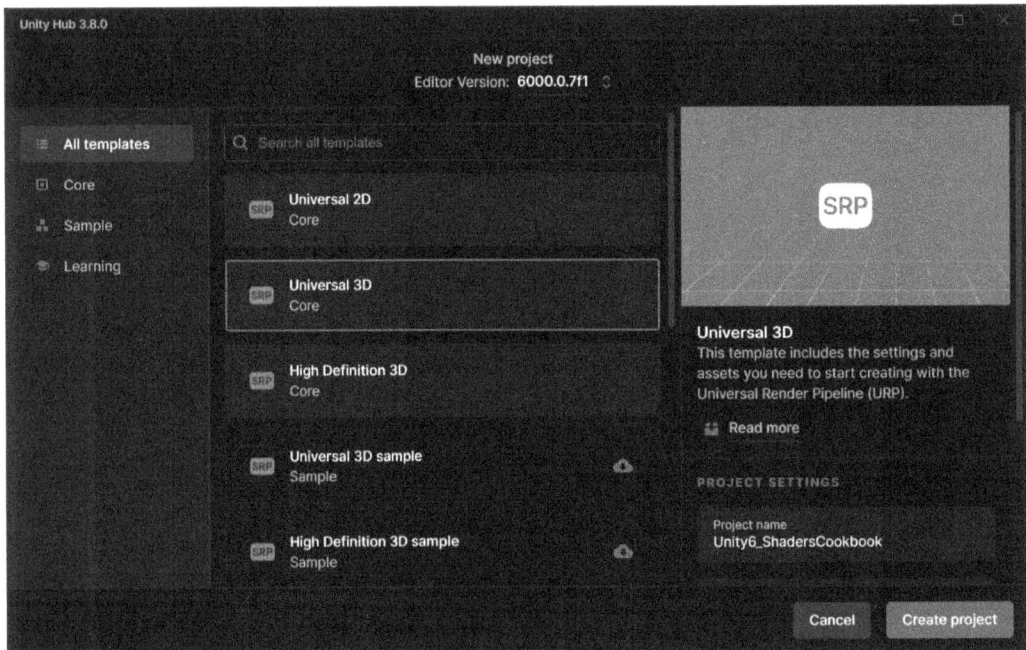

Figure 6.1 – Universal 3D (URP) project

The code files for this chapter can be found on GitHub at https://github.com/PacktPublishing/Unity-6-Shaders-and-Effects-Cookbook. The necessary files for this chapter are organized in the Unity project in a folder named Chapter 06 (https://github.com/PacktPublishing/Unity-6-Shaders-and-Effects-Cookbook/tree/main/Unity6_ShadersCookbook/Assets/Chapter%20 06) on GitHub.

Accessing a vertex color in a Shader Graph

Let's start this chapter by taking a look at how we can access information about a model's vertex using the vertex function in a Shader Graph. This will arm us with the knowledge to start utilizing the elements contained within a model's vertex to create really useful and visually appealing effects.

Each vertex in a model contains useful data that can be accessed in Shader Graph. You can retrieve a vertex's position and normal direction as a float3, which allows for various shading and lighting effects. The **Position** node provides the vertex position in different coordinate spaces, while the **Normal Vector** node gives the direction the vertex is facing. Additionally, if the model has stored per-vertex colors, these can be accessed as a float4 using the **Vertex Color** node. Many 3D modeling tools allow artists to paint vertex colors directly onto a model, which can then be used in Shader Graph to drive material effects such as blending textures or modifying emissive properties. However, Shader Graph itself does not store vertex colors dynamically; it can only retrieve and process the data already assigned to the model. In this recipe, we will explore how to retrieve vertex color information and use it within a shader.

Getting ready

In order to write this shader, we need to prepare a few assets.

To view the colors of a vertex, we need to have a model that has had color applied to its vertices. While you could use Unity to apply colors, you would have to write a tool to allow an individual to apply the colors or write some scripts to achieve the color application.

For this recipe, you can use a 3D modeling tool such as Maya or Blender to apply the colors to our model. If you prefer to use a ready-made asset, a sample model is available in the example code provided with this book. You can find it in the Chapter 06/Models folder (VertexColorObject. fbx), which can be downloaded from the book's GitHub page.

The following steps will set us up to create this vertex shader:

1. Create a new scene and place the imported model (**VertexColorObject**) in the scene.
2. Create a new Unlit Shader Graph by right-clicking in the **Project** window and selecting **Create | Shader | URP | Unlit Shader Graph** (SimpleVertexColor) and **Material** (SimpleVertexColorMat).

   When completed, assign the shader to the material and then the material to the imported model.

Your scene should now look similar to this:

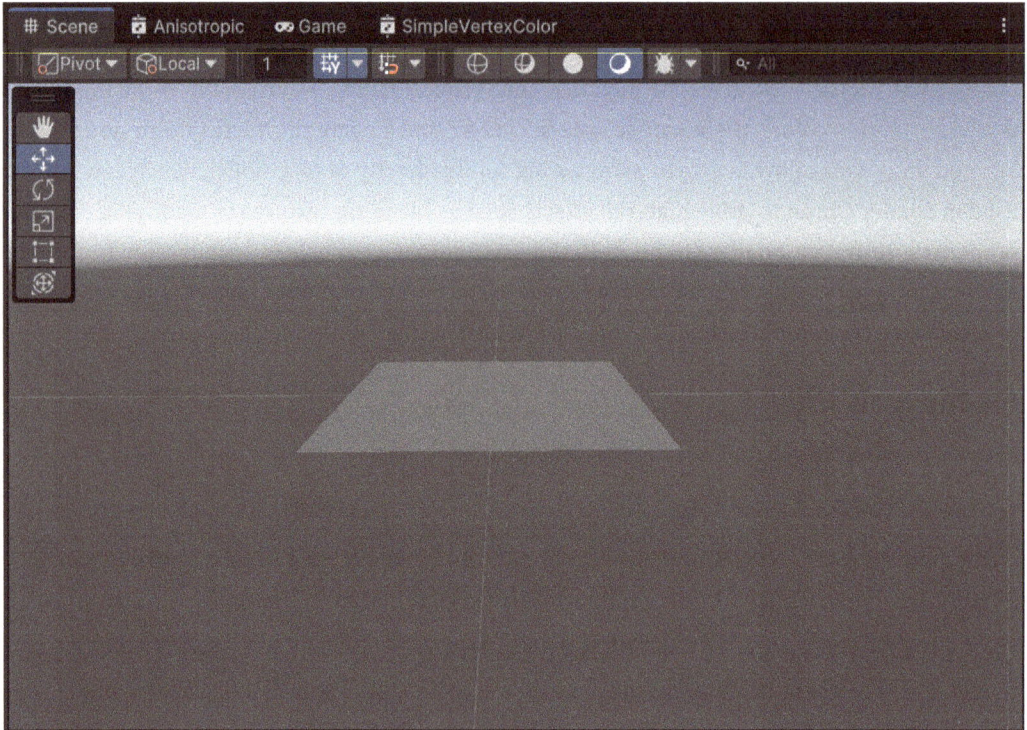

Figure 6.2 – Recipe setup

How to do it...

In the Shader Graph, we will add nodes to access the vertex color and use it in the shader:

1. Double-click **SimpleVertexColorShader** to open it in the Shader Graph editor.

    As we are creating a very simple shader, we technically don't need to add any additional properties to the **Blackboard**. However, to have some flexibility in the output, we will include a tint that we will apply onto to normal result as well.

2. From **Blackboard**, click on the + button to add a **Color** property. Name it Global Color Tint. From **Graph Inspector** set **Default Value** to white (from the **Color** window, I set the **Hexadecimal** set to FFFFFF).

3. Drag and drop **Global Color Tint** onto the graph. Below it, create a **Vertex Color** node to access the vertex color data from the model.

4. To the right of the two nodes, create a **Multiply** node and connect their outputs to the **A** and **B** inputs of the **Multiply** node. Finally, connect **Out(4)** of the **Multiply** node to **Base Color(3)** of the **Fragment** part of the **Master Stack**.

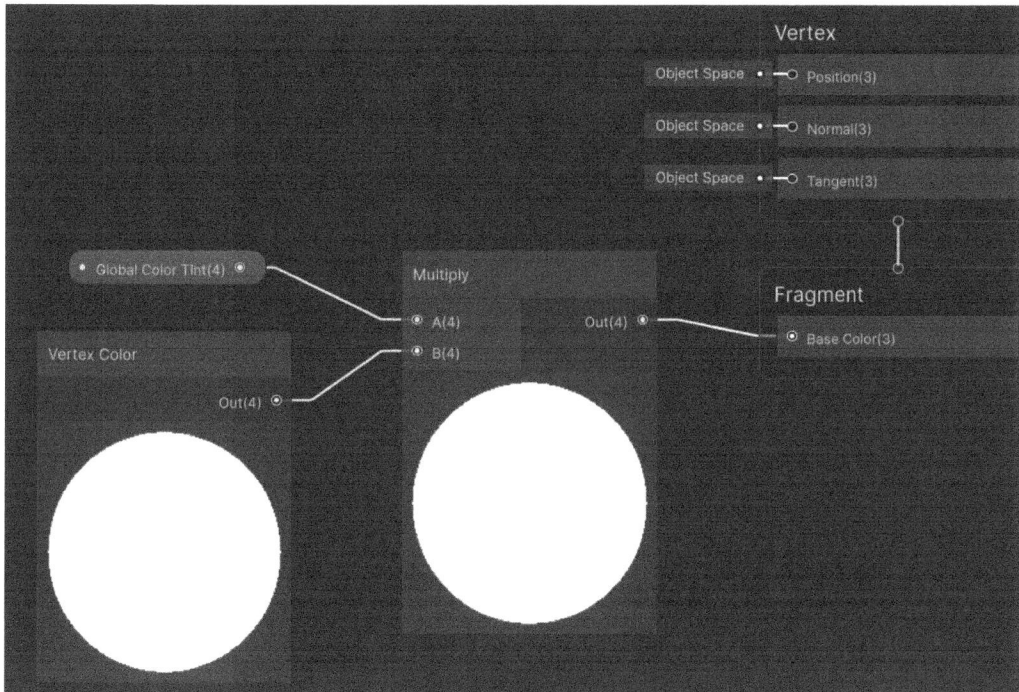

Figure 6.3 – Accessing Vertex Color

5. Save the Shader Graph and return to the Unity Editor. If all goes well, you should see something like this:

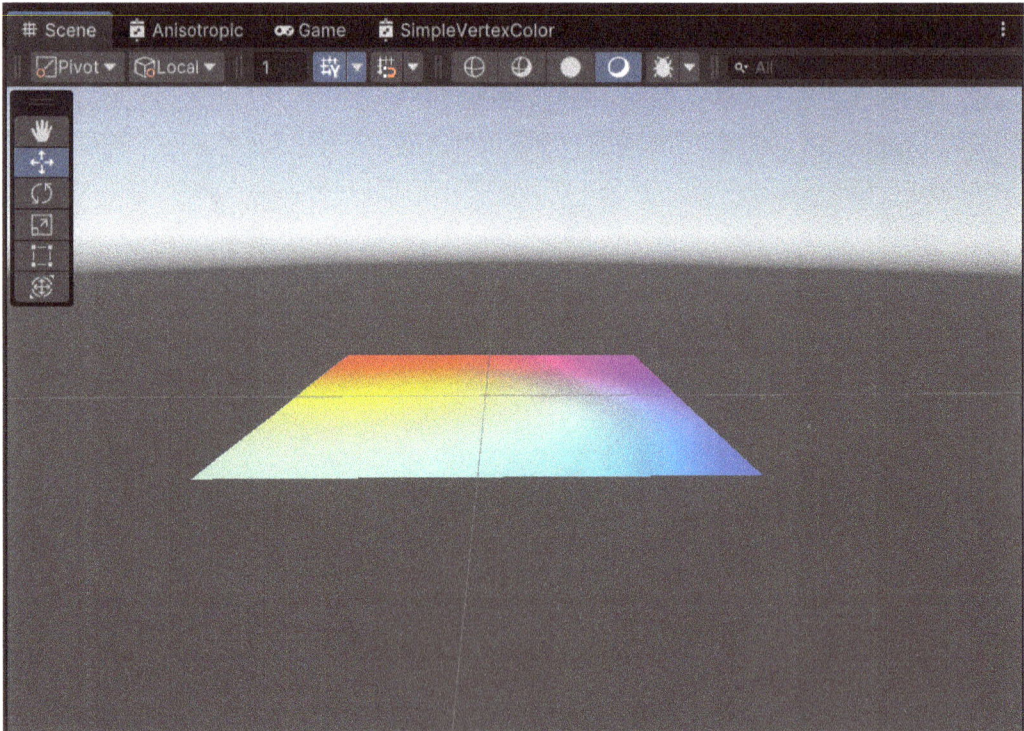

Figure 6.4 – Shader result

How it works...

Unity provides us with a way to access the vertex information of the model to which a shader is attached. This gives us the power to modify things such as the vertices' position and color. With this recipe, we imported a mesh from Maya (although just about any 3D software application can be used), where vertex colors were added to **Verts**. You'll notice that by importing the model, the default material will not display the vertex colors. By using our Shader Graph, we can access and manipulate vertex information directly in the shader. The **Vertex Color** node allows us to retrieve the color data stored in each vertex of our model. By multiplying this color with **Global Color Tint**, we can modify the appearance of the model based on the vertex colors.

There's more...

Additionally, the **Vertex Color** node has data that includes a fourth component – the alpha value. This alpha value can be used in various ways, such as for creating transparency effects or providing an extra mask for blending textures.

Whether or not you choose to utilize this fourth component depends on the needs of your production. It's a valuable tool that offers flexibility for achieving different visual effects, so it's worth considering how it can enhance your shaders.

Animating vertices in a Shader Graph

Now that we know how to access data on a per-vertex basis, let's expand our knowledge set to include other types of data and the position of a vertex.

Using a vertex function, we can access the position of each vertex in a mesh. This allows us to actually modify each individual vertex while the shader does the processing.

In this recipe, we will create a shader that will allow us to modify the positions of each vertex on a mesh with a sine wave. This technique can be used to create animations for objects such as flags or waves in an ocean.

Getting ready

Let's gather our assets together so that we can create the code for our vertex shader. Follow these steps:

1. Create a new scene and place a plane mesh in the center of the scene (**GameObject** | **3D Object** | **Plane**).

   The **Plane** object created may seem to be a single quad but, in fact, has 121 verts that we are going to be moving. Using a quad would provide unexpected results. To check for yourself, select the circle to the right of the **Plane** object from the **Inspector** tab on the **Mesh Filter** component and note the properties displayed when selected in the **Select Mesh** menu.

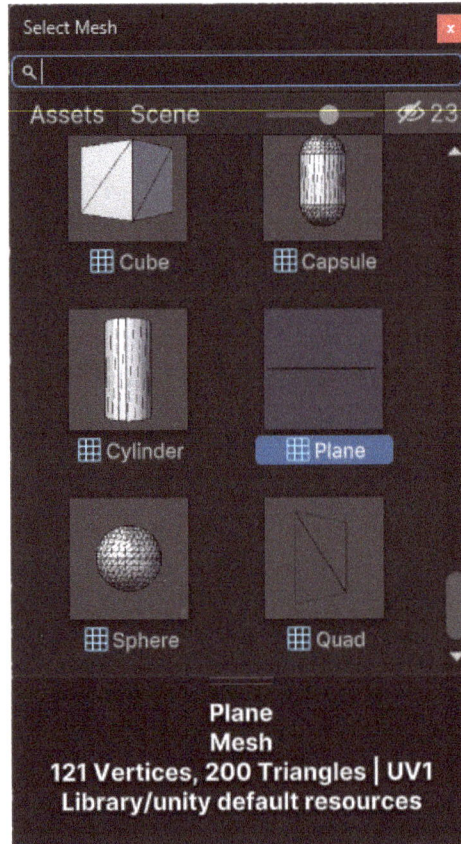

Figure 6.5 – The Plane mesh's properties

2. Create a new shader (VertexAnimation) and material (VertexAnimationMat).

3. Finally, assign the shader to the material and the material to the plane mesh.

Your scene should look similar to this:

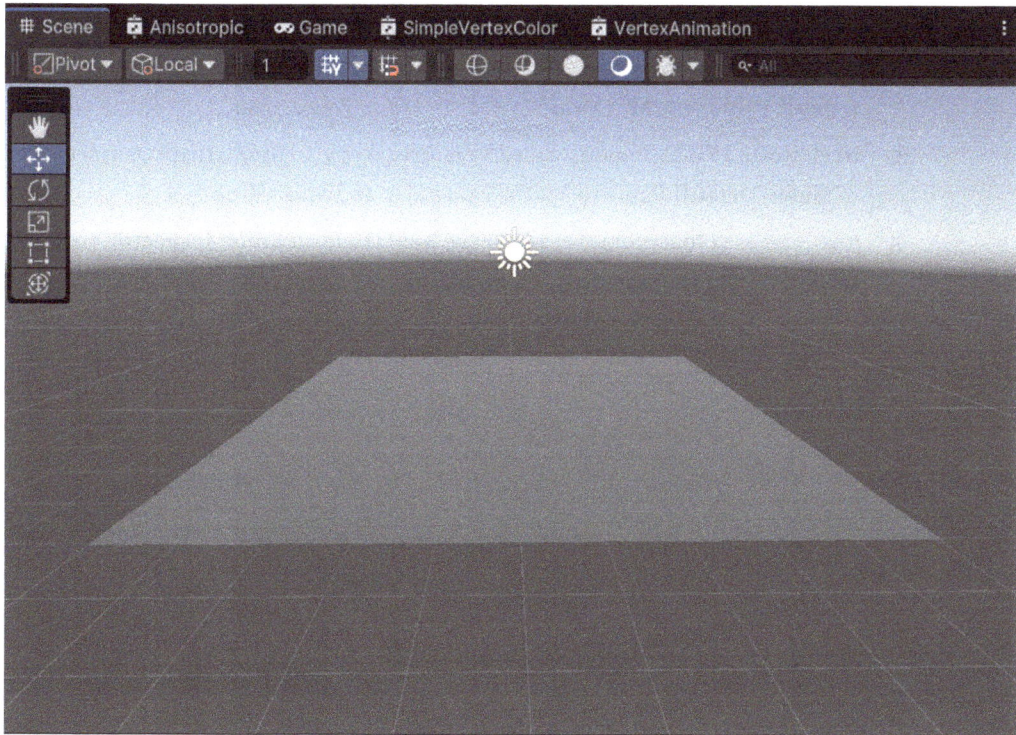

Figure 6.6 – Recipe setup

How to do it...

After setting up the scene, perform the following steps:

1. Open up the Shader Graph and go to **Blackboard**. We will start off by creating several properties that we will need to work with. Hit the + button and select **Texture2D**. Name this first property Base (RGB), and in **Graph Inspector**, set **Default Value** to the UVChecker texture found in the sample code for this chapter.

2. Next, create a **Float** property called Tint Amount. In **Graph Inspector**, set **Mode** to **Slider**, **Default Value** to 0.5, **Min Value** to 0, and **Max Value** to 1.

3. Next, create two **Color** properties: **Color A** and **Color B**. Set **Default Value** to two different colors. I used red and blue.

4. After that, create a **Category** called Wave Properties, which we will put the following three properties into:

    1. Create a **Float** property called Wave Speed. In **Graph Inspector**, set **Mode** to **Slider**, **Default Value** to 5, **Min Value** to 0.1, and **Max Value** to 80.

    2. Next, create a **Float** property called Wave Frequency. In **Graph Inspector**, set **Mode** to **Slider**, **Default Value** to 3, **Min Value** to 0, and **Max Value** to 5.

    3. Next, create a **Float** property called Wave Amplitude. In **Graph Inspector**, set **Mode** to **Slider**, **Default Value** to 0.25, **Min Value** to -1, and **Max Value** to 1.

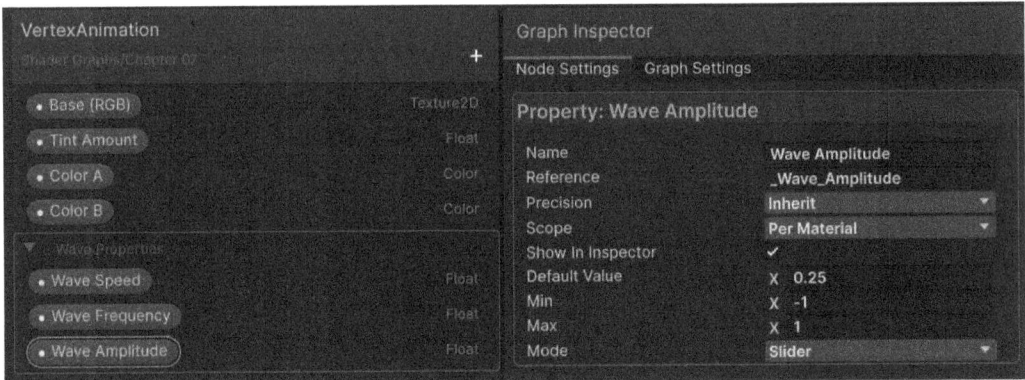

Figure 6.7 – Blackboard properties

We will start off by doing a sine wave calculation, which we will use in both the position and color calculations.

5. Create a **Time** node. Below that, drag and drop the **Wave Speed** variable from the **Blackboard** onto the graph. To the right of that, create a **Multiply** node and connect the **Time(1)** output of the **Time** node to **A** of the **Multiply** node and the **Wave Speed(1)** output to **B**.

6. Below those nodes, create a **Position** node and change **Space** to **Object**. To the right of it, create a **Split** node and connect **Out(3)** of the **Position** node to the input of the **Split** node. To the right of **Split**, create a **Multiply** node and connect **R(1)** of the **Split** node to **A** of the **Multiply** node.

> Note
>
> Note that, in reality, the **R(1)** output is the X position of our object.

7. Drag and drop **Wave Frequency** onto the graph and connect it to **B** of the **Multiply** node.

8. To the right of both **Multiply** nodes, create an **Add** node. Connect the result of the top **Multiply** node to **A** of the **Add** node. Connect **Out(1)** of the bottom **Multiply** node to **B(1)** of the **Add** node.

9. Finally, to the right of the **Add** node, create a **Sine** node. Connect **Out(1)** of the **Add** node to **In(1)** of the **Sine** node. To make it easier to understand what this grouping of nodes is doing, you can select them all and then hit *Ctrl + G* to make a group. Once you do so, you can give them a name such as Sine Wave Calculation.

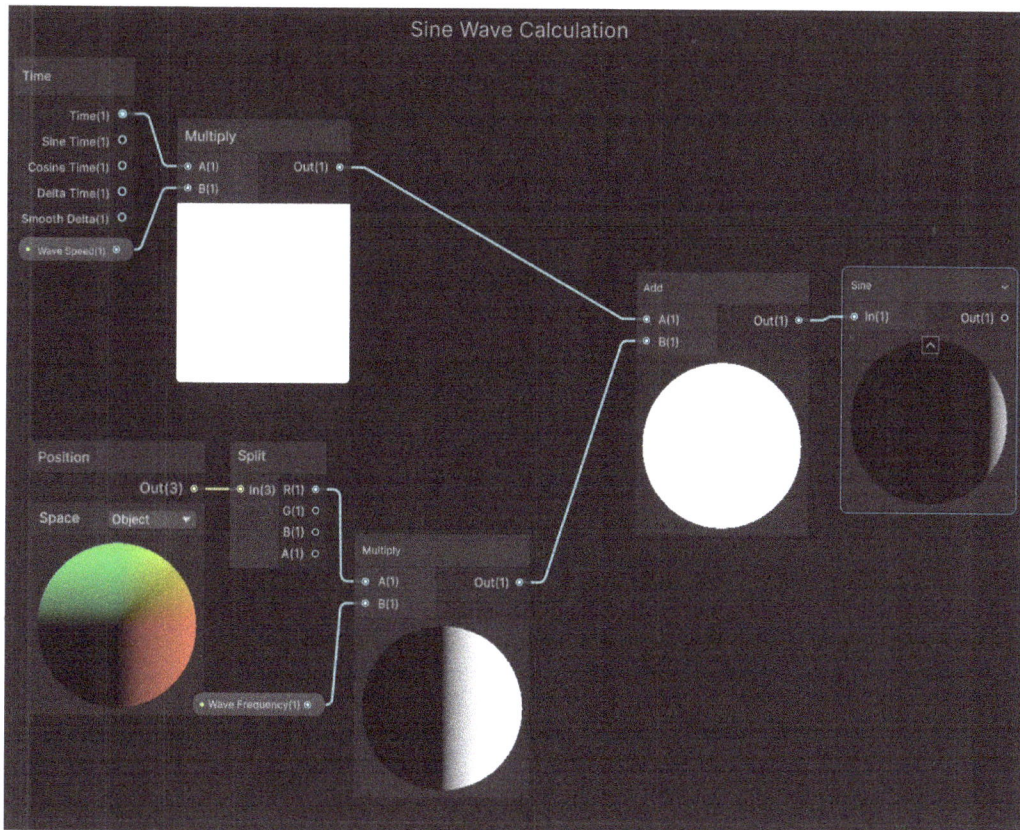

Figure 6.8 – Sine Wave Calculation

Now, this sine result will be used in two places, so feel free to use reroute nodes or create additional float nodes if needed. We will start off by doing the vertex position modification before doing the color modification.

10. Create a **Multiply** node and connect the **Out(1)** output of the **Sine** node to **B** of the **Multiply** node. Then, from the **Blackboard**, drag **Wave Amplitude** onto the graph and assign it to **A** of the **Multiply** node.

11. We will need to get the object's position again, so above those nodes, create a **Position** node and change **Space** to **Object**. To the right of it, create a **Split** node and connect **Out(3)** of the **Position** node to the input of the **Split** node. To the right of the **Split** node, create an **Add** node and connect **G(1)** of the **Split** node to **A** of the **Add** node. Then connect **Out(1)** of the **Multiply** node to **B** of the **Add** node.

    Here, we are changing the Y position of the vertices by adding the result of the sine wave scaled by **Wave Amplitude**. But after making the change, we need to combine it all together.

12. To the right of the **Add** node, create a **Combine** node. Connect **R** and **B** of the **Split** node to the **Combine** node. Then connect **Out(1)** of the **Add** node to **G** of the **Combine** node. Finally, connect **RGBA(4)** or **RGB(3)** of the **Combine** node to **Position(3)** of the **Vertex** section of the **Master Stack**.

13. Afterward, you can select the newly created nodes. Hit *Ctrl + G* to create a group and name it Vertex Position Modification to help group your nodes.

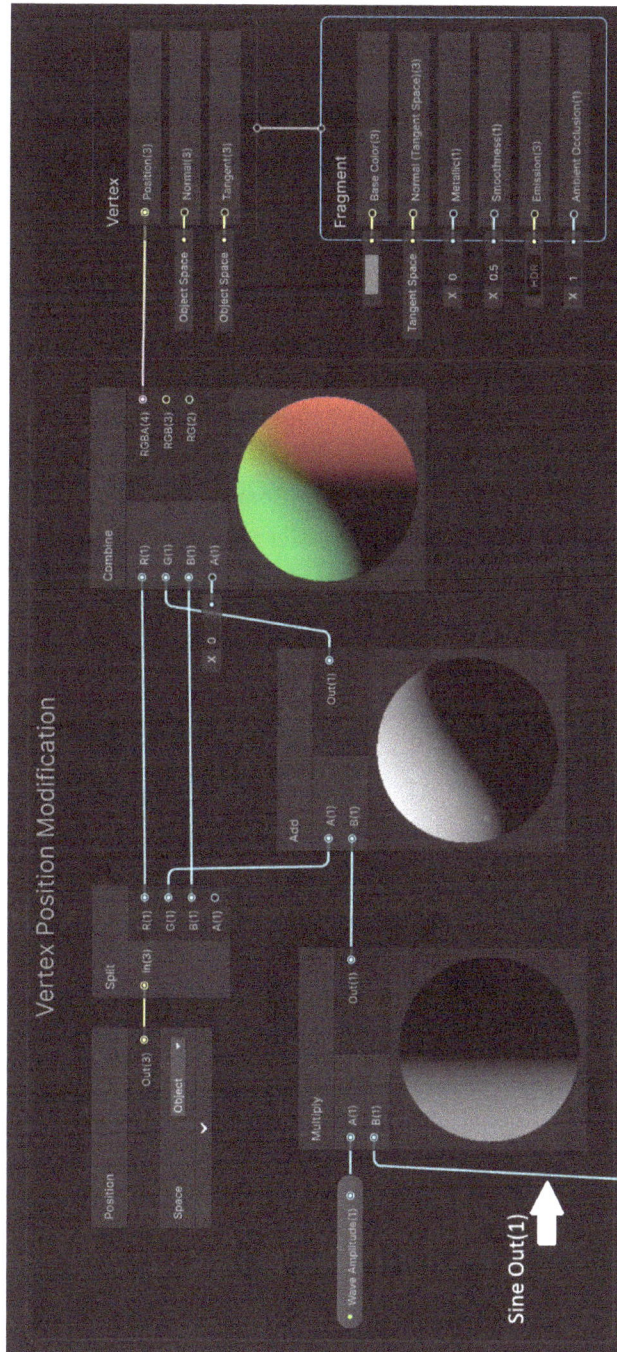

Figure 6.9 – Vertex Position Modification

Now that the **Vertex** section is finished, we can set **Base Color**:

14. From the **Blackboard**, drag and drop the **Color A** and **Color B** properties onto the graph. To the right of them, create a **Lerp** node and connect **Color A** to **A(4)** and **Color B** to **B(4)**. Connect **Out(1)** from the **Sine** node we created previously to the **T(1)** property.

15. To the right of that, create a **Multiply** node and connect the output of the **Lerp** node to the **A** of the **Multiply** node. From the **Blackboard**, drag and drop the **Tint Amount** property to the graph and connect it to **B** of the **Multiply** node.

16. To the right of that, create another **Multiply** node and connect **Out** of the previous **Multiply** node to the **B** input of the new **Multiply** node. Drag and drop the **Base RGB** texture onto the graph and to the right of it, create a **Sample Texture 2D** node, connecting the output of **Base RGB** to the **Texture(T2)** input. Connect the **RGBA(4)** output of the **Sample Texture 2D** node to **A** of the **Multiply** node. Finally, connect **Out(4)** of the **Multiply** node to **Base Color(3)** of the **Fragment** part of the **Master Stack**.

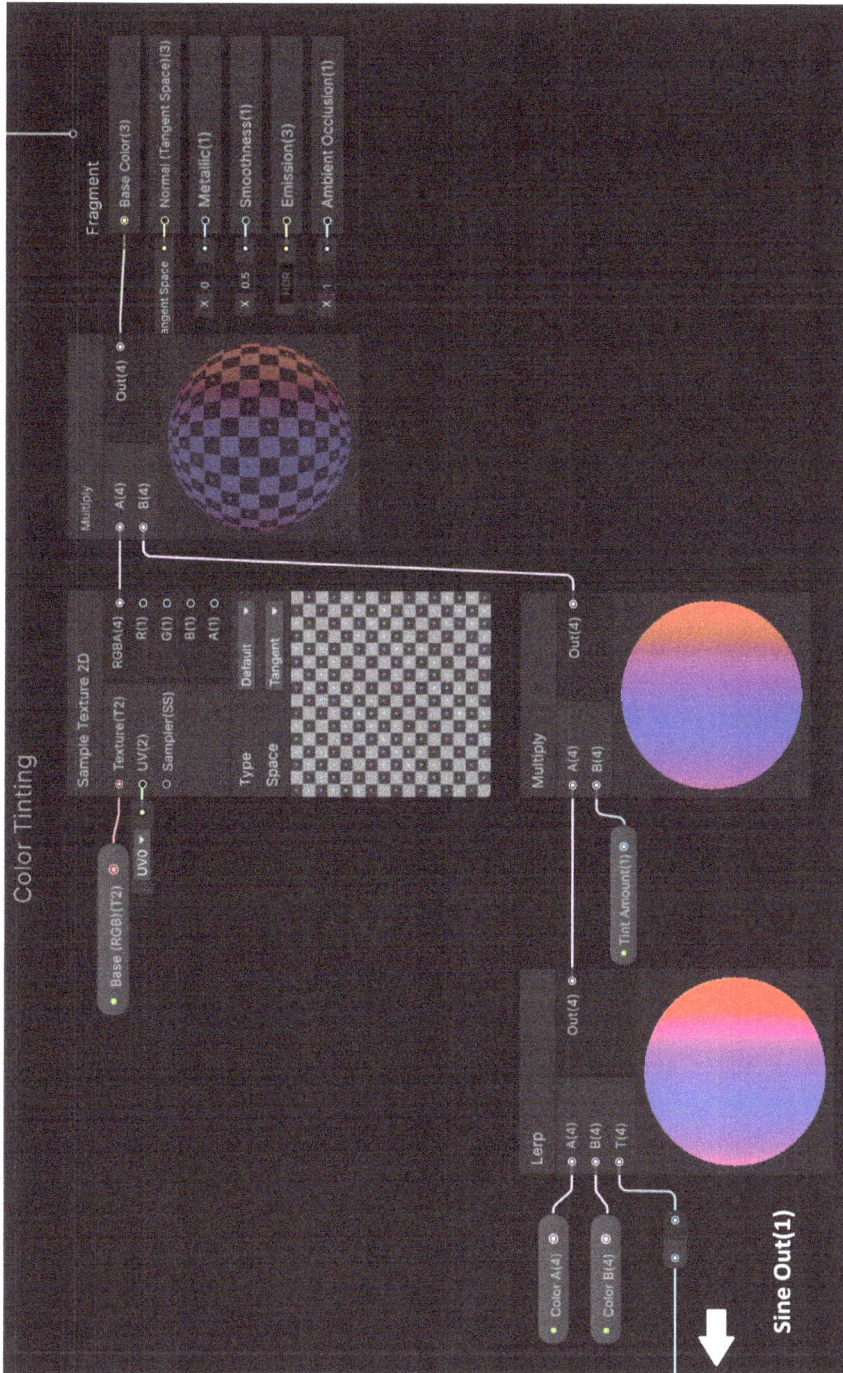

Figure 6.10 – Color tinting

17.   Save your Shader Graph and return to the Unity Editor.

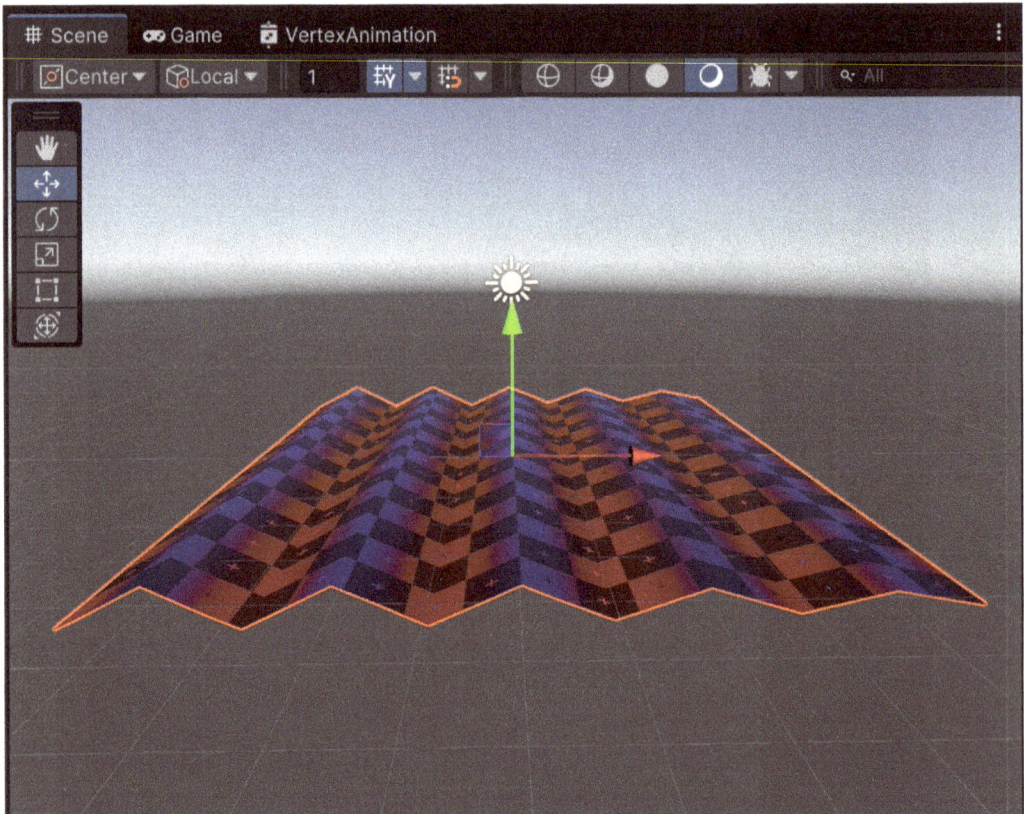

Figure 6.11 – Shader result

Play the game, and you should notice how, over time, the shader will affect the vertices of the given plane object! Also, feel free to adjust the properties to see how it'll affect how things look. For instance, you can see how this looks here with some adjustments:

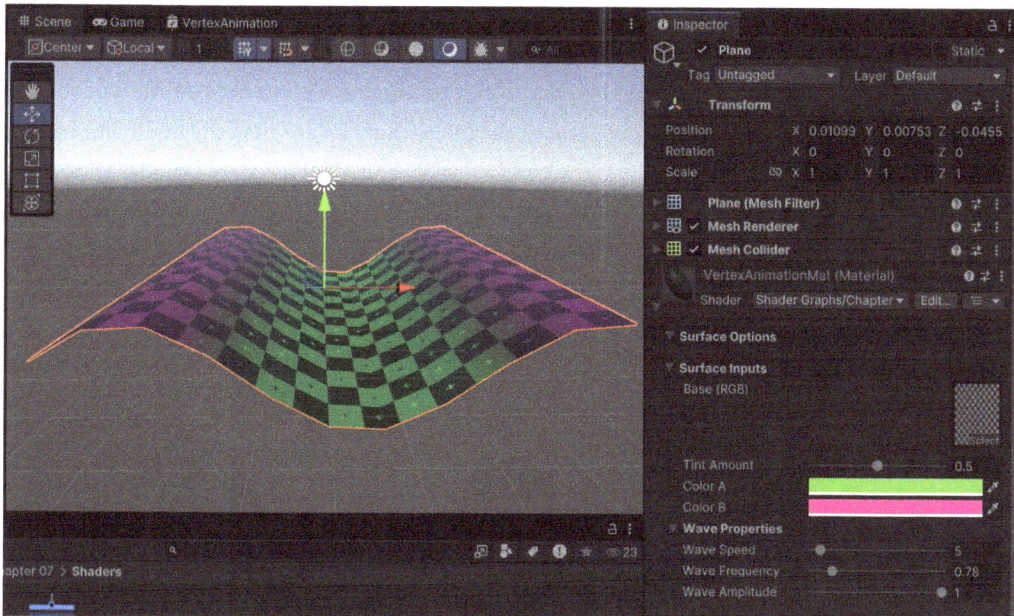

Figure 6.12 – Adjusting properties

How it works...

This particular shader uses the same concept from the last recipe, except that this time, we are modifying the positions of the vertices in the mesh. This is really useful if you don't want to rig up simple objects such as a flag, and then animate them using a skeleton structure or hierarchy of transforms. By leveraging the **Sine** node that utilizes the sin() function that is built into the Cg language, we create a wave pattern that animates the vertices over time. This involves calculating the sine wave value based on the vertex position and time and then adding this value to the Y-component of each vertex position. This approach results in a wave-like animation effect across the surface of the mesh.

The shader also incorporates color tinting to enhance the visual effect. By interpolating between two colors based on the sine wave value, we dynamically change the color of the vertices. This interpolation, achieved using the **Lerp** node, allows us to tint the vertices at the peaks and valleys of the wave differently, adding depth and interest to the animation.

The shader's ability to animate vertices without requiring a skeletal structure or complex animations makes it particularly useful for creating dynamic effects on simple objects such as flags or ocean waves. By utilizing the built-in vertex parameters provided by Shader Graph, we can easily create more complex vertex effects.

Extruding your models

One of the biggest problems in games is repetition. Creating new content is a time-consuming task, and when you have to face thousands of enemies, chances are that they will all look the same. A relatively cheap technique to add variation to your models is using a shader that alters their basic geometry. This recipe will show you a technique called normal extrusion, which can be used to create a chubbier or skinnier version of a model, as shown in the following screenshot of a soldier from the Unity camp demo:

Figure 6.13 – The results of modifying the Extrusion Amount parameter

For ease of use, I have provided a prefab of the soldier in the example code for this book under the Chapter 06/Prefabs folder.

Getting ready

For this recipe, you need to have access to the shader used by the model that you want to alter. Once you have it, we'll duplicate it so that we can edit it safely. This is how it can be done:

1. Find the Shader Graph your model (in our case, the soldier) is using and, once selected, duplicate it by pressing *Ctrl* + *D*. If it is just using the Lit Universal Pipeline Shader, as in this example, it is also possible to just create a new **Lit Shader Graph**. Either way, rename this new Shader Graph NormalExtrusion.

2. Duplicate the original material of the model and assign the cloned shader to it.

3. Assign the new material to your model (NormalExtrusionMat) and start editing it.

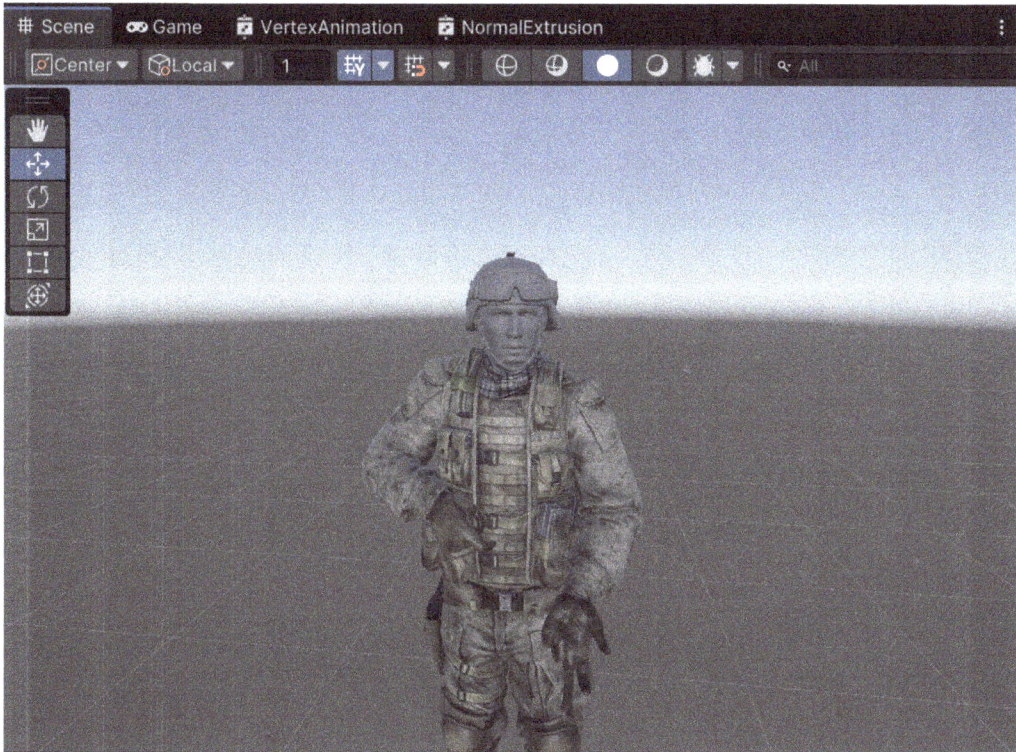

Figure 6.14 – Recipe setup

In order for this effect to work, your model should have normals.

1. In our case, from the **Blackboard** we are going to create two **Texture 2D** properties to hold the two textures that are currently used: **MainTex** and **Normal Map**. To make it easier to see, I also set **Default Value** to the **Soldier Head** and **Soldier Head Normal Map** textures.

2. Then we'll take care of the standard textures. Drag and drop **MainTex** to the graph, create a **Sample Texture 2D** node to connect to it, and then connect the output to the **Base Color(3)** aspect of the **Main Stack**. Then do the same thing for **Normal Map** to **Normal (Tangent Space)(3)**.

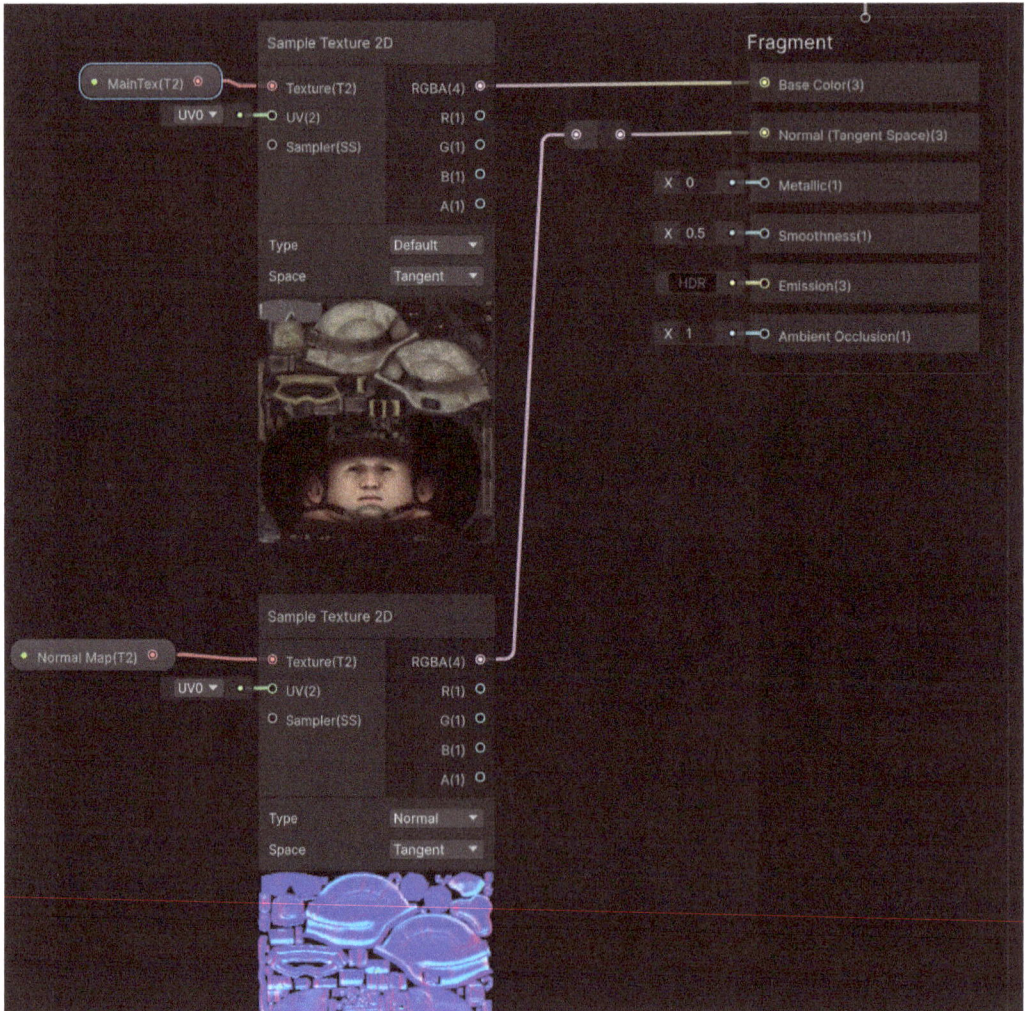

Figure 6.15 – Texture setup

How to do it...

Let's start by adding a property to our shader, which will be used to modulate its extrusion.

From the **Blackboard,** click on the + button to create a **Float** property called **Extrusion Amount.** Change **Mode** to **Slider.** Then change **Min** to -0.0001 and **Max** to 0.0001, but you might have to adjust this according to your own needs.

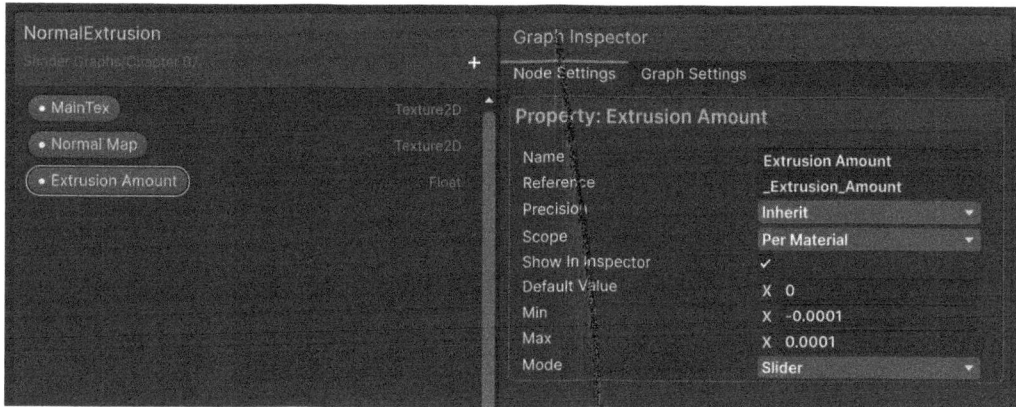

Figure 6.16 – Blackboard properties

Now we can start the actual vertex position manipulation:

1. Create a **Position** node. Change **Space** to **Object.** To the right of that, create an **Add** node and connect **Out(3)** of the **Position** node to **A** of **Add.**

2. Below the **Position** node, create a **Normal Vector** node. Change **Space** to **Object.**

3. Below that, drag and drop the **Extrusion Amount** property from the **Blackboard.** Then create a **Multiply** node and connect **Normal Vector** to the **A** input and **Extrusion Amount** to **B.** Finally, connect **Out(3)** of the **Multiply** node to **B(3)** of the **Add** node.

4. Afterward, connect **Out(3)** of the **Add** node to **Position(3)** of the **Vertex** section of the **Master Stack.**

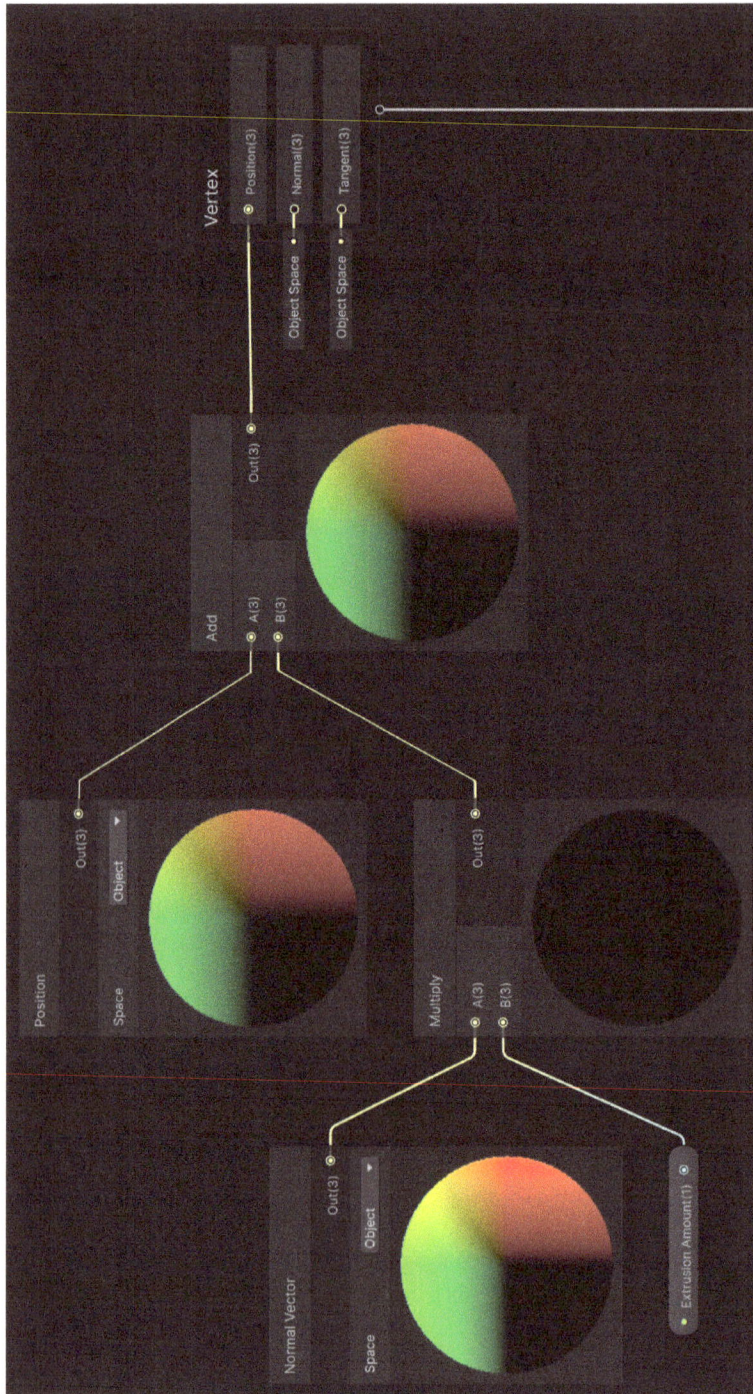

Figure 6.17 – Vertex manipulation

The shader is now ready; you can use the **Extrusion Amount** slider in the material's **Inspector** tab to make your model skinnier or chubbier. Also, feel free to create a clone of the material in order to have different extrusion amounts for each character:

Figure 6.18 – The results of modifying the Extrusion Amount parameter

How it works...

A Shader Graph allows you to manipulate vertex positions by altering them along their normal vectors. By multiplying the normal vectors by an extrusion amount and adding the result to the original vertex positions, you can effectively alter the geometry of your model.

This technique, called **normal extrusion**, can add a lot of variation to your models. Small values for the extrusion amount create subtle changes, while larger values can significantly alter the appearance of the model. The position of a vertex is displaced by **Extrusion Amount** units toward the vertex normal. If **Extrusion Amount** gets too high, the results can be quite unpleasant. With smaller values, however, you can add a lot of variation to your models.

There's more...

If you have multiple enemies and want each one to have its own weight, you have to create a different material for each one of them. This is necessary as materials are normally shared between models, and changing one will change all of them. There are several ways in which you can do this; the quickest one is to create a script that automatically does it for you. Note that in the **Blackboard** there is always a property called **Reference**, which is how the variable will be referred to in code. In our case, **Extrusion Amount** is _Extrusion_Amount. The following script, once attached to an object with a renderer, will duplicate the object's first material and set the _Extrusion_Amount property automatically:

```
using UnityEngine;
public class NormalExtruder : MonoBehaviour
{
    [Range(-0.0001f, 0.0001f)]
    public float amount = 0;
    // Use this for initialization
    void Start()
    {
        Material material =
        GetComponent<Renderer>().sharedMaterial;
        Material newMaterial = new Material(material);
        newMaterial.SetFloat("_Extrusion_Amount", amount);
        GetComponent<Renderer>().material = newMaterial;
    }
}
```

This technique can actually be improved even further. We can add an extra texture (or use the alpha channel of the main one) to indicate the amount of extrusion. This allows for much better control over which parts are raised or lowered. The following shows you how it is possible to achieve such an effect:

1. From the **Blackboard**, add a new **Texture 2D** property called Extrusion Map. From **Graph Inspector**, assign it to the extrusion map you'd like to use (in our example code, it can be found as Assets/Chapter 06/Textures/Unity_soldier_Head_DIF_01_extrusion.tga).

2. Next, select the connection between **Extrusion Amount** and **B** of the **Multiply** node and use the *delete* key to remove it.

3. Drag and drop the **Extrusion Map** property from the **Blackboard** to the graph. To the right of it, create a **Sample Texture 2D LOD** node (note the **LOD** – it is part of the node's name and is required for vertex outputs). Connect **Extrusion Map** to the **Texture (T2)** input of the **Sample Texture 2D LOD** node.

4. To the right of it, create a **Multiply** node and connect **R(1)** of the **Sample Texture 2D LOD** node. Ensure **B(1)** of **Multiply** is set to 2. To the right of the **Multiply** node, create a **Subtract** node. Connect **A** of **Subtract** to the **Multiply** node and leave **B** at 1.

5. To the right of the **Subtract** node, create an **Absolute** node. Connect **Out(1)** to **In(1)** of the **Absolute** node. To the right of that, create a **Multiply** node. Connect our previously created **Extrusion Amount** output to the **A** and **Out(1)** of **Absolute** to **B(1)**. Finally, connect **Out(1)** of this newly created **Multiply** node to the original connection we deleted earlier.

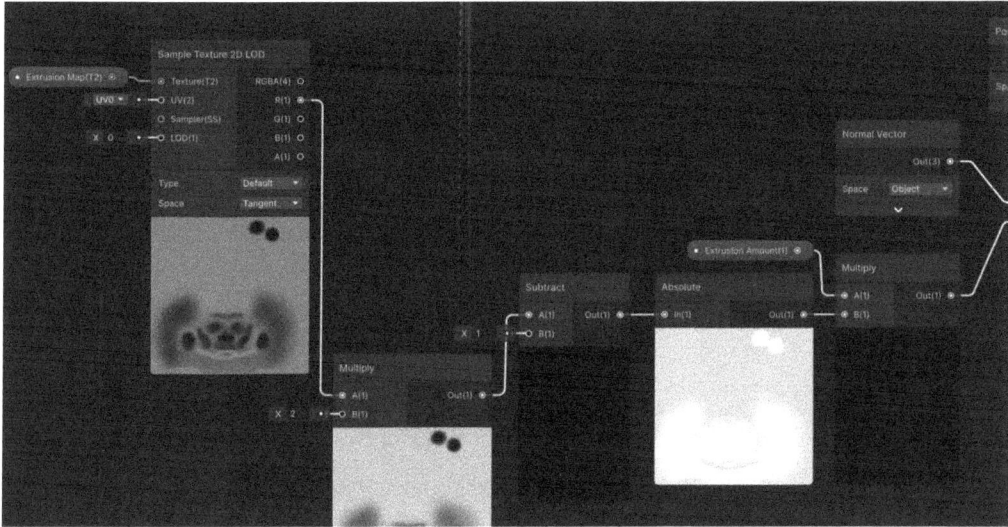

Figure 6.19 – Using an extrusion map

The red channel of the **Extrusion Map** texture is used as a multiplying coefficient for normal extrusion. A value of 0.5 leaves the model unaffected; darker or lighter shades are used to extrude vertices inward or outward, respectively. You should note that, in order to sample a texture within a vertex modifier, the **Sample Texture 2D LOD** node should be used instead of **Sample Texture 2D**.

> **Note**
>
> In shaders, color channels go from 0 to 1, although sometimes you need to represent negative values as well (such as inward extrusion). When this is the case, treat 0.5 as 0; consider having smaller values as negative and higher values as positive. This is exactly what happens with normals, which are usually encoded in **red-green-blue** (**RGB**) textures. The **Normal Unpack** node is used to map a value in the range (0,1) on the range (-1,+1). Mathematically speaking, this is equivalent to the *channel value * 2 -1*, which is the calculation we are doing through the preceding nodes.

Extrusion maps are perfect for zombifying characters by shrinking the skin to highlight the shape of the bones underneath. The following screenshot shows you how a healthy soldier can be transformed into a corpse using just a shader and extrusion map. Compared to the previous example, you may notice how the clothing is unaffected. The shader used in the following screenshot also darkens the extruded regions to give an even more emaciated look to the soldier:

Figure 6.20 – The zombified character

Implementing a snow shader

The simulation of snow has always been a challenge in games. The vast majority of games simply include snow directly in the model's texture so that their tops look white. However, what if one of these objects starts rotating? Snow is not just a lick of paint on a surface; it is a proper accumulation of material and should be treated as such. This recipe shows you how to give a snowy look to your models using just a shader.

This effect is achieved in two steps. First, white is used for all the triangles facing the sky. Second, their vertices are extruded to simulate the effect of snow accumulation. You can see the result in the following screenshot:

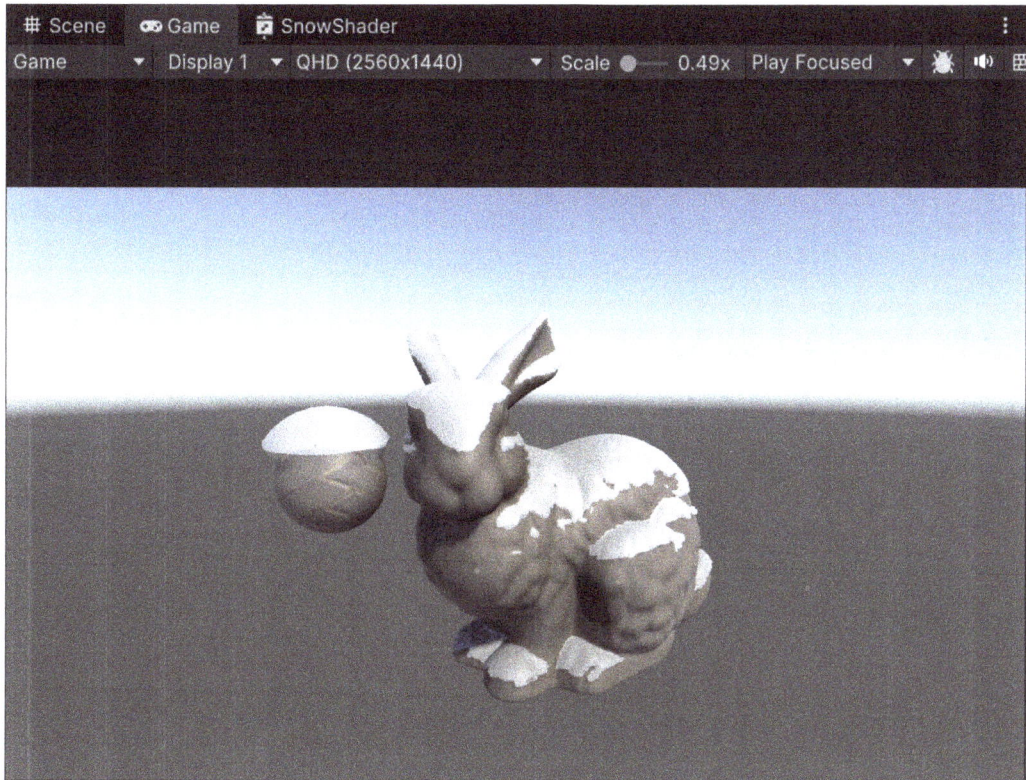

Figure 6.21 – Result of the recipe

Important note

Keep in mind that this recipe does not aim to create a photorealistic snow effect. It provides a good starting point, but it is up to you to create the right textures and find the right parameters to make it fit your game.

Getting ready

This effect is purely based on shaders. We will need to do the following:

1. Create a new Shader Graph for the snow effect (SnowShader).

2. Create a new material for the shader (SnowMat).

3.   Assign the newly created material to the object that you want to be snowy (in my case, I'm using the bunny from the sample code):

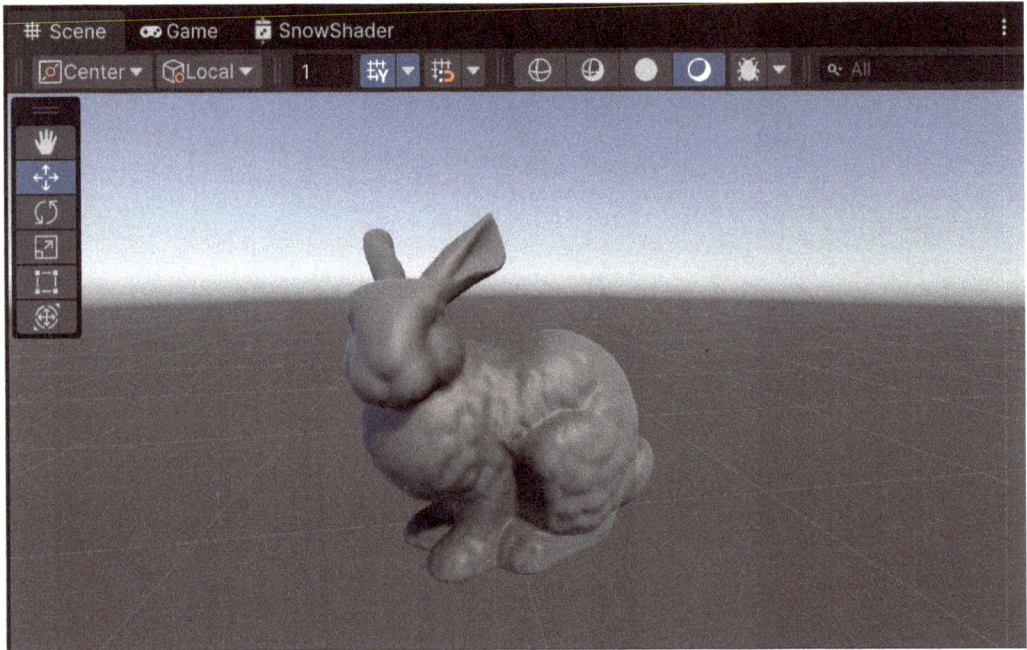

Figure 6.22 – Recipe setup

How to do it...

To create a snowy effect, open your Shader Graph and make the following changes:

1.   From the **Blackboard**, add two **Texture2D** properties, MainTex and Snow Texture. For **Default Value**, assign a material you'd like to use for each. I used the albedoMap texture we generated in Unity Muse in the last chapter for the MainTex property and provided a snow texture in the Textures folder for this chapter. If you'd prefer, you can also just use colors instead, without any other changes.

2.   Afterward, create a **Vector3** property called Direction of Snow with **Default Value** set to 0, 1, 0.

3.   Then create a **Float** property called Level of Snow. Set **Mode** to **Slider**. Give it a default value of 0.5, set **Min** to -1, and **Max** to 1.

4. Then create a **Float** property called Depth of Snow. Set **Mode** to **Slider**. Give it a default value of 0.25, set **Min** to 0, and **Max** to 1.

5. Create a **Normal Vector** node and set **Space** to **Object**. To the right of that, create a **Dot Product** node, connecting **Out(3)** of **Normal Vector** to **A(3)** of **Dot Product**.

6. From the **Blackboard**, drag and drop the **Direction of Snow** property onto the graph and connect it to **B(3)** of the **Dot Product** node. To the right of that, create a **Step** node. Connect **Out(1)** of the **Dot Product** node to **Edge(1)** of the **Step** node.

7. From the **Blackboard**, drag and drop the **Level of Snow** node onto the graph and connect it to **In(1)** of the **Step** node.

> Note
>
> This **Step** result will be used in two different places later on (*step 8* and *step 13*) so keep that in mind later on.

8. To the right of this, create a **Lerp** node. Connect **Out(1)** of the **Step** node to **T(1)** of the **Lerp** node.

9. Drag and drop **Snow Texture** and **MainTex** onto the graph and create two **Sample Texture 2D** nodes for them, connecting their **RGBA(4)** out values to **A** and **B** of the **Lerp** node.

10. Finally, connect **Out(4)** of the **Lerp** node to **Base Color(3)** of the **Fragment** aspect of the **Master Stack**.

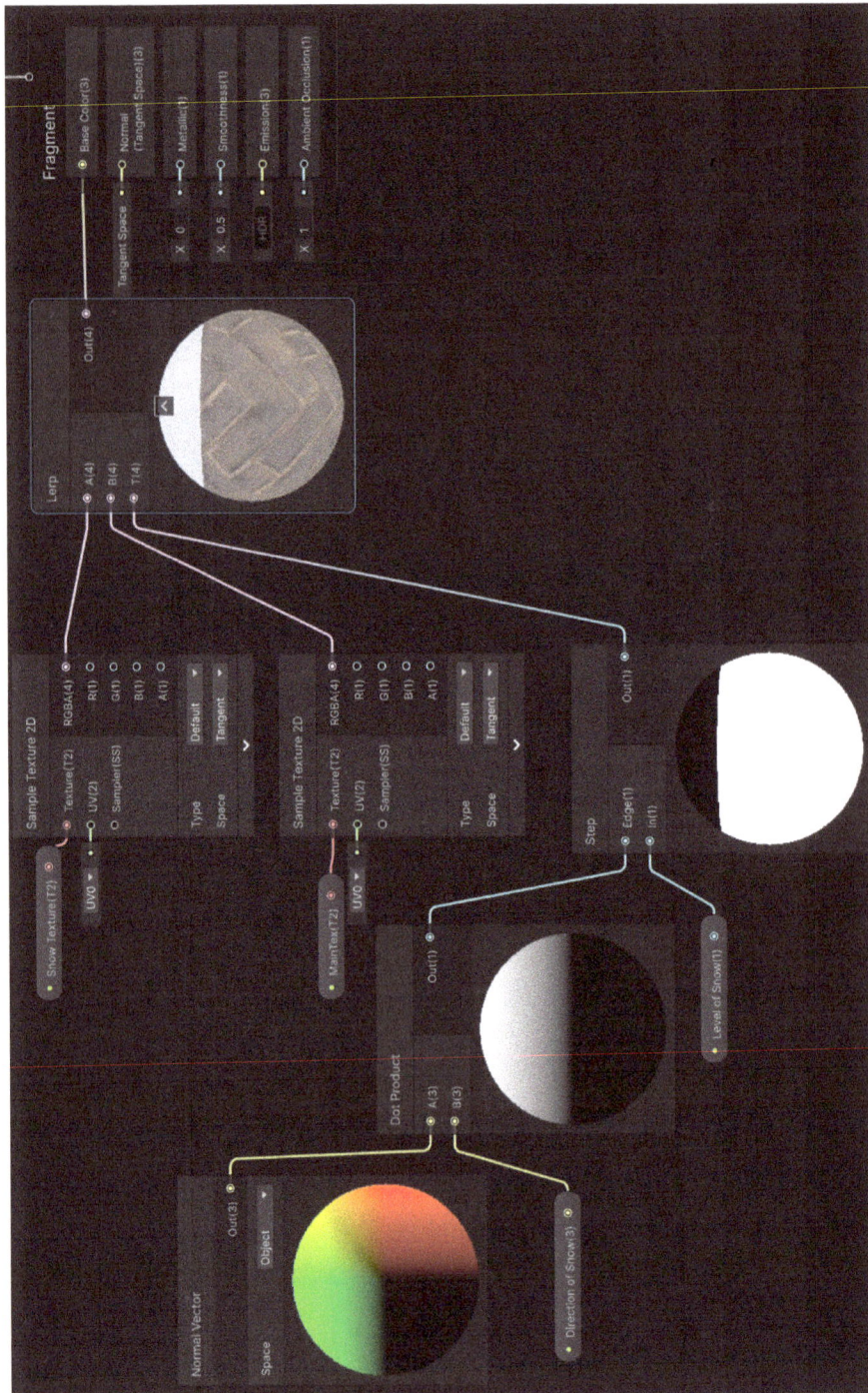

Figure 6.23 – Fragment setup

Now that the texture is done, let's alter the geometry of the snow portion:

1. Above where the **Vertex** section is, start off by creating a **Normal Vector** node. Set **Space** to **Object**. To the right of that, create a **Multiply** node, and connect **Out(3)** of **Normal Vector** to **A(3)** of the **Multiply** node.

2. Below the **Normal Vector** node, drag and drop the **Depth of Snow** variable from the **Blackboard** and connect it to **B** of the **Multiply** node. To the right of that, create another **Multiply** node and connect **Out** of the first **Multiply** node to **A** of the new **Multiply** node.

3. Below that, create an **Invert Colors** node. Connect **Out(1)** from the **Step** node to **In(1)** of the **Invert Colors** node. Check the **Red** channel. Connect **Out(1)** of the **Invert Colors** node to **B(3)** of the new **Multiply** node.

4. Above the **Multiply** node, create a **Position** node and set **Space** to **Object**. To the right of that, create an **Add** node. Connect **Out(3)** of **Position** to **A** of **Add** and **Out(3)** of **Multiply** to **B(3)** of the **Add** node. Finally, connect **Out(3)** of the **Add** node to **Position(3)** of the **Vertex** section of the **Master Stack**.

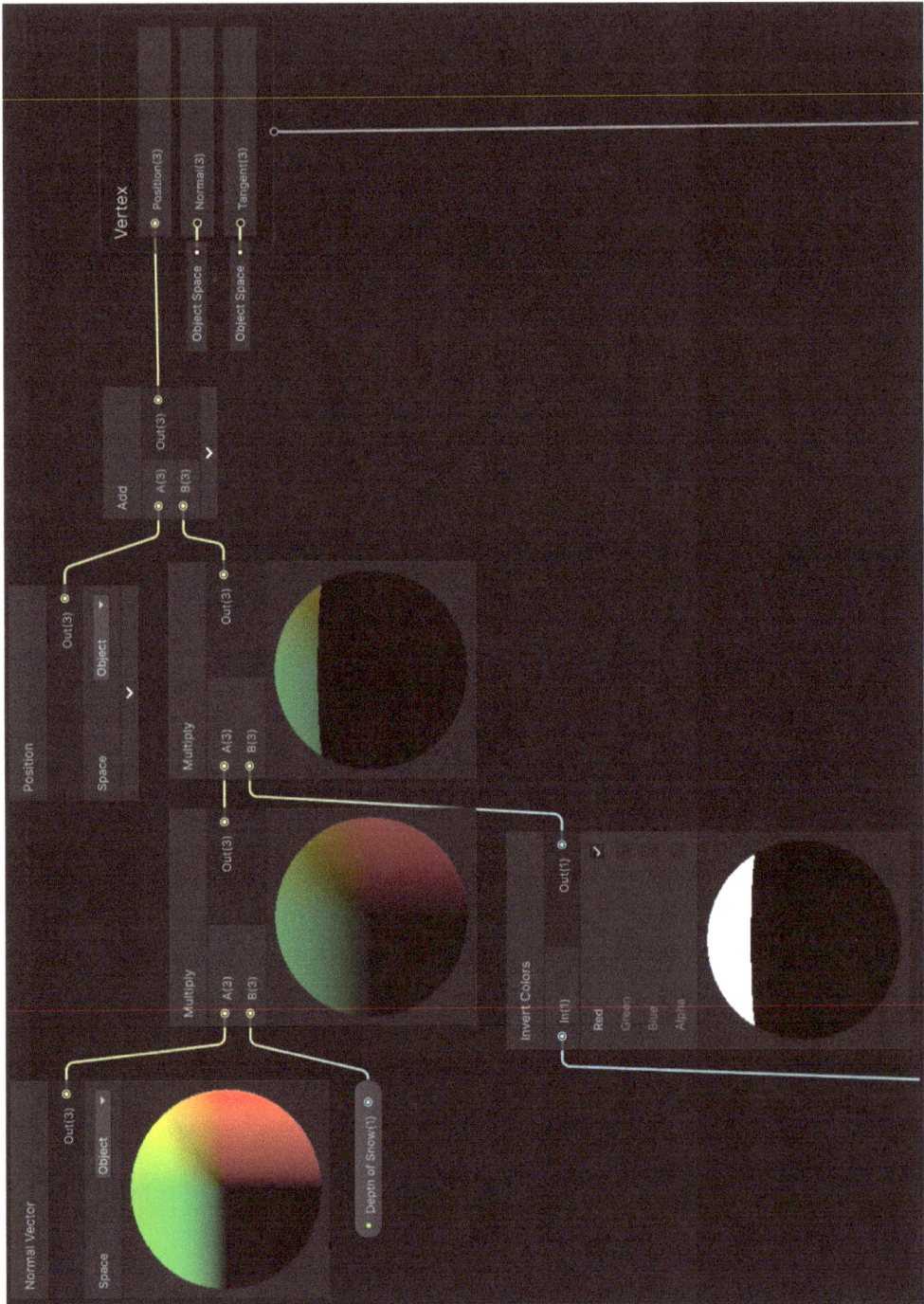

Figure 6.24 – Vertex setup

5. Save the graph and return to the Unity Editor. You can now use the material's **Inspector** window to select how much of your model is going to be covered and how thick the snow should be:

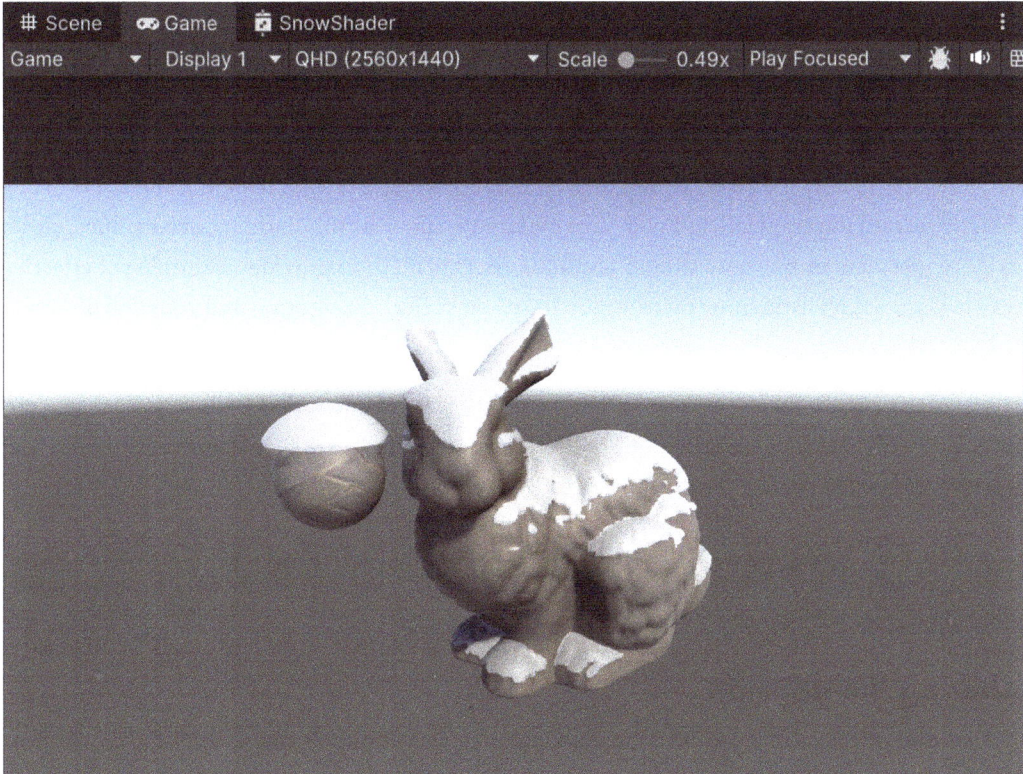

Figure 6.25 – Result of the recipe

How it works...

This shader works in two parts:

- **Fragment**: Coloring the surface
- **Vertex**: Altering the geometry

Coloring the surface

The first step alters the color of the triangles that are facing the sky. It affects all the triangles with a normal direction similar to **Direction of Snow**.

To calculate where snow should accumulate, we can use the dot product of two vectors: the surface **Normal Vector** and the **Direction of Snow** vector. The **dot product** gives us a measure of how aligned these two vectors are. The surface normal vector is perpendicular to the surface at a given point, indicating its orientation. The snowfall direction vector represents the direction from which the snow is falling, typically pointing downward due to gravity. The **Level of Snow** property is used to decide how aligned they should be in order to be considered as facing the sky.

The dot product gives us a measure of how aligned these two vectors are. When the angle is zero (i.e., the vectors are perfectly aligned), the dot product is 1, indicating the surface is facing directly toward the snowfall and will have maximum snow accumulation. Lower values, closer to -1, suggest less or no snow should accumulate. This method provides a simple yet effective way to simulate realistic snow distribution based on surface orientation and snowfall direction.

The dot product of these two vectors is calculated as the product of their magnitudes and the cosine of the angle between them. Shader Graph has a **Dot Product** node, which calls the Cg dot function, which implements the dot product extremely efficiently. It is important to note that the vectors need to be normalized for this to work correctly.

This shader simply colors the model with the snow texture; a more advanced shader should initialize itself with additional textures such as a normal map and parameters from a realistic snow material.

Altering the geometry

The second effect of this shader alters the geometry to simulate the accumulation of snow. Firstly, we identify which triangles have been colored white by using the same calculation we did previously; however, in our case, we want things that are white to be black and vice versa. This allows us to selectively apply the effect only where snow should accumulate while leaving other areas unchanged. To achieve this, we use the **Invert Colors** node which flips the color values.

By inverting the colors, we create a mask where snow-covered areas (previously white) become black, and non-snow areas (previously black) become white. We then multiply this mask against the displacement effect, ensuring that only areas originally marked as snow receive the modification while the rest of the geometry remains unaffected.

Once again, this is a very basic effect. You could use a texture map to control the accumulation of snow more precisely or give a peculiar, uneven look.

Implementing a volumetric explosion

The art of game development is a clever trade-off between realism and efficiency. This is particularly true for explosions; they are at the heart of many games, yet the physics behind them is often beyond the computational power of modern machines. Explosions are, essentially, nothing more than very hot balls of gas; hence, the only way to correctly simulate them is by integrating a fluid simulation into your game.

As you can imagine, this is unfeasible for a runtime application, and many games simulate them simply with particles. When an object explodes, it is common to simply instantiate fire, smoke, and debris particles so that together they can achieve believable results. This approach, unfortunately, is not very realistic and is easy to spot. There is an intermediate technique that can be used to achieve a much more realistic effect: volumetric explosions.

The idea behind this concept is that explosions are not treated like a bunch of particles; they are evolving 3D objects, not just flat **two-dimensional** (**2D**) textures.

Getting ready

To get started, we will begin this recipe with the following steps:

1. Create a new **Lit Shader Graph** for this effect (`VolumetricExplosion`).

2. Create a new material to host the shader (`VolumetricExplosionMat`).

3. Attach the material to a sphere. You can create one directly from the editor, navigating to **GameObject** | **3D Object** | **Sphere**:

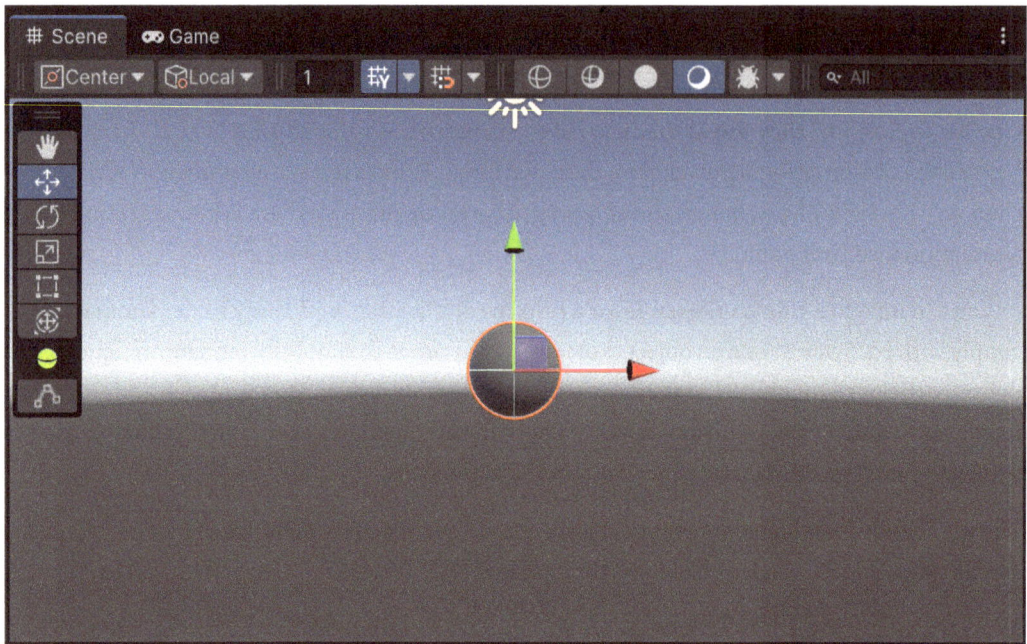

Figure 6.26 – Recipe setup

Tip

This recipe works well with the standard Unity **Sphere**, but if you need big explosions, you might need to use a high-poly sphere. In fact, a vertex function can only modify the vertices of a mesh. All the other points will be interpolated using the positions of the nearby vertices. Fewer vertices mean a lower resolution for your explosions.

4.   For this recipe, you will also need a ramp texture that has, in a gradient, all the colors your explosions will have. You can create a texture such as this one using **GNU Image Manipulation Program (GIMP)**, Paint.NET, Photoshop, or PhotoPea:

Figure 6.27 – The example ramp texture used in this recipe

Note

You can find this image (`explosionRamp`) in the `Chapter 06/Textures` folder in the example code provided with this book.

5. Once you have the picture, import it into Unity. Then, from its **Inspector** window, make sure that **Filter Mode** is set to **Bilinear** and that **Wrap Mode** is set to **Clamp**. These two settings make sure that the ramp texture is sampled smoothly:

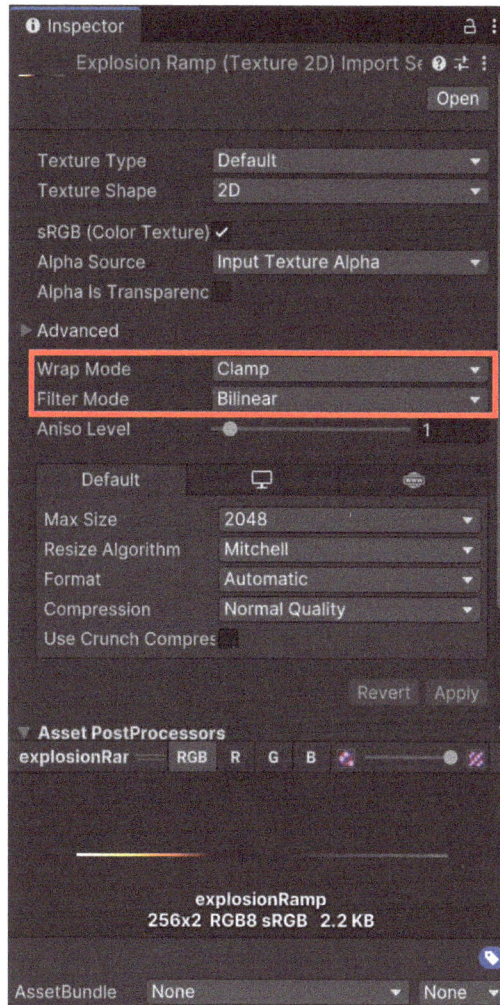

Figure 6.28 – Ramp texture setup

6. Lastly, you will need a noisy texture. While Shader Graph does have some nodes for randomness and noise, they don't work well for this particular recipe. You can search on the internet for freely available noise textures. The most commonly used ones are generated using Perlin noise. I have included an example in the `Chapter 06/Textures` folder for your use:

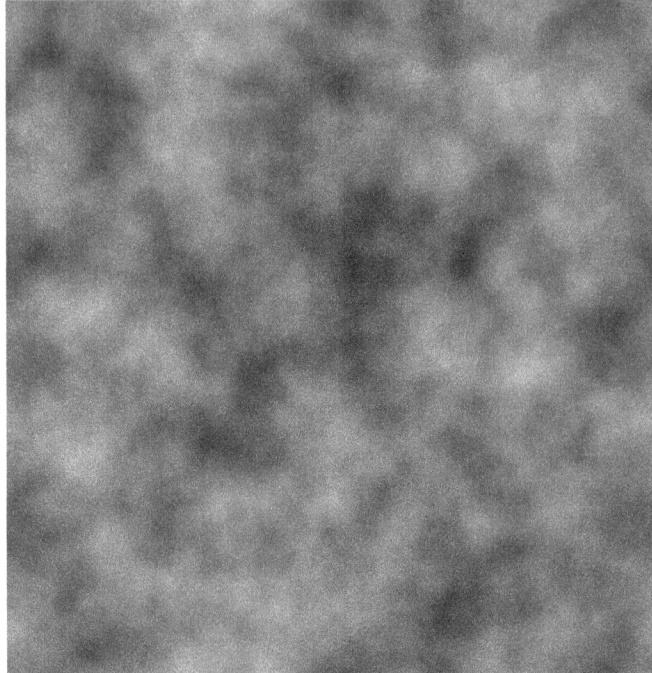

Figure 6.29 – Example of the noise texture

How to do it...

To get started, let's open the **Blackboard** and create some properties:

1. Create a **Texture2D** property named `Color Ramp`. Assign the `explosionRamp` texture that we prepared earlier.

2. Create another **Texture2D** property named `Noise Texture`. Assign the appropriate noise texture.

3. Create a **Float** property named `Ramp Offset`. Set **Mode** to **Slider**, with a default value of `0.2`, a **Min** value of `-0.5`, and a **Max** value of `0.5`.

4. Create another **Float** property named Period. Set **Mode** to **Slider**, with a default value of 0.2, a **Min** value of 0, and a **Max** value of 1.

5. Finally, create a **Float** property named Extrusion Amount. Set **Mode** to **Slider**, with a default value of 0.5, a **Min** value of 0, and a **Max** value of 1.

First, we're going to calculate some properties that we'll use in our vertex manipulation to cause the explosion effect:

1. To begin, drag and drop the **Noise Texture** property onto the graph from the **Blackboard**. To the right of that, drag and drop a **Sample Texture 2D LOD** node onto the graph and connect the **Noise Texture** property to the **Texture** input of the **Sample Texture 2D LOD** node. To the right of that, create a **Split** node and connect the **RGBA** output of the **Sample Texture 2D LOD** node to the input of the **Split** node.

> Note
>
> We'll be utilizing the **R** channel from this **Split** node in several different places, so keep that in mind.

2. First, create a **Multiply** node to the right of the **Split** node. Connect the **R** output of the **Split** node to the **A** input of the **Multiply** node, and set the **B** input to 10. To the right of the **Multiply** node, create an **Add** node. Connect the output of the **Multiply** node to the **A** input of the **Add** node.

3. Below that, create a **Time** node. To the right of the **Time** node, create another **Multiply** node. Connect the **Time** output of the **Time** node to the **A** input of this **Multiply** node. Drag and drop the **Period** property from the **Blackboard** onto the graph and connect it to the **B** input of this **Multiply** node. Then, take the output of the **Multiply** node and connect it to the **B** input of the **Add** node.

4. To the right of the **Add** node, create a **Sine** node and connect the output of the **Add** node to the input of the **Sine** node. To the right of the **Sine** node, create another **Multiply** node. Connect the output of the **Sine** node to the **A** input of this **Multiply** node, and connect the **R** channel of the **Split** node (from the noise texture) to the **B** input.

   To make it easier to understand, I grouped these calculations together by selecting them all and then pressing *Ctrl + G*, giving them the name Time Calculation.

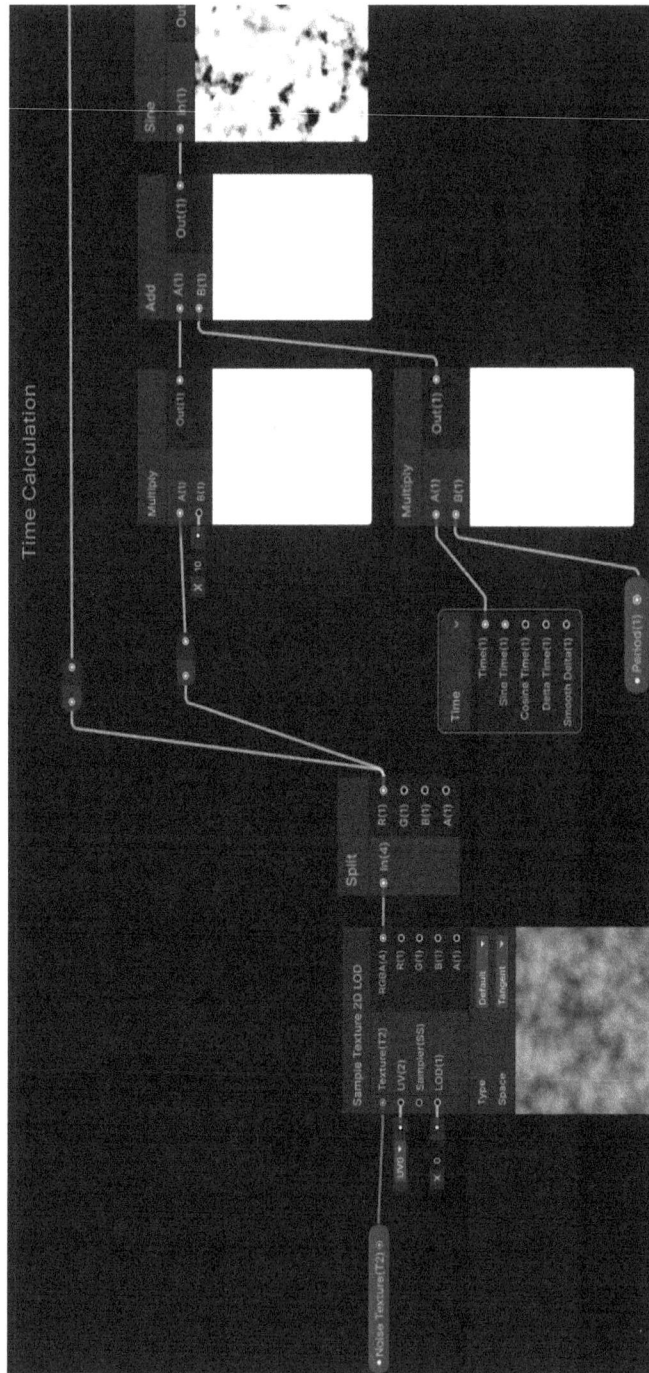

Figure 6.30 – Time Calculation

Next, let's take care of the vertex displacement part of the explosion:

1. First, create a **Normal Vector** node and set **Space** to **Object**. To the right of that, create a **Multiply** node and connect the output of the **Normal Vector** node to the **A** input of the **Multiply** node. Then, drag and drop the **Extrusion Amount** property from the **Blackboard** and assign it to the **B** input of the **Multiply** node.

2. To the right of that, create another **Multiply** node. Connect the output of the first **Multiply** node to the **A** input of this new **Multiply** node. Next, take the output from the multiply operation in our previous section (where we multiplied the sine result with the noise texture) and connect it to the **B** input of this second **Multiply** node.

    This will make it so that the texture is used to displace the object randomly, simulating an explosion.

3. To the right of the second **Multiply** node, create an **Add** node. Connect the output of the second **Multiply** node to the **B** input of the **Add** node. Above that, create a **Position** node and set the space to **Object**. Connect the output of the **Position** node to the **A** input of the **Add** node.

4. Finally, take the output of the **Add** node and connect it to the **Position** input on the **Vertex** section of the **Master Stack**.

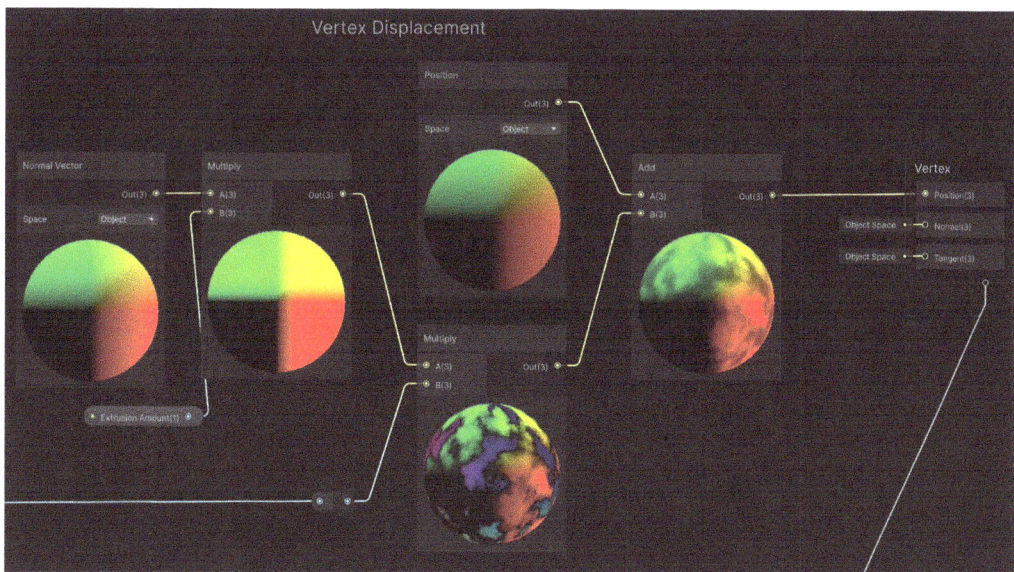

Figure 6.31 – Vertex displacement

This completes the vertex section of the explosion, but we still need to take care of the color section, which we will address next.

Below all the nodes that we've created so far, drag and drop the **Ramp Offset** property onto the graph. To the right of that, create an **Add** node. Connect the **Ramp Offset** property to the **B** input of the **Add** node. Then, take **Out** from the **Multiply** node (that combined the **Sine** and **R** channels we talked about previously) and connect it to the **A** input of the **Add** node.

1. To the right of the **Add** node, create a **Saturate** node to clamp our values. Then, to the right of the **Saturate** node, create a **Vector 2** node. Connect the output of the **Saturate** node to the **X** input of the **Vector 2** node and set the **Y** input to 0.5.

2. To the right of the **Vector 2** node, add a **Sample Texture 2D** node. Connect the output of the **Vector 2** node to the **UV** input of the **Sample Texture 2D** node. Drag and drop the **Color Ramp** texture from the **Blackboard** and assign it to the **Texture** input of the **Sample Texture 2D** node.

3. Finally, connect the **RGBA** output of the **Sample Texture 2D** node to the **Base Color** and **Emission** inputs of the **Fragment** part of the **Master Stack**.

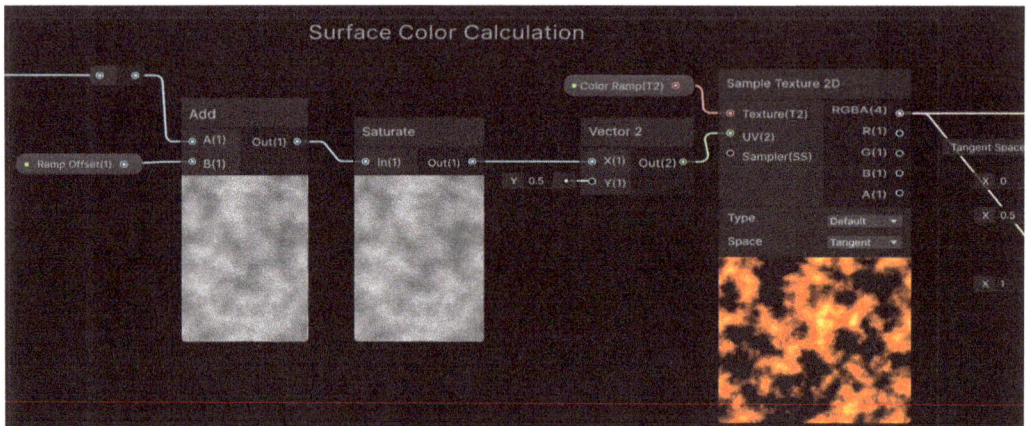

Figure 6.32 – Surface Color Calculation

4. Save your Shader Graph and return to the Unity Editor. If all goes well, you should be able to see the explosion effect when you play the game.

This is animated material, meaning that it evolves over time. You can watch the material changing in the editor by clicking on **Always Refresh** from the **Scene** window:

Figure 6.33 – Always Refresh option

How it works...

The main idea behind this effect is to alter the geometry of the sphere in a seemingly chaotic way, mimicking the behavior of a real explosion. This is achieved by manipulating vertex positions based on a combination of time and noise texture, resulting in dynamic and random deformations.

The vertex manipulation starts with calculating a time-based value using the sine function to introduce oscillation. The sine function creates a smooth, periodic change over time, which is then combined with noise texture values to ensure that each vertex moves independently. By multiplying the time-based sine value with the noise texture's red channel and an extrusion amount, we achieve the effect of vertices moving in and out, simulating an explosion.

The first step involves using a **Time** node to get the current time value. This value is multiplied by a **Period** property to control the speed of the explosion and further scaled by multiplying it by 10. Next, a noise texture is sampled, and its red channel is extracted. This noise value introduces randomness to the vertex movement.

The scaled time value is then added to the noise value, and the result is fed into a **Sine** node to create smooth oscillations. The output of the **Sine** node is multiplied by the noise value again to randomize the effect further. The final result from the sine and noise combination is used to displace the vertices along their normal direction, controlled by the **Extrusion Amount** property. This displacement causes the sphere to deform as if it were exploding.

The **Fragment** part of the **Main Stack** handles the visual aspect of the explosion. The noise texture is used to sample a color from the ramp texture, which represents the gradient of colors for the explosion, from bright fire to dark smoke. The **Ramp Offset** property shifts the color sampling point along the ramp texture, allowing control over the fire-to-smoke ratio. The red channel from the noise texture is combined with the ramp offset and clamped to ensure it stays within valid bounds. This combined value is used to sample the ramp texture, providing the final color for each pixel.

There's more...

The shader presented in this recipe makes a sphere look like an explosion. If you really want to use it, you should couple it with some scripts to get the most out of it. The best thing to do is to create an explosion object and make it into a prefab so that you can reuse it every time you need to. You can do this by dragging the sphere back into the **Project** window. Once this is done, you can create as many explosions as you want using the Instantiate() function.

One important thing to keep in mind is that all objects using the same material will share the same visual appearance. This means that if you have multiple explosions occurring simultaneously, they will all look identical unless they each have their own material instance. To ensure each explosion has a unique look, you should duplicate the material when instantiating a new explosion. You can achieve this with the following code snippet:

```
GameObject explosion = Instantiate(explosionPrefab) as GameObject;
Renderer = explosion.GetComponent<Renderer>();
Material = new Material(renderer.sharedMaterial);
renderer.material = material;
```

This should allow for more natural and varied effects since each one will have independent properties.

Lastly, if you are going to use this shader in a realistic way, you should attach a script to it that changes its size and _Ramp_Offset according to the type of explosion that you want to recreate. Likewise, you can also do things such as spawn particle effects and utilize post-processing effects as we did in *Chapter 1*, *Using Post-Processing with URP*, to give the explosion more depth.

7

Using Grab Passes

While previous chapters have explored the use of transparency to create effects where objects appear partially see-through, this approach doesn't allow for the modification of what is seen through the transparent areas. In other words, transparency alone merely reveals the scene behind an object but doesn't alter or distort it in any way. To go beyond simple transparency and create more complex visual effects—such as bending, distorting, or otherwise interacting with the background—a more advanced technique is required. This is where the **grab pass** comes into play.

The grab pass is a powerful technique traditionally used in shader programming to create effects that require knowledge of the scene behind a particular object, such as transparency, refraction, or other complex visual interactions. This technique captures the pixels of the scene that have already been rendered, allowing them to be reused within a shader to simulate how light and color behave as they pass through or interact with the object in question. Effects such as glass, water, or heat distortion often rely on grab passes to achieve realistic results, as they allow the shader to incorporate the background scene into the object's appearance dynamically.

In Shader Graph, the equivalent of a grab pass is achieved using the **Scene Color** node, which allows you to sample the color of the scene at specific points behind an object, essentially capturing the background and making it available for further manipulation within the shader.

In this chapter, we will cover several key recipes to help you master these techniques. First, you will learn how to use grab passes to draw behind objects, capturing and manipulating the background. Next, we will guide you through implementing a glass shader that simulates the appearance of stained glass, by adjusting the grab pass and altering its UV data to create a distortion. Finally, you will discover techniques for creating dynamic water effects in 2D games, enhancing the realism of your scenes by having animated distortions.

By the end of this chapter, you will have a deep understanding of the limitations of simple transparency and when more advanced techniques are necessary. You will gain proficiency in using grab passes (or the **Scene Color** node in Shader Graph) to capture and manipulate the background scene in real time. Moreover, you will be able to implement shaders that simulate complex materials, such as glass and water, incorporating background interactions to achieve realistic visual results. These skills will be invaluable in both 2D and 3D game development contexts, enabling you to enhance the visual fidelity of your projects.

In this chapter, we will cover the following recipes:

- Using grab passes to draw behind objects
- Implementing a glass shader
- Implementing a water shader for 2D games

Technical requirements

For this chapter, you will need Unity Editor version 6 Preview 6000.0.07f1. This chapter's instructions should work with minimal changes in future versions of the editor in projects that utilize the **Universal Render Pipeline** (**URP**). The chapter's sample project was created using the **Universal 3D Core** template.

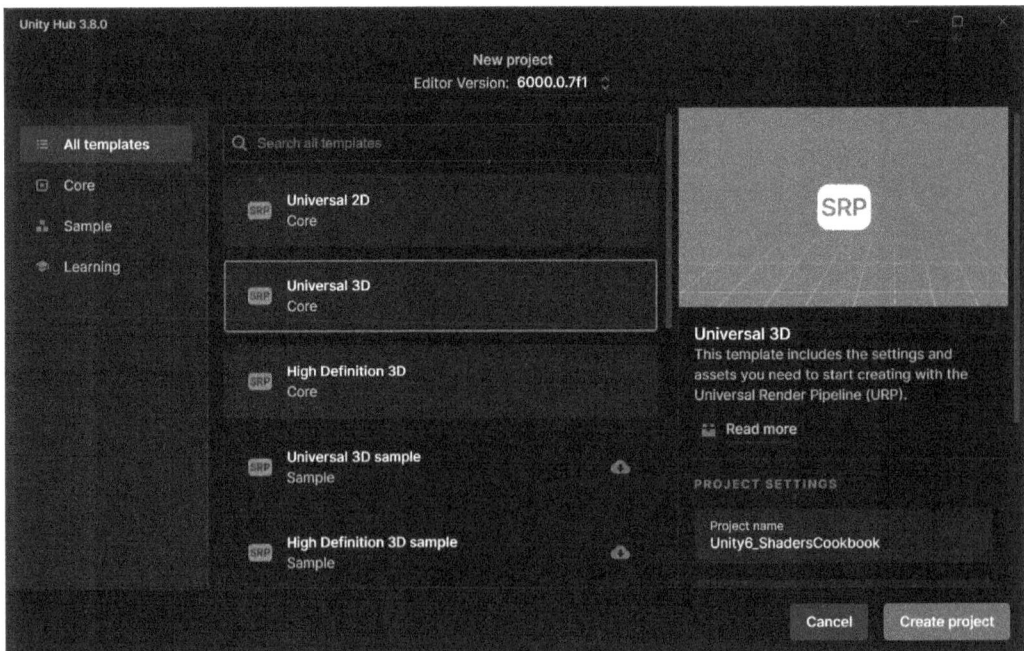

Figure 7.1 – Universal 3D (URP) project

The code files for this chapter can be found on GitHub at `https://github.com/PacktPublishing/` `Unity-6-Shaders-and-Effects-Cookbook`. The necessary files for this chapter are organized in the Unity project in a folder named `Chapter 07` (`https://github.com/PacktPublishing/Unity-` `6-Shaders-and-Effects-Cookbook/tree/main/Unity6_ShadersCookbook/Assets/Chapter%20` `07`) on GitHub.

Using grab passes to draw behind objects

In the *Adding transparency to PBR* recipe of *Chapter 5*, *Enhancing Realism: Unity Muse and Physically Based Rendering*, we learned how a material can be made transparent. Even if a transparent material can draw over a scene, it cannot change what has been drawn underneath it. This means that those transparent shaders cannot create distortions such as the ones typically seen in glass or water.

As mentioned above, to simulate distortions, we need to introduce another technique known as grab pass. This allows us to access what has been drawn onscreen so far so that a shader can use it (or alter it) with no restrictions. To learn how to use grab passes, we will create a material that grabs what's rendered behind it and draws it again on the screen. It's a shader that, paradoxically, performs several operations to show no changes at all.

Getting ready

For this recipe, you will need to do the following:

- Create a shader (`GrabShader`) that we will initialize later
- Create a material (`GrabMat`) that will host the shader

Attach the material to a flat piece of geometry, such as a quad. Place the quad in front of another object so that you cannot see through it. The quad will appear transparent as soon as the shader is complete:

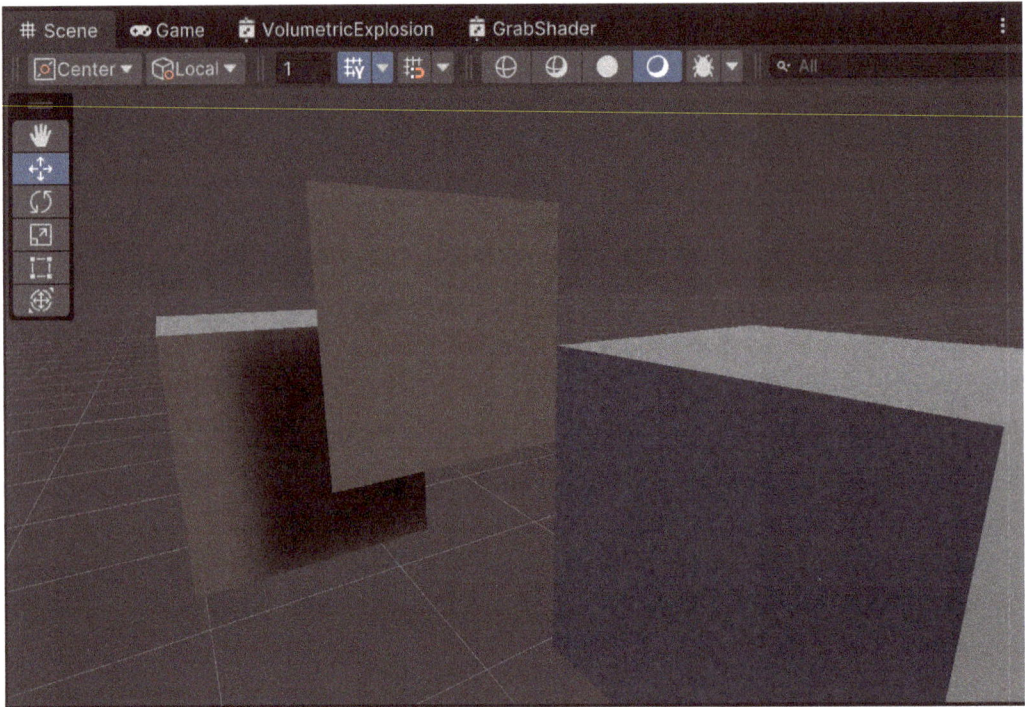

Figure 7.2 – Recipe setup

How to do it...

In Shader Graph, we will add nodes to access the data of what's on the screen and then use it in the shader:

1. Double-click **GrabShader** to open it in the Shader Graph editor.

2. From **Graph Inspector**, click on the **Graph Settings** tab to switch to it. And from there, change **Surface Type** to **Transparent** and then change **Render Face** to **Both**.

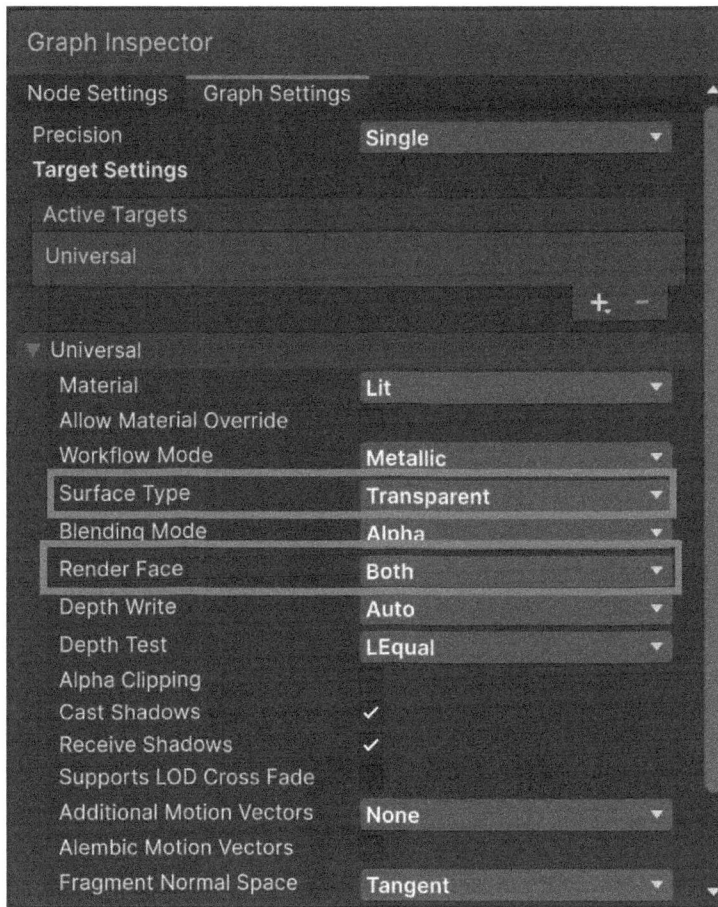

Figure 7.3 – Graph Settings

3. Then, from the graph, create a **Scene Color** node. To the right of that, create an **Add** node and connect **Out(3)** of the **Scene Color** node to **A** of the **Add** node. Then create a **Color** node and give it a value of (0.5, 0, 0,0) on the **RGB 0-1.0** scale. From there, connect **Out(4)** of the **Color** node to **B** of the **Add** node.

4. Finally, connect **Out(3)** of the **Add** node to **Base Color** on the **Fragment** part of the **Master Stack**.

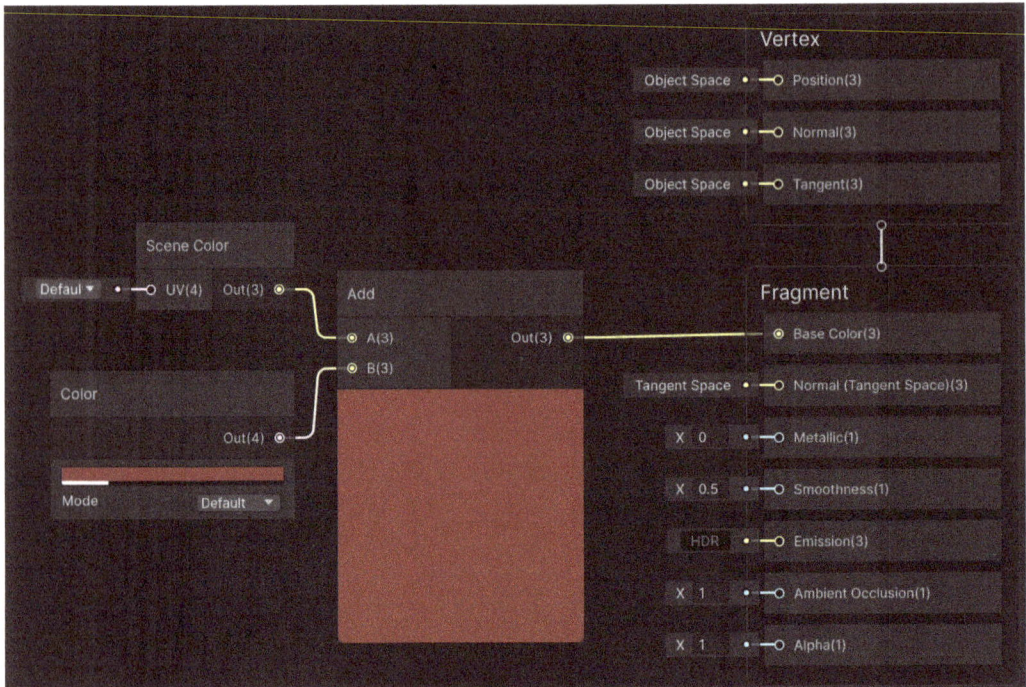

Figure 7.4 – Graph setup

5. Save your Shader Graph and return to the Unity Editor. You should notice now that the material now appears the way that we intend it to. This may be easier to see if we switch to the **Game** view.

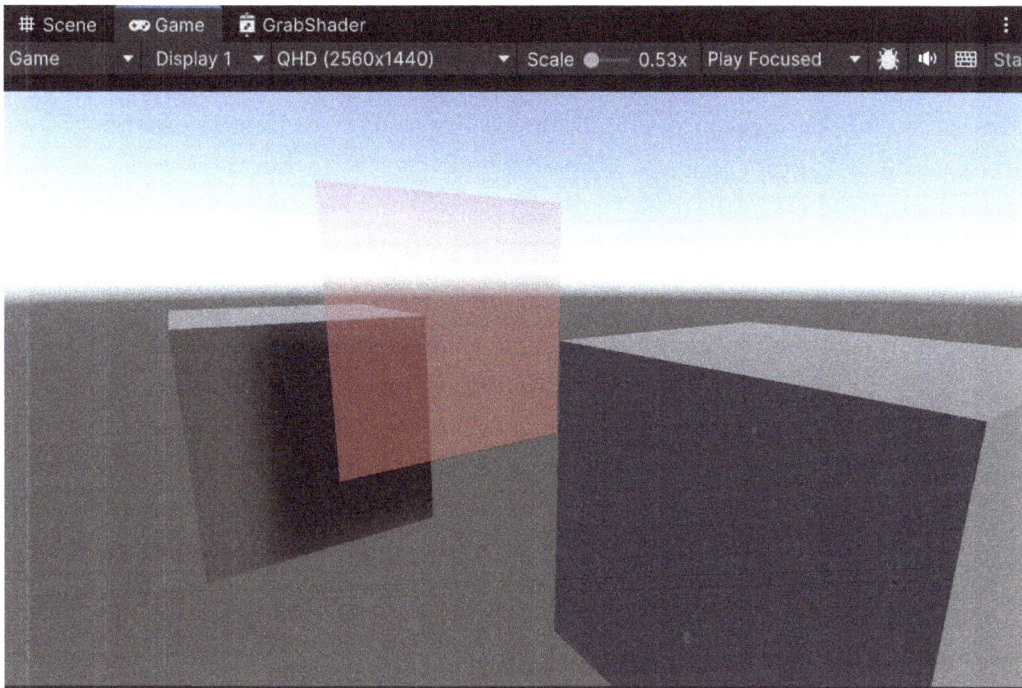

Figure 7.5 – Shader result

How it works...

In this recipe, we created a transparent shader using a grab pass. Unlike traditional transparent shaders that cannot alter what is rendered beneath them, a grab pass allows us to capture the screen's current content and use it within our shader. This technique is essential for creating effects like those seen in glass or water, which require the ability to distort or manipulate the scene behind the material.

We created a **Scene Color** node, which captures the current color information from the screen. This node serves as the basis for our grab pass operation. Since we would only see what is on the screen, we modify the screen a bit by tinting it red.

By following the preceding steps in the *How to do it...* section, we create a shader that captures the current screen content and adds a specific color to it, resulting in a material that can mimic complex visual effects. In the following recipes, we will see how this technique can be used to create materials such as water and glass.

There's more...

Every time you use a material with a grab pass, Unity will have to render the screen to a texture. This operation is very expensive and limits the number of grab pass instances that you can use in a game. Unity attempts to limit this problem by having objects with the same material do a single grab pass and share the texture with all of them. The main problem with this technique is that it doesn't allow effects that can be stacked. If you are creating glasses with this technique, you won't be able to have two glasses one after the other.

The reason behind this is that when Unity captures the screen for the grab pass, it only does so once for all objects using the same material. This means that subsequent objects cannot "see" or incorporate the effects of those rendered before them; they all reference the same pre-captured background texture. As a result, if you're creating an effect like glass using a grab pass, you won't be able to place two glass objects one after the other and have each interact with the other's effects—because the second object will only "see" the original, unmodified scene, not the first glass and its refractive effect.

Implementing a glass shader

Glass is a very complicated material; it should not be a surprise that we have already created shaders to simulate it, such as in the *Adding transparency to PBR* recipe of *Chapter 5, Enhancing Realism: Unity Muse and Physically Based Rendering*. We already know how to make our glasses semi-transparent to show the objects behind them perfectly, and this works for several applications.

However, most glasses are not perfect. For instance, if you look through a stained-glass window, you may notice distortions or deformations. This recipe will teach you how to achieve that effect. The idea behind this effect is to use a grab pass, and then sample the grab texture by changing its UV data to create a distortion. You can see this effect in the following screenshot. Here, we used the stained-glass textures that originally came from Unity's standard assets:

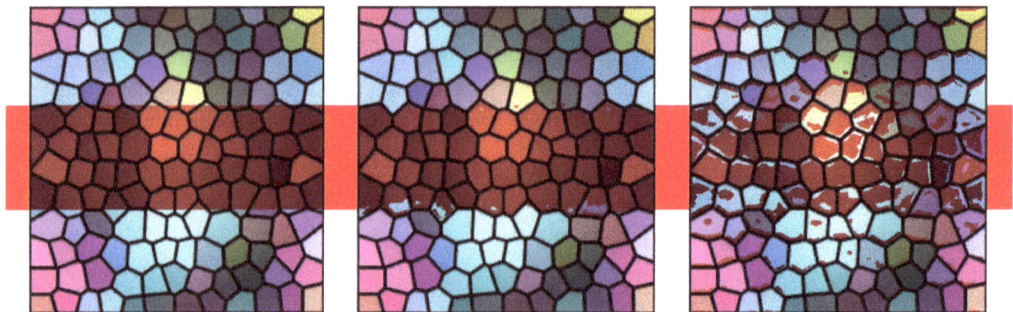

Figure 7.6 – The effect that will be created in this recipe

Getting ready

The setup for this recipe is similar to the one presented in the previous recipe:

1. Create a new Shader Graph. You can start by copying the one that we used in the previous recipe (*Using grab passes to draw behind objects*) as a base by selecting it and hitting *Ctrl + D* to duplicate it.

2. Once you have a Shader Graph duplicated, change its name to WindowShader.

3. Create a material that will use the shader (WindowMat).

4. Assign the material to a quad or another flat geometry that will simulate your glass.

5. Place some objects behind it so that you can see the distortion effect:

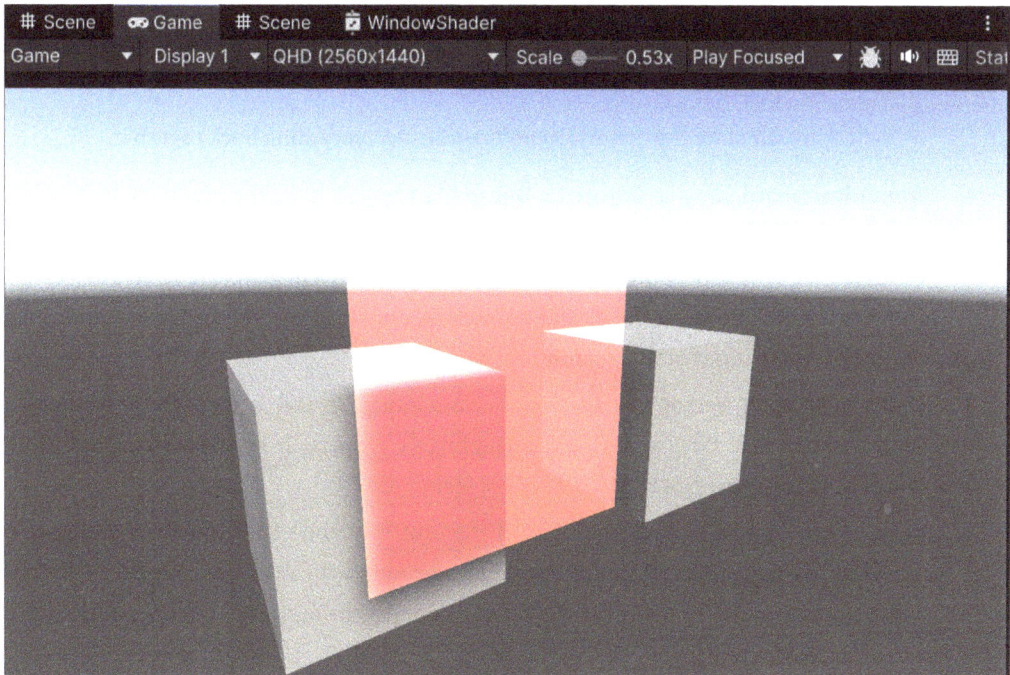

Figure 7.7 – Recipe setup

How to do it...

After setting up the recipe, perform the following steps:

1. Open up the Shader Graph and go to **Blackboard**. We will start off by creating several properties that we will need to work with. Hit the + button and select **Texture2D**. Give this first property a name of Base (RGB), and in **Graph Inspector**, set **Default Value** to the GlassStainedAlbedo texture found in the sample code for this chapter.

2. Create another **Texture2D** property. Give this property the name Bump Map, and in **Graph Inspector**, set **Default Value** to the GlassStainedNormals texture found in the sample code for this chapter.

3. Next, create a **Float** property called Magnitude. Set **Mode** to **Slider** and then set **Default Value** to 0.05. Leave the minimum at 0 and the max at 1. Then, lastly, create a **Color** property called Color. By default, we'll set this to white.

   We will then calculate the distortion before putting everything back together.

4. From **Blackboard**, drag and drop the **Bump Map** texture onto the graph. To the right of it, create a **Sample Texture 2D** node, set **Type** to **Normal**, and ensure that **Space** is set to **Tangent**. We only care about the **R** and **G** channels for the displacement, so next, create a **Vector 2** node. Connect the **R** channel to the **X** input of the **Vector 2** node and the **G** channel to the **Y** input of the **Vector 2** node.

5. To the right of the **Vector 2** node, create a **Multiply** node and connect the output of the **Vector 2** node to it. Drag and drop the **Magnitude** property from **Blackboard** into the **B** slot of the **Multiply** node to scale the displacement.

6. Next, create an **Add** node to the right of the **Multiply** node and connect the output of the **Multiply** node to the **B** slot of the **Add** node. Above the **Add** node, create a **UV** node to get the current UV data for this object and connect the output of the **UV** node to the **A** slot of the **Add** node.

7. Now that we have the displacement, add a **Sample Texture 2D** node to the right of the **Add** node. Drag and drop the **Base RGB** texture onto the graph, assign it to the **Texture** slot of the **Sample Texture 2D** node, and connect the output of the **Add** node to the **UV** slot of the **Sample Texture 2D** node.

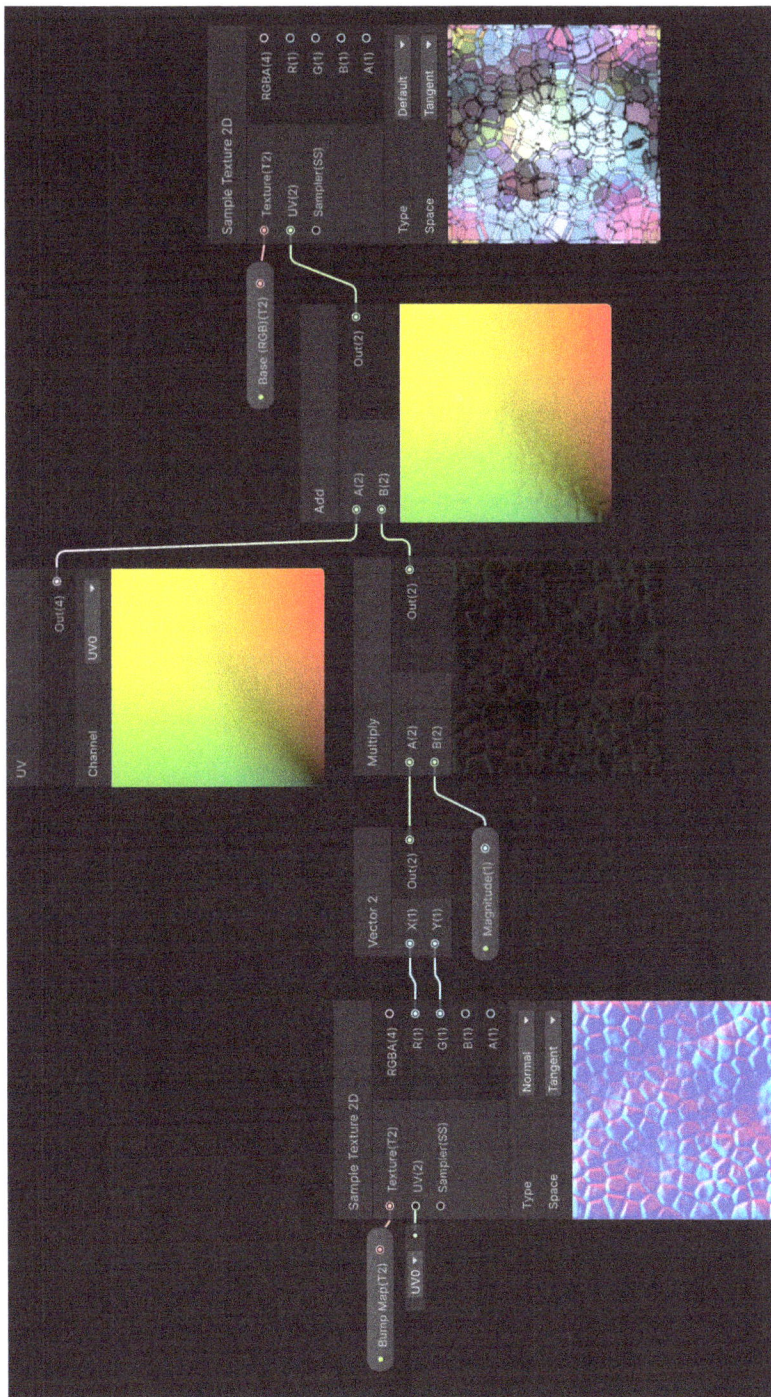

Figure 7.8 – Calculating distortion

We need to combine everything back together.

8. To the right of the **Sample Texture 2D** node, create a **Multiply** node. Above that, create another **Sample Texture 2D** node. Assign the **Base RGB** texture to the texture property of the second **Sample Texture 2D** node and connect both **Sample Texture 2D** nodes' outputs to the inputs of the **Multiply** node.

9. To the right of the **Multiply** node, create another **Multiply** node. Connect the **Scene Color** node's output, which we had created in the previous recipe, to the **B** input of this new **Multiply** node. Then, connect the output of the first **Multiply** node to the **A** input of the second **Multiply** node.

10. Next, we need to determine whether to keep the previous color calculation or use our new color variable. Drag and drop the color variable onto the graph, and to the right of the second **Multiply** node, create another **Multiply** node. Assign the color property to the **A** input and connect the output of the previous **Multiply** node to the input of this new **Multiply** node.

11. Finally, connect the output of this **Multiply** node to the **Base Color** section of the **Fragment** node in the **Master Stack**.

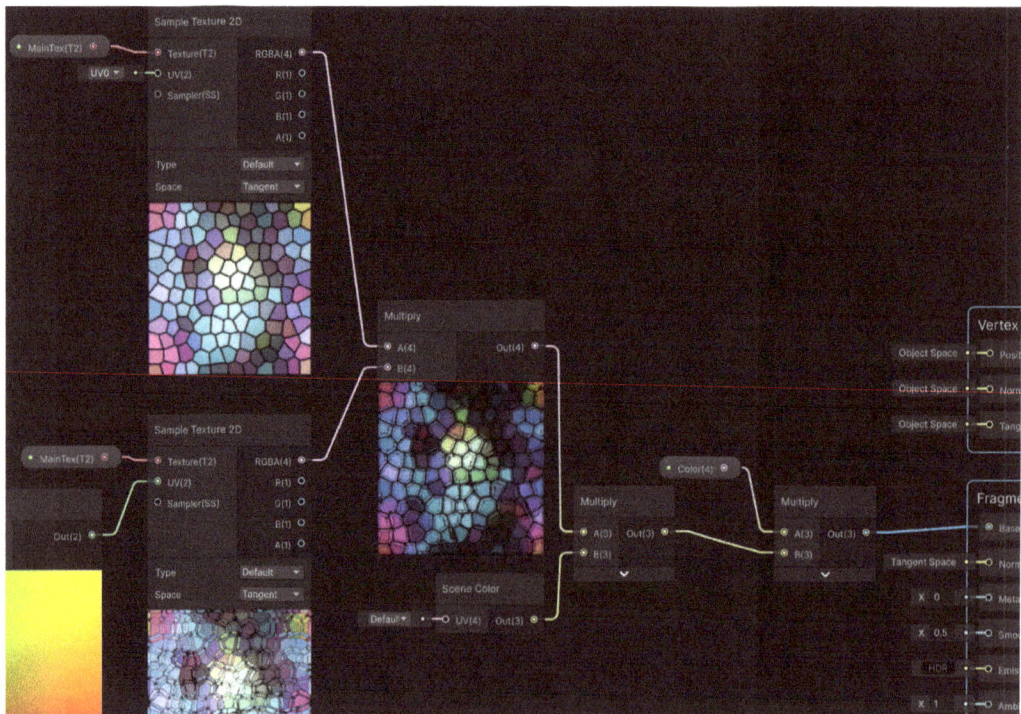

Figure 7.9 – Combining parts of the graph

If you prefer not to have this window cast a shadow, go into **Graph Inspector** and, from **Graph Settings**, set **Cast Shadows** to false. This will make it easier to see the objects behind the glass.

Once completed, save your Shader Graph, return to Unity, and you should see the stained-glass window effect working correctly.

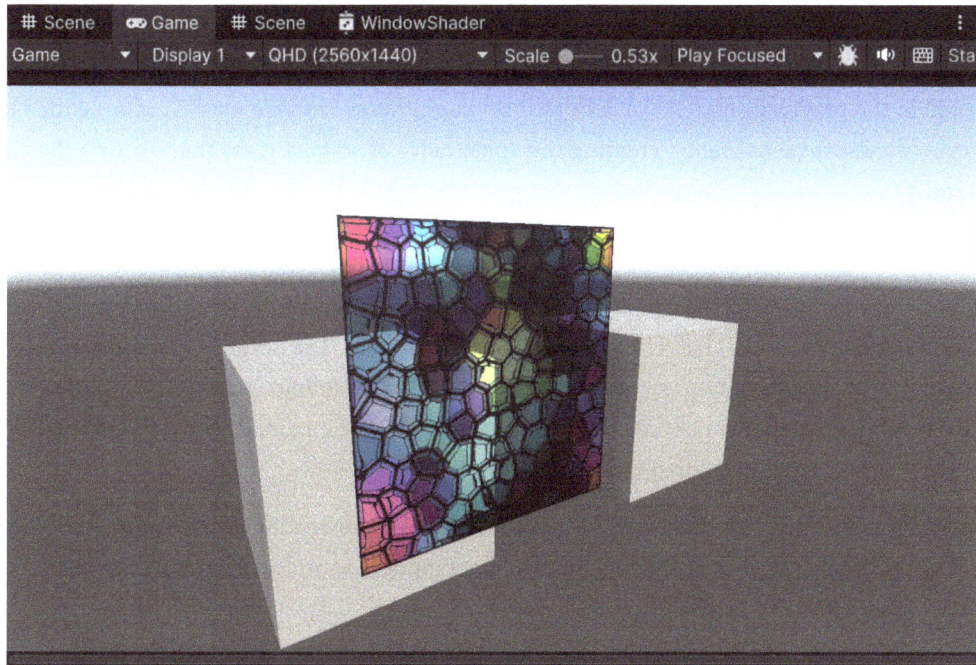

Figure 7.10 – Recipe result

How it works...

This shader uses a grab pass to take what has already been rendered on the screen.

The shader uses a normal map, specifically the `GlassStainedNormals` texture, to introduce distortion to the captured image. A normal map encodes surface detail, which in this case simulates the uneven surface of stained glass.

By unpacking the normal map's **R** and **G** channels, we obtain the necessary data to distort the UV coordinates of the texture that was grabbed from the screen. These UV coordinates determine how the texture is applied to the object's surface. Altering these coordinates creates the illusion of light being refracted through the uneven surface of the glass.

Distortion magnitude

The **Magnitude** property introduced in the Shader Graph plays a crucial role in controlling the intensity of this distortion. By adjusting the slider associated with this property, we can manipulate the strength of the UV offset, thereby determining how pronounced the refraction effect is on the stained glass. A higher magnitude results in more dramatic distortions, while a lower magnitude produces a subtler effect.

As seen in the provided shader, the distorted UV coordinates are then used to sample the base texture (GlassStainedAlbedo), creating the appearance of stained glass that distorts the view behind it.

Combining the effects

After calculating the distorted texture, the shader multiplies this result with the captured scene color to blend the stained-glass effect with the scene behind it. The **Color** property offers further flexibility by allowing a tint to be applied to the final output, enabling customization of the glass's color. This gives the shader not only the ability to create realistic stained-glass effects but also to simulate various types of colored glass.

Finally, by connecting this processed output to the **Base Color** section of the **Fragment** node in the **Master Stack**, the shader ensures that the final rendered surface accurately represents the stained-glass effect on the object.

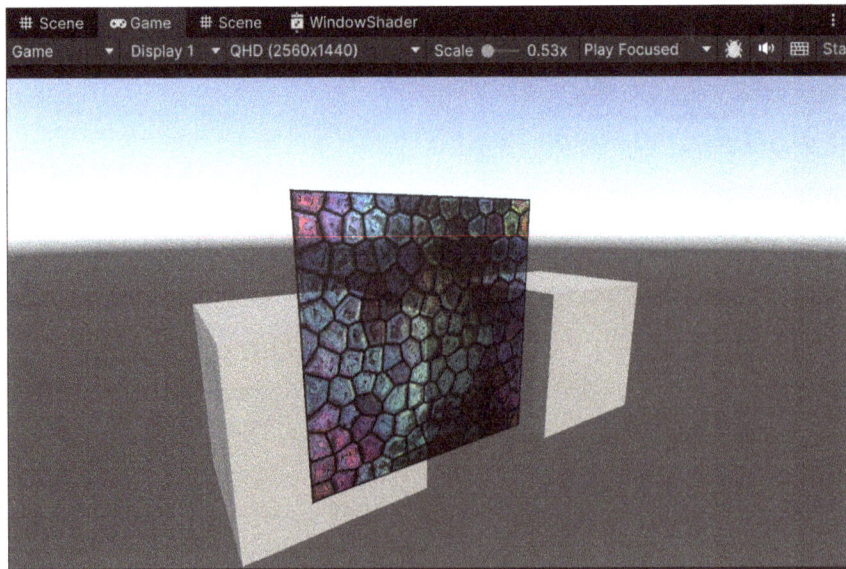

Figure 7.11 – Increasing the magnitude of the effect

There's more...

This effect is very generic; it grabs the screen and creates a distortion based on a normal map. There is no reason why it shouldn't be used to simulate more interesting things. Many games use distortions around explosions or other sci-fi devices. This material can be applied to a sphere and, with a different normal map, it would simulate the heatwave of an explosion perfectly.

Implementing a water shader for 2D games

The glass shader that we introduced in the previous recipe is static; its distortion never changes. It takes just a few changes to convert it into an animated material, making it perfect for 2D games that feature water. This recipe uses a similar technique to the one shown in *Chapter 6, Using Vertex Functions*, in the *Animating vertices in a Shader Graph* recipe:

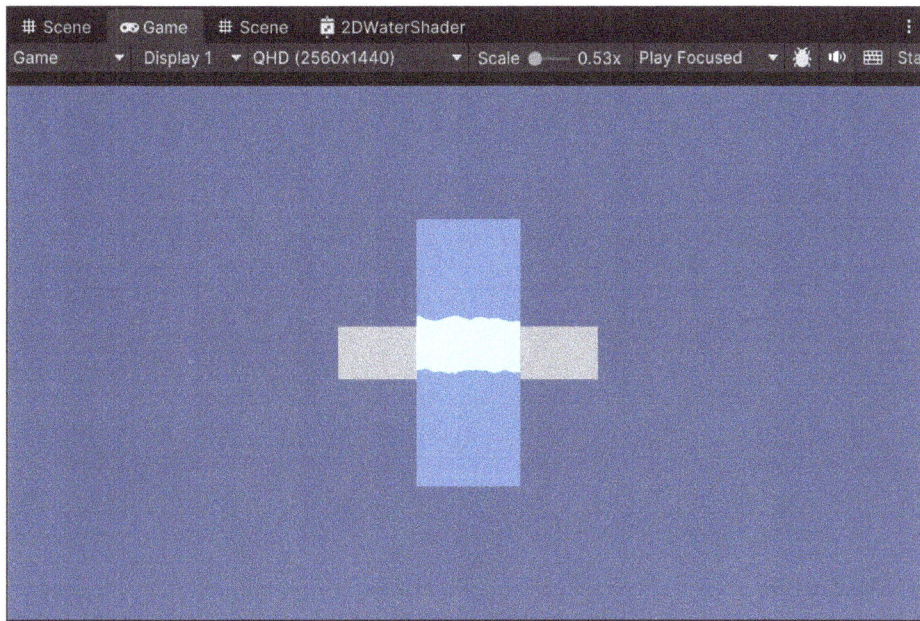

Figure 7.12 – The result of the following recipe

Getting ready

This recipe is based on the vertex and fragment shaders described in the *Using grab passes to draw behind objects* recipe, as it will rely heavily on the use of grab passes. Let's get started:

1. Create a new Shader Graph. You can start by copying the one that we used in the previous recipe (*Using grab passes to draw behind objects*) as a base by selecting it and hitting *Ctrl + D* to duplicate it.

2. Once duplicated, change its name to 2DWaterShader.

3. Create a material that will use the shader (2DWaterMat).

4. Assign the material to a flat geometry that will represent your 2D water (I used two **Quad** objects and also changed the **Main Camera**'s **Perspective** to **Orthographic** to look like a 2D game). For this effect to work, you should have something rendered behind it so that you can see the water-like displacement:

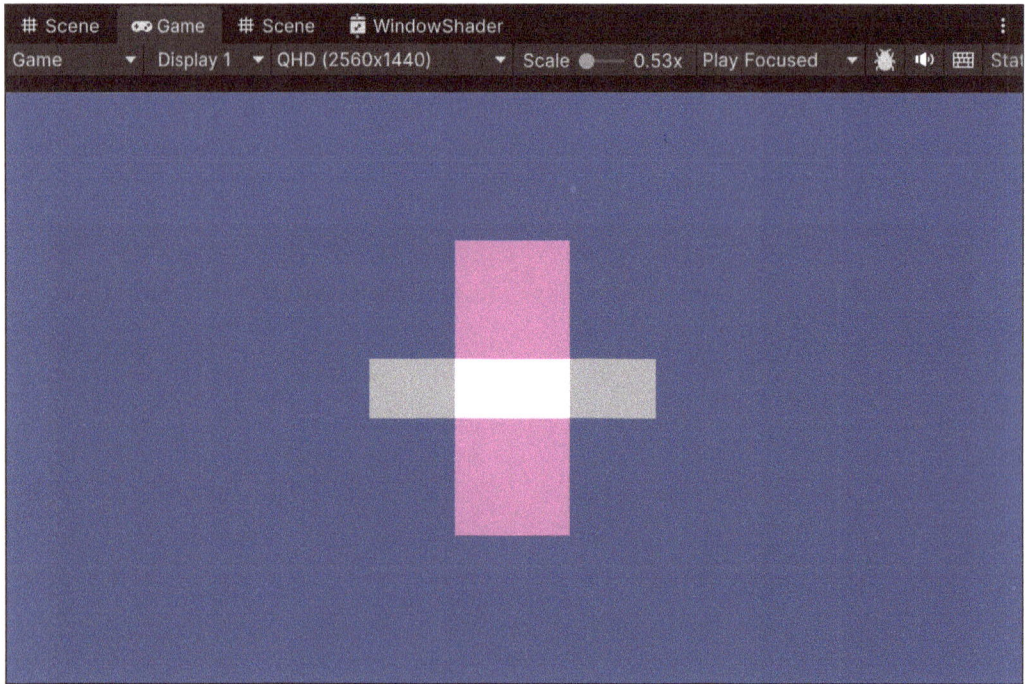

Figure 7.13 – Recipe setup

How to do it...

As usual, our first step will be to create the needed properties:

1. Open your Shader Graph and go to **Blackboard**. Click on the + button and select **Texture2D**. Name the texture NoiseTex and assign **Default Value** in **Graph Inspector** as the Noise texture that you used previously in the Chapter 06/Textures folder.

2. Create another property of type **Color** called `Color`. Set **Default Value** to light blue; the specific values I used are in the example code as well as in the following screenshot.

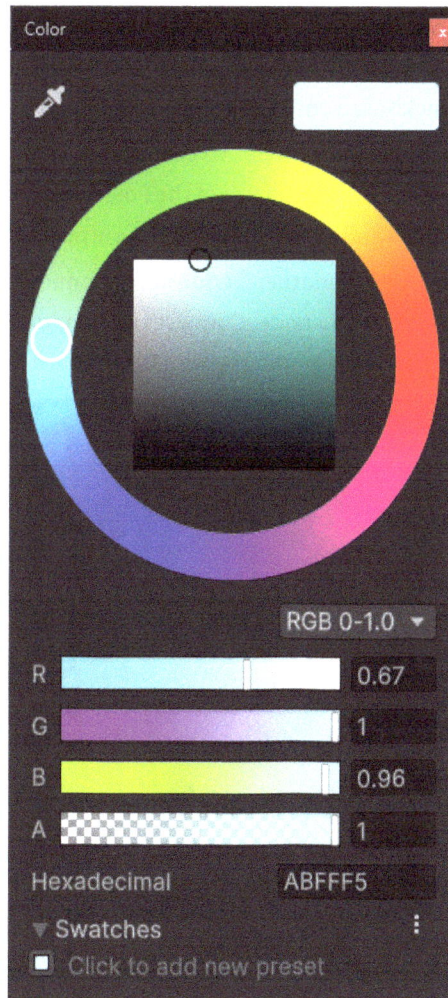

Figure 7.14 – Setting Default Value

3. Next, create a **Float** property called `Period`. Set **Mode** to **Slider** with a range of 0 to 50 and **Default Value** to 1. Then, create a **Float** property called `Magnitude` with a range of 0 to 5 and **Default Value** of 0.05. Finally, create a **Float** property called `Scale`, also set to **Slider**, with a range of 0 to 10 and **Default Value** of 1.

Now, we can start building the graph itself. We will begin by creating some variable values that we will need to use for both the *x* and *y* axes to create the distortions needed for the water effect:

1. First, create a **Time** node. To the right of that, create a **Divide** node. Connect the **Sine Time** output from the **Time** node to the **A** input of the **Divide** node. Drag and drop the **Period** property from **Blackboard** onto the graph, assigning it to the **B** input of the **Divide** node.

2. Below that, create a **Position** node. To the right of that, create a **Split** node, as we will only be using the **X** and **Y** coordinates of the **Position** node. To the right of the **Split** node, create a **Vector 2** node and connect the **R** and **G** outputs to the **X** and **Y** inputs, respectively.

3. To the right of that, create another **Divide** node. Connect the output of the **Vector 2** node to the **A** input of the **Divide** node. Connect the **B** input of the **Divide** node to the **Scale** property by dragging and dropping it from **Blackboard** as well.

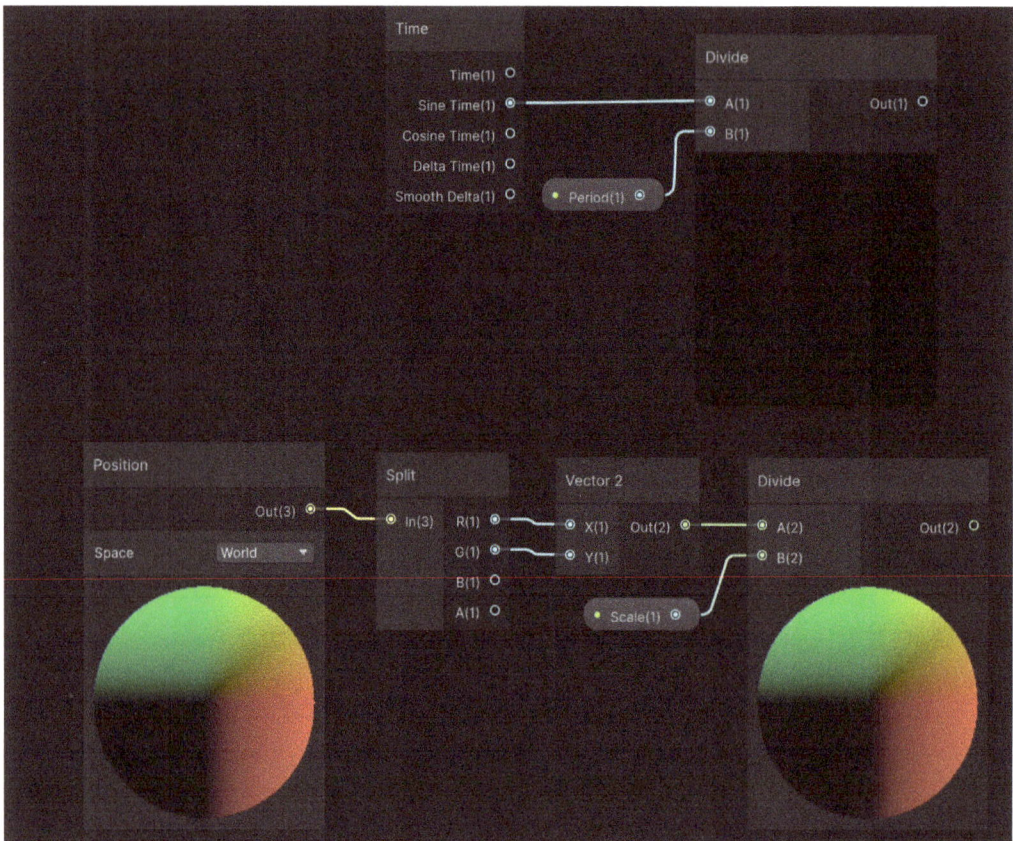

Figure 7.15 – Graph setup

We are next going to calculate the x and y displacements separately, so we'll be doing similar calculations on top of each other:

1. To the right of both the **Divide** node and the **Period** property, create two **Vector 2** nodes, one on top of the other. Connect the output of the **Divide** node to the **A** input of one **Vector 2** node and the **B** input of the other.

2. To the right of both **Vector 2** nodes, create an **Add** node. Connect the output of the **Divide** node to one of the inputs of each **Add** node. Connect the output of each **Vector 2** node to the other input of each **Add** node.

3. To the right of each **Add** node, create a **Sample Texture 2D** node. Drag and drop the **NoiseTex** property from the **Blackboard** onto the graph and connect it to both **Sample Texture 2D** nodes. Connect the output of each **Add** node to the UV input of each **Sample Texture 2D** node.

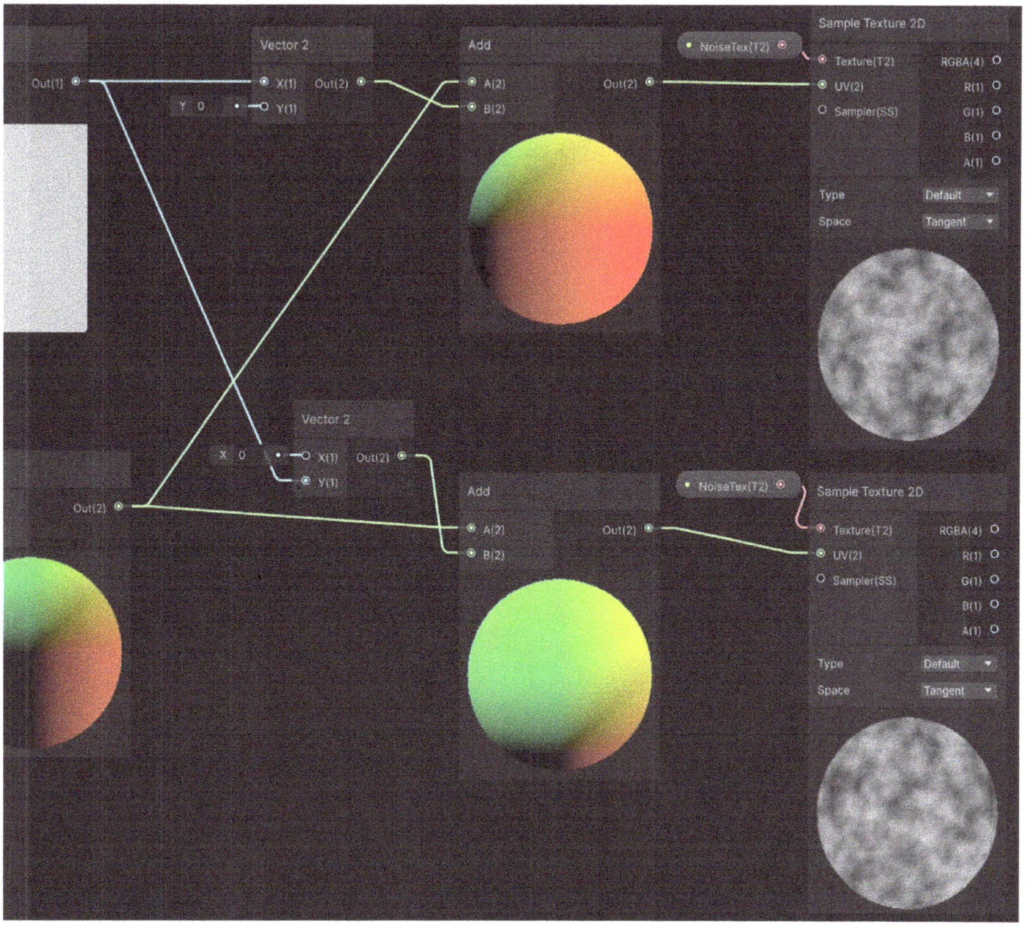

Figure 7.16 – Creating X and Y distortions

4. To the right of the **Sample Texture 2D** nodes, create two **Subtract** nodes. For each **Subtract** node, connect the **R** channel of the respective **Sample Texture 2D** node to the **A** input of the **Subtract** node. Set the **B** input of both **Subtract** nodes to 0.5.

5. Next, create a single **Vector 2** node. Connect the output of the top **Subtract** node to the **X** input of the **Vector 2** node and connect the output of the bottom **Subtract** node to the **Y** input of the **Vector 2** node.

   This step combines the *x* and *y* displacements together.

6. To the right of the **Vector 2** node, create a **Multiply** node. Connect the output of the **Vector 2** node to the **A** input of the **Multiply** node. Then, drag and drop the **Magnitude** property from **Blackboard** onto the graph and connect it to the **B** input of the **Multiply** node.

   This will allow us to scale the displacement in the final shader.

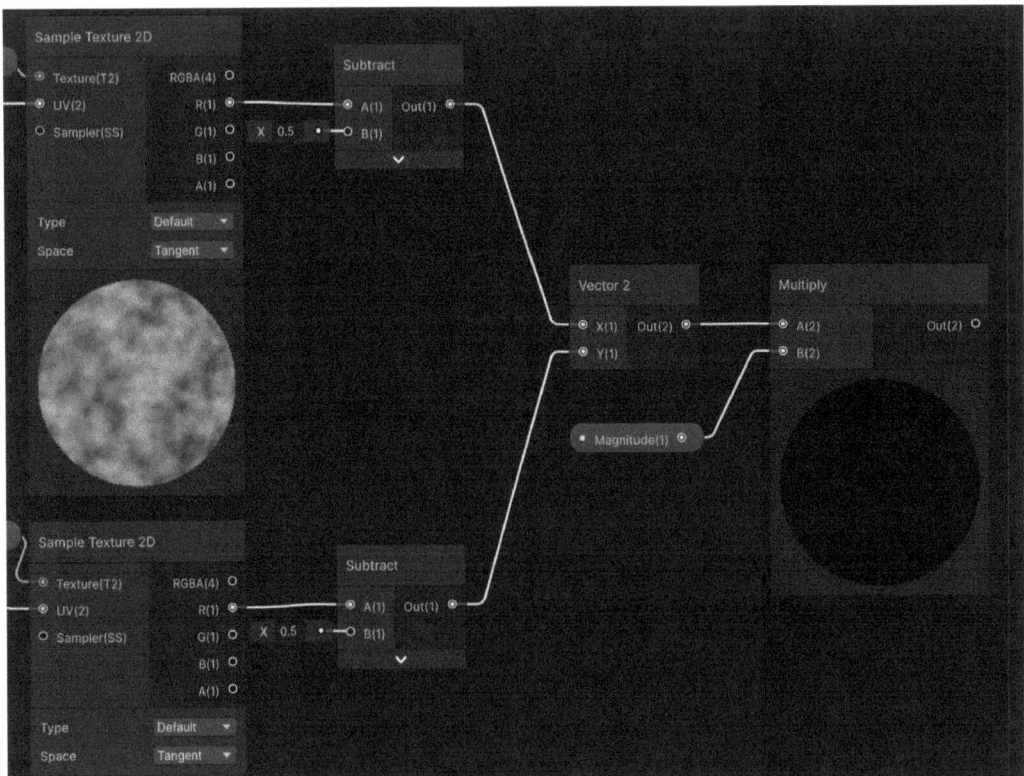

Figure 7.17 – Scaled displacement

Now we need to connect this displacement result to the actual thing that we see.

7. First, create a **Screen Position** node. To the right of that, create an **Add** node. Connect the output of the **Screen Position** node to the **A** input of the **Add** node and connect the output of the **Multiply** node (from the previous step) to the **B** input of the **Add** node.

At this point, you can remove the nodes we had previously for **Base Color** and build the rest of our graph from scratch or reuse nodes as needed. I'll write here as if we are creating the rest of the graph from scratch:

1. Next, create a **Scene Color** node. Connect the output of the **Add** node to the UV input of the **Scene Color** node.

2. To the right of the **Scene Color** node, create a **Multiply** node. Connect the output of the **Scene Color** node to the **A** input of the **Multiply** node. Then, drag and drop the **Color** property from **Blackboard** onto the graph and connect it to the **B** input of the **Multiply** node.

3. Finally, take the output of the **Multiply** node and connect it to the **Base Color** input of the **Fragment** section of the **Master Stack**.

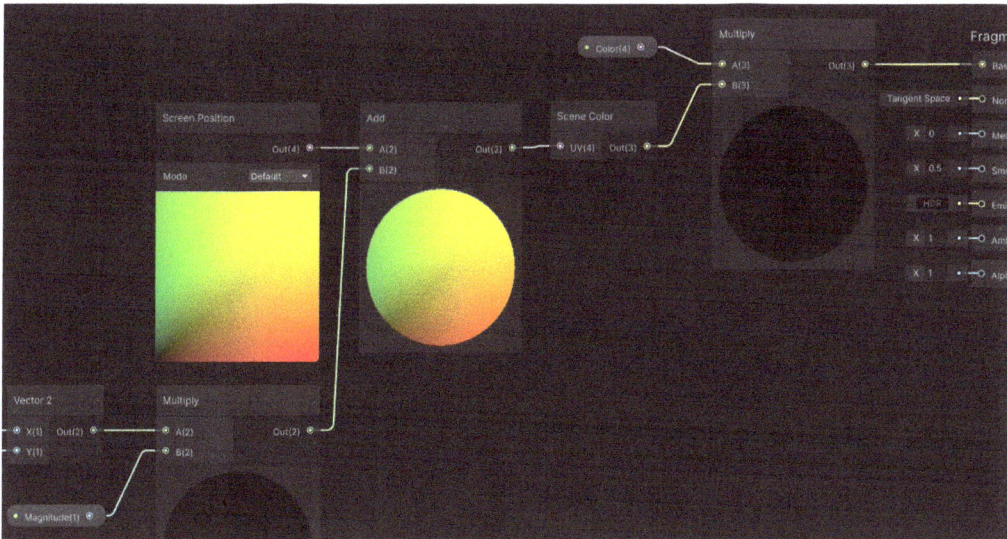

Figure 7.18 – Final recipe graph

If you prefer not to have this window cast a shadow, go into **Graph Inspector** and, from **Graph Settings**, set **Cast Shadows** to false by unchecking it.

Once that's completed, save your Shader Graph and return to the Unity Editor. Adjust the properties in your material to fine-tune the effect to your liking.

Figure 7.19 – Final recipe result

How it works...

This Shader Graph setup is very similar to the one introduced in the *Implementing a glass shader* recipe. The major difference is that this is an animated material; the displacement is not generated from a normal map but takes the current time into account to create a constant animation.

The displacement effect relies on a sinusoid function to make the water oscillate. The distortion generated by the shader evolves over time, which is achieved using the **Time** node. The **Period** property determines the period of the sinusoid, controlling how fast the waves appear.

In the Shader Graph, we use a **Time** node connected to a **Divide** node, where the **Sine Time** output is divided by the **Period** property. This setup creates a time-based oscillation. To avoid uniform displacement on both the *x* and *y* axes, which would cause a circular motion, we introduce randomness by using a noise texture.

We sample the noise texture at seemingly random positions to avoid an obvious sinusoid pattern. By using sine waves as offsets in the UV data of the **NoiseTex** texture, we achieve this randomness. The **Scale** property determines the size of the waves.

To ensure the waves are anchored to the background and not moving with the water quad, we use the world position of the current fragment as the initial position for the UV data. This is done by dividing the world position coordinates by the **Scale** property and adding sine wave offsets.

The **Subtract** nodes adjust the sampled noise values by subtracting `0.5` to center the distortion. We then combine the *x* and *y* distortions into a single **Vector 2** node. This combined distortion is scaled using the **Magnitude** property via a **Multiply** node.

The final displacement result is applied to the **Screen Position** UV coordinates, and the adjusted UVs are used to sample the scene color. The sampled scene color is then multiplied by the **Color** property to apply the final color adjustment.

The result is a pleasant, seamless distortion that simulates water-like movement.

> **Note**
>
> As with all these special effects, there is no perfect solution. We have shown a technique you can use for creating water-like distortion effects, but as with all special effects, you are encouraged to experiment and adjust the properties to fit the aesthetics of your game.

Join our community on Discord

Join our community's Discord space for discussions with the authors and other readers:

`https://packt.link/gamedevelopment`

Part 3

Performance Optimization and Fullscreen Effects

Performance is a key concern in game development, especially when working with real-time rendering. This part focuses on optimizing shaders for efficiency while maintaining visual fidelity across different platforms. You will learn how to reduce memory overhead, optimize calculations, and profile shaders to ensure smooth performance on everything from high-end PCs to mobile devices.

Beyond optimization, this part also explores Fullscreen shaders, which apply visual effects across the entire screen. Unlike object-based shaders, fullscreen shaders allow you to implement post-processing effects from scratch, giving you complete control over how the final frame is rendered. This knowledge will help you create cinematic effects, such as depth-based rendering and color grading.

We will conclude with a focus on gameplay-driven effects, such as old film filters and night vision, which respond to player actions or environmental triggers. By the end of this part, you will be equipped to integrate shaders seamlessly into gameplay, enhancing both visual appeal and player immersion.

This part has the following chapters:

- *Chapter 8, Optimizing Shaders*
- *Chapter 9, Creating Screen Effects with Fullscreen Shaders*
- *Chapter 10, Gameplay and Screen Effects*

8

Optimizing Shaders

In this chapter, we are going to take a look at making the shaders that we write performance-friendly for different platforms. We won't be talking about any one platform, but we'll be breaking down the elements of shaders that we can adjust to make them more optimized for mobile and efficient on any platform in general. The techniques employed include the use of Unity's built-in variables that reduce the overhead of the shader's memory as well as approaches to make our shader code more efficient.

Learning the art of optimizing your shaders will come up in just about any game project that you work on. There will always come a point in any production environment where a shader needs to be optimized, or maybe it needs to use fewer textures to produce the same effect. As a technical artist or shader programmer, you have to understand the core fundamentals to optimize your shaders so that you can increase the performance of your game while still achieving the same visual fidelity.

Having knowledge of how to optimize shaders can also help with how you write your shader from the start. For instance, by knowing that the game that was built using your shader will be played on a mobile device, we can automatically set all our lighting functions to use a half vector as the view direction, or we can even set all of our float variable types to fixed or half to reduce the amount of memory that's used. These, and many other techniques, all contribute to your shaders running efficiently on your target hardware.

This chapter will cover the following recipes:

- Techniques to make shaders more efficient
- Profiling your shaders
- Modifying our shaders for mobile

Technical requirements

For this chapter, you will need Unity Editor version 6 Preview 6000.0.07f1. This chapter's instructions should work with minimal changes in future versions of the editor in projects that utilize the **Universal Render Pipeline (URP)**. The chapter's sample project was created using the **Universal 3D Core** template.

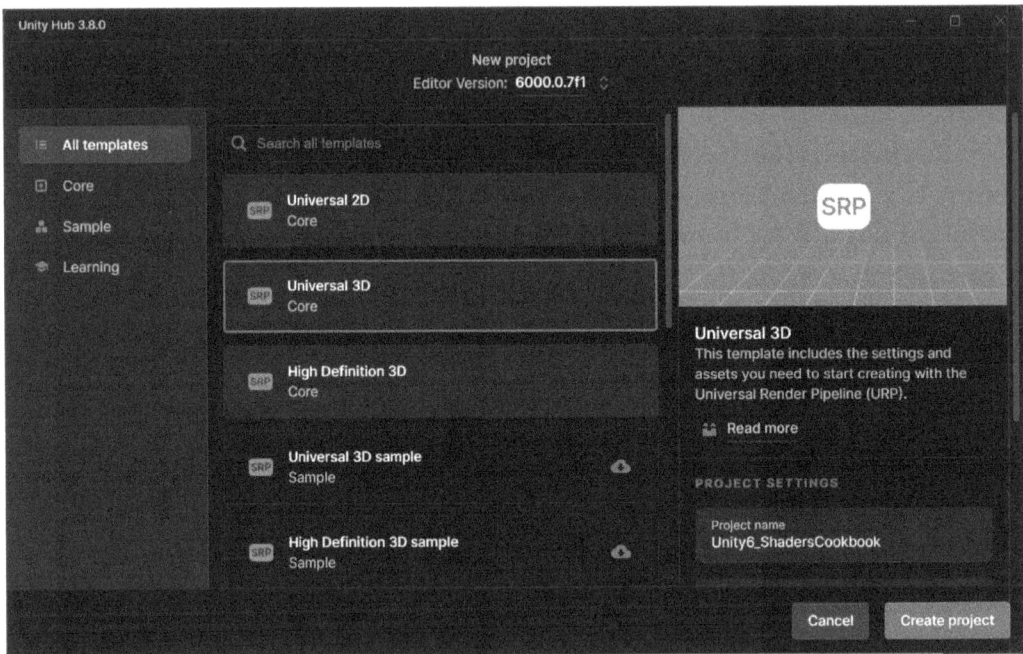

Figure 8.1 – Universal 3D (URP) project

The code files for this chapter can be found on GitHub at https://github.com/PacktPublishing/Unity-6-Shaders-and-Effects-Cookbook. The necessary files for this chapter are organized in the Unity project in a folder named Chapter 08 (https://github.com/PacktPublishing/Unity-6-Shaders-and-Effects-Cookbook/tree/main/Unity6_ShadersCookbook/Assets/Chapter%20 08) on GitHub.

Techniques to make shaders more efficient

When asked what makes a shader "cheap," the answer isn't always straightforward. Shader efficiency depends on several factors, including memory usage, the number of textures sampled, and the complexity of calculations performed per pixel or vertex. Sometimes, a shader may already function correctly, but we can achieve the same visual effect with half the data by reducing unnecessary computations, optimizing variable precision, or minimizing texture lookups.

In this recipe, we explore techniques to improve shader performance without sacrificing visual quality. Specifically, we cover precision optimization by adjusting variable types, reducing texture samples by reusing UVs, and minimizing unnecessary calculations with **Multiply**, **Step**, and **If** nodes. We also discuss disabling unnecessary features, such as shadow casting, optimizing mathematical expressions, and leveraging built-in Shader Graph optimizations. Finally, we touch on efficient color and texture handling and custom lighting models to further enhance performance.

By combining these techniques, we can create shaders that are fast, memory-efficient, and visually high-quality, ensuring smooth performance across both mobile devices and PCs.

Getting ready

To get started, we need to gather a few resources. So, let's perform the following tasks:

1. First, create a new scene in Unity. Navigate to **File** | **New Scene** and select the **Basic (URP)** option.

2. Next, add a sphere object and a directional light to the scene. In the **Hierarchy** window, right-click and select **3D Object** | **Sphere** to create a new sphere object. Position the sphere at the center of the scene (0, 0, 0). Then, if there isn't one there already, right-click again in the **Hierarchy** window and select **Light** | **Directional Light** to create a new directional light. Adjust the directional light to ensure it illuminates the sphere adequately.

3. Now, we need to create a new shader and material. In the **Project** window, right-click and select **Create** | **Shader** | **Unlit Shader**, and name it OptimizedShader. Then, right-click again and select **Create** | **Material**, and name it OptimizedShaderMat. In the **Inspector** window, select the newly created material and assign OptimizedShader to it by clicking the **Shader** dropdown and selecting your shader from the list.

4. Finally, assign the material to the sphere object. In the **Hierarchy** window, select the sphere object. In the **Inspector** window, locate the **Mesh Renderer** component. Assign **OptimizedShaderMat** to the sphere by dragging the material from the **Project** window into the **Element 0** field under **Materials** in the **Mesh Renderer** component.

By completing these tasks, you've set up the basic scene and materials required to start experimenting with shader optimization techniques.

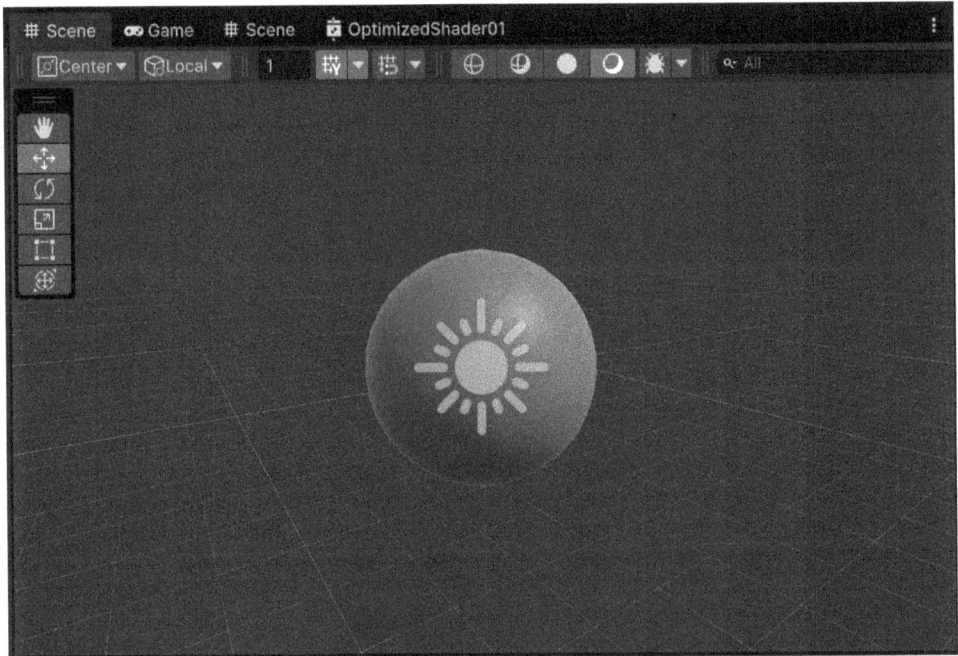

Figure 8.2 – Recipe setup

5. From the **Blackboard**, click on the + button to add a **Texture 2D** property. Name it Base (RBG). From **Graph Inspector**, set **Default Value** to a texture (I used the MudRocky texture, which is included in the assets for *Chapter 1, Using Post-Processing with URP*, in the Assets\ Chapter 01\Standard Assets\Environment\TerrainAssets\SurfaceTextures folder).

6. Afterward, create another **Texture 2D** property. Name it Normal Map. From **Graph Inspector**, set **Default Value** to a normal map texture.

7. Drag and drop both texture variables onto the graph and create two **Sample Texture 2D** nodes. Connect the **RGBA(4)** outputs to the **Base Color(3)** and **Normal (Tangent Space(3))** inputs, respectively. For **Type** of the normal map **Sample Texture 2D**, change it to **Normal**.

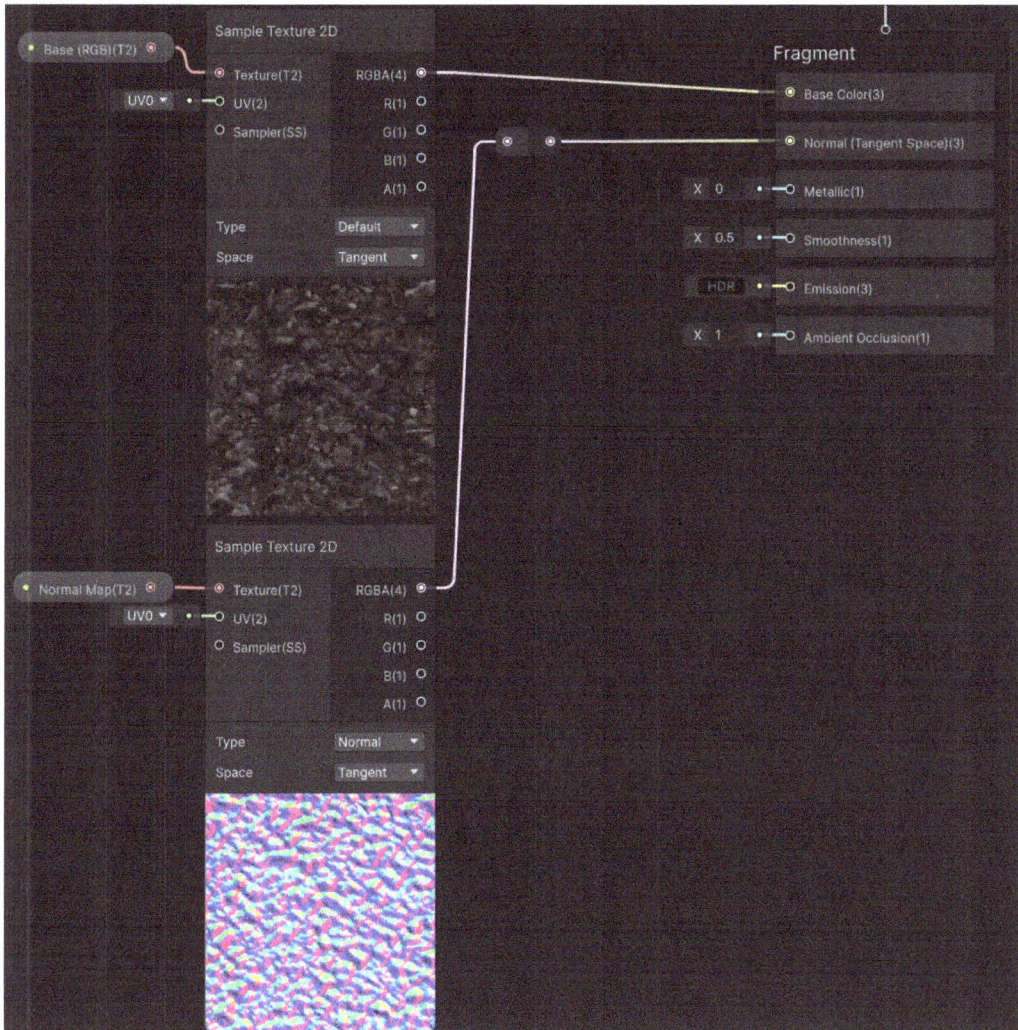

Figure 8.3 – Sampling textures

Save the Shader Graph and return to the Unity Editor. Assign the maps, if needed, from the **Inspector** or **Reset** the material.

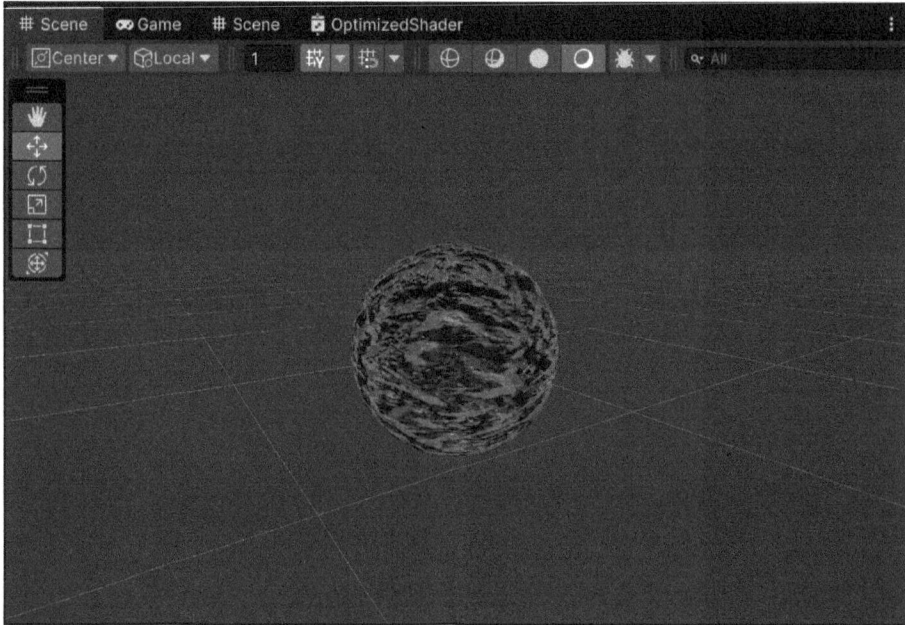

Figure 8.4 – Recipe setup

This setup will allow us to take a look at some of the basic concepts that go into optimizing shaders using Surface Shaders in Unity.

How to do it...

We are going to build a simple Diffuse shader to take a look at a few ways in which you can optimize your shaders in general.

First, we'll optimize our variable types so that they use less memory when they are processing data:

1. Double-click **OptimizedShader** to open it in the Shader Graph editor.

    In a Shader Graph, **Float**s provide the highest form of precision at a full 32 bits of memory. This is needed for complex trigonometry or exponents, but if you can handle less precision, it's much better to use half precision instead. Using half precision will have us use the half type under the hood, which provides up to three digits of precision using half the size or 16 bits of memory. Thankfully, Shader Graph makes it very easy to change the precision for all aspects of our graph with one setting.

2. Select **Graph Inspector** and, from there, change **Precision** from **Single** to **Half**.

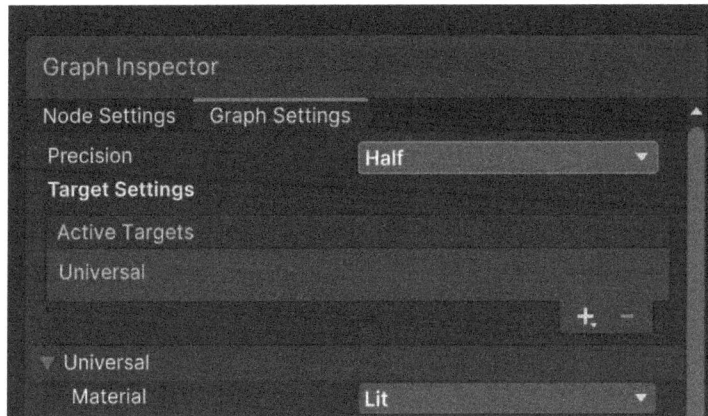

Figure 8.5 – Changing Precision

This will set the default precision that will be used for the entire graph. If there's a particular spot that you need more precision, you can select that aspect of the **Master Stack** and assign it. By default, the precision settings are set to **Inherit** whatever we set here.

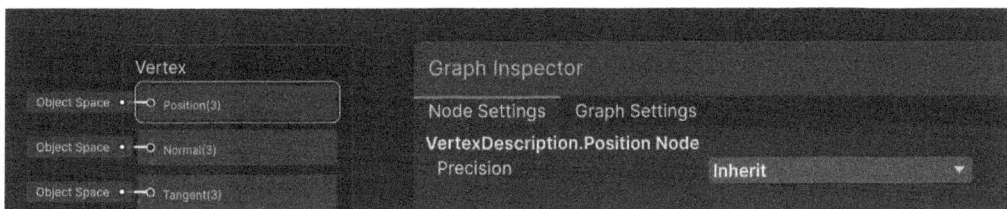

Figure 8.6 – Changing individual nodes

Another thing we can do if possible is disable receiving or casting shadows; this can cause the object to look not as nice, so you'll need to check how it looks before doing this.

You can reduce the number of texture samples by reusing UVs or sharing texture data where possible. For example, if your normal map and base texture share the same UVs, you can use a single UV node and connect it to both textures. We are doing this already since we are using the **UV0** channel. This approach not only simplifies your Shader Graph but also optimizes performance by minimizing the number of texture lookups required during rendering.

The result of our optimization passes doesn't indicate a difference in the visual quality, but we have reduced the amount of time it takes for this shader to be drawn to the screen. You will find out how much time it takes for a shader to render in the next recipe, but the idea to focus on here is that we can achieve the same result with less data being used. So, keep this in mind when you're creating your shaders.

> **Note**
>
> It's also important to note that when using `fixed`/`half` variables on a PC, you won't notice any difference at all because variable types will still use full precision.

The following screenshot shows the final result of our shader:

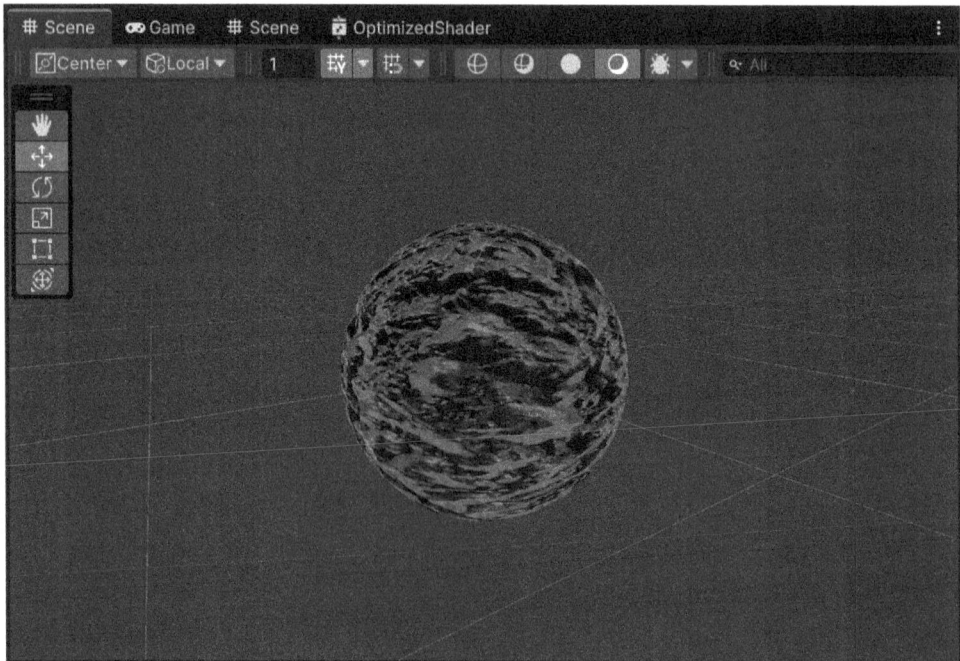

Figure 8.7 – Final result

How it works...

Now that we have seen how we can optimize our shaders, let's dive in a bit deeper and understand how all of these techniques work, why we should use them, and look at a couple of other techniques that you can try for yourself in your shaders.

First, let's focus our attention on the size of the data each of our variables is storing when we declare them. If you are familiar with programming, then you will understand that you can declare values or variables with different types of sizes. This means that a float has a maximum size in memory. In Shader Graph, these are represented as **Float**, **Vector2**, **Vector3**, and **Vector4** respectively and it is converted for us automatically based on what we set the precision to. The following list describes these variable types in much more detail, which may be useful if we look at compiled code or need to write code ourselves (something we will look at in the final chapter):

- **Float**: A float is a full 32-bit precision value and takes up the most memory of the three different types we will look at here. It also has corresponding vector types of `float2`, `float3`, and `float4`, which allow us to store multiple floats in one variable.
- **Half**: The half variable type is a reduced 16-bit floating-point value and is suitable for storing UV values and color values. It is much faster than using a float value. As with the float type, it has its corresponding values, which are `half2`, `half3`, and `half4`.
- **Fixed**: A fixed value is the smallest of the three types, but it can be used for lighting calculations and colors and has the corresponding values of `fixed2`, `fixed3`, and `fixed4`.

> Note
>
> For more information on working with array types for shaders, check out the *Accessing and modifying packed arrays* recipe from *Chapter 3, Working with Surfaces*.

By spending a bit of time on this, you will be amazed at how much a shader can be optimized – like how you have seen how we can pack grayscale textures into a single RGBA texture.

> Note
>
> You can see an example of how to create and use a lookup texture with the **Color Grading** attribute from the **Post Processing Stack** shown in *Chapter 1, Using Post-Processing with URP,* here: `https://www.youtube.com/watch?v=hYhL0qK_NC0`.

There are numerous ways to optimize a shader, making the question of how to approach optimization somewhat open-ended. However, by applying the right techniques, you can tailor your shaders to your game's specific needs and target platform, resulting in more efficient rendering, reduced computational overhead, and a consistently smooth frame rate.

There's more...

Optimizing lighting calculations in Shader Graph can be achieved by customizing the lighting model. By reducing the number of lights or opting for a less computationally expensive lighting model, you can streamline the shader's performance. We will learn how we can create our own custom lighting function in *Chapter 11, Understanding Lighting Models*.

When working in Shader Graph, it's beneficial to combine operations wherever possible to reduce the number of nodes and calculations. For example, using a **Multiply** node instead of multiple **Add** nodes can achieve the same effect with fewer operations. Additionally, instead of managing separate nodes for each color channel operation, you can utilize a single node, such as the **Combine** node, that handles all channels simultaneously, further simplifying your graph.

To reduce unnecessary calculations in Shader Graph, structure your node tree to only perform operations when needed. Utilizing **If** nodes or **Step** nodes allows you to conditionally process parts of the shader, ensuring that calculations are only executed when necessary. This approach can significantly improve the efficiency of your shaders by preventing needless computations. Likewise, wherever possible, Shader Graph will not add unused features to the output shader, so Shader Graph will attempt to optimize your code for you.

> Note
>
> Unity released a video, which is now slightly out of date, with some advice on the built-in optimizations and advice on making your shaders more efficient that may be useful: `https://youtu.be/Y6WfgFI5H90?t=1177`

Another way of optimizing shaders is to look at the math. Sometimes, it can be simplified or rewritten using algebra so that it's more efficient. Also, sometimes, complicated equations can be approximated by a polynomial such as a Maclaurin series.

Profiling your shaders

Now that we know how we can reduce the overhead that our shaders might take, let's explore how to identify shaders that could be slowing down your scene, especially when you have many shaders, objects, and scripts running simultaneously. Problematic shaders can lead to performance bottlenecks, resulting in slower frame rates and longer render times. Finding a single object or shader in a whole game can be quite daunting, but Unity provides us with its built-in **Profiler**. This allows us to see, on a frame-by-frame basis, what is happening in the game, and each item that is being used by the GPU and CPU.

Using the Profiler, we can isolate items such as shaders, geometry, and general rendering items using its interface to create blocks of profiling jobs. We can filter out items until we are looking at the performance of just a single object. This lets us see the effects that the object has on the CPU and GPU while it is performing its functions at runtime.

Let's take a look through the different sections of the **Profiler** and learn how to debug our scenes and, most importantly, our shaders.

Getting ready

Let's use the Profiler by getting a few assets ready and launching the **Profiler** window:

1. Let's use the scene from the previous recipe and launch the Unity Profiler from **Window | Analysis | Profiler** or by using *Ctrl + 7*. Feel free to drag and drop or move it so that you can see it well. I put it where the **Inspector** window is.

2. In the **Scene** view, duplicate the sphere a couple more times to see how that affects our rendering.

3. From the **Profiler** window, click on the **Deep Profile** option to get additional information about the project. Then, play your game!

You should see something similar to the following:

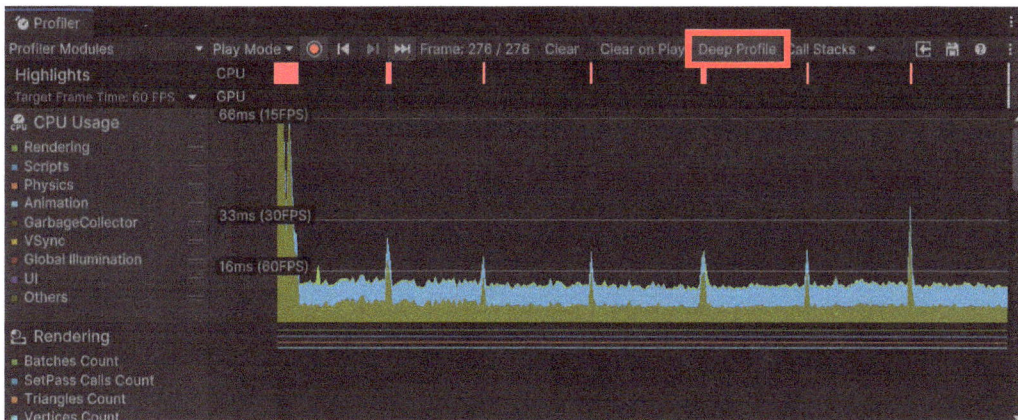

Figure 8.8 – Utilizing the Profiler

How to do it...

To use the Profiler, we will take a look at some of the UI elements of this window. Before we hit **Play**, let's take a look at how to get the information we need from **Profiler**:

1. First, click on the larger blocks in the **Profiler** window called **CPU Usage**, **Rendering**, and **Memory**. You will find these blocks on the left-hand side of the upper window:

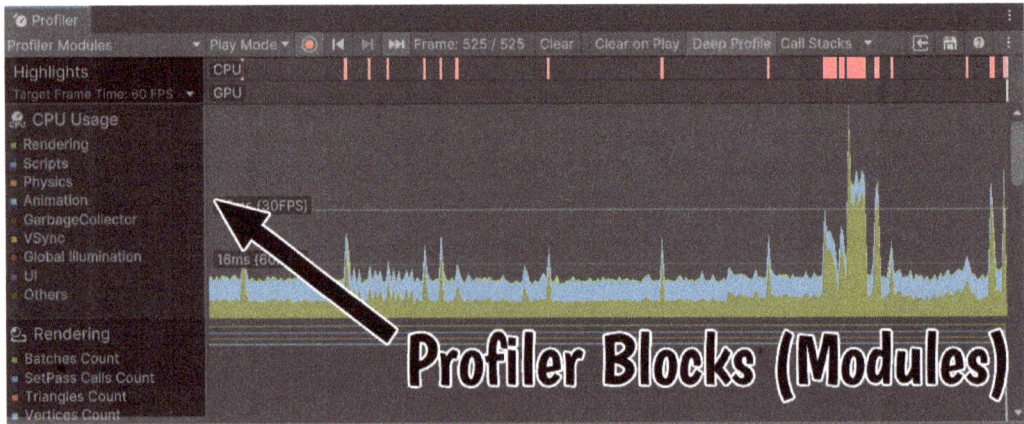

Figure 8.9 – Profiler blocks (modules) within the Profiler window

Using these blocks, we can see different data that's specific to those major functions of our game. **CPU Usage** is showing us what most of our scripts are doing, as well as physics and overall rendering. The **Rendering** block provides information about draw calls, which represent each request made by the CPU to the GPU to render objects. The more draw calls you have, the more work the CPU and GPU have to handle, which can lead to performance slowdowns. The **Rendering** block also shows us the amount of geometry present in our scene at any given frame. The **Memory** block shows the total memory being used, when allocations are happening, and when the garbage collector is being utilized. **Highlights** is a new addition, which shows us in a visual manner how often we are or aren't meeting our goal in regards to FPS.

> **Note**
>
> It's important to note that, when recording, our FPS will be lower than normal due to the fact that we will be doing a lot more than we normally are, so seeing this when doing a **Deep Profile** isn't necessarily cause for alarm.

The **Highlights** panel is used to give us detailed information about the elements that are specific to our lighting, shadows, and render queues.

2. Go to the top left of the window, to the **Profiler Modules** dropdown. From there, check the **GPU Usage** option if it isn't checked already:

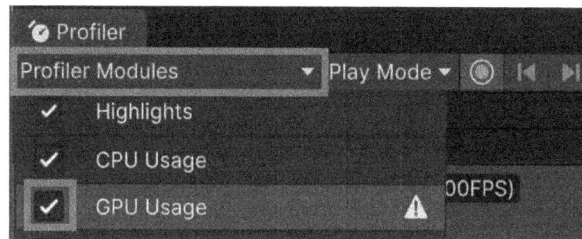

Figure 8.10 – Enabling the GPU Usage panel

The **GPU Usage** block gives us detailed information about the elements that are specific to our lighting, shadows, and render queues. It is disabled by default because collecting the GPU **Profiler** data may cause overhead and HDRP and URP renderers aren't fully supported. However, since this is information directly related to shaders, we will want to have it running.

Important note

The **GPU Usage** menu may not show up if your graphics card drivers are not up to date.

By clicking on each of these blocks, we can isolate the type of data we see during our profiling session.

3. Now, click on the tiny colored blocks in one of these **Profile** blocks and hit **Play**, or *Ctrl + P*, to run the scene.

4. This lets us dive even deeper into our profiling session so that we can filter out what is being reported back to us. While the scene is running, uncheck all of the boxes, except for **Shadows/Depth** in the **GPU Usage** block. We can now see just how much time is being used to render the shadows and depth of objects:

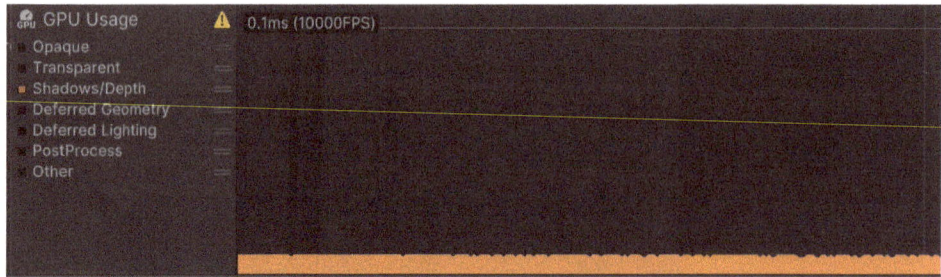

Figure 8.11 – The time required for rendering shadows and the depth of objects

5. Another great function of the **Profiler** window is the action of being able to click at any point of the timeline within the **Graph** view.

    This will automatically pause your game and draw a white line at that point so you know what is being looked at and you can analyze a certain spike in the graph. By doing this, you can find out exactly which item is causing a performance problem. Click and drag around in the **Graph** view to pause the game and see the effect of using this functionality:

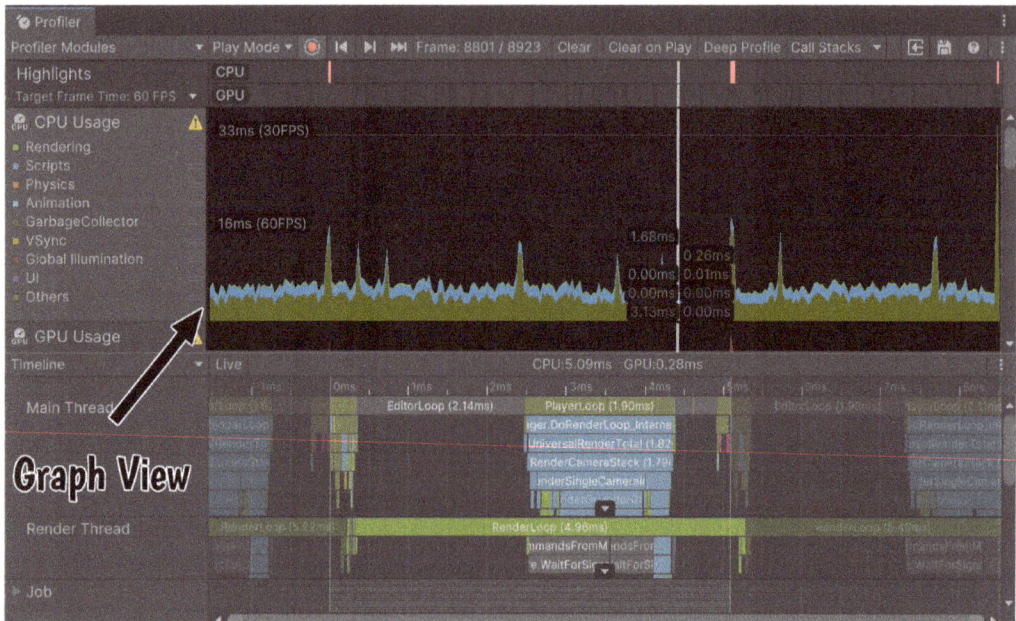

Figure 8.12 – The Graph view

6. Let's turn our attention to the lower half of the **Profiler** window. You will notice that there is a drop-down item available called **Timeline**, which lets us view the time spent in each part of the program, as a percentage. For a more detailed view, we can change the mode by clicking on the **Timeline** dropdown and selecting **Hierarchy**. From there, go to **Profiler Modules** and select **GPU Usage**.

At this point, you should be able to see a list of things detailing how the GPU is being used in a particular frame. We can expand this to get even more detailed information about the current active profiling session and, in this case, more information about what the camera is currently rendering and how much time it is taking up:

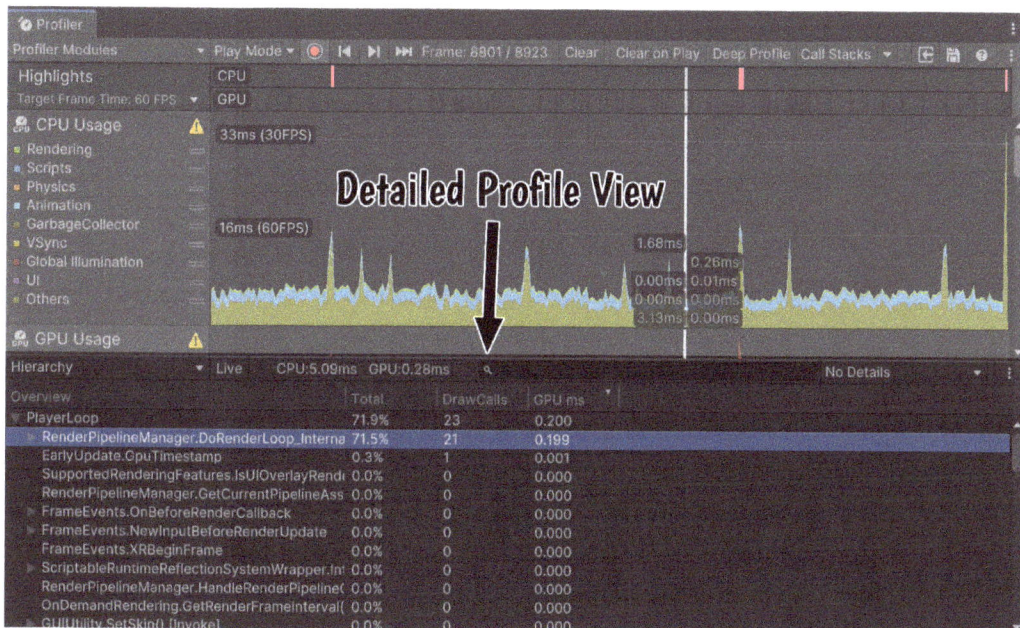

Figure 8.13 – Detailed profile view

It is also possible to sort the options using the tops of the columns. For instance, we can use **GPU ms** to measure the amount of time it takes to perform various actions:

Overview	Total	DrawCalls	GPU ms
▼ PlayerLoop	19.0%	23	0.156
▶ RenderPipelineManager.DoRenderLoop_Internal()	19.0%	21	0.156
▶ SupportedRenderingFeatures.IsUIOverlayRenderedBySRP()	0.0%	0	0.000
RenderPipelineManager.GetCurrentPipelineAssetType()	0.0%	0	0.000
▶ FrameEvents.OnBeforeRenderCallback	0.0%	0	0.000
▶ FrameEvents.NewInputBeforeRenderUpdate	0.0%	0	0.000
FrameEvents.XRBeginFrame	0.0%	0	0.000
▶ ScriptableRuntimeReflectionSystemWrapper.Internal_Scriptabl	0.0%	0	0.000
RenderPipelineManager.HandleRenderPipelineChange()	0.0%	0	0.000
▶ OnDemandRendering.GetRenderFrameInterval()	0.0%	0	0.000
▶ GUIUtility.SetSkin()	0.0%	0	0.000
▶ updateScene.Invoke	0.0%	0	0.000
▶ UIEvents.CanvasManagerEmitOffScreenGeometry	0.0%	0	0.000

Figure 8.14 – The total percentage and milliseconds used to do different operations

Note

If you click on the dropdown on the right-hand side of the view that says **No Details** and change the option to **Related Data**, you can see what objects are being used in the functions being called.

This gives us a complete look at the inner workings of what Unity is processing in this particular frame. In this case, we can see that our three spheres with our optimized shader are taking roughly 0.156 milliseconds to draw to the screen, they are taking up 21 draw calls, and that this process is taking 19.0% of the GPU's time in every frame (the numbers will likely be different, depending on what hardware you have for your computer).

7. We can use this information to diagnose and resolve performance issues related to shaders. To test the impact of adding an extra texture, we will blend two diffuse textures using a **Lerp** node in Shader Graph. The **Profiler** will allow us to observe how this modification affects rendering performance. From the **Blackboard**, add a new **Texture 2D** property called **Blend Texture** and assign it the texture you'd like to use. For this example, I'm using the grass texture from *Chapter 1, Using Post-Processing with URP* (Assets/Chapter 01/ Standard Assets/Environment/TerrainAssets/SurfaceTextures/GrassHillAlbedo. psd). Drag and drop **Blend Texture** onto the graph. To the right of it, add a **Sample Texture 2D** node and connect **Blend Texture** to the **Texture** input of this node.

8. Next, create a **Lerp** node. Connect the original **Base (RGB)** texture to the **A** input of the **Lerp** node and **Blend Texture** to the **B** input. Then, connect the **R** channel of **Blend Texture** to the **T** input of the **Lerp** node. Finally, connect the output of the **Lerp** node to the **Base Color (RGB)** input of the **Master Stack**, replacing the original output.

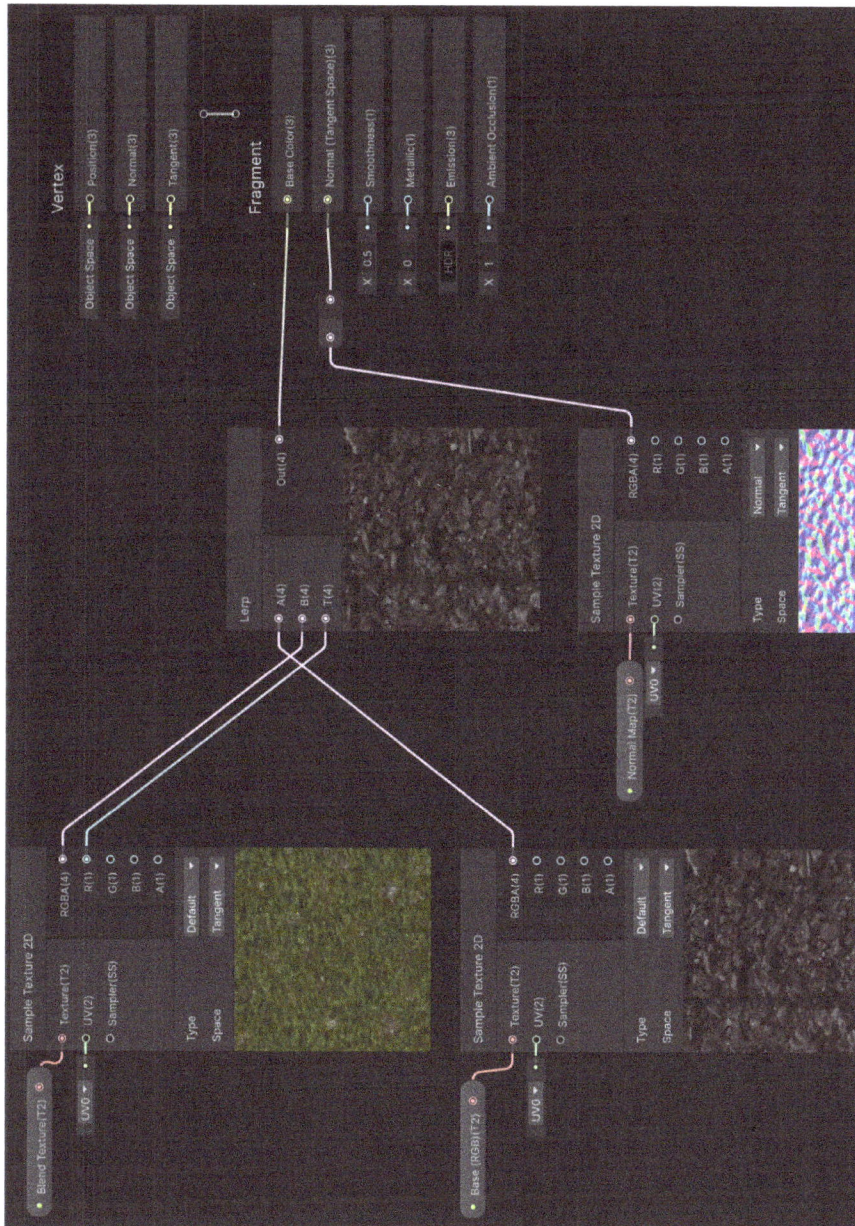

Figure 8.15 – Adjustments to the shader

Once you've saved your modifications in your shader and returned the Unity Editor, you can run the game and see the new shader's increase in milliseconds.

9. Click **Play** to start the game again with **Profiler** turned on. Click **Play** once you have returned to Unity. Now, let's take a look at the results in the Profiler:

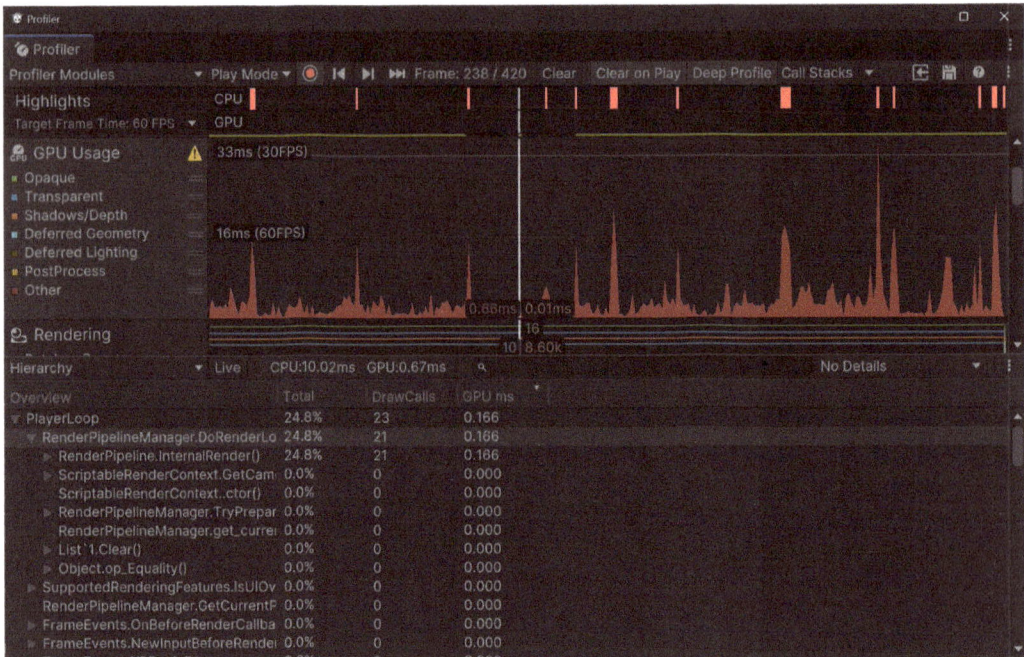

Figure 8.16 – New Profiler results

Here, you can see that the amount of time it takes to render our three spheres in this scene is 0.166 milliseconds, up from 0.156 milliseconds. By adding another texture and using the **Lerp** node along with a few other calculations, we increased the render time for our spheres. While this was a small change, imagine having 20 shaders all working in different ways on different objects.

Using the information given here, you can pinpoint areas that are causing performance decreases more quickly and solve these issues using the techniques shown in the previous recipe.

How it works...

While it is completely outside the scope of this book to describe how this tool works internally, we can surmise that Unity has given us a way to view the computer's performance while our game is running. This window is tied very tightly to the CPU and GPU to give us real-time feedback on how much time is being taken for each of our scripts, objects, and render queues. Using this information, we have seen that we can track the efficiency of our shader writing to eliminate problem areas and code.

Note that games running with **Profiler** open, as well as from within the editor in general, will make the game slightly slower than it would be when compiled and running in a normal situation. You may even notice **Editor**-related processes appearing in the **Profiler**'s list of CPU expenses, which can affect timing measurements. Keep this in mind when assessing shader performance, as the actual impact may differ when you build your project.

There's more...

It is also possible to profile specifically for mobile platforms. Unity provides us with a couple of extra features when the Android or iOS build target is set in **Build Settings**. We can get real-time information from our mobile devices while the game is running. This becomes very useful because you can profile directly on the device itself instead of profiling directly in your editor. To find out more about this process, refer to Unity's documentation at the following link: `https://docs.unity3d.com/Manual/profiler-profiling-applications.html`.

Profiling on a mobile device and PC may give completely different results, to the point where it may not be worth the time to perform profiling on a PC within the editor if you are making a mobile-only game. For example, there may be a situation where dynamic batching worked fine on a PC but was not working correctly on a mobile device. I recommend always profiling on the target device with a standalone build if possible.

Modifying our shaders for mobile

Now that we have looked at a broad set of techniques for making optimized shaders, let's take a look at writing a nice, high-quality shader targeted at a mobile device. It is quite easy to make a few adjustments to the shaders we have written so that they run faster on a mobile device. We can make adjustments such as reducing the number of textures, and even applying better compression to the textures we are using. By the end of this recipe, we will have a nicely optimized, normally mapped Specular shader that we can use in our mobile games.

Getting ready

Before we begin, let's create a fresh new scene and fill it with some objects that we will apply to our mobile shader:

1. Create a new scene and fill it with a default sphere and a single directional light.
2. Create a new material (`MobileMat`) and lit Shader Graph (`MobileShader`), and assign the shader to the material.

3.   Finally, assign the material to the sphere object in our scene.

Once you've done this, you should have a scene similar to the one shown in the following screenshot:

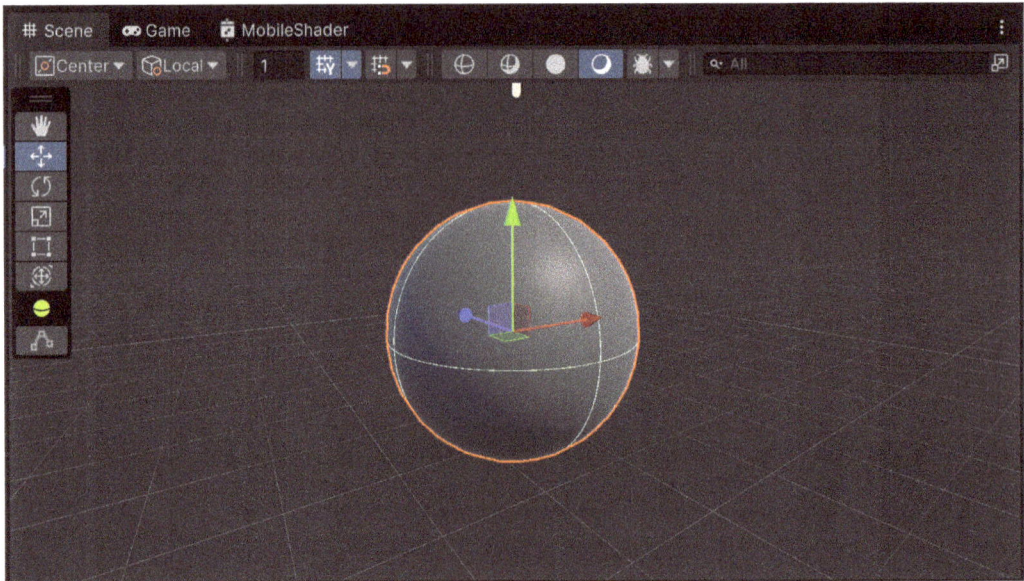

Figure 8.17 – Setup for this recipe

How to do it...

For this recipe, we will write a mobile-friendly shader from scratch and discuss the elements that make it more mobile-friendly:

1.   First, let's populate our **Blackboard** block with the required textures. In this case, we are going to use a single diffuse texture with the gloss map in its alpha channel, normal map, and a **Slider** for specular intensity:

2.   From the **Blackboard**, click on the + button to create a **Texture 2D** property with a name `Base (RGB) Specular Amount (A)`, and set **Default Value** to the `MudRockyAlbedoSpecular.bmp` texture (`Assets/Chapter 01/Standard Assets/Environment/TerrainAssets/SurfaceTextures/MudRockyAlbedoSpecular.bmp`).

3.   Then create a **Float** property called `Specular Intensity`. Change **Mode** to **Slider**. Then change **Min** to `0.01` and **Max** to 1, then set **Default Value** to `0.5`.

4.   Finally, create a **Texture 2D** property, give it the name `Normal Map`, and set **Default Value** to the `MudRockyNormals.bmp` texture (`Assets/Chapter 01/Standard Assets/Environment/TerrainAssets/SurfaceTextures/MudRockyNormals.bmp`). Also, set **Mode** to **NormalMap**.

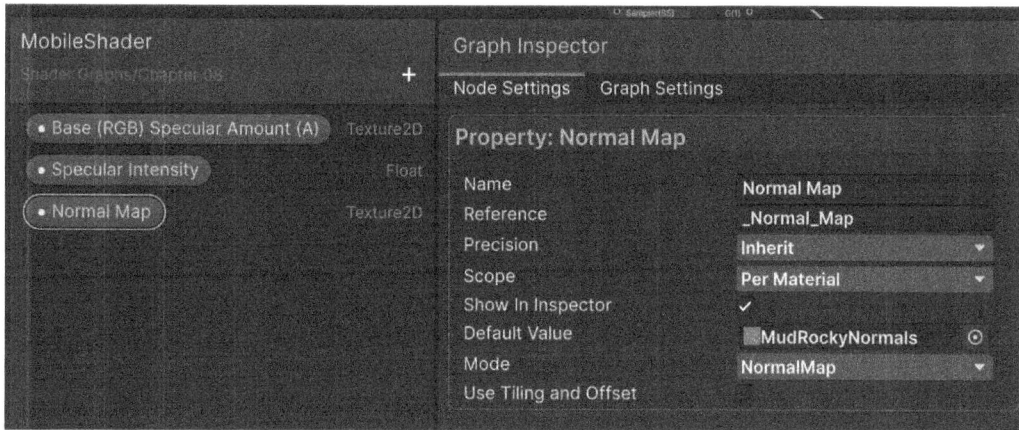

Figure 8.18 – Blackboard properties

Next, let's set up the shader. We will use **Specular** mode and change our precision so it will take up less memory:

1. From **Graph Inspector**, switch to the **Graph Settings** tab. Change **Workflow Mode** to **Specular**. Then change **Precision** to **Half**.

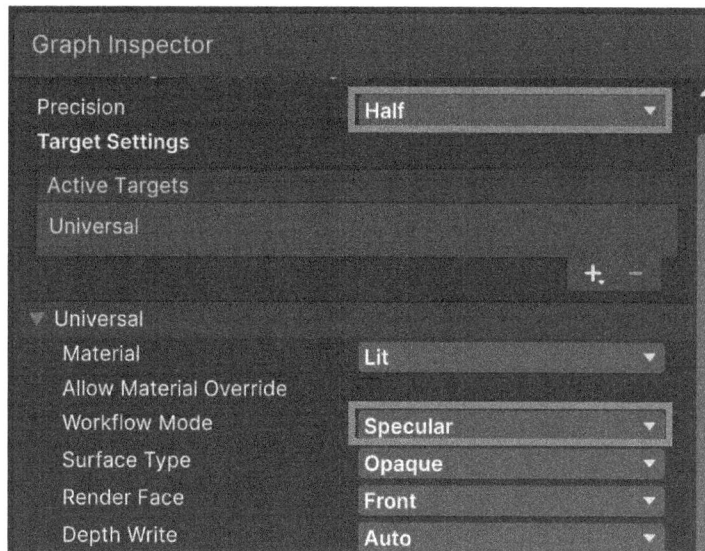

Figure 8.19 – Setting graph properties

2. Drag and drop both textures onto the graph. For each texture, create a **Sample Texture 2D** node and connect the texture to the **Texture** input of the corresponding node. For the normal map texture, ensure **Type** is set to **Normal** if it hasn't been done already.

3. Next, connect the **RGBA** output of the normal map's **Sample Texture 2D** node to the **Normal (Tangent Space)** input on the **Master Stack**. Then, connect the **RGBA** output of the other **Sample Texture 2D** node to the **Base Color** input on the **Master Stack**.

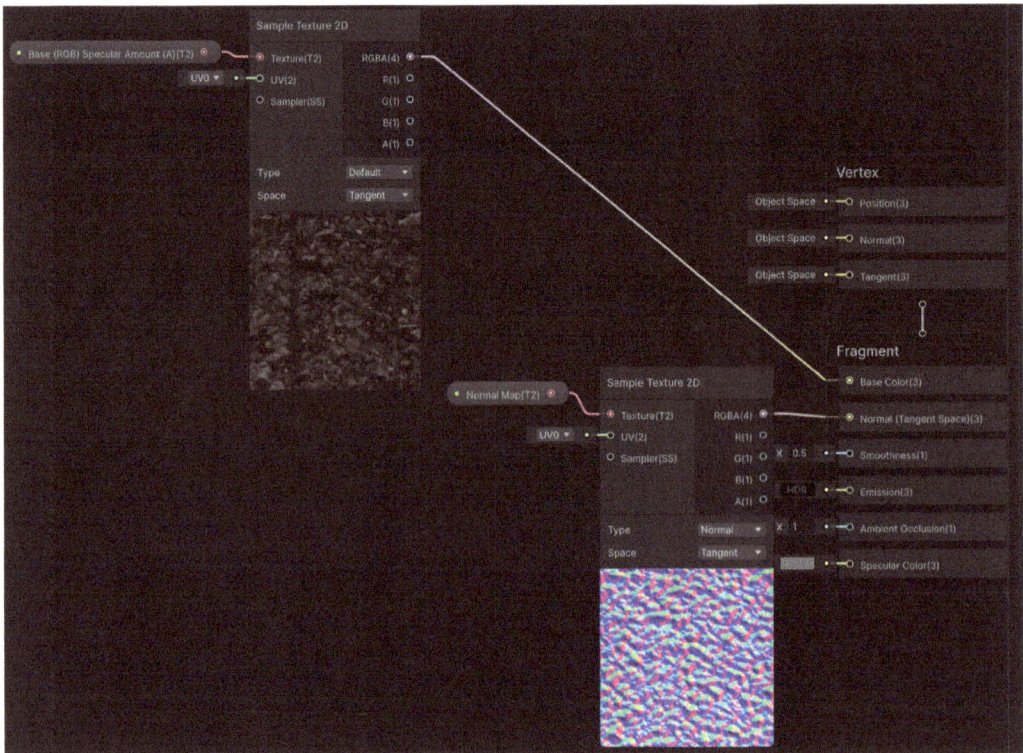

Figure 8.20 – Sampling textures

Now let's add specular support:

1. Start by taking the **RGBA** output of the **Base Color Sample Texture 2D** node and connect it to a new **Multiply** node. Below that, add the **Specular Intensity** variable to the graph and connect it to the **B** input of the **Multiply** node.

    In the preview window, you should see that only a portion of the image is being used for the specular effect.

2. Finally, connect the output of the **Multiply** node to the **Specular Color** input on the **Master Stack**.

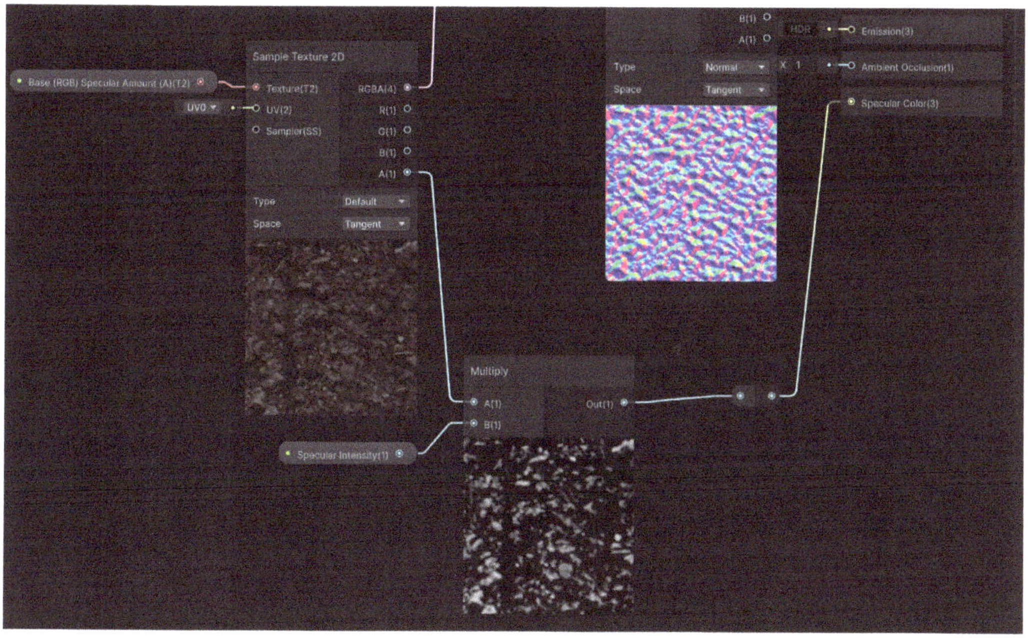

Figure 8.21 – Calculating specular result

3. Save your Shader Graph and return to the Unity Editor. Assign the textures to the material if needed.

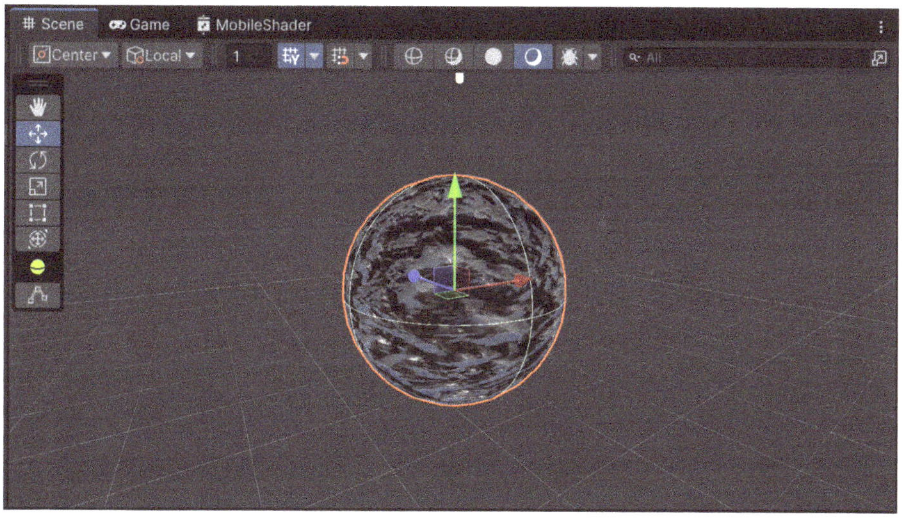

Figure 8.22 – Result of the shader

4. Add a few point lights and some copies of the new object. At this point, you should see a result similar to the following:

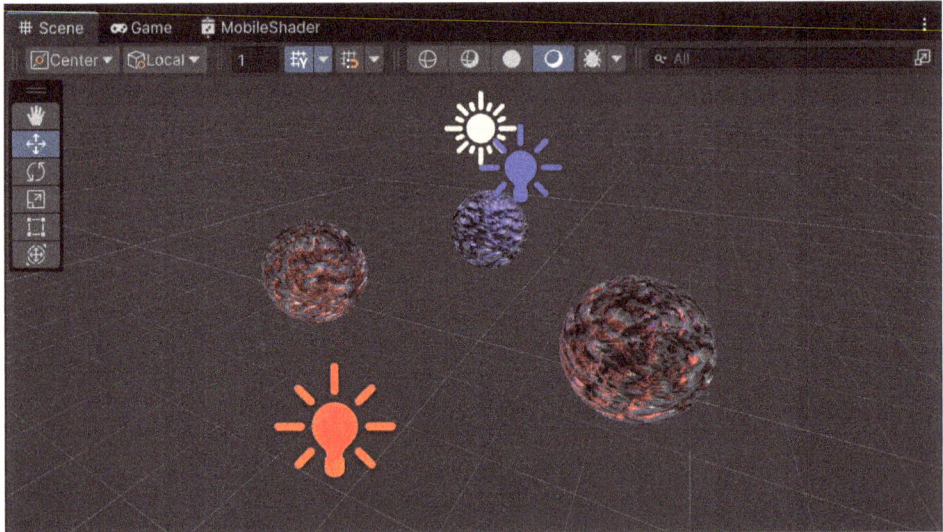

Figure 8.23 – The result of the created MobileShader

How it works...

This shader has been optimized for mobile devices by focusing on key techniques that reduce processing load while maintaining visual quality. One of the main optimizations is setting the precision to **Half**, which allows the shader to use less memory and computational resources. This is crucial for performance on mobile devices, where **Half** precision ensures that calculations remain lightweight without compromising the visual output.

In terms of texture optimization, we've reduced the number of textures by combining data into a single texture whenever possible. For example, the alpha channel of the base texture is used for specular intensity. This approach minimizes the number of texture samples needed, leading to improved performance by reducing the overall complexity of the shader.

This shader also utilizes the **Specular** workflow instead of the **Metallic** workflow to manage specular highlights. While both workflows are similar in terms of memory and computational resource requirements, the **Specular** workflow can offer slight optimizations in certain scenarios. For instance, by using a constant specular color or a simpler texture for specular highlights, we can reduce the memory footprint and potentially lower the computational load.

Additionally, the shader utilizes normal mapping to add surface detail without increasing geometric complexity. By using a **Multiply** node to blend the **A** channel of the base color with the **Specular Intensity** property, we can efficiently control specular highlights. This results in realistic lighting effects with minimal computational overhead.

The shader's design is specifically tailored for mobile devices, where hardware resources are more limited. By carefully managing inputs and optimizing rendering calculations, we've created a shader that provides high-quality visuals while remaining efficient. These techniques combine to produce a shader that balances visual fidelity and performance, making it ideal for mobile games. The adjustments ensure that the shader runs smoothly even on devices with lower processing power, without sacrificing the overall appearance.

9

Creating Screen Effects with Fullscreen Shaders

Fullscreen shaders, also known as fullscreen passes or post-processing effects, apply visual effects across the entire screen rather than being limited to individual objects. A key skill in shader development is learning to create these **screen effects** yourself. These effects, often referred to as post effects, allow for real-time enhancements such as bloom, motion blur, and **high-dynamic-range (HDR)** rendering. In modern games, such effects are commonly used to achieve depth-of-field, bloom, and color correction, significantly enhancing visual quality.

In *Chapter 1, Using Post-Processing with URP*, we discussed how to create screen effects with Unity's built-in Post Processing Stack, but in this chapter, you will learn how to build up a similar shader yourself by hand. This system will give you the control to create many kinds of screen effects. We will cover fullscreen shaders, show you what the depth buffer is, and teach you how to create effects that give you Photoshop-like control over the final rendered image of your game. By utilizing screen effects for your games, you will not only round out your shader writing knowledge, but you will also have the power to create your own incredible real-time renders with Unity from scratch.

In this chapter, we will cover the following recipes:

- Creating a simple fullscreen shader
- Creating a custom fullscreen camera depth effect
- Customizing brightness, saturation, and contrast with a fullscreen shader
- Making Photoshop-like Blend modes with a fullscreen shader
- Enabling and disabling render features with script

Technical requirements

For this chapter, you will need Unity Editor version 6 Preview 6000.0.07f1. This chapter's instructions should work with minimal changes in future versions of the editor in projects that utilize the **Universal Render Pipeline** (**URP**). The chapter's sample project was created using the **Universal 3D Core** template.

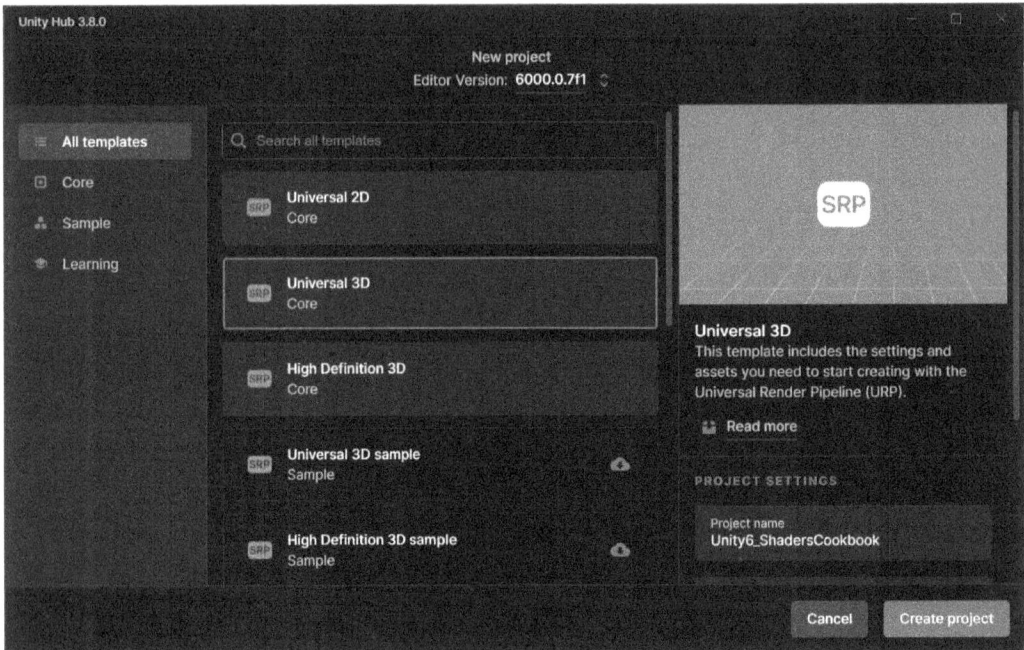

Figure 9.1 – Universal 3D (URP) project

The code files for this chapter can be found on GitHub at `https://github.com/PacktPublishing/Unity-6-Shaders-and-Effects-Cookbook`. The necessary files for this chapter are organized in the Unity project in a folder named `Chapter 09` (`https://github.com/PacktPublishing/Unity-6-Shaders-and-Effects-Cookbook/tree/main/Unity6_ShadersCookbook/Assets/Chapter%20 09`) on GitHub.

Creating a simple fullscreen shader

Creating screen effects involves capturing a fullscreen image (or texture) and processing its pixels using a fullscreen shader on the GPU. The processed result is then sent back to Unity's renderer, where it is applied to the entire game image. Fullscreen shaders allow us to perform real-time, per-pixel operations on the final output, giving us more global artistic control.

For instance, imagine needing to adjust the contrast of your game's appearance by modifying each material on every object—this would be a tedious and time-consuming task. In this recipe, we will explore how fullscreen shaders can address such challenges, simplifying global adjustments to enhance your game's overall look and feel.

With fullscreen shaders, we can apply these adjustments to the entire scene in a single step, offering Photoshop-like control over the game's final visual presentation.

For our first screen effect, we are going to create a very simple grayscale effect and make our game look black and white.

Getting ready

To get our screen effects system up and running, we need to create a few assets for our current Unity project. By doing this, we will set ourselves up for the steps in the following sections.

1. In the current project, create a new scene to work in.

2. Create a simple sphere in the scene and assign it a new material (I called mine RedMat). This new material can be anything, but for our example, we will make a simple red material using the default URP Lit Shader.

3. Finally, create a new directional light if one isn't there already and save the scene.

With all of our assets ready, you should have a simple scene set up that looks similar to this:

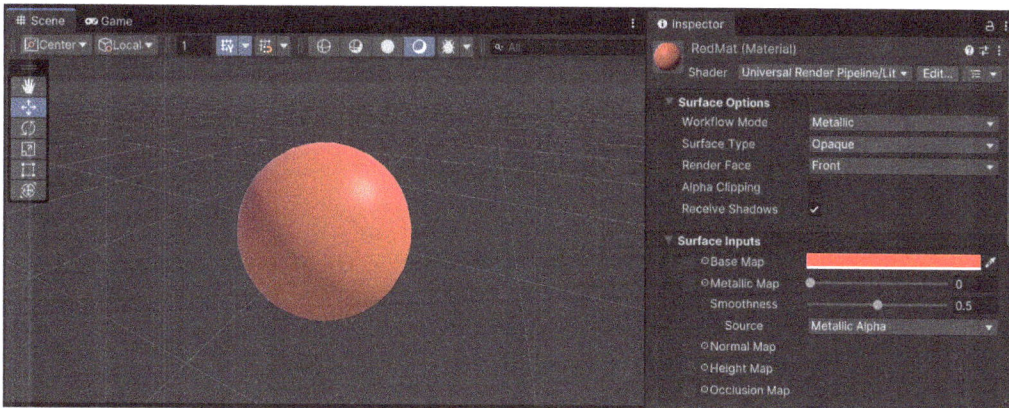

Figure 9.2 – Recipe setup

How to do it...

In order to make our grayscale screen effect work, we need a shader, and we need to add a feature to our renderer to support a fullscreen pass. We will start by creating the default shader and material, activate it, and then add the functionality.

1. Create a fullscreen shader graph by going to the **Project** window, going to your Shaders folder, and right-clicking. From there, select **Create** | **Shader Graph** | **URP** | **Fullscreen Shader Graph**. Give the newly created shader the name of ScreenGrayscale.

2. Just like all of our other shaders, we will need to create a material for it (ScreenGrayscaleMat) and assign our newly created shader to it.

   We now have a shader, but right now we are not actually using this shader in the game, and we will need to enable it within the renderer for the pipeline.

3. From the **Project** window, go to the Assets\Settings folder and select the PC_Renderer object. From there, go to the **Inspector** window, and at the bottom, click on the **Add Renderer Feature** button.

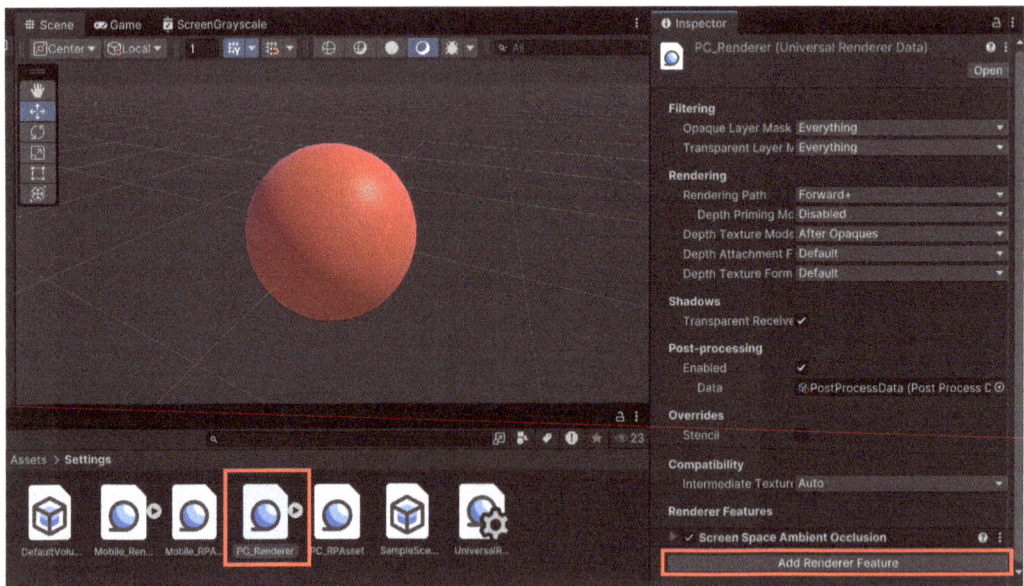

Figure 9.3 – Add Renderer Feature

4. From the menu that pops up, select the **Full Screen Pass Renderer Feature** option. You'll see the screen colors invert because, by default, **Pass Material** is set to `FullscreenInvertColors`.

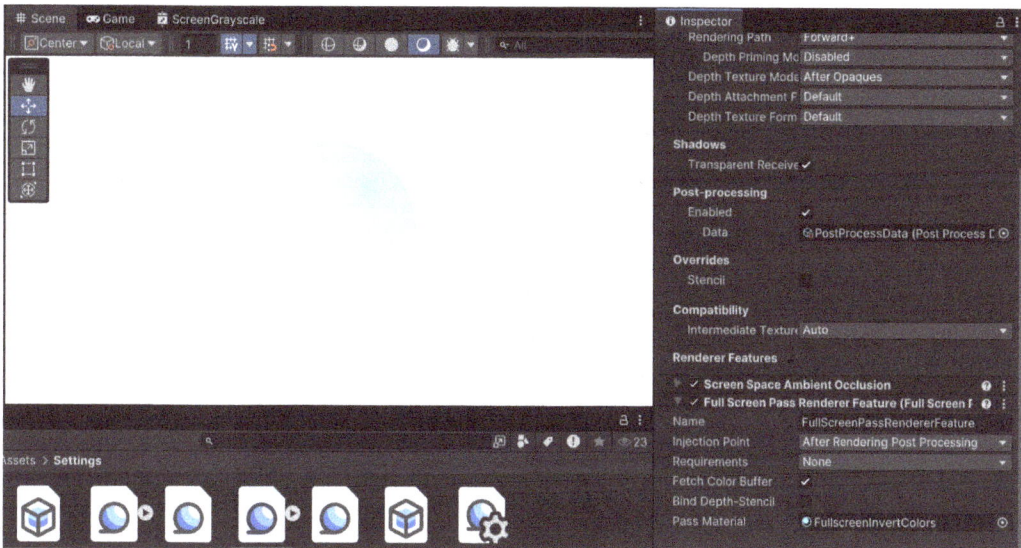

Figure 9.4 – Default Full Screen Renderer Feature

5. Change **Pass Material** to the `ScreenGrayscaleMat` option, and you should see the screen turn gray, which is the default behavior of fullscreen materials:

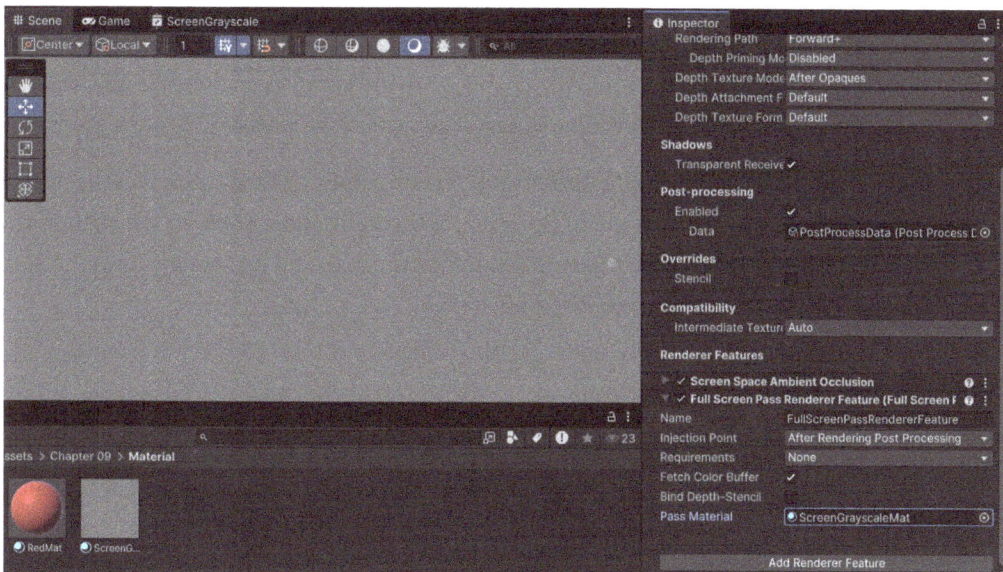

Figure 9.5 – Changing Pass Material

6.   Double-click the **ScreenGrayscale** graph to open it in the Shader Graph editor.

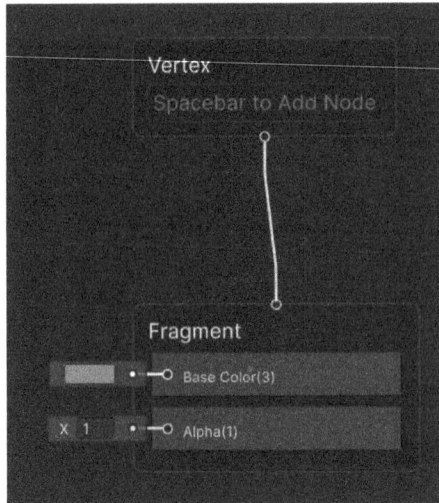

Figure 9.6 – Default fullscreen shader

You'll notice that the shader looks different than our previously created ones with only two nodes by default; the base color being that same gray we currently see in the game.

7.   From the graph, create a **URP Sample Buffer** node. Set **Source Buffer** to **Blit Source**.

If you were to connect **Output** of the **URP Sample Buffer** node to **Base Color** of the **Fragment** section of **Master Stack** right now, you'd see the game as we normally do, but so we can actually tell we are making changes, we are going to make some adjustments and make it so that the game can be in grayscale. That's what we will be doing next.

8.   To the right of the **URP Sample Buffer** node, create a **Split** node and connect the output of the **URP Sample Buffer** node to the input of the **Split** node. Then, to the right of the **Split** node, create three **Multiply** nodes. Connect the **R**, **G**, and **B** channels from the **Split** node to one input of each of the **Multiply** nodes.

9.   For the **R** channel's **Multiply** node, set the other input to 0.299. For the **G** channel's **Multiply** node, set the other input to 0.587. For the **B** channel's **Multiply** node, set the other input to 0.114.

These values represent how bright each color appears to the human eye (a concept called **relative luminance**). Our eyes see green as the brightest (which is why it has the highest value, 0.587), red is less bright (0.299), and blue is the dimmest (0.114). Using these values helps make sure the grayscale effect looks natural, keeping the brightness similar to how we see it in real life.

10. Next, add all these multiplications together to achieve the final grayscale effect. Create an **Add** node and connect the outputs of the red and green **Multiply** nodes to the **A** and **B** inputs of this **Add** node.

11. Then, create another **Add** node. Connect the output of the first **Add** node to the **A** input of this new **Add** node, and connect the output of the blue **Multiply** node to the **B** input.

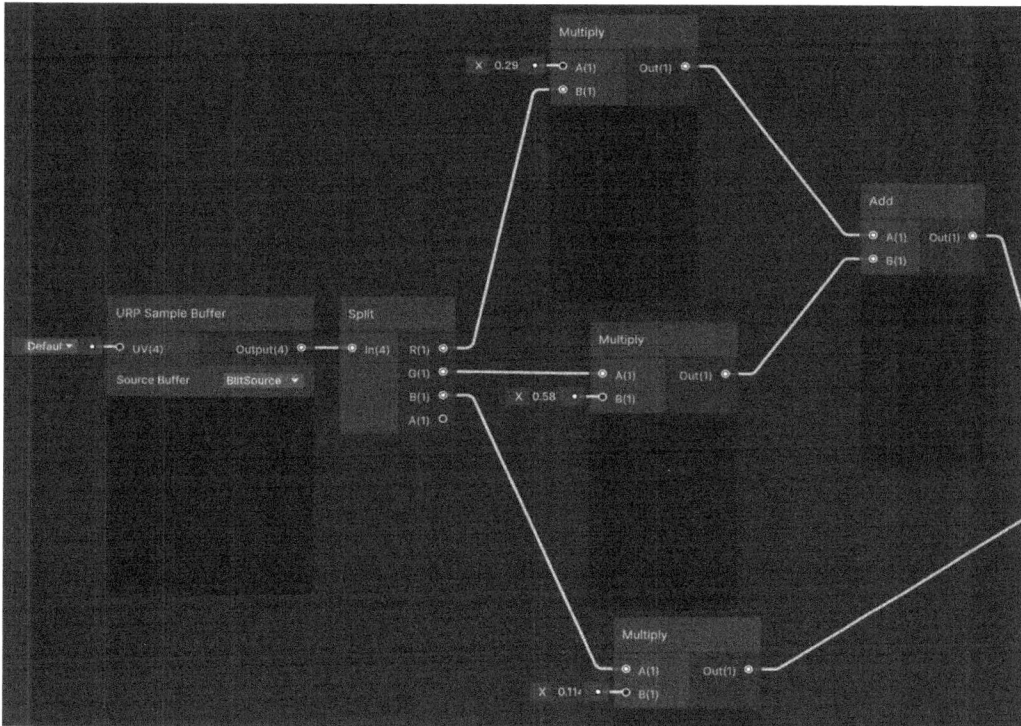

Figure 9.7 – Shader Graph

This setup gives you a grayscale version of your game's visuals. If we were to connect this output directly to **Base Color**, you would see the game in full grayscale. However, we want to create a way to blend between the original colors and the grayscale effect, allowing us to control the amount of grayscale applied. To achieve this, we'll use a **Lerp** node.

12. To the right of the final **Add** node, create a **Lerp** node. Connect the output of the **URP Sample Buffer** node to the **A** input of the **Lerp** node and the output of the final **Add** node (which represents the grayscale effect) to the **B** input. Then, from the **Blackboard**, drag and drop the **Grayscale Amount** variable onto the graph and assign it to the **T** input of the **Lerp** node.

13. Next, take the output of the **Lerp** node and connect it to the **Base Color** input on the **Fragment** section of **Master Stack**. Additionally, connect the **Alpha** channel from the **Split** node to the **Alpha** input on the **Fragment** section of **Master Stack**.

I've moved the **Add** node in the following screenshot to make the layout easier to follow, but feel free to use reroute nodes if you want to keep your graph organized and easy to read while building your version.

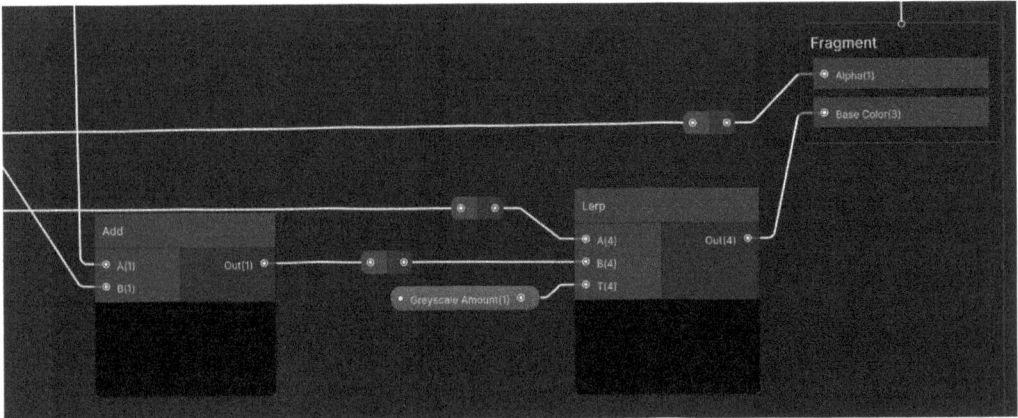

Figure 9.8 – Lerping between grayscale and color screens

Save your Shader Graph and return to the Unity Editor. You should now see your game displayed in grayscale:

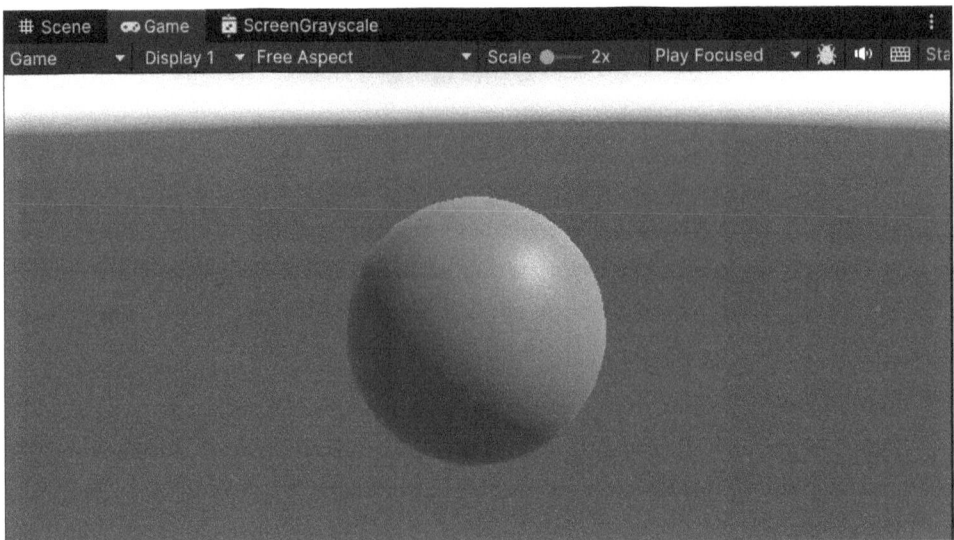

Figure 9.9 – Shader result

If you select your material, you'll also be able to adjust the **Grayscale Amount** slider to control the intensity of the grayscale effect within the game, blending between the original colors and the grayscale version.

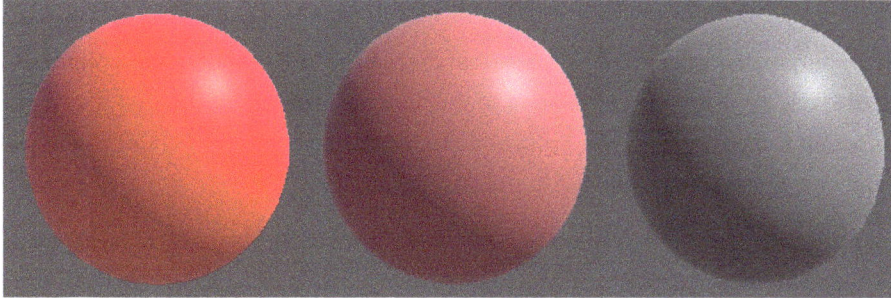

Figure 9.10 – Grayscale amount at 0, 0.5, and 1 (left to right)

Let's dive in a little deeper and learn about what's going on with fullscreen shaders and how they are processed throughout their existence.

How it works...

To create a fullscreen shader in URP, we created a **Fullscreen Shader Graph**. We then needed to integrate the shader into the URP pipeline by adding it to the URP asset in **Project Settings** by adding the custom render pass using **Full Screen Pass Renderer Feature**, ensuring that the fullscreen shader is applied at the correct stage in the rendering process, usually after all other rendering operations are complete.

This shader allows you to apply a grayscale effect to your game while giving you control over the intensity of the effect.

The process begins with the **URP Sample Buffer** node, which captures the scene's color information.

As mentioned previously, the grayscale values are calculated using a weighted sum of the RGB channels of the color image. This approach is based on how the human eye perceives brightness, exhibiting different sensitivities to each color. Human vision is more sensitive to green light than to red or blue, which means the green channel contributes more to the perceived brightness, or luminance, of an image.

To change the weights, this data is split into its **Red**, **Green**, **Blue**, and **Alpha** channels using a **Split** node. The red, blue, and green color channels are then multiplied by specific coefficients. The outputs of these multiplications are then summed together using **Add** nodes, producing the final grayscale version of the image.

To allow dynamic control over the grayscale effect, a **Lerp** node is introduced. This node blends between the original scene color and the grayscale version based on the **Grayscale Amount** variable. By adjusting this variable, you can control how much of the grayscale effect is applied, ranging from no effect (full color) to a complete grayscale.

Finally, the output of the **Lerp** node is connected to the **Base Color** input on the **Fragment** section of **Master Stack**, applying the color blend to the material. The **Alpha** channel is also preserved by connecting it directly from the **Split** node to the **Alpha** input on **Master Stack**, ensuring transparency is maintained if present in the original image.

This setup provides a flexible way to control the grayscale effect in your game, allowing for dynamic adjustments that can enhance gameplay visuals and create unique visual experiences. You can see how powerful this becomes as it gives us Photoshop-like control over the final rendered image of our game. These screen effects work sequentially like Photoshop layers, on top of what the camera sees. When you place these screen effects one after the other, they will be processed in that order.

Creating a custom fullscreen camera depth effect

Now that we have some experience creating a fullscreen shader, let's explore some useful information we can obtain from Unity's renderer. One valuable piece of data is the depth of everything in our current game. By enabling Unity's built-in Screen Depth shader, we can access this depth information. From there, we can create our own custom version to use in our shaders, allowing us to manipulate and visualize depth in creative ways.

In this recipe, we'll build a custom fullscreen shader that captures the depth of objects in the scene and gives us control over how it is displayed. We'll modify this depth information using a **Power** node to adjust its intensity, ultimately creating a flexible tool that can be used for effects such as fog, depth of field, and more.

Getting ready

To start, let's add some objects to our scene to make it easier to see the effect that depth has.

1. Create a scene with three spheres in it and a plane underneath. You can use the same sphere as in the previous recipe and duplicate it if you wish.

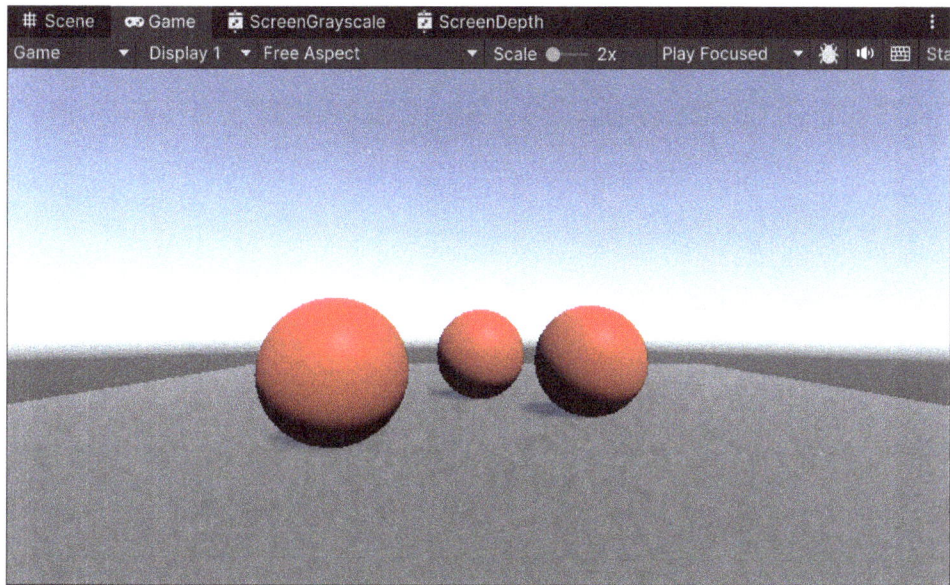

Figure 9.11 – Recipe setup

Now, let's set up a new **Full Screen Pass Renderer Feature** instance to display the new effect:

2. From the **Project** window, go to the Assets/Settings folder and select the PC_Renderer object. From there, go to the **Inspector** window and, at the bottom, click on the **Add Renderer Feature** button. Disable any currently enabled **Full Screen Pass Renderer Feature** instances to prevent conflicts.

3. From the menu that pops up, select the **Full Screen Pass Renderer Feature** option. You'll see the screen colors invert because, by default, **Pass Material** is set to FullscreenInvertColors.

4.   Change **Pass Material** to the ScreenDepth option by searching for it in the selection menu and you should see something similar to the following.

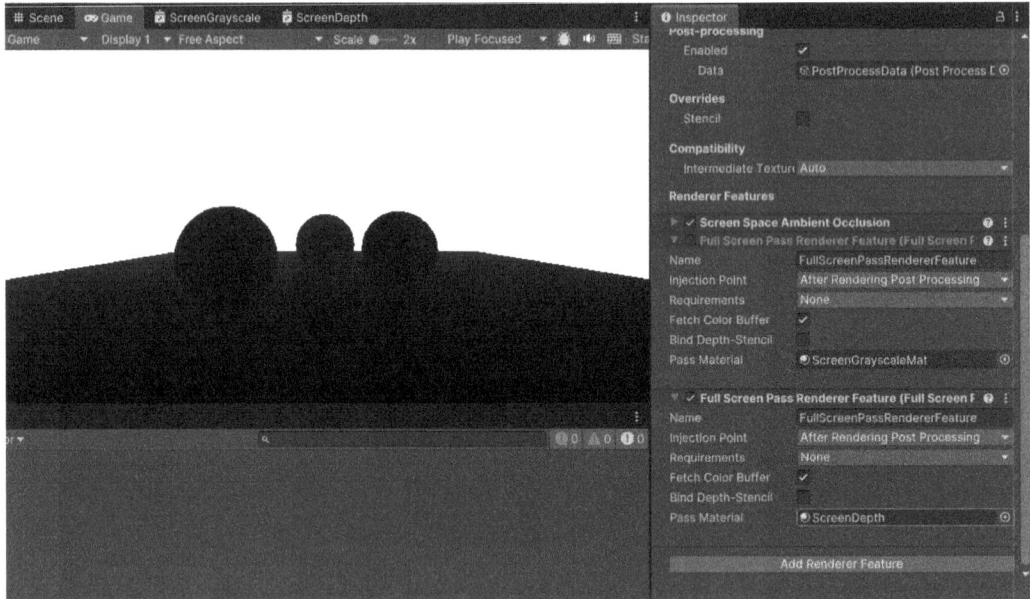

Figure 9.12 – Screen Depth shader

This is good to see, but we can create our own that we can customize and adjust to get more fine-tuned results, is more useful, and can be used for a ton of different effects.

How to do it...

To get started, let's create our new shader.

1.   Create a **Fullscreen Shader Graph** by going to the **Project** window, going to your Shaders folder, and right-clicking. From there, select **Create | Shader Graph | URP | Fullscreen Shader Graph**. Give the newly created shader the name of ScreenDepth.

2.   Just like all of our other shaders, we will need to create a material for it (ScreenDepthMat) and assign our newly created shader to it.

3.   Go back to the PC renderer and change **Pass Material** to the ScreenDepthMat option, and you should see the screen turn gray, which is the default behavior of fullscreen materials.

4. In the Shader Graph, start by creating a new **Float** property on the **Blackboard** named Depth Power. Set the mode to **Slider** with a **Default Value** of 0.2.

5. Next, add a **Scene Depth** node to the graph. To the right of this node, create a **Power** node. Connect the output of the **Scene Depth** node to the **A** input of the **Power** node.

6. Then, drag and drop the **Depth Power** property from the **Blackboard** onto the graph and connect it to the **B** input of the **Power** node. Finally, connect the output of the **Power** node to the **Base Color** input in the **Fragment** section of **Master Stack**.

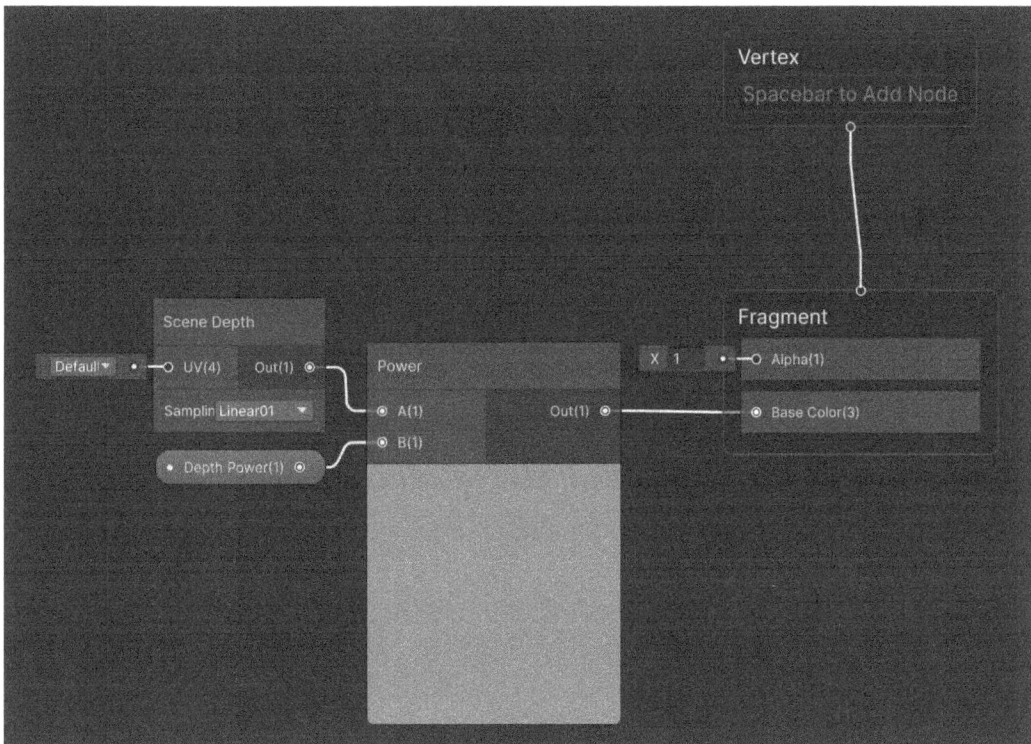

Figure 9.13 – Scene Depth Shader Graph

7. After completing these steps, save your Shader Graph and return to the Unity Editor. You should now be able to see the effects of the shader in your scene.

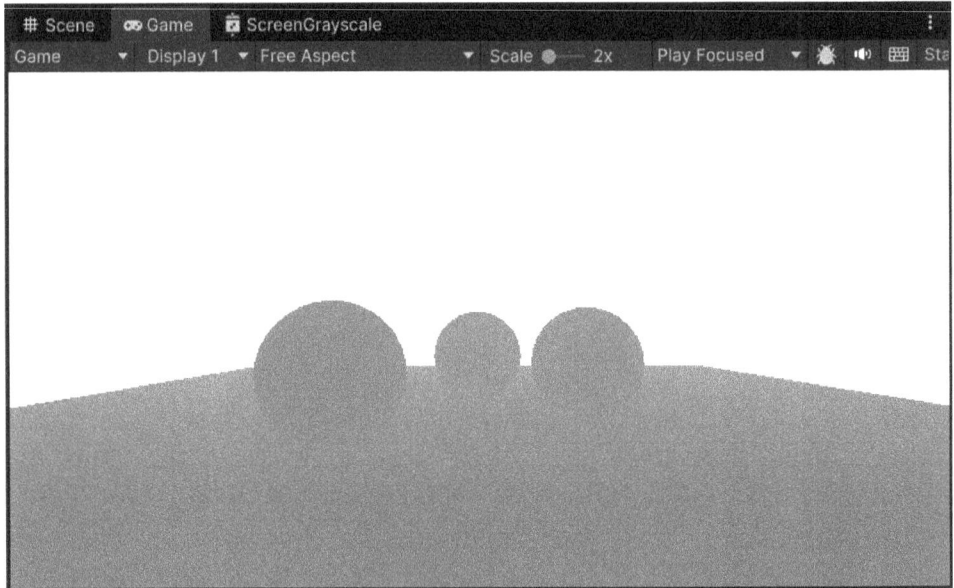

Figure 9.14 – Recipe result

Here's an example of what we can get if we tweak the values even more:

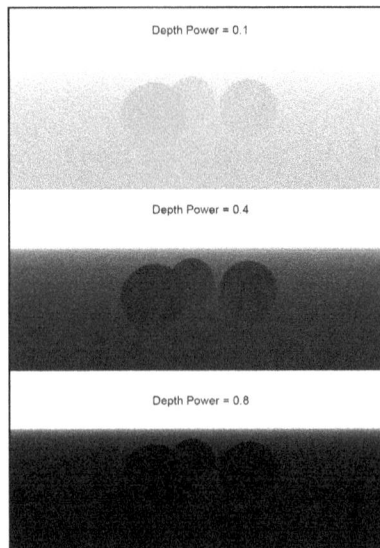

Figure 9.15 – The result with different depth power values

How it works...

The custom shader we create in this tutorial, named ScreenDepth, starts by capturing the scene's depth using the **Scene Depth** node in the Shader Graph. This node provides a grayscale value where closer objects are darker, and farther objects are lighter. We then manipulate this depth data using a **Power** node, which allows us to adjust the depth values non-linearly. The **Depth Power** property, which we expose in the **Blackboard**, controls how intensely the depth effect is applied, making it easy to tweak and experiment with different results.

By connecting the manipulated depth data to the **Base Color** input in the **Fragment** section of **Master Stack** of the shader, we effectively visualize the depth information on the screen. This grayscale visualization is a powerful tool for understanding how depth can be used creatively in various effects such as fog, depth of field, edge detection, heat vision, water depth, and more.

Customizing brightness, saturation, and contrast with a fullscreen shader

Now that we have our screen effects system up and running, we can explore how to create more involved pixel operations to perform some of the more common screen effects found in games today.

Using a screen effect to adjust the overall final colors of your game is crucial in giving artists global control over the final look of the game. Techniques such as color-adjustment sliders allow users to adjust the intensity of the reds, blues, and greens of the final rendered game. This concept is also used with techniques such as putting a certain tone of color over the whole screen, as seen in something such as a sepia film effect.

For this particular recipe, we are going to cover some of the more core color-adjustment operations we can perform on an image. These are brightness, saturation, and contrast. Learning how to make these color adjustments will give us a nice base from which we can learn the art of screen effects.

Getting ready

To get started, we will do some basic setup to have a scene to work with and disable any currently active full screen pass renderer features to avoid confusion with our effect.

1. From the **Project** window, go to the Assets/Settings folder and select the PC_Renderer object. Disable any currently enabled **Full Screen Pass Renderer Feature** instances.

2. Create a new scene by going to **File | New Scene** and use the **Basic (URP)** template.

3. Add a couple of new objects to the scene, set up some different colored diffuse materials, and randomly assign them to the new objects in the scene. This will give us a good range of colors to test with our new screen effect:

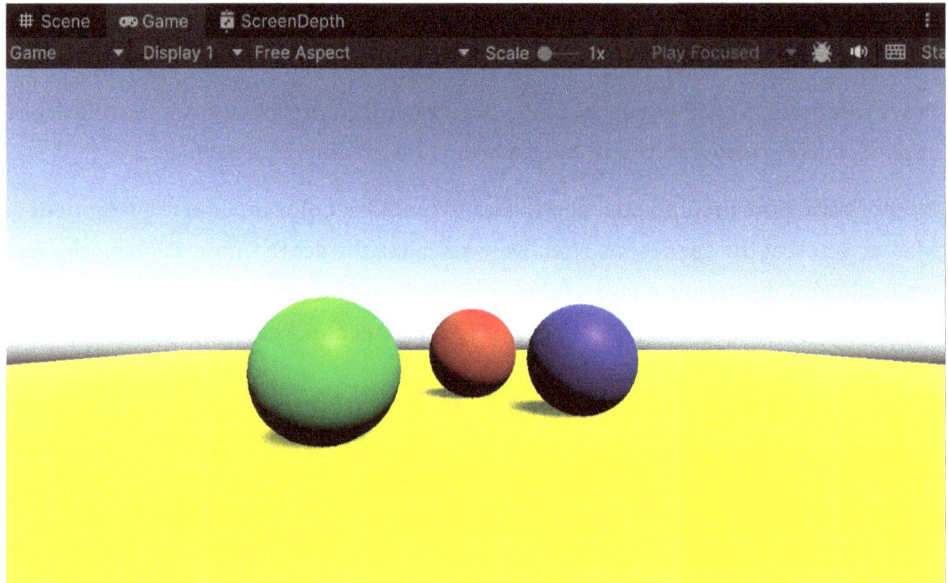

Figure 9.16 – Setup for this recipe

How to do it...

Now that we have completed our scene setup, we need to create our new shader and material:

1. Create a **Fullscreen Shader Graph** by going to the **Project** window, going to your Shaders folder, and right-clicking. From there, select **Create | Shader Graph | URP | Fullscreen Shader Graph**. Give the newly created shader the name of ScreenBSC.

2. Just like all of our other shaders, we will need to create a material for it (ScreenBSCMat) and assign our newly created shader to it.

3. From the **Project** window, go to the Assets/Settings folder and select the PC_Renderer object. From there, go to the **Inspector** window and, at the bottom, click on the **Add Renderer Feature** button.

4. From the menu that pops up, select the **Full Screen Pass Renderer Feature** option. You'll see the screen colors invert because, by default, **Pass Material** is set to FullscreenInvertColors. Change **Pass Material** to the ScreenBSCMat option, and you should see the screen turn gray, which is the default behavior of fullscreen materials.

5. From the **Blackboard**, click on the + button to create a **Float** property and give it a name of Brightness. Change **Mode** to **Slider**. Then change **Min** to 0 and **Max** to 2. Finally, set **Default Value** to 1.

6. Right-click on the **Brightness** variable and select **Duplicate**. Name this new variable Saturation. Then, do that again and create another variable called Contrast, changing **Max** to 3.

7. Finally, create a **Vector 3** property, give it a name of LuminanceCoeff, and set **Default Value** to 0.2135, 0.7154, 0.0721.

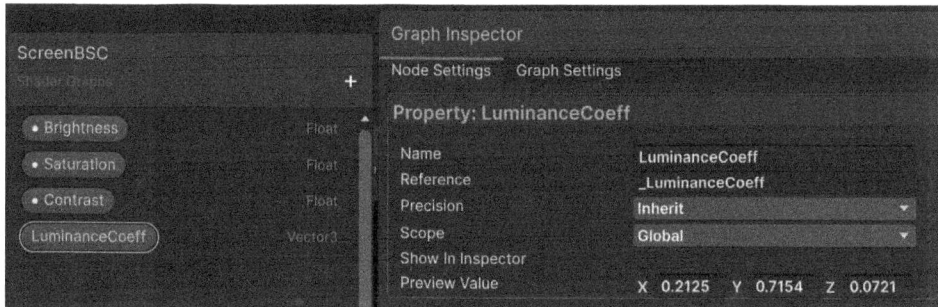

Figure 9.17 – Blackboard properties

Next, we'll focus on retrieving the color information from the screen and then adjusting the brightness.

8. To begin, create a **Scene Color** node in the Shader Graph. This node captures the color data from the entire screen, providing the base color information that we'll manipulate.

9. To adjust the brightness of the screen, add a **Multiply** node to the right of the **Scene Color** node. Connect the output of the **Scene Color** node to the **A** input of the **Multiply** node.

10. Finally, drag and drop the **Brightness** variable from the **Blackboard** onto the graph and connect it to the **B** input of the **Multiply** node.

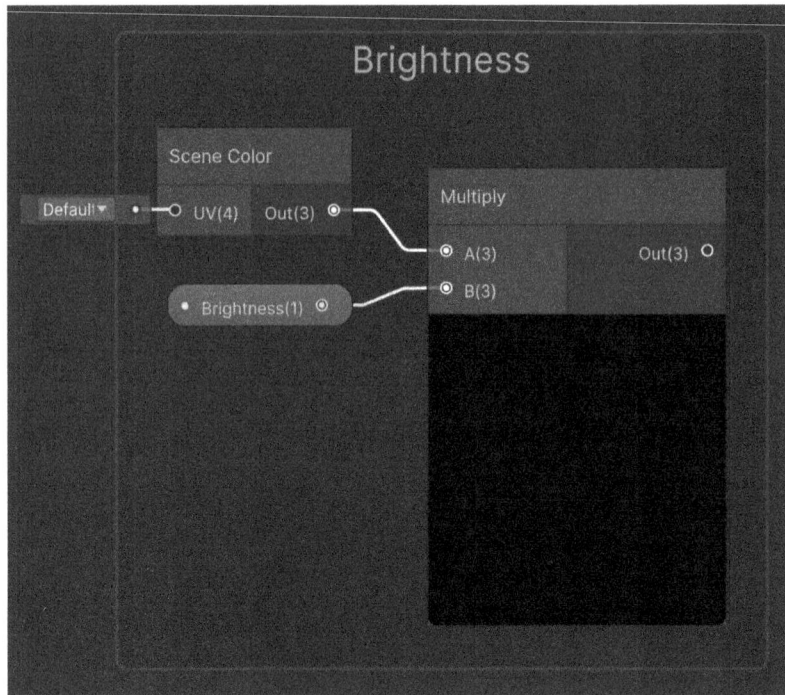

Figure 9.18 – Brightness

Next, we can calculate the saturation adjustment for our shader.

11. To begin, add a **Dot Product** node to the right of the **Multiply** node. Connect the output of the **Multiply** node to the **A** input of the **Dot Product** node.

12. Next, drag and drop the **Luminance Coefficient** variable from the **Blackboard** onto the graph and connect it to the **B** input of the **Dot Product** node.

    The **Luminance Coefficient** property helps in calculating the perceived brightness of the color, which is used to create a grayscale version of the image.

13. To apply the saturation effect, add a **Lerp** node to the right of the **Dot Product** node. Connect the output of the **Dot Product** node to the **A** input of the **Lerp** node, which represents the grayscale version of the color. Then, connect the output of the **Multiply** node (the original color) to the **B** input of the **Lerp** node.

14. Finally, drag and drop the **Saturation** variable from the **Blackboard** onto the graph and connect it to the **T** input of the **Lerp** node.

    This setup allows the shader to adjust the saturation dynamically, blending between the grayscale and the original colors based on the saturation value. If needed, use reroute nodes to keep the graph organized and connections clear.

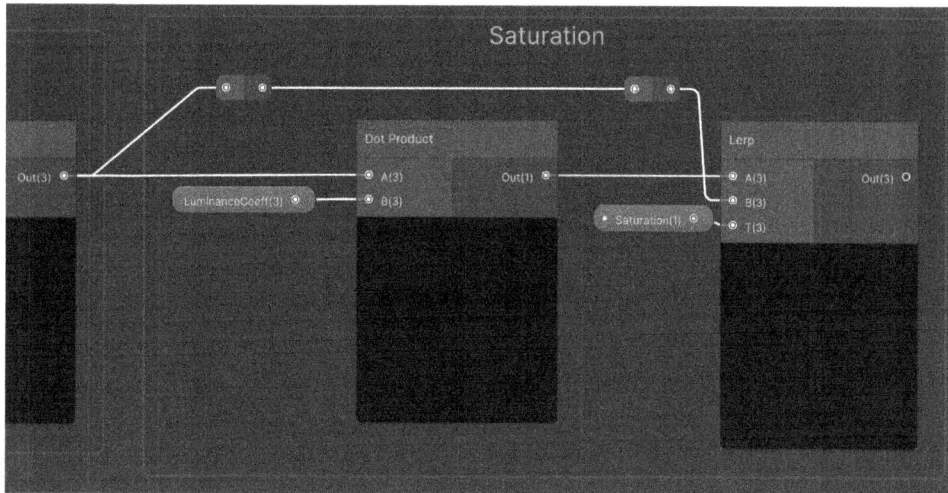

Figure 9.19 – Saturation

Next, we'll perform the contrast adjustment.

15. To do this, start by adding another **Lerp** node to the right of the previous **Lerp** node that handled saturation.

16. For the **B** input of this new **Lerp** node, connect the output of the previous **Lerp** node. In the **A** input, enter a constant value of (0.5, 0.5, 0.5). This represents the midpoint of the color range, which will be used to adjust the contrast.

17. Next, drag and drop the **Contrast** variable from the **Blackboard** onto the graph and connect it to the **T** input of this **Lerp** node.

    This setup allows the shader to dynamically adjust the contrast, blending between the mid-gray value and the output of the previous saturation adjustment.

18. Finally, connect the output of this **Lerp** node to the **Base Color** input of the **Fragment** section in the **Master Stack**.

This will apply the contrast-adjusted colors to the entire screen.

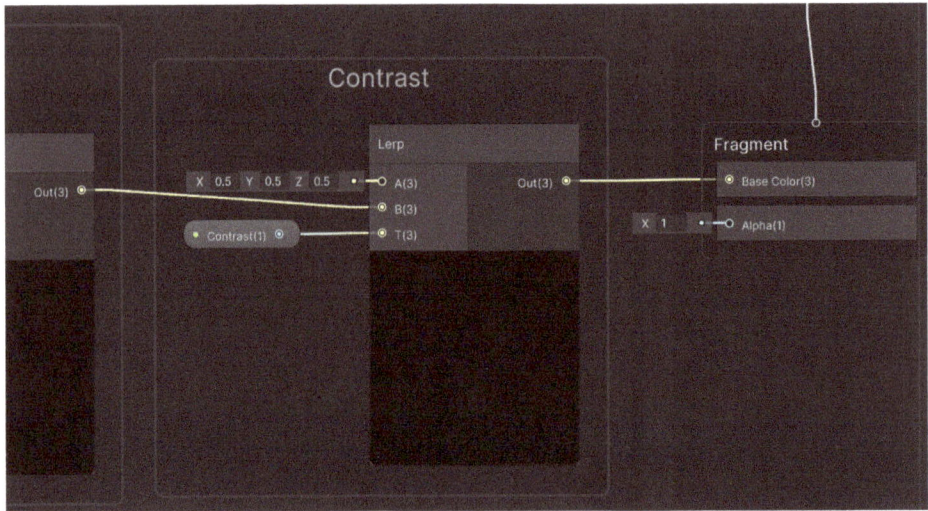

Figure 9.20 – Contrast

Once you've completed these steps, save your Shader Graph and return to the Unity Editor to see the results in your scene of brightness, saturation, and contrast by manipulating the property values to **Brightness** of 0.5, **Saturation** of 2.0, and **Contrast** of 1.75:

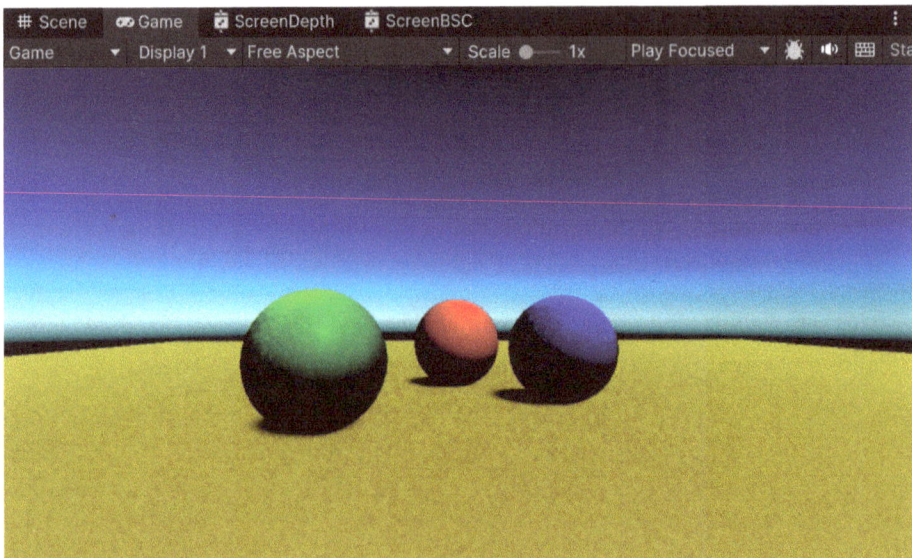

Figure 9.21 – Recipe result

The following screenshot shows another example of what can be achieved by adjusting the colors of the rendered image with **Brightness** of 1.64, **Saturation** of 0, and **Contrast** of 0.57:

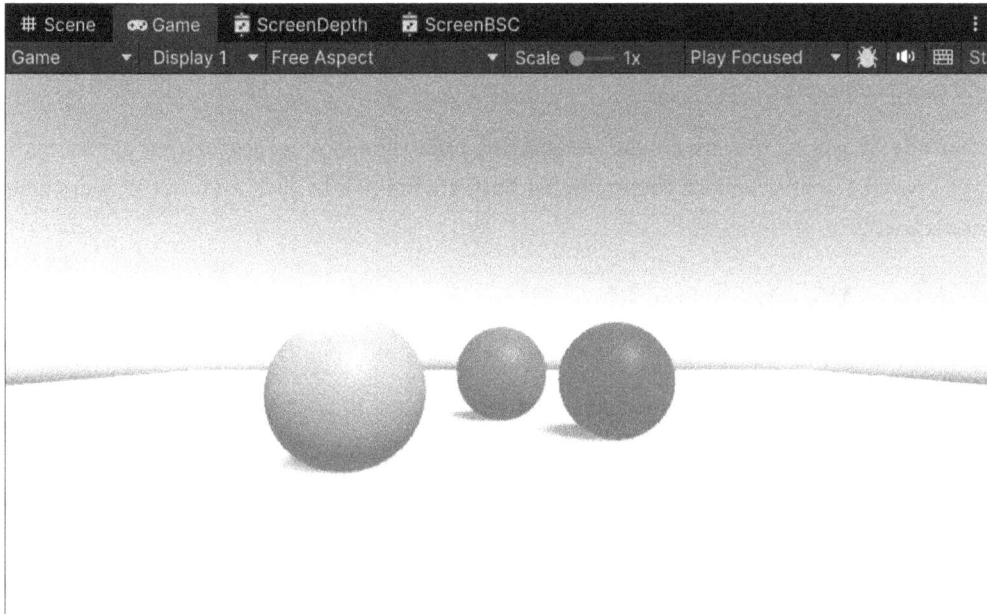

Figure 9.22 – Shader with adjusted values

How it works...

Since we now know how a fullscreen shader works, let's just cover the per-pixel operations we created for this shader. The shader operates by first capturing the color data from the entire screen using the **Scene Color** node. The brightness adjustment is handled by multiplying the captured scene color by a **Brightness** variable. This simple operation either increases or decreases the intensity of all colors, making the scene appear brighter or darker based on the user's input.

Next, the saturation adjustment is calculated. The shader uses a **Dot Product** operation between the scene colors and a predefined **Luminance Coefficient** vector, doing a similar calculation to our *Creating a simple fullscreen shader* recipe in fewer steps. The LuminanceCoeff coefficients are based on the **International Commission on Illumination** (**CIE**) color-matching functions and are pretty standard throughout the industry. This calculation extracts the perceived brightness of the colors, effectively converting them into a grayscale image. A **Lerp** node is then used to blend between this grayscale image and the original colors, with the blend controlled by the **Saturation** variable. This approach allows the saturation to be adjusted dynamically, either desaturating the image to grayscale or enhancing the vibrancy of the colors.

Finally, the contrast adjustment is implemented using another **Lerp** node. This node blends between a neutral gray value (representing no contrast) and the color output from the saturation adjustment. The **Contrast** variable determines the extent of this blend, allowing the shader to dynamically adjust the contrast, making the image appear either flatter (low contrast) or more vivid (high contrast).

Screen effects such as this are crucial to achieving high-quality graphics for your games as they let you tweak the final look of your game without having to edit each material in your current game scene.

Making Photoshop-like Blend modes with a fullscreen shader

The screen effects aren't just limited to adjusting the colors of a rendered image from our game. We can also use them to combine other images with our fullscreen shader. The technique involved is no different than creating a new layer in Photoshop and choosing a **Blend mode** to blend two images together—or, in our case, a texture on a material. This becomes a very powerful technique as it gives the artists in a production environment a way to simulate their blending modes in the game rather than just in Photoshop.

For this particular recipe, we are going to take a look at some of the more common Blend modes, such as **Multiply**, **Add**, and **Overlay**. You will see how simple it is to have the power of Photoshop Blend modes in your game.

Getting ready

To begin, we have to get our assets ready. So, let's follow the next few steps to get our screen effects system up and running for our new Blend mode screen effect:

We will need another texture to perform our **Blend mode** effect. In this recipe, we will use a grunge-type texture. This will make the effect very obvious when we are testing it out.

The following screenshot shows the grunge map used in the making of this effect. Finding a texture with enough detail and a nice range of grayscale values will make for a nice texture to test our new effect:

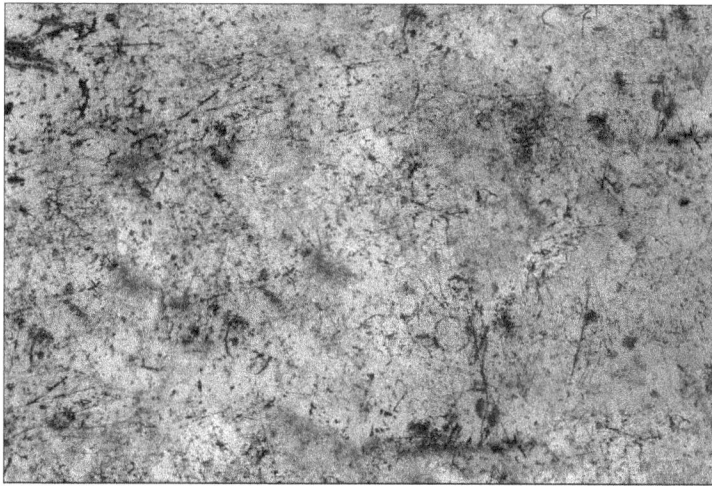

Figure 9.23 – The grunge map used in this recipe

Note

The preceding texture is available in the example code for this book in the `Chapter 09/Textures` folder.

We will also do some basic setup to have a scene to work with and disable any currently active full screen pass renderer features to avoid confusion with our effect.

1. From the **Project** window, go to the `Assets/Settings` folder and select the `PC_Renderer` object. Disable any currently enabled **Full Screen Pass Renderer Feature** instances.

2. Reuse the scene from the previous recipe or create a new scene by going to **File | New Scene** and use the **Basic (URP)** template.

   If using a new scene, add a couple of new objects to the scene, set up some different colored diffuse materials, and randomly assign them to the new objects in the scene. This will give us a good range of colors to test with our new screen effect:

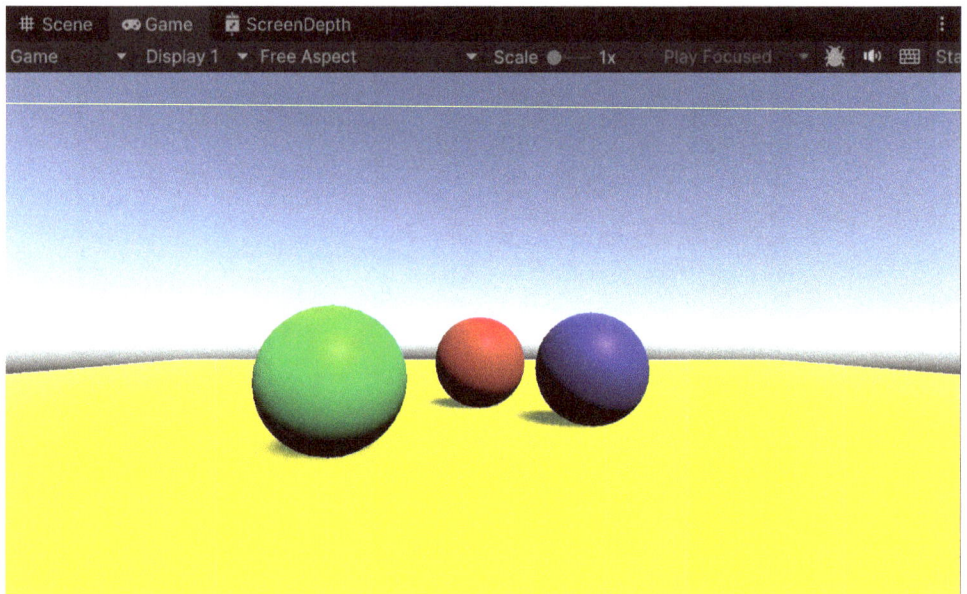

Figure 9.24 – Setup for this recipe

How to do it...

Now that we have completed our scene setup, we need to create our new shader and material:

1. Create a **Fullscreen Shader Graph** by going to the **Project** window, going to your Shaders folder, and right-clicking. From there, select **Create | Shader Graph | URP | Fullscreen Shader Graph**. Give the newly created shader the name of ScreenBlendMode.

2. Just like all of our other shaders, we will need to create a material for it (ScreenBlendModeMat) and assign our newly created shader to it.

3. From the **Project** window, go to the Assets/Settings folder and select the PC_Renderer object. From there, go to the **Inspector** window and, at the bottom, click on the **Add Renderer Feature** button.

4. From the menu that pops up, select the **Full Screen Pass Renderer Feature** option. You'll see the screen colors invert because, by default, **Pass Material** is set to FullscreenInvertColors. Change **Pass Material** to the ScreenBlendModeMat option, and you should see the screen turn gray, which is the default behavior of fullscreen materials.

5. From the **Blackboard**, click on the + button to create a **Float** property and give it the name Opacity. Change **Mode** to **Slider**. Then change **Min** to 0 and **Max** to 2. Finally, set **Default Value** to 1.

6. Finally, create a **Texture2D**property , give it the name Blend Texture, and set **Default Value** to the grunge texture you'd like to use (I'm using Assets/Chapter 09/Textures/ grunge_gray_12.jpg).

Now we can start building the shader properly.

7. Begin by creating a **Scene Color** node in the Shader Graph, which captures the color information from the entire screen. To the right of the **Scene Color** node, add a **Blend** node. Connect the output of the **Scene Color** node to the **Base** input of the **Blend** node.

8. Next, drag and drop **Blend Texture** from the **Blackboard** onto the graph, placing it below the **Scene Color** node. To the right of **Blend Texture**, create a **Sample Texture 2D** node and connect **Blend Texture** to the **Texture** input of this node. Then, connect the **RGBA** output of the **Sample Texture 2D** node to the **Blend** input of the **Blend** node.

9. Back in the **Blackboard**, drag and drop the **Opacity** variable onto the graph and connect it to the **Opacity** input of the **Blend** node. Set **Mode** of the **Blend** node to **Multiply** to start. Finally, connect the output of the **Blend** node to the **Base Color** input of the **Fragment** section in the **Master Stack**.

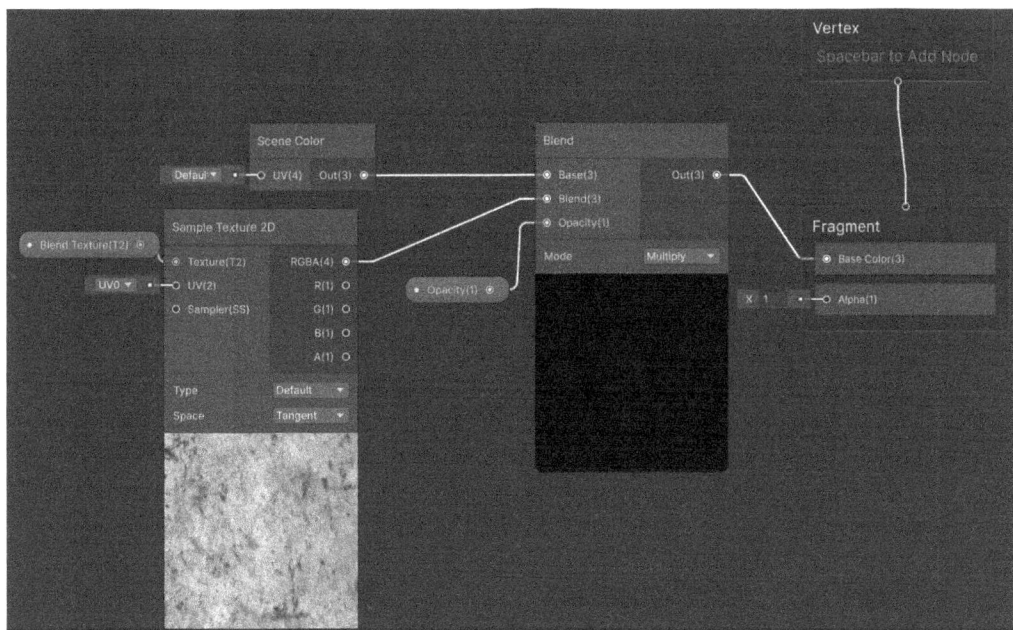

Figure 9.25 – Blend Shader Graph

Once you've made these connections, save your Shader Graph and return to the Unity Editor to see the results of your shader in action. You can assign any texture to the **Texture** field in the **Inspector** tab for the screen effects script. Once this texture is in place, you will see the effect of multiplying this texture over the game's rendered screenshot:

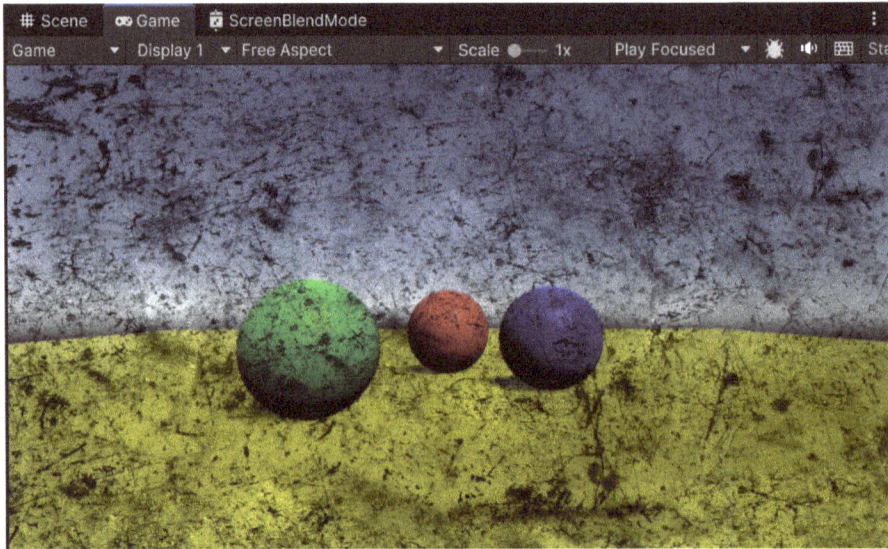

Figure 9.26 – Recipe result

The following screenshot demonstrates the screen effect with a lower Blend **Opacity** value (0.5):

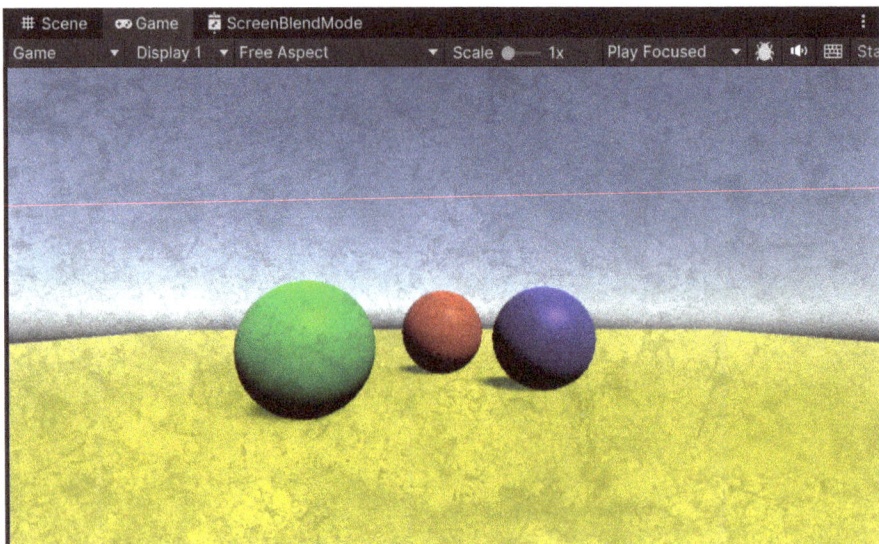

Figure 9.27 – Lower opacity example

With our first Blend mode set up, we can begin to add a couple of simpler Blend modes to get a better understanding of how easy it is to add more effects and really fine-tune the final result in your game. However, let's first break down what is happening here.

How it works...

With the creation of this fullscreen shader, we are beginning to unlock significant power and flexibility in our screen effects programming within Unity. This system allows us to replicate the effects of Photoshop layer-blending modes directly in our game, providing artists with the tools they need to achieve high-quality graphics quickly and efficiently.

In this shader, we utilize the **Blend** node, a powerful tool that allows you to combine two images or color inputs using various blending modes. Similar to the blending options found in image editing software such as Photoshop, the **Blend** node provides a range of operations that determine how one image (or color) interacts with another when layered together. This flexibility is crucial for creating complex visual effects in games, such as overlays, lighting effects, and texture combinations, all of which contribute to the overall aesthetic and mood of the scene.

The **Blend** node offers several modes, including **Multiply**, **Add**, **Screen**, **Overlay**, and others. When working with the **Blend** node, it's crucial to think on a per-pixel level. For instance, with the **Multiply** blend mode (which is the mode we are using in the preceding recipe), each pixel from the original screen render (captured by the **Scene Color** node) is multiplied by the corresponding pixel from the **Blend Texture** property. This simple mathematical operation darkens the image, creating a rich, moody effect. On the other hand, the **Screen** mode brightens the image by inverting, multiplying, and then inverting again. The node also allows you to control the opacity of the blend, giving you the ability to adjust the intensity of the effect. In our case, the opacity of this effect is controlled by an **Opacity** variable, allowing for dynamic adjustments that can be fine-tuned in real time.

As you continue to experiment with different blend modes, you'll see just how powerful this system can be. It offers an incredible level of control, enabling artists to push the visual boundaries of their games and achieve stunning results with relatively simple mathematical operations.

There's more...

Let's continue this recipe by seeing how a couple more Blend modes work:

- **Lighten**: Back in the Shader Graph, change the **Blend** node's **Mode** to **Lighten**, save it, and return to the Unity Editor:

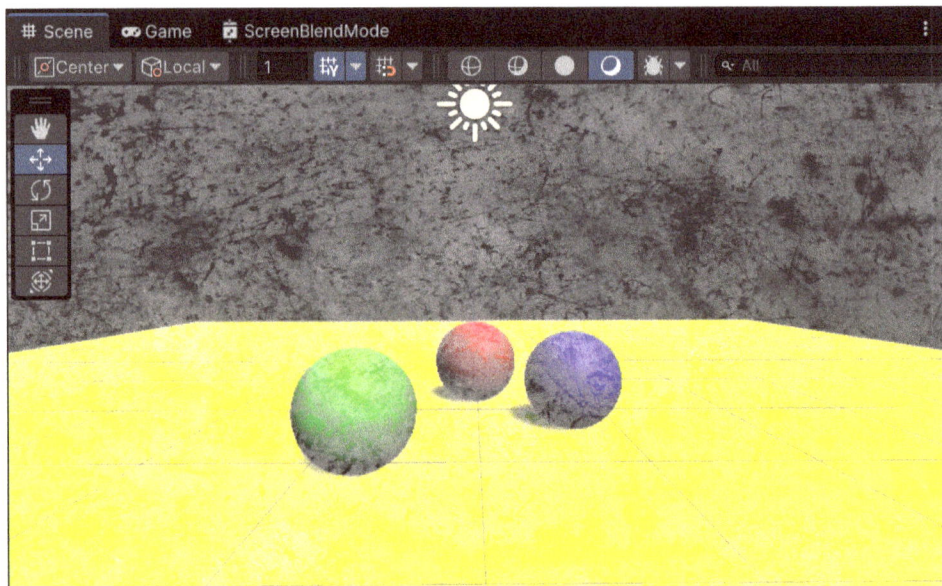

Figure 9.28 – Lighten

As you can see, this has the opposite effect of multiplying because we are adding the two images together.

Next, let's see one more mode, called **Screen**. This one is a little bit more involved from a mathematical standpoint but is still simple to implement.

- **Screen**: Back in the Shader Graph, change the **Blend** node's **Mode** to **Screen**, save it, and return to the Unity Editor.

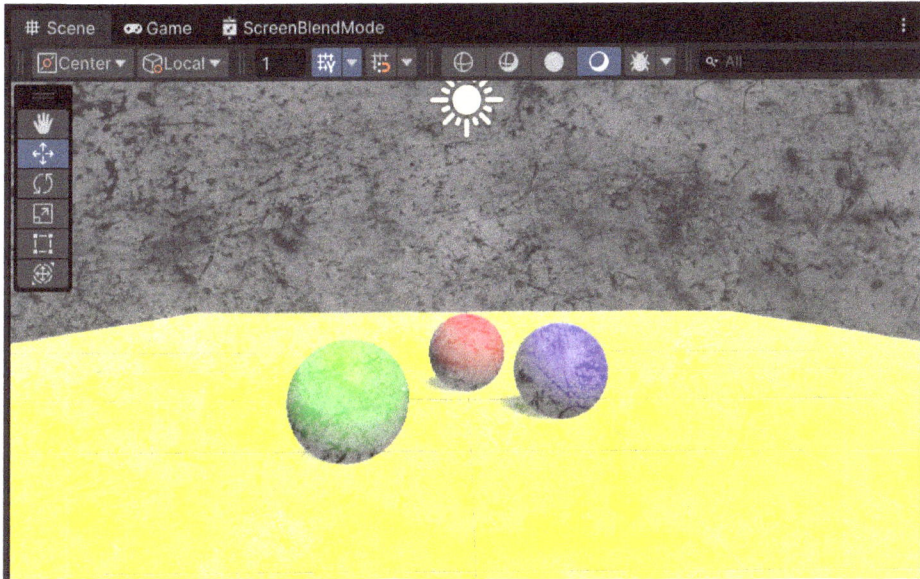

Figure 9.29 – Screen

In the case of the **Screen** blend mode, the process is a bit more involved. Here, both the original image and the blend texture are inverted, multiplied together, and then inverted again to produce the final effect. This process brightens the image, creating a soft, glowing appearance that is often used for highlights and glow effects. Just as Photoshop blends its layers using similar mathematical operations, we can replicate those same effects in our game through this shader as simply as changing the **Mode** we'd like to use.

- **Overlay**: Finally, let's look at the **Overlay** blend mode. Back in the Shader Graph, change the **Blend** node's **Mode** to **Overlay**, save it, and return to the Unity Editor. Back in **Material**, increase **Opacity** to 1.

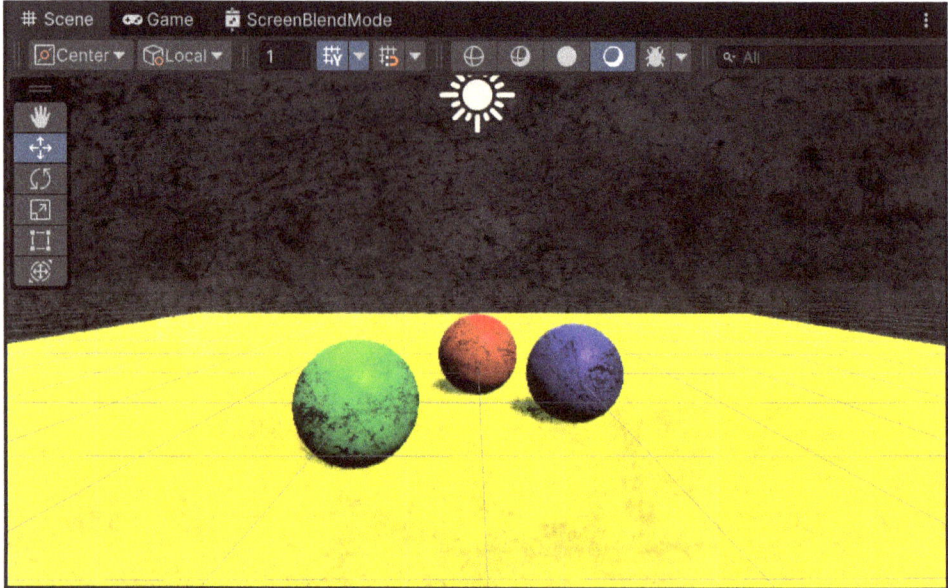

Figure 9.30 – Overlay

The **Overlay** blend mode is commonly used in shaders to mix two images or colors in a way that preserves both the highlights and shadows of the base layer. The **Overlay** blend mode is essentially a combination of the **Multiply** and **Screen** blend modes we saw earlier, which allows for a more dynamic blending effect that adjusts based on the brightness of the base color. The darker parts of the image use the **Multiply** effect to deepen shadows, while the lighter parts use the **Screen** effect to maintain highlights. The final color is then adjusted according to the specified opacity, providing control over the intensity of the overlay effect.

The Shader Graph manual for the **Blend** node includes all of the generated code for each of the different modes in case you are interested in the computations required to achieve the result: `https://docs.unity3d.com/Packages/com.unity.shadergraph@17.0/manual/Blend-Node. html`.

As you can see, many things can be done with screen effects. It really just depends on the platform and the amount of memory you have allocated for screen effects. Usually, this is determined throughout the course of a game project, so have fun and get creative with your screen effects!

Enabling and disabling render features with script

While it's fantastic to have the ability to use fullscreen shaders, it's equally important to be able to toggle them on and off as needed. This functionality is particularly useful when exploring and testing the various example recipes provided in the book. Being able to enable and disable these shaders allows you to better understand their effects and see the results of each recipe in action. In this recipe, we'll explore an example of how to implement a system that allows you to easily toggle fullscreen shaders when you enter a scene in the editor, giving you greater flexibility and control over your visual effects.

Getting ready

To start, ensure that you have completed at least one of the previous recipes in this chapter. This is necessary because you need to have a **Full Screen Pass Renderer** already set up and functioning. Additionally, it's crucial to disable all currently active **Full Screen Pass Renderer Feature** instances as we will now be controlling their activation and deactivation through code.

How to do it...

To get started, we need to create a script that will manage the feature we want to use. This script will allow us to control the fullscreen shader or other effects in our scene.

1. Begin by navigating to the **Project** window. If you haven't done so already, create a new folder within the Chapter 09 folder, and name it Scripts.

2. Next, right-click within the Scripts folder and select **Create | MonoBehaviour Script**. When prompted, name the script SceneFeature. After creating the script, double-click on it to open it in your preferred code editor, and use the following code:

```
using UnityEngine;
using UnityEngine.Rendering.Universal;

public class SceneFeature : MonoBehaviour
{
    public ScriptableRendererFeature feature;
}
```

3. Once you've finished writing the script, save it, and return to the Unity Editor.

4. Next, create a blank, empty GameObject in your scene by navigating to **GameObject |
    Create Empty**. Rename this GameObject to something descriptive, such as Scene Feature.
    Attach the **SceneFeature** component that you just created to this GameObject by dragging
    and dropping the script onto the object in the **Hierarchy** window.

5. In the **Inspector**, you'll see the **Feature** property of the **SceneFeature** component. Assign
    this property to the feature that you want to be enabled when this scene is active. Repeat
    this process for all the scenes where you want a specific feature to be enabled.

Now that this is set up, the next step is to create a script that will handle enabling or disabling
the feature when you enter or exit a scene.

1. To do this, return to your Chapter 09 folder in the **Project** window. Create a new folder
    called Editor. Inside this folder, create another MonoBehaviour script, and name it
    ToggleRendererFeature.

2. After naming the script, double-click on it to open it in your preferred code editor.

    You can then proceed to write the code that will manage the enabling and disabling of
    the renderer feature as you transition between scenes:

    ```
    using UnityEditor;
    using UnityEditor.SceneManagement;
    using UnityEngine;
    using UnityEngine.Rendering.Universal;
    using UnityEngine.SceneManagement;

    /// <summary>
    /// Automatically toggles a ScriptableRendererFeature when
    /// switching scenes in the Unity Editor.
    /// </summary>
    [InitializeOnLoad]
    public static class ToggleRendererFeature
    {
        /// <summary>
        /// Stores the reference to the renderer feature
        /// from the previous scene.
        /// </summary>
    ```

```
static ScriptableRendererFeature oldFeature;

/// <summary>
/// Static constructor subscribes to the
/// scene change event in edit mode.
/// </summary>
static ToggleRendererFeature()
{
    EditorSceneManager.activeSceneChangedInEditMode +=
        OnActiveSceneChanged;
}


/// <summary>
/// Called when the active scene is changed in edit mode.
/// </summary>
/// <param name="oldScene">The previous active scene.</param>
/// <param name="newScene">The new active scene.</param>
private static void OnActiveSceneChanged(Scene oldScene,
                                         Scene newScene)
{
    // Disable the renderer feature from the old scene
    if (oldFeature != null)
    {
        oldFeature.SetActive(false);
        oldFeature = null;
    }

    // Find the target component in the new scene
    var targetComponent = GameObject
        .FindAnyObjectByType<SceneFeature>();

    if (targetComponent != null)
    {
        // Enable the renderer feature in the new scene
        targetComponent.feature.SetActive(true);
```

```
                    // Store the reference to disable it later
                    oldFeature = targetComponent.feature;
            }
        }
    }
```

This script will ensure that the correct features are active based on the scene you're currently in.

3. Save your script and return to the Unity Editor.

As you navigate between scenes, you should notice that the script successfully enables the feature associated with the scene you're entering. When you leave that scene, the script will automatically disable the feature, and enable the appropriate feature for the next scene. This ensures that the correct visual or functional feature is active based on the scene you're currently in, providing a seamless transition and consistent experience across your project.

How it works...

In this recipe, we implemented a system that allows you to toggle fullscreen shaders or other features on and off as you navigate between scenes in Unity. This functionality is particularly useful when you need to test and explore various visual effects or screen shaders, ensuring that each scene in your project only activates the relevant features. By doing so, you gain greater flexibility and control over the visual presentation of your game, making it easier to manage and fine-tune the effects you've implemented.

The process begins with the creation of a SceneFeature script, which serves as a container for the specific renderer feature you want to enable in each scene. By attaching this script to an empty GameObject in your scene, you can assign the desired renderer feature via the **Inspector**. This setup allows each scene to have its own unique feature that will be enabled when the scene is active.

To manage the activation and deactivation of these features as you transition between scenes, we created a second script called ToggleRendererFeature. This script is designed to work in the Unity Editor and is automatically triggered whenever the active scene changes. It listens for scene changes and ensures that the renderer feature from the previous scene is disabled while enabling the feature assigned to the new scene.

The key to this system is the EditorSceneManager.OnActiveSceneChanged method, which handles the toggling of features. When a new scene becomes active, the script first disables the feature from the previous scene. It then looks for the SceneFeature component in the new scene, enabling its associated renderer feature. This ensures that only the relevant feature is active at any given time, maintaining a clean and organized workflow as you develop your project.

> Note
>
> I used the EditorSceneManager since we are working in the editor. If you wanted to switch between features at runtime within a game, you would use the SceneManager class instead and subscribe to the SceneManager.sceneLoaded method to handle scene changes dynamically.

By saving the script and testing it in Unity, you'll see that the system works seamlessly: as you move from one scene to another, the appropriate features are automatically enabled and disabled. This approach not only helps in testing and debugging but also contributes to optimizing the game's performance by ensuring that unnecessary effects are not active when they aren't needed. Overall, this method provides a robust way to manage visual effects across multiple scenes, giving you precise control over the look and feel of your game.

Join our community on Discord

Join our community's Discord space for discussions with the authors and other readers:

`https://packt.link/gamedevelopment`

10

Gameplay and Screen Effects

When it comes to creating believable and immersive games, material design is not the only aspect we need to take into account. The overall feeling of a game can be altered using screen effects. This is very common in movies, for instance, when colors are corrected in the post-production phase. You can implement these techniques in your games, too, using the knowledge from *Chapter 9, Creating Screen Effects with Fullscreen Shaders*. Two interesting effects are presented in this chapter; you can, however, adapt them to fit your needs and create your very own screen effects.

If you are reading this book, you are most likely a person who has played a game or two in your time. One of the features of real-time games is the effect of immersing a player in a world to make it feel as if they are actually playing in the real world. Modern games make heavy use of screen effects to achieve this immersion.

With screen effects, we can turn the mood of a certain environment from calm to scary, just by changing the look of the screen. Imagine walking into a room that is contained within a level; then, the game takes over and goes into a cinematic clip. Many modern games will turn on different screen effects to change the mood of a scene. Understanding how to create effects triggered by gameplay is next in our journey through shader writing.

In this chapter, we are going to take a look at some of the more common gameplay screen effects. You are going to learn how to change the look of a game from normal to an old movie effect, and we are going to take a look at how many first-person shooter (FPS) games apply night vision effects to the screen. In each of these recipes, we are going to look at how to hook these effects up to game events so that they are turned on and off as the game requires.

In this chapter, we will be covering the following recipes:

- Creating an old movie screen effect
- Creating a night vision screen effect

Technical requirements

For this chapter, you will need Unity Editor version 6 Preview 6000.0.07f1. This chapter's instructions should work with minimal changes in future versions of the editor in projects that utilize the Universal Render Pipeline (URP). The chapter's sample project was created using the **Universal 3D Core** template.

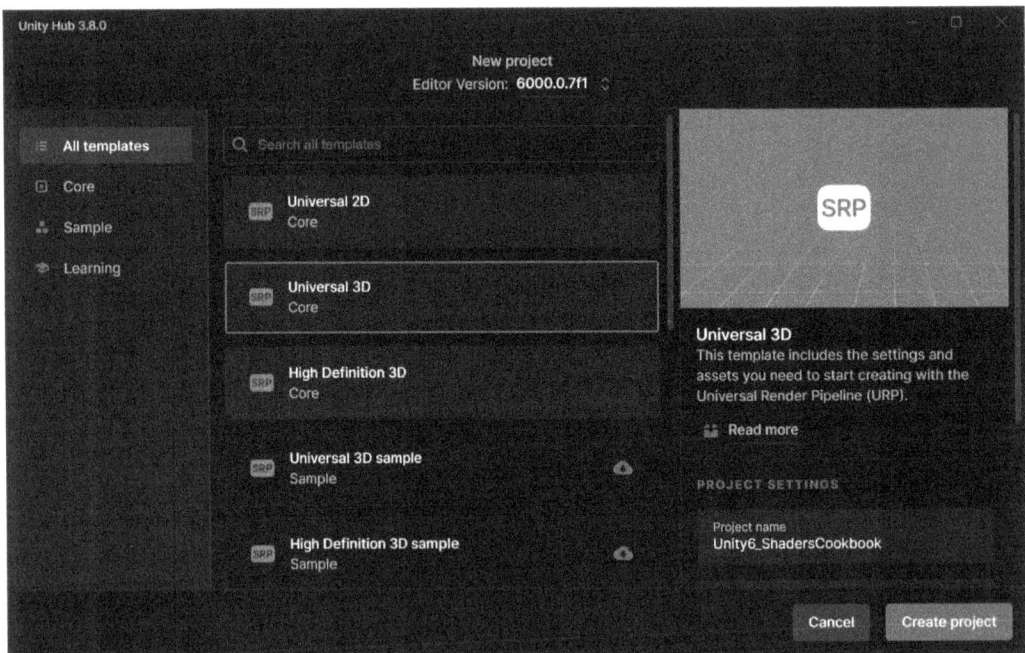

Figure 10.1 – Universal URP project

The code files for this chapter can be found on GitHub at https://github.com/PacktPublishing/Unity-6-Shaders-and-Effects-Cookbook. The necessary files for this chapter are organized in the Unity project in a folder named Chapter 10 (https://github.com/PacktPublishing/Unity-6-Shaders-and-Effects-Cookbook/tree/main/Unity6_ShadersCookbook/Assets/Chapter%20 10) on GitHub.

Creating an old movie screen effect

Games are set in many different times and places. Some take place in fantasy worlds or future sci-fi worlds, and some even take place in the Old West, where film cameras were just being developed and the movies that people watched were black and white or sometimes tinted with what is called a sepia effect. The old movie screen look is very distinct, and we are going to replicate this look using a screen effect in Unity.

There are a few steps to achieving this look. To make the whole screen black and white or grayscale, we need to break down this effect into its component parts. If we analyze some reference footage of an old movie, we can begin to do this. Before starting this recipe, I put together an example capturing the aesthetic that we will be going for:

Figure 10.2 – A demonstration of an old movie look

I constructed this screenshot using a few reference images found online. When designing visual effects, it's helpful to prototype them in an image editor such as Photoshop. This allows us to experiment with blending modes, layer composition, and color adjustments before implementing them in a shader. By doing this, we can better plan our approach and understand how different elements combine to create the final effect.

Getting ready

Now that we know what we have to make, let's take a look at how the layers are combined to create the final effect and gather some resources for our shader and screen-effects script:

- **Sepia tone**: This is a relatively simple effect to achieve because we just need to bring all the pixel colors of the original render texture into a single-color range. This is easily achieved using the luminance of the original image and adding a constant color. Our first layer will look like this:

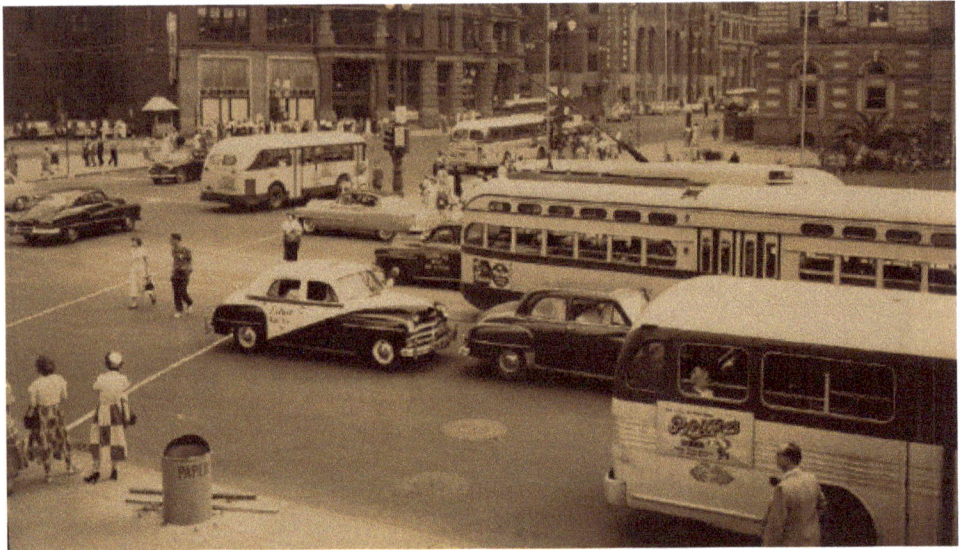

Figure 10.3 – Original image with added color

- **Vignette effect**: We can always see some sort of soft border around old films when they are being projected using an old movie projector. This is because the bulb that is used for the movie projector has more brightness in the middle than it does at the edges of the film. This effect is generally called a vignette effect and is the second layer in our screen effect. We can achieve this with a texture overlaid over the whole screen. The following screenshot demonstrates what this layer looks like, isolated as a texture:

Figure 10.4 – Vignette texture

- **Dust and scratches**: The third and final layer in our old movie screen effect is dust and scratches. This layer will utilize two different tiled textures— one for scratches and one for dust. The reason is that we will want to animate these two textures over time at different tiling rates. This will give the effect that the film is moving along and there are small scratches and dust on each frame of the old film. The following screenshot demonstrates this effect isolated to its own texture:

Figure 10.5 – Dust and scratches texture

Let's get our screen-effects system ready with the preceding textures. Perform the following steps:

1. Gather textures for the vignette (`OldFilmVignette`), dust (`OldFilmDust`), and scratches (`OldFilmScratches`) aspect of the effect. If you'd like to use the ones I am using, you can find them in the `Assets/Chapter 10/Textures` folder in the example code for the book.

2. We will also need a scene for which we want to emulate the effect we're trying to build. I have created a sample scene, which you can use, in the `Chapter 10/Scenes` folder of the example code called `10.1 Starting Point`:

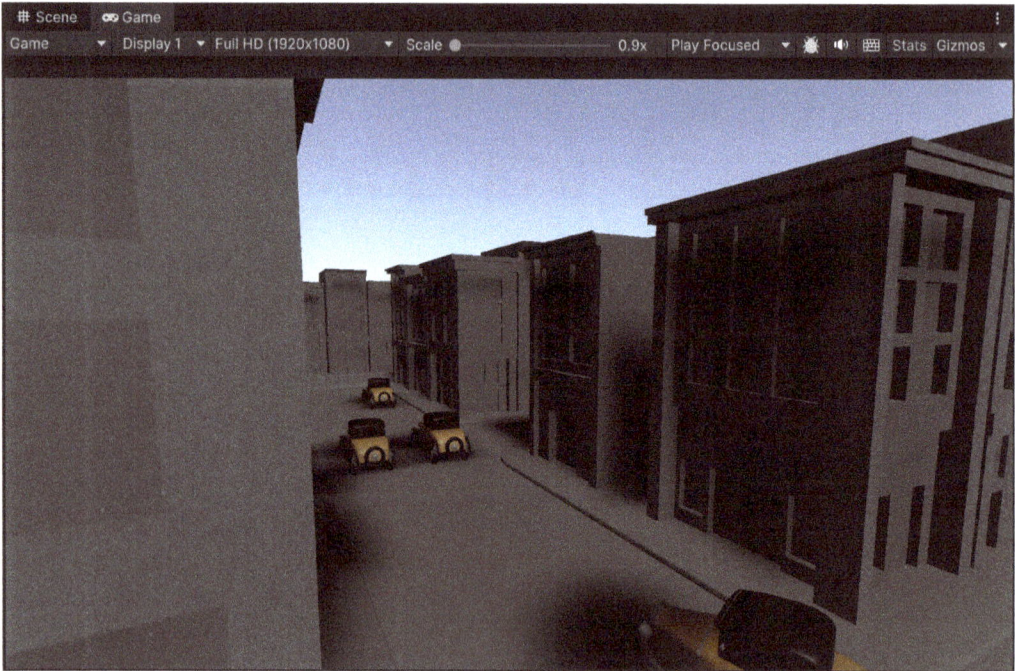

Figure 10.6 – Starting Point scene

To get our screen effects system up and running, we need to create a few assets for our current Unity project. By doing this, we will set ourselves up for the steps in the following sections.

3. Create a full-screen Shader Graph by going to the **Project** window and then going to your `Shaders` folder and right-clicking. From there, select **Create** | **Shader Graph** | **URP** | **Fullscreen Shader Graph**. Call the newly created shader `ScreenOldFilm`.

4. Just like all of our other shaders, we will need to create a material for it (`ScreenOldFilmMat`). Assign our newly created shader to it.

5. From the **Project** window, go to the `Assets/Settings` folder and select the `PC_Renderer` object. Then, go to the **Inspector** window and, at the bottom, click on the **Add Renderer Feature** button. Disable any currently enabled **Full Screen Pass Renderer Features**.

6. From the menu that pops up, select the **Full Screen Pass Renderer Feature** option. You'll see the screen colors are inverted because, by default, the **Pass Material** is set to `FullscreenInvertColors`. Change the **Pass Material** to `ScreenOldFilmMat`, and you should see the screen turn gray, which is the default behavior of full-screen materials. Change the **Name** of the property to `Screen Old Film` to make it easy to tell the difference between all the other features, if any.

7. Optionally, to make it easier to switch between renderer features, you may add a game object to the scene by going to **GameObject | Create Empty** and renaming it `Scene Feature`. From the `Chapter 09/Scripts` folder, add the **SceneFeature** component to the **Scene Feature** object and then assign your newly added feature to the **Feature** property.

Finally, with our screen-effects system up and running and our textures gathered, we can begin the process of recreating this old movie effect.

How to do it...

Let's get started by opening the **Blackboard** and creating our variables.

1. Open up the `ScreenOldFilm` Shader Graph. From the **Blackboard**, first, hit the + button, create a **Float** property named `Contrast`, and set its **Default Value** to 3. Next, create another **Float** property called **Effect Amount**. Set its **Default Value** to 1; then, change its **Mode** to **Slider** with a **Min** value of 0 and a **Max** value of 1.

2. Now, click the + button again and create a **Category** called `Vignette`. Inside this category, we will add the next three properties that we will be creating in *steps 3* and *4*.

> Tip
>
> Once you create a category, any new properties will automatically be added to it until you select elsewhere. To streamline your workflow, consider creating all the properties for a category first, then setting their default values afterward. Or, ensure you have selected the category again before creating new properties for them to appear there.

3.   Create a **Color** named Sepia Color, to which we'll assign a brown shade similar to the example below (**Hexadecimal**: 7D6144):

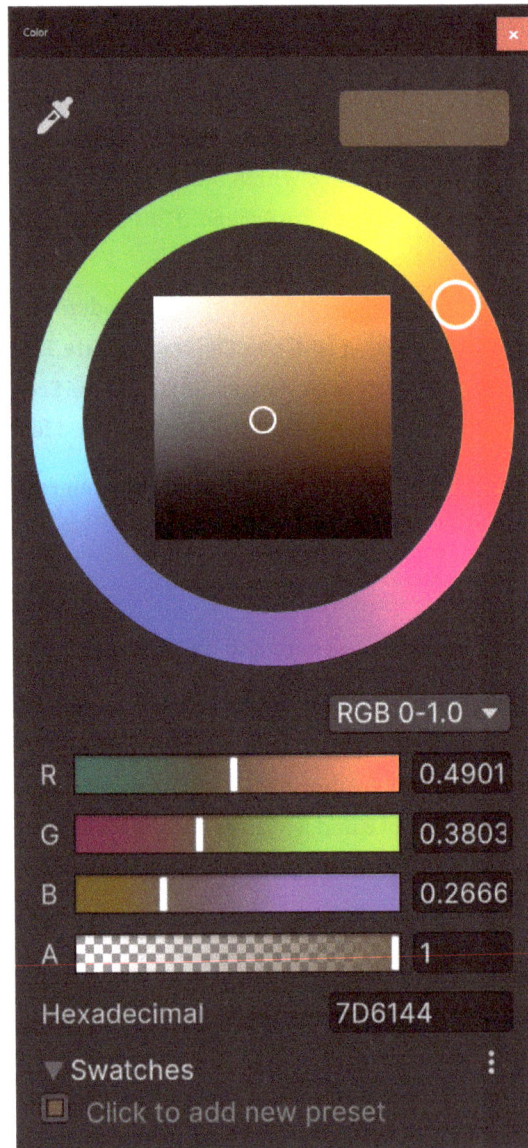

Figure 10.7 – Sepia color

4.   Next, create a **Texture2D** called Vignette Texture set to the **Old Film Vignette** texture we obtained in *step 1*, and a **Float** named Vignette Amount with **Mode** set to **Slider**, a **Min** value of 0, a **Max** value of 1, and a **Default Value** of 1.

5. Next, we'll create another category named Scratches. Inside the **Scratches** category, we will add a **Texture2D** called Scratches Texture set to the **Old Film Scratches** texture, and a **Vector2** named Scratches Speed with a default value of 10, 10.

6. Finally, we'll create one last **Category** named Dust. In this category, we will add a **Texture2D** called Dust Texture set to the **Old Film Dust** texture, and a **Vector2** named Dust Speed with a default value of 10, 10.

At the end, your **Blackboard** should look like this:

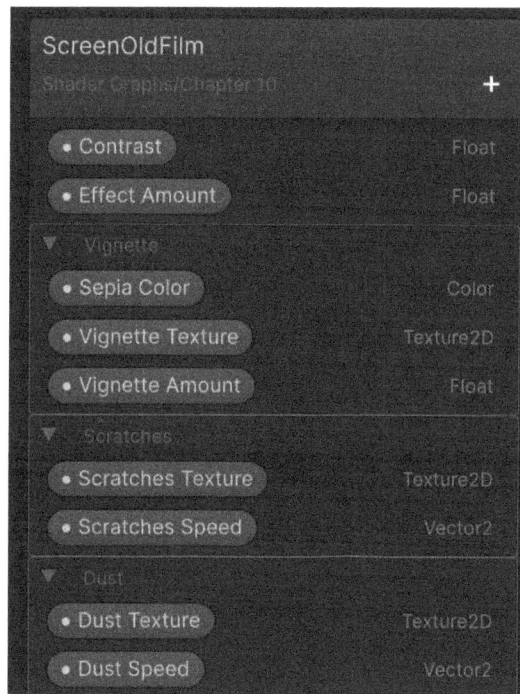

Figure 10.8 – Blackboard setup

Let's start with the flickering sepia effect:

1. Begin by adding a **Scene Color** node.

2. To the right of the **Scene Color** node, create a **Saturation** node and connect the output of the **Scene Color** node to the input of the **Saturation** node.

3. Change the **Saturation** input value to 0. This will turn the image from the **Scene Color** node black and white, removing all color saturation.

4. Next, add an **Add** node to the right of the **Saturation** node. Connect the output of the **Saturation** node to input **A** of the **Add** node.

5. To the left of the **Add** node, we'll add new nodes to generate the flickering sepia color. Start by creating a **Lerp** node and connect its output to input **B** of the **Add** node.

6. For the **A** input of the **Lerp** node, drag and drop the **Sepia Color** property from the **Blackboard**.

7. For the **B** input of the **Lerp** node, create another **Add** node. In this new **Add** node, add the **Sepia Color** property in one input and set the **X**, **Y**, and **Z** properties to 0.1 in the other input, making it a slightly lighter sepia color.

For the **T** input of the **Lerp** node, we'll add randomness to create the flickering effect.

1. Create a **Random Range** node and connect its output to the **T** input of the **Lerp** node.

2. By default, this won't have any effect yet. To provide a constantly changing seed value, create a **Time** node and connect its **Time** output to the **Seed** property of the **Random Range** node.

3. Finally, change the **Min** value of the **Random Range** node to -1. Because **Lerp** is clamped from 0–1, when it gets a negative number, it will keep the normal **Sepia Color** value half of the time.

4. To preview the result, connect the output of the final **Add** node to the **Base Color** of the fragment section of the **Master Stack**.

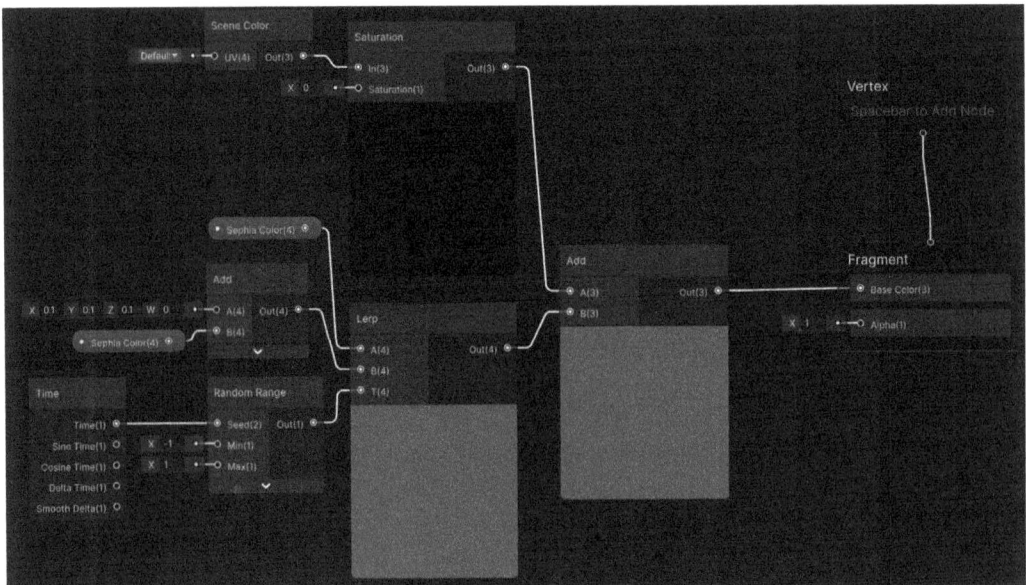

Figure 10.9 – Sepia effect

5.   Save the shader and return to the Unity Editor to see the effect in action.

Figure 10.10 – Sepia in action

As you can see, we have the flickering sepia effect, but there is still more we can do:

1.   Open up the `ScreenOldFilm` Shader Graph. Select all of the nodes to the right of the **Fragment** and hit *Ctrl* + *G* to group them. Give them the name `Flickering Sepia` so you can remember what they do.

2.   Then disconnect the connection between the **Out** of the **Add** node and the **Base Color** of the **Fragment**. Then drag the **Flickering Sepia** group to the left as we will need space for our next section of nodes.

3.   To the right of the **Add** node, create a **Contrast** node and connect the output of the **Add** node to the input of the **Contrast** node. Then, drag the **Contrast** property from the **Blackboard** onto the graph and connect it to the **Contrast** input of the **Contrast** node.

4. Next, drag the **Vignette Texture** from the **Blackboard** onto the graph. Drag out from the **Vignette Texture** and create a **Sample Texture 2D** node, assigning the texture to its **Texture** property.

5. To the right of that, create a **Multiply** node. Connect the **RGBA** output of the **Sample Texture 2D** node to the **B** input of the **Multiply** node and connect the **A** input of the **Multiply** node to the output of the **Contrast** node.

6. Now, to the right of the **Multiply** node, create a **Lerp** node. Connect the **A** input of the **Lerp** node to the output of the **Contrast** node and the **B** input to the output of the **Multiply** node.

7. To control the intensity of the vignette, drag the **Vignette Amount** property from the **Blackboard** onto the graph and connect it to the **T** input of the **Lerp** node. If needed, you can double-click any connection and drag it outward to make the connections easier to see.

8. Lastly, press *Ctrl + G* to group these nodes and name this group `Vignette`. Connect the output of the **Lerp** node to the **Base Color** of the **Fragment** section of the **Master Stack**.

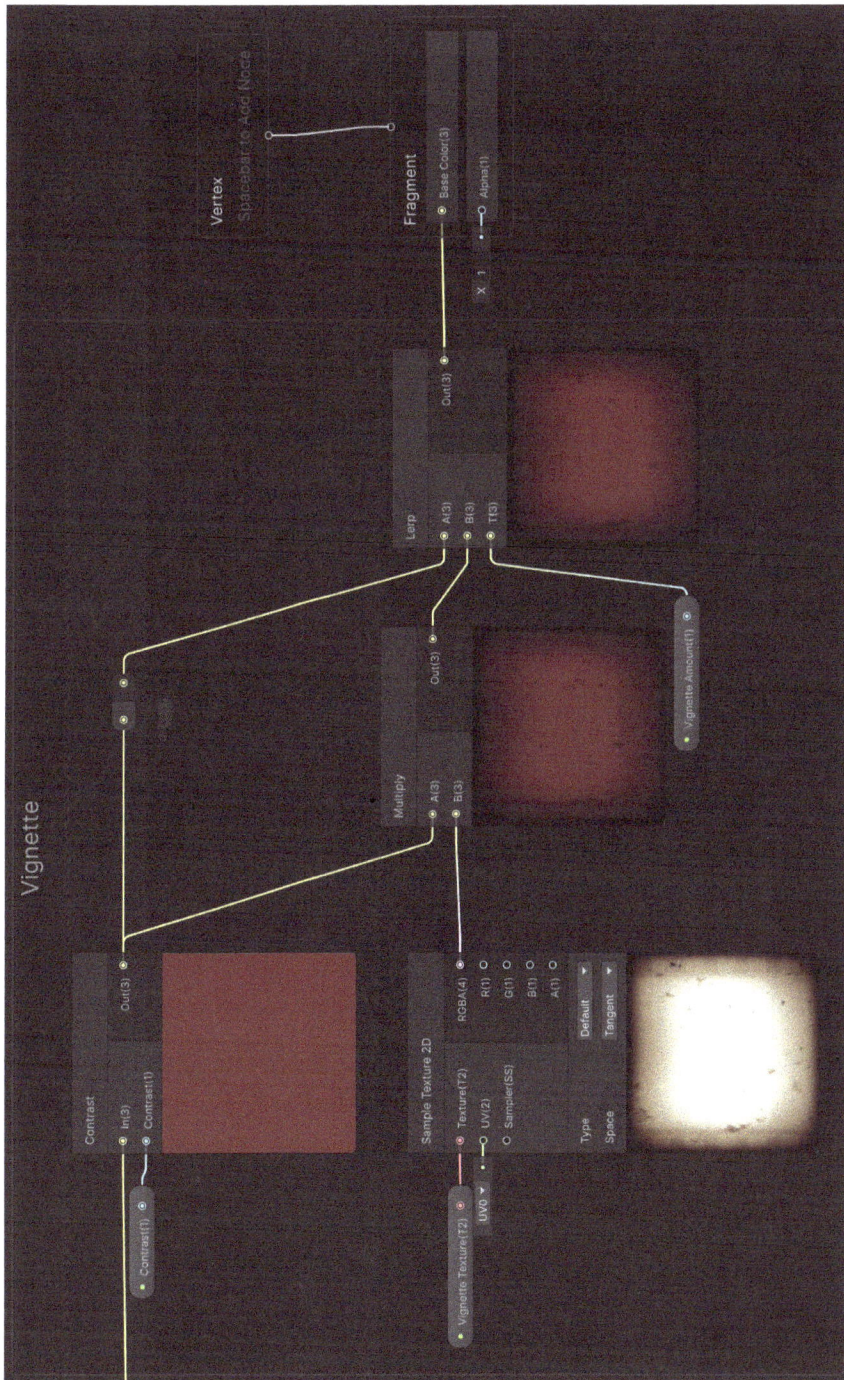

Figure 10.11 – Vignette effect

9.   Save your Shader Graph and return to the Unity Editor to see the changes.

Figure 10.12 – Vignette effect in action

At this point, you can see that our vignette texture has now been applied on top of our prior effect and can be tweaked using the **Contrast** and **Vignette Amount** properties.

As our shader grows more complex, adding more nodes directly to the main graph can make it difficult to manage. A **sub-graph** is a reusable, self-contained section of a Shader Graph that helps keep the main graph organized and easier to read. By grouping multiple nodes into a sub-graph, we can simplify our workflow, reduce clutter, and make debugging and adjustments more efficient.

In this case, the next step of our project involves adding the scratches aspect to simulate an old movie projector. Since this effect requires many nodes, we will create a sub-graph to handle the scratches separately, then integrate its result into the main Shader Graph:

1. From the **Project** window, open up the Shaders folder, right-click, and select **Create |
   Shader Graph | Sub Graph**. Name the sub-graph OldFilmScratches.

2. Double-click on it in order to open up its Shader Graph.

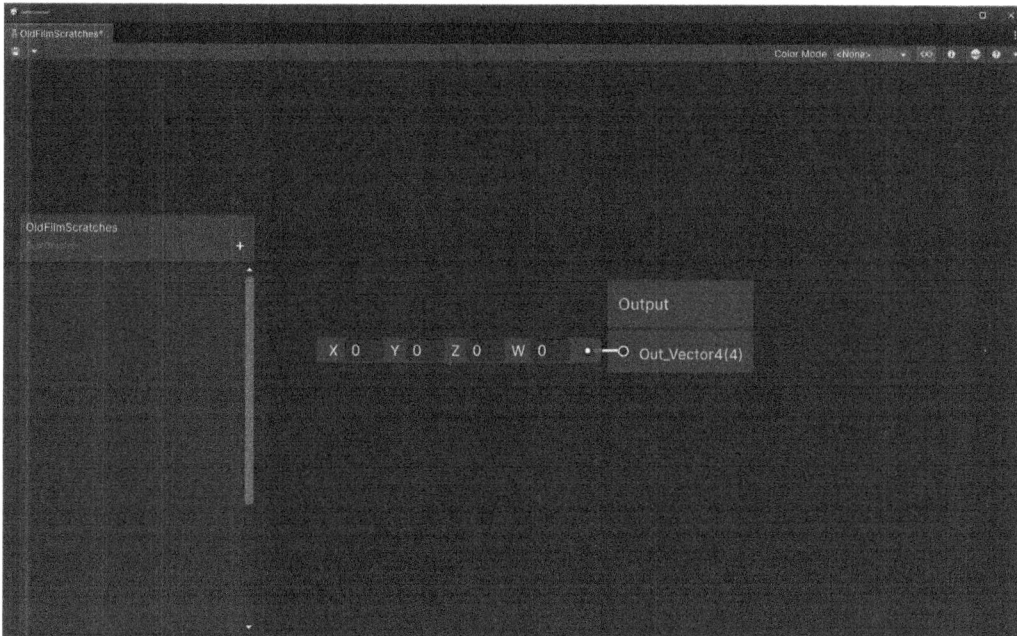

Figure 10.13 – Sub-graph

You'll notice that, by default, it looks quite similar to our normal Shader Graph except instead of a **Master Stack**, it has an **Output** node.

3. From the graph, select the **Output** node, and from **Graph Inspector**, go to the **Inputs** section. Since we only need the color of our output, which is the first three channels, change the **Vector 4** property to **Vector 3**. For the sake of readability, you can also change the name of our output to Final_Output if you'd like.

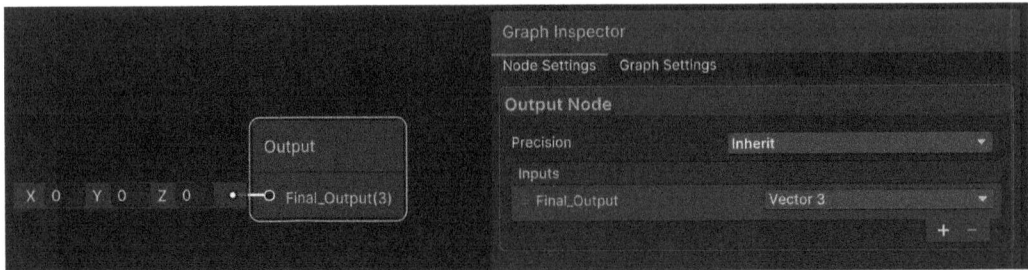

Figure 10.14 – Sub-graph output

4. Next, there are some properties that we will want to have to work with. From the **Blackboard** section, create a **Texture2D** property called Texture and a **Vector 2** called Speed. We will be assigning these properties through our main graph, but you are also welcome to set their **Default Values** if you'd like to see some visuals during setup (I used **OldFilmScratches** for the **Texture** and 10, 10 for Speed).

5. Drag and drop the **Texture** onto the graph from the **Blackboard**. To the right of that, create a **Sample Texture 2D** node and connect the Texture property to the **Texture** input. Then, to the right of the **Sample Texture 2D** node, add a **Lerp** node.

6. Connect the **RGBA** output of the **Sample Texture 2D** node to the **A** input of the **Lerp** node. For the **B** input of the **Lerp** node, set the value to 1, 1, 1, 1 to keep it plain white.

7. Next, below the **Lerp** node and to the left, create a **Random Range** node and connect its output to the **T** input of the **Lerp** node. To ensure that the **Random Range** node continuously generates random values, create a **Time** node and connect its **Time** output to the **Seed** input of the **Random Range** node.

8. Once everything is set up, the **Lerp** node will flash between showing the texture, not showing the texture, and various percentages in between.

9. Finally, connect the output of the **Lerp** node to the **Output** node of the sub-graph.

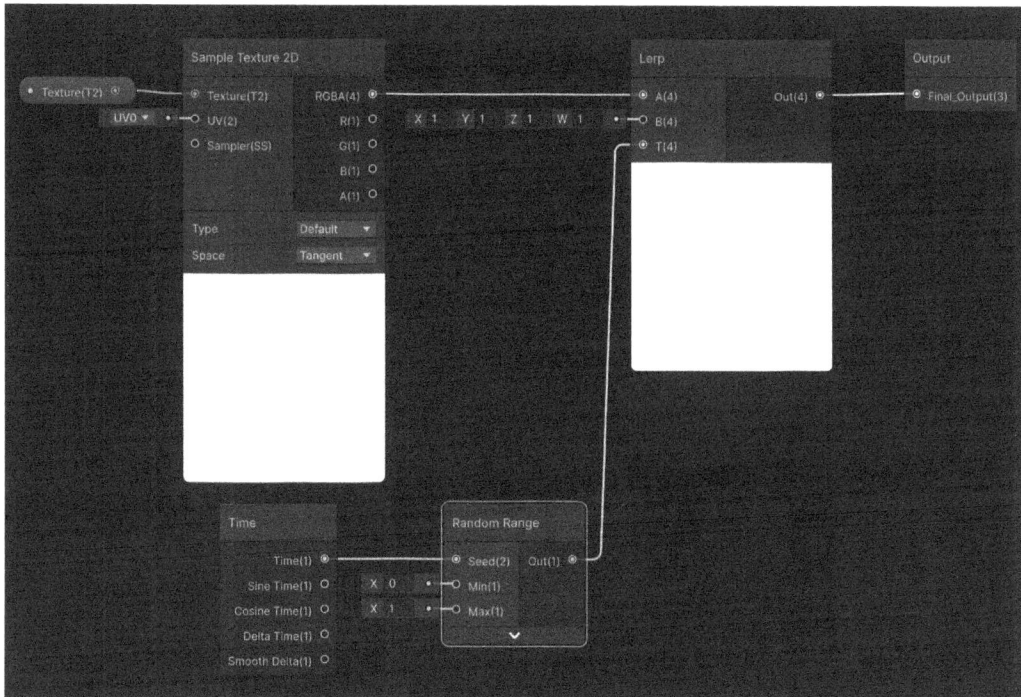

Figure 10.15 – Randomly flashing texture

This setup can now be integrated into the main Shader Graph to preview the result before adding additional randomness and adjusting speed for the final version.

10. Save this sub-graph and then open up the ScreenOldFilm Shader Graph.

11. Then disconnect the connection between the **Out** of the **Lerp** node and the **Base Color** of the **Fragment**. Then drag the **Flickering Sepia** and **Vignette** groups to the left as we will need space for our next section of nodes.

12. To the right of the **Lerp** node, create an **Old Film Scratches** node. The **Old Film Scratches** node includes the properties defined in the **Blackboard** as inputs and produces an output based on its internal **Output** node.

13. Drag and drop the **Scratches Texture** and **Scratches Speed** properties onto the graph and connect them to the **Texture** and **Speed** properties of the **Old Film Scratches** node.

14. To the right of the **Lerp** node, create a **Multiply** node. Connect the **A** to the output of the previous **Output** of the **Lerp** node. Then connect the **Final_Output** of the **OldFilmScratches** node to the **B** of the **Multiply** node and then connect the **Out** of the **Multiply** node to the

Base Color of the **Fragment** portion of the **Master Stack**.

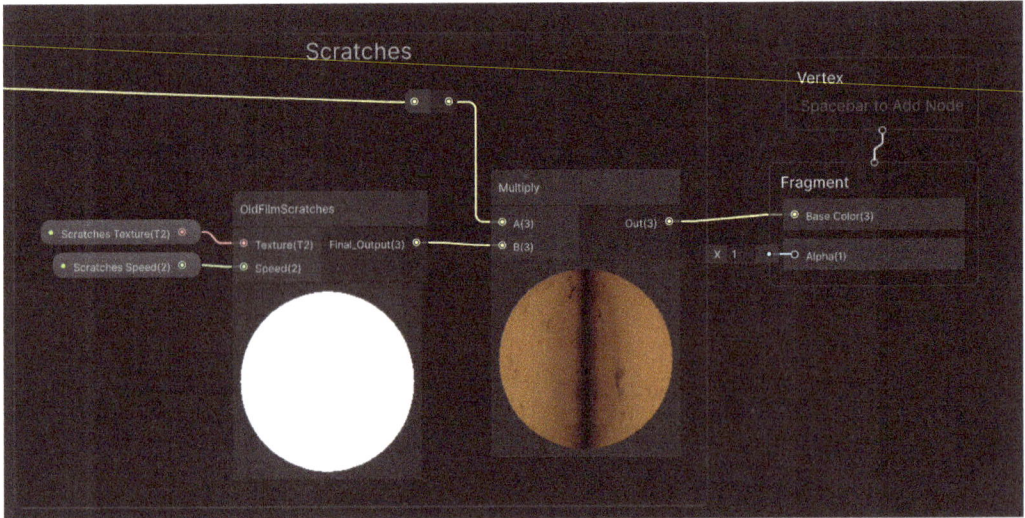

Figure 10.16 – Adding scratches to the shader

15. Save the Shader Graph and return to the Unity Editor.

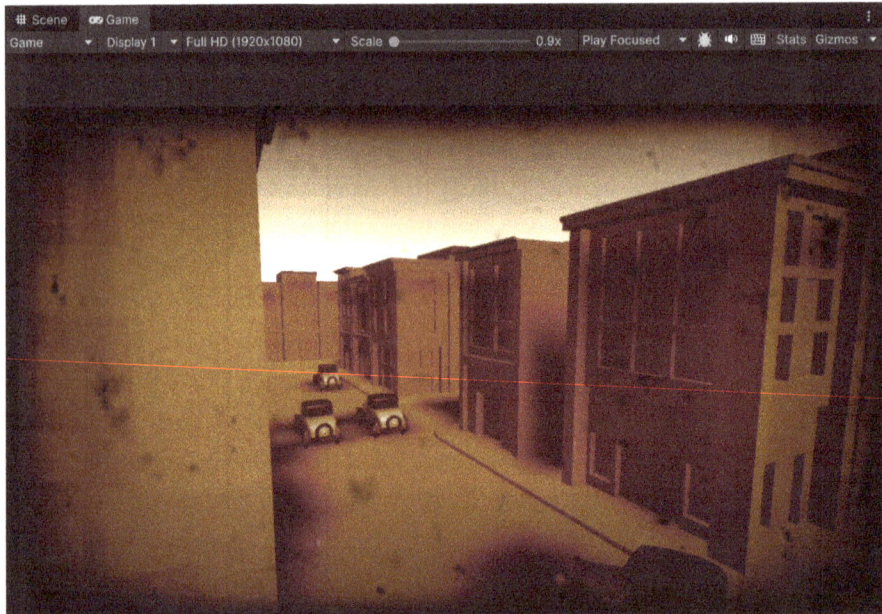

Figure 10.17 – Scratches in the Game view

At this point, we have the dust on the screen with a random opacity, which is great; but old film scratches weren't always in the same place. We will need to randomly move them as well, and that's what we're going to be doing next:

1. Open the `OldFilmScratches` sub-graph. To the left of all the nodes created so far, add a **UV** node, and to the right of it, create a **Split** node. The **R** and **G** channels will represent the **U** and **V** axes for the texture.

2. To the right of this **Split** node, drag and drop the **Speed** property from the **Blackboard**. Then, create another **Split** node to the right of the **Speed** property. We will be using the **R** and **G** channels of this split as well.

3. Since we want to modify the UV coordinates over time, create a **Time** node to the right of the second **Split** node.

4. Next, create two **Multiply** nodes. Connect the **R** of the **Speed Split** to input **A** of the first **Multiply** node and connect the **G** of the **Speed Split** to input **B** of the second **Multiply** node.

5. For the time-based movement, connect the **Sine Time** from the **Time** node to the **B** input of the **R** channel's **Multiply** node, and connect the **Time** output of the **Time** node to the **A** input of the second **Multiply** node. This setup will make the UV coordinates continuously move along the x and y axes as time progresses.

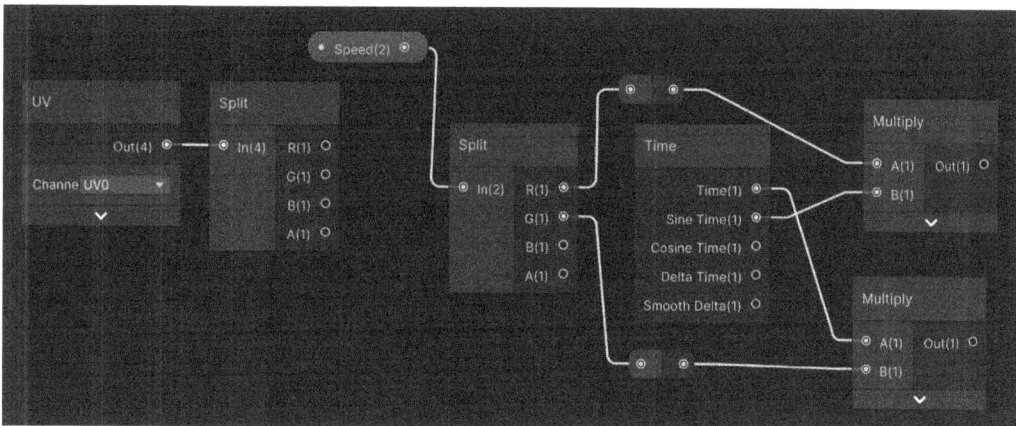

Figure 10.18 – Moving over time

6. To introduce some randomness, add a **Random Range** node above the two **Multiply** nodes. Set the **Min** property of the **Random Range** node to -1. Then, connect the **Time** output of the **Time** node to the **Seed** input of the **Random Range** node.

7. Connect the output of the **Random Range** node to the **A** input of the first **Multiply** node, and the output of the **Multiply** node to input **B** of the second **Multiply** node.

8. Now, create two **Add** nodes. Connect the output of the first **Multiply** node to the **B** input of the first **Add** node. Similarly, connect the output of the second **Multiply** node to the **B** input of the second **Add** node.

9. For the **A** input of the top **Add** node, connect the **R** output of the **UV Split** node. For the **A** input of the bottom **Add** node, connect the **G** output of the **UV Split** node. This will give the final offset values for the UVs.

10. To the right of these **Add** nodes, create a **Vector 2** node. Connect the output of the top **Add** node to the **X** input of the **Vector 2** node, and the output of the bottom **Add** node to the **Y** input of the **Vector 2** node.

11. Finally, connect the output of the **Vector 2** node to the **UV** input of the **Sample Texture 2D** node.

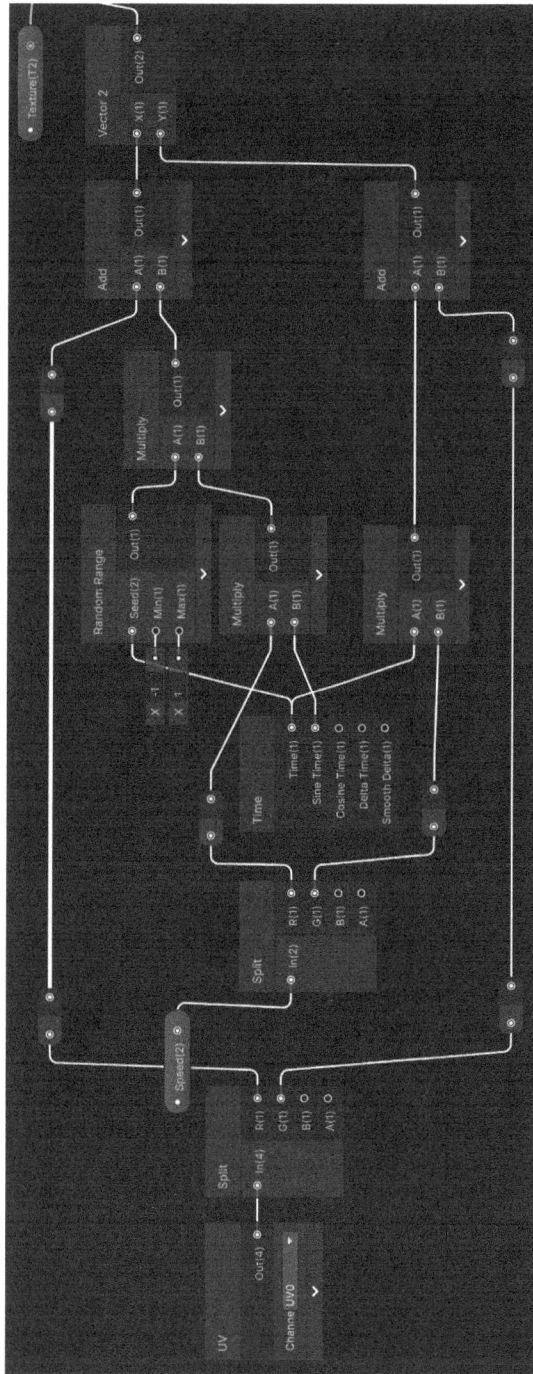

Figure 10.19 – Scratch random movement

12. Save the sub-graph and return to the Unity Editor as no further changes are needed in the master graph.

Figure 10.20 – Scratch random movement in the Game view

If everything is set up correctly, the old film scratches should now appear to randomly move over time. To create the Dust effect, we are going to duplicate the Scratches sub-graph and make some tweaks.

1. In the **Project** window, navigate to the Shaders folder and locate the OldFilmScratches sub-graph. Duplicate it by pressing *Ctrl + D* and rename the new sub-graph OldFilmDust.

2. Double-click on the newly created **OldFilmDust** sub-graph to open it for editing.

3. Inside the **Blackboard**, update the properties to reflect the new **Default Values** if you'd like to see a preview of the changes before applying them in the main Shader Graph.

4. In this version, unlike the scratches, which only have randomness on the **X** axis, the dust effect will have randomness on both the **X** and **Y** axes (or the **U** and **V** channels, since we are dealing with UVs).

5. Similar to how randomness was applied to the **R** (X-axis) channel, the same approach will now be used for the **G** (Y-axis) channel.

6. Locate the **Add** node between the **Multiply** node and the **Add** node in the **G** channel. First, remove the connection between the **Multiply** and **Add** nodes in the **G** channel.

7. Insert a new **Multiply** node between them. Connect the output of the **Random Range** property to the **A** input of this new **Multiply** node.

8. Then, take the output of the previously existing **Multiply** node and connect it to the **B** input of the new **Multiply** node.

9. Finally, connect the output of the new **Multiply** node to the **A** input of the previously connected **Add** node.

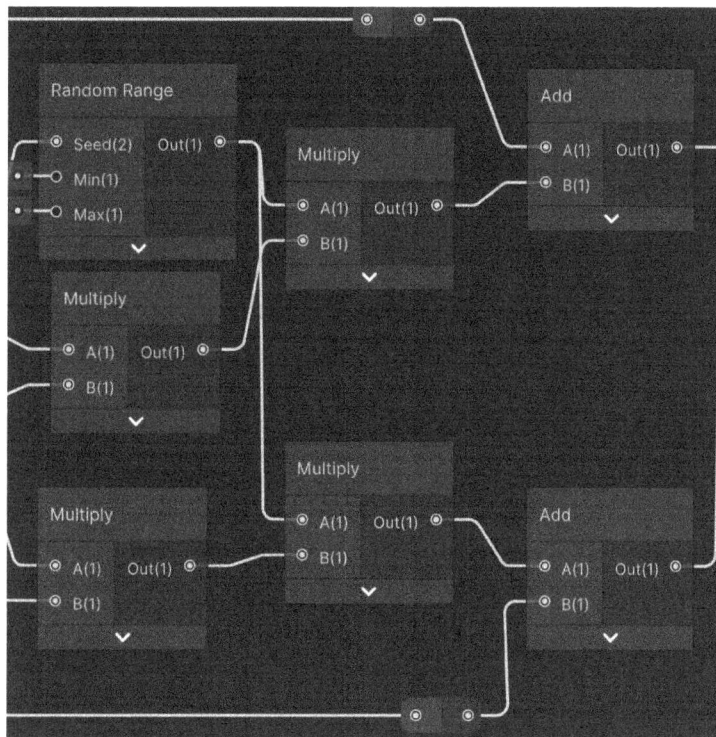

Figure 10.21 – Dust random movement

10. To the right of the **Sample Texture 2D** node, locate the **Random Range** node.

11. Disconnect the connection between the output of the **Random Range** node and the **T** input of the **Lerp** node.

12. To the right of the **Random Range** node, create a **Multiply** node.

13. Connect the output of the **Random Range** node to the **A** input of the **Multiply** node.

14. Then, connect the **Sine Time** output of the **Time** node to the **B** input of the **Multiply** node. If you see the window for the **Multiply** node you should notice this change causes periods where the flickering effect occurs and periods where it does not.

15. Finally, connect the output of the **Multiply** node to the **T** input of the **Lerp** node.

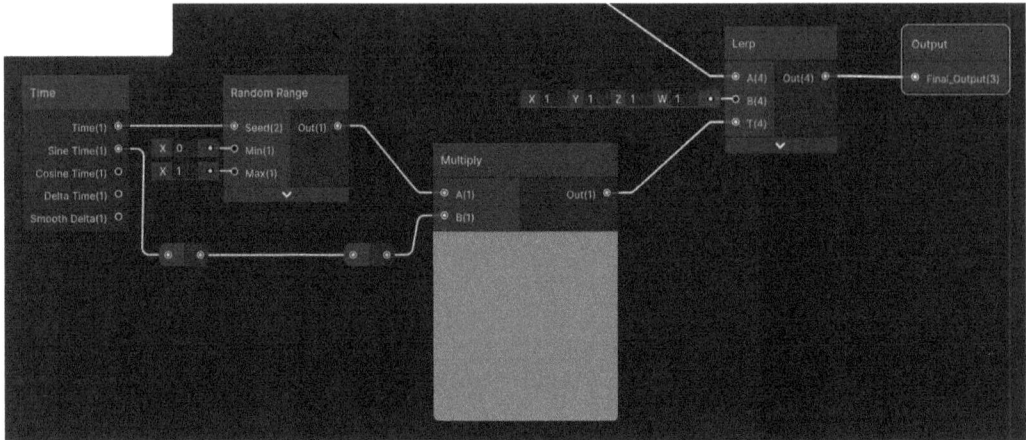

Figure 10.22 – Adjusting time effect on Lerp

16. Save this sub-graph and then open up the ScreenOldFilm Shader Graph.

17. Then disconnect the connection between the **Out** of the **Multiply** node and the **Base Color** of the **Fragment**.

18. To the right of the **Multiply** node, create an **Old Film Dust** node.

    Note that it has the items from the **Blackboard** as its inputs and an output based on the **Output** node.

19. Drag and drop the **Dust Texture** and **Dust Speed** properties onto the graph and connect them to the **Texture** and **Speed** properties of the **Old Film Dust** node.

20. To the right of the **Multiply** node, create another **Multiply** node. Connect the **A** to the output of the previous **Output** of the **Multiply** node. Then connect the **Final_Output** of the **OldFilmMultiply** node to the **B** of the **Multiply** node and then connect the **Out** of the **Multiply** node to the **Base Color** of the **Fragment** portion of the **Master Stack**.

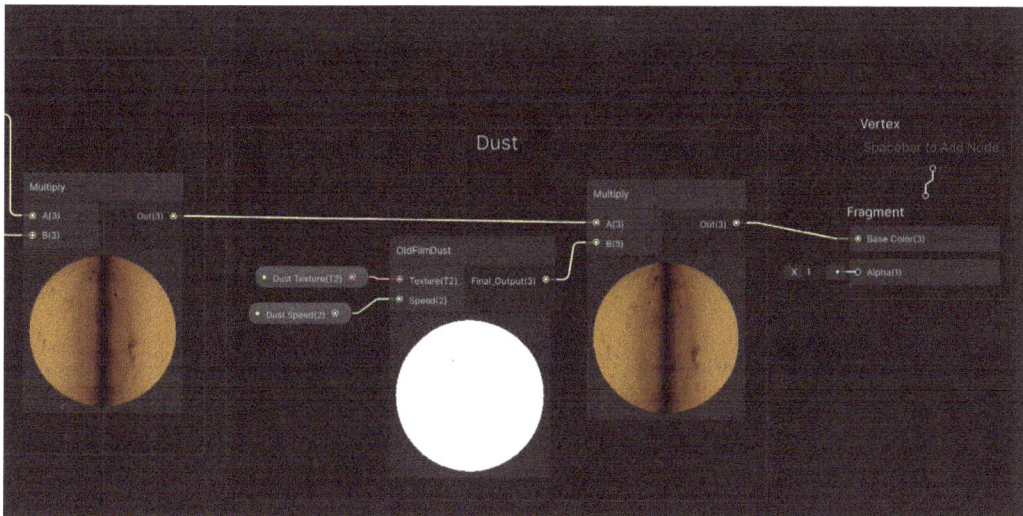

Figure 10.23 – Adding the dust effect to the graph

21. Save the Shader Graph and return to the Unity Editor.

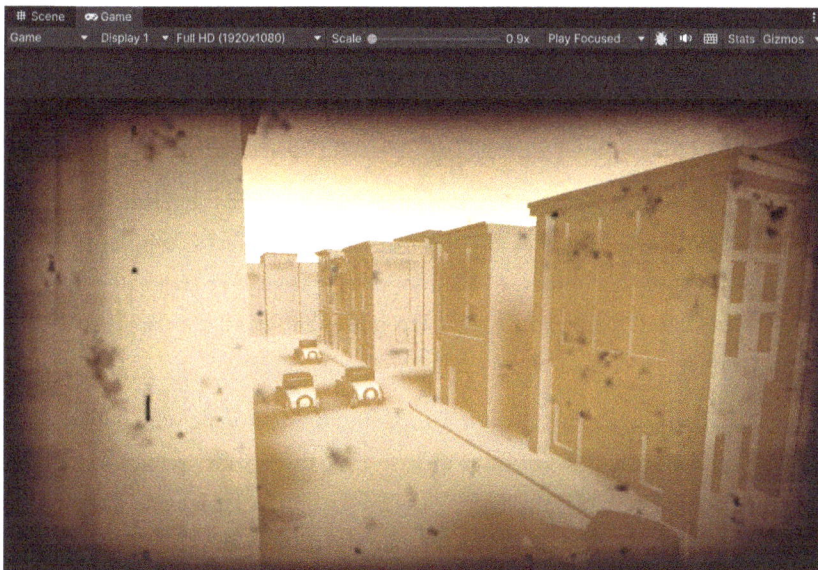

Figure 10.24 – Final result

And with that, we have all of our different effects being applied on top of each other, creating a compelling and interesting effect!

How it works...

In this recipe, we combined multiple visual effects to simulate an old film look by manipulating textures and colors and introducing randomness over time using Unity's Shader Graph.

We began by creating a flickering sepia effect by desaturating the image using a **Scene Color** and **Saturation** node, effectively removing all colors and turning the scene black and white. To add the sepia tone, we used a **Lerp** node to blend between a sepia color and a lighter version of it. The flickering effect was introduced by connecting a **Random Range** node to the **T** input of the **Lerp** node. This random value, influenced by a **Time** node, causes the sepia color to flicker over time, mimicking the inconsistent color quality seen in old films.

Next, we implemented the **Vignette** effect by overlaying a vignette texture on top of the sepia image. The **Multiply** node allowed us to blend the vignette texture with the contrast-adjusted image, creating the darkened edges typical of old films. We controlled the intensity of this effect using a **Lerp** node connected to the **Vignette Amount** property. This gave us the flexibility to adjust how strong the vignette appeared on the screen, enhancing the vintage film aesthetic.

To recreate the scratches and dust effects, we created a separate **sub-graph** for each effect. These sub-graphs generate textures representing scratches and dust, with dynamic movement applied to simulate their random appearance. The UV coordinates of the textures were adjusted using the **Multiply** and **Add** nodes, which allowed the textures to move unpredictably across the **U** and **V** axes. **Random Range** and **Time** nodes ensured that these movements were random, adding to the authentic feel of scratches and dust seen in old film reels.

All the effects—sepia, vignette, scratches, and dust—were layered together using **Multiply** and **Lerp** nodes. This sequential blending ensured the different effects complemented each other and resulted in a cohesive final image. **Multiply** nodes were used to combine the scratches and dust with the sepia-toned image, while the **Lerp** nodes provided control over the balance and intensity of each effect.

At the core of this shader are the **Random Range** and **Time** nodes, which introduce dynamic randomness into the effects. These nodes ensure that the visual artifacts, such as flickering, scratches, and dust, change constantly, making the final result feel more organic and less repetitive. This randomness is essential for mimicking the imperfections that naturally occur in old film footage.

By breaking the effects into sub-graphs, we kept the Shader Graph organized and manageable. This modular approach also makes it easier to customize and reuse individual effects like scratches and dust for other projects. The combination of color adjustments, texture manipulation, and dynamic randomness in this shader effectively recreates the nostalgic aesthetic of old film reels.

Creating a night vision screen effect

Our next screen effect is definitely a more popular one. A night vision screen effect is seen in *Call of Duty* (first published in 2003), *Halo* (first published in 2001), and just about any FPS out in the market today. It is the effect of brightening the whole image using that very distinct lime-green color.

In order to achieve our night vision effect, we need to break down our effect using Photoshop. This is a simple process of finding some reference images online and composing a layered image to see what kinds of blending modes you will need or in which order we will need to combine our layers. The following screenshot shows the result of doing this in Photoshop:

Figure 10.25 – The result we are trying to achieve in this recipe

Let's begin to break down our rough Photoshop composite image into its component parts so that we can better understand the assets we will have to gather. In this recipe, we will cover the process of doing this.

Getting ready

Using Photoshop, we constructed a layered image to better illustrate how we can go about capturing the effect of night vision. Let's begin this screen effect by again breaking down our effect into its component layers:

- **Tinted green**: Our first layer in our screen effect is the iconic green color, found in just about every night vision image. This will give our effect that signature night vision look, as shown in the following screenshot:

Figure 10.26 – A tinted green visual

- **Scan lines**: To increase the effect of this being a new type of display for the player, we include scan lines over the top of our tinted layer. For this, we will use a texture created in Photoshop and let the user tile it so that the scan lines can be bigger or smaller.

- **Noise**: Our next layer is a simple noise texture that we tile over the tinted image and scan lines to break up the image and add even more detail to our effect. This layer simply emphasizes that digital readout effect:

Figure 10.27 – A noise texture

- **Vignette**: The last layer in our night vision effect is the vignette. If you look at the night vision effect in *Call of Duty*, you will notice that it uses a vignette that fakes the effect of looking down a scope. We will do that for this screen effect:

Figure 10.28 – A vignette texture

Now that we have an understanding of the aspects involved, let's start creating the shader:

1. Create a **Fullscreen Shader Graph** by going to the **Project** window, going to your Shaders folder, and right-clicking. From there, select **Create | Shader Graph | URP | Fullscreen Shader Graph**. Give the newly created shader the name of ScreenNightVision.

2. Just like all of our other shaders, we will need to create a material for it. (ScreenNightVisionMat). Assign our newly created shader to it.

3. From the **Project** window, go to the Assets/Settings folder and select the PC_Renderer object. From there, go to the **Inspector** window and, at the bottom, click on the **Add Renderer Feature** button. Disable any currently enabled **Full Screen Pass Renderer Features**.

4. From the menu that pops up, select the **Full Screen Pass Renderer Feature** option. You'll see the screen colors are inverted because, by default, the **Pass Material** is set to FullscreenInvertColors. Change the **Pass Material** to the ScreenNightVisionMat option and you should see the screen turn gray, which is the default behavior of full-screen materials. Change the **Name** of the feature to Screen Night Vision to make it easy to tell the difference between all the other features, if any.

5. Optionally, to make it easier to switch between renderer features, you may add a game object to the scene by going to **GameObject | Create Empty** and renaming it Scene Feature. From the Chapter 09/Scripts folder, add the **SceneFeature** component to the **Scene Feature** object and then assign your newly added feature to the **Feature** property.

Finally, with our screen-effects system up and running and our textures gathered, we can begin the process of recreating this night vision effect.

How to do it...

Let's get started by opening the **Blackboard** and creating some variables for the first part of this effect:

1. Open up the ScreenNightVision Shader Graph. From the **Blackboard**, first, hit the + button and create a **Color** property called Night Vision Color. Set the value to green (I used 00FF00). Then create a **Float** property named Contrast and set its **Default Value** to 3. Then, change its **Mode** to **Slider** with a **Min** value of 0 and a **Max** value of 4. Next, create another **Float** property called Brightness. Set its **Default Value** to 0.1, then change its **Mode** to **Slider** with a **Min** value of 0 and a **Max** value of 2.

2. Now, click the + button again and create a **Category** called Barrel Distortion.

3. Afterwards, create another **Float** called Scale (Zoom) set to 0.8 and another **Float** called Distortion set to 2.

Figure 10.29 – Initial blackboard properties

4. From the graph, create a **Custom Function** node. With it selected, go to **Graph Inspector** and, under **Inputs**, press the + button and create three properties: a **Vector 2** called Coordinates, a **Float** called Distortion, and a **Float** called Scale. Click the + on **Outputs** and set it to a **Vector 2** called Out.

5. Then, change the **Type** to **String**.

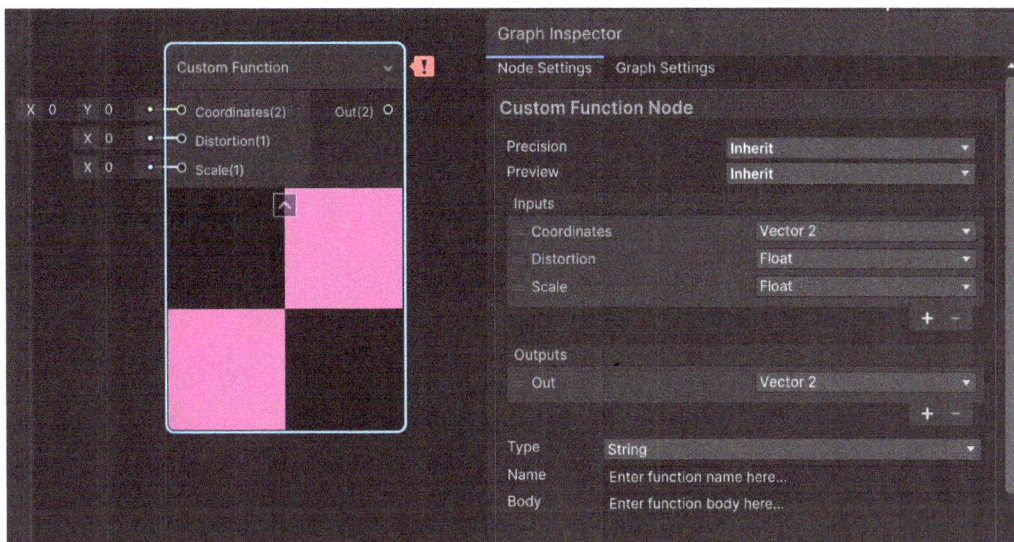

Figure 10.30 – Custom function setup

Right now, it'll show the pink and black checker box due to a compiler error since Out hasn't been set to anything. We'll need to fix that shortly.

6. Under **Name**, change the value to `BarrelDistortion` and, in the **Body** use the following code:

```
// lens distortion algorithm see
// http://www.ssontech.com/content/lensalg.htm

float2 h = Coordinates.xy - float2(0.5, 0.5);
float r2 = h.x * h.x + h.y * h.y;
float f = 1.0 + r2 * (Distortion * sqrt(r2));

Out = f * Scale * h + 0.5;
```

At this point, the code should compile and the error should go away.

7. To the left of our **Custom Function** node, create a **UV** node. Connect the **Out** of the **UV** node to the **Coordinates** of the **BarrelDistortion (Custom Function)** node. Then drag and drop the **Distortion** and **Scale (Zoom)** values from the **Blackboard** and assign them.

8. To the right of the **BarrelDistortion** node, create a **Scene Color** node and connect the **Output** of the **BarrelDistortion** to the **UV** of the **Scene Color** node. Connect the **Out** of the **Scene Color** to the **Base Color** of the **Fragment** part of the **Master Stack**.

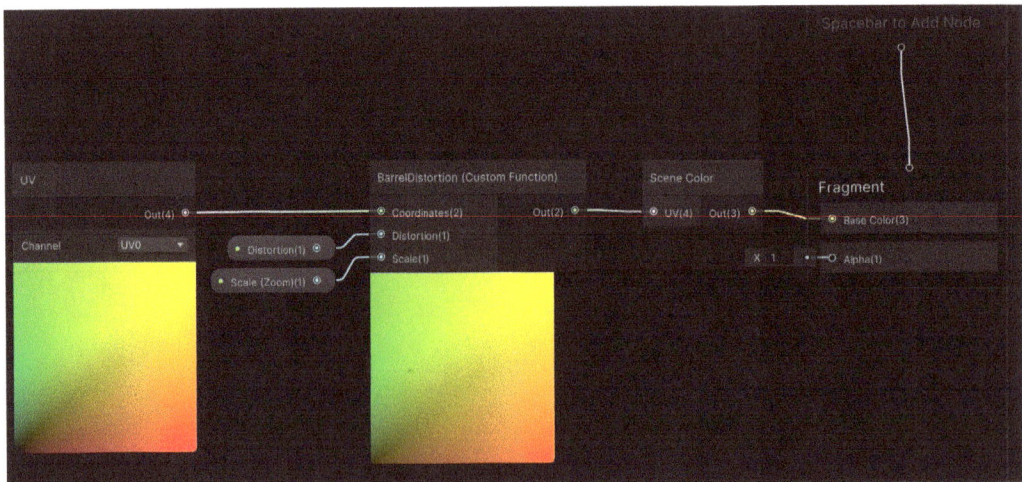

Figure 10.31 – Connecting Custom Function to Scene Color node

9. Save the shader and return to the Unity Editor.

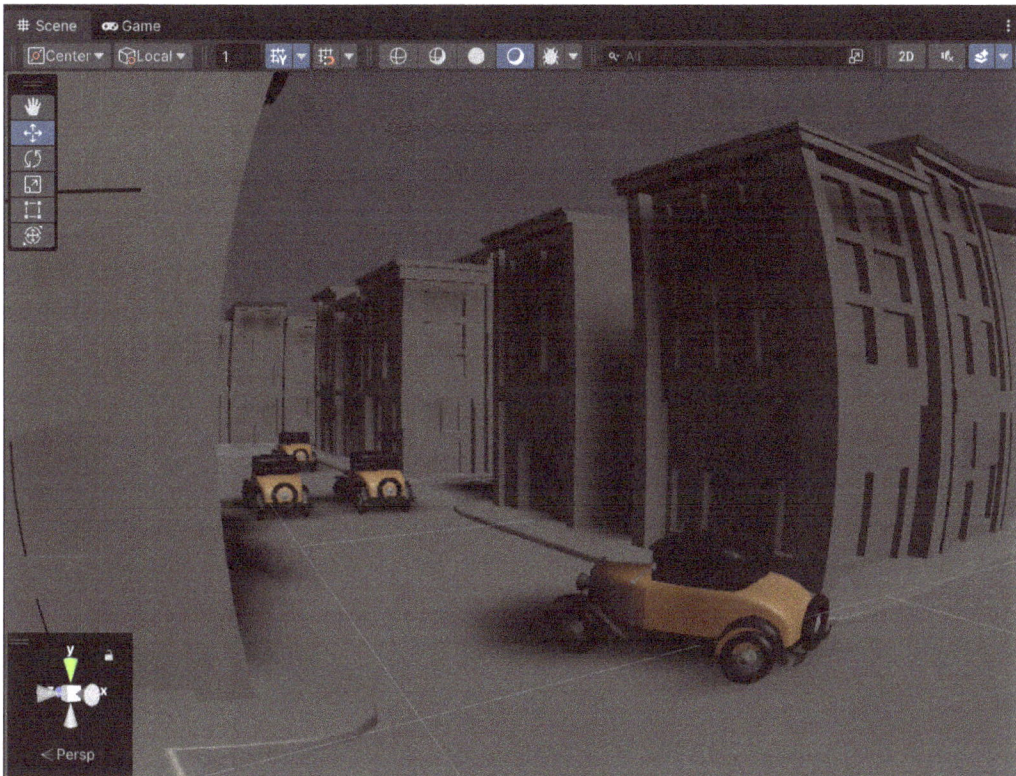

Figure 10.32 – Barrel distortion effect

At this point, you should notice a distortion effect applied to the UVs of the **Scene Color** node, distorting the final result. Let's continue applying more effects to enhance the overall effect.

1. Return to the Shader Graph and remove the connection between the output of the **Scene Color** node and the **Base Color** of the **Fragment** part of the **Master Stack**. Select the nodes we've created so far to the left of the **Fragment** and press *Ctrl + G* to group them. Name this group `Barrel Distortion` and move them to the left to make space for new additions.

2. To the right of the **Scene Color** node, create a **Saturation** node. Connect the output of the **Scene Color** node to the input of the **Saturation** node and set its **Saturation** value to 0 (to make the image grayscale).

3. To the right of the **Saturation** node, create an **Add** node. Connect the **A** input of the **Add** node to the output of the **Saturation** node.

4. From the **Blackboard**, drag and drop the **Brightness** property onto the graph and connect it to the **B** input of the **Add** node. This will help adjust the brightness.

5. To further brighten the color, create a **Multiply** node to the right of the **Add** node. Set the **A** input of this **Multiply** node to 2, 2, 2. Connect the output of the **Add** node to the **B** input of the **Multiply** node.

6. To the right of this **Multiply** node, create another **Multiply** node. Drag the **Night Vision Color** property from the **Blackboard** onto the graph and connect it to the **A** input of the new **Multiply** node. Then, connect the output of the previous **Multiply** node to the **B** input of the new **Multiply** node.

7. To the right of the second **Multiply** node, create a **Power** node. Connect the output of the second **Multiply** node to the **A** input of the **Power** node.

8. From the **Blackboard**, drag and drop the **Contrast** property onto the graph. Connect it to the **B** input of the **Power** node.

9. Finally, group all the newly created nodes together and name this new group Night Vision Color.

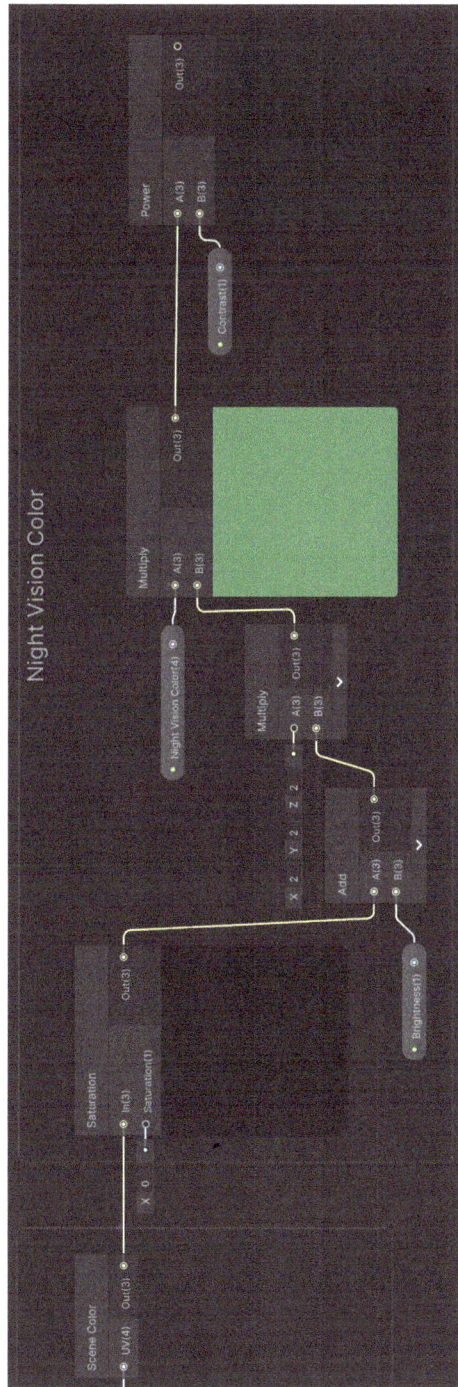

Figure 10.33 – Night Vision Color

10. Connecting to the **Base Color** on the **Master Stack** would show us something like the following:

Figure 10.34 – Night Vision Color in the Scene view

11. Back in the graph, to the right of the **Power** node, create a **Multiply** node and connect the output of the **Power** node to the **A** input of the **Multiply** node.

12. In the **Blackboard**, create a new **Texture 2D** property named **Vignette Texture**. Assign the texture you want to use for the vignette (in this case, **NightVisionVignette**).

13. Drag and drop the **Vignette Texture** property from the **Blackboard** onto the graph.

14. From the **Vignette Texture** property node, create a **Sample Texture 2D** node and connect it to the **Texture** input.

15. Connect the **RGBA** output of the **Sample Texture 2D** node to the **B** input of the **Multiply** node.

16. Group the two nodes (the **Multiply** and **Sample Texture 2D** nodes) together and name the group Vignette.

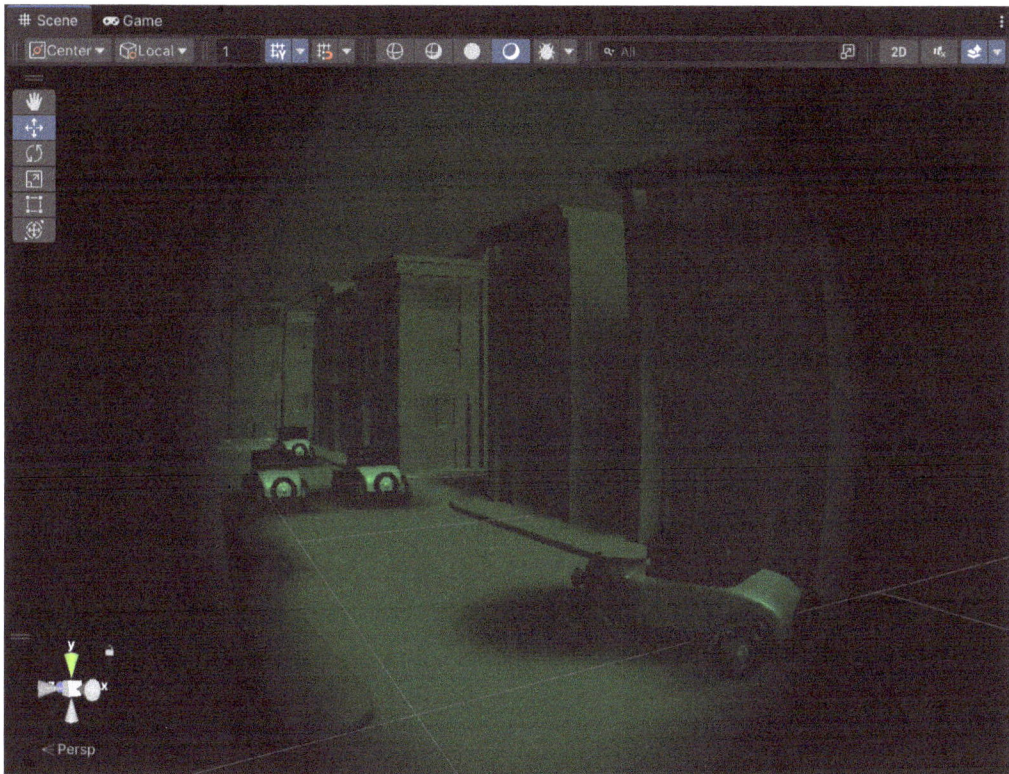

Figure 10.35 – Vignette effect in the Scene view

Tip

If you see your screen gray at this point, there's a good chance a texture property wasn't initialized correctly in the material. One quick way to fix this is to select your material, and from **Inspector**, right-click and select **Reset** to set the textures to their **Default Values** if needed.

Now that we have the vignette in, we can start to add the scan lines:

1. From the **Blackboard**, create a new category called Scan Lines. Inside this category, create the following properties:

    - A **Float** called Scanline Tile Amount, with its **Default Value** set to 4
    - A **Texture 2D** called Scanline Texture, with its **Default Value** set to **NightVisionScanLines**

2. To the right of the **Multiply** node created for the vignette effect, create another **Multiply** node. Connect the output of the previous **Multiply** node (from the vignette) to the **A** input of this new **Multiply** node.

3. To the left of this **Multiply** node, create a **Sample Texture 2D** node and connect the **Scanline Texture** to the **Texture** input of the **Sample Texture 2D** node. Connect the **RGBA** output of the **Sample Texture 2D** node to the **B** input of the new **Multiply** node.

4. To make the scan lines tile correctly, drag out from the **UV** input of the **Sample Texture 2D** node and create a **Tiling And Offset** node.

5. From the **Tiling** input of the **Tiling And Offset** node, create a **Multiply** node. Connect the **Scanline Tile Amount** property from the **Blackboard** to the **A** input of this **Multiply** node.

6. Finally, create a **Vector 2** node and set its values to 1, 1. Then, connect it to the **B** input of the **Multiply** node.

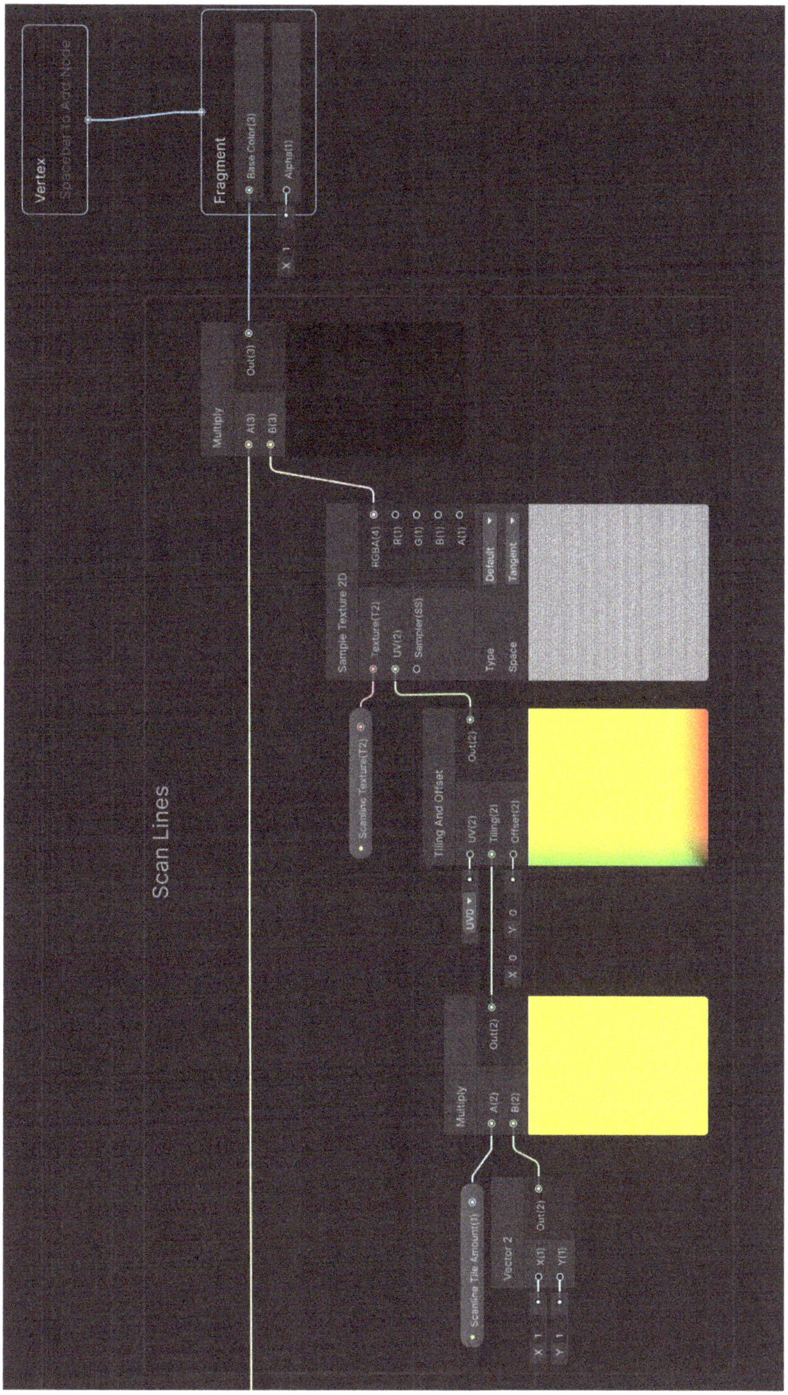

Figure 10.36 – Adding scan lines effect to the graph

This will add the scanlines to our screen.

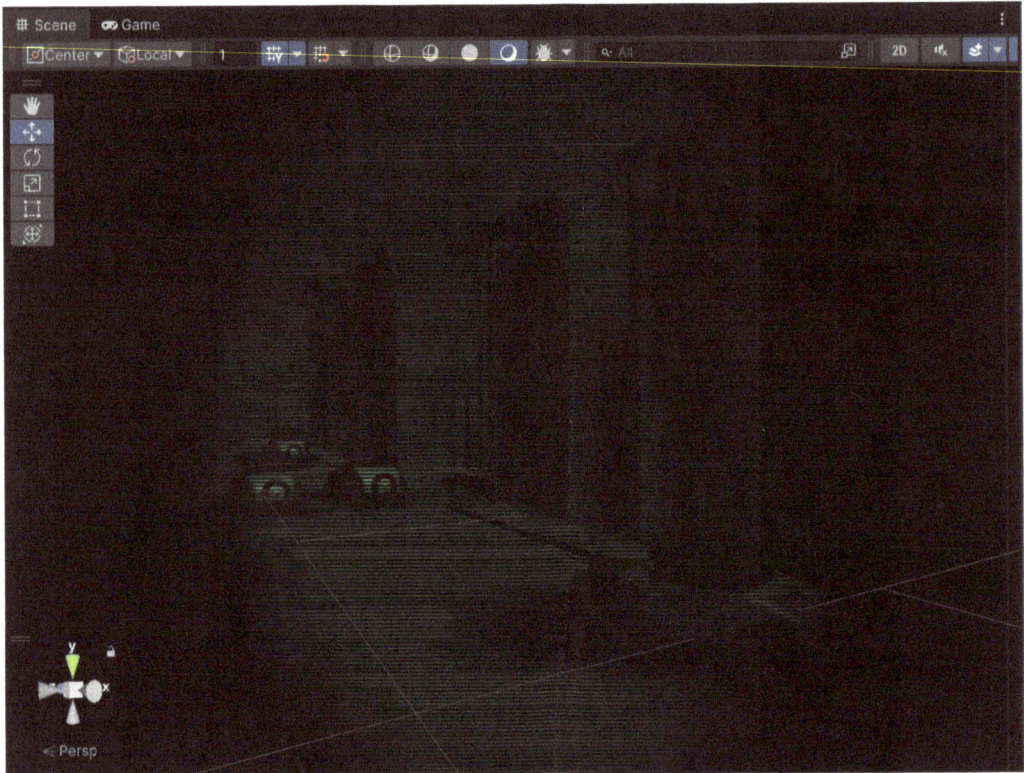

Figure 10.37 – Scan lines effect in the Scene view

In the previous implementation, a **sub-graph** was used to organize complex node structures. This time, a **Custom Function** will be used to generate noise, allowing us to write custom High-Level Shader Language (HLSL) code directly within our graph:

1. To the right of the **Scanline Multiply** output, disconnect the connection to the **Base Color** if there is one.
2. Create another **Multiply** node. Connect the output of the previous **Multiply** node to the **A** input of this new **Multiply** node.
3. Next, create a **Sample Texture 2D** node, similar to the one used for the scan lines, and connect it to the **B** input of the new **Multiply** node.

4. In the **Blackboard**, create a new category called `Noise`. Inside this category, create two properties:

   - A **Texture 2D** property called `Noise Texture` with the **Default Value** of **Night Vision Noise**
   - A **Vector 2** property called `Noise Speed` with a **Default Value** of `100, 100`

5. Drag the **Noise Texture** property from the **Blackboard** onto the graph and assign it to the **Texture** input of the **Sample Texture 2D** node.

6. To the left of the **Sample Texture 2D** node, create a **Custom Function** node. This function will handle the UV manipulation for the noise.

7. In the **Custom Function** node, create three inputs:

   - A **Vector 2** called `UV`
   - A **Vector 2** called `NoiseSpeed`
   - A **Float** called `RandomValue`

8. For the **Output** of the **Custom Function**, make a **Vector 2** and call it `noiseUV`.

9. Connect the output of the **Custom Function** node to the **UV** input of the **Sample Texture 2D** node.

10. Change the **Custom Function Mode** to **String**, set the function's **Name** to `Noise UVs`, and use the following code for the **Body** function:

    ```
    noiseUV.x = UV.x + (RandomValue * _SinTime.z * NoiseSpeed.x);
    noiseUV.y = UV.y + (_Time.x * NoiseSpeed.y);
    ```

11. Create a **UV** node and connect it to the **UV** input of the **Custom Function** node.

12. Drag and drop the **Noise Speed** property from the **Blackboard** onto the graph and connect it to the **Noise Speed** input of the **Custom Function** node.

13. Create a **Random Range** node and connect its output to the **Random Value** input of the **Custom Function** node.

14. Create a **Time** node, connect its **Time** output to the **Seed** input of the **Random Range** node, and set **Min** to `-1`.

15. Once everything is set up, you should see the **Sample Texture 2D** node produce a static noise effect that is propagated through the rest of the nodes.

16. Finally, connect the output of the **Multiply** node to the **Base Color** of the **Fragment** section of the **Master Stack**.

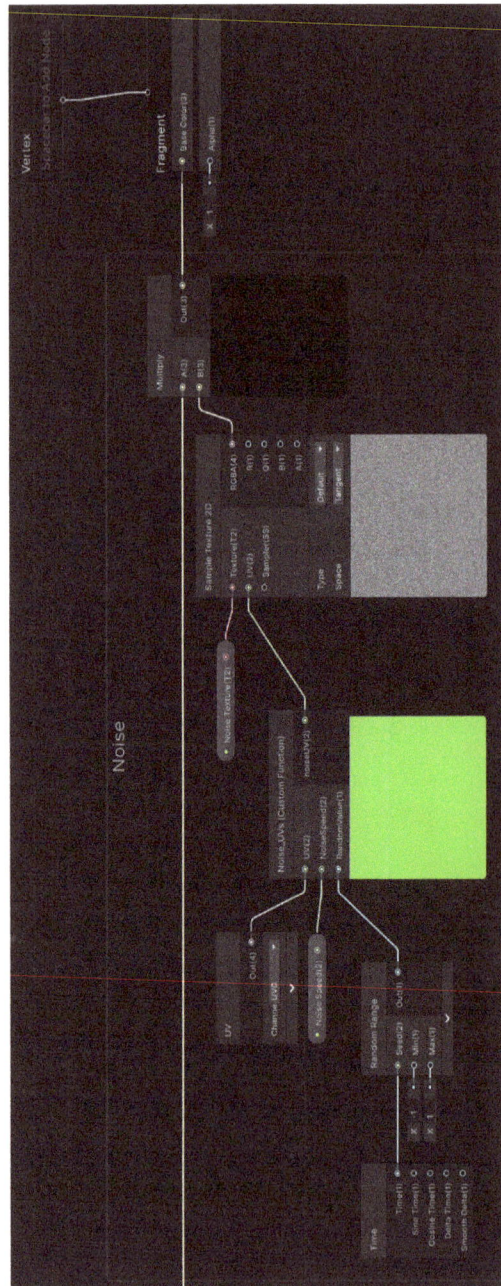

Figure 10.38 – Adding noise effect

17. Save the **Screen Night Vision** shader and return to the Unity Editor.

Figure 10.39 – Final result

The night vision effect, complete with noise, scan lines, and vignette, should now be fully functional. Play around with the values in the **Inspector** window and see how it changes the look!

How it works...

This night vision effect is created by layering multiple visual components, each adding a key element to the overall look. By combining color adjustments, texture overlays, and dynamic effects, we achieve a cohesive and realistic night vision effect.

First, we added **barrel distortion** to simulate the curved lens effect seen in night vision goggles or scopes. Using a **Custom Function**, we applied a distortion formula that warps the UV coordinates based on their distance from the image's center.

Using a **Custom Function** is particularly useful when:

- A complex effect would require too many nodes, making the graph difficult to manage.
- You need better performance, as custom HLSL code can be more efficient than a node-based setup.
- A specific operation isn't available as a built-in Shader Graph node.

The following code snippet illustrates the code used in processing our lens distortion. It is a snippet of code provided to us by the makers of **SynthEyes**, and the code is freely available to use in your own effects:

```
float2 barrelDistortion(float2 coord)
{
    // Lens distortion algorithm
    // See http://www.ssontech.com/content/lensalg.htm
    float2 h = coord.xy - float2(0.5, 0.5);
    float r2 = h.x * h.x + h.y * h.y;
    float f = 1.0 + r2 * (_distortion * sqrt(r2));

    return f * _scale * h + 0.5;
}
```

The **distortion** and **scale** properties allow us to control the strength of this effect, giving the impression of viewing the scene through a specialized lens, enhancing the immersion.

The green tint and vignette are similar to our previous recipe, so I won't dwell on it too much, but the blending of the green tint with the scene's image helps to give it the characteristic night vision look. The vignette effect adds a dark border around the screen, which helps focus attention toward the center. This simulates the limited field of view, which is typical of night vision equipment.

To enhance the digital look of the night vision, we added **scan lines**. These lines, applied via a **Tiling And Offset** node, simulate an electronic display. By tiling the **Scanline Texture**, we can control the density of the lines to mimic a display's grid-like appearance.

Finally, we added **noise** to simulate the static interference often seen in electronic displays or old film footage. Instead of using a sub-graph like in the previous recipe, we implemented a custom function that dynamically manipulates the UVs to apply a noise texture that changes over time. The **Noise Speed** and **Random Value** properties control the speed and variation of the noise, mimicking the unpredictable flickering of static. This adds imperfection to the display, which is a hallmark of night vision imagery.

These layers—green tint, barrel distortion, vignette, scan lines, and noise—were blended together in Shader Graph using a series of **Multiply**, **Add**, and **Lerp** nodes. By combining these effects, the shader created a final image that is both visually cohesive and realistic. Each component can be customized, making the night vision effect adaptable to different scenarios.

Part 4

Section Custom Lighting and Advanced Shader Programming

Lighting is one of the most important aspects of rendering. In previous chapters, we worked within Unity's built-in lighting models, but this part explores custom lighting models, allowing you to control how light interacts with surfaces. You will learn how to create custom diffuse and specular models, toon shading, and advanced reflection techniques to achieve both realistic and stylized visuals.

For those seeking greater control over shaders, this part also introduces ShaderLab and HLSL, enabling direct shader programming beyond Shader Graph's capabilities. Writing `.shader` files gives you more flexibility and optimization potential, allowing for effects that would be difficult or impossible with a purely node-based workflow.

Finally, we will explore the High-Definition Render Pipeline (HDRP), Unity's most advanced rendering system designed for high-end graphics on powerful PCs and consoles. You'll learn how to create cinematic-quality materials and lighting effects while leveraging HDRP's Physically Based Rendering system.

By the end of this part, you will have the skills to build custom lighting models, write shaders in code, and work with high-end rendering techniques, allowing you to push the visual quality of your projects to the next level.

This part has the following chapters:

- *Chapter 11, Understanding Lighting Models*
- *Chapter 12, Developing Advanced Shading Techniques*
- *Chapter 13, Utilizing the HDRP*

11

Understanding Lighting Models

In the previous chapters, we introduced Surface Shaders and explained how we can change physical properties to simulate different materials. So, how does this actually work? Well, at the heart of every Surface Shader is its lighting model. This is the feature that takes these properties and calculates the final shade of each pixel. Usually, Unity hides the lighting model from developers because, in order to write a lighting model, you have to understand how light reflects and refracts onto surfaces. This chapter will finally show you how lighting models work and present you with the basics that you need to know to create your own.

Simulating the way light works is a very challenging and resource-consuming task. For many years, video games have used very simple lighting models, which, despite lacking in realism, were very believable. Even if most 3D engines are now using physically based renderers, it is worth exploring some simpler techniques for simulating light. The ones presented in this chapter are reasonably realistic and have been widely adopted on devices with low resources such as mobile phones. Understanding these simple lighting models is also essential if you want to create your own.

In this chapter, we will cover the following recipes:

- Creating a custom diffuse lighting model
- Creating a toon shader
- Adding shadows with custom functions
- Adding support for multiple lights and a Blinn-Phong specular
- Creating an anisotropic specular type

Technical requirements

For this chapter, you will need Unity Editor version 6 Preview 6000.0.7f1. This chapter's instructions should work with minimal changes in future versions of the editor in projects that utilize the **Universal Render Pipeline** (**URP**). The chapter's sample project was created using the **Universal 3D Core** template.

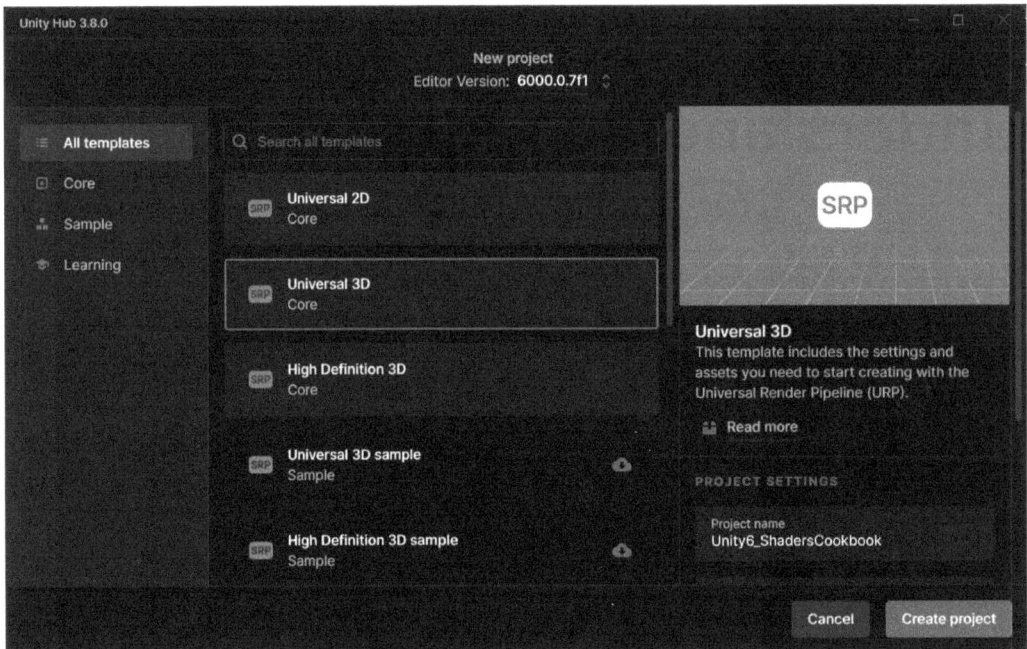

Figure 11.1 – Universal 3D (URP) project

The code files for this chapter can be found on GitHub at https://github.com/PacktPublishing/
Unity-6-Shaders-and-Effects-Cookbook. The necessary files for this chapter are organized in
the Unity project in a folder named Chapter 11 (https://github.com/PacktPublishing/Unity-
6-Shaders-and-Effects-Cookbook/tree/main/Unity6_ShadersCookbook/Assets/Chapter%20
11) on GitHub.

Creating a custom diffuse lighting model

If you are familiar with Unity 4, you might know that the default shader it provided was based on a lighting model called Lambertian reflectance. This recipe will show you how it is possible to create a Shader Graph that has a custom lighting model. Additionally, we will explain the mathematics involved and the implementation. The following diagram shows the same geometry rendered with a diffuse Lambert Shader (on the left-hand side) and a Standard one (on the right-hand side):

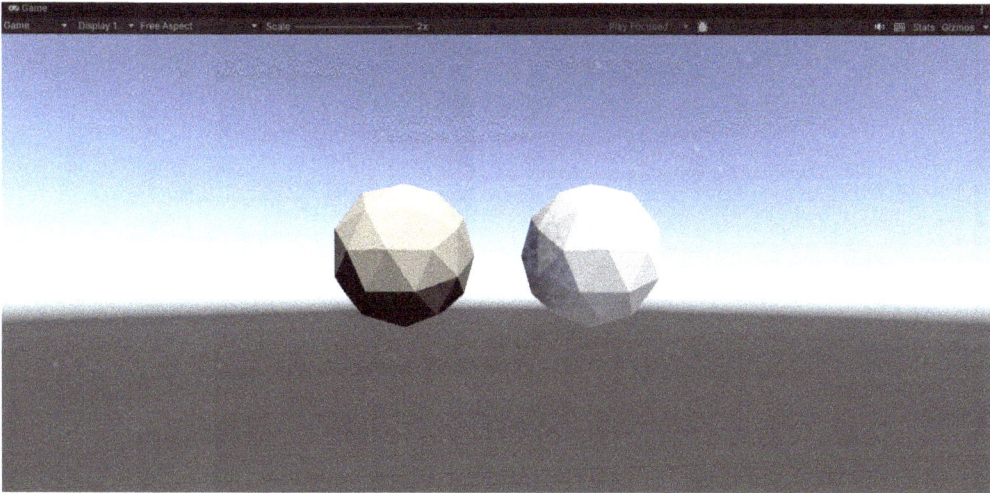

Figure 11.2 – A diffuse Lambert shader (left) versus a Standard Shader (right)

Shaders based on the Lambertian reflectance are classified as non-photorealistic; no object in the real world actually looks like this. However, Lambert shaders are still often used in low-poly games, as they produce a neat contrast between the faces of complex geometries. The lighting model used to calculate the Lambertian reflectance is also very efficient, making it perfect for mobile games.

Lighting in Shader Graph has come a long way, and there have been some newly added nodes to make our lives easier, as we will see; however, if we wish to have custom lighting in our games, we currently will need to create an Unlit Shader and do the calculation to create the lighting ourselves by hand in Shader Graph. Here, we will go into depth and explain where the data is coming from and why the custom light is working in the manner that it is. This will help you to get a nice grounding in how to set up custom lighting models; the knowledge gained here will set us up nicely for future recipes in this chapter.

Getting ready

Let's start by carrying out the following steps:

1. Create a new scene by navigating to **File** | **New Scene**. Select the **Basic (URP)** scene, and then hit **Create**.

   We won't be able to use Unity's default calculations for lighting for this shader, so we will use an Unlit Shader and then write it ourselves instead.

2. Create a new unlit shader (**Create** | **Shader Graph** | **URP** | **Unlit Shader Graph**) and give it a name (for example, `SimpleLambert`).

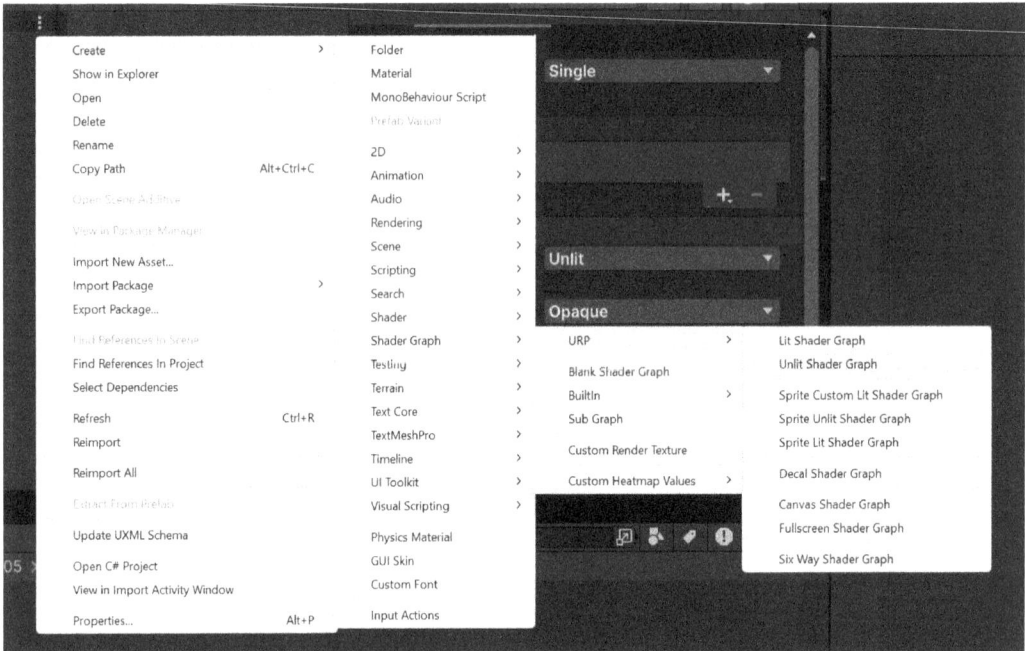

Figure 11.3 – Creating an Unlit Shader Graph

3. Create a new material, give it a name (for example, `SimpleLambertMat`), and assign the new shader to its shader property.

4. Then, create a sphere object and place it roughly in the center of the scene. Attach the new material to it.

5. Finally, let's create a directional light to cast some light on our object if one hasn't been created already.

Once your assets have been set up in Unity, you should have a scene that resembles the following screenshot:

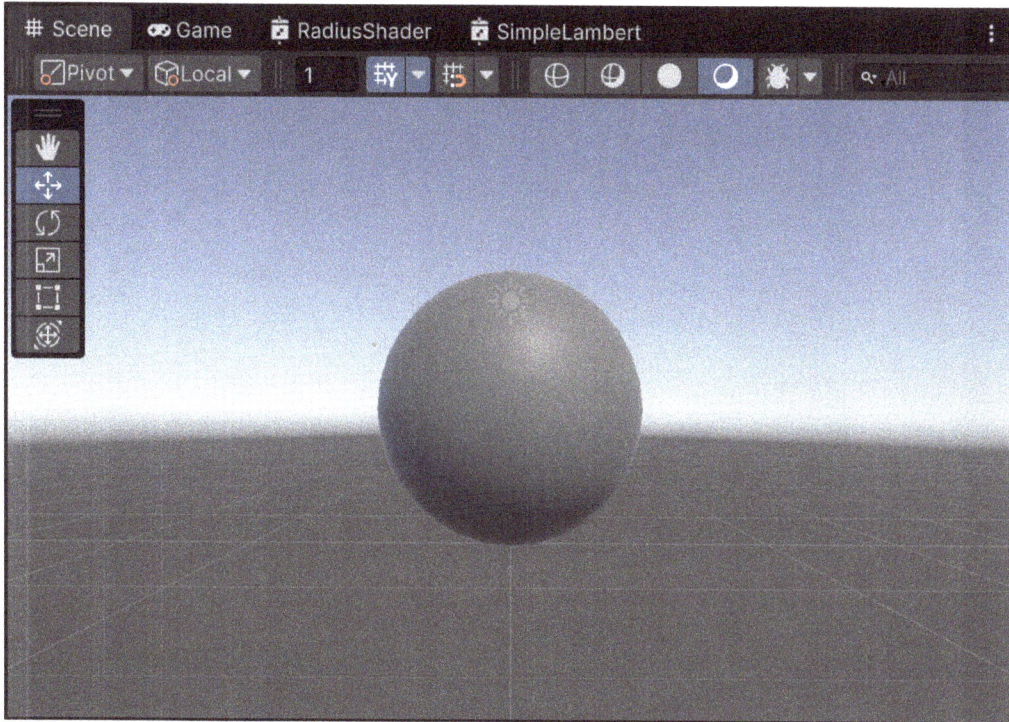

Figure 11.4 – The initial scene

How to do it...

The Lambertian reflectance can be achieved via the following steps in Shader Graph:

1. Double-click on the **SimpleLambert** Shader Graph to open it.

2. In the **Shader Graph** editor, start by creating a property for the main texture. Click the + button on the **Blackboard** and choose **Texture2D**. Name it Base Texture.

3. Drag the **Base Texture** property from the **Blackboard** to the graph.

4. Create a **Sample Texture 2D** node and ensure that **Main Texture(T2)** is connected to the **Texture(T2)** input of the **Sample Texture 2D** node.

5. Below those nodes, create a **Main Light Direction** node. To the right of it, create a **Negate** node. Connect **Direction(3)** of the **Main Light Direction** node to the **Negate** node.

6. Below those nodes, create a **Normal Vector** node (**Input** | **Geometry** | **Normal Vector**).

7. Create a **Dot Product** node. Connect **Out(3)** of the **Negate** node to **A** of the **Dot Product** node. Connect **Out(3)** of the **Normal Vector** node to **B** of the **Dot Product** node.

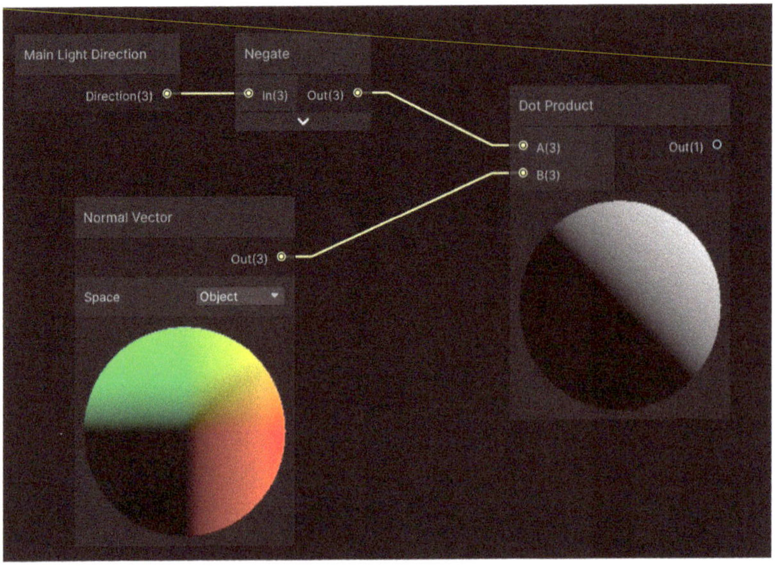

Figure 11.5 – Connections to Dot Product

8. To the right of the **Dot Product** node, create a **Saturate** node and connect **Out(1)** of **Dot Product** to **In(1)** of the **Saturate** node. Change the **Normal Vector** node's **Space** to **World**.

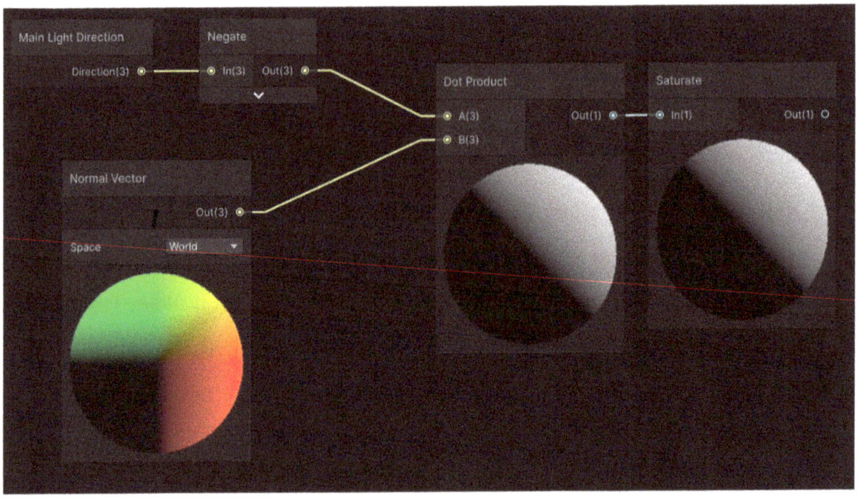

Figure 11.6 – Saturating the Dot Product result

We must clamp the **Dot Product** output to remain non-negative on the dark side.

9. To the right of the **Saturate** node, create a **Multiply** node. Connect **RGBA(4)** of the **Sample Texture 2D** node to **A** of the **Multiply** node. Connect **Out(1)** of the **Saturate** node to **B(4)** of the **Multiply** node.

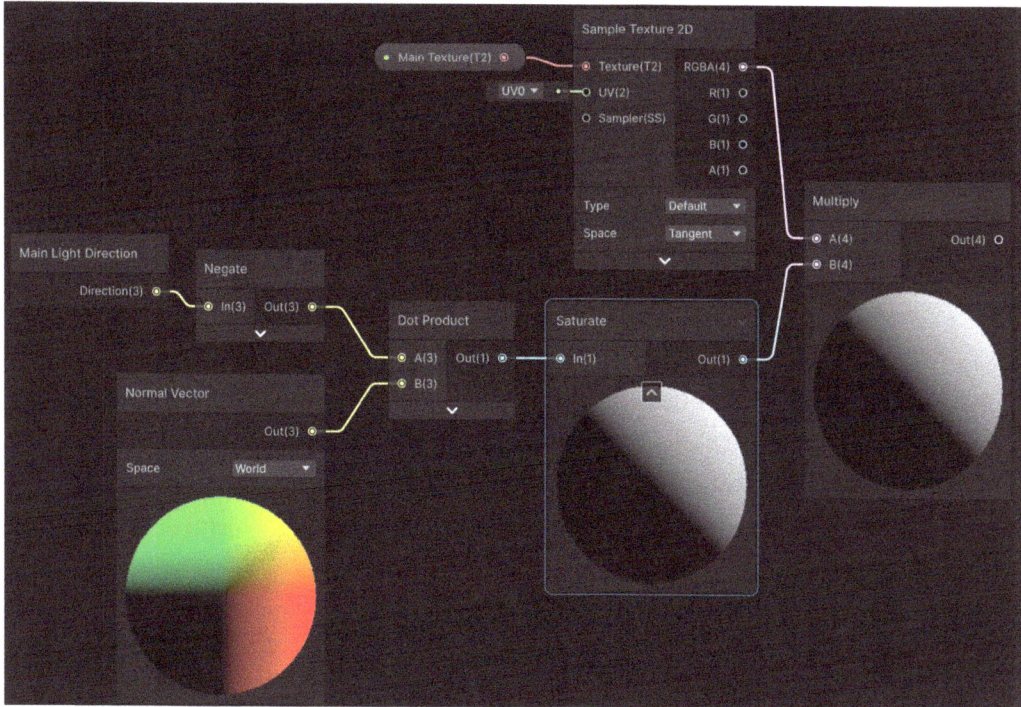

Figure 11.7 – Multiplying the Saturate results with the texture data

The preceding setup would give us a result that would take our light's direction into account but not the color. We can make use of Unity's built-in shader variables to get the color of our directional light.

10. On the **Blackboard**, create a new **Vector3** called LightColor0. In **Graph Settings**, ensure that **Reference** is set to _LightColor0 and uncheck the **Show In Inspector** property. To make it easier to see the effect, you can change **Default Value** to something other than the default of 0,0,0. For a yellowish color like the default directional light, you could use 1,0.9,0.8.

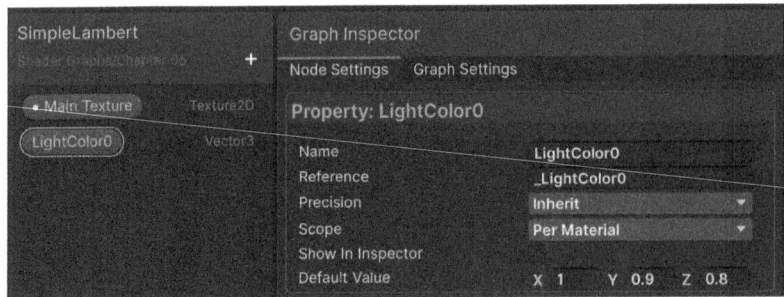

Figure 11.8 – LightColor0 property setup

Note that when changing the **Default Value** property, you will get a warning that says `Trying to set builtin parameter "_LightColor0". Will be ignored`, which is fine since we are only using it for preview purposes.

11. Drag and drop the **LightColor0** node onto the graph and create a **Multiply** node. Connect **LightColor(3)** to **A** of the new **Multiply** node and connect **Out(4)** of the first multiplication between **Sample Texture 2D** and **Dot Product** to **B** of the new **Multiply** node.

12. Finally, connect **Out(3)** of the newly created **Multiply** to **Base Color(3)** of the **Fragment** part of **Master Stack**.

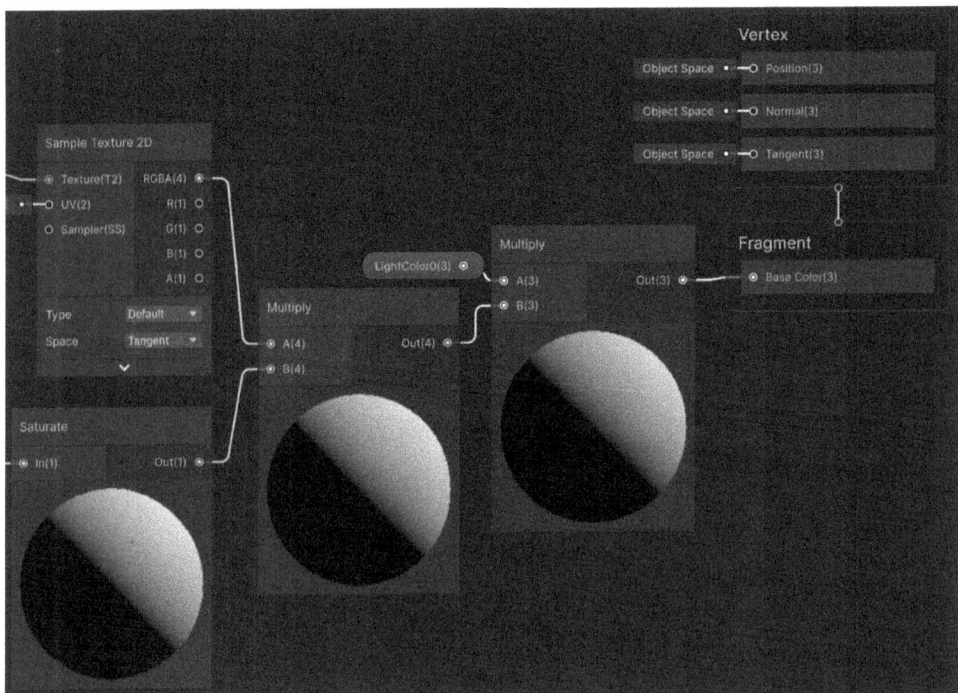

Figure 11.9 – Setting the base color

13. Save your graph and return to the Unity Editor.

You should now see the effect of the Lambertian reflectance on your object in the Unity Editor or in the **Game** view:

Figure 11.10 – The initial effect of the simple Lambert Shader Graph

The effect is even easier to view if we use the sphere object included within the Assets/Chapter 11/Models folder within the example code for this book:

Figure 11.11 – A simple Lambert Shader Graph (left) versus a normal diffuse shader (right)

Additionally, you can observe an even greater difference if you view it isometrically by selecting **Main Camera** and changing **Projection** to **Orthographic**:

Figure 11.12 – Orthographic view

How it works...

According to the Lambertian reflectance, the amount of light a surface reflects depends on the angle between the incident light and the surface normal. If you have played pool or billiards, you will be familiar with this concept; the direction of movement of a ball depends on its incident angle against the wall. If you hit the ball against a wall at a 90-degree angle, the ball will come back at you; if you hit it with a very low angle, its direction will be mostly unchanged. The Lambertian model makes the same assumption; if the light hits a triangle at a 90-degree angle, all the light gets reflected back. The lower the angle, the less light that is reflected back to you. This concept is shown in the following diagram:

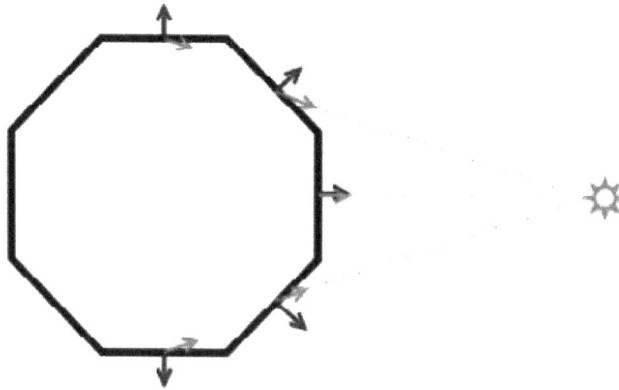

Figure 11.13 – A demonstration of the Lambertian model

This simple concept has to be translated into a mathematical form. In vector algebra, which is a part of the study of linear algebra, the angle between two unit vectors can be calculated via an operator called the **dot product**. When the dot product is equal to 0, the two vectors are orthogonal. This means that they make a 90-degree angle. When it is equal to 1 (or -1), they are parallel to each other. Shader Graph has a **Dot Product** node, which calls the Cg dot function, which implements the dot product extremely efficiently. It is important to note that the vectors need to be normalized for this to work correctly.

The following diagram shows a light source (the sun) shining on a complex surface. *L* indicates the light direction (the result of the **Main Light Direction** node after being negated in our shader) and *N* is the normal to the surface. The light is reflected at the same angle that it hits the surface:

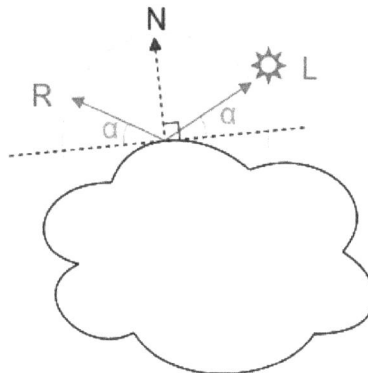

Figure 11.14 – A light source shining on a complex surface

Note

For more information on normals and what they mean mathematically, please refer to `https://en.wikipedia.org/wiki/Normal_(geometry)`.

The Lambertian reflectance simply uses the **NdotL** dot product as a multiplicative coefficient for the intensity of light:

$$I = N \cdot L$$

When N and L are parallel, all the light is reflected back to the source, causing the geometry to appear brighter. The **_LightColor0** variable contains the color of the light that is calculated.

When the dot product is negative, the light is coming from the opposite side of the triangle. This is not a problem for opaque geometries, as triangles that are not facing the camera frontally are culled (that is, discarded) and not rendered.

This basic Lambert is a great starting point when you are prototyping your shaders. This is because you can get a lot accomplished in terms of writing the core functionality of the shader while not having to worry about the basic lighting functions.

We lastly create a variable to hold whatever **_LightColor0** is set to, which is a built-in shader variable that Unity has that is set to whatever the directional light in the scene is set to.

Note

For a list of all of the built-in shader variables that Unity has, check out `https://docs.unity3d.com/Manual/SL-UnityShaderVariables.html`.

However, if we add a plane to the ground to both objects, you'll notice that right now, the default shader will have shadows, but our shader currently doesn't support it or additional lights; this is something that we will solve in a later recipe through the use of custom functions and subgraphs.

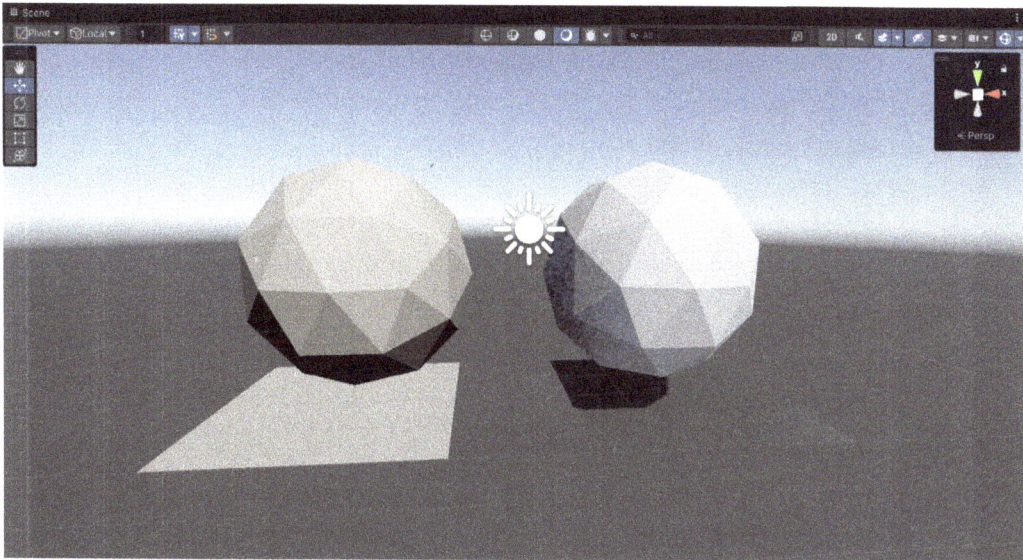

Figure 11.15 – Missing shadows

Creating a toon shader

One of the most commonly used effects in games is **toon shading**, which is also known as **celluloid** (**CEL**) shading. This is a non-photorealistic rendering technique that makes 3D models appear flat. Many games use it to give the illusion that the graphics are being drawn by hand rather than modeled in 3D. In the following diagram, you can view a sphere rendered with a standard shader (on the left-hand side) and a sphere rendered with a toon shader (on the right-hand side):

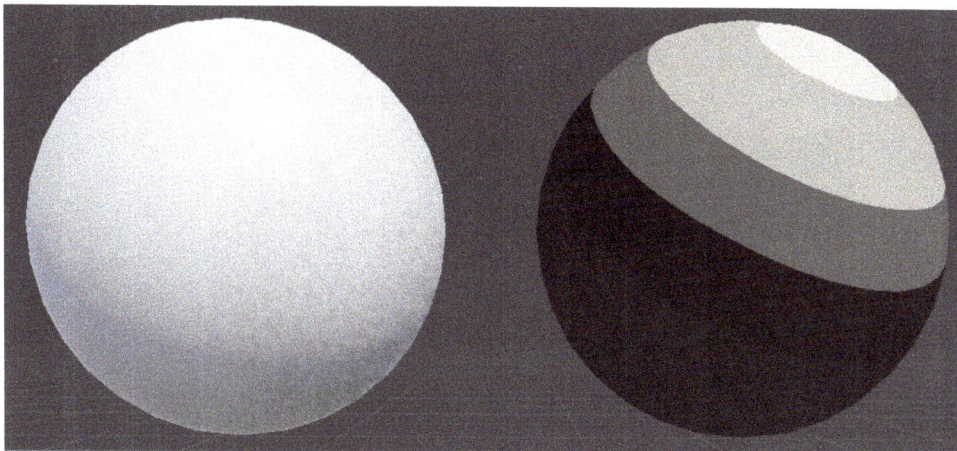

Figure 11.16 – A standard shader (left) versus a toon shader (right)

Achieving this effect using just surface functions is not impossible, but it would be extremely expensive and time-consuming. In fact, the surface function only works on the properties of the material, not its actual lighting condition. As toon shading requires us to change the way light reflects, we need to create a custom lighting model instead.

Getting ready

Let's start this recipe by creating a shader and its material and importing a special texture. Perform the following steps:

1. Create a new scene by going to **File** | **New Scene**. Select the **Basic (URP)** scene, and then hit **Create**.

2. Then, create a sphere object and place it roughly within the center of the scene.

3. Next, create a new Shader Graph; in this example, we will duplicate the one that we made in the *Creating a custom diffuse lighting model* recipe (that is, **SimpleLambert**) by selecting it in the **Project** tab and then hitting *Ctrl + D*. We will change the name of this new shader to ToonShader.

> Note
>
> You can rename an object in the **Project** window by clicking once on the name or by selecting it and hitting *F2* on the keyboard.

4. Create a new material for the shader (**ToonShaderMat**) and attach it to a 3D model. Toon shading works best on curved surfaces.

5. This recipe requires an additional texture called a ramp map, which will be used to dictate when we want to use certain colors depending on the shade received:

Figure 11.17 – An example of a ramp map

Our ramp maps were made in Adobe Photoshop, but they can be made using any other image editing application, such as GIMP.

An example texture can be found in the Chapter 11/Textures folder of this book. If you decide to import your own, it is important that you select your next texture, and from the **Inspector** tab, change the ramp map's **Wrap Mode** property to **Clamp**. If you want the edges between the colors to be sharp, the **Filter Mode** option should also be set to **Point (no filter)**.

6. Finally, hit the **Apply** button:

Figure 11.18 – Setup for the ToonRamp texture

Note

The example project included with this book already has *steps 5* and *6* completed in the Assets/Chapter 11/Texture/ToonRamp file, but it is a good idea to verify that this is the case before moving forward.

How to do it...

The toon aesthetic can be achieved by making the following changes to the shader:

1. Double-click on **ToonShader** to open Shader Graph.

2. Select the connection between the **Saturate** and **Multiply** nodes and delete it by tapping the *delete* key. Drag the nodes to the left of the connection to the left to make space for our new additions.

3. In the **Blackboard** (the panel on the left), click the + button and choose **Texture2D**. You should see the property show up. Change the name of the property to Ramp Texture and press *Enter*.

4. With the newly created **Texture** property selected, we can now go to **Graph Inspector** on the right side and set **Default Value** to the ramp texture example from this chapter by either dragging and dropping it from the **Project** window or clicking on the button on the right-hand side and then selecting it from the menu that pops up.

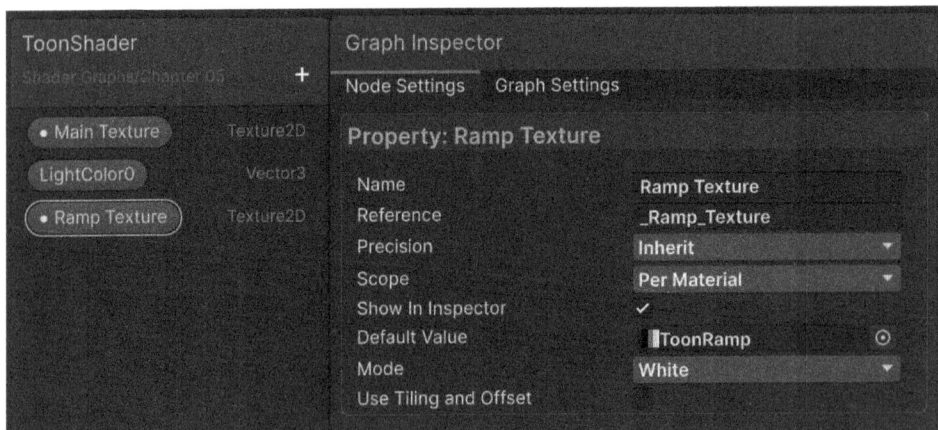

Figure 11.19 – Assigning Ramp Texture's Default Value

5. Drag the **Ramp Texture** property from the **Blackboard** to the graph area.

6. Drag from the output of the **Base Texture(T2)** node and create a **Sample Texture 2D** node. Then, connect **Ramp Texture(T2)** to **Texture(T2)** of the **Sample Texture 2D** node.

7. To the right of the **Saturate** node, create a **Vector 2** node. Connect **Out(1)** of the **Saturate** node to **X(1)** of the **Vector 2** node. You can set **Y(1)** to any value; I used 0.5. Connect **Out(2)** of the **Vector 2** node to **UV(2)** of the **Sample Texture 2D** node. Then, connect **RGBA(4)** of the **Sample Texture 2D** node to **B(2)** of the original **Multiply** node.

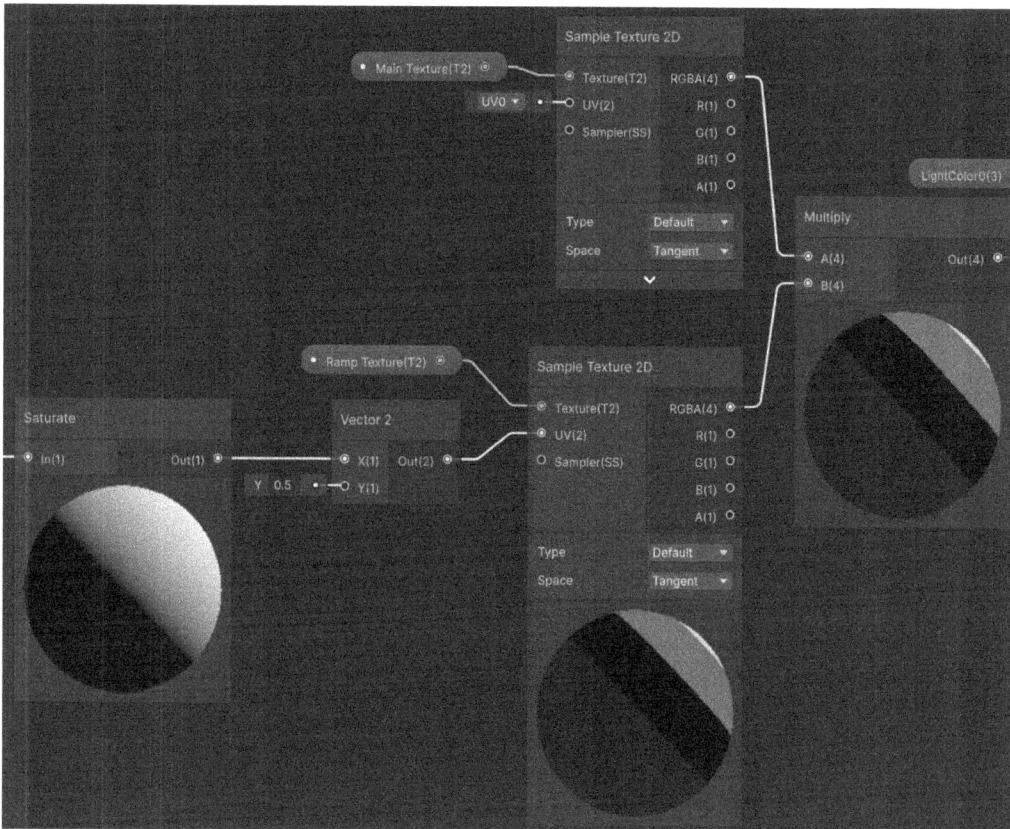

Figure 11.20 – Toon Shader Graph

8. Save Shader Graph by clicking on the **Save** icon (the one that looks like a floppy disk) in the top-left corner of the Shader Graph editor and return to the Unity Editor.

After making the changes, you'll get the following result:

Figure 11.21 – Toon Shader result

How it works...

The main characteristic of toon shading is the way the light is rendered; surfaces are not shaded uniformly. To achieve this effect, we need a ramp map. Its purpose is to remap the Lambertian light intensity, **NdotL**, to another value. Using a ramp map without a gradient, we can force the lighting to be rendered in steps. The following diagram shows how the ramp map is used to correct the light intensity:

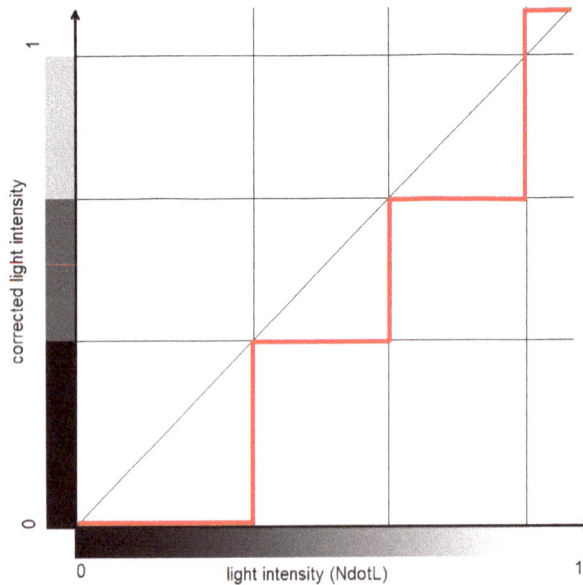

Figure 11.22 – How a ramp map is used to correct the light intensity

Any negative values from **NdotL** are clamped to the border pixel because the **Texture Wrap** mode is set to **Clamp**.

There's more...

There are many different ways whereby you can achieve a toon shading effect. Using different ramps can produce dramatic changes to the way your models look, so you should experiment in order to find the best one.

An alternative to ramp textures is to snap the NdotL light intensity so that it can only assume a certain number of values equidistantly sampled from 0 to 1:

1. Follow this shader's steps again, including those in the *Getting ready* section and those up to *step 2* in the *How to do it...* section, before creating the ramp texture, except this time we've named the shader ToonShaderSeeMore.

2. In the **Blackboard** (the panel on the left), click the + button and choose **Float**. You should see the property show up. Change the name of the property to Cel Shading Levels and press *Enter*.

3. With the newly created **Float** property selected, we can now go to **Graph Inspector** on the right side and set **Default Value** to 5:

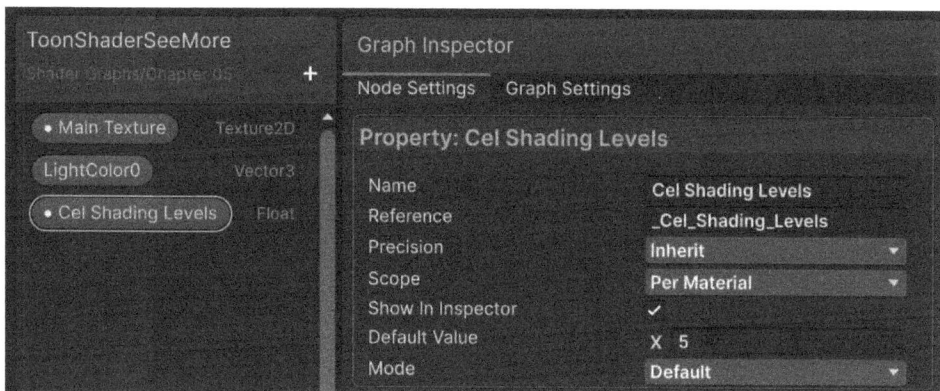

Figure 11.23 – Creating the Cel Shading Levels variable

4. Drag and drop the **Cel Shading Levels** variable onto the graph. Then, create a **Multiply** node to the right of it.

5. Connect **Cel Shading Levels** to the **B** input of the newly created **Multiply** node, and then connect the output of the **Saturate** node to the **Multiply** node in the **A** input.

6. To the right of the output of the **Multiply** node, create a **Floor** node. Connect the output of the **Multiply** node to the input of the **Floor** node to clamp any decimal values.

7. Create a **Divide** node to the right of the **Floor** node. Connect the output of the **Floor** node to the **A** input of the **Divide** node.

8. Below all these nodes, create a **Subtract** node. Connect the output of the **Subtract** node to the **B** input of the **Divide** node.

9. For the **A** input of the **Subtract** node, connect the **Cel Shading Levels** variable by either creating a new variable or using the one we created previously. For the **B** input of the **Subtract** node, input the value 0.5.

10. Finally, connect the output of the **Divide** node to the **B** input of the original **Multiply** node to link our additions to the sample texture and the multiplications with the light color.

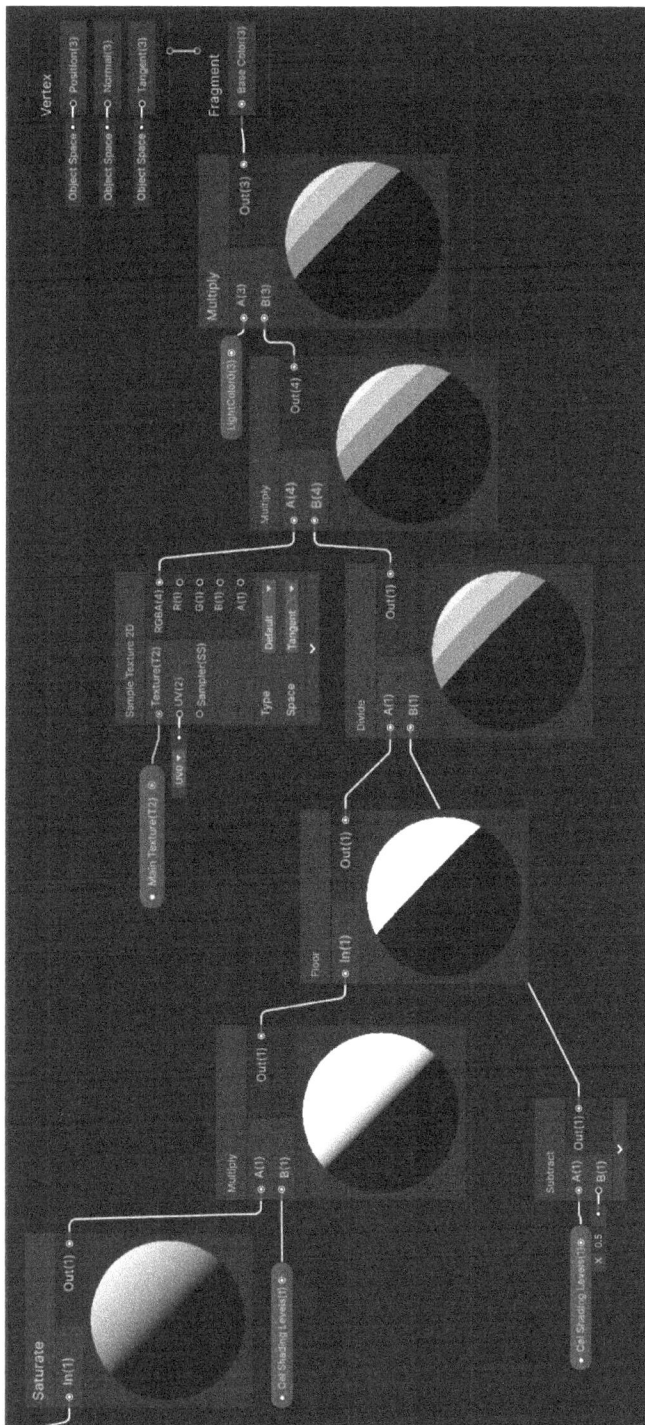

Figure 11.24 – Final version of the levels shader

11. Save Shader Graph by clicking on the **Save** icon (the one that looks like a floppy disk) in the top-left corner of the Shader Graph editor and return to the Unity Editor.

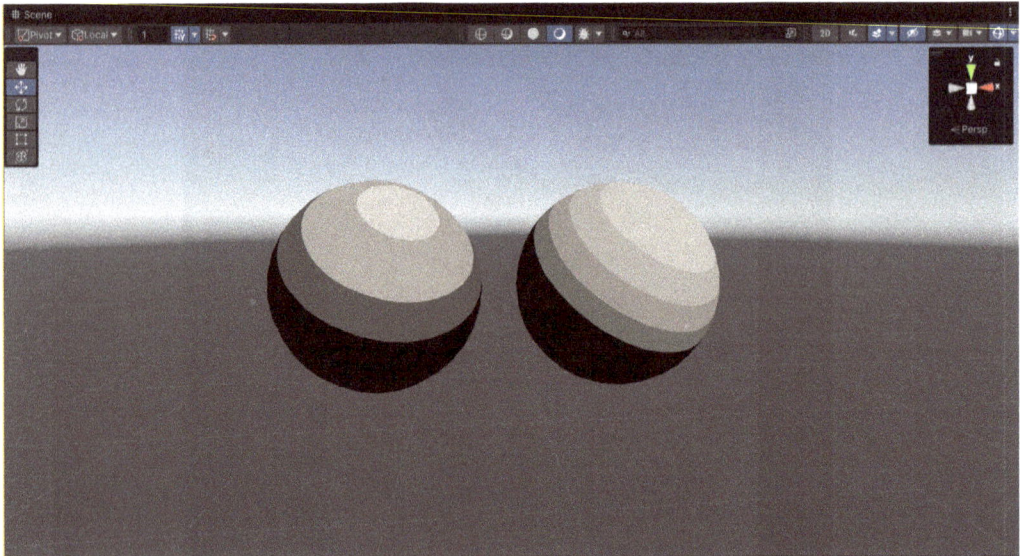

Figure 11.25 – The original implementation (left) versus the levels version (right)

To snap a number, first, we multiply the result of the dot product saturated by the **Cel Shading Levels** variable, round the result to an integer through the floor function, and then divide it back. This rounding is done by the **Floor** node, which will effectively remove the decimal point from a number. By doing this, the quantity is forced to assume one of the **Cel Shading Levels** equidistant values from 0 to 1. This removes the need for a ramp texture and makes all the color steps the same size. If you are going for this implementation, remember to add a property called **Cel Shading Levels** to your shader. Try changing the **Levels** property to view how it affects the object, as shown in the following screenshot:

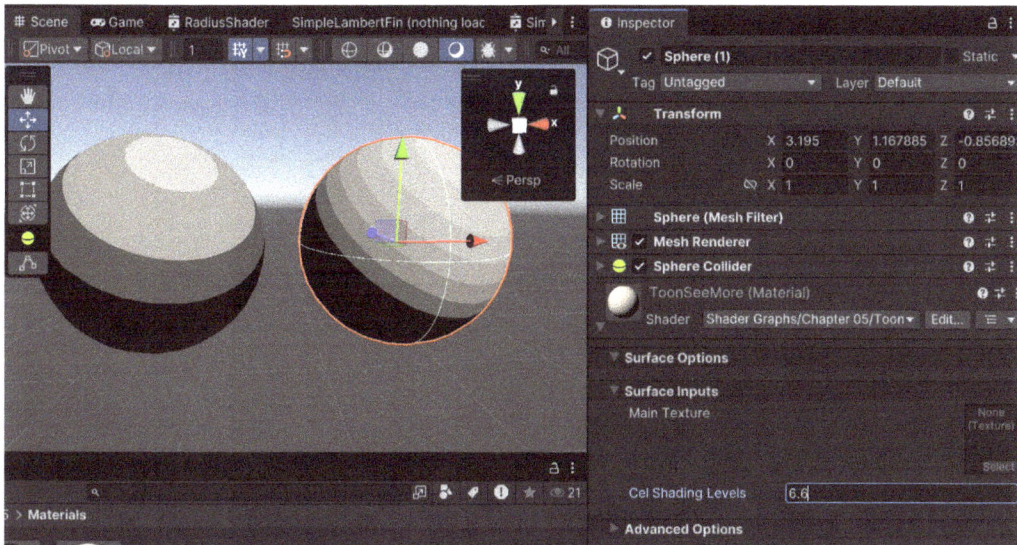

Figure 11.26 – Setting Cel Shading Levels

Adding shadows with custom functions

One of the things you may have noticed in the previous examples is that while we are getting the visual effects we are looking for on individual objects, when we start to introduce additional objects to our scene, we no longer see the desired effects when those objects interact with each other. Namely, we're not seeing shadows.

This is because Shader Graph, when using an unlit shader, doesn't include data from other lights or shadows by default. To achieve this interaction, we need to write some additional code using **High-Level Shading Language** (**HLSL**).

Thankfully, Unity has added a node in Shader Graph called **Custom Function**, which allows us to call a function from an HLSL file or a string to execute custom code.

Getting ready

Let's start this recipe by creating a shader and its material and importing a special texture. Perform the following steps:

1. Create a new scene by going to **File | New Scene**. Select the **Basic (URP)** scene and then hit **Create**.

2. Then, create a sphere object and place it roughly within the center of the scene. Then, create a plane below it in such a way that you can see a shadow below it.

3. Next, create a new Shader Graph; in this example, we will duplicate the one that we made in the *Creating a custom diffuse lighting model* recipe (that is, **SimpleLambert**) by selecting it in the **Project** tab and then hitting *Ctrl + D*. We will change the name of this new shader to Shadows.

> Note
>
> You can rename an object in the **Project** window by clicking once on the name or by selecting it and hitting *F2* on the keyboard.

4. Create a new material for the shader (**ShadowMat**) and attach it to both models. You should notice that the shadow disappears.

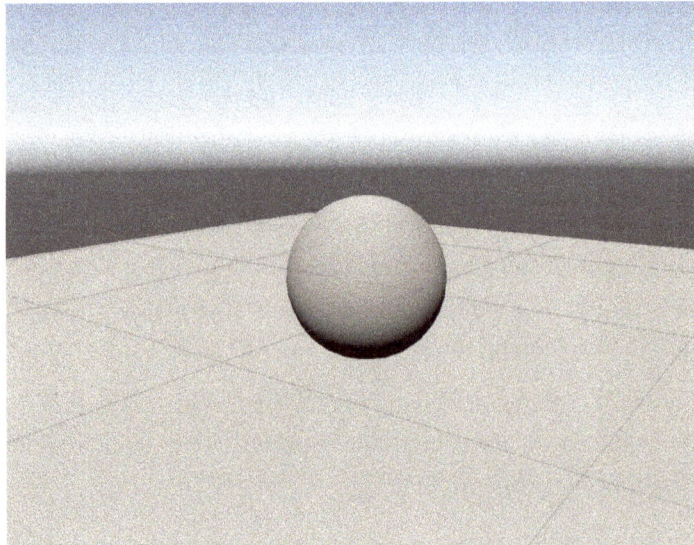

Figure 11.27 – Recipe setup

How to do it...

Unity no longer allows us to create HLSL files within the editor, so we will need to create the file by hand:

1. Go to the **Project** window and open the Shaders folder. From there, right-click and select **Show in...** (for those using Windows, select **Explorer**; for those using a Mac, select **Finder**).

    This will open up the window where the Shader Graph files have been created.

2. Create a text file. For those using Windows, you can right-click and select **New | New Text Document**. From there, rename the file to CustomLighting.hlsl. Afterward, we can return to the Unity Editor and double-click on the file to open your code editor of choice (in my case, Visual Studio).

3. Then, at the top of the file, we are going to include a #define preprocessor directive so the file will only be included once when the code is compiled:

```
/* If CUSTOM_LIGHTING_INCLUDED is not defined, define it */
#ifndef CUSTOM_LIGHTING_INCLUDED
#define CUSTOM_LIGHTING_INCLUDED
```

4. Below that, we need to start adding the content that we will be calling inside of Shader Graph itself, a function called GetShadowAtten that will calculate the shadow attenuation given a position in the world. First, let's add a section for when we are in preview mode:

```
/* Main function to calculate Shadow Attenuation for a given world
position */
void GetShadowAtten_float(float3 WorldPos,
                          out float ShadowAtten)
{
#if SHADERGRAPH_PREVIEW
    /* Set shadow attenuation for preview mode */
    ShadowAtten = 1.0;
```

5. Next, if we are not in preview mode, we can actually use Unity's functions to get the real data:

```
#else
    // Transform the world position to shadow coordinates
    float4 shadowCoord = TransformWorldToShadowCoord(WorldPos);

#if !defined(_MAIN_LIGHT_SHADOWS) || defined(_RECEIVE_SHADOWS_OFF)
    /* No shadow attenuation if shadows are disabled */
    ShadowAtten = 1.0h;
#else
    /* Get shadow sampling data for the main light */
    ShadowSamplingData shadowSamplingData =
        GetMainLightShadowSamplingData();
```

```
        /* Get shadow strength for the main light */
        float shadowStrength = GetMainLightShadowStrength();

        // Sample the shadow map to get the shadow attenuation
        ShadowAtten = SampleShadowmap(shadowCoord,
                TEXTURE2D_ARGS(_MainLightShadowmapTexture,
                        sampler_MainLightShadowmapTexture),
                                shadowSamplingData,
                                shadowStrength,
                                false
    );
#endif  /* End of shadow check */
#endif  /* End of SHADERGRAPH_PREVIEW check */
}


#endif  /* End of CUSTOM_LIGHTING_INCLUDED check */
```

Note

In the preceding code, I used `1.0h` to create a half-precision float, but Unity treats it as a high-precision float instead because it doesn't support HLSL floating-point suffixes. For more information, check out `https://docs.unity3d.com/6000.0/Documentation/Manual/SL-DataTypesAndPrecision.html`.

6. Next, save the script and return to the Unity Editor. Then, double-click on the **Shadows** Shader Graph to open it up.

7. Create a new **Custom Function** node. Select it and then go to **Graph Inspector**. In the **Inputs** section, click on the + button and then set the type to **Vector3** and the name of the input to WorldPos. Under **Outputs**, click on the + button, and under **Type**, set the dropdown to **float**. Change **Name** to ShadowAtten.

8. Leave **Type** as **File**, then change **Source** to the CustomLighting.hlsl file we created. Then, set **Name** to GetShadowAtten. If all goes well, you should see the preview box change from the pink-and-black box to a nice white preview:

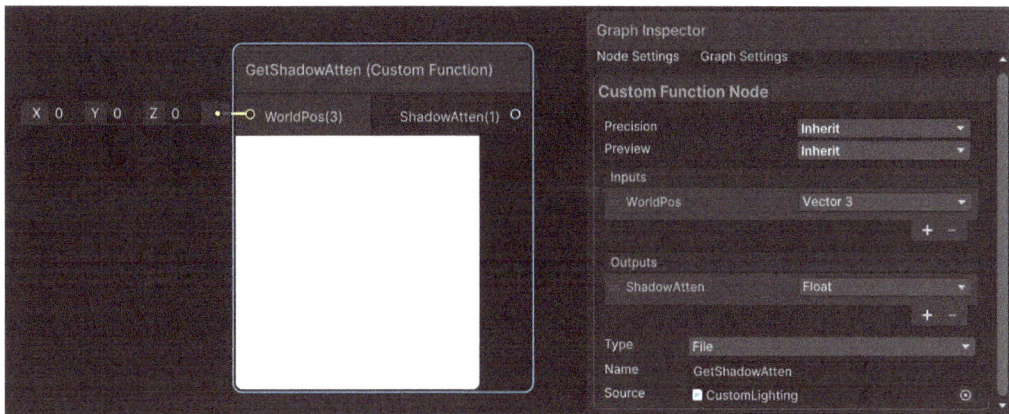

Figure 11.28 – Custom function setup

9. To get the correct information, we will need the correct position, so to the left of the
    Custom Function node (**GetShadowAtten**), create a **Position** node. Leave **Space** as **World**.
    Then, create a **Multiply** node. Connect the **ShadowAtten** output to **B** of the **Multiply**
    node, then disconnect the final **Multiply** output from the **Base Color** node and connect
    its output to **A** of the **Multiply** node. Then, connect our new **Multiply** node's output to
    the final **Base Color(3)** input.

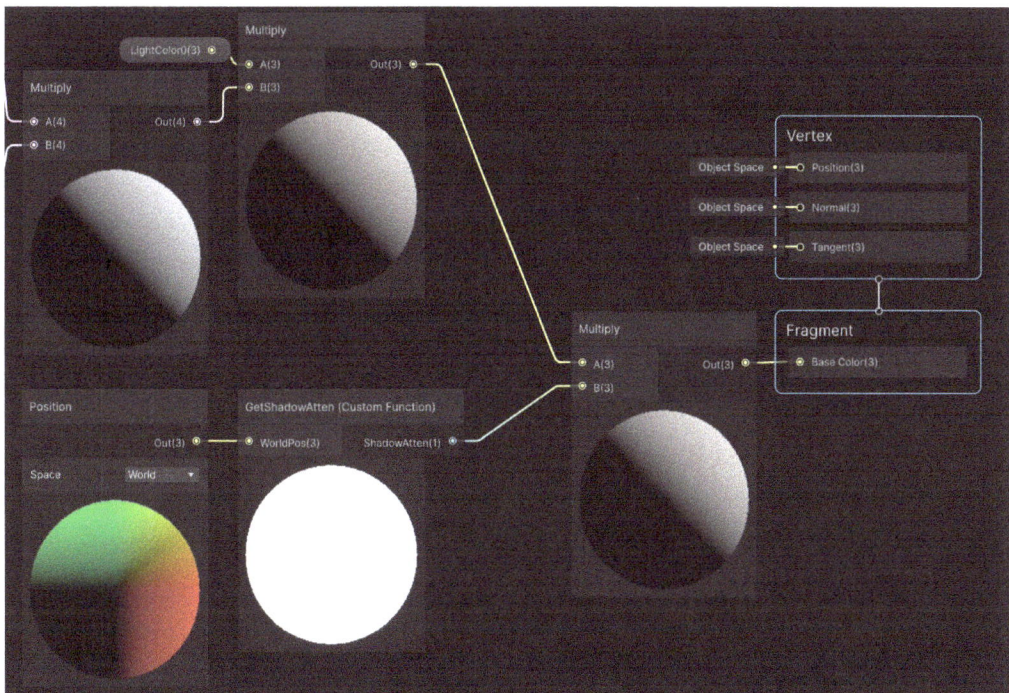

Figure 11.29 – Shadows Graph

This should work, but if we return to the editor, we'll see the shadows still won't work. This is because there are certain keywords that need to be enabled by Unity to enable shadows.

10. In the **Blackboard**, hit the + button and then select **Keyword | Boolean**. I gave it the name Enable Shadows. Then, go to **Graph Inspector** and change **Default Value** to true by checking it, and then set **Reference** to _MAIN_LIGHT_SHADOWS.

11. Save the graph and return to the editor.

Figure 11.30 – Shadows result

How it works...

The **Custom Function** node in Shader Graph allows you to write custom HLSL code directly within Shader Graph. This node provides flexibility to implement specific functionalities or effects that might not be available through the standard nodes.

The **Custom Function** node allows you to do the following:

- **Write custom HLSL code**: Insert custom HLSL code snippets to define how the node should behave

- **Define input and output ports**: Create custom input and output ports that interface with other nodes in Shader Graph

- **Include external HLSL files**: Reference external HLSL files if your custom code is extensive or reused across multiple shaders

In our case, we wrote a function inside of a file that we then called within Shader Graph. The GetShadowAtten function had the following function signature:

```
void GetShadowAtten_float(float3 WorldPos,
                          out float ShadowAtten)
```

These suffixes indicate the precision type, such as _float for high precision, _half for medium precision, and _fixed for low precision. When defining your custom HLSL function, you must include the appropriate precision suffix in the function name. For example, if your function uses high precision, the function name should end with _float, such as GetShadowAtten_float. However, when configuring the **Custom Function** node in Shader Graph, you should not include the precision suffix in the function's **Name** field. Instead, simply name the function GetShadowAtten. Shader Graph will handle the suffix internally based on the precision requirements. Additionally, ensure that the input and output ports in the **Custom Function** node match the parameters and return types of your HLSL function.

Likewise, the parameters of the function note the inputs and outputs we will need to set within the **Custom Function** node. In our case, this is a Vector3 property to relate to the float3 value of WorldPos and a Float property for ShadowAtten.

The code begins with preprocessor directives to ensure the custom lighting code is only included once. This is done using #ifndef to check that the CUSTOM_LIGHTING_INCLUDED macro is not defined, followed by #define CUSTOM_LIGHTING_INCLUDED to define it. This pattern prevents multiple inclusions of the same code, which can lead to redefinition errors.

The GetShadowAtten_float function is designed to calculate shadow attenuation for a given world position. It accepts a 3D world position (WorldPos) as input and outputs a shadow attenuation value (ShadowAtten). The function first checks whether the SHADERGRAPH_PREVIEW macro is defined. If it is, the function sets ShadowAtten to 1.0, indicating full light with no shadow attenuation, suitable for preview mode in Shader Graph.

If SHADERGRAPH_PREVIEW is not defined, the function transforms the world position to shadow coordinates using TransformWorldToShadowCoord, storing the result in shadowCoord. It then checks that either _MAIN_LIGHT_SHADOWS is not defined or _RECEIVE_SHADOWS_OFF is defined. If either condition is true, it sets ShadowAtten to 1.0, meaning shadows are effectively disabled, and full light is applied. This is one of the reasons we need to add the _MAIN_LIGHT_SHADOWS keyword to the **Blackboard**.

When shadows are enabled, the function retrieves shadow sampling data for the main light using `GetMainLightShadowSamplingData` and the shadow strength using `GetMainLightShadowStrength`. It then samples the shadow map using `SampleShadowmap`, which takes the shadow coordinates, shadow map texture, shadow sampling data, and shadow strength as inputs. The resulting shadow attenuation value is stored in `ShadowAtten`.

The code ends with `#endif` directives to close the conditional blocks, ensuring proper conditional compilation and preventing errors related to multiple inclusions or incorrect compilation paths.

There's more...

At this point, we now have shadows, but they are a bit pixelated. Thankfully, there are some additional keywords we can add that can make things a bit nicer.

Keyword	Description
`_MAIN_LIGHT_SHADOWS`	This keyword enables shadows for the main directional light in your scene. When this keyword is defined, the shader will include code to handle shadows cast by the main light.
`_SHADOWS_SOFT`	This keyword enables soft shadows, which are shadows with softened edges. Soft shadows are typically achieved by filtering the shadow map, resulting in a more natural and realistic shadow appearance compared to hard-edged shadows.
`_MAIN_LIGHT_SHADOW_CASCADE`	This keyword enables the use of cascaded shadow maps for the main directional light. Cascaded shadows improve the quality of shadows by using multiple smaller shadow maps, which cover different portions of the view frustum, providing higher-resolution shadows closer to the camera.
`_ADDITIONAL_LIGHT_SHADOWS`	This keyword enables shadows for additional lights in the scene, such as point lights and spotlights. When this keyword is defined, the shader will include code to handle shadows cast by these additional lights, not just the main directional light.

Table 11.1 – Keywords for light and shadow effects

Turning the keywords on, you can see the shadow looks nicer:

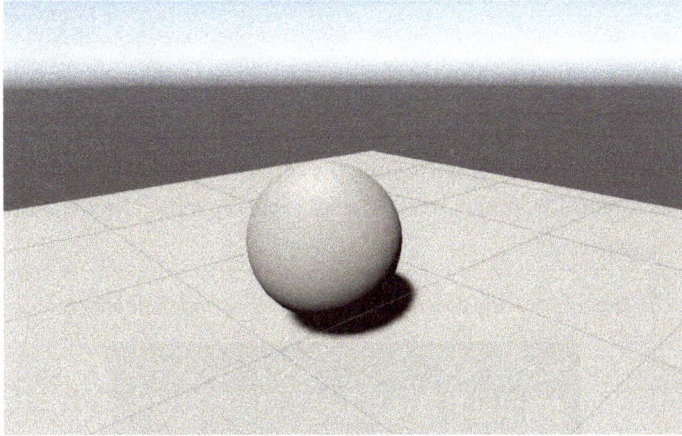

Figure 11.31 – Softer shadows

If you are using Cascade, you can tweak the settings further by going to your **Project** window and then going to the Settings folder and opening your render pipeline asset (in our case, PC_RPAsset, but you can double check in your **Project Settings** under the **Graphics** section what **Render Pipeline** is set to). Once selected, open the **Shadows** section and you can tweak the properties.

Property	Description
Max Distance	Defines the furthest distance from the camera at which shadows will be rendered. Objects beyond this distance will not cast or receive shadows. Balances shadow quality and performance.
Cascade Count	Determines the number of cascades used in the shadow map. More cascades can improve shadow quality near the camera but increase rendering complexity and impact performance.
Split 1	Defines the position where the view frustum is divided into the first cascade, expressed in meters or as a percentage of **Max Distance**.
Split 2	Defines the position where the view frustum is divided into the second cascade, expressed in meters or as a percentage of **Max Distance**.
Split 3	Defines the position where the view frustum is divided into the third cascade, expressed in meters or as a percentage of **Max Distance**.
Last Border	Sets the distance for the final cascade split, ensuring smooth transitions between cascades. Helps maintain shadow consistency across different distances.

Property	Description
Depth Bias	Offsets the depth values of shadow map samples to reduce shadow acne (self-shadowing artifacts). Must be fine-tuned to prevent shadows from appearing detached from objects.
Normal Bias	Offsets shadow map samples along the surface normal to reduce shadow acne. Needs careful adjustment to avoid noticeable separation between shadows and their casting objects.

Table 11.2 – Shadow mapping properties and their effects

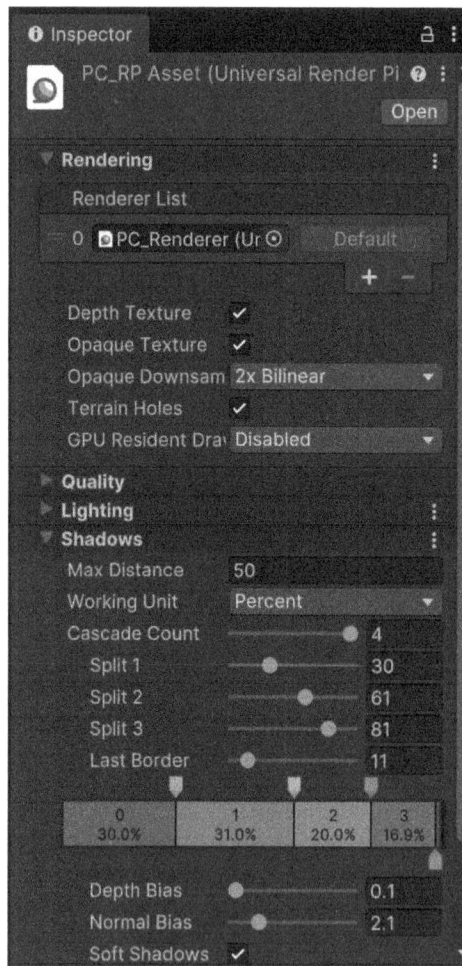

Figure 11.32 – Cascade adjustments

For instance, using the preceding properties gave me something that I was happier with:

Figure 11.33 – Final cascade shadows result

Adding support for multiple lights and a Blinn-Phong specular

Having shadows is great, but Unity currently lacks support for additional lights in our scene with our custom lighting model. In this recipe, we will address this limitation by adding support for multiple lights and incorporating Blinn-Phong, which is an efficient method for simulating shiny surfaces in real-time graphics as a way to enhance our lighting model.

This recipe serves as a complementary piece to the previous one, allowing us to build upon the foundation we established. Adding multiple lights to our scene also requires the use of custom functions since Shader Graph currently does not support looping.

Getting ready

Let's start this recipe by creating a shader and its material and importing a special texture. Perform the following steps:

1. Create a new scene by going to **File | New Scene**. Select the **Basic (URP)** scene and then hit **Create**.

2. Then, create a sphere object and place it roughly within the center of the scene. Then, create a plane below it in such a way that you can see a shadow below it. Add some point lights where you can see that it is affecting both objects. I used a *red*, *blue*, and *green* light to help show the differences in color. Also, feel free to increase the intensity to make it easier to see.

Figure 11.34 – Placing objects and lights

3. Next, create a new Shader Graph; in this example, we will duplicate the one that we made in the *Adding shadows with custom functions* recipe (that is, **Shadows**) by selecting it in the **Project** tab and then hitting *Ctrl + D*. We will change the name of this new shader to AdditionalLights.

4. Create a new material for the shader (AdditionalLightMat) and attach it to both models. You should notice that the effect of the lights disappears.

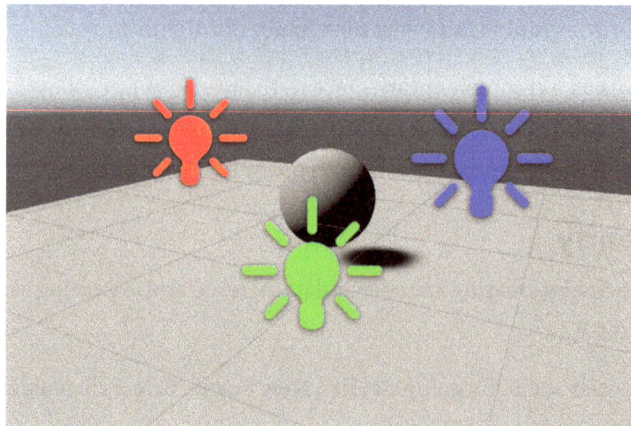

Figure 11.35 – Recipe setup

How to do it...

To get started, we will need to add our function for calculating additional lights in our shader:

1. From the Unity Editor, go to the **Project** window and double-click on our CustomLighting. hlsl file to open it in the code editor of your choice. Begin by declaring the function and its parameters:

```
/* Function to calculate additional light contributions */
void AdditionalLights_float( float3 WorldPosition,
                             float3 WorldNormal,
                             float3 WorldView,
                             float3 SpecColor,
                             float Smoothness,
                             float SpecPower,
                             out float3 Diffuse,
                             out float3 Specular)
```

2. Next, initialize the variables that will accumulate the diffuse and specular light contributions:

```
{
    /* Diffuse and specular color accumulators */
    float3 diffuseColor = 0;
    float3 specularColor = 0;
```

3. Then, we need to start the block that will occur if we are not in preview mode. To start, we will set the smoothness, retrieve the count of additional lights, and prepare the input data for light calculations:

```
#ifndef SHADERGRAPH_PREVIEW
    /* Adjust Smoothness for better visual results */
    Smoothness = exp2(10 * Smoothness + 1);

    /* Get count of lights affecting the pixel */
    uint pixelLightCount = GetAdditionalLightsCount();

    /* Prepare inputData for Forward+ */
    InputData inputData = (InputData) 0;
    float4 screenPos =
ComputeScreenPos(TransformWorldToHClip(WorldPosition));
```

```
inputData.normalizedScreenSpaceUV = screenPos.xy /
screenPos.w;
   inputData.positionWS = WorldPosition;
```

4. Loop through the additional lights and calculate the lighting contributions using a Blinn-
    Phong shading model:

```
/* Begin light loop for additional lights */
LIGHT_LOOP_BEGIN(pixelLightCount)

/* Get the properties of the current light */
Light light = GetAdditionalLight(lightIndex,
                                    WorldPosition);

/* Blinn-Phong shading model */
float3 attenuatedLightColor =
        light.color *
        (light.distanceAttenuation *
            light.shadowAttenuation);

/* Accumulate diffuse lighting contribution */
diffuseColor += LightingLambert(attenuatedLightColor,
                                    light.direction,
                                    WorldNormal);

/* Accumulate specular lighting contribution */
specularColor += LightingSpecular(attenuatedLightColor,
                                        light.direction,
                                        WorldNormal,
                                        WorldView,
                                    float4(SpecColor,
                                        SpecPower),
                                        Smoothness);
LIGHT_LOOP_END
```

5. Finally, we will output the accumulated diffuse and specular colors:

```
#endif /* End of SHADERGRAPH_PREVIEW check */

/* Output the accumulated colors */
```

```
        Diffuse = diffuseColor;
        Specular = specularColor;
    }


    #endif  /* End of CUSTOM_LIGHTING_INCLUDED check */
```

6. Save the script and return to the Unity Editor.

7. From the **Project** window, go to the Shader folder and double-click on the **AdditionalLights** shader to open Shader Graph.

8. Below all of the current nodes, add a **Custom Function** node. Add the following inputs for the function: **WorldPos (Vector 3)**, **WorldNormal (Vector 3)**, **World View (Vector 3)**, **SpecColor (Vector 3)**, **Smoothness (Float)** and **SpecPower (Float)**. Then, add the following outputs: **Diffuse (Vector 3)** and **Specular (Vector 3)**. Then, set **Type** to **File**, **Name** to **AdditionalLights**, and **Source** to our CustomLighting.hlsl file.

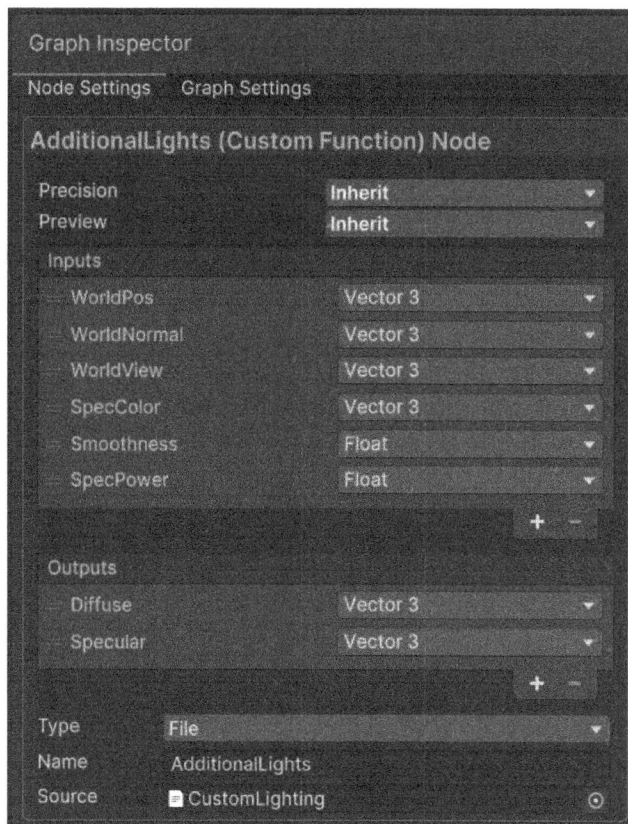

Figure 11.36 – AdditionalLights node setup

9. Connect **Out** from the **Position** node to **WorldPos** of the **AdditionalLights** node. To the left of **Custom Function**, create a **Normal Vector** node and connect **Out(3)** to **World Normal** of the **AdditionalLights** node.

10. Then, create a **View Direction** node. From there, connect **Out(3)** to the **WorldView** connection.

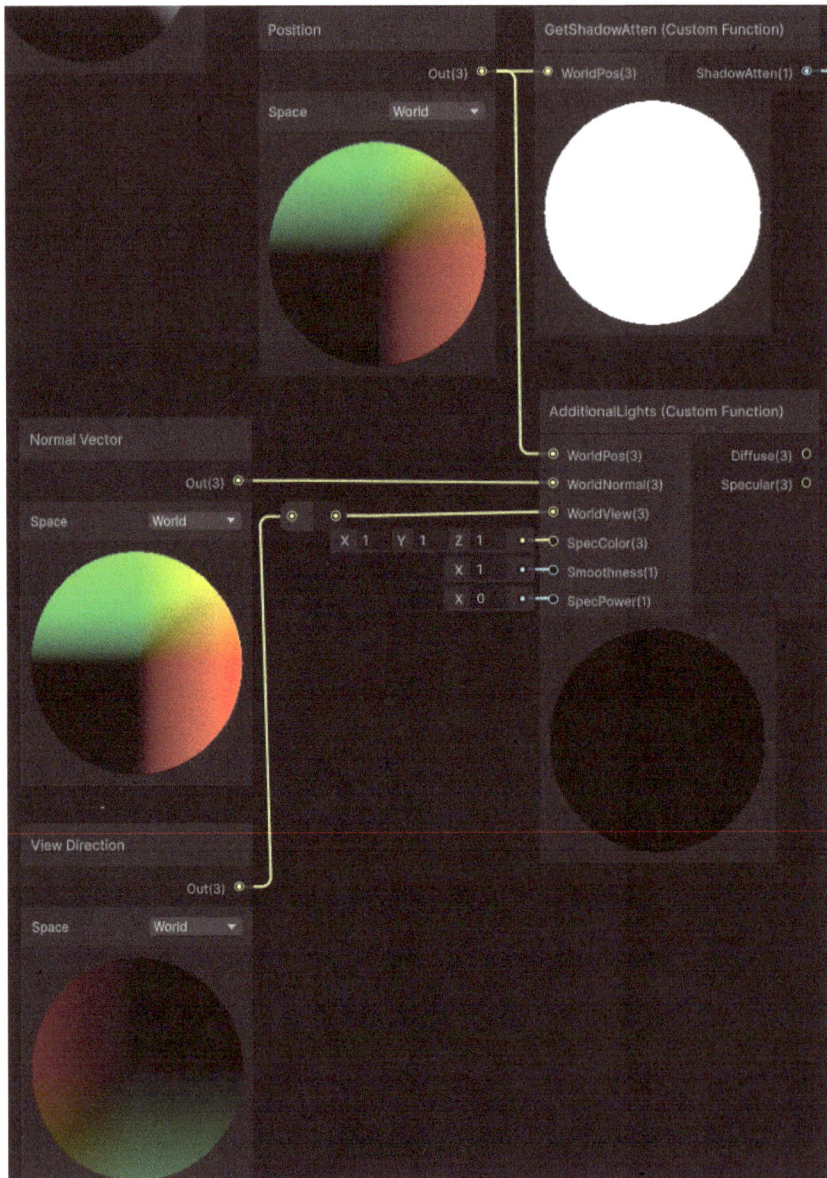

Figure 11.37 – Calling the AdditionalLights function

11. To the right of the **AdditionalLights** node, create an **Add** node. Add the **Diffuse** and **Specular** outputs together. Then, create another **Add** node and add the result from that node to the result of the **Multiply** node that is currently connected to **Base Color** of the **Master Stack** node. Then, replace the output with ours.

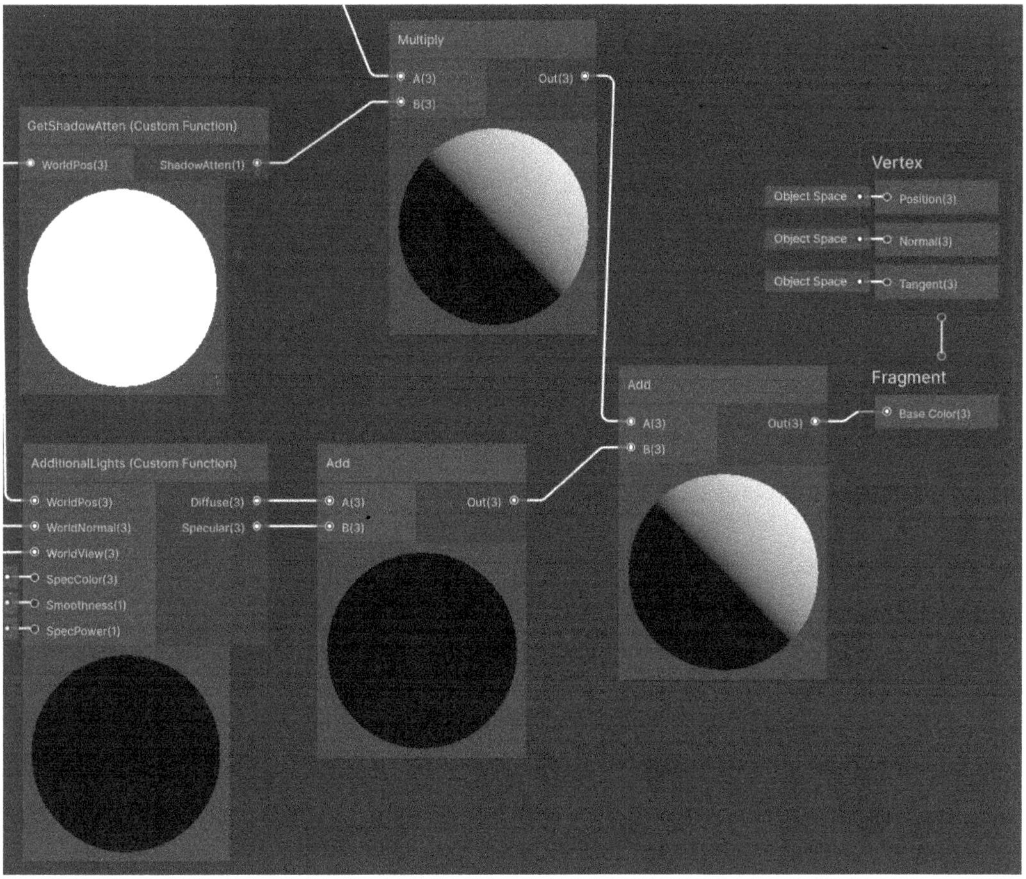

Figure 11.38 – Finishing the graph

12. Lastly, go to the **Blackboard** and click on the + icon. Then, select **Keyword | Boolean**. From **Graph Inspector**, set **Reference** to _FORWARD_PLUS, **Definition** to **MultiCompile**, and **Default Value** to true by checking it.

13. Then, right-click on your newly added **Boolean Keyword** property and duplicate it. Set the new property's reference to _ADDITIONAL_LIGHTS.

14. Save your Shader Graph and return to the Unity Editor.

Figure 11.39 – Shader recipe result

And with that, we now have support for additional lights, and if we turn them on, we have shadows for those additional lights as well.

How it works...

In this recipe, we continued exploring what can be done with custom functions.

The `AdditionalLights_float` function calculates the contributions of additional lights to a pixel's diffuse and specular lighting in a 3D scene.

The specularity of an object's surface simply describes how shiny it is. In the shader world, these types of effects are often referred to as view-dependent effects. This is because in order to achieve a realistic specular effect in your shaders, you need to include the direction of the camera or the user who is facing the object's surface.

In this case, we are using the Blinn-Phong specular model, which is an efficient method for simulating shiny surfaces in real-time graphics. It is an improvement over the Phong specular model, which calculates the reflection vector to determine the intensity of the specular highlight. This reflection vector calculation can be computationally expensive. The Blinn-Phong specular model simplifies the calculation of specular highlights by using the half vector, which is halfway between the view direction and the light direction. This approach is both efficient and physically accurate. Before the introduction of physically based rendering, this approach was the default choice for specular reflection in Unity 4.

Calculating the reflection vector, *R*, is generally expensive. The Blinn-Phong specular replaces it with the half vector, *H*, between the view direction, *V*, and the light direction, *L*:

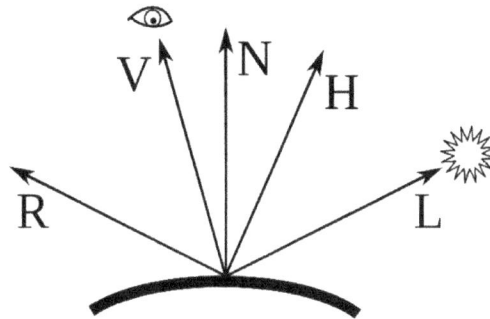

Figure 11.40 – The components of the Blinn-Phong model

Instead of calculating our own reflection vector, we are simply going to get the vector halfway between the view direction and the light direction, essentially simulating the reflection vector.

$$S_{Phong} = (R \cdot V)^p, S_{Blinnphong} = (N \cdot H)^p$$

According to vector algebra, the half vector (*H*) can be calculated as follows:

$$H = \frac{V + L}{|V + L|}$$

Here, $|V + L|$ is the length of the vector, $V + L$. We simply need to add the view direction and the light direction together and then normalize the result into a unit vector

Then, we simply need to dot the vertex normal with this new half vector to get our main specular value. Following this, we just take it to a power of _SpecPower and multiply it by the specular color variable. It's much lighter on the code and math; however, it still gives us a nice specular highlight that will work for many real-time situations.

In our case, the Blinn-Phong calculation is computed for us through the `LightingSpecular` function that Unity provides.

Initially, the function sets up accumulators for diffuse and specular colors. If not in `SHADERGRAPH_PREVIEW` mode, the function adjusts the smoothness for better visual results and retrieves the number of additional lights affecting the pixel. It also prepares the input data necessary for **Forward+** rendering techniques.

Forward+ rendering is used for efficiently handling a large number of dynamic lights in real-time rendering. It divides the screen into tiles and assigns lights to each tile based on their influence, reducing the number of light calculations per pixel and improving performance. This method involves a two-pass approach: constructing a light list for each tile and then performing shading calculations using these precomputed lists.

Within a loop (defined in the light helpers in the `Lighting.hlsl` file found in the `Editor/Data` folder of our Unity installation), the function processes each additional light source by fetching its properties, such as color, direction, and attenuation factors. The diffuse lighting contribution is calculated using the Lambertian reflectance model that was discussed in the *Creating a custom diffuse lighting model* recipe, while the specular lighting is computed using the Blinn-Phong specular model that we just discussed. These contributions are accumulated for each light source. Finally, the accumulated diffuse and specular colors are assigned to the output parameters, providing the combined lighting effects from all additional light sources to the calling context.

See also

The light models that you have viewed in this chapter are extremely simple; no real material is perfectly matte or perfectly specular. Moreover, it is not uncommon for complex materials such as clothing, wood, and skin to require knowledge of how light scatters in the layers beneath the surface. Use the following table to recap the different lighting models that we have encountered so far:

Technique	Type	Light Intensity (I)
Lambertian	Diffuse	$I = N \cdot L$
Blinn-Phong	Specular	$I = N \cdot L + (N \cdot H)^P$ $H = \dfrac{V + L}{|V + L|}$

Table 11.3 – Different lighting models

There are other interesting lighting models, such as the Oren-Nayar, Ward, Cook-Torrance, and Ashikhmin-Shirley lighting models for rough surfaces. For more information, please refer to `https://www1.cs.columbia.edu/CAVE/projects/oren/`.

Creating an anisotropic specular type

Anisotropic is a type of specular or reflection that simulates the directionality of grooves in a surface and modifies/stretches the specular in a perpendicular direction. This is very useful when you want to simulate brushed metals, that is, metals without a clear, smooth, and polished surface. Imagine the specular that you see when you look at the data side of a CD or DVD or the way the specular is shaped at the bottom of a pot or pan. Note that if you carefully examine the surface, there is a direction to the grooves, usually in the way that the metal was brushed. When you apply a specular to this surface, you get a specular stretched in a perpendicular direction.

This recipe will introduce you to the concept of augmenting your specular highlights to achieve different types of brushed surfaces. In future recipes, we will look at the various ways in which we can use the concepts of this recipe to achieve other effects, such as stretched reflections and hair; however, first, you are going to learn about the fundamentals of this technique. We will be using a shader as a reference for our own custom anisotropic shader, which you can find at https://web.archive.org/web/20200917032623/https://wiki.unity3d.com/index.php/Anisotropic_Highlight_Shader.

The following diagram shows examples of different types of specular effects that you can achieve using anisotropic shaders in Unity:

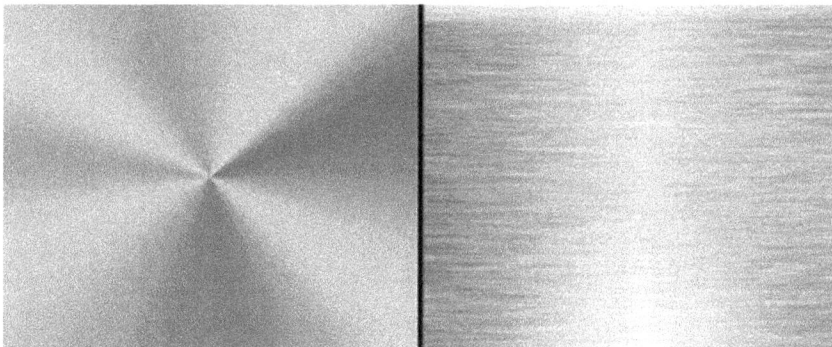

Figure 11.41 – Radial (left) vs horizontal (right) anisotropy

Getting ready

To get started, you should have already completed the *Adding support for multiple lights and a Blinn-Phong specular* recipe in this chapter. Let's start this recipe by creating a shader, its material, and some lights for our scene:

1. Create a new scene with some objects and lights so that we can visually debug our shader. In this case, we will be using some capsules, a sphere, and a cylinder.

2. Following this, create a new shader (**Anisotropic**) by duplicating our **Additional Lights** shader and material (**AnisotropicMat**). Then, hook them up to your objects:

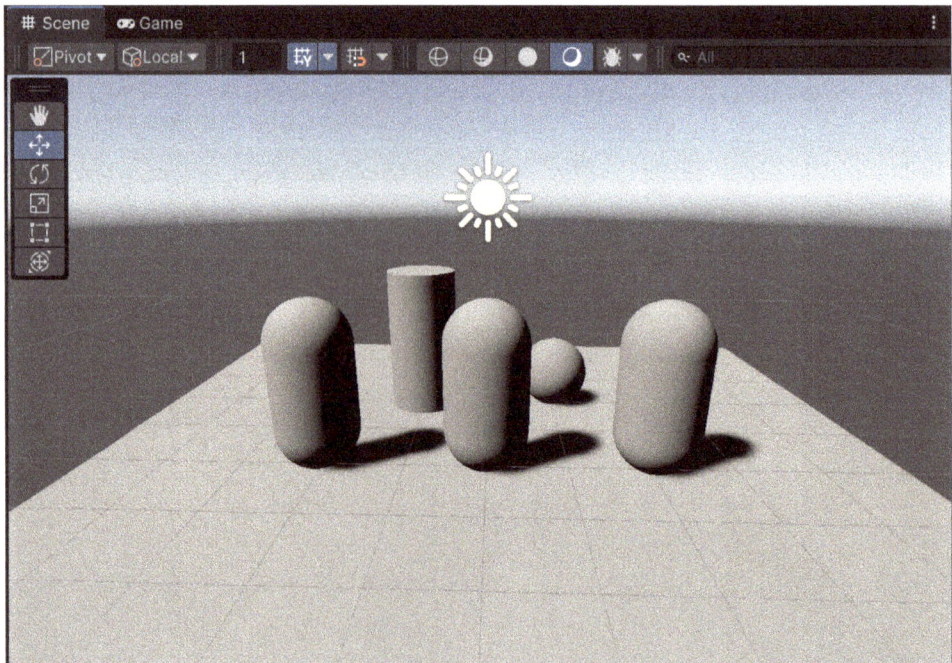

Figure 11.42 – The scene setup

3. Finally, we will need some sort of a normal map that will indicate the directionality of our anisotropic specular highlight.

The following screenshot shows the anisotropy normal map that we will be using for this recipe. It is available from the code sample provided for this book.

Figure 11.43 – Anisotropy normal map

How to do it...

To get started, let's create what we can before introducing the new variables needed for this type of specular effect:

1. From the **Anisotropic** Shader Graph, move below the material that we created before and to the left of that area. Begin by creating a **Main Light Direction** node. To the right of that, create a **Negate** node.

2. Next, create a **Normalize** node to the right of the **Negate** node. Connect the output from the **Negate** node to the input of the **Normalize** node.

3. To the right of the **Normalize** node, create an **Add** node. Connect the output of the **Normalize** node to input **A** of the **Add** node.

4. Below and to the left of the **Add** node, create a **View Direction** node. To the right of the **View Direction** node, create another **Normalize** node. Connect the output of the **View Direction** node to the input of this **Normalize** node.

5. Then, connect the output of the **Normalize** node (which normalizes the view direction) to input **B** of the **Add** node.

6. Finally, to the right of the **Add** node, create another **Normalize** node and connect the output of the addition to the input of the newly created **Normalize** node.

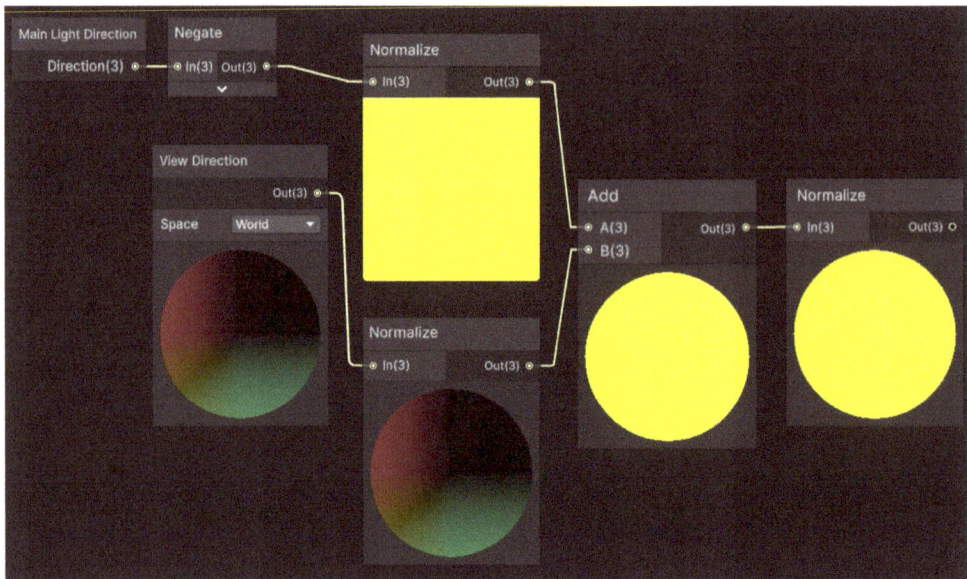

Figure 11.44 – Initial graph

7. To the right of the last node, create a **Dot Product** node. Connect the output of the previous **Normalize** node to input **A** of the **Dot Product** node.

Next, we need to calculate the input for **B** of the **Dot Product** node, which requires several nodes to set up.

8. Open the **Blackboard** and create a new variable called Anisotropic Direction, which will be a **Texture2D** variable. In **Graph Inspector**, go to the **Default Value** property and assign it the texture discussed earlier. Drag and drop this variable into the graph. To the right of this, create a **Sample Texture 2D** node and connect the **Anisotropic Direction** variable to the **Texture** input slot of the **Sample Texture 2D** node.

9. To the right of the **Sample Texture 2D** node, create a **Normal Unpack** node. Connect the **RGBA** output of the **Sample Texture 2D** node to the input of the **Normal Unpack** node. Next, to the right of the **Normal Unpack** node, create an **Add** node. Connect the output of the **Normal Unpack** node to input **B** of the **Add** node.

10. Above the **Normal Unpack** node, create a **Normal Vector** node. Set its **Space** to **Object** if it's not already set. Connect the output of the **Normal Vector** node to input **A** of the **Add** node. To the right of the **Add** node, create another **Normalize** node. Finally, connect the output of this **Normalize** node to input **B** of the **Dot Product** node that we created earlier.

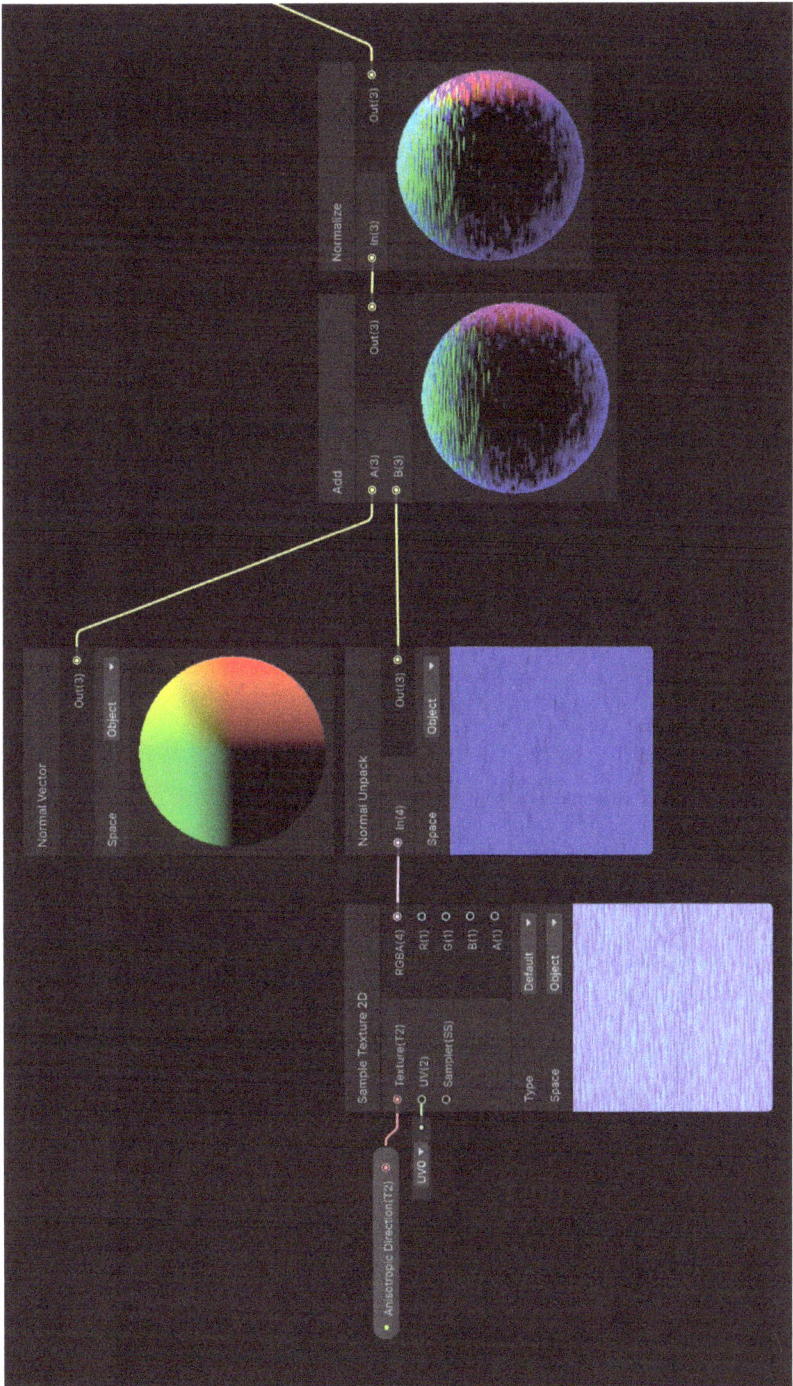

Figure 11.45 – Calculating the anisotropic effect

Next, let's create some new variables that we will use to control the property:

1. Open up the **Blackboard** and create three floats named Anisotropic Offset (**Mode** set to **Slider**, **Min** to -1, **Max** to 1, and **Default Value** to -0.2), Specular Amount (**Mode** set to **Slider**, **Min** to 0, **Max** to 1, and **Default Value** to 0.5), and Specular Power (**Mode** set to **Slider**, **Min** to 0, **Max** to 1, and **Default Value** to 0.5). Then, create a color called Specular Color and set **Default Value** to red.

2. To make it easier to see, click the + icon and select **Category** to create a new category. Double-click on the name to name it Specular. Drag the **Specular Amount**, **Specular Power**, and **Specular Color** properties into it. Do the same for the **Lighting** properties.

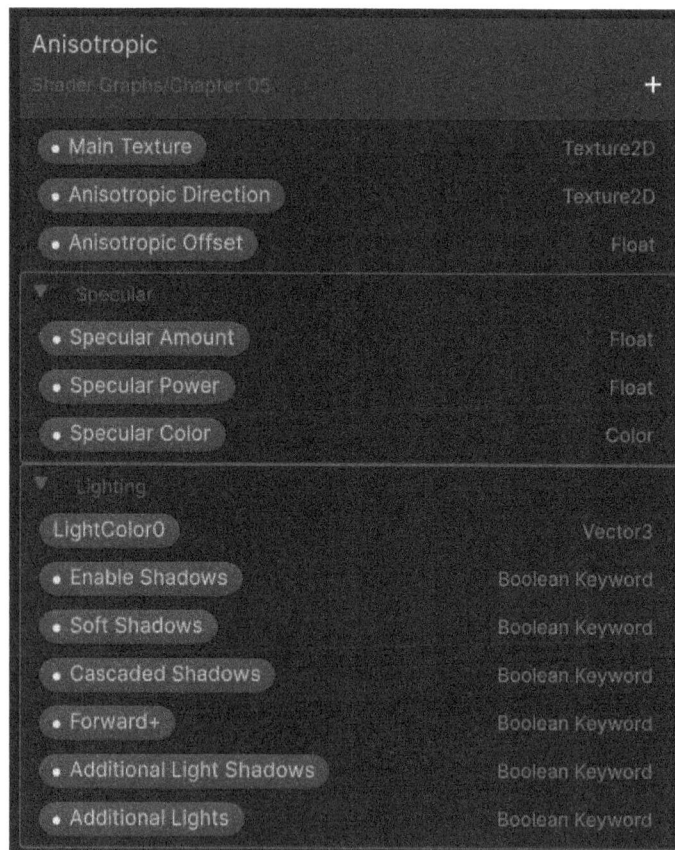

Figure 11.46 – Properties setup

Now, if you return to the Unity Editor, you'll see the properties have drop-down menus that will make it easier to work with.

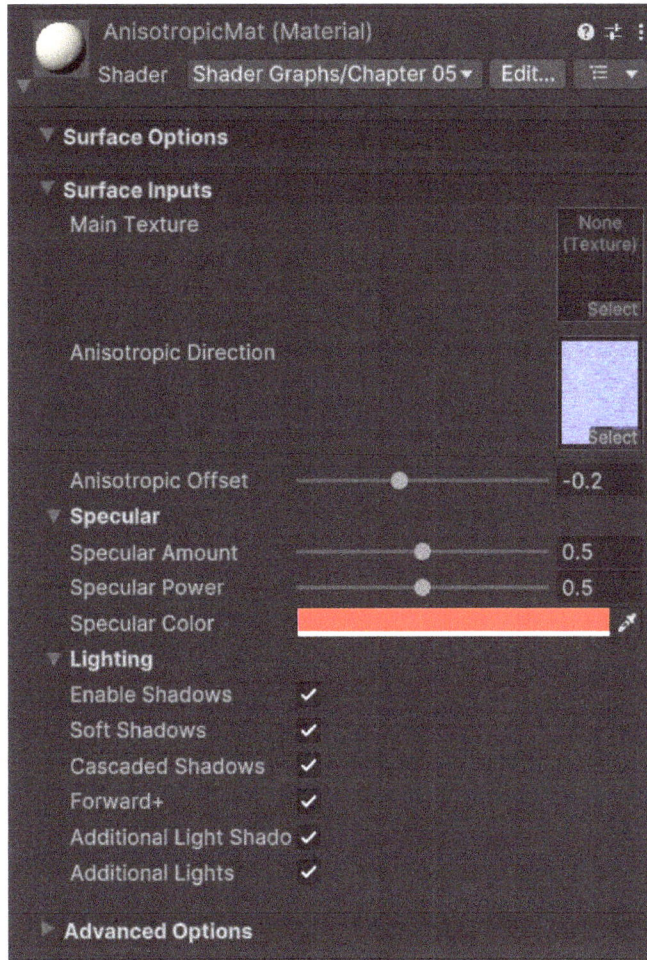

Figure 11.47 – Categories view in Inspector window

3.   Return to Shader Graph if you left it previously. Drag and drop **Anisotropic Offset** onto the graph below the **Dot Product** node. Create an **Add** node to the right of it. Connect the output of **Dot Product** to input **A** of the **Add** node. Connect **Anisotropic Offset** to input **B** of the **Add** node.

4.   To the right of the **Add** node, create a **Degrees to Radians** node. Connect the output of the **Add** node to the input of the **Degrees to Radians** node. To the right of that node, create a **Sine** node and connect the output of the **Degrees to Radians** node to the input of the **Sine** node.

5.   To the right of the **Sine** node, create a **Multiply** node. Connect the output of the **Sine** node to input **A** of the **Multiply** node. Below the **Sine** node, create another **Multiply** node. For the **B** input, type in 180. For the **A** input, drag and drop the **Specular Amount** variable onto the graph and connect it to the **A** input of this **Multiply** node.

6.   To the right of that, create a **Maximum** node. Connect the output of the **Multiply** node to input **A** of the **Maximum** node. Set the **B** input of the **Maximum** node to 0.

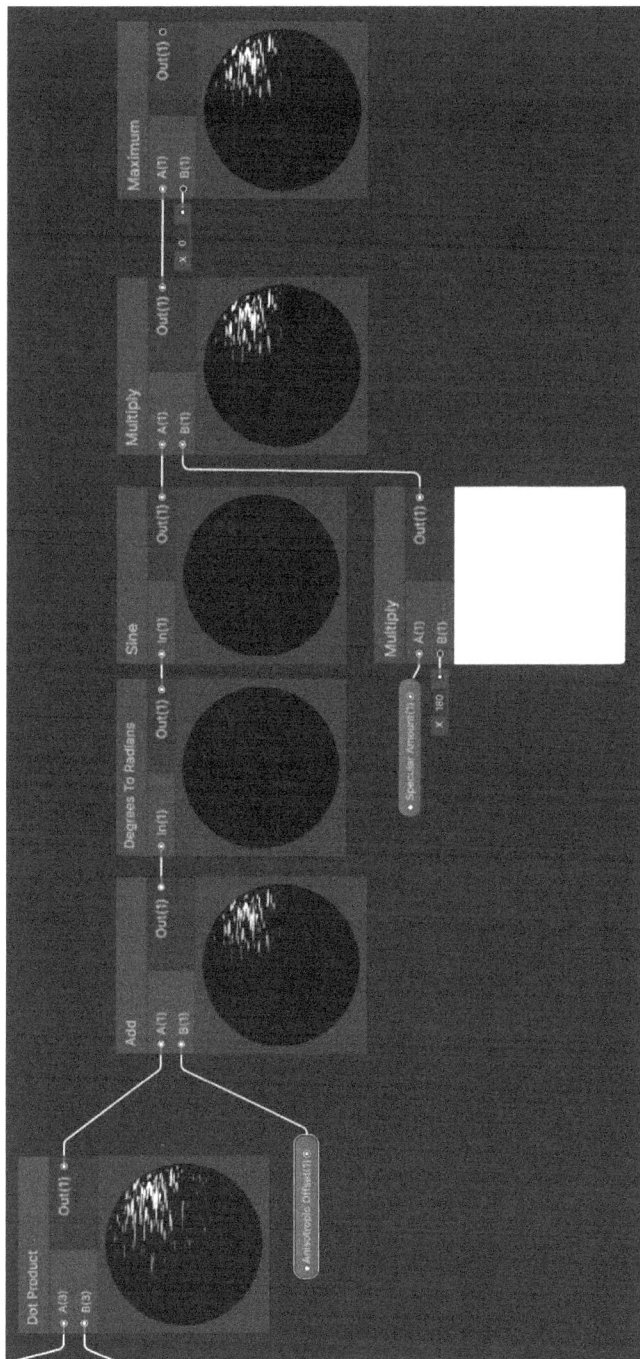

Figure 11.48 – Scaling the anisotropic effect

7. To the right of the **Maximum** node, create a **Power** node. Connect the output of the **Maximum** node to input **A** of the **Power** node and leave the **B** input of the **Power** node set at 2. Drag out from the **Power** node's output and create a **Saturate** node.

8. To the right of the **Saturate** node, create a **Multiply** node. Connect the output of the **Saturate** node to input **A** of the **Multiply** node. From the **Blackboard**, drag and drop the **Specular Power** property onto the graph and connect it to input **B** of the **Multiply** node.

9. To the right of the **Multiply** node, create another **Multiply** node and connect it to the **B** output. Then, from the **Blackboard**, drag and drop the **Specular Color** property and connect that to the **A** input.

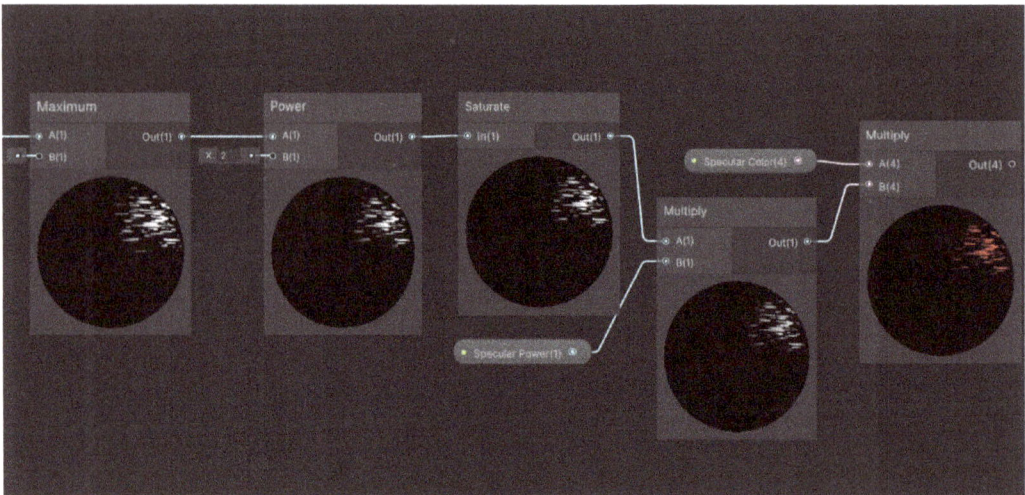

Figure 11.49 – Adding color to the anisotropic effect

Now we need to connect this to the final output of our previous recipe.

10. From **AdditionalLights (Custom Function)**, disconnect the **Specular** output of the **Add** node by selecting it and pressing the *delete* key.

11. Grab the output (**Specular**) from the **AdditionalLights** node and create a new **Add** node. Connect the **Specular** output to input **A** of this new **Add** node.

12. Take the output from our **Multiply** node (the one connected to **Specular Power**) and assign that to input **B** of the new **Add** node.

13. Finally, connect the output of this new **Add** node to the **Add** node that we previously disconnected from the **Specular** output. This re-establishes the connection with the updated specular calculations.

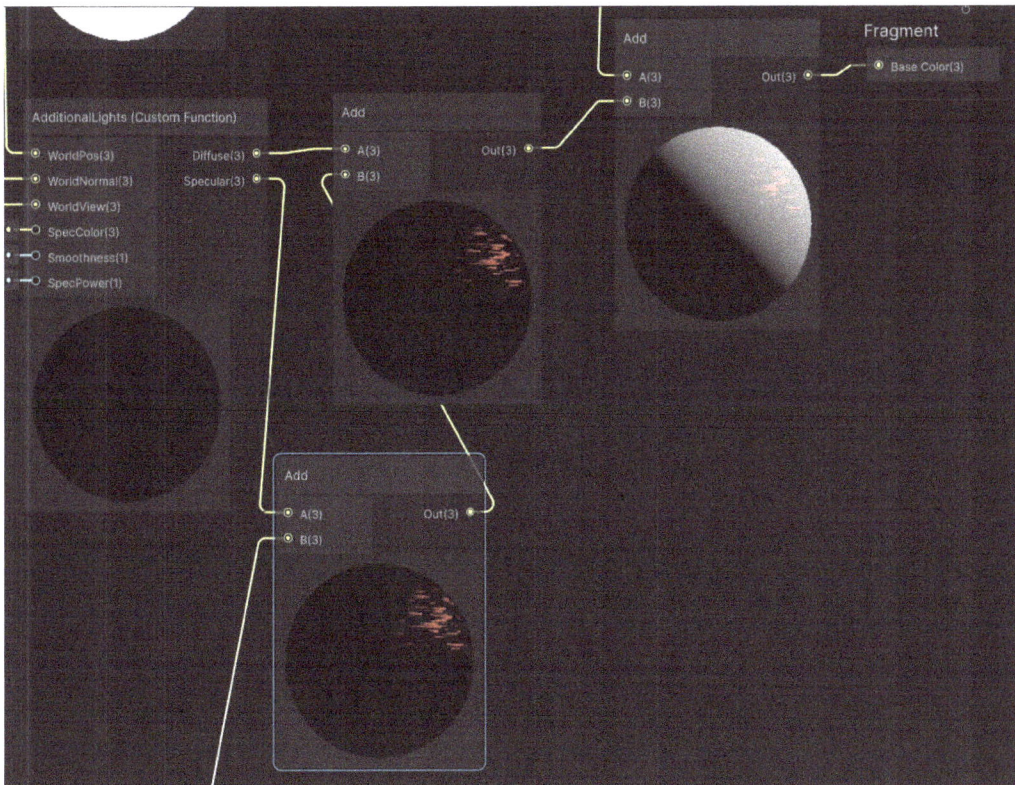

Figure 11.50 – Connecting to the main graph

14. Save the graph and return to the Unity Editor. Afterward, adjust the **Anisotropic Offset** property using the slider and make a note of the changes.

    The **Anisotropic Direction** normal map allows us to give the surface direction and helps us to disperse the specular highlight around the surface.

15. Next, try adjusting the other properties to observe how this will affect the final result. For instance, the following settings are what I used within the example code for this book:

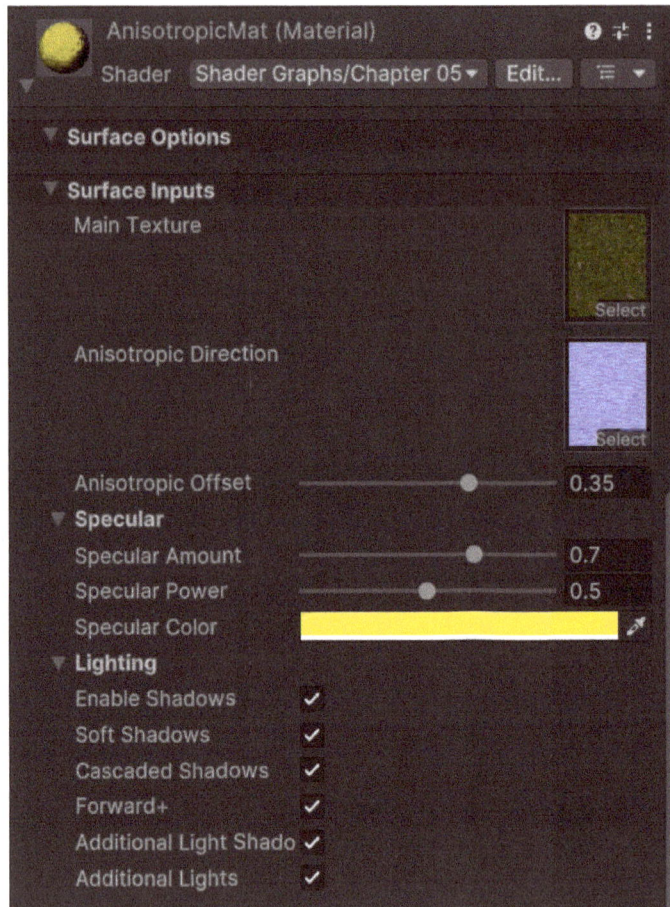

Figure 11.51 – Tweaked parameters within the anisotropic material

The following screenshot shows the result of our anisotropic shader:

Figure 11.52 – Result of the anisotropic Shader

How it works...

Let's break down this shader into its core components and explain why we are getting this effect. We will mostly be covering the custom lighting function here, as, at this point, the rest of the shader should be pretty self-explanatory.

It begins by getting the usual out of the way, that is, the half vector. This is so that we don't have to do the full reflection calculation and diffuse lighting, which is the vertex normal dotted with the light vector or direction. The **Saturate** node clamps the value within it so that it is never larger than 1.0 and never smaller than 0.0.

Then, we start the actual modification to **Specular** to get the right look. First, we dot the normalized sum of the vertex normal and per-pixel vectors from our **Anisotropic** normal map with the half vector value that was calculated in the previous step. This gives us a float value that shows a value of 1 as the surface normal, which is modified by the **Anisotropic Direction** normal map as it becomes parallel with the half vector, and 0 as it is perpendicular. The result of the dot product is adjusted by adding the **Anisotropic Offset** value and converting the result from degrees to radians using a **Degrees to Radians** node. The sine of this value is then calculated to create the desired anisotropic effect. This manipulation helps in achieving the characteristic ring-like highlight so that, essentially, we can get a darker middle highlight and, ultimately, a ring effect based on a half vector.

The sine output is scaled by multiplying it with a constant (e.g., 180) and the specular amount. The result is clamped using a **Saturate** node to ensure it stays within the range of 0.0 to 1.0. This value is further adjusted by raising it to a power (specular power) and multiplied to determine the final specular intensity. The final adjusted specular value is combined with the base specular output from the additional lights called from the custom function we created in the previous recipe. This combined value represents the anisotropic specular highlight, which is then used in the final shading calculations.

This effect is great for creating more advanced metal types of surfaces, especially the ones that are brushed and appear to have some directionality to them. It also works well for hair or any sort of soft surface with directionality.

Join our community on Discord

Join our community's Discord space for discussions with the authors and other readers:

`https://packt.link/gamedevelopment`

12

Developing Advanced Shading Techniques

This chapter covers some advanced shader techniques that you can use for your game while also giving you a chance to write several shaders using `.shader` files. Unlike Shader Graph, which provides a node-based workflow for creating shaders, `.shader` files blend ShaderLab and **High-Level Shading Language (HLSL)** code.

ShaderLab is Unity's proprietary scripting language used to define the structure of shaders, such as rendering properties, passes, and tags, while HLSL is a standard shading language used for writing the actual logic of vertex and fragment shaders.

By combining ShaderLab and HLSL, you have more direct control over how your shaders function compared to Shader Graph. This approach enables you to access lower-level functionality, optimize performance, and implement custom effects that may not be possible through the Shader Graph interface.

Remember that many of the most eye-catching effects that you see in games are made by testing the limits of what shaders can do. This book provides you with the technical foundations to modify and create shaders, but you are strongly encouraged to play and experiment with them as much as you can.

After all, making a good game is not a quest for photorealism; you should not approach shaders with the intention of replicating reality because that is unlikely to happen. Instead, you should try to use shaders as a tool to make your game truly unique. With the knowledge you gain in this chapter, you will be able to create the materials that you want.

In this chapter, we will cover the following recipes:

- Using the Universal Render Pipeline's shader library files
- Making your shader modular with HLSL include files
- Implementing a Fur shader
- Implementing heatmaps with arrays

Technical requirements

For this chapter, you will need Unity Editor version 6 Preview 6000.0.07f1. This chapter's instructions should work with minimal changes in future versions of the editor in projects that utilize the **Universal Render Pipeline** (URP). Note that the chapter's sample project was created using the **Universal 3D Core** template.

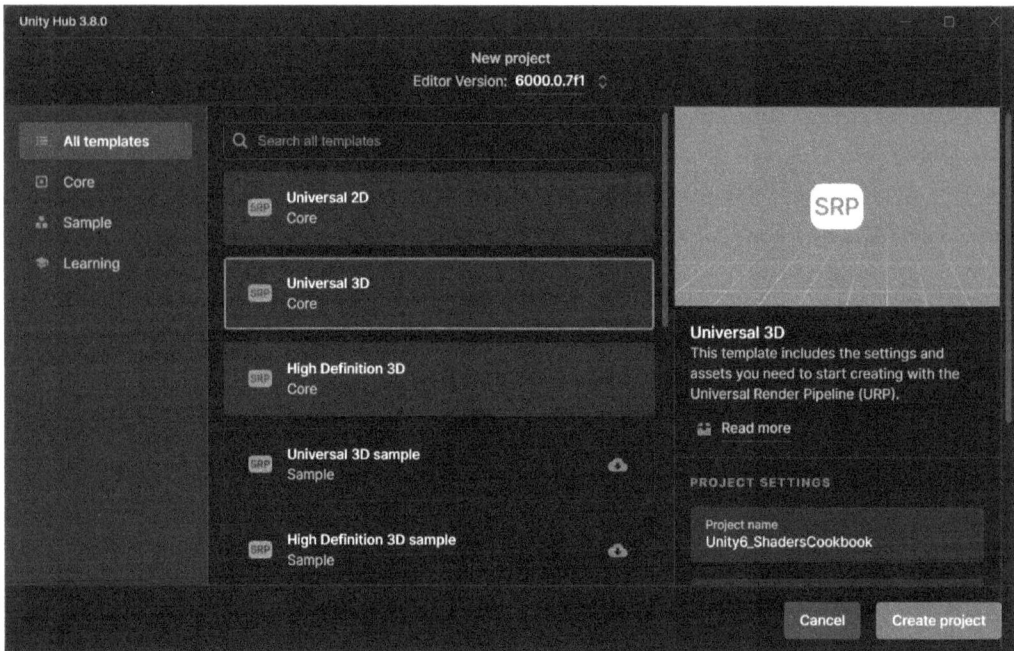

Figure 12.1 – Universal URP project

The code files for this chapter can be found on GitHub at https://github.com/ PacktPublishing/Unity-6-Shaders-and-Effects-Cookbook. The necessary files for this chapter are organized in the Unity project in a folder named Chapter 12 (https://github. com/PacktPublishing/Unity-6-Shaders-and-Effects-Cookbook/tree/main/Unity6_ ShadersCookbook/Assets/Chapter%2012) on GitHub.

Important note

Note that the code files include additional spacing and comments that will improve the understanding and readability of some scripts within this chapter. It is recommended to reference it carefully while following the recipes.

Using the Universal Render Pipeline's shader library files

When developing shaders in the URP, Unity provides a comprehensive collection of ShaderLibrary files that can streamline the process. These HLSL-based files, included as part of the URP package, contain pre-written functions and utilities for handling common tasks such as lighting calculations, surface shading, and platform-specific adjustments. By leveraging these files, you can reduce the amount of custom code you need to write while ensuring your shaders align with URP's modern rendering framework.

Although URP promotes the use of Shader Graph and HLSL-based shaders, its ShaderLibrary files encourage a modular approach to shader development and can be used by both if needed. These files allow you to reuse URP's optimized utilities while also seeing how to create a shader completely from scratch with code rather than Shader Graph, customizing your shaders for specific needs.

In this recipe, we will explore how to access and utilize the ShaderLibrary files included in the URP package. We will build a simple desaturation shader using URP's lighting functions and helper methods. This modular approach will serve as a foundation for future recipes, where we'll create custom HLSL include files and advanced effects, such as fur rendering.

Getting ready

Before diving into shader development, we need to set up a basic scene and put a few items into our scene.

Follow these steps to get everything ready for this recipe:

1. Start by creating a new scene in Unity using **Basic (URP) Template**. Add a basic sphere model to the scene by going to **GameObject** | **3D Object** | **Sphere**.

2. We will then create a shader, but this time we will create it using code. To do this, go to your **Project** window and create a new shader by selecting **Create** | **Shader** | **Unit Shader**. Name the shader Desaturate.

In URP, if you are not using Shader Graph, shaders are typically written in HLSL rather than using Unity's legacy Surface Shaders.

3. Create a new material for our shader and assign the **Desaturate** shader to it. This can be done simply by right-clicking on the shader, selecting **Create | Material**, and giving it a name (DesaturateMat). Attach the material to the sphere in the scene.

With the scene and resources set up, you are now ready to proceed to the shader implementation.

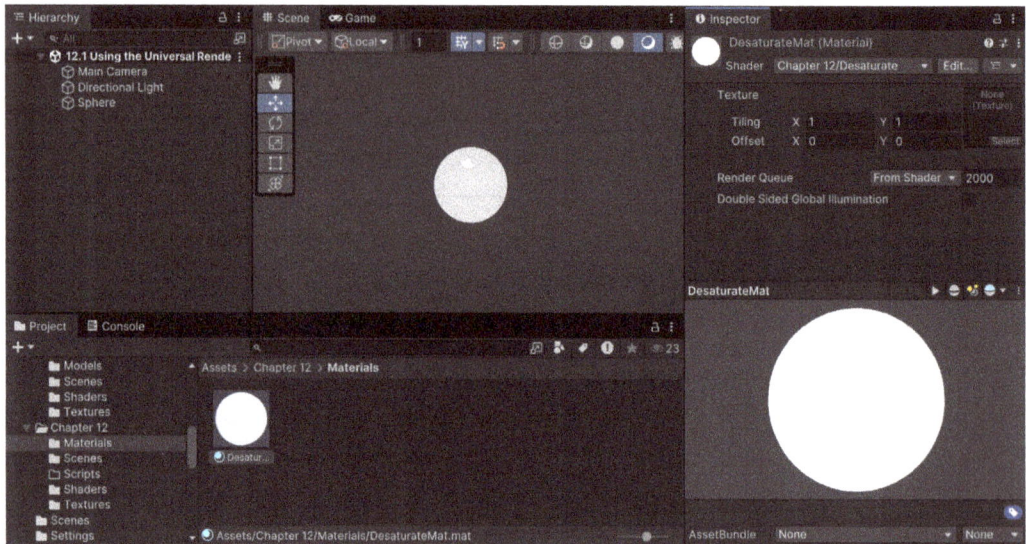

Figure 12.2 – Desaturate shader setup

How to do it...

With the scene prepared, we can now begin the process of experimenting with some of the built-in helper functions included with the ShaderLibrary. Double-click on the shader that was created for this scene to open it in your IDE of choice and insert the code given in the following steps:

1. Add the following code to the Properties block of the new shader file. We will need a single texture and slide for our example shader:

```
Properties
{
    _MainTex ("Base (RGB)", 2D) = "white" {}
    _DesatValue ("Desaturate", Range(0,1)) = 0.5
}
```

2. Next, we need to update the CGPROGRAM and ENDCG sections of the code to say HLSLPROGRAM and ENDHLSL. This ensures compatibility with HLSL syntax.

> Tip
>
> Unity originally used Cg, a variant of HLSL, for writing shaders. However, it has since transitioned to using HLSL exclusively. Despite this change, you may still encounter legacy keywords such as CGPROGRAM and file extensions such as .cginc. These remain in use to maintain backward compatibility and prevent shader breakage when upgrading Unity versions. For future-proofing our project, we should adopt modern HLSL conventions while being aware of these legacy elements.

We then need to create the data connection between our Properties and the HLSLPROGRAM blocks.

3. Add the following bolded line after the declaration of the two _MainTex and _MainTex_ST variables:

```
sampler2D _MainTex;
float4 _MainTex_ST;
float _DesatValue;
```

4. Next, we have to update the shader to update the definition of the appdata structure to pass vertex data to the shader. Update it to include the normal in addition to the position and texture coordinates:

```
struct appdata
{
    float4 vertex : POSITION;
    float2 uv : TEXCOORD0;
    float3 normal : NORMAL;
};
```

5. Now, we need to update the definition of the v2f structure to pass data from the vertex shader to the fragment shader. Add world space normals and positions for lighting calculations:

```
struct v2f
{
```

```
        float2 uv : TEXCOORD0;
        float4 vertex : SV_POSITION;
        float3 worldNormal : TEXCOORD1;
        float3 worldPos : TEXCOORD2;
    };
```

6. Next, we will implement the vert function to process vertex data. To do so, replace the current vert function with the following:

```
v2f vert (appdata v)
{
    v2f o;

    o.vertex = TransformObjectToHClip(v.vertex.xyz);
    o.uv = v.uv;
    o.worldNormal = TransformObjectToWorldNormal(v.normal);
    o.worldPos = TransformObjectToWorld(v.vertex.xyz);

    return o;
}
```

7. The above code uses URP's helper functions for transformations, but we will need to replace the current #include line with the following instead to get access to these functions:

```
#include "Packages/com.unity.render-pipelines.universal/
ShaderLibrary/Core.hlsl"
```

This ensures access to URP's core shader functions.

8. Modify the frag function to implement the desaturation effect using the built-in Luminance function:

```
float4 frag (v2f i) : SV_Target
{
    // sample the texture
    float4 col = tex2D(_MainTex, i.uv);

    // Calculate the luminance for desaturation
    float luminance = Luminance(col.rgb);
    col.rgb = lerp(col.rgb, luminance.xxx, _DesatValue);
```

```
    return col;
}
```

You'll have noticed that we are using the Luminance function, but it doesn't exist by default, and if we return to the editor, we will get an error. So to fix it, we will need to add an additional include to it.

9. Add an additional include directive for color utilities:

```
#include "Packages/com.unity.render-pipelines.core/ShaderLibrary/
Color.hlsl"
```

10. Save the script and return to the Unity Editor. From there, you should be able to assign a texture to the **Base (RGB)** value of **DesaturateMat** (I used the TerrainBlend texture from the Chapter 04/Textures folder):

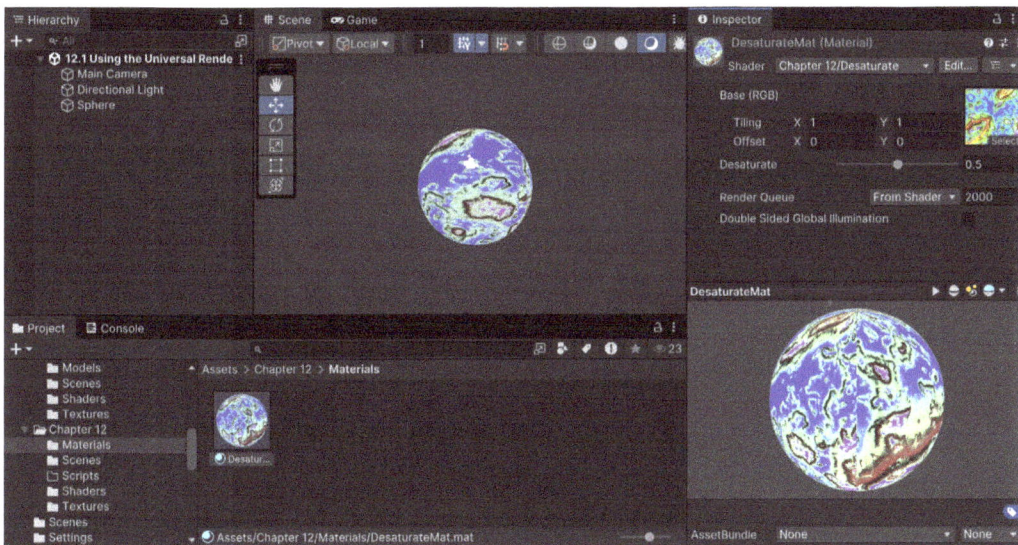

Figure 12.3 – Assigning a texture

11. With the shader code modified, you should see something similar to the preceding screenshot. We have simply used a helper function, built into Unity's CgInclude file, to give us the effect of desaturating the main texture of our shader. Notice that if we change the value to 1, all of the color leaves, giving us a grayscale effect:

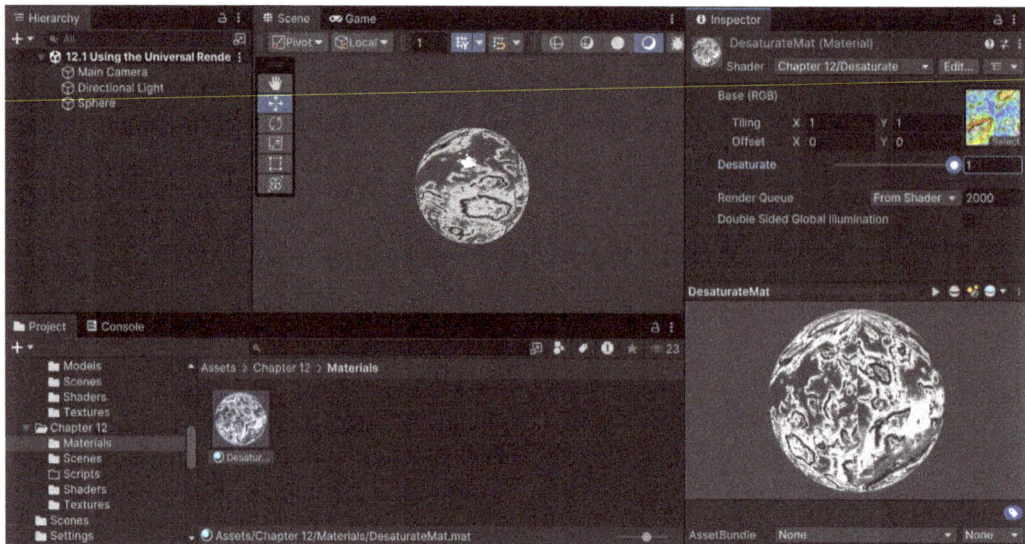

Figure 12.4 – Activating a grayscale effect

12. Next, we can extend the `frag` function to include lighting calculations:

```
float4 frag (v2f i) : SV_Target
{
    // sample the texture
    float4 col = tex2D(_MainTex, i.uv);

    // Calculate the luminance for desaturation
    float luminance = Luminance(col.rgb);
    col.rgb = lerp(col.rgb, luminance.xxx, _DesatValue);

    // Fetch main light direction and color
    Light mainLight = GetMainLight();
    float3 lightDir = normalize(mainLight.direction);

    // Calculate diffuse lighting
    float3 normal = normalize(i.worldNormal);
    float NdotL = max(0.0, dot(normal, lightDir));
    float3 diffuse = mainLight.color * NdotL;
```

```
    // Apply lighting to the base color
    col.rgb *= diffuse;

    return col;
}
```

This enhances the shader's interaction with the scene's lighting.

13. Save the shader again and return to the editor.

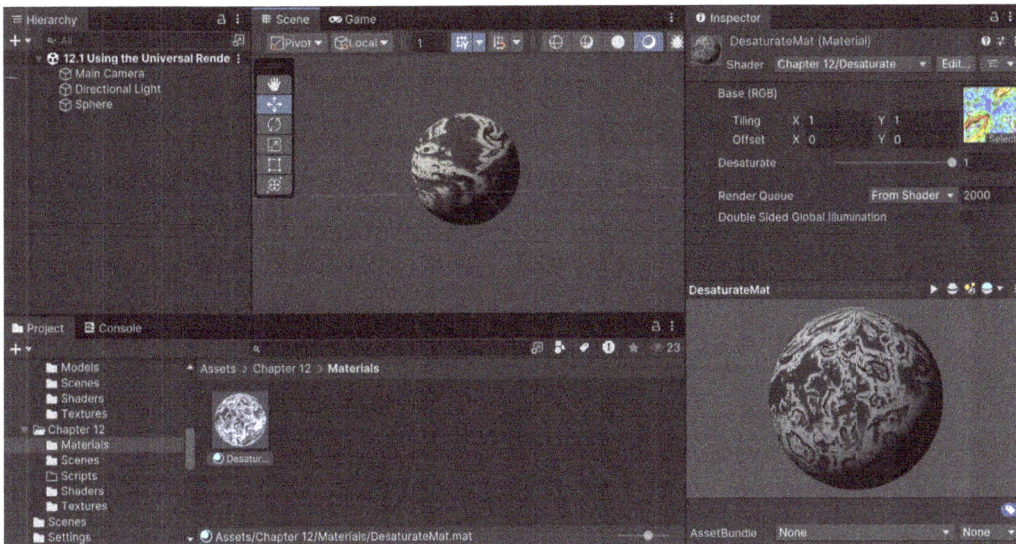

Figure 12.5 – Desaturation effect with lighting

The scene will now display the desaturation effect with dynamic lighting.

How it works...

Since this is our first full-blown shader written in HLSL code, let's examine some general shader aspects before jumping into the details specific to this particular recipe.

Every Unity shader has a built-in structure that it is looking for in its code. The **Properties** block is one of those functions that is expected by Unity. The reason behind this is to give you, the shader programmer, a means of quickly creating GUI elements that tie directly into your shader code. These properties (variables) that you declare in the **Properties** block can then be used in your shader code to change values, colors, and textures.

The syntax for defining a property is as follows:

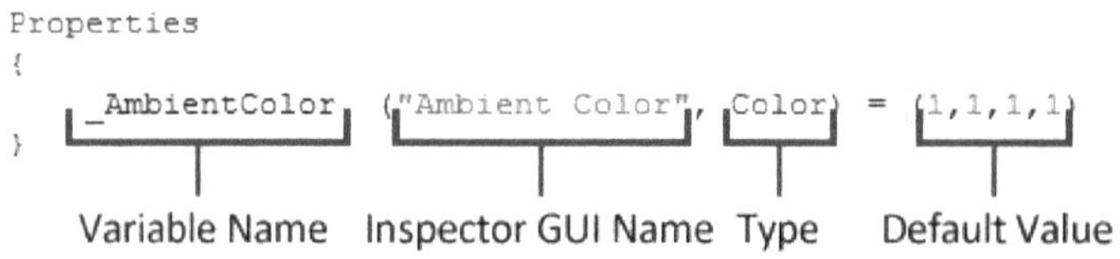

```
Properties
{
    _AmbientColor  ("Ambient Color",  Color) = (1,1,1,1)
}
```

        Variable Name   Inspector GUI Name   Type   Default Value

Figure 12.6 – Properties syntax

When you first s tart writing a new property, you will need to give it a **Variable Name**. The variable name is going to be the name that your shader code is going to use to get the value from the GUI element. This saves us a lot of time because we don't have to set up this system ourselves.

The next elements of a property are the **Inspector GUI Name** and the **Type** of the property, which are contained within parentheses. Here, the **Inspector GUI Name** is the name that is going to appear in the material's **Inspector** tab when the user is interacting with and tweaking the shader. The **Type** is the type of data that this property is going to control. There are many types that we can define for properties inside Unity shaders, including `Integer`, `Float`, `Texture2D`, `Cubemap`, `Color`, `Vector`, and `Texture2D/CubemapArrays`, which we've already been using in Shader Graph; they're just defined in a different way.

Further reading

Shader property types are documented in the Unity manual at `http://docs.unity3d.com/Documentation/Components/SL-Properties.html`.

Finally, there is the **Default Value**, which, just like in Shader Graph, simply sets the value of this property to the value that you placed in the code. So, in the previous example diagram, the default value for the `_DesatValue` property, which is of the `float` type, is set to a value of `0.5`.

Note

Default values are only set the first time a shader is assigned to a new material. After that, the material's values are used. Changing the default value will not affect the values of existing materials that use the shader. This is a good thing, of course, but often forgotten. So, if you change a value and notice something not changing, this could be the reason for this.

Shader code structures

When writing shader code, appdata and v2f structures are used to pass information between the vertex shader and the fragment shader.

The appdata structure represents the data associated with each vertex, such as its position, UV coordinates, and normals. It's where you declare the input data format for the vertex shader. For example, it might contain fields for the vertex position (POSITION), texture coordinates (TEXCOORD0), and normal vector (NORMAL).

The v2f structure defines the data passed from the vertex shader to the fragment shader, including world-space transformations, lighting information, or any other data needed for rendering. This separation ensures a clear flow of data between the vertex and fragment shaders.

> Important note
>
> The appdata and v2f structures are common naming conventions in Unity's shader examples, but they are not fixed or required names. These are just user-defined structures, and you can name them whatever makes sense for your shader. For example, you might see them referred to as VertexInput (instead of appdata) or FragmentInput (instead of v2f) in other examples or tutorials.

Shader code functions

The #pragma vertex and #pragma fragment directives are used in Unity shaders to explicitly tell the compiler which functions should be used as the **vertex shader** and **fragment shader**, respectively. In our case, we are using the default values of vert and frag.

The vert function processes each vertex in the scene and calculates its transformed position, normals, and other data for use by the fragment shader. It outputs a v2f structure containing this processed data. Using URP's ShaderLibrary functions like TransformObjectToHClip or TransformObjectToWorld, the vert function simplifies common transformations such as converting object space to clip space or world space.

Meanwhile, the frag function processes the pixel data passed from the vertex shader. It calculates the final color of each pixel, taking into account textures, lighting, and custom effects.

The #include directive allows us to incorporate external files containing pre-written functions and utilities into our shader. Effectively, it acts like copying/pasting the file into our file, and if we open that file in our editor, we can see what it is doing. In this case, we are including the Core.hlsl file from the URP, which provides access to essential transformation and rendering helper functions used throughout our shader, such as TransformObjectToHClip, TransformObjectToWorldNormal, and TransformObjectToWorld.

Using the built-in helper function named Luminance(), we are able to quickly get a desaturation or grayscale effect on our shaders. This is all possible because of the Color.hlsl file that was brought into our file when we added it via our #include directive.

If you open the Color.hlsl file in your project's Library\PackageCache\com.unity.render-pipelines.core\ShaderLibrary folder, you'll see that the code for the Luminance function is located on line 172. The following snippet is taken from the file:

```
// Convert rgb to Luminance
// with rgb in linear space with sRGB primaries and D65 white point
#ifndef BUILTIN_TARGET_API
real Luminance(real3 linearRgb)
{
    return dot(linearRgb, real3(0.2126729, 0.7151522, 0.0721750));
}
#endif
```

As this function is included in the file and Unity automatically compiles with this file, we can use the function in our code as well, thereby reducing the amount of code that we must write over and over again.

Notice there is also a Lighting.hlsl file, which Unity comes with. This file houses all the lighting models that we use when we add lighting. Sifting through this file reveals that all the built-in lighting models are defined here for reuse and modularity.

There's more...

Like any other programming language, our code cannot have mistakes. As such, your shader will not work if you have a typo in your code. When this happens, your materials will be rendered in unshaded magenta:

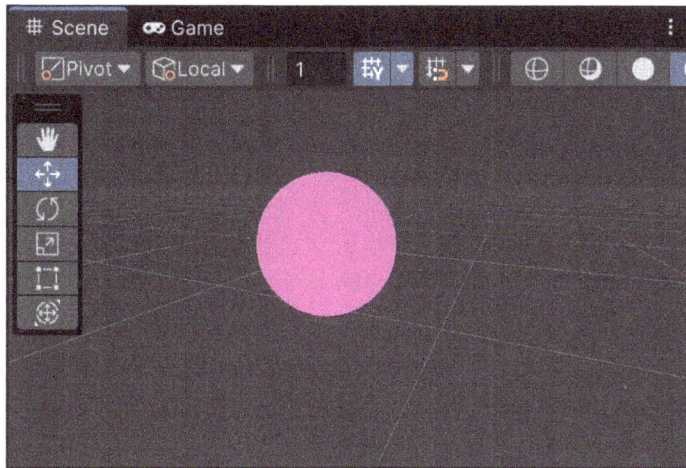

Figure 12.7 – Example of ErrorShader

When a script does not compile, Unity prevents your game from being exported or even executed. Conversely, errors in shaders do not stop your game from being executed. If one of your shaders is magenta, it is time to investigate where the problem is. If you select the incriminating shader, you will see a list of errors in its **Inspector** window or the **Console** window:

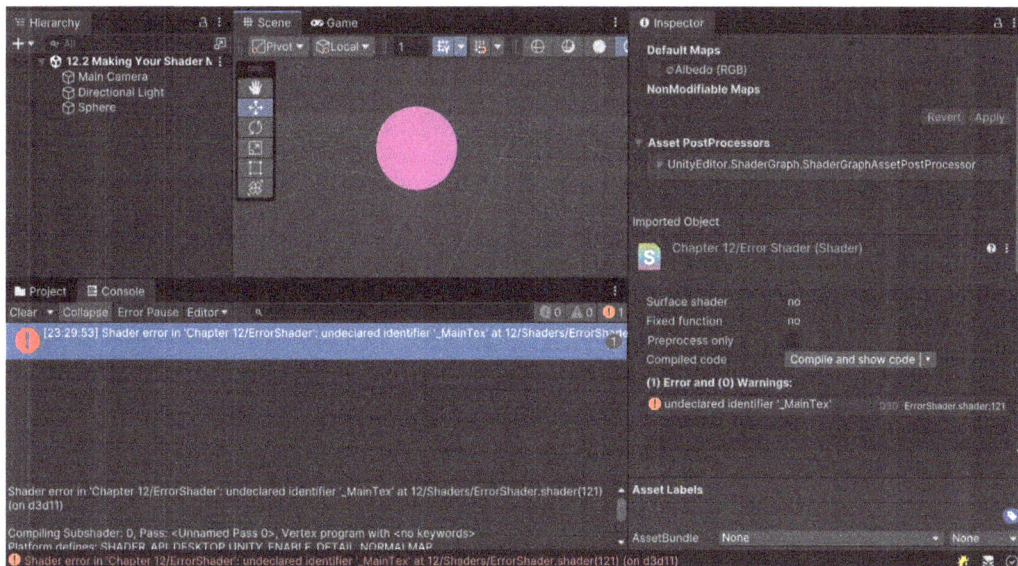

Figure 12.8 – Errors example

Despite showing the line that raised the error, this rarely means that this is the line that must be fixed. The error message shown in the previous screenshot was generated by deleting the `sampler2D _MainTex` variable from the `SubShader{}` block. However, the error is raised by the first line that tries to access such a variable. Finding and fixing what's wrong with code is a process called **debugging**. The most common mistakes that you should check for are as follows:

- A missing bracket. If you forgot to add a curly bracket to close a section, the compiler is likely to raise errors at the end of the document, at the beginning of the document, or in a new section.

- A missing semicolon. This is one of the most common mistakes but luckily one of the easiest to spot and fix. When looking at the error definition, check whether the line above it contains a semicolon or not.

- A property that has been defined in the `Properties` section but has not been coupled with a variable in the `SubShader{}` block.

- Compared to what you might be used to in C# scripts, the floating-point values in ShaderLab and HLSL do not need to be followed by an `f`. It's `1.0`, not `1.0f`.

> Tip
>
> The error messages raised by shaders can be very misleading, especially due to their strict syntactic constraints. If you are in doubt about their meaning, it is best to search the internet. The Unity forums are filled with other developers who are likely to have encountered (and fixed) your problem before.

Making your shader modular with HLSL include files

Knowing about Unity's ShaderLibrary is a great start, but what if we want to create our own files to store custom lighting models and helper functions? When working with shaders, reusing and organizing code efficiently can significantly improve your workflow. Unity's HLSL include files allow you to modularize your shader development by consolidating reusable functions and variables in external files. This approach not only reduces redundancy but also simplifies the maintenance and expansion of your shaders over time.

In *Chapter 11*, *Understanding Lighting Models*, we explored how to call code from a `.hlsl` file within Shader Graph. But how do we achieve similar modularity when working with `.shader` files? In this recipe, we'll dive into the process of creating custom HLSL include files for organizing your shader code. By the end of the recipe, you'll have the tools to make your shaders more modular, organized, and easier to manage.

Getting ready

Before starting this recipe, ensure you've completed the previous recipe, *Using the Universal Render Pipeline's shader library files*. This will give you a foundational understanding of how Unity's built-in shader utilities work and provide you with the Desaturate shader to build upon.

Once you've completed the previous recipe, follow these steps to prepare for creating a custom HLSL include file:

1. In Unity, right-click on the Chapter 12/Shaders folder in the **Project** window and select **Show in Explorer**. This will open the project folder. Navigate to the **Assets** folder and create a new text file by right-clicking and selecting **New | Text Document**.

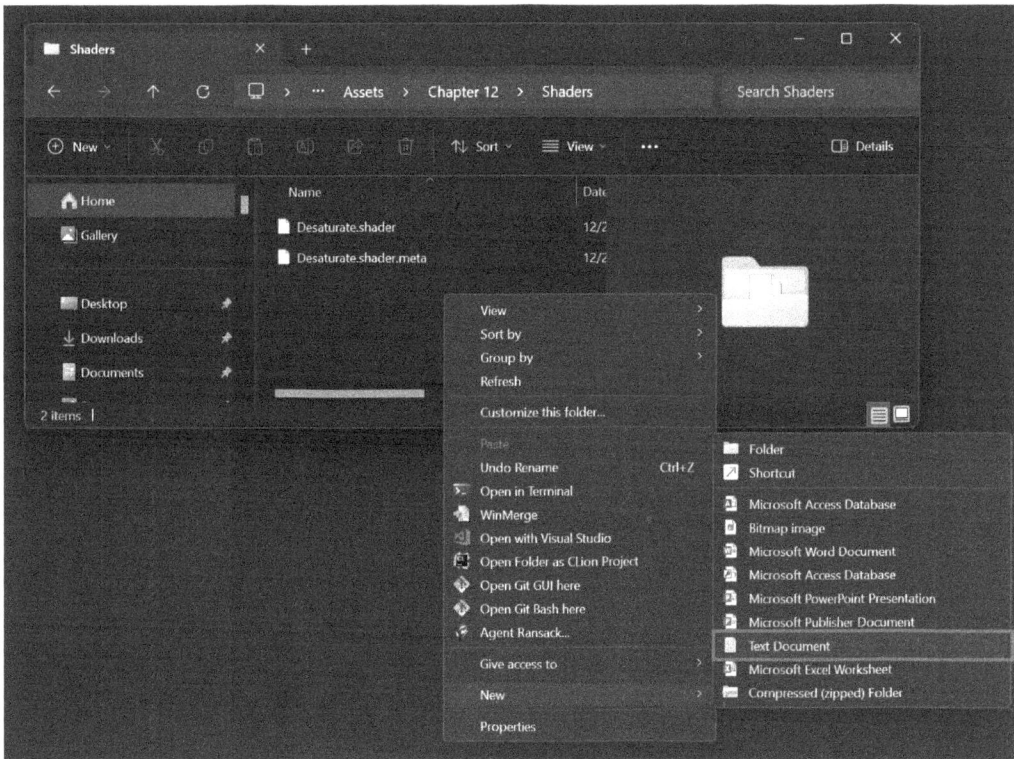

Figure 12.9 – Creating a new text document

2.   Rename the text file `MyHLSLInclude` and replace the `.txt` extension with `.hlsl`:

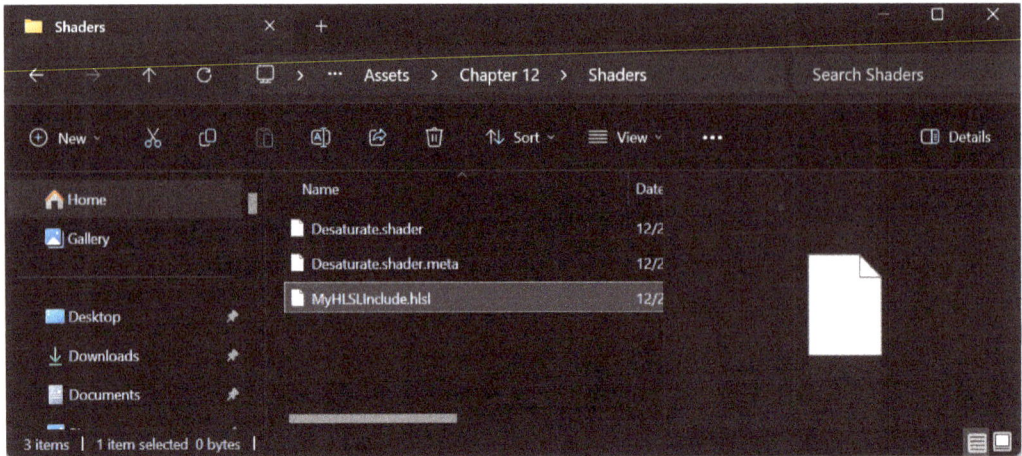

Figure 12.10 – Renaming the text file

3.   Your operating system may warn you about the extension change making the file unusable. Confirm the change, as Unity will recognize it as an HLSL file.

4.   When you return to the editor, Unity will recognize it as a valid HLSL include file.

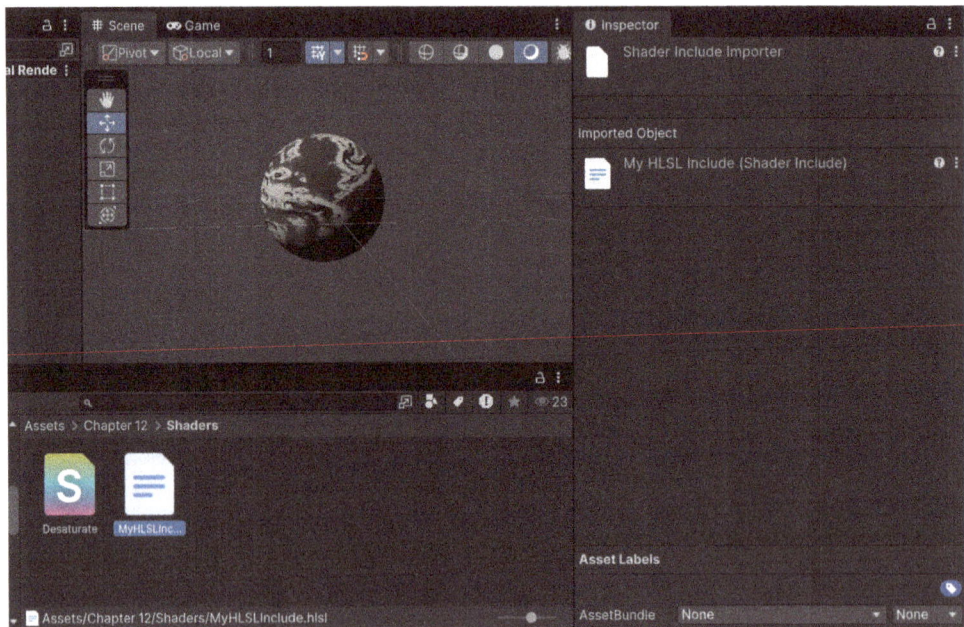

Figure 12.11 – The newly created file is now part of our Unity project

5. Next, duplicate the **Desaturate** shader and rename it Colorize. Create a new material for the **Colorize** shader and assign it to a sphere within a scene.

With the file ready, let's begin writing reusable shader code.

How to do it...

Now that the HLSL include file is prepared, we'll add custom code to make it usable across multiple shaders:

1. First, we need to add the preprocessor directives to ensure the file is included only once during compilation:

```
#ifndef MY_HLSL_INCLUDE
#define MY_HLSL_INCLUDE
```

2. Then at the bottom of the file, add a #endif to indicate the end of the file.

3. Next, we will add a custom lighting function and any necessary variables between the #define and #endif:

```
float4 _MyColor;
inline float3 LightingHalfLambert(float3 normal,
                                  float3 lightDir,
                                  float3 lightColor,
                                  float3 baseColor,
                                  float atten)
{
    // Calculate Half-Lambert diffuse factor
    float diff = max(0, dot(normal, lightDir));
    diff = (diff + 0.5) * 0.5;

    // Calculate final color
    float3 resultColor;

    resultColor = baseColor * lightColor * diff *
                  atten * _MyColor.rgb;

    return resultColor;
}
```

4. Save the file and now open up the **Colorize** shader. We need to first add a new property:

```
Shader "Chapter 12/Colorize"
{
    Properties
    {
        _MainTex ("Base (RGB)", 2D) = "white" {}
        _DesatValue ("Desaturate", Range(0,1)) = 0.5
        _MyColor ("My Color", Color) = (1,1,1,1)
    }
```

5. Next, we need to include our new function in our **Colorize** shader by adding the following directive within the HLSLPROGRAM block:

```
#include "Packages/com.unity.render-pipelines.universal/
ShaderLibrary/Core.hlsl" // TransformObjectToHClip
#include "Packages/com.unity.render-pipelines.core/ShaderLibrary/
Color.hlsl" // Luminance
#include "Packages/com.unity.render-pipelines.universal/
ShaderLibrary/Lighting.hlsl"
#include "MyHLSLInclude.hlsl"
```

6. Next, integrate the custom function into the frag function to replace the existing lighting logic:

```
float4 frag (v2f i) : SV_Target
{
    // sample the texture
    float4 col = tex2D(_MainTex, i.uv);

    // Calculate the Luminance for desaturation
    float luminance = Luminance(col.rgb);
    col.rgb = lerp(col.rgb, luminance.xxx, _DesatValue);

    // Fetch main light direction and color using URP functions
    Light mainLight = GetMainLight();
    float3 lightDir = normalize(mainLight.direction);
    float3 lightColor = mainLight.color;
    float3 customDiffuse = LightingHalfLambert(normalize(i.
worldNormal), lightDir, lightColor, col.rgb, 1.0);
```

```
        // Apply custom lighting to the base color
        col.rgb *= customDiffuse;

        return col;
    }
```

7. Save the script and return to the Unity Editor. This replaces the manually written diffuse lighting calculation with the reusable `LightingHalfLambert` function from the include file.

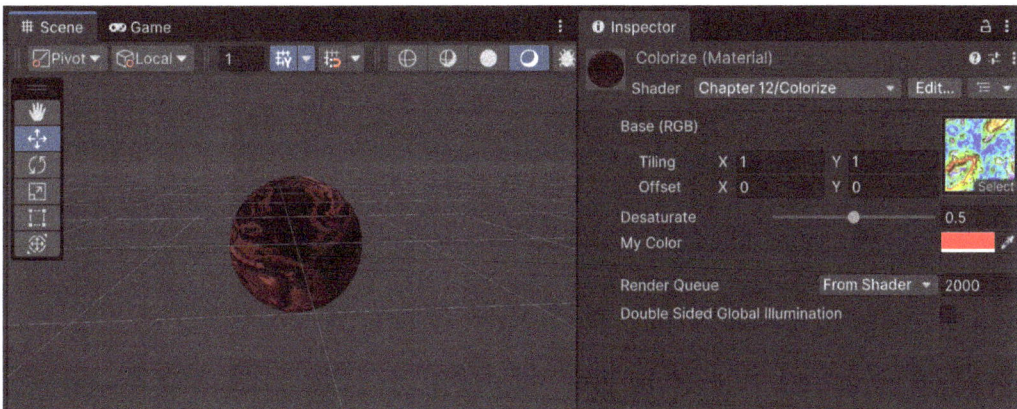

Figure 12.12 – Finished Colorize shader

How it works...

The updated `Colorize` shader leverages URP's ShaderLibrary for transformation functions, luminance calculations, and main light data, while also incorporating a custom lighting function from our newly created `MyHLSLInclude.hlsl` file. The `#include` directive integrates this external file, enabling modularity and the ability for us to reuse the code across multiple shaders in our project.

Once we have declared the `#include` directive and Unity is able to find the file in the project, Unity will then look for code snippets that have been defined. This is where we start to use the `#ifndef` and `#endif` directives. When we declare the `#ifndef` directive, we are simply saying, *if not defined, define something with the name*. This helps avoid multiple inclusion of the same code, which can lead to errors.

In this recipe's case, we said we wanted to `#define MY_HLSL_INCLUDE`. So, if Unity doesn't find a definition called `MY_HLSL_INCLUDE`, it goes and creates it when the HLSL file is compiled, thereby giving us access to the code that follows. The `#endif` method simply says that this is the end of this definition, so stop looking for more code.

The `LightingHalfLambert` function centralizes lighting calculations, allowing for consistent logic and reducing repetitive code. You can expand `MyHLSLInclude.hlsl` with additional functions, such as specular calculations or unique effects, and reuse them across your shaders, making your workflow more efficient.

This modular approach simplifies maintenance and encourages experimentation, helping you create shaders that enhance your game's visual identity.

Implementing a Fur shader

The look of a material depends on its physical structure. The shaders attempt to simulate them, but, in doing so, they oversimplify the way light behaves. Materials with a complex macroscopic structure are particularly hard to render. This is the case for many fabrics and animal furs.

This recipe will show you how it is possible to simulate fur and other materials (such as grass) that are more than just a flat surface. In order to do this, the same material is drawn multiple times over and over, increasing in size every time. This creates the illusion of fur. The shader presented here is based on the work of Jonathan Czeck and Aras Pranckevičius:

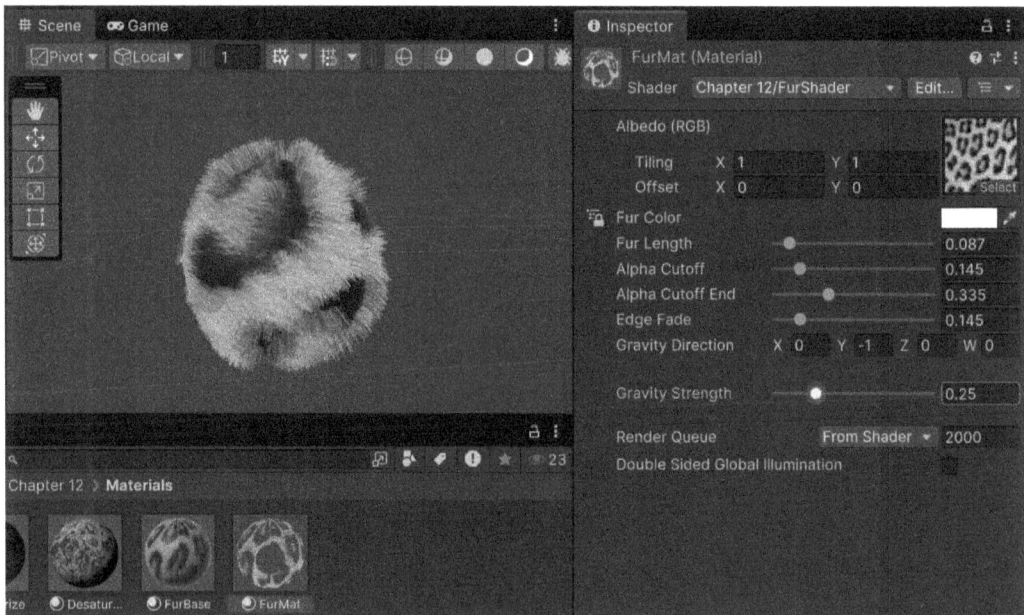

Figure 12.13 – Our end result

Getting ready

In order for this recipe to work, you will need a texture that shows how you wish to have your fur displayed:

Figure 12.14 – The fur texture

I have provided two examples (Faux Fur and panda) in the Chapter 12/Textures folder with the book's example code.

Like all the other shaders before, you will need to create a new Standard Surface shader (Fur) and a material (FurMat) to host it, and attach it to a sphere for demonstration purposes.

Follow these steps to complete the setup for this recipe:

1. Start by creating a new scene in Unity using **Basic (URP) Template**. Add a basic sphere model to the scene by going to **GameObject | 3D Object | Sphere**.

2. We will then create a shader but this time we will create it using code. To do this, go to your **Project** window and create a new shader by selecting **Create | Shader | Unit Shader**. Name the shader FurShader.

3. Create a new material for our shader and assign the **Fur** shader to it. This can be done simply by right-clicking on the Shader, selecting **Create | Material**, and giving it a name (FurMat). From that **Material**'s properties, asset the **Texture** property to one of the fur options (I used Faux Fur, for example) and then attach the material to the sphere in the scene.

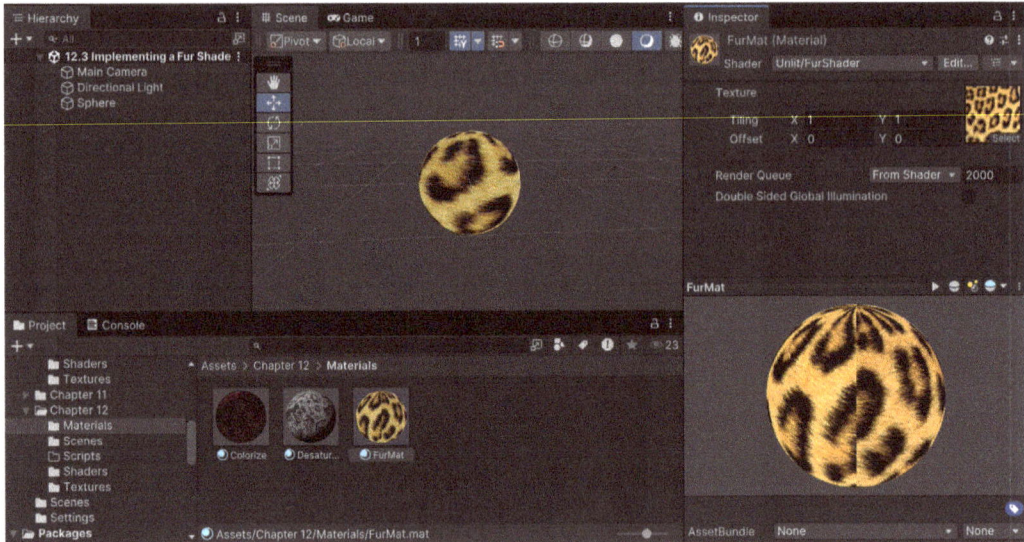

Figure 12.15 – Fur map setup

With the scene and resources set up, you are now ready to proceed to the shader implementation.

How to do it...

With the scene prepared, we can now begin the process of creating the base fur material. Double-click on the shader that was created for this scene to open it in your IDE of choice and insert the code given in the following steps:

1. To define the controls for our Fur shader, we need to populate the `Properties` block. Replace the current content of the `Properties` block with the following code:

```
Properties
{
    _MainTex ("Albedo (RGB)", 2D) = "white" {}
    _Color ("Fur Color", Color) = (1, 1, 1, 1)
    _FurLength ("Fur Length", Range(0.01, 1.0)) = 0.1
    _Cutoff ("Alpha Cutoff", Range(0, 1)) = 0.5
    _CutoffEnd ("Alpha Cutoff End", Range(0, 1)) = 0.5
    _EdgeFade ("Edge Fade", Range(0, 1)) = 0.5
    _Gravity ("Gravity Direction", Vector) = (0, -1, 0, 0)
    _GravityStr ("Gravity Strength", Range(0, 1)) = 0.25
}
```

2. Next, we will update the `Tags` to work with the URP:

```
SubShader
{
    Tags { "RenderPipeline"="UniversalPipeline"
"RenderType"="Transparent" }
    LOD 100
```

This step tells Unity to use the URP rendering pipeline and sets the transparency and rendering order for our fur material.

3. The next step is to replace the `#include` statement for `UnityCG.cginc` with the URP-specific shader libraries.

```
#include "Packages/com.unity.render-pipelines.universal/
ShaderLibrary/Core.hlsl"
#include "Packages/com.unity.render-pipelines.universal/
ShaderLibrary/Lighting.hlsl"
```

These files provide functions for working with URP's lighting system and shading.

4. Now, we'll expand the `appdata` and `v2f` structures to include fields for world-space transformations and fur-specific data. Replace the existing structures with the following:

```
struct appdata
{
    float4 vertex : POSITION;
    float2 uv : TEXCOORD0;
    float3 normal : NORMAL;
    float4 color : COLOR; // Vertex color for alpha
};

struct v2f
{
    float2 uv : TEXCOORD0;
    float4 vertex : SV_POSITION;
    float3 worldPos : TEXCOORD1;
    float3 worldNormal : TEXCOORD2;
    float3 viewDir : TEXCOORD3;
};
```

5. Next, we need to update the `CGPROGRAM` and `ENDCG` sections of the code to say `HLSLPROGRAM` and `ENDHLSL`. This ensures compatibility with HLSL syntax.

    We then need to create the data connection between our `Properties` and the `HLSLPROGRAM` blocks.

6. Add the following bolded line after the declaration of the two `_MainTex` and `_MainTex_ST` variables:

```
sampler2D _MainTex;
float4 _MainTex_ST;
float4 _Color;
float _FurLength;
float _Cutoff;
float _CutoffEnd;
float _EdgeFade;
float4 _Gravity;
float _GravityStr;
```

7. Now we need to modify the `vert` function to include calculations for world-space transformations, gravity, and fur offset:

```
v2f vert(appdata v)
{
    v2f o;

    // Transform normal and position to world space
    float3 normalWS = TransformObjectToWorldNormal(v.normal);
    float3 worldPos = TransformObjectToWorld(v.vertex.xyz);

    // Calculate view direction in world space
    float3 viewDirWS = normalize(TransformWorldToViewDir(worldPos));

    // Normalize gravity direction
    float3 gravityDir = normalize(_Gravity.xyz);

    // Compute fur offset
    float3 furOffset = CalculateFurOffset(normalWS, gravityDir,
v.color.a);
    worldPos += furOffset;
```

```
        // Pass data to fragment shader
        o.vertex = TransformWorldToHClip(worldPos);
        o.worldPos = worldPos;
        o.worldNormal = normalWS;
        o.viewDir = viewDirWS;
        o.uv = v.uv;

        return o;
    }
```

This function computes the fur offset based on gravity and applies it to the vertex positions

8. In the above code snippet, we use a function called CalculateFurOffset but that function doesn't actually exist, so we have to create it ourselves. Above the vert function, add the CalculateFurOffset function to compute the fur offset based on the normal and gravity:

```
    float3 CalculateFurOffset(float3 normalWS, float3 gravityDir, float
    alpha)
    {
        float3 direction = lerp(normalWS,
            normalize(gravityDir * _GravityStr + normalWS * (1.0 -
    _GravityStr)), _FUR_MULTIPLIER
        );
        return direction * _FurLength * _FUR_MULTIPLIER * alpha;
    }
```

Note that we have to put the function above vert or put a function declaration above the vert function, or our code will not compile.

9. Now we will modify the frag function to incorporate alpha fade and color tint:

```
    float4 frag(v2f i) : SV_Target
    {
        // Sample the base texture
        float4 texColor = tex2D(_MainTex, i.uv);

        // Apply alpha fade
        float alpha = texColor.a;
        alpha *= CalculateAlphaFade(alpha, i.viewDir,
                            normalize(i.worldNormal));
```

```
// Discard fragments below cutoff
if (alpha < _Cutoff)
    discard;

// Apply color tint
texColor.rgb *= _Color.rgb;

return texColor;
}
```

10. Above the `frag` function, add the `CalculateAlphaFade` function to handle edge fading:

```
float CalculateAlphaFade(float alpha, float3 viewDir, float3
normalWS)
{
    float edgeFade = 1.0 - _EdgeFade;
    edgeFade += dot(normalize(viewDir), normalize(normalWS));
    return saturate(alpha * edgeFade);
}
```

11. Save your script and return to the Unity Editor. If you select the `FurMat` and adjust the **Alpha Cutoff**, you should notice the closer you get to 0, the more of the material shows.

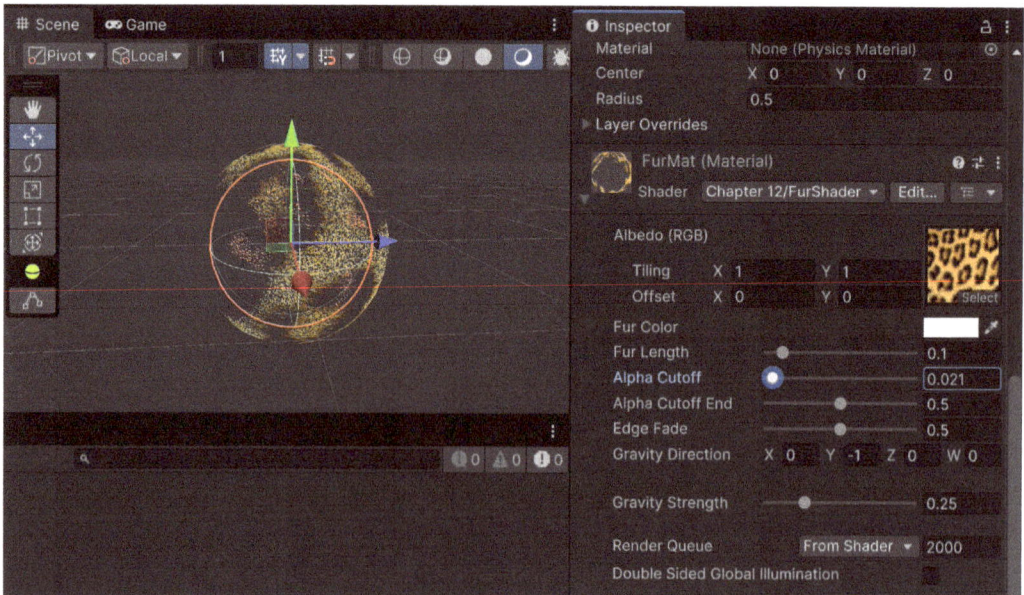

Figure 12.16 – Single pass of the fur material

This gives us a single pass of our fur material. As shown in the figure, the shader effectively renders some parts of the fur with some transparency.

1. Back in the FurShader file, add a new variable:

```
float _GravityStrength;
float _FUR_MULTIPLIER;          // Multiplier for fur layering
```

Note that because we didn't put this in the Properties block at the top, we won't see it in the **material**. But we can still access it via code.

2. Inside the CalculateFurOffset function, update it to the following:

```
float3 CalculateFurOffset(float3 normalWS, float3 gravityDir, float
alpha)
{
    float3 direction = lerp(
        normalWS,
        normalize(gravityDir * _GravityStrength + normalWS * (1.0 -
_GravityStrength)),
        _FUR_MULTIPLIER
    );
    return direction * _FurLength * alpha * _FUR_MULTIPLIER;
}
```

3. Next, update CalculateAlphaFade to the following:

```
float CalculateAlphaFade(float alpha, float3 viewDir, float3
normalWS)
{
    float edgeFade = 1.0 - (_FUR_MULTIPLIER *
                        _FUR_MULTIPLIER);
    edgeFade += dot(normalize(viewDir),
                        normalize(normalWS)) - _EdgeFade;
    return saturate(alpha * edgeFade);
}
```

4. Next, go into the frag function and update the alpha variable to be set to the following:

```
float4 frag(v2f i) : SV_Target
{
    // Sample the base texture
```

```
float4 texColor = tex2D(_MainTex, i.uv);
// Apply alpha fade
float alpha = step(lerp(_Cutoff,_CutoffEnd,_FUR_MULTIPLIER),
texColor.a);
alpha *= CalculateAlphaFade(alpha, i.viewDir, normalize(i.
worldNormal));
//... rest of the frag function
```

5. Save the script and return to the Unity Editor. Because _FUR_MULTIPLIER is **0**, we won't be able to do much right now, but we will be fixing that shortly.

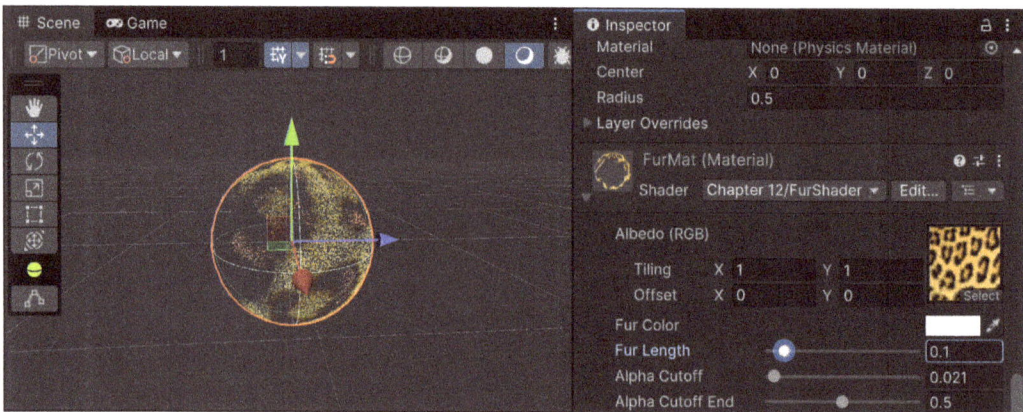

Figure 12.17 – Added _FUR_MULTIPLIER effect

Expanding the Fur shader with a fur layer generator

To fix our issue, we are going to be creating several child GameObjects and giving them each a different multiplier to expand them out to create fur. So we don't have to do it manually, we're going to create a script to take care of all of that for us:

1. Go to the **Project** window and create a `Scripts` folder for the chapter if it doesn't exist. Then, create a new MonoBehaviour script called `FurLayerGenerator`. Open up your code editor.

2. At the top of the file, add the following variables:

```
public Material baseMaterial;
public float startValue = 0.05f;
public float stepSize = 0.05f;

private int baseRenderQueue = 3000;
```

3. Add the following function to handle fur layer creation:

```
[ContextMenu("Generate Fur Layers")]
public void GenerateFurLayers()
{
    if (baseMaterial == null)
    {
        return;
    }
    ClearExistingFurLayers();

    int layerCount = Mathf.CeilToInt((1 - startValue) /
stepSize);
    CreateFurLayers(layerCount);
}
```

This function calculates how many layers are needed and calls other helper methods to generate them.

4. Then we will add a helper function to remove any previously generated layers:

```
private void ClearExistingFurLayers()
{
    for (int i = transform.childCount - 1; i >= 0; i--)
    {
        Transform child = transform.GetChild(i);
        if (child.name.Contains("FurLayer"))
        {
            DestroyImmediate(child.gameObject);
        }
    }
}
```

5. Then we will add a function to create the fur layers:

```
private void CreateFurLayers(int layerCount)
{
    MeshFilter parentMeshFilter = GetComponent<MeshFilter>();
    if (parentMeshFilter == null || parentMeshFilter.sharedMesh ==
null)
```

```
    {
        Debug.LogWarning("No parent MeshFilter or sharedMesh found.
Cannot generate fur layers.");
        return;
    }
    for (int i = 0; i < layerCount; i++)
    {
        float furMultiplier = startValue + (stepSize * i);
        if (furMultiplier > 1.0f)
        {
            break;
        }
        CreateSingleFurLayer(i, furMultiplier, parentMeshFilter.
sharedMesh);
    }
}
```

This function loops through each layer, calculating its _FUR_MULTIPLIER and creating a new child object for it.

6. To make it easier to break apart the functionality, add the following function to handle the creation of individual fur layers:

```
private void CreateSingleFurLayer(int index, float furMultiplier,
Mesh mesh)
{
    GameObject layer = new GameObject($"FurLayer_{index}");
    layer.transform.SetParent(transform);
    layer.transform.localPosition = Vector3.zero;
    layer.transform.localRotation = Quaternion.identity;
    layer.transform.localScale = Vector3.one;

    MeshFilter meshFilter = layer.AddComponent<MeshFilter>();
    meshFilter.sharedMesh = mesh;

    MeshRenderer meshRenderer = layer.AddComponent<MeshRenderer>();
    Material layerMaterial = CreateLayerMaterial(furMultiplier,
index);
```

```
        meshRenderer.sharedMaterial = layerMaterial;
    }
```

Each layer is created as a child object with its own material and mesh.

7. The function uses the `CreateLayerMaterial` function, so now we need to create it:

```
    private Material CreateLayerMaterial(float furMultiplier, int index)
    {
        Material layerMaterial = new Material(baseMaterial);
        layerMaterial.SetFloat("_FUR_MULTIPLIER", furMultiplier);
        layerMaterial.renderQueue = baseRenderQueue + index;
        return layerMaterial;
    }
```

8. Save the script and return to the Unity Editor. Attach the script to the `Sphere` and assign the `FurMat` to the **Base Material**. Then, right-click on the component attached to the object and select the **Generate Fur Layers** function:

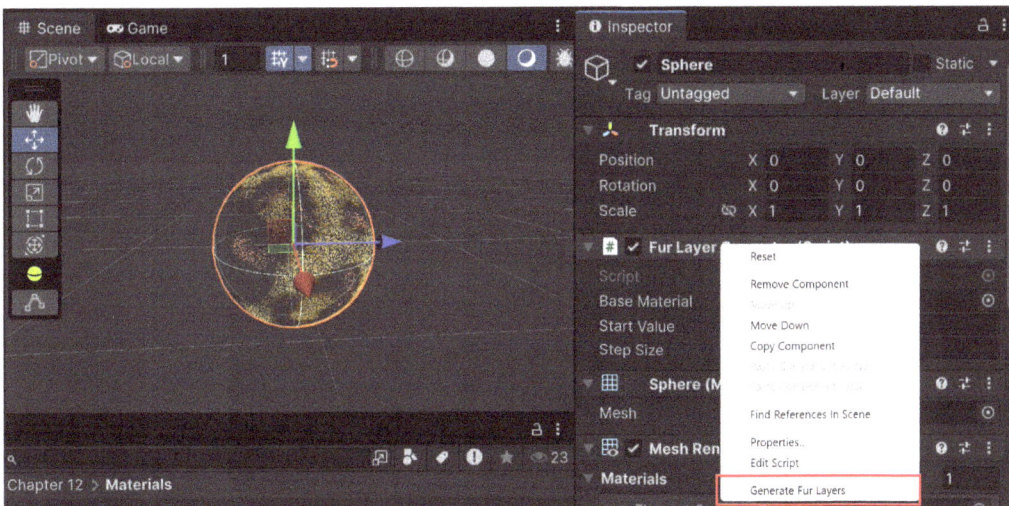

Figure 12.18 – Selecting Generate Fur Layers

And with that, we can now see the fur appearing on our object:

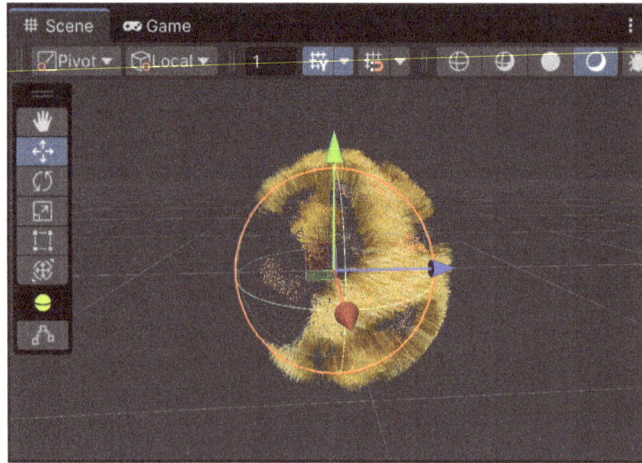

Figure 12.19 – Fur layers created

9. To make it look nicer, we can right-click on our sphere object and create a child sphere object, which I named `Base Layer`. From there, create a basic `FurBase` material with the Standard Shader with **Base Color** set to our fur and assign it to the sphere.

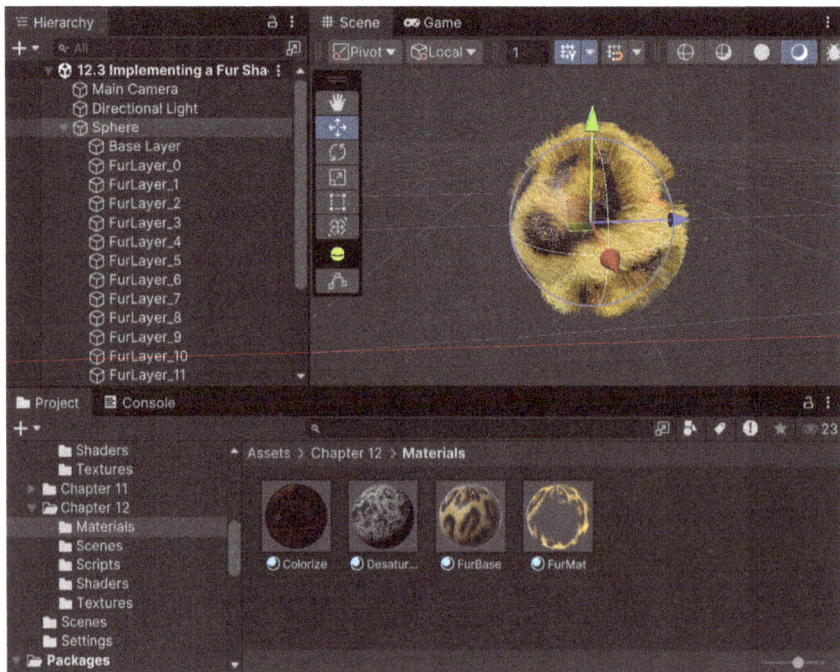

Figure 12.20 – Added base fur layer

Now, this looks nice; but any time we want to make a change, we have to regenerate our layers. It would be nice if it would automatically regenerate for us, but we don't want to do it all the time for efficiency reasons. With that in mind, let's create a debug mode where users can automatically run the code.

1. In our script, add the following new variables:

    ```
    public bool debugMode = true;
    private float updateInterval = 0.1f;
    private float timeSinceLastUpdate = 0.0f;
    ```

2. Next, inside of Update, add the following:

    ```
    private void Update()
    {
        if (debugMode && isActiveAndEnabled)
        {
            timeSinceLastUpdate += Time.deltaTime;
            if (timeSinceLastUpdate >= updateInterval)
            {
                GenerateFurLayers();
                timeSinceLastUpdate = 0.0f;
            }
        }
    }
    ```

3. In the Start method, call the function so we get the fur loaded in case it's been removed:

    ```
    public void Start()
    {
        GenerateFurLayers();
    }
    ```

4. Lastly, to have the script run in the editor mode as well, we can add the following attribute above the class:

    ```
    [ExecuteAlways]
    public class FurLayerGenerator : MonoBehaviour
    ```

5. Save the script and return to the editor.

Now, we should be able to test out the properties in both the material and the **Fur Layer Generator** component and we should be able to see them modify at runtime or at edit time as long as **Debug Mode** is checked.

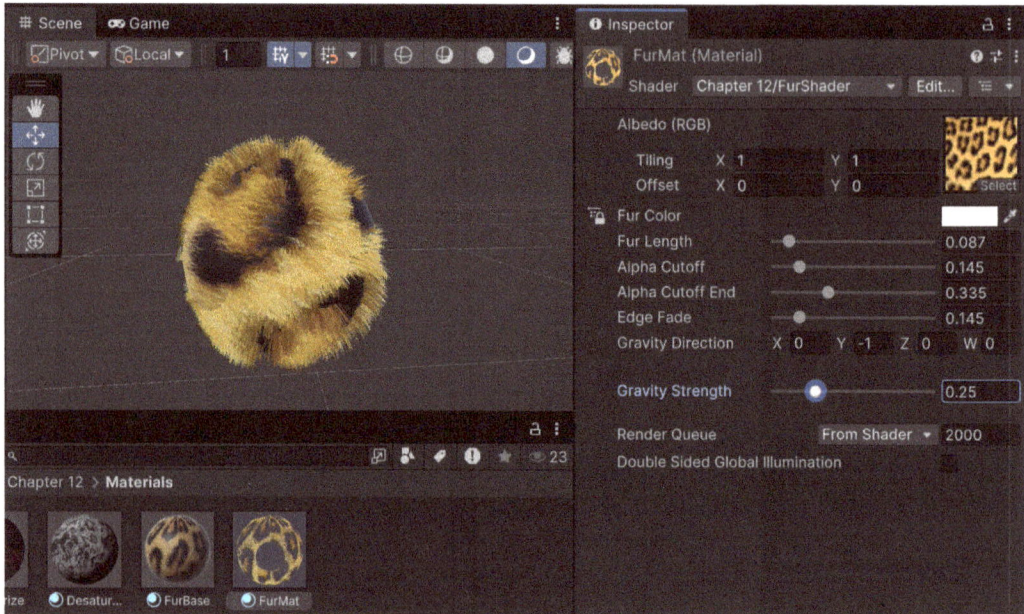

Figure 12.21 – Adjusting fur properties

Let's take a closer look at each property and its role:

- The **Fur Length** property determines the space between the fur shells, which will alter the length of the fur. Longer fur might require more passes to look realistic.

- **Alpha Cutoff** and **Alpha Cutoff End** are used to control the density of the fur and how it gets progressively thinner.

- **Edge Fade** determines the final transparency of the fur and how fuzzy it looks. Softer materials should have a high **Edge Fade** value.

- Finally, **Gravity Direction** and **Gravity Strength** curve the fur shells to simulate the effect of gravity.

How it works...

The technique presented in this recipe is known as **Lengyel's concentric fur shell technique**, or simply the **shell technique**. It works by creating progressively bigger copies of the geometry that needs to be rendered. With the right transparency, it gives the illusion of a continuous thread of hair:

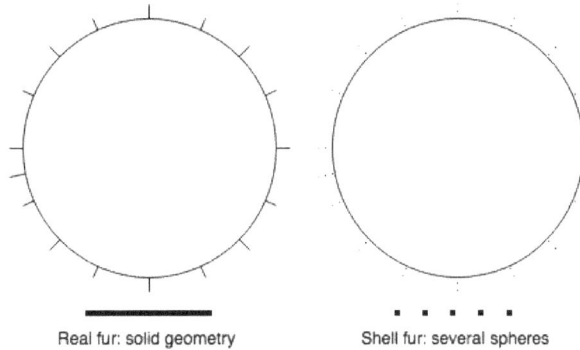

Real fur: solid geometry   Shell fur: several spheres

Figure 12.22 – Real fur versus shell fur

The shell technique is extremely versatile and relatively easy to implement. Realistic fur requires not only extruding the geometry of the model but also altering its vertices. This is possible with tessellation shaders, which are much more advanced and not covered in this book.

In this recipe, we achieve this by combining a custom shader with a script that automates the generation of fur layers. The shader defines how each layer looks, while the script handles the creation of these layers dynamically in Unity.

Each layer is rendered with a unique material, and the _FUR_MULTIPLIER property determines how far the layer is offset and how transparent it appears. Together, these layers simulate the fuzzy appearance of fur.

Each time we create a layer, it creates a slightly bigger version of the model, which is based on the **principle of normal extrusion**. Additionally, the effect of gravity is taken into account, so that it gets more intense the further we are from the center, which is calculated in the CalculateFurOffset function.

```
float3 direction = lerp(
    normalWS,
    normalize(gravityDir * _GravityStr + normalWS * (1.0 - _GravityStr)),
    _FUR_MULTIPLIER
);
return direction * _FurLength * _FUR_MULTIPLIER * alpha;
```

In this example, the `alpha` channel is used to determine the final length of the fur. This allows for more precise control.

Finally, the `surface` function reads the control mask from the `alpha` channel. It uses the `cutoff` value to determine which pixels to show and which ones to hide. This value changes from the first to the final fur shell to match the alpha `_Cutoff` and alpha `_CutoffEnd`:

```
float alpha = step(lerp(_Cutoff,_CutoffEnd,_FUR_MULTIPLIER), texColor.a);

alpha *= CalculateAlphaFade(alpha, i.viewDir, normalize(i.worldNormal));
```

The final `alpha` value of the fur also depends on its angle from the camera, giving it a softer look.

There's more...

The Fur shader has been used to simulate fur. However, it can be used for a variety of other materials. It works very well for materials that are naturally made of multiple layers, such as forest canopies, fuzzy clouds, human hair, and even grass.

Some additional examples of the same shader being used by just tweaking the parameters can be seen in the book's example code, within the `Chapter 12/Scenes/12.3 Implementing a Fur Shader.unity` scene in the GitHub repository (see the *Technical requirements* section):

Figure 12.23 – Additional examples using this shader

There are many other improvements that can dramatically increase its realism. You can add a very simple wind animation by changing the direction of gravity based on the current time. If calibrated correctly, this can give the impression that the fur is moving because of the wind.

Additionally, you can make your fur move when the character is moving. All these little tweaks contribute to the believability of your fur, giving the illusion that it is not just a static material drawn on the surface. Unfortunately, this shader comes at a price: 20 passes are very heavy to compute. The number of passes determines roughly how believable the material is. You should play with the fur length and passes to get the effect that works best for you.

Given the performance impact of this shader, it is advisable to have several materials with different numbers of passes; you can use them at different distances and save a lot of computation.

See also

If you are interested in exploring fur shaders more, you can see another implementation of shell-based fur using Unity's URP that includes multi-pass and physical hair at: `https://github.com/jiaozi158/ShellFurURP/tree/main`.

Implementing heatmaps with arrays

One characteristic that makes shaders hard to master is the lack of proper documentation. Most developers learn how to use shaders by messing around with the code, without having a deep knowledge of what's going on. The problem is amplified by the fact that HLSL makes a lot of assumptions, some of which are not properly advertised. Unity3D allows C# scripts to communicate with shaders using methods such as `SetFloat`, `SetInt`, and `SetVector`. Unfortunately, Unity3D doesn't have a `SetArray` method, which leads many developers to believe that HLSL doesn't support arrays either.

This is not true. This recipe will show you how it's possible to pass arrays to shaders. Just remember that GPUs are highly optimized for parallel computations, and using for loops in a shader will dramatically decrease its performance.

For this recipe, we will implement a heatmap, as shown in the following screenshot:

Figure 12.24 – Heatmap example

Getting ready

The effect in this recipe creates a heatmap from a set of points. This heatmap can be overlaid on top of another picture, like in *Figure 12.24*.

The following steps are necessary:

1. Create a quad with the texture that you want to use for the heatmap (**GameObject** | **3D Object** | **Quad**). In this example, a map of London has been used. To put the texture on the quad, create a new material (Map) using the **Unlit/Texture** shader, and assign the image to the **Base (RGB)** property. Once created, drag and drop that material onto the quad. The position of the quad object must be set to (0, 0, 0). I scaled the image to fit the aspect ratio better (2, 1, 1), but that's not required.

2. Create another quad and place it on top of the previous one. Our heatmap will appear on this quad.

3. Attach a new shader (**Heatmap**) and material (**HeatmapMat**) to the second quad:

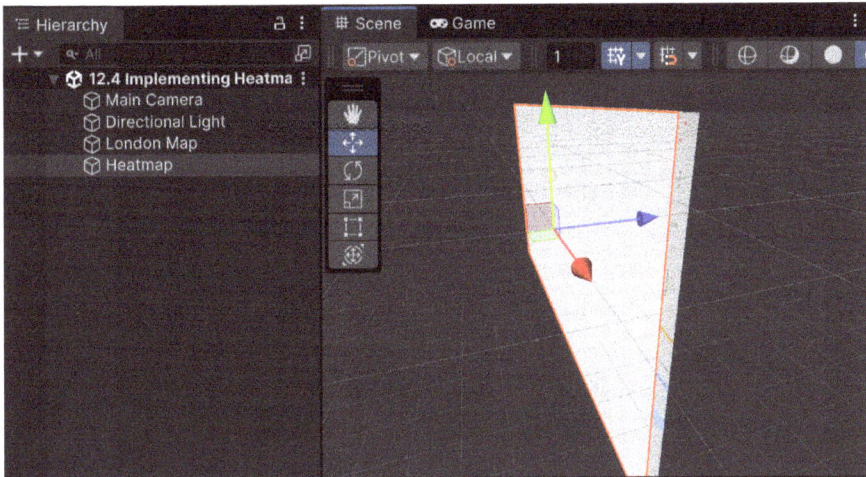

Figure 12.25 – Recipe setup

4. For ease of visualization, select the **Main Camera** and change the object's position to (0, 0, -10), and under the **Camera** component, change the **Projection** property to **Orthographic** and the **Size** property to 0.5 (half the height of the screen).

In the **Game** view, you'll now only see a *white box* due to the second quad covering the map; but we will be changing that shortly.

How to do it...

This shader is quite different from the ones created before, yet the code for it is relatively short. For this reason, the entire code is provided in the following steps:

1. Copy this code to the newly created shader:

```
Shader "CookbookShaders/URP/Heatmap"
{
    Properties
    {
        _HeatTex("Gradient Texture", 2D) = "white" {}
    }
    SubShader
    {
        Tags { "RenderPipeline" = "UniversalPipeline" "RenderType" =
"Transparent" "Queue" = "Transparent"}
```

```
        LOD 100

        Pass
        {
            Tags { "LightMode" = "UniversalForward" }
            Blend SrcAlpha OneMinusSrcAlpha
            HLSLPROGRAM

            #pragma vertex vert
            #pragma fragment frag

            #include "Packages/com.unity.render-pipelines.universal/
ShaderLibrary/Core.hlsl"

            struct appdata
            {
                float4 vertex : POSITION;
            };

            struct v2f
            {
                float4 vertex : SV_POSITION;
                float3 worldPos : TEXCOORD0;
            };

            // Heatmap data
            uniform int _Points_Length = 0;
            uniform float3 _Points[20];
            uniform float2 _Properties[20];

            sampler2D _HeatTex; // Gradient texture

            // Vertex shader
            v2f vert(appdata v)
            {
                v2f o;
                o.vertex = TransformObjectToHClip(v.vertex.xyz);
```

```
                    o.worldPos = TransformObjectToWorld(v.vertex.xyz);
                    return o;
                }

                // Fragment shader
                half4 frag(v2f i) : SV_Target
                {
                    half h = 0.0;

                    // Calculate heatmap contribution
                    for (int j = 0; j < _Points_Length; j++)
                    {
                        half di = distance(i.worldPos,
                                            _Points[j].xyz);
                        half ri = _Properties[j].x; // Radius

                        // Heat intensity
                        half hi = 1.0 - saturate(di / ri);

                        // Add weighted intensity
                        h += hi * _Properties[j].y;
                    }

                    h = saturate(h); // Clamp heat value to 0-1
                    half4 color = tex2D(_HeatTex, float2(h, 0.5)); //
        Map to gradient
                    return color;
                }

            ENDHLSL
        }
    }
}
```

2. Once you have attached this script to your material, you should provide a ramp texture for the heatmap. It is important to configure it so that **Wrap Mode** is set to **Clamp**:

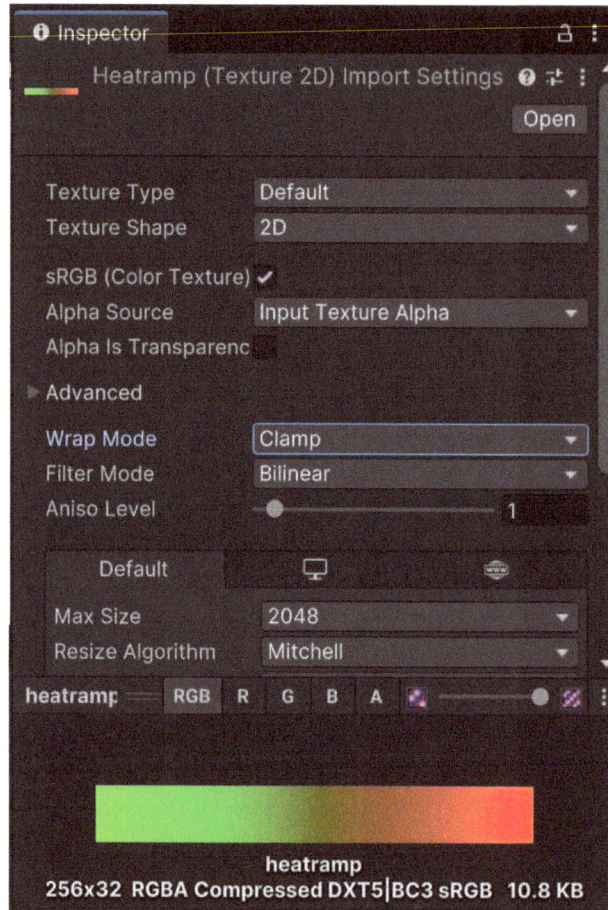

Figure 12.26 – Setting Wrap Mode to Clamp

Note

If your heatmap is going to be used as an overlay, then make sure that the ramp texture has an alpha channel and the texture is imported with the **Alpha Is Transparency** option checked.

3.   Afterward, assign the **Texture** property of the **Heatmap** material to the **Heatramp** texture and you should notice the *white box* is now gone:

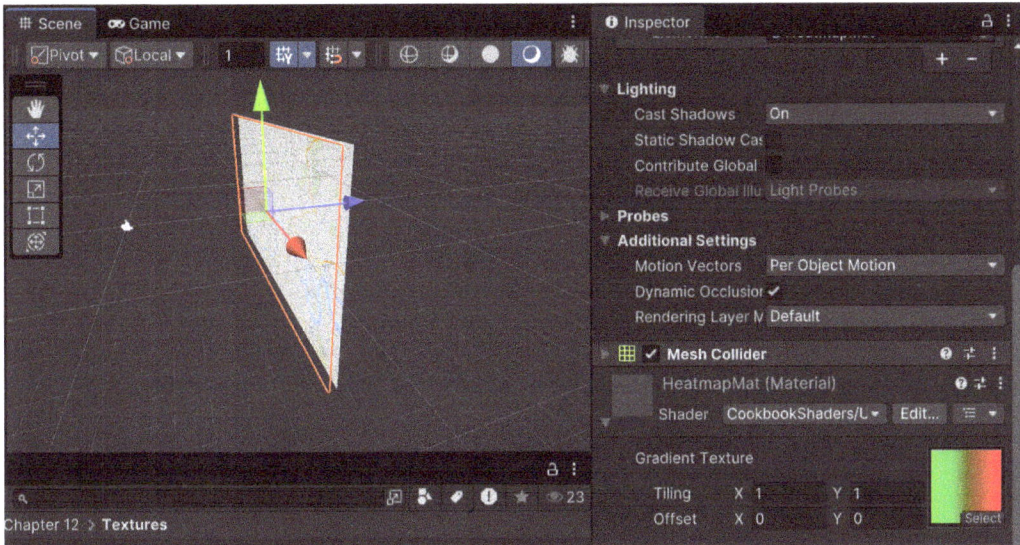

Figure 12.27 – Setting the heatmap material

To have points show up, we will now create a new script to display the points we want to draw.

1.   Create a new script called `HeatmapDrawer` using the following code:

```
using UnityEngine;

public class HeatmapDrawer : MonoBehaviour
{
    public Vector4[] positions;
    public float[] radiuses;
    public float[] intensities;
    public Material material;

    void Start()
    {
        UpdateHeatmap();
    }
```

```
    void UpdateHeatmap()
    {
        if (material == null || positions.Length != radiuses.Length
|| positions.Length != intensities.Length)
        {
            Debug.LogWarning("HeatmapDrawer: Invalid data!");
            return;
        }
        material.SetInt("_Points_Length", positions.Length);
        material.SetVectorArray("_Points", positions);

        Vector4[] properties = new Vector4[positions.Length];
        for (int i = 0; i < positions.Length; i++)
        {
            properties[i] = new Vector4(radiuses[i], intensities[i],
0, 0);
        }
        material.SetVectorArray("_Properties", properties);
    }
}
```

2. Save the file and return to the Unity Editor. Attach the script to an object in your scene, preferably to the Heatmap quad. Then, drag the material created for this effect to the Material slot of the script. By doing this, the script will be able to access the material and initialize it.

3. Lastly, expand the **Positions**, **Radiuses**, and **Intensities** fields of your script and fill them with the values of your heatmap:

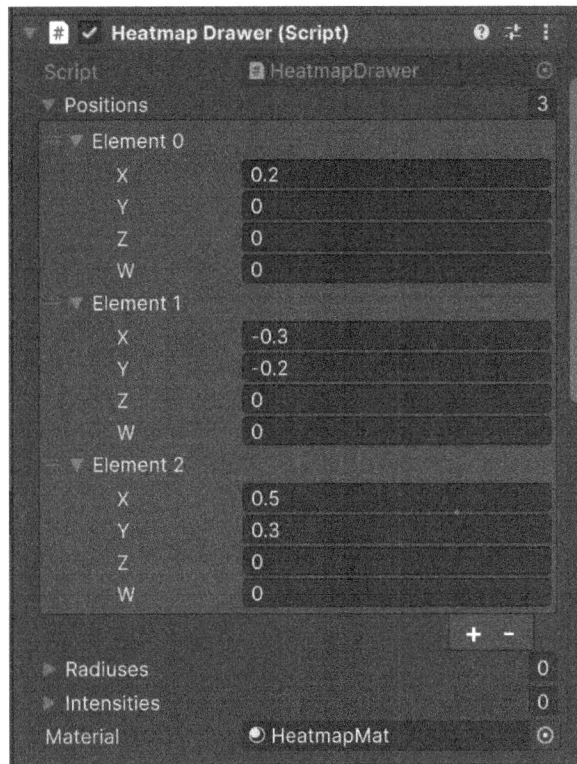

Figure 12.28 – Example values for Heatmap Drawer

Positions indicates the points (in world coordinates) of your heatmap. **Radiuses** indicates their size, and **Intensities** indicates how strongly they affect the surrounding area:

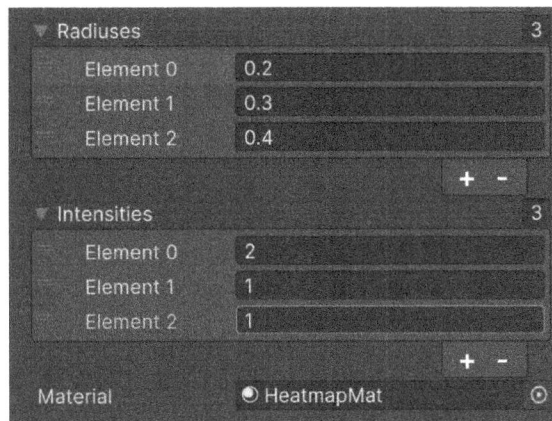

Figure 12.29 – Radiuses and Intensities settings for Heatmap Drawer

4.   If all goes well, once you play the game, you should notice something similar to the following screenshot:

Figure 12.30 – Recipe result

If you do not see this, make sure that the heatmap is placed in front of the map quad and that both objects are in front of the camera. Also, be sure that you are playing the game; the effect does not show up when in **Edit Mode**.

> Note
>
> If you get a warning saying the number of points has changed, go into your shader, modify the script by adding a space, and then save it again.

How it works...

This shader relies on several advanced concepts, including arrays and heatmap rendering, which we have not covered in depth before. **Arrays** in HLSL allow us to store a collection of values, but they come with certain limitations. In HLSL, arrays must have a predefined size, meaning we cannot dynamically adjust their length at runtime. For example, the following line in our shader declares an array of 20 elements:

```
uniform float3 _Points[20];
```

This creates a fixed-size array to store the world positions of up to 20 points. Similarly, we use another array to store the properties of these points, such as their radii and intensities. Unity allows us to pass arrays to shaders using methods like SetVectorArray, SetColorArray, and SetFloatArray. These functions enable us to populate the arrays defined in the shader code from a C# script.

Note on SetVectorArray

It is important to note that Unity's SetVectorArray method only works with Vector4 values. This limitation is not a problem for our shader because Vector3 values can be automatically converted to Vector4 by appending a default 0 for the fourth element. This makes it possible to store the positions of our heatmap points as Vector3 while seamlessly passing them to the shader as Vector4.

Although we could update the arrays in real-time using an Update loop in our C# script, doing so would be computationally expensive, especially with a large number of points. Instead, we initialize the arrays once during the Start method for better performance.

Calculating heatmap contributions

In the shader's fragment function (frag), we calculate the heatmap intensity for each pixel by iterating through all the points in the array. For each point, the contribution to the heatmap is determined based on the distance between the pixel's world position (i.worldPos) and the point's position (_Points[i]). The contribution decreases as the distance increases, following this formula:

```
half di = distance(i.worldPos, _Points[j].xyz);
half ri = _Properties[j].x; // Radius
half hi = 1.0 - saturate(di / ri); // Heat intensity
```

In this code snippet:

- di is the distance from the pixel to the point.
- ri is the radius of influence for the point.
- hi is the heat intensity contributed by the point, calculated as 1.0 - saturate(di / ri). This ensures that the contribution decreases smoothly as the pixel moves further away from the point, with values clamped between 0 and 1.

The total heat intensity (h) for a pixel is the sum of all the contributions, weighted by the intensity of each point (`_Properties[i].y`):

```
h += hi * _Properties[i].y;
```

It is then used to look up which color to use from the ramp texture.

While shaders and arrays provide powerful tools for rendering dynamic heatmaps, their extensive use can introduce a significant computational bottleneck. Each pixel requires the shader to cycle through all points to compute contributions, potentially slowing down performance as the number of points increases, so keep that in mind as you utilize these tools in the future, and use them wisely.

13

Utilizing the HDRP

In the previous chapters of this book, we explored URP, used Shader Graph, and wrote shaders with pure code using ShaderLab and HLSL. In this chapter, we will dive into more advanced Shader Graph techniques, focusing on utilizing the **High-Definition Render Pipeline (HDRP)**.

The HDRP is designed for high-end hardware, targeting platforms such as powerful PCs and modern consoles such as the Xbox Series X and PlayStation 5. It is the go-to choice for projects that demand cutting-edge visuals, including AAA games, architectural visualizations, and cinematic experiences. HDRP unlocks access to state-of-the-art graphics features, such as physically based rendering, real-time global illumination, and advanced volumetric effects, all of which provide unparalleled visual fidelity.

That said, the HDRP is not without its challenges. It requires significantly more resources—both in terms of hardware and development effort. Creating assets for the HDRP typically involves generating additional texture maps and leveraging more complex material setups, which can increase the workload for artists and developers. As a result, the HDRP is most suitable for large teams or projects with sufficient budgets to support the additional effort. For smaller teams or less graphically intensive projects, it might be overkill.

It's important to remember that great visuals are not solely about technical fidelity. Art direction and cohesive aesthetics often have a great impact on how a game looks and feels. The HDRP gives us the tools for stunning graphics, but it's the creative application of those tools that bring a project to life.

The main advantage the HDRP offers lies in its lighting and rendering systems. Features such as real-time global illumination, physically accurate lighting models, volumetric fog, and ray tracing allow for more immersive and realistic scenes. While computationally expensive, these features bring a level of detail and realism that is unmatched in other Unity rendering pipelines.

In this chapter, we'll harness the power of the HDRP and Shader Graph to create visually stunning effects that take full advantage of this high-end pipeline.

In this chapter, we'll cover the following recipes:

- Implementing a glowing highlight system
- Using Portal Shaders in Unity

By the end of this chapter, you'll be equipped to create sophisticated visual effects that leverage the HDRP's advanced features, providing the tools to craft cinematic-quality visuals and immersive 3D experiences. Whether you're aiming for photorealism or stylized graphics, the HDRP combined with Shader Graph will open up a world of possibilities.

Technical requirements

For this chapter, you will need Unity Editor version 6 Preview 6000.0.07f1. This chapter's instructions should work with minimal changes in future versions of the editor in projects that utilize the **Universal Render Pipeline** (**URP**). The chapter's sample project was created using the **High Definition 3D Core** template.

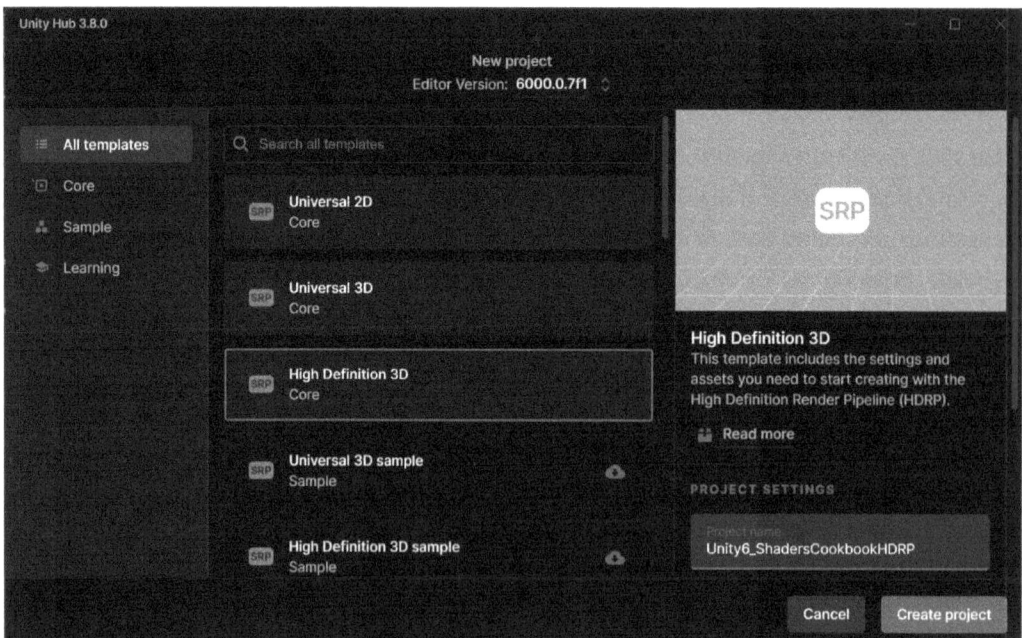

Figure 13.1 – Universal URP project

The code files for this chapter can be found on GitHub at `https://github.com/PacktPublishing/` `Unity-6-Shaders-and-Effects-Cookbook`. The necessary files for this chapter are organized in the Unity project in a folder named `Unity6_ShadersCookbookHDRP` (`https://github.` `com/PacktPublishing/Unity-6-Shaders-and-Effects-Cookbook/tree/main/Unity6_` `ShadersCookbookHDRP/Assets/Chapter%2013`) on GitHub.

Implementing a glowing highlight system

When playing certain kinds of games, you may notice that when the player faces an object they can interact with, the object may glow.

Recent examples of this can be seen in CD Projekt Red's *Cyberpunk 2077* (2020), where interactive objects are highlighted in neon colors to match the game's aesthetic; Arkane Studios' *Deathloop* (2021), which uses outlines and glows to guide players; and FromSoftware's *Elden Ring* (2022), where glowing objects indicate items of interest in the vast open world.

This effect is also commonly found in mobile games such as miHoYo's *Genshin Impact* (2020), where interactive elements are subtly highlighted to draw the player's attention.

This glowing effect can be implemented using Shader Graph, giving us a chance to explore its power and versatility while working through a non-trivial example of the HDRP in action.

Getting ready

Follow these steps to get everything ready for this recipe:

1. Start by creating a new scene in Unity. For the purposes of this chapter, we will be using the HDRP, so you can select **Basic Indoors (HDRP)** instead of the basic options when creating the new project.

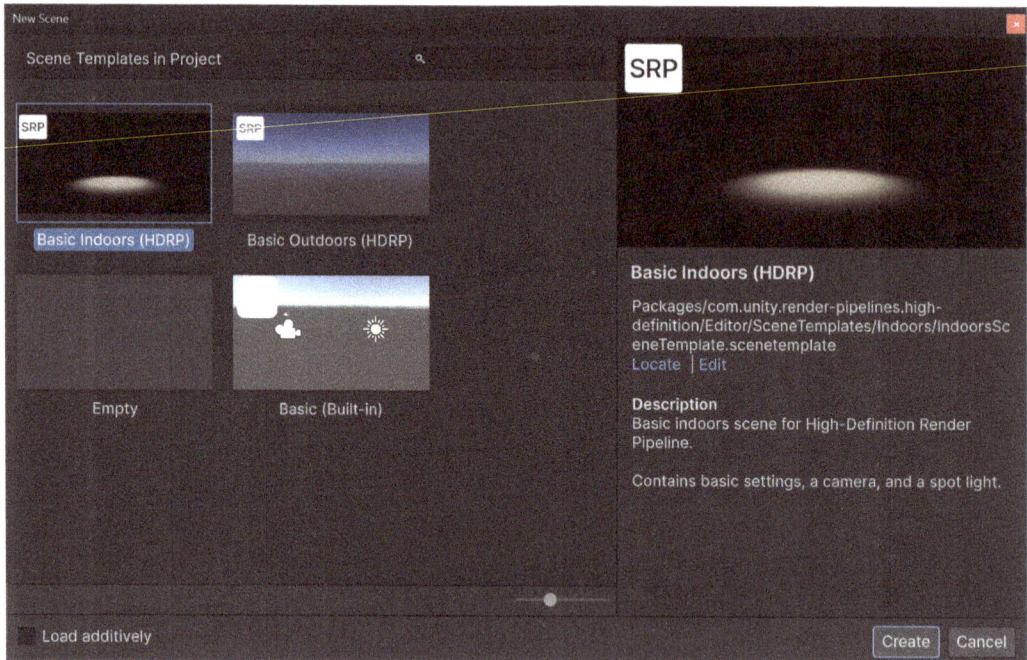

Figure 13.2 – Basic Indoors scene

2.   Add a basic sphere model to the scene by going to **GameObject** | **3D Object** | **Sphere**. I
     then raised the sphere so it'd be above the plane, 0.5 in the **Y** axis.

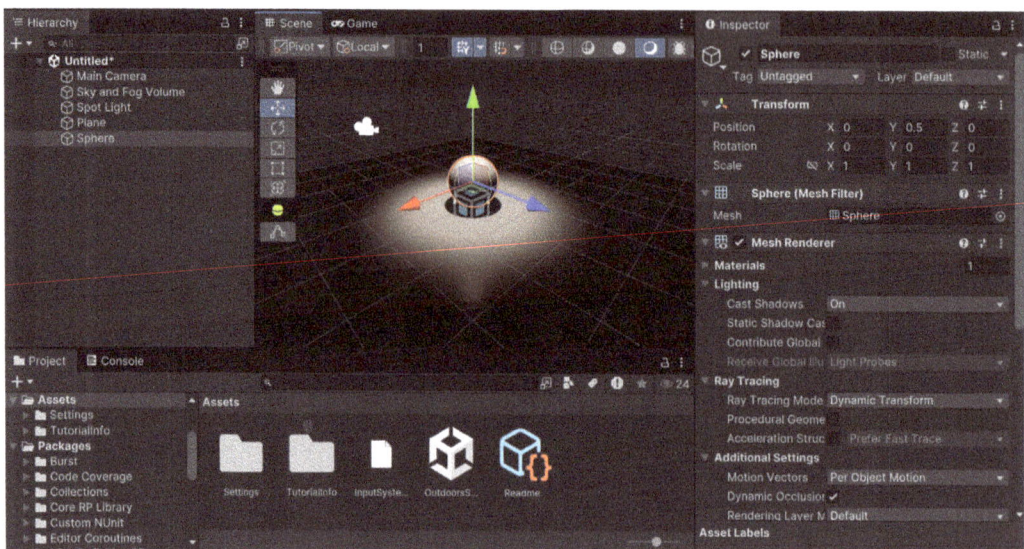

Figure 13.3 – Recipe setup

How to do it...

With the scene prepared, we can now begin the process of creating our first shader graph within the HDRP:

1. In the Project window, create a new shader by navigating to **Create | Shader Graph | HDRP | Lit Shader Graph** and name it GlowGraph.

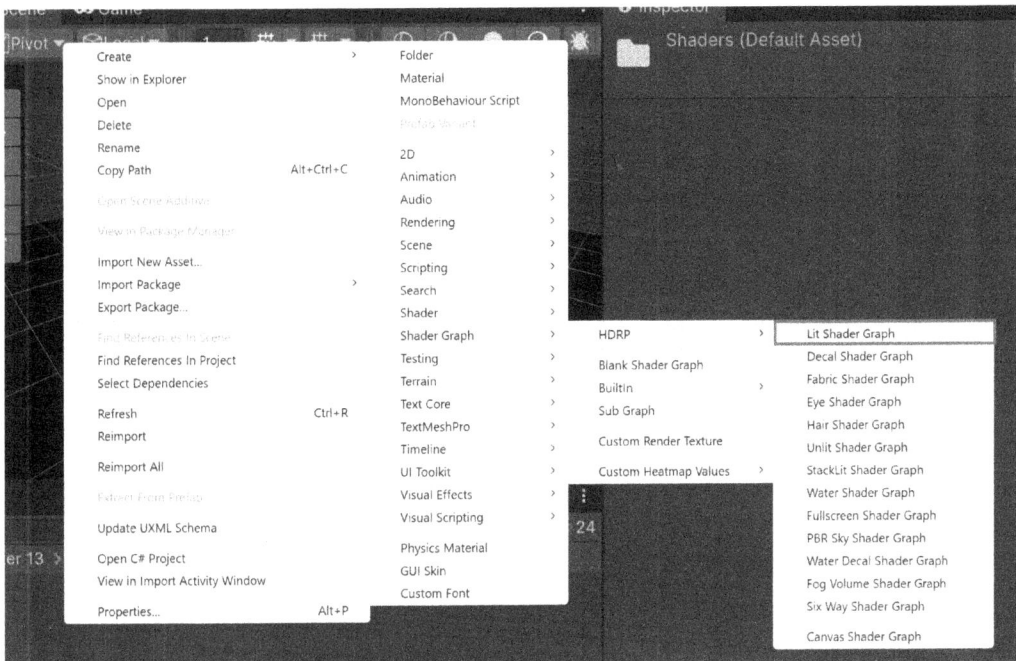

Figure 13.4 – Creating a HDRP Lit Shader Graph

2. Create a new material by going to **Create | Material**. Name it GlowGraphMat.

3. Assign the GlowGraph shader to the material by selecting the material, and then, in the **Inspector**, select the **Shader** dropdown at the top and choose Shader Graphs/GlowGraph.

4. Apply this material to your sphere object by dragging and dropping the material onto it in the **Scene** view.

5. Select the GlowGraph shader in the **Project** window. In the **Inspector**, click the **Open Shader Editor** button to open the Shader Graph editor.

6. Firstly, we will add a new node called **Fresnel** (pronounced *fer-nel*) **Effect**. To add it, go to the left-hand side of the **Fragment** node, right-click, and select **Create Node**. From there, type in Fresnel, and once it has been selected, press the *Enter* key.

Note

The **Fresnel Effect** is often used to provide rim lighting for objects. For more information on this, check out `https://docs.unity3d.com/Packages/com.unity.shadergraph@17.0/manual/Fresnel-Effect-Node.html`.

7. Once the node has been created, connect the **Out** of the **Fresnel Effect** node to the Emission property of the PBR Master node.

8. To make it easier to tell what each node does, click on the gray color to the left of the **Base Color** property and change it to a different color, such as bright *pink*.

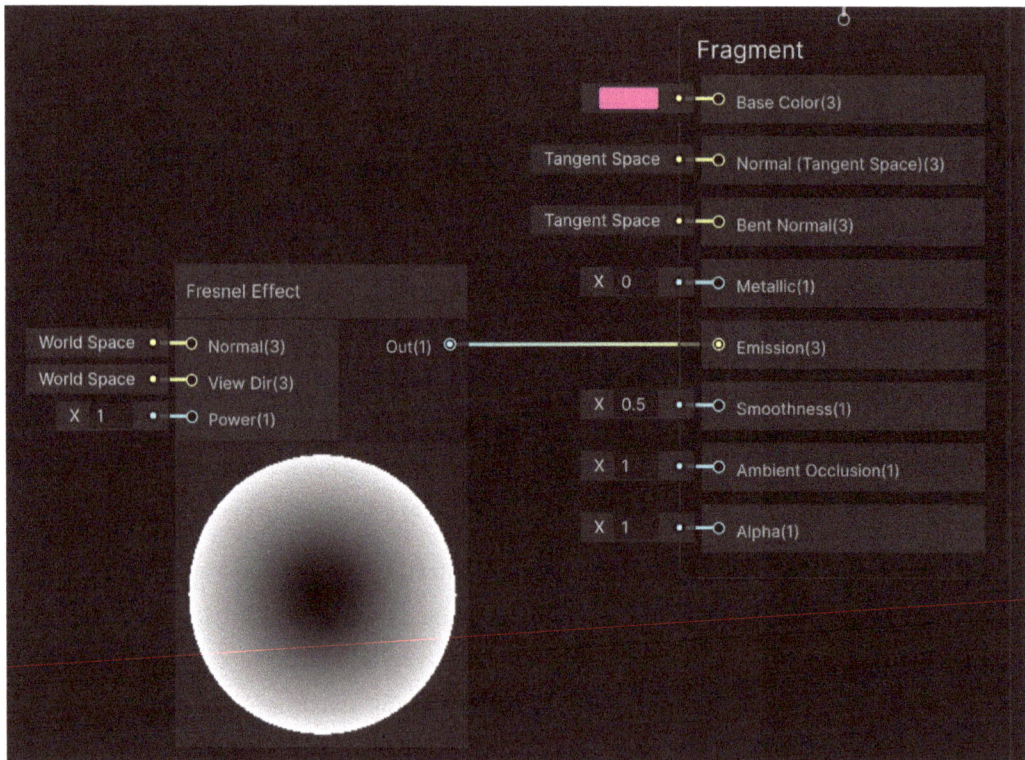

Figure 13.5 – Setting up Base Color

Notice how the **Fresnel Effect** is applied on top of the Albedo color due to it using that value for the **Emission** property.

9. We just want the edges of our object to glow, so change the **Power** property of the **Fresnel Effect** node to 4.

The **Power** value controls how sharply the **Fresnel Effect** fades from the center of the object to its edges. A lower value results in a very broad glow across the object's surface, while a higher value creates a narrow, sharper glow concentrated at the very edges. Setting it to 4 provides a good middle ground, making the glow visually distinct without being overly harsh or too subtle. You can tweak this value to match the visual intensity you want, but 4 is a solid starting point for readability and effect clarity in most lighting environments.

Currently, the light around our object is *white*, but we can make it a different color instead by multiplying it by a color.

10. To do this, go to the **Blackboard** and create a new color by clicking on the + icon and then selecting **Color**. Once the color has been created, give it a name (HoverColor), then go to the **Graph Inspector** and change **Mode** to **HDR**. Then, set the **Default Value** color to something else; I used a *light blue color*. Make sure to set **A** to 255.

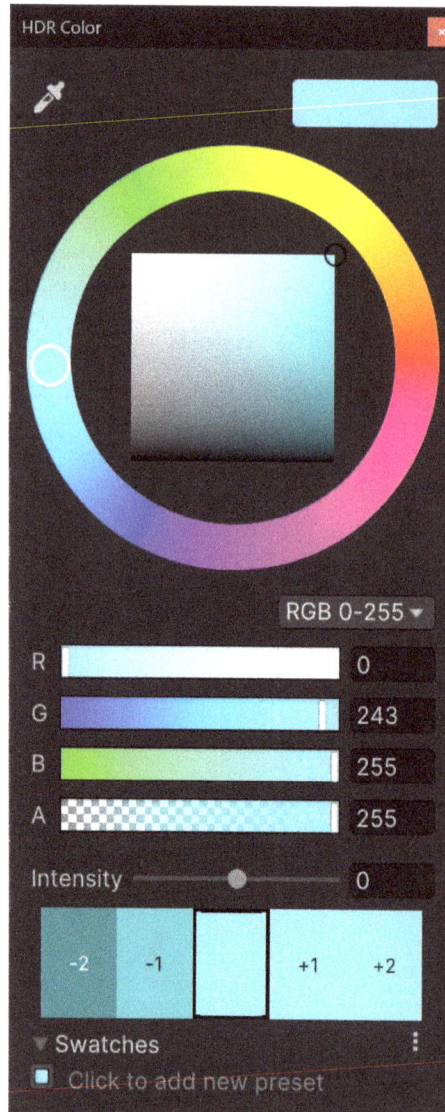

Figure 13.6 – Changing the default hover color

Important note

Remember to note the name HoverColor as we will be using it in code later; if it's not exactly the same, the code will not work correctly.

11. Once it has been created, drag and drop the property beneath the **Fresnel Effect** node in the same way we learned previously.

    Now, we need to multiply the **Fresnel Effect** by the **HoverColor** value before connecting it to the **Emission** input.

    This multiplication serves two key purposes. By default, the **Fresnel Effect** produces a grayscale output, indicating how strongly the effect applies at each pixel. Multiplying it by a color lets us tint that effect, essentially painting the glow with our desired color. Also, because we're working in HDRP, which uses physically based lighting, materials, and emissive surfaces need more intensity to stand out, especially in well-lit environments. That's why we use **HDR Color** (enabled in the **Graph Inspector**) instead of standard color. HDR color allows us to go beyond the typical 0–1 color range and specify values that contribute to the visible light emission, making the glow pop even under strong directional lights.

    This means the **HoverColor** doesn't just define hue; it also acts as a brightness multiplier. If the glow is too faint, increase the intensity (the color's value) in HDR mode.

12. Create a new node between them by selecting **Math | Basic | Multiply** from the node creation menu. Connect the **Out** pin of the **Fresnel Effect** node to the **A** pin of the **Multiply** node. Then, connect the **HoverColor** property to the **B** pin of the **Multiply** node. Afterward, connect the **Out** pin of the **Multiply** node to the **Emission** property.

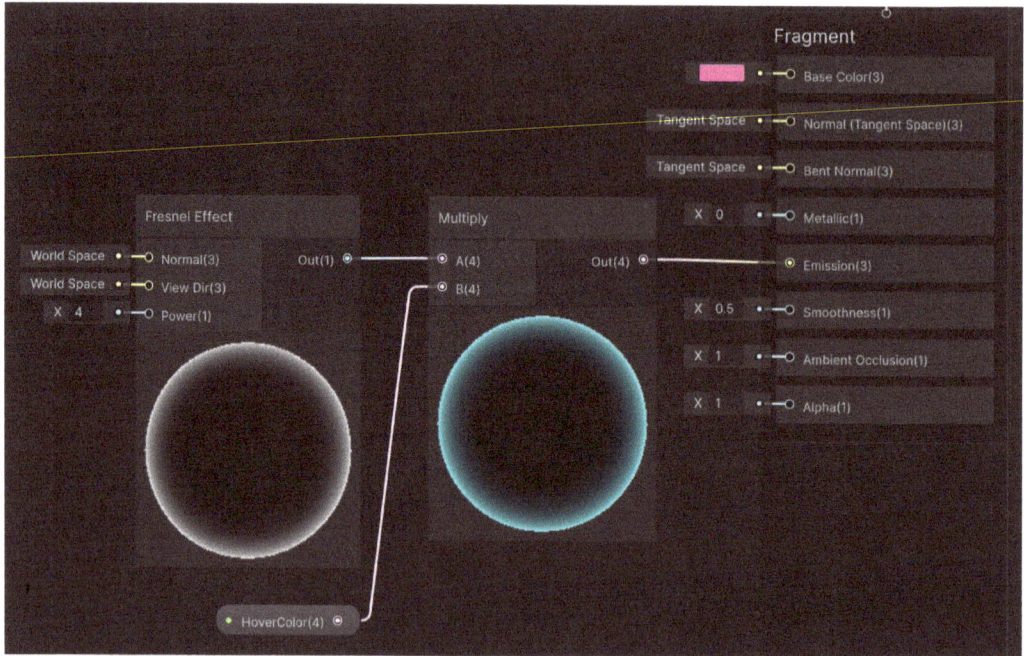

Figure 13.7 – Connecting to Emission

13. Save the graph and dive back into the Unity Editor.

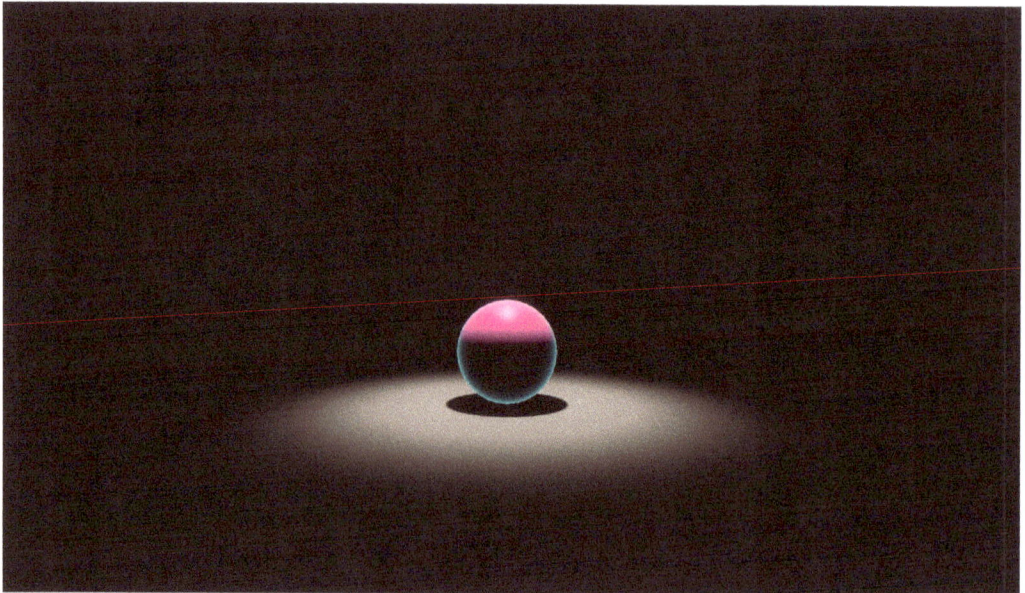

Figure 13.8 – Shader result

At this point, you may notice if you return to the scene that the hover effect will show up if you're in a dark room; but if we add a directional light or if we are in the outdoor scene, it does not appear. HDRP scene lights are physically based, which means the lights are much stronger than the default emissive weight. With that in mind, you may need to increase the effect to see it in those scenes:

1. Create a new MonoBehaviour script called HighlightOnHover. Double-click on it to enter your IDE, and use the following code:

```
using UnityEngine;
using UnityEngine.EventSystems;

public class HighlightOnHover : MonoBehaviour,
                                IPointerEnterHandler,
                                IPointerExitHandler
{
    public Color highlightColor = Color.red;
    private Material material;

    void Start()
    {
        material = GetComponent<MeshRenderer>().material;
        OnPointerExit(null); // Turn off glow initially
    }

    public void OnPointerEnter(PointerEventData eventData)
    {
        material.SetColor("_HoverColor", highlightColor);
    }

    public void OnPointerExit(PointerEventData eventData)
    {
        material.SetColor("_HoverColor", Color.black);
    }
}
```

2. Save the script and return to the Unity Editor. Attach the **HighlightOnHover** script to your sphere.

3. Then **Next**, click on the **Main Camera** game object. From the **Inspector** window, click **Add Component** and select the **Physics Raycaster** option.

4. Afterward, click on **GameObject | UI | Event System**.

5. Save your scene and start the game.

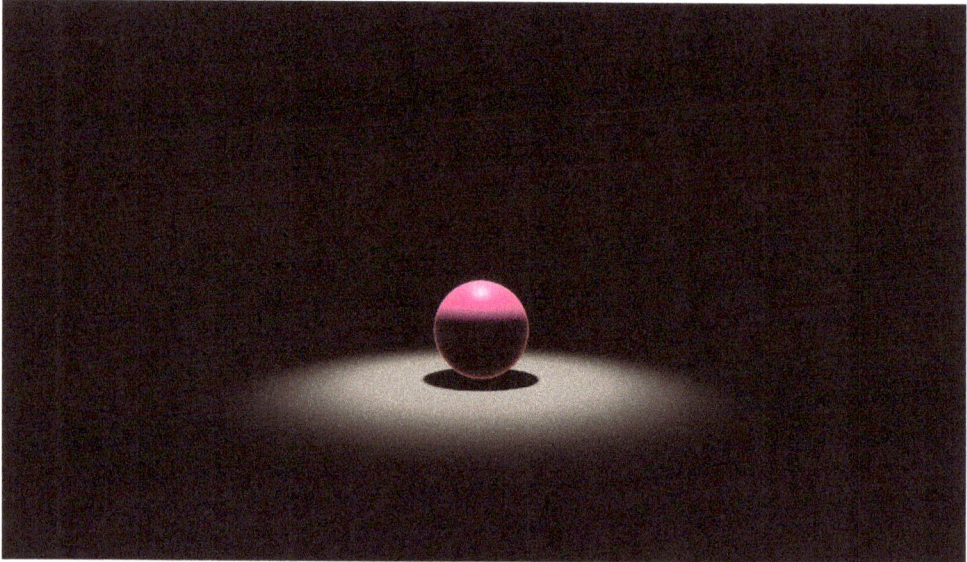

Figure 13.9 – Final result

Now, when we highlight the object with the mouse, we will see the hover effect, but otherwise, it will turn itself off!

How it works...

In this shader, we use a **Fresnel Effect** to simulate a rim light that responds to the object's orientation relative to the camera. We then multiply this effect by a user-defined HDR color, which allows us to tint and intensify the glow using values beyond the standard 0–1 color range. This is especially important in HDRP, where lighting is physically based, and emissive materials need strong intensity values to remain visible under bright environmental lights. Finally, we plug the result into the **Emission** input to make it appear as if the object is glowing.

The **Emission** property is reflective of the light that an object emits or receives. If the **Emission** value is set to *white*, the object will appear fully lit in that color, independent of the surrounding light. Conversely, if the **Emission** value is *black*, the property effectively becomes *off*, and the object emits no light. In this recipe, we make use of this behavior by setting the **Emission** to *black* by default and changing it dynamically when a hover event occurs.

By default, the HDRP template project uses Unity's new input system, which no longer supports older methods such as OnMouseOver and OnMouseUp. Instead, we use a PhysicsRaycaster, which performs a **Raycast**—a virtual line cast from the camera's perspective—at every frame against the 3D objects in the scene. This allows Unity to detect which objects the mouse cursor is hovering over and to send messages to objects that implement **event interfaces**.

Introduction to interfaces

An **interface** in programming is a contract that defines a set of methods or properties that a class must implement, but it does not define how these methods work. In Unity, interfaces are often used to standardize event handling.

For example, when we add IPointerEnterHandler and IPointerExitHandler after the MonoBehaviour class, we are agreeing to implement the OnPointerEnter and OnPointerExit methods. These methods are automatically triggered when the corresponding pointer events occur, as long as the object has the appropriate components.

Interfaces such as IPointerEnterHandler and IPointerExitHandler are part of Unity's Event System. They allow developers to define behavior for events such as mouse or pointer interactions in a structured and predictable way.

Unity's Event System

To enable these event interfaces to function, Unity requires an **Event System** in the scene. This system manages input events and ensures that interactions, such as mouse or pointer hover events, are properly dispatched to the relevant objects.

Putting it all together

With these changes added, when the mouse hovers over the object, the OnPointerEnter function is triggered, causing the object to use the specified hover color. Similarly, when the mouse leaves the object, the OnPointerExit function is triggered, resetting the **Emission** property to *black*.

Using Portal Shaders in Unity

Portals are something that are used quite often in games in order to allow users to travel to different locations quickly. They also give us an opportunity to see how we can utilize time to adjust our shaders and utilize both the **Twist** and **Voronoi** nodes to great effect. In this recipe, we will create a portal shader using **Shader Graph** and the **HDRP**. We will begin by setting up a shader that applies a **Twist** effect to distort the portal's appearance and use **Voronoi** noise to generate a dynamic, animated texture. Then, we will introduce time-based movement to make the portal feel alive. Finally, we will refine the effect by masking the edges, adding HDR color control, and ensuring proper transparency and blending for a polished look.

Getting ready

Follow these steps to get everything ready for this recipe:

1. Start by creating a new scene in Unity. For the purposes of this chapter, we will be using the HDRP, so you can select **Basic Indoors (HDRP)** instead of the basic options when creating the new project.

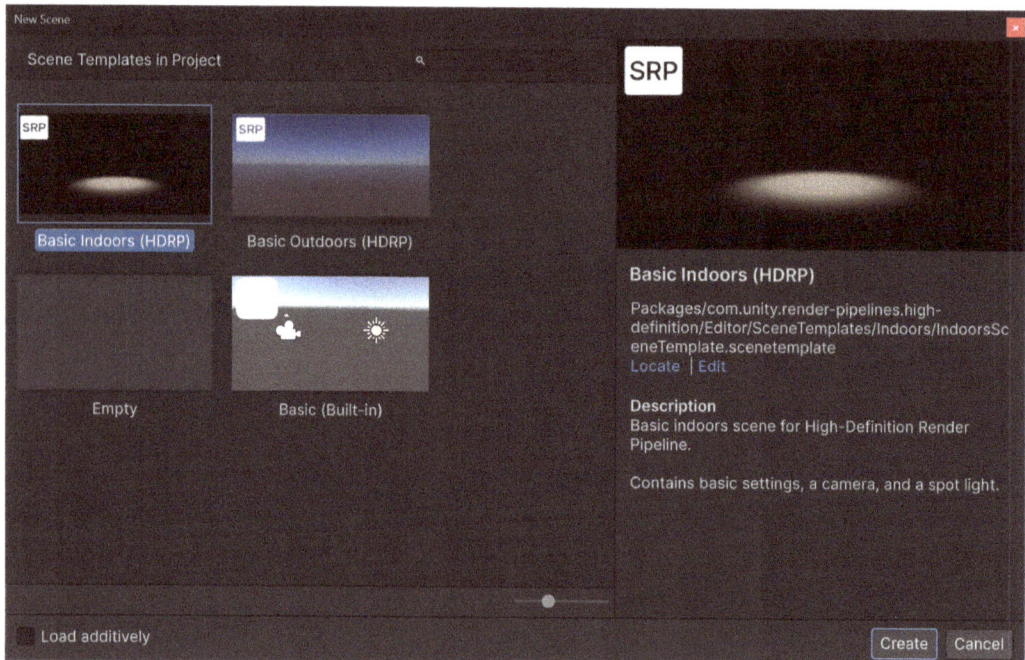

Figure 13.10 – Basic Indoors scene

2. Add a basic sphere model to the scene by going to **GameObject** | **3D Object** | **Plane**. Then, rotate and scale the plane to face the camera nicely in the scene.

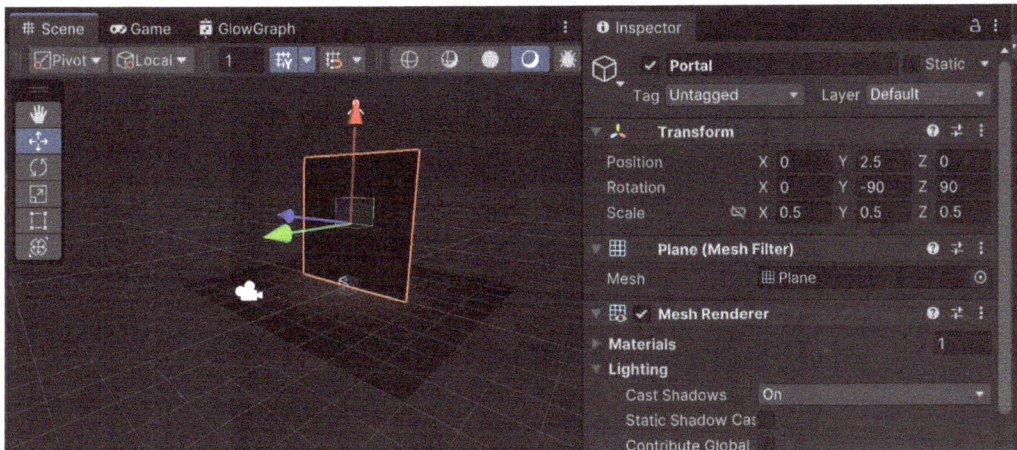

Figure 13.11 – Recipe setup

How to do it...

With the scene prepared, we can now begin the process of experimenting with some of the built-in helper functions included with the ShaderLibrary. Double-click on the shader that was created for this scene to open it in your IDE of choice and insert the code given in the following steps:

1. In the Project window, create a new shader by navigating to **Create | Shader Graph | HDRP | Lit Shader Graph** and name it `PortalGraph`.

2. Afterward, create a new material by going to **Create | Material** (I named mine `PortalGraphMat`). With the material selected, in the **Inspector** window, under **Surface Options**, check the **Double-Sided** option and set **Surface Type** to **Transparent**.

3. Next, assign the shader to the material by selecting the material, and then, from the **Inspector** tab, you should select the **Shader** dropdown at the top and select **Shader Graphs/PortalGraph**. Then, drag and drop the material onto our sphere object in the scene so we can see our shader being used in action.

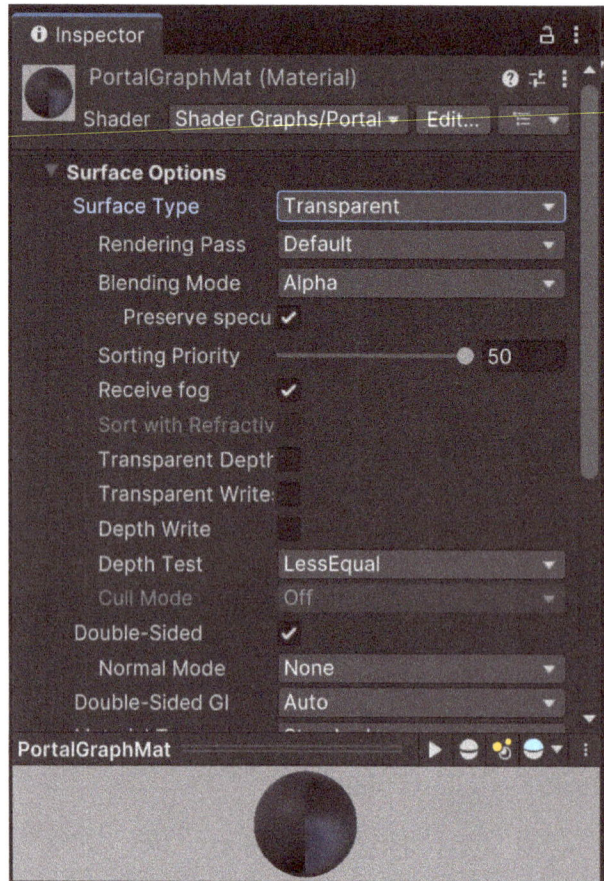

Figure 13.12 – Setting Surface Type

4. Now that the setup is done, we can start creating the graph. If you select the shader, you should see that, from the **Inspector** tab, there will be a button that says **Open Shader Editor**. Click on the button and the Shader Graph editor will open automatically.

5. First, add a **Twirl** node to the graph. Afterward, add a **Voronoi** node. Connect the **Out** pin
    of the **Twirl** node to the **UV** input of the **Voronoi** node.

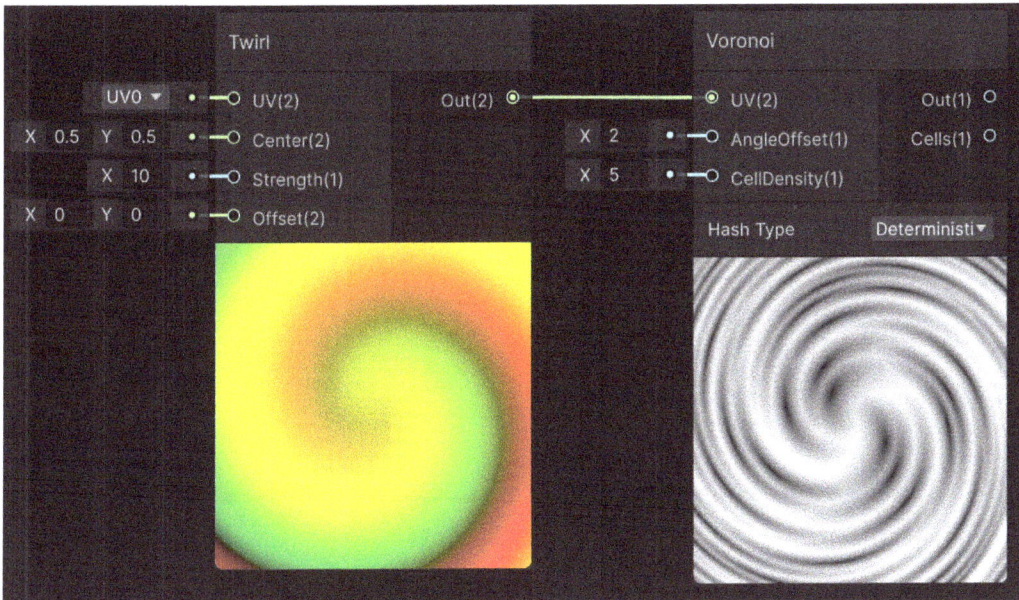

Figure 13.13 – Basic portal texture

6. This provides a good static portal, but we want the portal to move. Open the **Blackboard**
    and add a **Float** variable called PortalSpeed, and from the **Graph Inspector**, set its **Default
    Value** to 0.25.

7. To the left of the **Twirl** node, add the **PortalSpeed** variable and a **Time** node. To the right
    of those two newly created nodes, add a **Multiply** node. Connect the **PortalSpeed** value
    to the **A** pin of the **Multiply** node and connect the **Time** output to the **B** input.

8. Connect the **Out** pin of the **Multiply** node to the **Offset** pin of the **Twirl** node. If all goes well, you should notice that the **Voronoi** node's preview is twisting in a portal-like manner.

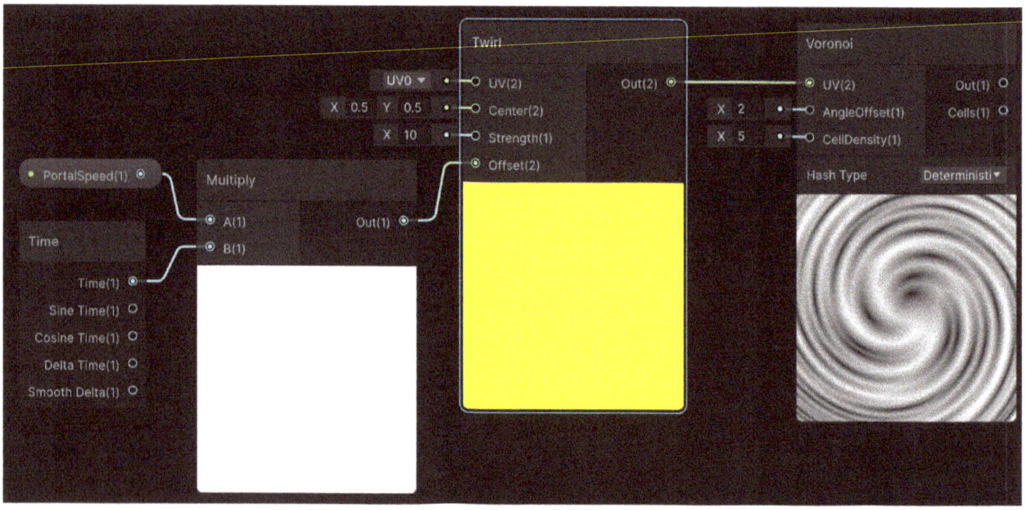

Figure 13.14 – Moving portal texture

9. To hide the edges and mask the effect, add a **Texture Sample 2D** (or **Sample Texture 2D**) node. Change the **Texture** property to the **Default Particle** texture. Then, add a **Multiply** node and connect the **RGBA** value of the **Texture Sample 2D** node to the **A** input of the **Multiply** node and connect **Out** of the **Voronoi** node to the **B** input.

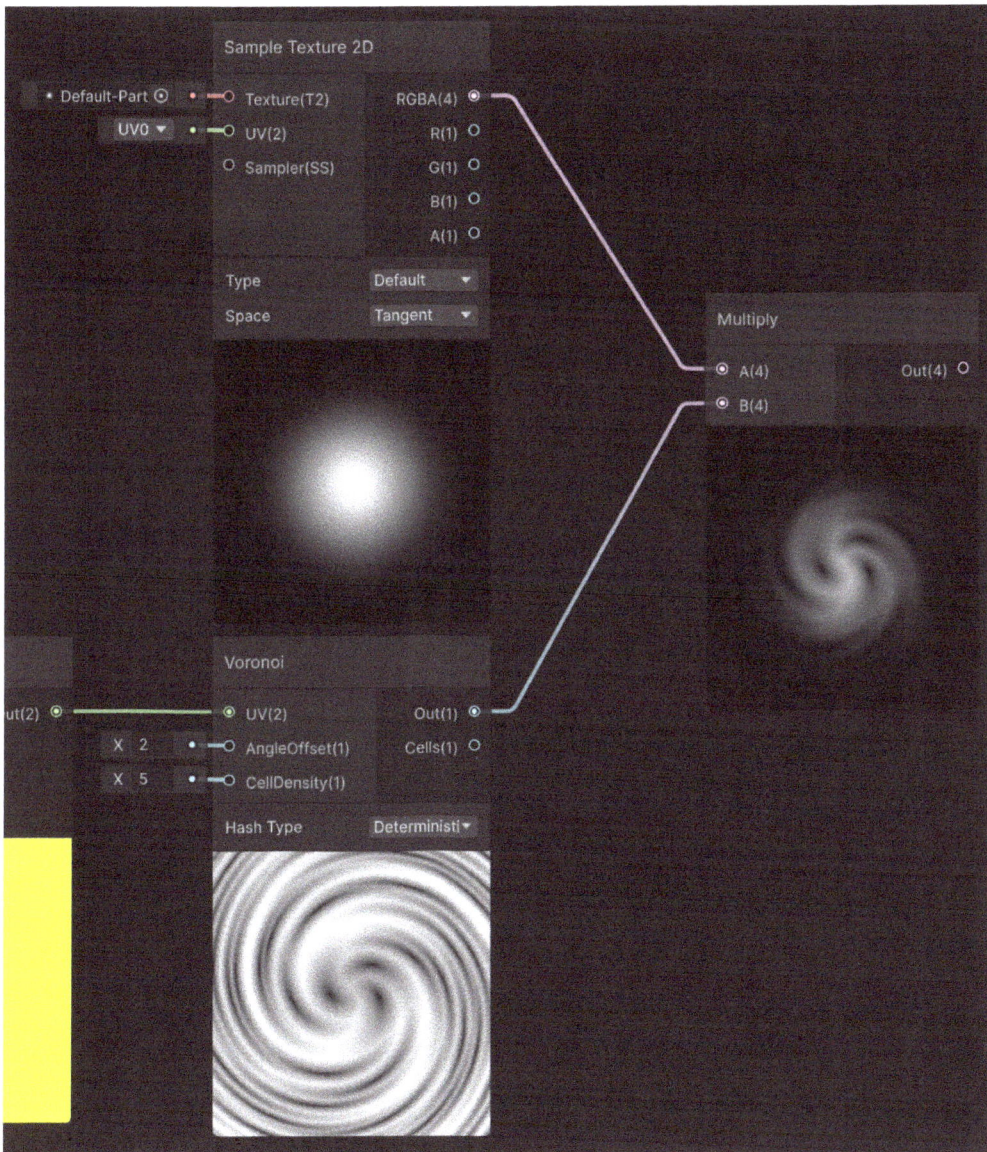

Figure 13.15 – Masking the portal effect

10. Now, we want the portal to have color. Open the **Blackboard** and add a **Color** variable called **PortalColor** and, from the **Graph Inspector**, set its **Default** value to a *green* color and set **Mode** to **HDR**.

11. Bring the **PortalColor** variable into the graph. Then, create another **Multiply** node to multiply the result of the masking to the new color.

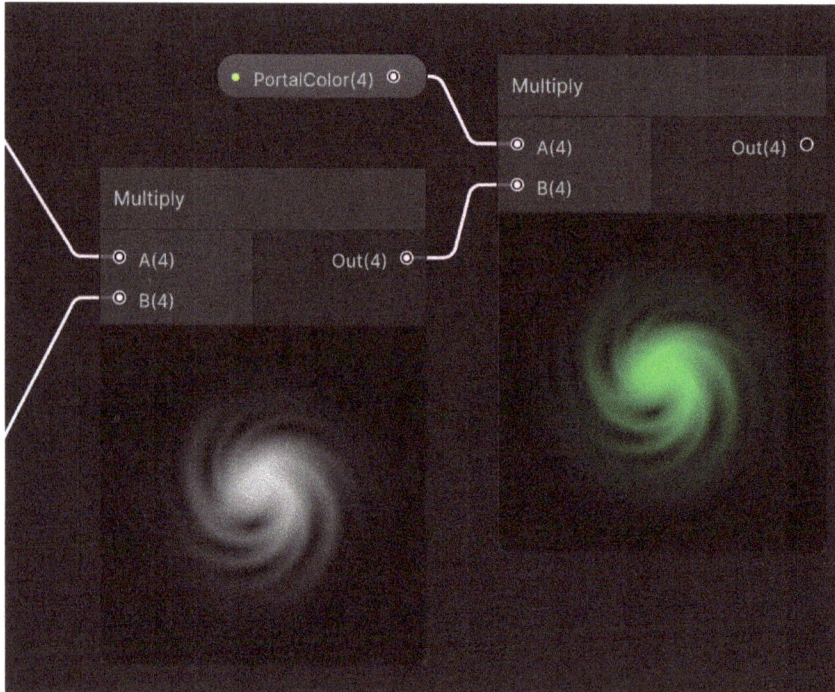

Figure 13.16 – Adding color to the portal

12. We will need to scale the effect to work well on HDRP projects. To do this, create a **Power** node and then set the values to 10 and 2. Then, create a **Multiply** node and combine the **Out** pin of the **Power** node and the **Out** pin of the last **Multiply** node. Take this final **Out** pin and connect it to the **Base Color**, **Emission**, and **Alpha** channels of **Fragment**.

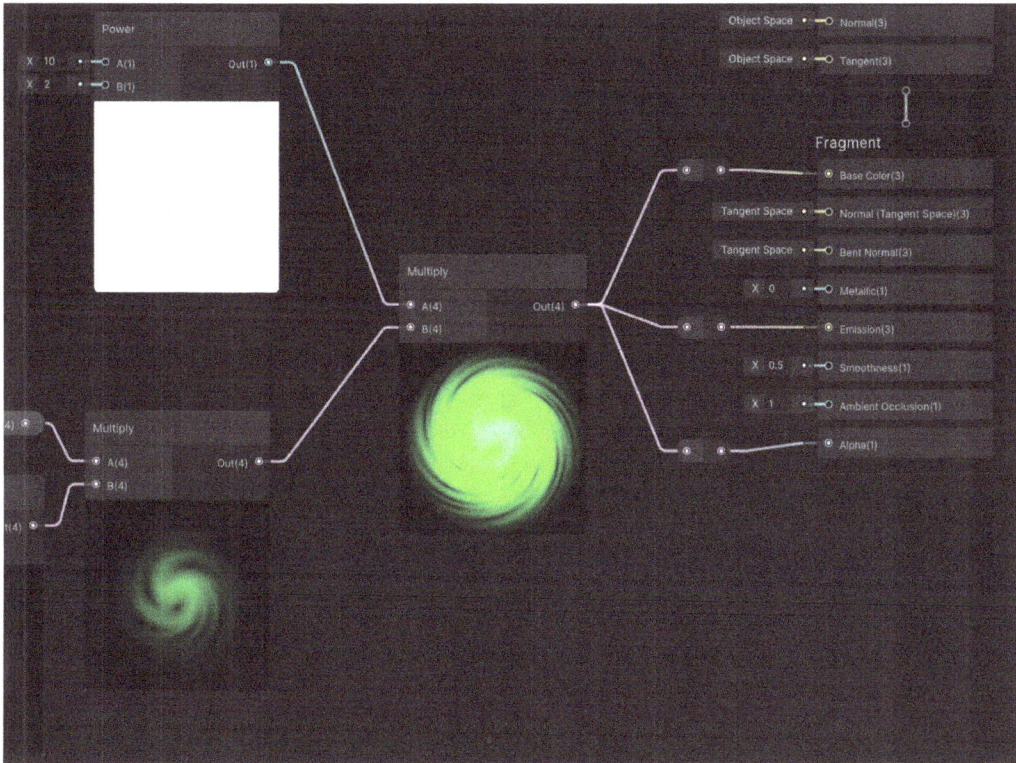

Figure 13.17 – Scaling the effect

13. Save the graph and return to the scene. You should notice faint transparency on the plane. To remove this, select the material and, from the **Inspector** window, uncheck the **Preserve** specular lighting option. Lastly, change the **Blending Mode** to **Premultiply**.

14. It may take a bit of time to compile so it may appear in solid light blue at first but once it finishes, go ahead and play the game.

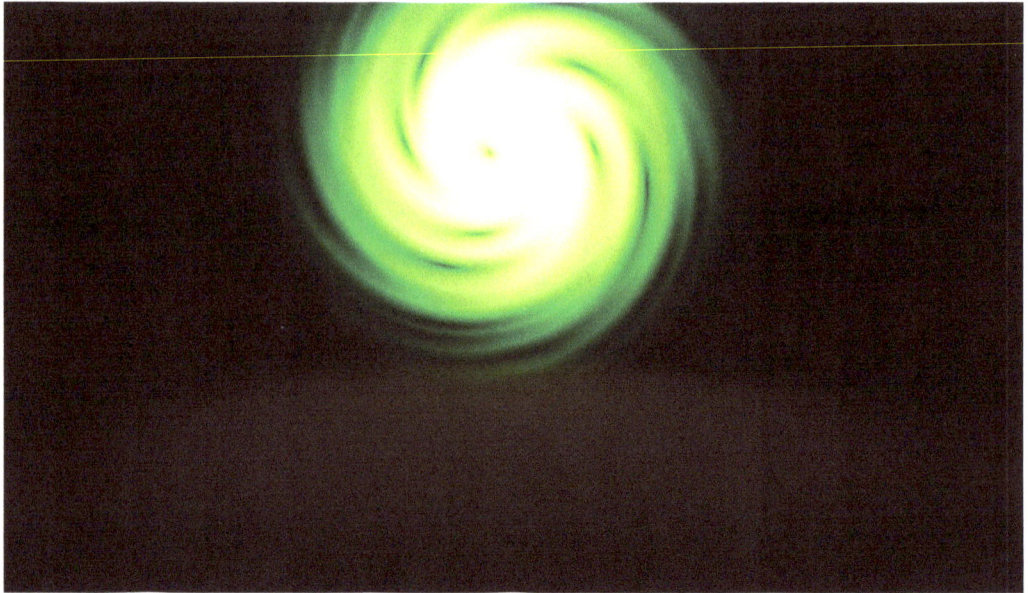

Figure 13.18 – Final result

How it works...

Marking the shader as **Double-Sided** means that it will show up on both sides of the plane; this is very useful with regard to how portals typically work in games.

The **Twirl** node applies a warping effect similar to being affected by a black hole.

Voronoi, or **Worley**, noise is generated by calculating distances between a pixel and a lattice of points. By offsetting these points by a pseudo-random number, controlled by input **Angle Offset**, a cluster of cells can be generated that, for our purposes, allows us to have a procedural texture to work with.

> Note
>
> For more information, check out `https://docs.unity3d.com/Packages/com.`
> `unity.shadergraph@17.0/manual/Voronoi-Node.html`.

Join our community on Discord

Join our community's Discord space for discussions with the authors and other readers:

```
https://packt.link/gamedevelopment
```

‹packt›

Subscribe to our online digital library for full access to over 7,000 books and videos, as well as industry leading tools to help you plan your personal development and advance your career. For more information, please visit our website.

Why subscribe?

- Spend less time learning and more time coding with practical eBooks and Videos from over 4,000 industry professionals
- Improve your learning with Skill Plans built especially for you
- Get a free eBook or video every month
- Fully searchable for easy access to vital information
- Copy and paste, print, and bookmark content

At www.packt.com, you can also read a collection of free technical articles, sign up for a range of free newsletters, and receive exclusive discounts and offers on Packt books and eBooks.

Other Books You May Enjoy

If you enjoyed this book, you may be interested in these other books by Packt:

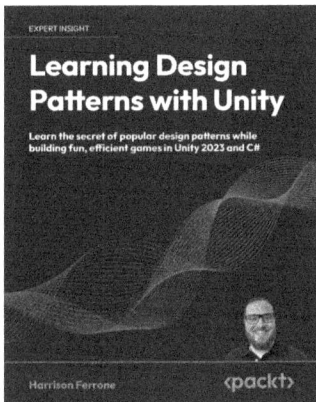

Learning Design Patterns with Unity

Harrison Ferrone

ISBN: 978-1-80512-028-5

- Implement a persistent game manager using the Singleton pattern
- Spawn projectiles efficiently with Object Pooling for optimized performance
- Build a flexible crafting system using the Factory Method pattern
- Design an undo/redo system for player movement with the Command pattern
- Implement a state machine to control a two-person battle system
- Modify existing character objects with special abilities using the Decorator pattern

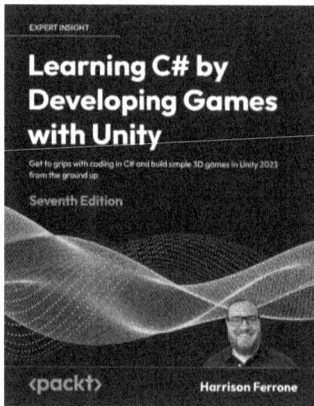

Learning C# by Developing Games with Unity, Seventh Edition

Harrison Ferrone

ISBN: 978-1-83763-687-7

- Understanding programming fundamentals by breaking them down into their basic parts

- Comprehensive explanations with sample codes of object-oriented programming and how it applies to C#

- Follow simple steps and examples to create and implement C# scripts in Unity

- Divide your code into pluggable building blocks using interfaces, abstract classes, and class extensions

- Grasp the basics of a game design document and then move on to blocking out your level geometry, adding lighting and a simple object animation

- Create basic game mechanics such as player controllers and shooting projectiles using C#

- Become familiar with stacks, queues, exceptions, error handling, and other core C# concepts

- Learn how to handle text, XML, and JSON data to save and load your game data

Packt is searching for authors like you

If you're interested in becoming an author for Packt, please visit authors.packtpub.com and apply today. We have worked with thousands of developers and tech professionals, just like you, to help them share their insight with the global tech community. You can make a general application, apply for a specific hot topic that we are recruiting an author for, or submit your own idea.

Share Your Thoughts

Now you've finished *Unity 6 Shaders and Effects Cookbook, Fifth edition*, we'd love to hear your thoughts! Scan the QR code below to go straight to the Amazon review page for this book and share your feedback or leave a review on the site that you purchased it from.

https://packt.link/r/1835468578

Your review is important to us and the tech community and will help us make sure we're delivering excellent quality content.

Index

Download a free PDF copy of this book

Thanks for purchasing this book!

Do you like to read on the go but are unable to carry your print books everywhere?

Is your eBook purchase not compatible with the device of your choice?

Don't worry, now with every Packt book you get a DRM-free PDF version of that book at no cost.

Read anywhere, any place, on any device. Search, copy, and paste code from your favorite technical books directly into your application.

The perks don't stop there, you can get exclusive access to discounts, newsletters, and great free content in your inbox daily

Follow these simple steps to get the benefits:

1. Scan the QR code or visit the link below

https://packt.link/free-ebook/9781835468579

2. Submit your proof of purchase
3. That's it! We'll send your free PDF and other benefits to your email directly

www.ingramcontent.com/pod-product-compliance
Lightning Source LLC
Chambersburg PA
CBHW072007230326
41598CB00082B/6815